Stephen Walther
Jonathan Levine

SAMS
Teach Yourself

E-Commerce
Programming
with ASP

in 21 Days

SAMS

A Division of Macmillan USA
201 West 103rd St., Indianapolis, Indiana, 46290 USA

Sams Teach Yourself E-Commerce Programming with ASP in 21 Days
Copyright © 2000 by Sams

International Standard Book Number: 0672318989

Library of Congress Catalog Card Number: 99-068489

Printed in the United States of America

First Printing: April, 2000

02   01   00   4   3   2   1

Trademarks

All terms mentioned in this book that are known to be trademarks or service marks have been appropriately capitalized. Sams cannot attest to the accuracy of this information. Use of a term in this book should not be regarded as affecting the validity of any trademark or service mark.

Warning and Disclaimer

Every effort has been made to make this book as complete and as accurate as possible, but no warranty or fitness is implied. The information provided is on an "as is" basis. The author(s) and the publisher shall have neither liability nor responsibility to any person or entity with respect to any loss or damages arising from the information contained in this book or from the use of the CD or programs accompanying it.

ASSOCIATE PUBLISHER
Bradley L. Jones

EXECUTIVE EDITOR
Chris Webb

DEVELOPMENT EDITOR
Kevin Howard

MANAGING EDITOR
Charlotte Clapp

PROJECT EDITOR
Elizabeth Roberts

COPY EDITOR
Rhonda Tinch-Mize

INDEXER
Erika Millen

PROOFREADER
Jill Mazurczyk

TECHNICAL EDITOR
Jia Wang

TEAM COORDINATOR
Meggo Barthlow

MEDIA DEVELOPER
Dan Scherf

INTERIOR DESIGNER
Gary Adair

COVER DESIGNER
Aren Howell

COPYWRITER
Eric Borgert

LAYOUT TECHNICIAN
Eric S. Miller

Contents at a Glance

Introduction   1

WEEK 1 At a Glance   **5**

Day 1   Introduction to E-Commerce   7

Day 2   Interacting with the Customer   21

Day 3   Using Application and Session Objects in E-Commerce Applications   47

Day 4   Working with Files in Your E-Commerce Application   69

Day 5   Building Your Product Catalog Database   89

Day 6   Displaying Your Products   119

Day 7   Searching for Products   143

WEEK 1 In Review   **163**

WEEK 2 At a Glance   **167**

Day 8   Building the Transaction Databases   169

Day 9   Building the Shopping Cart   191

Day 10   Checking Out   213

Day 11   Working with Credit Cards   237

Day 12   Letting Customers Track Their Orders   259

Day 13   Creating a Subscription-Based Site   273

Day 14   Customizing the Shopping Experience   297

WEEK 2 In Review   **319**

WEEK 3 At a Glance   **323**

Day 15   Securing Your Store   325

Day 16   Debugging Your E-Commerce Applications   345

Day 17   Administering Your Store Remotely with ASPs   377

Day 18   Using Email from Active Server Pages   409

Day 19   Generating Store Reports   441

Day 20   Working with Wallets   467

Day 21   Promoting Your Site and Managing Banner Advertising   495

WEEK 3 In Review   **519**

Appendix A   Quiz Answers   523

Appendix B   Frequently Asked Questions About Active Server Pages   545

Appendix C   SQL Reference   559

Index   571

Contents

Introduction   **1**

WEEK 1 At A Glance   **5**

DAY 1 Introduction to E-Commerce   **7**

What Is E-Commerce? 8
Microsoft Technologies for E-Commerce 9
    Microsoft Personal Web Server 10
    Microsoft Internet Information Server 10
    Microsoft Access 11
    Microsoft SQL Server 11
    Microsoft Visual InterDev 12
What Is an ASP Page? 13
    Active Server Pages Contain Scripts 14
    Active Server Pages Contain Objects and Components 15
    Active Server Pages and Database Access 17
Summary 17
Q&A 18
Workshop 18
    Quiz 18

DAY 2 Interacting with the Customer   **21**

Working with the Response Object 22
    Outputting Long Strings 23
    Displaying Special Characters 23
    Displaying Quotation Marks 24
    Using the <%= and %> Output Delimiters 26
    Ending Script Execution with the Response Object 26
Working with the Request Object 27
    Using Query Strings 28
    Using the Form Collection 31
Retrieving Query String and Form Variables 38
    Working with Server Variables 39
    Retrieving the Customer's Internet Address 41
Summary 43
Q&A 43
Workshop 44
    Quiz 44
    Exercise 45

**DAY 3 Using Application and Session Objects in E-Commerce
Applications**   **47**

Tracking Customers with Cookies 48
   Adding a Cookie to a Customer's Browser 50
   Reading Cookies from a Customer's Browser 51
Tracking Customers with Session Variables 52
   Storing Arrays in Session Variables 54
   Tracking a Session with a SessionID 56
   Ending a User Session 56
Using Application Variables 57
   Storing Arrays in Application Variables 60
   Removing Application Variables From Memory 61
Using the Global.asa File 62
Summary 65
Q&A 66
Workshop 67
   Quiz 67
   Exercise 68

DAY 4 Working with Files in Your E-Commerce Application   **69**

Including Files in an ASP Page 69
   Dynamically Including Files 73
Using File Redirection 75
Using the File Access Component 77
   Managing Text Files 81
   Displaying the Contents of a Folder 83
   Sample Application: Recording Marketing Data 84
Summary 85
Q&A 86
Workshop 86
   Quiz 87
   Exercise 87

DAY 5 Building Your Product Catalog   **89**

Creating the Store Database 89
Creating the Products Table 91
Connecting to a Database 93
Adding Products to the Products Table 95
   Creating the AddProducts Form 97
   A Problem with Databases and Quotation Marks 102
Updating Product Information in the Products Table 104
   Displaying the List of Products to Update 106
   Creating the updateProduct Form 109

A Problem with HTML Forms and Quotation Marks 112

Updating a Database Record 113

Summary 117

Q&A 117

Workshop 118

Quiz 118

Exercises 118

DAY 6 Displaying Your Products   **119**

Using Recordsets 119

Using the SQL SELECT Statement 121

Recordset Cursor Types 122

Displaying Products 123

Selecting Product Categories 125

Displaying the List of Products 126

Creating the Main Store Page 128

Displaying Product Details 130

Paging Through A Recordset 134

Making Your Store More Scalable 137

Summary 140

Q&A 140

Workshop 140

Quiz 140

Exercise 141

DAY 7 Searching for Products   **143**

Displaying a Rotating List of Featured Products 143

Selecting the List of Featured Products 144

Retrieving the List of Featured Products 146

Optimizing the Display of Featured Products 149

Creating a Search Page 152

Optimizing the Search Page 157

Creating Indexable Web Pages 158

Summary 160

Q&A 160

Workshop 160

Quiz 160

Exercise 161

WEEK 1 In Review   **163**

Bonus Project 163

Creating a Customer Feedback Form 163

Week 2 At A Glance   **167**

Day 8 Building the Transaction Databases   **169**

The Transaction Database Tables 170
Creating the Users Database Table 171
Registering Users 172
    Creating the cart.asp Page 172
    Creating the register.asp Page 174
    The Registration Functions 176
Gracefully Handling Form Errors 181
Using the Secure Sockets Layer 183
    Enabling SSL on Your Web Server 185
    Applying for a Server Certificate 186
    Installing Your Server Certificate 187
    Using SSL in an ASP Page 187
Summary 188
Q&A 189
Workshop 189
    Quiz 189
    Exercise 190

Day 9 Building the Shopping Cart   **191**

Using Session Variables to Create
    a Shopping Cart 191
    Creating the SessionCart.asp Page 193
Using Native ADO Methods 200
    Creating Updateable Recordsets 200
    Adding New Records with AddNew 201
    Updating Existing Records 202
    Deleting Records with Delete 203
Using a Database Table to Create
    a Shopping Cart 204
    Creating the addCart.asp Page 206
Summary 211
Q&A 211
Workshop 212
    Quiz 212
    Exercise 212

Day 10 Checking Out   **213**

Understanding Transactions 213
    ASP Page Transactions 214
    ADO Transactions 218
    Database Transactions 219

Completing the Order 219
　　　Retrieving Address and Payment Information 220
　　　Updating Address and Payment Information 221
　　　Transferring the Shopping Cart 224
　　Processing Orders 226
　　Summary 234
　　Q&A 234
　　Workshop 235
　　　Quiz 235
　　　Exercises 235

DAY 11 Working with Credit Cards　　　　　　　　　　　**237**

　　Methods of Processing Credit Cards 237
　　　Offsite Payment Processors 238
　　　Payment Terminal Solutions 239
　　　Component-Based Solutions 239
　　　Choosing a Method of Processing Credit Cards 240
　　Preparing for CyberCash 240
　　　Opening a Credit Card Merchant Account 241
　　　Registering at CyberCash 242
　　　Installing the CyberCash Software 243
　　Authorizing a Credit Card Transaction 245
　　　Integrating the Authorization Script into Your Store 248
　　Settling Credit Card Transactions 254
　　Summary 256
　　Q&A 256
　　Workshop 257
　　　Quiz 257

DAY 12 Letting Customers Track Their Orders　　　　　**259**

　　Enabling Customers to Track Orders with a Web Page 260
　　Calculating Shipping Costs 264
　　　Installing the iisCARTship Component 265
　　　iisCARTship Properties and Methods 265
　　　iisCARTship Component Sample Application 269
　　Summary 271
　　Q&A 272
　　Workshop 272
　　　Quiz 272

DAY 13 Creating a Subscription-Based Site　　　　　　**273**

　　Using HTTP Authentication 274
　　　Enabling HTTP Authentication 275
　　　When You Should Use HTTP Authentication 276

Using Database Authentication 276
    Passing Security Information From Page to Page 285
Using Hybrid Authentication 287
    Understanding How Basic Authentication Works 288
    Forcing a Password Dialog to Appear 288
    Decoding the AUTHORIZATION Header 290
Summary 294
Q&A 295
Workshop 295
    Quiz 295

DAY 14 Customizing the Shopping Experience   **297**

Retrieving the Existing User Settings 297
    Creating `mypage.asp` 298
Showing Past Purchases 302
Advertising Items Your Customers Would Like 307
    Updating the Users Table for Favorites 307
    Building the `favorites.asp` Page 308
    Building the `savefavorites.asp` Page 311
    Updating the `featured.asp` Page 313
    Updating the `default.asp` Page 315
Summary 316
Q&A 316
Workshop 317
    Quiz 317
    Exercise 317

WEEK 2 In Review   **319**

Bonus Project 320
    Creating a Transactional Customer Feedback Form 320

WEEK 3 At A Glance   **323**

DAY 15 Securing Your Store   **325**

Registering Your Own Domain 326
    Domain Names and Marketing 326
    Registering Your Domain Name Yourself 327
Making Your Server More Secure 329
    Use NT Server or Windows 2000 Server, not NT Workstation
    or Windows 2000 Professional 329
    Make Sure That the Latest Service Packs and Hotfixes Are Applied
    to Your System 330
    Change the Name and Password of Your System's Administrator
    Account 331

Use NTFS 332
Use a Firewall 334
Keep Your Server Locked Up 334
Keep Your Server Running 335
Protecting Your Users' Private Information with SSL 335
Protecting Your Database 337
Registering with the Better Business Bureau Reliability Program 338
Establishing a Privacy Policy and Joining a Privacy Seal Program 339
The Better Business Bureau's Children's Advertising Review Unit
  Guidelines 341
Summary 342
Q&A 343
Workshop 343
Quiz 343
Exercise 343

DAY 16 Debugging Your E-Commerce Applications   **345**
Keeping Your Development and Production Systems Separate 346
Creating a Second IP Address 347
Creating a Second Web Site 349
Deploying Your Application Using Visual InterDev 350
Debugging Your Application Using Visual InterDev's Integrated Debugger 354
Getting Ready to Debug 355
Debugging a Site 357
Debugging Your Application on a Production Server 361
Creating and Maintaining a Session Variable for Debugging 362
Using the Session-level Debugging Variable 364
Creating a Debug Library 366
Recovering from and Capturing Errors 366
Capturing Errors into a Log File 369
Testing for Scalability 372
Summary 373
Q&A 374
Workshop 375
Quiz 375
Exercise 375

DAY 17 Administering Your Store Remotely with ASPs   **377**
The IIS Administration Pages 378
Installing the Administration Pages 378
Securing the Administration Pages 379
Using the Administration Pages 384
Installing and Administering the IIS FTP Service 385
Uploading Files to Your Site Using FTP 387

Advanced Web-Based Product Catalog Maintenance 389
How the Posting Acceptor Makes it Easier for the User and
the Programmer 391
Uploading Pictures from addProduct.asp and updateProduct.asp 396
Moving Form Processing Logic from manageProducts.asp to the New
donePost.asp 401
Integrating the Pages into the Administration Web 405
Summary 407
Q&A 408
Workshop 408
Quiz 408

DAY 18 Using Email from Active Server Pages   **409**

The Basics of Internet Mail 410
Configuring the SMTP Service 411
The Collaboration Data Objects for NT Server (CDONTS) 414
Sending Email from an ASP Page 415
The CDONTS Constants 417
Send Yourself Email on Errors 419
Sending New Users Email 421
Sending HTML Mail 423
Sending Batches of Email 428
Selecting Customers 429
Composing the Message 432
Sending the Messages 435
Doing Email Marketing 438
Summary 438
Q&A 438
Workshop 439
Quiz 439

DAY 19 Generating Store Reports   **441**

Reporting on Site Usage 441
Site Usage Logs 443
Analyzing Your Logs 455
Other Ways to Analyze Logs 464
Summary 465
Q&A 465
Workshop 465
Quiz 465

DAY 20 Working with Wallets   **467**

Physical Commerce Versus Electronic Commerce 468
Electronic Wallets 469
Client-Side Wallets 469

Server-Side Wallets 471
General Server-Side Wallets 472
Wallet Standards 475
Your Own Store Wallet 476
Accepting Information from Wallets 492
Summary 492
Q&A 493
Workshop 493
Quiz 493
Exercises 493

DAY 21 Promoting Your Site and Managing Banner Advertising 495

Search Engines 496
How Do They Work? 496
What's the Best Way to Get Listed? 496
Web Rings 508
Try It Out! 508
Banner Ads 510
Link Exchanges 510
Paying for Banner Ads 513
Participating in Reward Programs 513
Other Ways to Increase Revenue 514
Affiliate Programs 514
Running Your Own Advertising 514
Summary 517
Q&A 517
Workshop 517
Quiz 518
Exercises 518

WEEK 3 In Review 519

Bonus Project 520
Sending Customer Feedback Acknowledgement Emails 520

Appendixes

APPENDIX A Quiz Answers 523

APPENDIX B Frequently Asked Questions About Active Server Pages 545

APPENDIX C SQL Reference 559

Index 571

About the Authors

STEPHEN WALTHER is the host of Superexpert (`www.superexpert.com`), the community of computer experts. He actively moderates the Active Server Pages community at Superexpert, where you can get the answers to all your Active Server Pages questions.

He was the past Chief Technical Officer of CityAuction (recently acquired by Ticketmaster Online-CitySearch), where he developed the auction Web site used by both Snap! and CitySearch. Previously, he was the Chief Technical Officer of Collegescape (acquired by Peterson's), where he built an online college application Web site used by over 200 colleges, including Harvard University and the Massachusetts Institute of Technology.

He received his Bachelor of Arts from the University of California at Berkeley. He was a Ph.D. candidate in Linguistics and Philosophy at the Massachusetts Institute of Technology when he became involved with the World Wide Web. He can be contacted in the Active Server Pages forum at `www.superexpert.com`.

JONATHAN LEVINE is a San Francisco-based strategic technology consultant. He has been designing and building innovative software for more than 15 years.

His current consulting engagements are as "virtual CTO" for several Bay Area Internet startups. Previously, he was Vice President, Engineering, for ePhysician, where he architected and led implementation of an ASP-based application for medical professionals. Previously, he was Director, Engineering at PointCast, where he founded and directed the Program Management Group, and was responsible for client deployment, content development, and quality assurance. He also founded and directed PointCast's International Engineering group, and was responsible for all technical aspects of PointCast networks in Japan, Greater China, and seven vertical markets.

From 1991–1996, Jonathan was the fourth employee of Approach Software Corporation (later acquired by Lotus Development Corporation). At Approach and Lotus, he designed and implemented the user interface for the critically acclaimed first two releases of Approach for Windows and provided technical and managerial direction in developing innovative features such as drill-downs, Approach Assistants, and context-sensitive user interfaces.

Prior to joining Approach, Jonathan held a variety of technical positions at Oracle, Martin-Marietta Data Systems, IBM, and the SRI-David Sarnoff Research Center. He holds three patents on the user interfaces that he helped design while at Lotus, and has patents pending on various aspects of the technology he designed at ePhysician. He is a co-author of the 1996 publication, *Making Sense of Java*.

Dedication

This book is dedicated to my father, Jon Walther.
- Stephen Walther

For Susan
- Jonathan Levine

Acknowledgments

I'd like to thank Ruth Johnson, who provided so much help with this book that I decided to marry her.

- Stephen Walther

Many thanks to Chris Webb and the staff at Macmillan for their help and patience, and to everyone at Waterside Productions. Thanks to Philipe, Owen, and Giles at Xenote for providing the resources that allowed me to write Days 16–21. Also, thanks to my family for encouraging me to spend most of my waking hours on researching, programming, and writing.

A special thanks to my wife, Susan Lin, who has little interest in programming, but who spent hours proofreading hundreds of pages of my writing on programming in ASP. Finally, a million thanks to all the folks who spend their spare time building Web-based resources on ASP programming: you folks are awesome, and without your hard work the research for this book would have been much, much more difficult. Of course, I remain solely responsible for any errors or omissions within.

- Jonathan Levine

Tell Us What You Think!

As the reader of this book, *you* are our most important critic and commentator. We value your opinion and want to know what we're doing right, what we could do better, what areas you'd like to see us publish in, and any other words of wisdom you're willing to pass our way.

As a Associate Publisher for Sams, I welcome your comments. You can fax, email, or write me directly to let me know what you did or didn't like about this book—as well as what we can do to make our books stronger.

Please note that I cannot help you with technical problems related to the topic of this book, and that due to the high volume of mail I receive, I might not be able to reply to every message.

When you write, please be sure to include this book's title and author as well as your name and phone or fax number. I will carefully review your comments and share them with the author and editors who worked on the book.

Fax: 317-581-4770

Email: adv_prog@mcp.com

Mail: Bradley L. Jones
          Associate Publisher
          Sams
          201 West 103rd Street
          Indianapolis, IN 46290 USA

Introduction

This book teaches you everything you need to know to create a Web site that generates money. You'll learn how to build a commercial Web site using Microsoft's Active Server Pages technology; the same technology used to create many of the most successful commercial Web sites on the Internet including Dell Online (`http://www.dell.com`), Eddie Bauer (`http://www.eddiebauer.com`), Nasdaq (`http://www.nasdaq.com`), and Barnes and Noble (`http://www.bn.com`).

Each chapter in this book is presented as a lesson. In each lesson, you'll be presented with code samples that you can use in your own Web projects (many of these code samples are included on the CD-ROM that accompanies this book). All the lessons end with a quiz so that you can test your knowledge of the material covered in the lesson.

In the first week of lessons, you'll learn how to place a store on the Internet and sell products online. You'll begin by learning how to build Active Server Pages to display your catalog of products. Next, you'll learn how to create a virtual shopping cart that customers can use to select products from your store. Finally, you'll learn how to securely perform credit card transactions over the Internet.

In the second week, you'll learn how to create a subscription Web site. You'll build a user registration system to password protect sections of your Web site. This registration system can be used to restrict certain sections of your Web site to paying customers.

In the final week, you'll learn several important skills for maintaining and promoting your commercial Web site. First, you'll learn several valuable techniques for debugging your Web site. You'll also learn how to remotely administer your Web site over the Internet. Last, you'll learn how to promote your Web site and build customer traffic through email marketing.

What Do I Need to Know to Use This Book?

The lessons in this book assume that you have a good understanding of HTML and Visual Basic Scripting Edition (VBScript). If you are not familiar with VBScript, don't worry. VBScript is a subset of Microsoft Visual Basic. So, if you know Visual Basic, you should be able to quickly understand the VBScript code samples in this book.

To get the most out of the lessons in this book, you should also be familiar with SQL. You'll need to use SQL when completing the lessons that discuss database access. If you need to learn SQL, I recommend that you buy the book *Sams Teach Yourself SQL in 21 Days* (ISBN: 0-672-31674-9).

What Software Do I Need to Use This Book?

To complete the lessons in this book, you'll need access to a computer with a Microsoft Web server and a database. At the very minimum, you'll need a computer that has Windows 95 or Windows 98 installed with the Microsoft Personal Web Server. If you don't have the Microsoft Personal Web Server, you can download it from Microsoft at the following Web address:

```
http://www.microsoft.com/windows/ie/pws/default.htm
```

To complete many of the advanced lessons in this book, you'll need access to a computer running Windows NT or Windows 2000 with Internet Information Server installed. Internet Information Server is included as a component of both the Windows NT and Windows 2000 operating systems. However, if you are using Windows NT, you should download the latest version of Internet Information Server by downloading the Windows NT Server 4.0 Option Pack at

```
http://www.microsoft.com/ntserver/nts/downloads/recommended/NT4OptPk/default.asp
```

Many of the lessons in this book assume that you have a database installed on your computer. To complete the basic lessons, you can use Microsoft Access. However, I recommend that you use Microsoft SQL Server 7.0 for a live commercial Web site.

For the database lessons, you should download the latest version of the Microsoft Data Access Components (MDAC). You can download the MDAC at the Microsoft Universal Data Access Web Site at

```
http://www.microsoft.com/data/
```

Finally, you should download the latest version of the Microsoft Scripting Engines. The Microsoft Scripting Engines contain the latest versions of VBScript and JScript. You can download the Microsoft Scripting Engines at the Microsoft Windows Script Technologies Web site at

```
http://msdn.microsoft.com/scripting/
```

Conventions Used in This Book

This book uses different typefaces to differentiate between code and regular English, and also to help you identify important concepts.

Text that you type and text that should appear on your screen is presented in monospace type.

```
It will look like this to mimic the way text looks on your screen.
```

Placeholders for variables and expressions appear in `monospace italic` font. You should replace the placeholder with the specific value it represents.

This arrow (➥) at the beginning of a line of code means that a single line of code is too long to fit on the printed page. Continue typing all characters after the ➥ as though they were part of the preceding line.

Note
A Note presents interesting pieces of information related to the surrounding discussion.

Tip
A Tip offers advice or teaches an easier way to do something.

Caution
A Caution advises you about potential problems and helps you steer clear of disaster.

INPUT The Input icon identifies code that you can type in yourself. It usually appears next to a listing.

OUTPUT The Output icon highlights the output produced by running a program. It usually appears after a listing.

ANALYSIS The Analysis icon alerts you to the author's line-by-line analysis of a program.

WEEK 1

At A Glance

This week, you'll begin building your online store. In the first lesson, you'll be introduced to E-Commerce and Active Server Pages programming. You'll learn about three different models of E-Commerce. You'll also be given an overview of the Microsoft technologies for creating commercial Web sites.

The next three lessons, Days 2 through 4, provide you with a crash course in Active Server Pages programming as it relates to creating commercial Web sites. You'll learn how to write Active Server Pages scripts that retrieve customer information. You'll also learn how to track customer information by using cookies and Session variables. Finally, you'll learn how to work with files in an Active Server Page.

On Day 5, you'll begin building your online store. First, you'll learn how to create Active Server Pages to manage your catalog of products. Next, on Day 6, you'll create the product pages for your store. Finally, in the lesson on Day 7, you'll learn some techniques for enabling customers to search through your product catalog.

By the end of the week, you'll be ready to place your catalog of products on the Web.

1

2

3

4

5

6

7

DAY 1

Introduction to E-Commerce

The explosive growth of Internet commerce has captured the public's imagination. It's not hard to understand why.

No small part of the public's fascination with the Internet is caused by the vast fortunes that it's created. People are making money, and lots of it. According to a recent study funded by Cisco Systems, the Internet economy is projected to reach $507 billion in the year 2000 (see http://www.internetindicators.com). E-Commerce is already generating more money than the telecommunications and the airline industries.

eBay, a company started less than five years ago by a man trying to find a more efficient method of selling his wife's Pez dispensers, recently bought Butterfield & Butterfield, a 135 year-old auction house. And Amazon, a company that started a scant five years ago, is selling more than five times as many books online than the long established bookseller Barnes and Noble.

The world is changing in other ways. Not so long ago creating Web sites, especially commerce enabled Web sites, was a task best left to MIT graduate students. You had no choice but to wrestle with the impenetrable syntax of a language like Perl or work with a low-level programming language like C++.

Fortunately, Microsoft has developed a technology that enables you to quickly create commercial Web sites: Active Server Pages (ASP). Using Active Server Pages, you can create Web sites of the same quality as Dell.com or BarnesandNoble.com. (Both sites were created with Active Server Pages.)

In today's lesson, you will be introduced to the two subjects of this book: E-Commerce and Active Server Pages. We'll discuss the following questions:

- What does it mean for a business to engage in E-Commerce?
- What are the Microsoft technologies for creating a commerce enabled Web site?
- What is an ASP page?

What Is E-Commerce?

E-Commerce refers to the process of buying or selling a product or service over an electronic network. The most popular medium in which E-Commerce is conducted is the Internet.

E-Commerce encompasses three types of business transactions. First, a transaction can occur between a business and consumer. When you think of E-Commerce, this type of transaction is the first thing that springs to mind. A prime example of a business that engages in business-to-consumer E-Commerce is Amazon. Amazon promotes itself as the "place to find and discover anything you want to buy online" by selling books, CDs, electronics, and videos to consumers.

Business-to-consumer E-Commerce can also include services. A subscription Web site that doesn't sell any tangible goods can also be engaged in E-Commerce. For example, Match.com—the online dating service—sells subscriptions to their Web site to enable customers to browse their listings for potential romantic partners.

A second general form of E-Commerce involves transactions between one business and another. A business that engages in this type of E-Commerce is typically less visible to consumers and, therefore, to the general public. A good example of a company that engages in business-to-business E-Commerce is Cisco Systems. Cisco Systems creates much of the physical infrastructure of the Internet that allows businesses to communicate.

Finally, a form of E-Commerce that has become very popular over the past couple of years involves consumer-to-consumer transactions. The best-known example of a company that engages in this type of E-Commerce is eBay. eBay enables its customers to auction items to other customers. (eBay collects a fee from every transaction.)

Note E-Commerce has its roots in Electronic Data Interchange (EDI). EDI is a structured method of transmitting information from one computer to another. EDI was developed to enable businesses to automate the process of transmitting business documents such as invoices and purchase orders. EDI can also be used to transfer many other types of information. For example, colleges use EDI to transfer student transcripts, and health care providers use EDI to transfer patient records.

When you think of E-Commerce, you typically think of a customer selecting a product from a Web site and paying for it online with a credit card. In other words, credit card transactions would appear to be an essential part of E-Commerce. However, E-Commerce might encompass only the activities leading up to the purchase and not the final purchase itself.

For example, suppose that you have a store (I mean a real, physical store and not a virtual store) that sells kitchen appliances such as stoves and refrigerators. You might decide it makes sense to create a Web site that lists the appliances you sell at your store even if you don't offer a method for consumers to actually purchase your products online. The only purpose of the Web site would be to entice customers to visit your existing store. This is also a valid form of E-Commerce.

Note A good source of information on E-Commerce is the United States Government Electronic Commerce Policy Web site at http://www.ecommerce.gov. It has a number of interesting reports on E-Commerce paid for by your tax dollars.

Microsoft Technologies for E-Commerce

The lessons in this book focus on using Microsoft technologies for creating commerce enabled Web sites. The lessons assume that you are using both a Microsoft Web server and a Microsoft database.

Microsoft offers two Web servers: the Personal Web Server and Internet Information Server. You'll need to have one or the other of these Web servers installed on your computer to complete the lessons. (Some of the advanced lessons require Internet Information Server.)

You'll also need access to a database to complete the lessons. The lessons assume that you are using either Microsoft Access or Microsoft SQL Server. However, with minor modifications, most of the lessons should also work with other database servers such as Oracle.

The following sections provide a brief overview of the differences between these programs and additional Microsoft tools for building commercial Web sites.

Microsoft Personal Web Server

The Microsoft Personal Web Server works with Windows 95, Windows 98, or Windows NT Workstation. You can download the Personal Web Server (for free) at the following Internet address:

```
http://www.microsoft.com/windows/ie/pws/default.htm
```

Note   For some mysterious reason, Microsoft includes the Personal Web Server as part of the Windows NT Option Pack. This is confusing because the Personal Web Server was designed to work with Windows 95 or Windows 98.

The Personal Web Server was created for two purposes. You can use it to host a very low traffic Web site (for example, to share documents on your company's intranet). Alternatively, you can use the Personal Web Server to prototype a Web site before you transfer the content of the site to Internet Information Server.

It should be emphasized that the Personal Web Server isn't an appropriate Web server to use for hosting a live site on the Internet. It cannot handle very many concurrent users. However, unless specifically noted, you can use the Personal Web Server with all the lessons discussed in this book.

Microsoft Internet Information Server

When you are ready to launch your Web site on the Internet, you'll need to use Microsoft Internet Information Server. Unlike the Personal Web Server, Internet Information Server can support hundreds or even thousands of simultaneous users.

Some of the largest Web sites on the Internet use Internet Information Server. Not surprisingly, Microsoft uses Internet Information Server for its own Web site at `http://www.microsoft.com`. The Microsoft site is the fourth busiest site on the Internet. (It receives about 5 million visitors a day.)

The Internet Information Server isn't compatible with Windows 95 or Windows 98. You'll need to use it with Windows NT Server or Windows 2000 Server. It's included as part of both operating systems.

Note

If your plans for your Web site are very ambitious, you can use Internet Information Server with Windows 2000 Advanced Server. Windows 2000 Advanced Server includes support for server clustering, which enables you to distribute your Web site over many machines.

Microsoft Access

To create a commercial Web site, you'll need to use a database to store product and order information. Unless noted otherwise, the lessons in this book assume that you will be using Microsoft Access as your database. Microsoft Access is part of the Microsoft Office family of products and can be purchased from almost any software store.

Microsoft Access is a desktop database and not a client/server database like SQL Server (discussed in the next section). Because Microsoft Access is a desktop database, you should use it only for prototyping your Web site or for creating a low traffic Web site. In general, a Microsoft Access database cannot support more than about 30 concurrent users.

After you create your Web site with Microsoft Access, you can upgrade to Microsoft SQL Server. (Microsoft refers to this process as "upsizing.") Microsoft has a tool, named the Upsizing Tools, which enables you to convert a Microsoft Access database to a Microsoft SQL Server database. (It converts tables and common queries.)

If you are using Microsoft Access 97, you can download the Upsizing Tools from `http://www.microsoft.com/accessdev/prodinfo/aut97dat.htm`. When using Microsoft Access 2000, there is no need to download anything. The Upsizing Tools are included with Microsoft Access 2000.

Microsoft SQL Server

Unlike Microsoft Access, Microsoft SQL Server 7.0 can scale to support thousands of concurrent users and terabyte sized databases. For all intents and purposes, SQL Server can enable you to support an online store of any size. Some of the largest commercial Web sites on the Internet are using SQL Server including Dell, Buy.com, Barnes and Noble, and 1-800-flowers.com.

There are three versions of SQL Server 7.0: SQL Server Desktop, SQL Server Standard Edition, and SQL Server Enterprise Edition. SQL Server Desktop will work with Windows 95, Windows 98, and Windows NT Workstation. SQL Server Standard Edition was designed to work with Windows NT Server or Windows 2000 Server. Finally, the Enterprise Edition is an enhanced version of the standard edition that supports more memory, more processors, clustering, and Online Analytical Processing (OLAP) services.

Unless you need to create an extremely high volume commercial Web site, you should use the standard edition of Microsoft SQL Server with the Windows NT Server operating system. You can download or order an evaluation version of SQL Server from Microsoft by visiting the following Internet address (the evaluation edition automatically stops functioning after 120 days):

```
http://www.microsoft.com/sql/productinfo/evalcd.htm
```

To use Microsoft SQL Server on the Web, you will need to buy the correct licenses. Microsoft requires you to buy the Internet Connector license if any person from the Internet accesses SQL Server. You must buy an additional license for each processor on each server that is running SQL Server.

I strongly recommend that you upgrade to SQL Server before publicly launching your Web site on the Internet. The current version isn't much more difficult to use than Microsoft Access. And, SQL Server is both more dependable and scalable than Microsoft Access.

Microsoft Visual InterDev

Microsoft Visual InterDev is a development environment for building Web sites. At its most basic level, it's a very fancy text editor that allows you to create and modify Web pages on a remote or local server. You can use Visual InterDev to write both Active Server Pages and normal HTML pages.

Visual InterDev is tightly integrated with Microsoft SQL Server. You can use Visual InterDev to design and modify database tables and create stored procedures. Visual InterDev works with any ODBC or OLE DB compliant database.

You don't need Visual InterDev to create an ASP page. You can create Active Server Pages using any standard text editor. Notepad, the text editor included with all versions of the Windows operating system, works perfectly well. However, Visual InterDev makes it much easier to manage the pages of a large Web site. Visual InterDev also includes several debugging tools.

Note   Microsoft has another product for creating Web sites: Microsoft FrontPage. I wouldn't recommend using Microsoft FrontPage to create Web sites that contain Active Server Pages. Microsoft FrontPage has a tendency to modify the source code of a page without asking. This means that it can often garble an ASP script that you have just spent hours writing.

What Is an ASP Page?

The lessons in the days that follow describe how to create commercial Web sites using Active Server Pages. But, you might ask, what exactly is an ASP page?

An ASP page is any file located on your Web server that has the extension .ASP. This special extension distinguishes an ASP page from a normal HTML file that ends with the extension .HTML or .HTM.

When a user visits a Web site and requests a normal HTML file, the Web server simply retrieves the file from the computer's hard drive or memory and sends the file to the user's browser. The browser interprets the HTML content of the file and the visitor sees the Web page.

When someone requests a normal HTML page, the Web server doesn't care about the content of the file. The Web server's role is to simply retrieve the appropriate file without processing it. All the work of interpreting the content of the file is performed by the user's Web browser.

On the other hand, when someone requests an ASP page, the Web server takes a more active role. Before the file is sent to the user's Web browser, it is first processed by the Web server. The Web server interprets and executes any scripts in an ASP page before sending it to the user's browser.

For example, the file in Listing 1.1 contains a very simple ASP page named showtime.asp. This page displays the current time.

LISTING 1.1   Display Current Time

```
1 <HTML>
2 <HEAD><TITLE>Show Time</TITLE></HEAD>
3 <BODY>
4 At the tone, the time will be: <%=TIME()%>
5 </BODY>
6 </HTML>
```

If someone requests the showtime.asp file from a Web server, the Web server will recognize the file as an ASP page because the name of the file ends with the extension .ASP. Before sending the file to the user's browser, the Web server will first process any scripts in the file. In the case of the showtime.asp file, the text <%=TIME()%> in line 4 is replaced with the current time.

The actual file sent to the Web browser is included in Listing 1.2. Notice that this file is a normal HTML file. All the scripts are processed on the Web server before the file is sent to the browser. Because an ASP page is processed on the server rather than the browser, an ASP page is compatible with all Web browsers.

LISTING 1.2   Content After Processing

```
1 <HTML>
2 <HEAD><TITLE>Show Time</TITLE></HEAD>
3 <BODY>
4 At the tone, the time will be: 4:55:36 AM
5 </BODY>
6 </HTML>
```

Active Server Pages Contain Scripts

Active Server Pages include server-side scripts. In the lessons in this book, we will be using Microsoft Visual Basic Scripting Edition (VBScript) as the scripting language. However, an ASP page can contain scripts written in other scripting languages such as Microsoft JScript (Microsoft's brand of JavaScript) or PerlScript.

Note | Microsoft bundles JScript with Active Server Pages. PerlScript isn't produced by Microsoft. To use PerlScript, you must first download it from http://www.activestate.com.

Scripting languages, such as VBScript, differ from full-fledged programming languages, such as Visual Basic and Java, in the simplicity of their rules and syntax. For example, VBScript doesn't require you to declare variables with particular data types.

Furthermore, unlike Visual Basic or Java, you don't need to compile an ASP page into a separate file before you can execute it. When you change an ASP page, the page is automatically recompiled the next time it is requested.

The advantage of using a scripting language to build Web pages is that it makes it easy to modify a Web site even after it has been launched. If you discover a bug on your Web site, you can quickly load the offending page into Notepad and fix the problem.

You shouldn't conclude that because an ASP page uses a scripting language that Active Server Pages are slow or don't scale well. ASP scripts run in the same process as the Web server, and they are multithreaded. This allows an ASP page to efficiently support large numbers of concurrent users.

Active Server Pages Contain Objects and Components

An ASP page would be severely limited if it could only contain scripts. You could display the current time and output interesting messages, but you would have no way of retrieving information from users, storing data in a database, or creating files on the server. Fortunately, an ASP page can contain server-side components.

A component is something that typically has methods, properties, and collections. A component's methods determine the actions you can take with the object. A component's properties can be read or set to specify the state of the component. A component's collections are sets of key and value pairs related to the component.

This book, *Sams Teach Yourself E-Commerce Programming with ASP in 21 Days*, is an example of a component. The component has certain methods that determine what you can do with it. For example, you can read the book, use it as a doorstop, or (please don't do this!) tear it into shreds. The book has certain properties. It weighs a certain amount and has a certain number of pages. Finally, it has a collection of key and value pairs. Each page number (the key) has a corresponding page of text (the value).

Active Server Pages includes two types of components: the built-in objects and the installable components.

Here is a brief description of the six built-in Active Server Pages objects:

- Application Object—The Application object represents information that can be shared among all users of an Active Server Pages Application.
- ObjectContext Object—The ObjectContext object is used with transactional Active Server Pages.
- Request Object—The Request object represents all information sent from a browser to a server including form variables and query strings.
- Response Object—The Response object represents all information sent from a server to a browser including HTML content sent by an ASP page.
- Server Object—The Server object enables the use of various utility functions on the server.
- Session Object—The Session object represents information about a particular user session.

Note

The new version of Active Server Pages included with Windows 2000 includes an additional built-in object named the ASPError object. The ASPError object represents information about an error that has occurred in an ASP page.

For example, Listing 1.3 demonstrates how you can use the `Response` object to output the text `"Hello World!"` to the browser.

LISTING 1.3   Hello World!

```
1 <HTML>
2 <HEAD><TITLE>Hello World!</TITLE></HEAD>
3 <BODY>
4 <%
5 Response.Write "Hello World!"
6 %>
7 </BODY>
8 </HTML>
```

In addition to the built-in objects, several installable components are bundled with Active Server Pages. Here is a list of some of the more useful of these components:

- Ad Rotator Component—The Ad Rotator component is used to display banner advertisements on the Web pages of a Web site. You can use this component to specify how frequently different banner advertisements should be displayed.
- Browser Capabilities Component—The Browser Capabilities component can be used to display different HTML content, according to the capabilities of different browsers. For example, you can use this component to display Web pages with frames only to frames-compliant browsers.
- Content Linking Component—The Content Linking component can be used to link together several HTML pages so that they can be navigated easily. For example, you can use this component to link together the pages of an online book.
- File Access Component—The File Access component allows you to work with your computer's file system. You can use this component to read and write text files.

Unlike the built-in Active Server Pages objects, you must create an instance of an installable component before you can use it in an ASP page. The ASP page in Listing 1.4 creates an instance of the Ad Rotator component and displays a banner advertisement.

LISTING 1.4   Using the Ad Rotator Component

```
1 <HTML>
2 <HEAD><TITLE>Ad Rotator Component</TITLE></HEAD>
3 <BODY>
4 <%
5 Set MyAd = Server.CreateObject( "MSWC.AdRotator" )
6 %>
7 <CENTER><%=MyAd.GetAdvertisement( "adrot.txt" )%></CENTER>
8 </BODY>
9 </HTML>
```

1

> **Note**
>
> What's the difference between a component and an object? An object is one instance of a component. The Active Server Pages built-in objects are called objects rather than components because they have already been implicitly created.

You aren't limited to using only the components bundled with Active Server Pages. There are hundreds of components created by third-party companies that you can include in your scripts. You can use these components to accept file uploads, transfer files between servers, or send and receive email. You can also create your own components by using a language such as Visual Basic, C++, or Java.

> **Note**
>
> To see an extensive list of third-party components, visit the software section of asp superexpert at http://asp.superexpert.com/software.

Active Server Pages and Database Access

A special set of objects are included with Active Server Pages that deserve to be discussed in a section of their own: the ActiveX Data Objects. The ActiveX Data Objects enable you to access a database from an ASP page.

You can use the ActiveX Data Objects to insert, update, and delete rows in a database table. You can also use these objects to retrieve a set of records from a database query, and represent these records in an ASP page.

In the lessons in this book, you will learn how to use the ActiveX Data Objects to store and retrieve data from both a Microsoft Access Database and a Microsoft SQL Server Database. However, the ActiveX Data Objects can be used with any Open Database Connectivity (ODBC) or any OLE DB compliant database. This includes Oracle, Sybase, Informix, DB2, and Ingres databases.

Summary

In today's lesson, you were introduced to the two main subjects of this book: E-Commerce and Active Server Pages. In the first section, you learned about the phenomenal growth of E-Commerce. Each of the different forms of E-Commerce was briefly discussed.

In the second section, you were introduced to the Microsoft Technologies for creating commercial Web sites. You learned about the Microsoft Personal Web Server and Internet Information Server. You also learned about Microsoft Access and Microsoft SQL Server.

The final section focused on Active Server Pages. You learned how an ASP page differs from a normal HTML file. You learned how Active Server Pages use scripts, objects, components, and the ActiveX Data Objects for database access.

Q&A

Q What are the limitations of Active Server Pages? Can I use Active Server Pages to develop any type of commercial Web site?

A As you discovered in today's lesson, Active Server Pages has already been used to develop some of the largest and most successful commercial Web sites on the Internet. For example, Dell currently sells over $18 million worth of products online a day. The Dell Web site was created with Internet Information Server and Active Server Pages.

Active Server Pages is an extremely flexible technology. If it lacks any functionality, an ASP script can always be extended with custom components.

Q Which operating systems are compatible with Active Server Pages?

A Active Server Pages runs natively on Microsoft Windows NT Server 4.0, Microsoft Windows NT Workstation 4.0 with Peer Web Services, and Windows 95/98 with the Personal Web Server.

Using Chili!Soft's Chili!ASP (see `http://www.chilisoft.com`), you also can use Active Server Pages with SUN Solaris and IBM AIX. Chili!ASP enables Active Server Pages to run on Apache servers, Netscape Enterprise and FastTrack servers, the Lotus Domino Go Webserver, and O'Reilly Website Pro.

Microsoft created a version of the Personal Web Server and Active Server Pages for the Macintosh. Sadly, however, they no longer support it.

Workshop

The Quiz questions are designed to test your knowledge of the material covered in this chapter. The answers are in Appendix A, "Quiz Answers."

Quiz

1. What are the three types of E-Commerce?

2. Can Microsoft Personal Web Server be used to create a commercial Web site that supports thousands of visitors a day?

3. Can Microsoft Access be used in a commercial Web site that supports thousands of visitors a day? *NO*

4. Do you need Visual InterDev to create Active Server Pages? *Yes - No*

5. How does a Web server distinguish an ASP page from a normal HTML page?

6. Are Active Server Pages compatible with all Web browsers? *yes*

7. Can you create Active Server Page scripts using any other language than VBScript? *yes*

1

DAY **2**

Interacting with the Customer

In today's lesson, you'll begin learning how to create an E-Commerce Web site using Active Server Pages. Today's lesson introduces you to two of the most important Active Server Page objects: the Response and the Request objects. You can use these objects to interact with the customers who visit your Web site.

Today, you will learn

- How to use the Response object to send content to a Web browser
- How to use the Request object to work with HTML query strings
- How to use the Request object to retrieve information that customers enter into HTML forms
- How to use the Request object to retrieve browser headers and server variables

Working with the Response Object

In yesterday's lesson, you were introduced to Active Server Pages. You learned that an ASP page is a normal HTML page that contains scripts. You can use these scripts to send dynamic content to the browser.

What is dynamic content? A normal HTML page contains static content. Every time an HTML page is requested, the content displayed by the page remains the same. An ASP page, on the other hand, can contain content that changes whenever the page is requested.

When operating a commercial Web site, there are many situations in which you'll need to send dynamic content to a customer. For example, if you enable customers to browse the products in your store by category, then you'll need to dynamically generate the list of products for the appropriate category. After a customer places an order, you'll need to dynamically generate a receipt with the customer's order information.

You can send dynamic content from an ASP page by using the Response object, a built-in ASP object. It represents all the information sent from the Web server to a Web browser.

For example, the ASP page in Listing 2.1 displays the current date and time. Each time a customer requests the ASP page in Listing 2.1, a different date and time is displayed.

INPUT   **LISTING 2.1**   Displaying Dynamic Content

```
1 <HTML>
2 <HEAD><TITLE>Date and Time</TITLE></HEAD>
3 <BODY>
4 <%
5 Response.Write NOW()
6 %>
7 </BODY>
8 </HTML>
```

ANALYSIS   You will notice that the majority of the ASP page in Listing 2.1 consists of a normal HTML page. The dynamic content is generated in the body of the HTML page.

Lines 4–6 contain a very simple ASP script. The beginning and end of the script are marked with the script delimiters <% and %>.

In line 5, the Write method of the Response object is used to output the current date and time, which is displayed by using the VBScript NOW() function.

Typically, you use the Write method of the Response object to output the value of a function, the value of a variable, or a string literal. For example, the ASP page in Listing 2.2 displays the text "Welcome to our store!" with the Response object.

LISTING 2.2   Welcome to Our Store

```
1 <HTML>
2 <HEAD><TITLE>Welcome</TITLE></HEAD>
3 <BODY>
4 <%
5 Response.Write "Welcome to our store!"
6 %>
7 </BODY>
8 </HTML>
```

2

Outputting Long Strings

If you need to use the Response object to output really long strings, you can break the string into multiple lines by using the underscore character. For example, the ASP page in Listing 2.3 displays the first paragraph of the Declaration of Independence.

LISTING 2.3   Outputting a Long String

```
1 <HTML>
2 <HEAD><TITLE>Long String</TITLE></HEAD>
3 <BODY>
4 <%
5 Response.Write "When in the Course of human events, " &_
6    "it becomes necessary for one people to " &_
7    "dissolve the political bands which have " &_
8    "connected them with another, and to assume " &_
9    "among the powers of the earth, the separate " &_
10   "and equal station to which the Laws of " &_
11   "Nature and of Nature's God entitle them, " &_
12   "a decent respect to the opinions of " &_
13   "mankind requires that they should declare " &_
14   "the causes which impel them to the separation. "
15 %>
16 </BODY>
17 </HTML>
```

In the ASP script contained in lines 4–15, the Write method is used to display a single string that spans multiple lines. The character combination & is used to indicate that the string is continued on the next line.

Displaying Special Characters

Certain characters will not be displayed correctly when outputted with the Write method of the Response object. These characters include the greater than sign, >; the less than sign, <; and quotation marks.

The problem results from the fact that these characters have a special meaning in HTML. For example, the < and > characters are used to mark the beginning and end of an HTML tag. When a browser comes across these characters in a page, it attempts to interpret them as part of an HTML tag.

To get around this problem, you need to encode the characters before you display them. Fortunately, this is very easy to do with Active Server Pages. You can use the HTMLEncode() method of the Server object to HTML-encode the string before it is displayed.

For example, the ASP page in Listing 2.4 correctly encodes the string "We sell the <<BEST!>> products!" before the string is displayed.

INPUT   **LISTING 2.4**   HTML-Encoding a String

```
1 <HTML>
2 <HEAD><TITLE>Long String</TITLE></HEAD>
3 <BODY>
4 <%
5 Response.Write Server.HTMLEncode( "We sell the <<BEST!>> products!" )
6 %>
7 </BODY>
8 </HTML>
```

You'll discover that you'll need to HTML-encode strings quite often when working with HTML forms. Later in today's lesson, you will learn how to use the HTMLEncode() method with an HTML form (see the section titled "Using the Form Collection").

Displaying Quotation Marks

The VBScript language uses quotation marks to mark the beginning and end of a string. If the string itself contains quotation marks, then problems occur. VBScript will misinterpret a quotation mark contained in a string as marking the end of a string.

For example, the ASP page in Listing 2.5 will generate an error.

INPUT   **LISTING 2.5**   Bad Use of Quotation Marks

```
1 <HTML>
2 <HEAD><TITLE>Bad Quotes</TITLE></HEAD>
3 <BODY>
4 <%
5 Response.Write "He said, "This doesn't work!" "
6 %>
7 </BODY>
8 </HTML>
```

ANALYSIS The ASP page in Listing 2.5 will generate an error because of the quotation marks included in the string on line 5. VBScript will assume that the second quotation mark indicates the end of the string.

There are two ways around this problem with outputting quotation marks. First, you can write two quotation marks in a row. VBScript will interpret two consecutive quotation marks in a string as a single quotation mark. The ASP page in Listing 2.6 demonstrates how to use this method:

INPUT **LISTING 2.6** Good Use of Quotation Marks

```
1 <HTML>
2 <HEAD><TITLE>Good Quotes</TITLE></HEAD>
3 <BODY>
4 <%
5 Response.Write "He said, ""This does work!"" "
6 %>
7 </BODY>
8 </HTML>
```

ANALYSIS Line 5 passes the string `"He said, ""This does work!"" "` to the `Write` method of the Response object. When this string is outputted to the browser, the correct number of quotation marks is displayed:

```
He said, "This does work!"
```

There is a second method of including quotation marks in a VBScript string. You can represent a quotation mark by using the VBScript `CHR()` function. Listing 2.7 uses this method to display quotation marks.

INPUT **LISTING 2.7** Another Good Use of Quotation Marks

```
1 <HTML>
2 <HEAD><TITLE>Good Quotes</TITLE></HEAD>
3 <BODY>
4 <%
5 Response.Write "He said, " & CHR( 34 ) & "This does work!" & CHR( 34 )
6 %>
7 </BODY>
8 </HTML>
```

Both methods of displaying quotation marks work perfectly well. The method you choose is completely a matter of personal preference.

Using the <%= and %> Output Delimiters

Instead of using the Write method of the Response object to send content to the browser, you can use the <%= and %> output delimiters. For example, the ASP page in Listing 2.8 uses the output delimiters instead of the Write method to display the current time.

INPUT   **LISTING 2.8**   Using the Output Delimiters

```
1 <HTML>
2 <HEAD><TITLE>Output Delimiters</TITLE></HEAD>
3 <BODY>
4 <%=TIME()%>
5 </BODY>
6 </HTML>
```

ANALYSIS   The current time is displayed in line 4. Line 4 uses <%= and %> to output the value of the VBScript TIME() function to the browser.

It is important not to confuse the <%= and %> output delimiters with the <% and %> script delimiters. The <%= and %> output delimiters are used to display content to the browser. On the other hand, the <% and %> script delimiters are used to mark the beginning and end of a script.

When should you use the <%= and %> output delimiters and when should you use the Write method of the Response object? You can use these two methods of outputting content interchangeably. However, it is often more convenient to use the <%= and %> output delimiters when displaying the values of multiple variables or functions within an ASP page.

For example, although you can write the ASP page in Listing 2.9 using the Write method, the code is easier to read when the <%= and %> output delimiters are used.

INPUT   **LISTING 2.9**   Displaying Multiple Values

```
1 <HTML>
2 <HEAD><TITLE>Output Delimiters</TITLE></HEAD>
3 <BODY>
4 <br>The current date is: <%=DATE()%>
5 <br>The current time is: <%=TIME()%>
6 </BODY>
7 </HTML>
```

Ending Script Execution with the Response Object

Up to this point, you have learned how to use a single method of the Response object. You've learned how to use the Write method to send output to a customer's Web browser. In this section, you'll learn about a second useful method of the Response object: the End method. You can use the End method to stop the execution of a script.

For example, the script in Listing 2.10 displays two messages. However, the second message is never seen because the End method of the Response object is called before the second message is displayed.

INPUT   **LISTING 2.10**   Ending Script Execution

```
1   <HTML>
2   <HEAD><TITLE>Output Delimiters</TITLE></HEAD>
3   <BODY>
4   <%
5   Response.Write "I am the first message!"
6   Response.End
7   Response.Write "I am the second message!"
9   %>
10  </BODY>
11  </HTML>
```

ANALYSIS   The first message is displayed in line 5. On line 6, the End method of the Response object is called. When this method is called, processing of the page comes to an immediate stop. Only the content produced in lines 1–5 is sent to the browser.

Working with the Request Object

Whereas the Response object represents all content sent from the Web server to a Web browser, the Request object represents all content sent from a Web browser to the Web server. Whenever you need to retrieve information from a customer, you'll need to use the Request object.

The Request object has four very useful collections:

- QueryString collection—Represents query string variables
- Form collection—Represents HTML form fields
- ServerVariables collection—Represents browser headers and server variables
- Cookies collection—Represents browser cookies

In the following sections, you will learn how to use the first three of these collections. In Day 3, "Using Application and Session Objects in E-Commerce Applications," you'll learn how to use the Cookies collection.

Using Query Strings

A *query string* is the portion of the URL that appears after a question mark. For example, the following URL contains a query string:

```
http://search.yahoo.com/bin/search?p=Active+Server+Pages
```

In this example, the query string contains a variable named p that has the value "Active Server Pages". If you entered this string into the address bar of your Web browser, all the listings from Yahoo! related to Active Server Pages would be returned.

Query strings are used to pass information to the server from a browser. Typically, you do not enter a query string directly into the address bar of a browser. Instead, you create a link in a page that contains the query string.

You can use query strings to enable customers to make choices. For example, using query strings, you can enable customers to click on different product categories at your store to view different types of products. The ASP page in Listing 2.11 enables customers to choose between two product categories: red delicious apples and McIntosh apples.

INPUT   **LISTING 2.11**   Choosing Apples

```
1 <HTML>
2 <HEAD><TITLE>Apples</TITLE></HEAD>
3 <BODY>
4 Please choose a type of apple:
5 <p><a href="page2.asp?apple=red">Red Delicious</a>
5 <p><a href="page2.asp?apple=mcintosh">McIntosh</a>
6 </BODY>
7 </HTML>
```

ANALYSIS   The ASP page in Listing 2.11 contains two hypertext links to a page named page2.asp. The first link passes a query string named apple that has the value red. The second query string, also named apple, has the value mcintosh. By clicking on one or another of the two links, the customer can choose the type of apples to view.

Within page2.asp, you can determine which link the customer clicked by accessing the QueryString collection of the Request object. Listing 2.12 contains the page2.asp page.

INPUT   **LISTING 2.12**   Retrieving a Query String

```
1 <HTML>
2 <HEAD><TITLE>Page 2</TITLE></HEAD>
3 <BODY>
4 <%
```

```
5 apple = Request.QueryString( "apple" )
6 Response.Write "You have selected " & apple & " apples"
7 %>
8 </BODY>
9 </HTML>
```

ANALYSIS In line 5, the QueryString collection of the Request object is used to retrieve the query string variable named apple. The query string variable is assigned to a local VBScript variable named apple. Next, in line 6, the value of the apple variable is displayed.

Passing Multiple Query String Variables

You can pass multiple query string variables in a single query string. To pass multiple variables, you separate each variable with the & character. For example, the ASP page in Listing 2.13 passes two query string variables named fruit and type.

INPUT   **LISTING 2.13**   Passing Multiple Query String Variables

```
1 <HTML>
2 <HEAD><TITLE>Fruit</TITLE></HEAD>
3 <BODY>
4 Please choose a type of fruit:
5 <p><a href="page2.asp?fruit=orange&type=mandarin">Mandarin Orange</a>
6 <p><a href="page2.asp?fruit=apple&type=red">Red Delicious Apple</a>
7 <p><a href="page2.asp?fruit=apple&type=mcintosh">McIntosh Apple</a>
8 </BODY>
9 </HTML>
```

ANALYSIS The hypertext links in Listing 2.13 contain query strings that include two variables. Each query string contains both a variable named fruit and a variable named type. When any of the three hypertext links are clicked, both query string variables are passed to the page2.asp page.

When multiple query string variables are passed to a page, you can retrieve any of the variables by name from the QueryString collection. The Active Server Page in Listing 2.14 retrieves both the fruit and the type query string variables.

INPUT   **LISTING 2.14**   Retrieving Multiple Query String Variables

```
1 <HTML>
2 <HEAD><TITLE>Get Fruit</TITLE></HEAD>
3 <BODY>
4 You selected:
5 <p>Fruit: <%=Request.QueryString( "fruit" )%>
```

continues

LISTING 2.14   continued

```
6 <p>Type: <%=Request.QueryString( "type" )%>
7 </BODY>
8 </HTML>
```

ANALYSIS   Line 5 uses the <%= and %> output delimiters to display the value of the query string variable named `fruit`. Line 6 displays the value of the query string variable named `type`.

Passing Special Characters in Query Strings

You cannot include spaces or other special characters in the name or value of a query string variable. For example, suppose that you wanted to pass the string `"red delicious apples"` in a query string variable. You might be tempted to do this by using the ASP page contained in Listing 2.15.

INPUT   **LISTING 2.15**   Passing a Query String with Spaces

```
1 <HTML>
2 <HEAD><TITLE>Get Fruit</TITLE></HEAD>
3 <BODY>
4 <a href="page2.asp?fruit=red delicious apples">Apples</a>
5 </BODY>
6 </HTML>
```

Line 4 contains a hypertext link with a query string variable named `fruit`. If you click on this link, however, the value of the query string will not be correctly passed to the `page2.asp`. The value of the query string will be truncated at the first space.

Before you can pass a query string that contains spaces or special characters, you must first URL-encode the query string. When a string is URL-encoded, any problematic characters are replaced. For example, spaces are replaced with + signs.

You can URL-encode a query string by using the `URLEncode()` method of the Server object. The Active Server Page in Listing 2.16 correctly passes the string `"red delicious apples"` by URL-encoding the string before it is passed.

INPUT   **LISTING 2.16**   URL-Encoding a Query String

```
1  <HTML>
2  <HEAD><TITLE>Get Fruit</TITLE></HEAD>
3  <BODY>
4  <%
5  theValue = "red delicious apples"
6  theValue = Server.URLEncode( theValue )
7  %>
```

```
8   <a href="page2.asp?fruit=<%=theValue%>">Apples</a>
9   </BODY>
10  </HTML>
```

ANALYSIS In Listing 2.16, the string `"red delicious apples"` is URL-encoded before it is added to the query string. In line 5, the string `"red delicious apples"` is assigned to a variable named `theValue`. Next, in line 6, the value of the variable is URL-encoded with the `URLEncode()` method of the Server object. In line 8, the variable is added to the query string.

Using the Form Collection

To enable a customer to register at your Web site, complete a marketing form, or enter a credit card number, you must use an HTML form. To retrieve the information a customer enters into an HTML form, you use the Form collection of the Request object.

For example, the page in Listing 2.17 contains a simple HTML form that asks the customer to enter his first name.

INPUT **LISTING 2.17**   Simple HTML Form

```
1   <HTML>
2   <HEAD><TITLE>Get Fruit</TITLE></HEAD>
3   <BODY>
4   Please enter your first name:
5   <FORM method="post" action="page2.asp">
6   <INPUT name="firstname" type="text">
7   <INPUT type="submit" value="OK">
8   </FORM>
9   </BODY>
10  </HTML>
```

ANALYSIS Listing 2.17 contains a simple HTML form with one field named `"firstname"`. Line 6 displays the single form field. Line 7 displays a submit button labeled `"OK"`.

When a customer enters his first name and clicks the button labeled OK, the form data is submitted to a page named `page2.asp`. Within the page, you can retrieve the value of the `firstname` form field by using the Form collection of the Request object. Listing 2.18 demonstrates how to use this collection.

INPUT **LISTING 2.18**   Retrieving a Form Field

```
1   <HTML>
2   <HEAD><TITLE>Get Fruit</TITLE></HEAD>
```

continues

LISTING 2.18   continued

```
3  <BODY>
4  <%
5  firstname = Request.Form( "firstname" )
6  %>
7   Hi <%=firstname%>!,
8   Welcome to our store!
9  </BODY>
10 </HTML>
```

ANALYSIS   In line 5, the HTML form field `"firstname"` is retrieved from the Form collection of the Request object. The value of the form field is assigned to a local
VBScript variable named `firstname`. In line 7, the `firstname` variable is used to personalize the output of the ASP page.

You can use the Form collection of the Request object to retrieve the value of most types
of HTML form element. You can use the Form collection to retrieve the value of a text
field, text area, check box, radio button, pick list, or password field.

 Note

> You cannot use the Form collection to retrieve a file uploaded within an
> HTML form using the `<INPUT TYPE="FILE">` tag. To accept file uploads, you
> must use the `BinaryRead()` method of the Request object or buy a third-
> party component. To see a list of file upload components, visit `http://`
> `asp.superexpert.com/software`.

For example, the page in Listing 2.19 contains an HTML form with four radio buttons.
Customers can provide feedback on your store by selecting one of the radio buttons.

INPUT   LISTING 2.19   Rate Our Store

```
1  <HTML>
2  <HEAD><TITLE>Rate Our Store</TITLE></HEAD>
3  <BODY>
4  Please rate our store:
5  <FORM METHOD="POST" ACTION="page2.asp">
6  <br><INPUT NAME="rating" TYPE="RADIO" VALUE="1" CHECKED>
7  Great!
8  <br><INPUT NAME="rating" TYPE="RADIO" VALUE="2">
9  Not Bad!
10 <br><INPUT NAME="rating" TYPE="RADIO" VALUE="3">
11 Mediocre
12 <br><INPUT NAME="rating" TYPE="RADIO" VALUE="4">
13 Needs Improvement!
14 <br><INPUT TYPE="SUBMIT" VALUE="OK">
```

```
15 </FORM>
16 </BODY>
17 </HTML>
```

The HTML form in Listing 2.19 submits the form data to a page named page2.asp. Within page2.asp, you can determine which radio button was selected by a customer by using the Form collection. Listing 2.20 demonstrates how you can retrieve the value of a radio button.

INPUT   **LISTING 2.20**   Retrieving the Value of a Radio Button

```
1  <HTML>
2  <HEAD><TITLE>Get Rating</TITLE></HEAD>
3  <BODY>
4  Thanks for rating our store!
5  <p>
6  <%
7  rating = Request.Form( "rating" )
8  rating = cINT( rating )
9  IF rating < 3 THEN
10   Response.Write "Glad you like us!"
11 ELSE
12   Response.Write "We'll try harder!"
13 END IF
14 %>
15 </BODY>
16 </HTML>
```

ANALYSIS   The ASP page in Listing 2.20 retrieves the value of the radio button the customer selected. In line 7, the value of the selected radio button is grabbed from the Form collection. Next, in line 8, the value is converted to an integer value.

Lines 9–13 conditionally display one of two messages. If the customer gives your store a good rating, then the message "Glad you like us!" is displayed. Otherwise, the message "We'll try harder!" is displayed.

Checking for Empty Form Fields

Whenever you have an HTML form, you need to check whether the customer has actually entered data into all the required form fields. For example, if you have asked the customer to enter a credit card number, you need to check whether the data was actually entered.

You can check whether a form field contains data by comparing the value of the form field to a zero length string. The page in Listing 2.21 contains an HTML form with fields for the customer's name, customer's credit card number, and credit card expiration date.

INPUT **LISTING 2.21**   Credit Card Form

```
1  <HTML>
2  <HEAD><TITLE>Credit Card Form</TITLE></HEAD>
3  <BODY>
4  <b>Please enter the following information:</b>
5  <FORM METHOD="POST" ACTION="page2.asp">
6  <p>Your Name:
7  <br><INPUT name="customer" SIZE="30">
8  <p>Your Credit Card Number:
9  <br><INPUT name="ccnumber" size="15">
10  <p>Credit Card Expiration Date:
11 <br><INPUT name="ccexpires" size="15">
12 <p><INPUT type="submit" value="OK">
13 </FORM>
14 </BODY>
15 </HTML>
```

If the customer neglects to enter her name, her credit card number, or her credit card expiration date, then you will lose an order. The ASP page in Listing 2.22 demonstrates how you can check for empty form fields.

INPUT **LISTING 2.22**   Checking for Empty Form Fields

```
1  <%
2  SUB errorForm( theError )
3  %>
4    <HTML>
5    <HEAD><TITLE>Error</TITLE></HEAD>
6    <BODY>
7    <%=theError %>
8    <FORM method="post" action="page1.asp">
9    <p><INPUT TYPE="submit" value="Return">
10   </FORM>
11   </BODY>
12   </HTML>
13 <%
14 Response.End
15 END SUB
16 ' Retrieve Form Fields
17 customer = TRIM( Request.Form( "customer" ) )
18 ccnumber = TRIM( Request.Form( "ccnumber" ) )
19 ccexpires = TRIM( Request.Form( "ccexpires" ) )
20 ' Check For Required Fields
21 IF customer = "" THEN
22   errorForm "You did not enter your name!"
23 END IF
24 IF ccnumber = "" THEN
25   errorForm "You did not enter a credit card number!"
```

```
26 END IF
27 IF ccexpires = "" THEN
28   errorForm "You did not enter an expiration date!"
29 END IF
30 %>
31 <HTML>
32 <HEAD><TITLE>Thank You</TITLE></HEAD>
33 <BODY>
34 Thank you for entering your credit card information!
35 </BODY>
36 </HTML>
```

ANALYSIS The ASP page in Listing 2.22 displays an error message if the customer does not enter data in all the required form fields. In lines 17–19, all the form fields are retrieved from the Form collection and assigned to local variables.

Notice that the VBScript TRIM() function is used when retrieving each of the form fields. The TRIM() function removes any leading or trailing spaces from a string. (Browsers have a tendency to add an extra space to each form field when it is submitted.)

Next, in lines 16–29, each variable is compared to a zero length string. If a variable does not have any content, a subroutine named errorForm is called. An error message is passed to the subroutine.

Contained in lines 2–15, the errorForm subroutine displays an HTML page that shows the error message passed to it. It also contains a form that displays a button which links back to page1.asp (the page in Listing 2.22).

Notice that the End method of the Response object is called in the last line of the errorForm subroutine (line 14). This stops the execution of the rest of the script and displays only the error message.

If the errorForm subroutine is not called, the HTML page contained in lines 31–36 is displayed. This page will be displayed only if the customer has entered information for all the required form fields. The page simply thanks the customer for entering all the form information.

Redisplaying Form Fields

There is nothing more irritating than completing a long form at a Web site only to receive an error message that forces you to enter all the form data again. When a customer fails to complete a required field, you should redisplay all the information that a customer has already entered. To do this, you will need to pass back all the data to the original form.

For example, in the previous section you created an HTML form that contains three form fields: the customer name, the customer credit card number, and the credit card expiration date. If a customer enters his credit card number and credit card expiration date, but fails to enter his name, an error message will be displayed with a button that links back to the original form. When the customer returns to the original form, the customer's credit card number and credit card expiration date will be lost.

To fix this problem, you need to modify both of the pages discussed in the previous section. First, you need to modify the errorForm subroutine so that it passes back all the information that the customer has entered into the form fields (see Listing 2.23).

INPUT   **LISTING 2.23**   Passing Back Form Fields   *Page2-asp*

```
1  <%
2  SUB errorForm( theError )
3  %>
4    <HTML>
5    <HEAD><TITLE>Error</TITLE></HEAD>
6    <BODY>
7    <%=theError %>
8    <FORM method="post" action="page1.asp">
9    <% FOR EACH item IN Request.Form %>
10    <INPUT name="<%=item%>" type="hidden"
11    value="<%=Server.HTMLEncode( Request.Form( item ) )%>">
12    <% NEXT %>
13    <p><INPUT TYPE="submit" value="Return">
14    </FORM>
15    </BODY>
16    </HTML>
17 <%
18 Response.End
19 END SUB
20 ' Retrieve Form Fields
21 customer = TRIM( Request.Form( "customer" ) )
22 ccnumber = TRIM( Request.Form( "ccnumber" ) )
23 ccexpires = TRIM( Request.Form( "ccexpires" ) )
24 ' Check For Required Fields
25 IF customer = "" THEN
26    errorForm "You did not enter your name!"
27 END IF
28 IF ccnumber = "" THEN
29    errorForm "You did not enter a credit card number!"
30 END IF
31 IF ccexpires = "" THEN
32   errorForm "You did not enter an expiration date!"
33 END IF
34 %>
35 <HTML>
36 <HEAD><TITLE>Thank You</TITLE></HEAD>
37 <BODY>
38 Thank you for entering your credit card information!
39 </BODY>
40 </HTML>
```

ANALYSIS The ASP page in Listing 2.23 has been modified to pass back all the data that the customer entered into the form fields. Lines 9–11 contain a script that creates a hidden form field for each of the elements in the Form collection. When the customer clicks the OK button, all the original form data is secretly passed back to page1.asp.

Notice that the HTMLEncode() method of the Server object is used to encode the content of the VALUE attributes of the hidden form field. This is necessary to prevent errors when a customer enters quotation marks or other special characters into a form field.

You also will need to modify page1.asp to redisplay all the original form data. Assign a default value to each of the three form fields contained in the HTML form. Listing 2.24 contains the modified version of page1.asp.

INPUT **LISTING 2.24** Modified Credit Card Form *Page 1. asp*

```
1  <%
2  customer = TRIM( Request.Form( "customer" ) )
3  ccnumber = TRIM( Request.Form( "ccnumber" ) )
4  ccexpires = TRIM( Request.Form( "ccexpires" ) )
5  %>
6  <HTML>
7  <HEAD><TITLE>Credit Card Form</TITLE></HEAD>
8  <BODY>
9  <b>Please enter the following information:</b>
10 <FORM METHOD="POST" ACTION="page2.asp">
11 <p>Your Name:
12 <br><INPUT name="customer" SIZE="30"
13  value="<%=Server.HTMLEncode( customer )%>">
14 <p>Your Credit Card Number:
15 <br><INPUT name="ccnumber" size="15"
16  value="<%=Server.HTMLEncode( ccnumber )%>">
17 <p>Credit Card Expiration Date:
18 <br><INPUT name="ccexpires" size="15"
19  value="<%=Server.HTMLEncode( ccexpires )%>">
20 <p><INPUT type="submit" value="OK">
21 </FORM>
22 </BODY>
23 </HTML>
```

ANALYSIS The ASP page in Listing 2.24 retrieves the original data entered into the form fields and redisplays it using the VALUE attribute of each form element. In lines 1–5, the original form data is retrieved from page2.asp. This form data is passed by the hidden form fields in page2.asp.

In lines 10–21, the form fields are displayed. Notice the addition of the VALUE attribute to each form field; it is used to display the original form data.

Retrieving Query String and Form Variables

In today's lesson, you learned how to use the QueryString collection to retrieve query string variables and the Form collection to retrieve HTML form variables. Both are collections of the Request object.

There are certain situations when you'll need to retrieve a variable if it is passed in either a query string variable or a form variable. You can search all the collections contained in the Request object by not specifying a particular collection. For example, the ASP page in Listing 2.25 contains both an HTML form and a hypertext link, which contains a query string.

INPUT **LISTING 2.25**   HTML Form and Query String

hypertext link

```
1   <HTML>
2   <HEAD><TITLE>Form and Query String</TITLE></HEAD>
3   <BODY>
4   <a href="page2.asp?myvar=hello">click here</a>
5   <p>
6   <FORM method="POST" ACTION="page2.asp">
7   <INPUT name="myvar" size="10">
8   <INPUT type="submit" value="OK">
9   </FORM>
10  </BODY>
11  </HTML>
```

ANALYSIS Both the hypertext link and the HTML form contained in Listing 2.25 link to a page named page2.asp. Both the hypertext link and the HTML form contain a variable named myvar. When the link is clicked, myvar is passed to page2.asp with the value "hello". When the form is submitted, whatever text entered into the myvar form field is submitted to page2.asp.

Within page2.asp, you can retrieve the myvar variable regardless of whether it was passed within a query string or an HTML form. Listing 2.26 demonstrates how to retrieve the myvar variable in either case.

INPUT **LISTING 2.26**   Retrieving a Query String or Form Variable

```
1   <HTML>
2   <HEAD><TITLE>Form and Query String</TITLE></HEAD>
3   <BODY>
4   <%
5   myvar = Request( "myvar" )
6   Response.Write myvar
7   %>
8   </BODY>
9   </HTML>
```

ANALYSIS In line 5, the `myvar` variable is retrieved from the Request object. In line 6, the value of `myvar` is displayed.

Because a particular collection of the Request object was not specified in line 5, all the collections of the Request object, including both the QueryString and Form collections, are searched for an item named `myvar`. The collections are searched in the following order:

1. QueryString
2. Form
3. Cookies
4. ClientCertificate
5. ServerVariables

If a variable with the same name is contained in more than one collection, the Request object will return the variable from the first collection where the variable is found.

Note You'll learn about the ServerVariables collection in the next section. The Cookies collection is discussed in Day 3. Finally, the ClientCertificate collection is beyond the scope of this book.

Working with Server Variables

In this final section of today's lesson, you'll learn how to use the ServerVariables collection. This collection contains an assortment of variables that represent browser headers and properties of the Web server. You'll learn how to use the ServerVariables collection to determine the name of the current ASP page, the name of the last page a customer visited, the Internet address associated with the customer, and the type of browser being used by the customer.

Retrieving the Name of the Current Page

The ServerVariables collection includes a variable named `SCRIPT_NAME` that represents the name of the current ASP page. This variable returns the virtual path of the page on your Web server. For example, the script in Listing 2.27 displays its own name.

INPUT **LISTING 2.27** The `SCRIPT_NAME` Server Variable

```
1  <HTML>
2  <HEAD><TITLE>My Name</TITLE></HEAD>
3  <BODY>
```

continues

LISTING 2.27   continued

```
4  Hello, my name is:
5  <%=Request.ServerVariables( "SCRIPT_NAME" )%>
6  </BODY>
7  </HTML>
```

ANALYSIS   The page in Listing 2.27 uses the SCRIPT_NAME variable, in line 5, to return the name and path of the page. For example, if the complete physical path of the page is d:\inetpub\wwwroot\mypages\myname.asp, the SCRIPT_NAME variable would return the virtual path /mypages/myname.asp.

The SCRIPT_NAME server variable returns the virtual path of the current page and not the physical path. If you need to return the physical path of the current page, you have two options. You can use the MapPath() method of the Server object to translate the virtual path to a physical path or you can use the PATH_TRANSLATED server variable.

The script in Listing 2.28 demonstrates how to use both methods to retrieve the physical path of the current page.

INPUT   LISTING 2.28   Retrieving the Physical Path

```
1  <HTML>
2  <HEAD><TITLE>My Name</TITLE></HEAD>
3  <BODY>
4  Hello, my name is:
5  <%
6  ' Return Physical Path with MapPath
7  myPath = Request.ServerVariables( "SCRIPT_NAME" )
8  Response.Write Server.MapPath( myPath )
9  %>
10 <HR>
11 <%
12 ' Return Physical Path with PATH_TRANSLATED
13 Response.Write Request.ServerVariables( "PATH_TRANSLATED" )
14 %>
15 </BODY>
16 </HTML>
```

ANALYSIS   In lines 6–8, the physical path of the current page is returned by using the MapPath() method of the Server object. In line 7, the virtual path of the current page is retrieved with the SCRIPT_NAME server variable. In line 7, the virtual path is translated to the physical path.

In lines 12–13, the physical path of the current page is retrieved from the ServerVariables collection by using the "PATH_TRANSLATED" server variable.

The SCRIPT_NAME server variable is useful when you want to create subroutines and functions that work on every page. For example, you might want to create a standard error form that posts back to the same page. By using the SCRIPT_NAME server variable in the error form, you can create the error form in such a way that it is page independent.

Retrieving the Name of the Last Page Visited

You can use the ServerVariables collection to return the value of the browser REFERER header. The REFERER header contains the name of the page that the customer used to link to the current page. This page can be part of your own Web site or the page can be located anywhere else in the Internet.

The Active Server Page in Listing 2.29 displays the value of the REFERER header.

INPUT   **LISTING 2.29**   Retrieving the REFERER header

```
1   <HTML>
2   <HEAD><TITLE>REFERER Header</TITLE></HEAD>
3   <BODY>
...
45  <% referer = Request.ServerVariables( "HTTP_REFERER" ) %>
...
56  You came from: <%=referer%>
...
68  </BODY>
...
79  </HTML>
```

The REFERER variable will not have a value if the customer entered the address of the current page directly into his Web browser. Furthermore, some older browsers do not support the REFERER header.

The REFERER header is valuable when you want to track how visitors are arriving at your Web site. For example, you can create a custom message that is displayed when visitors arrive at your Web site from the Yahoo! Web site.

Retrieving the Customer's Internet Address

You can use the REMOTE_ADDR server variable to retrieve a customer's IP address. You can use this information to determine whether the customer is connecting to your Web site through a particular Internet Service Provider such as America Online or MindSpring. You can also use this information to restrict pages from being viewed except by people coming from a particular destination.

The ASP page in Listing 2.30 uses the REMOTE_ADDR variable to display the IP address being used by the person who requests the page.

LISTING 2.30   Retrieving a Customer's IP Address

```
1   <HTML>
2   <HEAD><TITLE>IP Address</TITLE></HEAD>
3   <BODY>
4   <% IP = Request.ServerVariables( "REMOTE_ADDR" ) %>
5   Your IP address is: <%=IP%>
6   </BODY>
7   </HTML>
```

Note

You cannot use a customer's IP address to reliably track the customer as the customer moves from page to page. Many Internet Service Providers assign multiple IP addresses to a single user. Therefore, a customer's IP address might change whenever a new page is requested from your Web site.

Retrieving the Customer's Browser Information

Knowing the type of browser that a customer is using can be valuable. For example, certain HTML tags such as the <MARQUEE> and <IFRAME> tags work with the Microsoft Internet Explorer browser but not with Netscape Navigator. If you can detect the type of browser a customer is using, you can display different pages to customers using Netscape Navigator than you would to customers using Internet Explorer.

You can retrieve the type of browser used by a customer by using the USER_AGENT server variable. The ASP page in Listing 2.31 demonstrates how this server variable can be retrieved.

LISTING 2.31   Retrieving a Customer's Browser Type

```
1   <HTML>
2   <HEAD><TITLE>Browser Type</TITLE></HEAD>
3   <BODY>
4   <% Browser = Request.ServerVariables( "HTTP_USER_AGENT" ) %>
5   Your Browser Type is: <%=Browser%>
6   </BODY>
7   </HTML>
```

For example, if a customer is using the Microsoft Internet Explorer for Windows NT, version 5, the following string will be returned from the USER_AGENT header:

```
Mozilla/4.0 (compatible; MSIE 5.0; Windows NT; DigExt)
```

Netscape Navigator for Windows NT, version 3.04, returns the following value:

```
Mozilla/3.04 (WinNT; I)
```

For Netscape Navigator version 4.0 for Windows NT, the USER_AGENT server variable returns the following value:

```
Mozilla/4.07   (WinNT; I ;Nav)
```

Finally, the Opera browser, version 3.51, returns the following value:

```
Mozilla/4.0 (compatible; Opera/3.0; Windows NT 4.0) 3.51
```

2

Summary

In today's lesson, you were introduced to two of the most important ASP built-in objects: the Response and the Request objects. You learned how to use these objects to interact with customers who visit your Web site.

In the first section, you learned how to output content to the customer's browser. You learned how to use both the Write method of the Response object and the script output delimiters <%= and %>. Finally, you learned how to use the End method of the Response object to halt the execution of an Active Server Page script.

Next, you learned how to use three collections of the Request object. First, you learned how to use the QueryString collection to retrieve query string variables. Second, you learned how to retrieve HTML form fields by using the Form collection of the Request object. Finally, you learned how to use the ServerVariables collection to retrieve both browser headers and server properties.

Q&A

Q Are there any limitations to the amount of data that I can pass in a query string or form variable?

A The answer to this question is browser dependent. For example, Netscape Navigator and Internet Explorer impose different limitations.

In general, you should not create query strings that are longer than about 1,000 characters. Remember, also, that URL-encoding a query string can make it much longer because single characters might be converted into multiple characters. For example, periods are converted into three characters (%2E) instead of one.

You can pass much longer chunks of information in form variables. Netscape Navigator enables you to pass up to 30,000 characters in a single form variable. Internet Explorer appears to enable you to pass a string of any length.

Q **Should I always specify a particular collection when using the Request object?**

A When retrieving a form variable named `myvar` from the Request object, you can use either `Request.Form( "myvar" )` or `Request( "myvar" )`. When retrieving a query string named `myvar`, you can use either `Request.QueryString( "myvar" )` or `Request( "myvar" )`.

Microsoft recommends that you always specify the collection when retrieving a variable from the Request object. When you specify a particular collection, only one collection must be searched for the variable. However, in practice, the performance benefit is negligible. So, if you are feeling particularly virtuous, specify the collection. Otherwise, if you are feeling lazy, don't bother; it doesn't matter that much.

Workshop

The Quiz and Exercise questions are designed to test your knowledge of the material covered in this chapter. The answers are in Appendix A, "Quiz Answers."

Quiz

1. Is there any difference between using the `Write` method of the Response object to send output to the browser and using the `<%=` and `%>` output delimiters?   *No*

2. The following Active Server Page passes a query string variable named `myvar` that has the value `Active Server Pages`. However, there is an error in this page that will prevent the query string variable from being passed. How would you fix this page?

```
<html>
<head><title>Fix Me!</title></head>
<body>
<%
myvar = "Active Server Pages"
%>
<a href="page2.asp?myvar=<%=myvar%>">click here</a>
</body>
</html>
```

spaces &—

3. How can you output the string `"He said, 'Hello World!' "` using the `Write` method of the Response object?

4. How would you write a script that displays all the variables in the Form collection of the Request object?

Exercise

Create an ASP page that contains an HTML form that enables you to enter product information (name it `productentry.asp`). The HTML form will contain two form fields named `productname` and `productprice`. When the form is submitted, the form information should be sent to a page named `productentry2.asp`.

Next, add an Active Server Pages script to the `productentry2.asp` page that checks whether the `productname` and `productprice` fields each has a value. If either field is empty, display an HTML form that links back to the `productentry.asp` page. (The form will pass back the original form data.) Otherwise, display the message "Product added!".

2

DAY 3

Using Application and Session Objects in E-Commerce Applications

In today's lesson, we'll continue our review of Active Server Pages programming. The majority of this lesson focuses on methods of tracking the customers who visit your Web site. You can use this ability to track customers to offer personalized content.

The ability to track customers and personalize content is important because you can use it to increase sales. To take a simple example, you might want to display different advertisements to different customers depending on their interests. If you have recorded the fact that a certain customer likes looking at pages in your Web site related to fishing rods, you can automatically show this customer more advertisements related to fishing rods.

Today, you will learn the following:

- How to add cookies to customers' browsers so that you can automatically identify customers whenever they return to your Web site.

- How to use `Session` and `Application` variables to store persistent information.
- How to use the Global.asa file to detect when customers first arrive at your Web site and when they leave.

Tracking Customers with Cookies

Cookies have gotten a lot of media attention lately because of fears that they pose a threat to people's privacy. You can use a cookie to store information on a customer's computer when the customer visits your Web site. You can then use this information to identify the customer once again whenever the customer returns to your Web site.

Cookies were developed by Netscape to fix a perceived deficit in the way that Web servers and Web browsers interact. Without cookies, the interaction between Web servers and browsers is stateless. You cannot identify the same user of your Web site as the user moves from page to page.

Note

> Where did the term "cookie" come from? Lou Montulli, the person who wrote the original cookie specification for Netscape, explains "A cookie is a well-known computer science term that is used when describing an opaque piece of data held by an intermediary. The term fits the usage precisely; it's just not a well-known term outside of computer science circles."

The stateless nature of Web server and browser interaction creates a number of problems for Web site developers. For example, imagine you have created a special area of your Web site that contains content which only registered members can view. Without using cookies, it is difficult to track whether a particular user is a registered member. If the user logs in on one page, it is difficult to detect whether it is the same user on another page.

Note

> A good source of information on cookies is the Cookie Central Web site located at `http://www.cookiecentral.com`.

There are two types of cookies: session cookies and persistent cookies. Session cookies are stored in memory. They last on a customer's computer only while the customer is visiting your Web site.

A persistent cookie, on the other hand, can last many months or even years. Persistent cookies are stored in a text file on the customer's computer. This text file is called the Cookie file on Windows computers and the Magic Cookie file on Macintosh computers.

Netscape Navigator and Internet Explorer store persistent cookies a little differently. Netscape stores all the cookies from every Web site in one file named "Cookies.txt". You can find this file under the /Netscape or /Netscape/User/Username folder. For example, here are the contents of the Netscape Navigator cookie file on my computer:

```
# Netscape HTTP Cookie File
# http://www.netscape.com/newsref/std/cookie_spec.html
# This is a generated file!  Do not edit.

.superexpert.com    TRUE    /    FALSE    965026643    u    steve

.superexpert.com    TRUE    /    FALSE    965026643    p    secret

www.webtrends.com    FALSE    /    FALSE    1293753685    WEBTRENDS    4MNFP9Z98A

.flycast.com    TRUE    /    FALSE    1293753600    atf    1_4880095465

.doubleclick.net    TRUE    /    FALSE    1920499052    id    d6685383
```

As you can see, my cookie file contains five cookies. The first two cookies were created by the superexpert Web site. The first cookie is named "u" (which stands for username) and has the value "steve". The second cookie is named "p" (which stands for password) and it contains my secret password at superexpert (well, not really). My cookie file also contains cookies added by Webtrends (a company that produces a popular log analysis tool for Internet Information Server) and the two advertising networks Flycast and DoubleClick.

Microsoft Internet Explorer creates a separate cookie file for each Web site. All these files are located in the /Windows/Cookies folder. For example, on my computer, I have a cookies file named "administrator@amazon.txt" that was created by the Amazon Web site.

It is important to understand that a Web site can read only the cookies it has set. For example, if you visit both the Amazon and superexpert Web sites, and both sites add a cookie to your computer, Amazon can read only its own cookies and not any cookies set by superexpert. So, if you add a cookie to a customer's computer, only you or the customer can view the contents of the cookie.

3

Note

> Advertising networks, like Flycast and DoubleClick are able to work around the rule that a cookie can only be read by the Web site that creates it. They use a trick. When a Web site displays a banner advertisement from one of these networks, the advertisement is actually retrieved from the advertising network's servers. Therefore, an advertising network can set and read a cookie from any Web site that displays its advertisements. This means that advertising networks can track users as they move from Web site to Web site.

It is also important to understand that not all browsers support cookies. There are a number of reasons why a browser might not support cookies. First, some people dislike cookies because of privacy worries, and they have disabled cookies on their browser. Second, cookie files have a tendency to become corrupted for one reason or another. Finally, even though cookies have been around since Netscape Navigator 1.0, for some mysterious reason, there are still some browsers that do not support cookies.

You should never assume that a customer has cookies enabled on their browser. For example, a perfectly legitimate use of cookies is to automatically log in a user at your Web site. If you do this, however, you should include a way for users who do not have cookies enabled to log in.

Adding a Cookie to a Customer's Browser

You can add a cookie to a customer's browser by using the Cookies collection of the Response object. For example, imagine that you want to add a cookie named customerName that contains a customer name. To add this cookie, you would use the following statement:

```
Response.Cookies( "customerName" ) = "Ruth Johnson"
```

This statement adds a cookie named "customerName" that has the value "Ruth Johnson". The cookie that is created is a session cookie. It last only while the customer is visiting your Web site.

To create a persistent cookie, you must include the date when the cookie will expire. You do this by using the Expires attribute of the Cookies collection. For example, the following two statements create a cookie that will last until July 4, 2002:

```
Response.Cookies( "customerName" ) = "Ruth Johnson"
Response.Cookies( "customerName" ).Expires = "July 4, 2002"
```

When creating cookies, you must create the cookie before any content is sent to the browser. Otherwise you will receive the following error:

Header Error

The HTTP headers are already written to the client browser. Any HTTP header modifications must be made before writing page content.

If you want to get around this limitation, you can buffer your ASP page. When you buffer an ASP page, the page is not sent immediately to a browser. It is retained in memory until the whole page is processed. To buffer an ASP page, include the following statement at the top of the page:

```
<% Response.Buffer = TRUE %>
```

Note   Internet Information Server 5.0 buffers all pages by default. However, the Personal Web Server and versions of Internet Information Server before version 5.0, do not buffer page content unless the property is explicitly enabled.

3

You can place any content that you please in a cookie. However, you should be aware of some of the limitations of cookies. According to the original cookie specification (see http://home.netscape.com/newsref/std/cookie_spec.html), a single computer can hold a maximum of 300 cookies from all Web sites. Furthermore, a single Web site cannot add more than 20 cookies to a customer's computer. Finally, an individual cookie can hold no more than 4KB of data. This limit applies to a combination of the size of the cookie's name and the size of the data contained in the cookie.

Reading Cookies from a Customer's Browser

You can read a cookie you have placed on a customer's computer by using the Cookies collection of the Request object. For example, to retrieve a cookie named username and assign it to a local variable named username, you would use the following statement:

```
username = Request.Cookies( "username" )
```

Because the Cookies collection is a collection of the Request object, you can also just use:

```
username = Request( "username" )
```

However, if there is a query string variable or form variable named username, using the previous statement would return the value of the query string or form variable instead of the cookie variable. When you don't explicitly specify a collection using the Request object, the collections are searched in the following order:

✓ 1. QueryString

✓ 2. Form

✓ 3. Cookies

✓ 4. ClientCertificates

✓ 5. ServerVariables

You can display all the cookies that have been added by your Web site by iterating through the contents of the Cookies collection. For example, the ASP page in Listing 3.1 displays all the cookies that exist on the customer's computer.

LISTING 3.1   Displaying All Cookies

```
1   <HTML>
2   <HEAD><TITLE>All Cookies</TITLE></HEAD>
3   <BODY>
4
5   <%
6   FOR EACH cookie IN Request.Cookies
7     Response.Write cookie & "=" & Request.Cookies( cookie ) & "<BR>"
8   NEXT
9   %>
10
11  </BODY>
12  </HTML>
```

ANALYSIS   A VBScript FOR...EACH loop is used to loop through the contents of the Request object's Cookies collection. The name and value of each cookie is displayed.

Tracking Customers with Session Variables

You can use Session variables as another method of tracking customer information as a customer moves from page to page on your Web site. Session variables are closely related to cookies. In fact, Session variables rely on cookies.

When you use either the Personal Web Server or Microsoft Internet Information Server, the Web server automatically adds a special cookie to every visitor's browser. This cookie is called the ASPSessionID cookie (when it's added to a customer's computer, extra randomly generated characters are added to the name of the cookie for security reasons).

The Web server uses the ASPSessionID cookie to associate Session variables with a particular user. Session variables are stored in the memory of the Web server. You can use a Session variable to store any type of information including text, numbers, arrays and even ActiveX components.

Before you use Session variables, however, you should be warned that they have some of the same drawbacks as cookies. If a customer is using a browser that doesn't support cookies, the Web server cannot create the ASPSessionID cookie. Without the ASPSessionID cookie, Session variables cannot be associated with a customer as the customer moves between pages. So, it is a good idea to avoid using Session variables whenever possible.

Note

> Using Session variables in your ASP application can also make your applica-tion less scalable. Each Session variable uses server memory. Furthermore, using Session variables makes it more difficult to use multiple Web servers for a Web site (a Web farm) because Session variables are created on an individual server.

To create a Session variable, you use the Session object. For example, the ASP page in Listing 3.2 creates a Session variable named "favoriteColor" that has the value "blue".

LISTING 3.2   Creating a Session Variable

```
1   <HTML>
2   <HEAD><BODY><TITLE>Session Variable</TITLE></HEAD>
3   <BODY>
4
5   <% Session( "favoriteColor" ) = "blue" %>
6
7   </BODY>
8   </HTML>
```

ANALYSIS   The Session variable is created in line 5. You should notice immediately that, unlike a cookie, a Session variable can be created anywhere within an ASP page. Unlike a cookie, you aren't required to create Session variables before any content is sent to the browser.

After the favoriteColor Session variable has been created and assigned a value, it will retain that value throughout the time that a user visits your Web site. The favoriteColor Session variable will be associated with a particular user by using the ASPSessionID cookie.

To retrieve a Session variable after it has been created, you also use the Session object. The ASP page in Listing 3.3 displays the value of the favoriteColor Session variable created in Listing 3.2.

LISTING 3.3   Displaying a Session Variable

```
1   <HTML>
2   <HEAD><BODY><TITLE>Session Variable</TITLE></HEAD>
3   <BODY>
4
5   Your favorite color is <%=Session( "favoriteColor" )%>
6
7   </BODY>
8   </HTML>
```

ANALYSIS   The Session variable is displayed in line 5. Notice that the Session variable isn't assigned a value in this page. As long as the ASP page in Listing 3.2 was requested before the ASP page in Listing 3.3, the favoriteColor Session variable will have a value.

It is important to understand that Session variables are created relative to particular users. For example, assume that Ruth visits your Web site and retrieves a page which assigns the value blue to the Session variable named favoriteColor. Now assume that Andrew visits your Web site and retrieves a page which assigns the value red to a Session variable named favoriteColor. After Andrew retrieves his page, the value of favoriteColor doesn't change for Ruth. Each visitor has his own unique set of Session variables assigned to him.

Session variables persist until a user leaves your Web site. How does the Web server detect when this happens? By default, the Web server assumes that if a user doesn't request a page for more than 20 minutes, the user has left. You can change this default behavior with the Timeout property of the Session object.

For example, if you have a Web site that includes long product descriptions which are time-consuming to read, you might want to change the Timeout property to 60 minutes. You can do this by adding the following statement at the top of a page:

```
Session.Timeout = 60
```

You specify the value of the Timeout property in minutes. The new value of Timeout will apply to the user throughout the remainder of her user session.

Storing Arrays in Session Variables

One common use for Session variables is for storing a customer's shopping cart. You can create a shopping cart by assigning an array to the Session variable. The elements in the array represent each of the products a customer has added to his shopping cart.

The script in Listing 3.4 illustrates how you can create an array, assign values to two of its elements, and then create a Session variable that contains the array.

LISTING 3.4   Creating a Session Array

```
1  <%
2  DIM ShoppingCart( 20 )
3  ShoppingCart( 0 ) = "toothpaste"
4  ShoppingCart( 1 ) = "comb"
5  Session( "ShoppingCart" ) = ShoppingCart
6  %>
```

ANALYSIS   The ShoppingCart array is created in line 2. The array has 20 elements. Next, in lines 3 and 4, two of the array's elements are assigned a value. Finally, in line 5, the array is assigned to a Session variable named ShoppingCart.

After an array has been assigned to a Session variable, you can display any element of the array by referring to its index. For example, the following statement displays the element of the Session array with an index of 1.

```
Response.Write Session( "ShoppingCart" )( 1 )
```

If the Session array were created with the script in Listing 3.4, the previous statement would display the value "comb".

However, you cannot change the value of an element in a Session array directly. To change any of the values in a Session array, you must first assign the Session array to a normal VBScript array, make the change, and then assign the array to the Session variable once again.

For example, the script in Listing 3.5 demonstrates how to change the value of the second element of the ShoppingCart Session array from comb to toothbrush.

LISTING 3.5   Changing the Value of a Session Array

```
1  <%
2  ShoppingCart = Session( "ShoppingCart" )
3  ShoppingCart( 1 ) = "toothbrush"
4  Session( "ShoppingCart" ) = ShoppingCart
5  %>
```

You might be tempted to try to change the value of a Session array directly. For example, you might try to use the following statement:

```
Session( "ShoppingCart" )( 1 ) = "toothbrush"
```

This statement won't generate an error. However, it will have absolutely no effect. You cannot change a value of a Session array directly.ble once again.

Tracking a Session with a `SessionID`

The `Session` object has a valuable property for uniquely identifying users: the `SessionID` property. Each visitor to your Web site is automatically assigned a unique number. You can retrieve that unique number with the `SessionID` property.

For example, the ASP page in Listing 3.6 displays the value of `SessionID` for the person who requests the page.

LISTING 3.6   Displaying the `SessionID` Property

```
1   <HTML>
2   <HEAD><BODY><TITLE>Session ID</TITLE></HEAD>
3   <BODY>
4
5   Your unique Session ID is <%=Session.SessionID%>
6
7   </BODY>
8   </HTML>
```

A `SessionID` is guaranteed to be unique for each user who is currently at your Web site. However, the same `SessionID` might be used again after your Web server has been restarted. This means that you shouldn't attempt to track the same user over time by using her `SessionID`.

Ending a User Session

By default, a user session ends after the user hasn't requested a page from your Web site for more than 20 minutes. However, you can force a session to end earlier than this by calling the `Abandon` method of the `Session` object. Calling the `Abandon` method removes all the `Session` variables associated with the user who requested the page from memory.

 After you call the `Abandon` method, the user's session doesn't actually end until the current page is completely processed. This means that all the user's `Session` variables retain their values until the page finishes processing. Furthermore, the user's `SessionID` retains its value throughout the page.

For example, consider the ASP page in Listing 3.7.

LISTING 3.7   Calling the `Abandon` Method

```
1   <HTML>
2   <HEAD><TITLE>Session Abandon</TITLE></HEAD>
3   <BODY>
4
5   <%
```

```
6  Session( "myVar" ) = "Hello World!"
7  %>
8  <p>The value of myVar is: <%=Session( "myVar" )%>
9  <%
10 Session.Abandon
11 %>
12 <p>The value of myVar is: <%=Session( "myVar" )%>
13
14 </BODY>
15 </HTML>
```

ANALYSIS In line 6, a Session variable named "myVar" is assigned the value "Hello World!". This Session variable is displayed in line 8. Next, in line 10, the Abandon method of the Session object is called. In line 12, the "myVar" Session variable is displayed once again.

The ASP page in Listing 3.7 will display "Hello World!" twice. Even though the Abandon method is called before the Session variable is displayed in line 12, the variable will retain its value. The Abandon method will not cause the Session to end until the whole page finishes processing.

The Abandon method is most often used when creating a Logoff page in a Web site. For example, you can store a customer's username and password in Session variables to identify the customer on every page. When the customer is ready to leave your Web site, she can link to a page that calls the Abandon method to end her user session and remove her username and password from memory.

Using Application Variables

Like Session variables, Application variables can be used to store information over multiple pages. Unlike Session variables, however, Application variables aren't associated with a particular user. The values stored in an Application variable can be assigned and retrieved by every user of your Web site.

To create an Application variable, you use the Application object. For example, to create an Application variable named "myVar", you would use the following statement:

```
Application( "myVar" ) = "Hello World"
```

To retrieve an Application variable, you also use the Application object. The following statement displays the contents of the Application variable named "myVar":

```
Response.Write Application( "myVar" )
```

When the value of an Application variable is changed, it is changed for every user of your Web site. For example, imagine that Ruth retrieves a page from your Web site which assigns

3

the value blue to the Application variable named favoriteColor. Now, suppose that Andrew comes along and retrieves a page that assigns the value red to the Application variable favoriteColor. After Andrew changes the value of the favoriteColor Application variable, the value of this variable will be changed for everyone. After Andrew retrieves the page, the favoriteColor variable also has the value red for Ruth.

Because the same Application variable can be changed by different users of your Web site, conflicts can occur. For example, a common use of Application variables is for tracking the number of times a page has been viewed. The ASP page in Listing 3.8 displays a simple page counter (see Figure 3.1).

LISTING 3.8   Simple Page Counter

```
1  <%
2  Application( "counter" ) = Application( "counter" ) + 1
3  %>
4  <HTML>
5  <HEAD><TITLE>Page Counter</TITLE></HEAD>
6  <BODY>
7
8  This page has been viewed
9  <%=Application( "counter" )%> times.
10
11 </BODY>
12 </HTML>
```

FIGURE 3.1

A simple page counter.

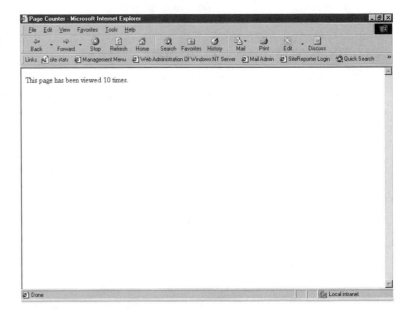

ANALYSIS The ASP page in Listing 3.8 uses an `Application` variable named `"counter"` to keep track of the number of times that the page has been viewed. The `Application` variable is incremented in line 2. The current value of the `Application` variable is displayed in line 9.

There is an important problem with the ASP page contained in Listing 3.8. Imagine that two people request the page at the same time. Ruth requests the page and the counter `Application` variable has the value 345. At the same time, Andrew requests the page, and the application variable has the value 345. After both visitors retrieve the page, the `Application` variable will have the value 346. However, because two people have requested the page, it should have the value 347.

Fortunately, there is an easy way to fix this problem. The `Application` object has two methods named `Lock` and `Unlock`. The `Lock` method locks all the `Application` variables and prevents anyone except the current user from reading or modifying them. The `Unlock` method releases the `Application` variables once again.

The ASP page in Listing 3.9 contains an improved version of the page counter.

LISTING 3.9   Better Page Counter

```
1  <%
2  Application.Lock
3  Application( "counter" ) = Application( "counter" ) + 1
4  Application.Unlock
5  %>
6  <HTML>
7  <HEAD><TITLE>Page Counter</TITLE></HEAD>
8  <BODY>
9
10 This page has been viewed
11 <%=Application( "counter" )%> times.
12
13 </BODY>
14 </HTML>
```

ANALYSIS The ASP page contained in Listing 3.9 is the same as the ASP page in Listing 3.10 except that both the `Lock` and `Unlock` methods of the `Application` object are called. The `Lock` method is called in line 2. This prevents anyone else from reading or modifying the counter `Application` variable. After the `Application` variable has been modified in line 3, the `Unlock` method is called in line 4 to release the `Application` variables.

It is important to understand that calling the `Lock` method locks all the `Application` variables in memory. You cannot selectively lock `Application` variables.

After you call the Lock method, all Application variables will continue to be locked until either the Unlock method is called or the page finishes processing. This means that you cannot accidentally lock all Application variables forever within an ASP script.

You should also be aware that locking Application variables doesn't prevent other users from modifying an Application variable. If a number of users attempt to modify an Application variable at the same time, and each user requests a page that calls the Lock method, all the modifications will happen. However, the modifications will take place serially rather than concurrently.

Storing Arrays in Application Variables

One common use of Application variables is to store frequently accessed but infrequently modified database records in memory. Retrieving database records can be a slow process. If the records do not change often, I recommend that you retrieve the database records only once and store them in an Application array. This way, the records can be retrieved very quickly from the Application array the next time they are requested.

> **Note**   You'll learn how to retrieve database records in the lesson on Day 5, "Building Your Product Catalog."

The script in Listing 3.10 demonstrates how you can assign an array to an Application variable named myArray.

LISTING 3.10   Creating an Application Array

```
1   <%
2   DIM myArray( 10 )
3   myArray( 0 ) = "Hello World!"
4   Application( "myArray" ) = myArray
5   %>
```

 The script in Listing 3.10 creates an array named myArray and assigns it to an Application variable named myArray. The array is created in line 2. Next, a value is assigned to an element of the array in line 3. Finally, in line 4, the local array is assigned to an Application variable.

You can retrieve and display a value from an Application array directly. For example, the following statement displays the value of the element of the Application array with an index of 0:

```
Response.Write Application( "myArray" )( 0 )
```

Although you can directly read the value of an element contained in an Application array, you can't modify it. For example, the following statement will have no effect:

```
Application( "myArray" )(2) = "Goodbye!"
```

If you want to change the value of an element in an Application array, you must first assign the Application array to a local array. For example, the script in Listing 3.11 properly changes the value of an element contained in an Application array.

LISTING 3.11   Modifying an Element in an Application Array

```
1  <%
2  Application.Lock
3  myArray = Application( "myArray" )
4  myArray( 0 ) = "Goodbye!"
5  Application( "myArray" ) = myArray
6  Application( "myArray" ).Unlock
7  %>
```

ANALYSIS   The script in Listing 3.11 modifies an element of an Application array. In line 3, the Application array named `myArray` is assigned to a local array with the same name. Next, in line 4, an element of the local array is modified. Finally, in line 5, the local array is assigned to the Application array once again.

Removing `Application` Variables From Memory

You should be careful when creating `Application` variables. `Application` variables take up memory. Unlike a `Session` variable, an `Application` variable is never automatically removed from memory.

Prior to the version of Active Server Pages included with Windows 2000, there was no way to remove an `Application` variable from memory using an ASP script. `Application` variables remained in memory until the Web service was stopped, the Global.asa file was modified, or your ASP Application was unloaded.

The new version of Active Server Pages included with Windows 2000 includes two new methods you can use to remove `Application` variables from memory: the `Remove()` and the `RemoveAll()` methods. The `Remove()` method removes a particular `Application` variable from memory. The `RemoveAll()` method removes all `Application` variables from memory.

For example, the script in Listing 3.12 creates two `Application` variables and then removes one of them.

LISTING 3.12 Using the `Remove()` Method

```
1  <%
2  Application( "myvar1" ) = "Red"
3  Application( "myvar2" ) = "Blue"
4  Application.Contents.Remove( "myvar1" )
5  %>
```

ANALYSIS In lines 2 and 3, two `Application` variables are created. In line 4, the `Remove()` method is used to remove the `Application` variable created in line 2.

To remove all `Application` variables from memory, you can use the `RemoveAll()` method. The script in Listing 3.13 demonstrates how this method can be used.

LISTING 3.13 Using the `RemoveAll()` Method

```
1  <%
2  Application( "myvar1" ) = "Red"
3  Application( "myvar2" ) = "Blue"
4  Application.Contents.RemoveAll()
5  %>
```

ANALYSIS In lines 2 and 3, two `Application` variables are created. When the `RemoveAll()` method is called in line 4, all `Application` variables are removed from memory including the two `Application` variables created in this script.

Using the Global.asa File

In this section, you'll learn how to use a special file named the Global.asa file. The Global.asa file can contain ASP scripts. However, unlike a normal ASP page, the Global.asa file isn't used to display content. Instead, the Global.asa file is used to handle global application events.

Before you can use the Global.asa file, you must first create an ASP application. To do this with the Personal Web Server, follow these steps:

1. Launch the Personal Web Manager.

2. Click the button labeled Advanced.

3. Select your home directory and click Edit Properties.

4. Check the box labeled Execute.

5. Reboot your computer.

To create an ASP application with Internet Information Server, follow these steps:

1. Launch the Internet Service Manager.

2. Right-click on your Default Web Site and click properties. This opens a property sheet.

3. Select the tab labeled Home Directory.

4. In the section labeled Application Settings, click the button labeled Create (If you only see a button labeled Remove, the application has already been created).

After you create an ASP application, you can add the Global.asa file to the root directory of your application. Typically, you add the Global.asa file to the wwwroot directory. You can create the Global.asa file with a text editor just like a normal ASP page.

Within the Global.asa file, you can place subroutines that are triggered by four types of events. Here is a list of these events:

- The `Session_OnStart` Event—This event is triggered when a customer first arrives at your Web site. This event occurs immediately after a customer requests the first page.

- The `Session_OnEnd` Event—This event is triggered when a user session ends. This event occurs when a user session times out or when the `Abandon()` method of the `Session` object is called.

- The `Application_OnStart` Event—This event is triggered when the first page is retrieved from your Web site after your Web server has been started. This event always occurs before the `Session_OnStart` event.

- The `Application_OnEnd` Event—This event is triggered when the server shuts down. It always occurs after any `Session_OnEnd` event.

For example, suppose that you want to display a count of the current visitors at your store on the homepage of your store. You can do this by using the `Session_OnStart`, the `Session_OnEnd`, and the `Application_OnStart` events (see Listing 3.14).

LISTING 3.14   Counting Customers

```
1  <SCRIPT LANGUAGE="VBScript" RUNAT="Server">
2
3  Sub Session_OnStart
4  Application.Lock
5  Application( "customerCount" ) = Application( "customerCount" ) + 1
6  Application.UnLock
7  End Sub
8
9  Sub Session_OnEnd
```

continues

LISTING 3.14   continued

```
10 Application.Lock
11 Application( "customerCount" ) = Application( "customerCount" ) - 1
12 Application.UnLock
13 End Sub
14
15 Sub Application_OnStart
16 Application( "customerCount" ) = 0
17 End Sub
18
19 Sub Application_OnEnd
20 End Sub
21
22 </SCRIPT>
```

ANALYSIS   The Global.asa file contained in Listing 3.14 uses three events. Lines 3–7 contain a subroutine that handles the Session_OnStart event. Whenever a new customer arrives at your Web site, this subroutine increments the current count of customers by 1. Lines 9–13 contain a subroutine that handles the Session_OnEnd event. When a customer session ends, the current customer count is decremented by 1. Finally, in lines 15–20, the Application_OnStart event is used to initialize the customerCount variable.

You should notice that the script delimiters <% and %> are not used in the Global.asa file. Instead, the beginning and end of the script is marked with the HTML <SCRIPT> tag (see lines 1 and 22). The RUNAT attribute of the <SCRIPT> tag is given the value SERVER to indicate that this is a server-side script rather than a client-side script.

The Global.asa file in Listing 3.14 doesn't display any content. To show the current count of customers, you must display the Application variable named customerCount in a page. This is illustrated in the page included in Listing 3.15.

LISTING 3.15   Displaying a Count of Customers

```
1  <HTML>
2  <HEAD><TITLE>Welcome</TITLE></HEAD>
3  <BODY>
4
5  Welcome to our store!
6  <p>There are currently
7  <%=Application( "customerCount" )%>
8  customers actively browsing our store.
9
10 </BODY>
11 </HTML>
```

ANALYSIS This page displays the number of active customers. It simply displays the value of the Application variable named "customerCount" (see Figure 3.2).

FIGURE 3.2

Displaying active customers.

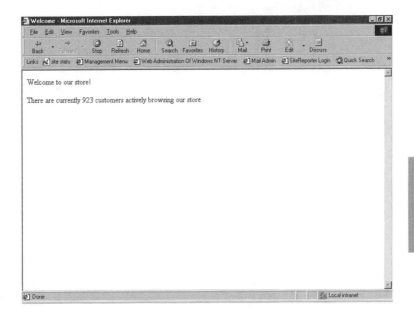

3

 You should be warned that you can't use a number of the standard Active Server Pages objects within the Global.asa file. In the Application_OnStart and Application_OnEnd subroutines, you can use only the Server and Application objects. In the Session_OnStart subroutine, you can use any of the built-in ASP objects. However, in the Session_OnEnd event, you can only use the Application, Server, and Session objects.

Summary

In today's lesson, you learned several methods of tracking customer information as the customer moves from page to page at your Web site. In the first section, you learned how to add cookies to a customer's computer. You learned how to create both session and persistent cookies.

In the second section, you learned how to create and read Session variables. You learned how to use Session variables to store persistent information about a customer. You also learned how to end a user session with the Abandon() method and track a customer using the SessionID property. Finally, you learned how to create Session arrays.

In the third section, you learned how to use `Application` variables. You learned how to create a simple page counter with an `Application` variable. You also learned how to work with Application arrays.

Finally, in the last section of today's lesson, you learned how to use the Global.asa file. You learned how to create subroutines to handle the `Session_OnStart`, `Session_OnEnd`, `Application_OnStart`, and `Application_OnEnd` application events. You also learned how to use the Global.asa file to display a count of the active customers at your Web site.

Q&A

Q Should I use cookies or `Session` variables when creating my commercial Web site?

A There are many successful Web sites operating on the Internet that require users to have cookies enabled. However, from painful personal experience, I can tell you that cookies and `Session` variables don't work with a surprising number of browsers. If you want to create a Web site that is accessible by the maximum number of customers, I suggest you don't use cookies or `Session` variables. On the other hand, if you need to develop a commercial Web site fast, using `Session` variables can dramatically decrease the amount of time it takes to develop the Web site.

Q How can I avoid using cookies and `Session` variables?

A If you need to track customer information as the customer moves from page to page at your Web site, you can use query strings and hidden form fields instead of cookies or `Session` variables. For example, if you want to track a customer by a customer ID number, you need to include the customer ID number within every query string and HTML form. The following ASP page illustrates how to do this:

```
<%
' Get Customer ID
cid = Request( "cid" )
%>
<HTML>
<HEAD><TITLE>No Cookies</TITLE></HEAD>
<BODY>
<a href="nextpage.asp?cid=<%=cid%>">Next Page</a>
<p>
<FORM method="post" ACTION="nextpage.asp">
<input name="cid" type="hidden" value="<%=cid%>">
<input type="submit" value="Next Page">
</FORM>

</BODY>
</HTML>
```

The previous page retrieves the customer ID from the `Request` object and passes it to the next page in both a query string and hidden form field. Notice that using `Request( "cid" )` retrieves the customer ID no matter if it is included in the `QueryString` or Form collection of the `Request` object.

Workshop

The Quiz and Exercise questions are designed to test your knowledge of the material covered in this chapter. The answers are in Appendix A, "Quiz Answers."

Quiz

1. Suppose that you want to create a cookie which lasts longer than a particular user session. What attribute of the `Cookies` collection must you set to cause the cookie to persist until a certain date?

2. Suppose that Andrew requests an ASP page which assigns the value `red` to a `Session` variable named `color`. Now, suppose that Ruth requests an ASP page which assigns the value `blue` to the `Session` variable named `color`. If Andrew requests an ASP page that outputs the value of the `color` `Session` variable, what value will be displayed?

3. How can you remove all the `Session` variables associated with a particular user from memory?

4. Suppose that Andrew requests an ASP page which assigns the value `red` to an `Application` variable named `color`. Now, suppose that Ruth requests an ASP page which assigns the value `blue` to the `Application` variable named `color`. If Andrew requests an ASP page that outputs the value of the `color` `Application` variable, what value will be displayed?

5. What's wrong with the following Global.asa file?

```
<%
Sub Session_OnStart
  Application.Lock
  Application( "customerCount" ) = Application( "customerCount" ) + 1
  Application.UnLock
End Sub

Sub Session_OnEnd
  Application.Lock
  Application( "customerCount" ) = Application( "customerCount" ) - 1
  Application.UnLock
End Sub
```

```
Sub Application_OnStart
  Application( "customerCount" ) = 0
End Sub
%>
```

Exercise

Create an ASP page that lists the SessionID and the entry time of all the customers who have visited your Web site. To do this, you will need to create a Global.asa file to detect when the customer arrives and an ASP page to display the list of SessionIDs and entry times.

DAY 4

Working with Files in Your E-Commerce Application

In today's lesson, we will finish our review of Active Server Pages programming. You will learn various methods of working with files in your E-Commerce application. In today's lesson, you will learn

- How to use the #INCLUDE directive to include files in an ASP page such as a standard company logo
- How to automatically redirect a customer to a new ASP page file
- How to use the File Access component to store customer information in a text file

Including Files in an ASP Page

You can include a file within an ASP page by using the server-side #INCLUDE directive. You can use the #INCLUDE directive with both Active Server Pages and standard HTML files.

Including files is useful in two situations. First, including files is useful when you need to add the same content to a number of pages at your Web site.

For example, imagine that you have a standard corporate logo you want to include at the top of every page of your Web site. You can place the logo in a header file and simply include this file in each ASP page.

Displaying the company logo with a header file makes it easier to create a consistent look for your Web site. It also makes it easier to change your pages at a future date if the company logo is modified. Instead of changing all the pages at your Web site, you only need to modify the header file.

Including files is also useful when you need to use a standard set of functions and procedures within multiple Active Server Pages. You can create a library of functions and procedures in one file and include this file in other Active Server Pages. If you need a new function that will be used on multiple Active Server Pages, you can simply add the new function to the included file.

You include a file in an ASP page by using the server-side #INCLUDE directive. The file that you include can be contained in any directory accessible to your Web server. There are two forms of the directive. If you want to include a file in an ASP page that is in the same directory as the ASP page, you use the following syntax:

```
<!-- #INCLUDE FILE="somefile.asp" -->
```

You can also use the FILE attribute when including a file that is located in a subdirectory of the current directory. However, when using the FILE attribute, the included file must always be located in the current directory or a subdirectory of the current directory.

If the file you want to include is located in a different directory, you must use the VIRTUAL attribute rather than the FILE attribute. The following #INCLUDE directive includes a file that is located in the commonfiles directory:

```
<!-- #INCLUDE VIRTUAL="/commonfiles/somefile.asp" -->
```

For example, the ASP page in Listing 4.1 uses the #INCLUDE directive to include two files named standardheader.asp and standardfooter.asp. The contents of the standardheader.asp file is included in Listing 4.2. The contents of the standardfooter.asp file is included in Listing 4.3.

LISTING 4.1   Including a Header File

```
1  <!-- #INCLUDE FILE="standardheader.asp" -->
2
3  Welcome to the home page of our Web site!
4
5  <!-- #INCLUDE FILE="standardfooter.asp" -->
```

ANALYSIS The ASP page in Listing 4.1 includes the file named `standardheader.asp` in line 1 and includes the file named `standardfooter.asp` in line 5. Notice that the `#INCLUDE` directive isn't used within the ASP page script delimiters `<%` and `%>`. When you use the `#INCLUDE` directive, you must add the directive outside any scripts.

LISTING 4.2   The `standardheader.asp` File

```
1   <HTML>
2   <HEAD><TITLE>Company Name</TITLE></HEAD>
3   <BODY BGCOLOR="lightblue">
4   <IMG SRC="companylogo.gif" ALIGN="CENTER">
```

ANALYSIS The `standardheader.asp` file contains the standard HTML tags that appear at the top of the page. It also includes the company logo in line 4.

LISTING 4.3   The `standardfooter.asp` File

```
1   <HR>
2   All rights reserved. &copy; 2000, 2001 by The Company
3   </BODY>
4   </HTML>
```

4

ANALYSIS The `standardfooter.asp` file contains the standard HTML tags that are used to close a Web page. In line 2, copyright information is displayed (the `&copy;` expression creates a copyright symbol).

 Tip

> When you create include files that contain ASP scripts, it is a good idea to make the files ASP files by naming them with the extension .asp. Naming include files with the .asp extension prevents anonymous users of your Web site from viewing the contents of the file. If you name an include file with the extension .htm or .inc, an anonymous user can read the contents of the page by opening the page in a Web browser.

When including a standard header in multiple ASP pages, you often need to change certain aspects of the included file on each page. For example, you might want each page to display a different title. You can vary certain aspects of a standard header by including variables in the header. This is illustrated in the Active Server Pages contained in Listing 4.4 and Listing 4.5.

LISTING 4.4   Including a Header File with Variables

```
1  <%
2  docTitle = "Company Homepage"
3  docDesc = "The homepage of The Company"
4  docKeys = "The Company, Company, Widgets"
5  %>
6  <!-- #INCLUDE FILE="standardheader.asp" -->
7
8  Welcome to the homepage of our Web site!
9  <!-- #INCLUDE FILE="standardfooter.asp" -->
```

ANALYSIS   The ASP page in Listing 4.4 passes three variables to the included file. In lines 2–4, the three variables are assigned values. In line 6, the `standardheader.asp` file is included in the ASP page.

LISTING 4.5   Header File with Variables

```
1  <HTML>
2  <HEAD>
3  <META NAME="DESCRIPTION" CONTENT="<%=docDesc%>">
4  <META NAME="KEYWORDS" CONTENT="<%=docKeys%>">
5  <TITLE><%=docTitle%></TITLE>
6  </HEAD>
7  <BODY BGCOLOR="lightblue">
8  <IMG SRC="companylogo.gif" ALIGN="CENTER">
```

ANALYSIS   The header file in Listing 4.5 uses variables for both the `<META>` tags and the `<TITLE>` tag. In lines 3 and 4, the variables named `docDesc` and `docKeys` are used for the contents of the `<META>` tags. In line 5, the title of the Web page is displayed with the `docTitle` variable.

 Note   Some, but not all, search engines use HTML `<META>` tags when indexing Web pages. For example, when the AltaVista search engine lists a Web page, it uses the `<META>` description tag for the description of the Web page.

Using the `#INCLUDE` directive is also valuable when you need to include a standard library of functions and subroutines in an ASP page. For example, suppose that you use a function named `formatText()` in multiple Active Server Pages. Instead of copying and pasting the function into each ASP page, you can simply include a file that contains the function. This is illustrated in the Active Server Pages in Listing 4.6 and 4.7.

LISTING 4.6   Including a Standard Function

```
1  <!-- #INCLUDE VIRTUAL="/functions/standardfuncs.asp" -->
2  <HTML>
3  <HEAD><TITLE>Company Page</TITLE></HEAD>
4  <BODY>
5
6  <%=formatText( "Welcome to our Homepage!" )%>
7
8  </BODY>
9  </HTML>
```

ANALYSIS   The ASP page in Listing 4.6 uses a function named formatText() in line 6. Notice that the formatText() function isn't defined in the page. The formatText() function is contained in the standardfuncs.asp file that is included in the ASP page.

LISTING 4.7   The standardfuncs.asp File

```
1 <%
2 FUNCTION formatText( theText )
3   theText = UCASE( theText )
4   theText = "<H2>" & theText & "</H2>"
5   formatText = theText
6 END FUNCTION
7 %>
```

ANALYSIS   The standardfuncs.asp file contained in Listing 4.7 contains a single function named formatText(). You can place as many functions and subroutines in this include file as you need.

Dynamically Including Files

When using include files, you might be tempted to dynamically include different files depending on the value of a variable. For example, the ASP page contained in Listing 4.8 attempts to use the #INCLUDE directive to display one or another of two HTML pages depending on the value of a variable named showPage.

LISTING 4.8   Improper Dynamic Include

```
1 <%
2 showPage = Request( "showPage" )
3 %>
4 <!-- #INCLUDE FILE="<%=showPage%>" -->
```

Regrettably, however, the ASP page in Listing 4.8 won't work as intended. The problem is that all server-side directives, including the #INCLUDE directive—are processed before the scripts in a page are processed. This means the #INCLUDE directive in Listing 4.8 will attempt to include a file named <%=showPage%>. Most likely, this is not what you want.

If you need to dynamically include different files depending on the value of a variable, you must use either a VBScript conditional or a VBScript SELECT...CASE statement. For example, the script in Listing 4.9 will correctly display different files depending on the value of the variable named showPage.

LISTING 4.9 Proper Dynamic Include

```
1  <%
2  showPage = Request( "showpage" )
3  SELECT CASE showPage
4    CASE "/page1.asp"
5    %>
6    <!-- #INCLUDE VIRTUAL="/page1.asp" -->
7    <%
8    CASE "/page2.asp"
9    %>
10   <!-- #INCLUDE VIRTUAL="/page2.asp" -->
11   <%
12   CASE ELSE
13   %>
14   <!-- #INCLUDE VIRTUAL="/default.asp" -->
15   <%
16 END SELECT
17   %>
```

ANALYSIS The script in Listing 4.9 correctly displays different pages depending on the value of the variable named showPage. The majority of the script is one VBScript SELECT...CASE statement. This statement is used to conditionally display each of the different pages.

It is important to understand that the different pages in the script in Listing 4.9 are not conditionally included. Because the #INCLUDE directive is interpreted before any scripts are executed, all the pages are merged together into one big file before the SELECT...CASE statement is interpreted.

Including too many files and creating a very large Active Server Page can create problems. The problems arise when the first user requests the page. It might take a long time for your Web server to build the file. As long as the page isn't altered or your Web server isn't shut down, subsequent requests should be satisfied much faster because the Web server will cache the page.

Using File Redirection

The `Request` object includes a method that can be used to automatically redirect a customer to a new file. I'm going to explain how to use this method in this section. You should know about it; many programmers use it. However, I will also suggest that you never use this method on your own Web site.

You can automatically redirect a customer to a new page by using the `Redirect` method of the `Response` object. For example, the script in Listing 4.10 will automatically transfer a customer to a page named `login.asp` if the customer's username and password cannot be retrieved from the `Request` object.

LISTING 4.10   Using Browser Redirection

```
1   <%
2   username = TRIM( Request( "username" ) )
3   password = TRIM( Request( "password" ) )
4   IF username = "" OR password = "" THEN
5     Response.Redirect "/login.asp"
6   END IF
7   %>
8   <HTML>
9   <HEAD><TITLE>Welcome</TITLE></HEAD>
10  <BODY>
11
12  Welcome registered user!
13
14  </BODY>
15  </HTML>
```

ANALYSIS   The script in Listing 4.10 begins by retrieving the username and password items from the `Request` object in lines 2 and 3. If a value for the username or password cannot be retrieved, the customer is redirected to a page named `login.asp` in line 5.

The `Redirect` method uses browser redirection. If a customer requests the page in Listing 4.10, and the customer hasn't logged in, the server sends a message to the browser telling the browser to request the `login.asp` page. So, the browser must request two pages before the `login.asp` page is shown.

You can pass query string variables with the `Redirect` method. However, you cannot use the `TARGET` attribute. This means that you cannot redirect a customer to a particular window or frame.

Finally, not all browsers fully support the `Redirect` method. If a customer is using a browser that doesn't support redirects, a page displaying a message similar to the following message will be displayed in the customer's browser:

```
302: Object has Moved
```

I recommend that you never use browser redirects when building your Web site for two reasons. First, using redirects places more strain on your Web server because it forces the browser to retrieve two pages instead of one. Second, redirects aren't fully supported by all browsers. When a browser doesn't support redirects, the customer will get the previous confusing message.

Instead of using browser redirects, you can use a VBScript conditional or SELECT...CASE statement to conditionally display different include files. Using the #INCLUDE directive in this manner has the same effect as using a redirect without any of the drawbacks. For example, the script in Listing 4.11 does exactly the same thing as the script in Listing 4.10 without using the Redirect method.

LISTING 4.11   Avoiding Browser Redirection

```
1   <%
2   username = TRIM( Request( "username" ) )
3   password = TRIM( Request( "password" ) )
4   IF username = "" OR password = "" THEN
5   %>
6   <!-- #INCLUDE VIRTUAL="/login.asp" -->
7   <%
8   Response.End
9   END IF
10  %>
11  <HTML>
12   <HEAD><TITLE>Welcome</TITLE></HEAD>
13  <BODY>
14
15  Welcome registered user!
16
17  </BODY>
18  </HTML>
```

ANALYSIS The ASP page in Listing 4.11 displays the login.asp page if a customer's username and password cannot be retrieved from the Request object. Otherwise, the page contained in lines 11–18 is displayed.

Instead of using the Redirect method to redirect to the login.asp page, the page is included in line 6 with the #INCLUDE directive. Notice that the End method of the Response object is used in line 8 to prevent the rest of the page from being displayed if the login.asp page is displayed.

Note

The version of Active Server Pages included with Windows 2000 has new and better methods for redirecting a user to a new file. The new `Transfer` method of the `Server` object has exactly the same effect as the `Redirect` method without any of the `Redirect` method's shortcomings. The `Transfer` method transfers a customer to a new page without forcing the Web browser to request a new page. All the action takes place on the Web server.

A second new method of the `Server` object, the `Execute` method, enables you to execute one ASP page from within another. Again, the `Transfer` method doesn't rely on the capabilities of a customer's browser. All the work happens on the server.

Using the File Access Component

In this section, you'll learn how to use the File Access component to create and read text files. You can use the File Access component to record information that customers input into HTML forms at your Web site.

Note

Before you can use the File Access component to create a text file with Windows NT or Windows 2000, you must first grant the anonymous Internet user account Write permission on a directory. If you receive the following cryptic error while using the File Access component, you will know that you haven't granted the necessary permissions:

```
Server object error 'ASP 0177 : 800a004c'
Server.CreateObject Failed
/test.asp, line 7
The operation completed successfully.
```

4

The File Access component actually represents a collection of objects. These objects are listed as follows:

- `FileSystemObject`—Includes all the basic methods for working with the file system.

- `TextStream`—Used for reading and writing to a text file.

- `File`—Represents an individual file. For example, you can use this object to determine the date that a file was last modified or to retrieve the full path to a file.

- `Folder`—Represents a file folder (a directory). For example, you can use this object to list all the files in a folder.

- Drive—Represents a disk drive or network share. You can use the properties of this object to retrieve such information as the amount of disk space available or the type of file system being used on a drive.

For example, to create a text file, you use the FileSystemObject object and the TextStream object. You use the FileSystemObject to return an instance of the TextStream object and you use the methods of the TextStream object to write content to the file.

The script in Listing 4.12 illustrates how you can use these two objects to create a new text file.

LISTING 4.12   Creating a Text File

```
1  <%
2  Set fs = Server.CreateObject( "Scripting.FileSystemObject" )
3  Set textFile = fs.CreateTextFile( "c:\mydir\test.txt" )
4  textFile.WriteLine( "Hello World!" )
5  textFile.Close
6  %>
```

ANALYSIS   The script in Listing 4.12 creates a simple text file named test.txt in the mydir directory. In line 2, an instance of the FileSystemObject is created. Next, in line 3, the CreateTextFile() method of the FileSystemObject object is used to create a text file named test.txt. The CreateTextFile() method returns an instance of the TextStream object.

In line 4, the WriteLine() method of the TextStream object is used to write the text Hello World! to the text file. Finally, in line 5, the TextStream object is closed. When the script finishes processing, you should have a new text file named test.txt on your hard drive that contains the text Hello World!.

The CreateTextFile() method of the FileSystemObject object is used to create the new text file and return a reference to the TextStream object. The CreateTextFile() method has one required parameter and two optional ones:

- FileSpecifier—Required parameter that specifies the path of the file to create. If the directory in the path doesn't exist, the error File Not Found is returned.
- Overwrite—This parameter is optional. By default, it has the value TRUE. A call to CreateTextFile() automatically overwrites any preexisting file with the same name. If this parameter is set to FALSE, an error occurs if the file already exists.
- Unicode—This parameter is optional. By default, it has the value FALSE, which indicates that a file using the ASCII character set should be created. If set to TRUE, a file using the Unicode character set will be created.

For example, to create a text file that won't overwrite a preexisting file with the same name and that uses the Unicode characters set, you would use the following statement:

```
textFile = fs.CreateTextFile( "c:\mydir\test.txt", FALSE, TRUE )
```

After you use the `CreateTextFile()` method to create an instance of the `TextStream` object, you use the methods of the `TextStream` object to actually write stuff to the file. The following three methods of the `TextStream` are useful when writing to a text file:

- `Write( string )`—This method writes a string to the text file.
- `WriteLine( [string] )`—This method writes a string to the text file and appends a newline character. The string argument is optional. If omitted, the method simply adds a newline character to the text file.
- `WriteBlankLines( lines )`—This method writes the indicated number of blank lines (newline characters) to the text file.

After you create a new text file, you'll want a method of reading it. Once again, you can use the `FileSystemObject` object and the `TextStreamObject` object. For example, the script in Listing 4.13 reads a text file and displays its contents in an ASP page.

LISTING 4.13 Reading a Text File

```
1  <HTML>
2  <HEAD><TITLE>File Contents</TITLE></HEAD>
3  <BODY>
4  <%
5  Set ts = Server.CreateObject( "Scripting.FileSystemObject" )
6  Set textFile = ts.OpenTextFile( "c:\mydir\test.txt" )
7  WHILE NOT textFile.AtEndOfStream
8    Response.Write textFile.ReadLine
9  WEND
10 textFile.Close
11 %>
12 </BODY>
13 </HTML>
```

ANALYSIS The contents of the test.txt file is displayed in lines 5–10. In line 5, an instance of the `FileSystemObject` object is created. Next, in line 6, the `OpenTextFile()` method is used to return an instance of a `TextStream` object. A `WHILE...WEND` loop in lines 7–9 displays each line of the text file. Finally, in line 10, the instance of the `TextStream` object is closed.

Notice that the `WHILE...WEND` loop in Listing 4.13 will continue to loop while the `AtEndOfStream` property of the `FileSystemObject` object has the value `FALSE`. The `AtEndOfStream` property is used to detect when the end of the file has been reached.

Note

If you need to convert between the virtual path and the physical path of a file, you can use the MapPath() method of the Server object. For example, the following statement displays the physical path of the default.asp page (typically, c:\inetpub\wwwroot\default.asp):

```
<% Response.Write Server.MapPath( "/default.asp" ) %>
```

The FileSystemObject has the following four properties that are useful when reading a text file:

- AtEndOfLine—This property indicates whether the end of a particular line in a text file has been reached. When the newline character is detected, this property has the value TRUE.

- AtEndOfStream—This property indicates whether the end of the entire text file has been reached. This property has the value FALSE before the end of the text file is reached, and the value TRUE afterwards.

- Column—This property indicates the current character position in a line. It returns an integer value.

- Line—This property indicates the current line in a file. It returns an integer value.

A particular line of text is retrieved from the text file in Listing 4.13 by using the ReadLine method of the TextStream object (see line 8). The TextStream object has four methods that are useful when reading from a text file:

- Read(characters)—This method reads the specified number of characters from the text file.

- ReadLine—This method reads a single line from the text file. (The newline character isn't returned.)

- ReadAll—This method returns the entire contents of the file.

- Skip(characters)—This method skips the specified number of characters in the text file.

- SkipLine—This method skips a single line in the text file.

You can use the ReadAll() method to grab the entire contents of a text file and assign it to a variable. You should be cautious when using this method with large text files. Using the method can devour a significant portion of your computer's memory.

So far, you have learned to create a text file and read the contents of a text file. You'll often discover that you'll need to append new text to an existing text file. You can do this by passing an optional parameter to the OpenTextFile() method.

For example, Listing 4.14 illustrates how to add the line `Goodbye!` to the end of the test.txt text file.

LISTING 4.14   Appending to a Text File

```
1  <%
2  Set ts = Server.CreateObject( "Scripting.FileSystemObject" )
3  Set textFile = ts.OpenTextFile( "c:\mydir\test.txt", 8, TRUE )
4  textFile.WriteLine( "Goodbye!" )
5  textFile.Close
6  %>
```

ANALYSIS   The script in Listing 4.14 adds a new line of text to the preexisting text file named test.txt. In line 2, an instance of the `FileSystemObject` object is created. Next, in line 3, the `OpenTextFile()` method of the `FileSystemObject` object is used to open a text file for appending. In line 4, the new line is added to the text file. In line 5, the text file is closed.

The crucial line in Listing 4.14 is line 3. This line uses an optional argument of the `OpenTextFile()` method to enable new text to be appended to the text file. The `OpenTextFile()` method accepts the following arguments:

- `FileSpecifier`—Required argument that specifies the path of the file to open.

- `IOMode`—Optional argument indicating whether the file should be opened for reading, writing, or appending. The default value is `1` for reading. To open a file for writing, set this value to `2`. To open a file for appending, set this value to `8`.

- `Create`—Optional argument indicating whether the file should be created if it doesn't already exist. By default, the value of this argument is `FALSE`.

- `Format`—Optional argument that specifies the format of the file. By default, a file uses the ASCII character set. However, you can use the Unicode character set by passing the value `-1`, or the system default by passing the value `-2`.

Managing Text Files

The `FileSystemObject` object has several valuable methods for managing text files. In this section, you'll learn how to use these methods to copy a file, move a file, delete a file, and check whether a file exists.

To copy a text file, you use the `CopyFile()` method of the `FileSystemObject` object. This method accepts two required arguments and one optional argument:

- `Source`—The full path and name of the file that you want to copy. You can use wildcard characters in the source argument to copy more than one file at a time.

4

- Destination—The full path and name of the new file to create.
- Overwrite—Optional argument that indicates whether existing files should be overwritten. This argument can have the value TRUE or FALSE.

For example, to copy a file named test.txt to a new file named test2.txt, you can use the script in Listing 4.15.

LISTING 4.15   Copying a File

```
1  <%
2  Set fs = Server.CreateObject( "Scripting.FileSystemObject" )
3  fs.CopyFile "c:\mydir\test.txt", "c:\mydir\test2.txt"
4  %>
```

To move a file, you use the MoveFile() method of the FileSystemObject object. The script in Listing 4.16 illustrates how you can move a file from a directory named mydir to a directory named myotherdir.

LISTING 4.16   Moving a File

```
1  <%
2  Set fs = Server.CreateObject( "Scripting.FileSystemObject" )
3  fs.MoveFile "c:\mydir\test.txt", "c:\myotherdir\test.txt"
4  %>
```

The MoveFile() method accepts the following two arguments:

- Source—The full path and name of the file that you want to move. You can use wildcard characters in the source argument to move more than one file at a time.
- Destination—The full path and name of the new file to create.

To delete a file, you use the DeleteFile() method of the FileSystemObject object. The script in Listing 4.17 deletes the file named test.txt.

LISTING 4.17   Deleting a File

```
1  <%
2  Set fs = Server.CreateObject( "Scripting.FileSystemObject" )
3  fs.DeleteFile "c:\mydir\test.txt"
4  %>
```

When specifying the file to delete, you can use wildcard characters. However, if no matches are found, an error is generated.

Finally, to check whether a file exists, you use the `FileExists()` method of the `FileSystemObject` object. The `FileExists()` method returns TRUE if the file exists and FALSE otherwise. Listing 4.18 contains a script that illustrates how to use the `FileExists()` method.

LISTING 4.18   Checking File Existence

```
1  <%
2  Set fs = Server.CreateObject( "Scripting.FileSystemObject" )
3  IF fs.FileExists( "c:\mydir\test.txt" ) THEN
4    Response.Write "File Exists!"
5  ELSE
6    Response.Write "Can't Be Found!"
7  END IF
8  %>
```

ANALYSIS   The `FileExists()` method is used in line 3 to detect whether a file named test.txt exists. If the file does exist, the message `File Exists!` is displayed. Otherwise, the message `Can't Be Found!` is displayed.

Displaying the Contents of a Folder

Suppose that you want to display a list of files contained in a folder. For example, these files could be customer support documents that you want to enable customers to download from your Web site. Or, they could be a list of pictures that you want to display.

You can retrieve a list of the files in a folder by using the `FileSystemObject` object and the `Folder` object. For example, Listing 4.19 displays a list of all the files in a folder named `mydir`. A download link is automatically created for each file that enables a customer to download the file.

LISTING 4.19   Listing Files in a Folder

```
1  <HTML>
2  <HEAD><TITLE>File List</TITLE></HEAD>
3  <BODY>
4  <%
5  Set fs = Server.CreateObject("Scripting.FileSystemObject" )
6  Set folder = fs.GetFolder( "c:\mydir" )
7  FOR EACH file IN folder.Files
8    %>
9    <br><a href="<%=file.Name%>"><%=file.Name%></a>
10   <%
11 NEXT
12 %>
13 </BODY>
14 </HTML>
```

ANALYSIS The files are listed in lines 5–11. In line 5, an instance of the `FileSystemObject` object is created. In line 6, an instance of the `Folder` object is created by calling the `GetFolder()` method of the `FileSystemObject` object.

Each file in the `mydir` folder is displayed within the `FOR...NEXT` loop in lines 7–11. The `Name` property of the `File` object is used to display the name of each file. This property is also used within the hypertext anchor to create a link to the file.

Sample Application: Recording Marketing Data

In this section, you'll learn how to create two Active Server Pages that illustrate how to use the File Access component in a real world application. In the first ASP page, we'll create a simple form that asks a customer information about how the customer discovered the current Web site. The second ASP page is used to retrieve and store the information that the customer enters into the HTML form.

The HTML form that gathers the information from the customer is contained in Listing 4.20.

LISTING 4.20   Marketing Form

```
1   <HTML>
2   <HEAD><TITLE>Customer Survey</TITLE></HEAD>
3   <BODY>
4
5   <H2>Customer Survey</H2>
6   <fORM method="post" action="saveform.asp">
7   <b>How did you find out about our Web site?
8   <br><input name="source" type="radio"
9     value="friend" CHECKED> A Friend
10  <br><input name="source" type="radio"
11    value="article"> Magazine Article
12  <br><input name="source" type="radio"
13    value="other"> Other
14  <p>How would you rate our Web site?
15  <br><input name="rate" type="radio"
16    value="great" CHECKED> Great!
17  <br><input name="rate" type="radio"
18    value="okay"> Okay
19  <br><input name="rate" type="radio"
20    value="bad"> Needs Improvement
21  <p><input type="submit" value="Submit Survey">
22  </FORM>
23
24  </BODY>
25  </HTML>
```

ANALYSIS The page in Listing 4.20 contains a simple customer survey form. When the HTML form is submitted, the data from the form is sent to a page named save-form.asp. The saveform.asp ASP page is contained in Listing 4.21.

LISTING 4.21   Saving the Form Data

```
 1  <%
 2  source = TRIM( Request( "source" ) )
 3  rate = TRIM( Request( "rate" ) )
 4  Set fs = Server.CreateObject( "Scripting.FileSystemObject" )
 5  Set textFile = fs.OpenTextFile( "c:\survey.txt", 8, TRUE )
 6  textFile.WriteLine "============="
 7  textFile.WriteLine "Answers submitted on " & NOW()
 8  textFile.WriteLine "Source=" & source
 9  textFile.WriteLine "Rating=" & rate
10  textFile.Close
11  %>
12  <HTML>
13  <HEAD><TITLE>Customer Survey</TITLE></HEAD>
14  <BODY>
15
16  Thank you for completing our customer survey!
17
18  </BODY>
19  </HTML>
```

ANALYSIS The ASP page in Listing 4.21 saves the survey results in a text file named sur-vey.txt. The form variables are retrieved in lines 2 and 3. Next, an instance of the FileSystemObject object is created in line 4.

In line 5, the text file named survey.txt is opened. The text file is opened for appending by passing the value 8 for the IOMODE argument.

After the text file is opened, the form variables are appended to the text file in lines 6–9. Finally, in line 10, the text file is closed. The remainder of the ASP page in Listing 4.21 is used to display a thank you message to the customer.

Summary

In today's lesson, you learned various methods of working with files. In the first section, you learned how to include one file in another file by using the server-side #INCLUDE directive. You also learned how to conditionally display the contents of different include files.

In the next section, you learned how to use browser redirection to automatically redirect a customer to a new file. You also learned about some of the drawbacks of using browser redirection.

Finally, you were introduced to the File Access component. You learned how to use the File Access component both to create a new text file and to read from an existing text file. You also learned how to copy a file, move a file, delete a file, and detect whether a file exists. Lastly, you learned how to create a customer survey form and save the survey data with the File Access component.

Q&A

Q **You recommend avoiding the Redirect method of the Response object and using #INCLUDE files instead. Is it really such a bad idea to use browser redirection?**

A Using browser redirection entails the same types of risks as using cookies or Session variables. Like cookies and Session variables, browser redirection depends on the properties of a customer's browser. If you want your Web site to be accessible to the broadest possible audience, you shouldn't use browser redirection.

Q **When saving customer data, is it better to save the information to a text file or a database table?**

A In today's lesson, you learned how to use the File Access component to save customer information to a text file. In tomorrow's lesson, you'll learn how to work with a database table in an ASP page. In general, you should store information in a database table instead of a text file.

Saving information in a database table has many advantages. One of the most important advantages is that a database provides you with more flexible methods of retrieving data. For example, when retrieving data from a database table, you can write database queries that select only the data that meet a certain criteria. Furthermore, using a database to store customer information is a more scalable solution than using a text file. Unlike a text file, a database is designed to be accessed by multiple users at a time.

Workshop

The Quiz and Exercise questions are designed to test your knowledge of the material covered in this chapter. The answers are in Appendix A, "Quiz Answers."

Quiz

1. What's the difference, if any, between using the FILE attribute of the #INCLUDE directive and the VIRTUAL attribute of the #INCLUDE directive?

2. There is a problem with the following script. How can the script be rewritten so that it works as intended?

```
<%
answer = Request( "answer" )
IF answer = "yes" THEN
  displayPage = "page1.asp"
ELSE
  displayPage = "page2.asp"
END IF
%>
<!-- #INCLUDE VIRTUAL="<%=displayPage%>" -->
```

3. How would you rewrite the following script so that it does not use the Redirect method?

```
<%
username = TRIM( Request( "username" ) )
IF username = "" THEN
  Response.Redirect "/login.asp"
END IF
%>
```

4. What method of the FileSystemObject object do you use to detect whether a file exists?

Exercise

Create an ASP page that displays its own source code. Use the FileSystem and TextStream objects in the page.

4

DAY 5

Building Your Product Catalog

In today's lesson, you will begin building your online store. You'll learn how to create and manage your store's inventory of products using ASP scripts. You'll also learn several valuable techniques for working with databases. Today, you will learn the following:

- How to create a database for your store
- How to create the Products table to contain your product information
- How to connect to a database within an ASP page
- How to use ASP scripts to add new products
- How to use ASP scripts to update existing product information

Creating the Store Database

The first step in creating your online store is to create a database to hold all the information about your products. In this book, we will be using Microsoft Access for our database. However, the ASP scripts in the following chapters should also work with other databases with little or no modification. For example, with minor modifications, you can use the same scripts with a Microsoft SQL Server or Oracle database.

Microsoft Access is an appropriate database to use for prototyping a Web site or running a low traffic Web site. However, if you expect heavy traffic at your online store, you should seriously consider upgrading to Microsoft SQL Server.

You can easily upgrade an Access database to a SQL Server database by using the Microsoft Upsizing Tools. These Upsizing Tools are included with Microsoft Access 2000. If you are using Microsoft Access 97, you can download the Upsizing Tools from `http://www.microsoft.com/accessdev/prodinfo/aut97dat.htm`.

Follow these steps to create a new Microsoft Access database:

1. Launch Microsoft Access by selecting Start, Programs, Microsoft Access.
2. From the initial dialog box, choose the option to create a new database using a blank Access database (see Figure 5.1).

FIGURE 5.1

Creating a new database.

3. Within the File New Database dialog box, name your new database **storeDB** and save the new database to your hard drive. (Remember where you save it.)

After you have completed these three steps, you should have a new file on your hard drive named storeDB.mdb. You will use this database to store information about your products, your users, and your orders.

Note

If you don't own Microsoft Access, don't worry. You can copy the storeDB file from the CD that accompanies this book to your computer's hard drive. This database already contains the Products table discussed in the next section.

Creating the Products Table

In the previous section, you created a new Access database. However, a database, all by itself, isn't particularly useful. Before you can begin storing information in a database, you must add one or more database tables to it.

A database table is structured like a spreadsheet or ledger. It contains one or more rows divided into one or more columns. Each column has a name, and it is used to store a particular type of information. Each row in a database table represents a distinct record.

We'll be storing our product information for our store in a database table named Products. This table will have the following eight columns:

product_id — This column contains a unique number for each product in the table.

product_name — This column contains the name of the product. For example, Holiday Gift Basket.

product_price — This column contains the product's current price. For example, $28.52.

product_picture — This column contains the path to the picture of the product.

product_category — This column contains the category of the product. For example, if you were creating an online bookstore, this column might contain values such as Science Fiction or Mystery.

product_briefdesc — This column contains a short description of the product. For example, This holiday gift basket contains three delicious cakes for the holiday season.

product_fulldesc — This column contains a full description of the product. This might be a full page of information.

product_status — This column contains information about the current status of the product. For example, it might indicate that the product should not be displayed currently.

5

To create the Products table, follow these steps:

1. If Microsoft Access isn't currently open, launch it by selecting Start, Programs, Microsoft Access. Select the option to open an existing file and select the database named storeDB.

2. After you open the storeDB database, double-click the item labeled Create table in Design view. The window in Figure 5.2 should appear.

FIGURE 5.2

Creating a table in Design view.

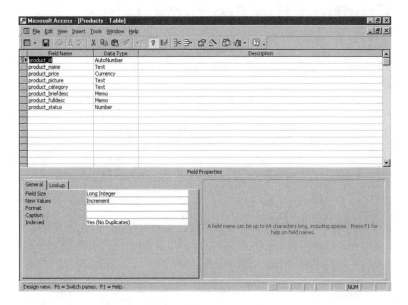

3. Enter the information from Table 5.1 into the Design view table grid. (You can safely ignore the Description field.)

TABLE 5.1 The Products Database Table

Field Name	Data Type
product_id	AutoNumber
product_name	Text
product_price	Currency
product_picture	Text
product_category	Text
product_briefdesc	Memo
product_fulldesc	Memo
product_status	Number

4. Make the `product_id` column into the table's primary key by selecting the column within the grid and clicking the icon of the key.

5. Save the new table by clicking Save (the disk icon) and entering the name **Products**.

After you complete these steps, you will have created a table named Products. Each row in this table will represent an individual product of your online store. In the remainder of this chapter, you will learn how to use ASP scripts to connect to the database and update the information in the Products table.

Connecting to a Database

In this section, you will learn how to open a connection to a database within an ASP script. Before you can open a database connection, however, you need to provide the ASP page with information about the physical location of the database. In other words, you need to provide the script with a method for finding the database on your hard drive. One way to do this is with a Data Source Name (DSN).

A couple of different types of DSNs can be created. If you create a File DSN, the database connection information is stored in a file. If you create a System DSN, the database connection information is stored within your computer's registry.

There is no particular reason to use one type of DSN rather than another. Both File and System DSNs work perfectly well, but we'll create a System DSN.

To create a System DSN, follow these steps:

1. Open the Control Panel by selecting Start, Settings, Control Panel.

2. Click on the ODBC Data Sources applet.

3. Select the tab labeled System DSN and click Add.

4. Select the Microsoft Access driver and click Finish.

5. In the ODBC Microsoft Access Setup dialog box, click the button labeled Select and navigate through your hard drive to the database named storeDB (the database that you created in the earlier section "Creating the Store Database"). Click OK.

6. Enter **accessDSN** for the Data Source Name and click OK (see Figure 5.3).

7. Click OK to close the ODBC Data Sources applet.

5

FIGURE 5.3

Creating a DSN.

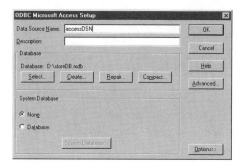

After you complete these steps, you will have created a new System DSN named accessDSN. You only need to create one DSN for each database that you use in your scripts. After you create the DSN, all your scripts can use the same DSN to connect with the database. However, if you ever move your database, you will need to update the DSN by using the ODBC Data Sources applet.

Note

The process for creating a DSN for an SQL Server database or Oracle database is very similar to the process of creating a DSN for an Access database. For example, to create a DSN for an SQL Server database, choose the SQL Server driver in step 4. You will also need to provide the name of a valid SQL Server login and password.

Now that you have created a DSN, you can use it to open a database connection. To create a connection, you must use one of the ActiveX Data Objects (ADO). The ADO is a collection of objects that allows you to work with databases within your ASP scripts. They are ActiveX objects that you can use in the same way as you would use any other ASP component such as the File Access Component.

A database connection is represented in an ASP page by the ADO Connection object. Listing 5.1 demonstrates how to use the Connection object with the DSN that we just created to open a database connection.

INPUT   **LISTING 5.1**   Connecting to a Database

```
1 <%
2 Set Con = Server.CreateObject( "ADODB.Connection" )
3 Con.Open "accessDSN"
4 %>
```

ANALYSIS This script opens a connection to the storeDB Microsoft Access database by using a DSN named accessDSN. In line 2, an instance of the Connection object is created. In line 3, the database connection is opened by calling the Open method of the Connection object.

Opening a database connection is very much like opening a phone connection. After the connection is open, messages can be passed back and forth between the ASP script and the database. For example, you can pass a message from the script to the database to tell the database to insert a certain record or update a particular bit of information. In the next two sections, you will learn how to pass these messages.

Adding Products to the Products Table

Databases speak their own language. To get a database to do something, you must send a message to the database in its language. Microsoft Access, like most modern databases, uses a language called the Structured Query Language (SQL).

For example, to add a new record to a database table from an ASP page, you must first open a connection to the database, and then send the database a string that tells it to insert a new record. To insert a new record into a database, use the SQL INSERT INTO statement.

The script in Listing 5.2 inserts a new record into the Products table.

INPUT   **LISTING 5.2**   Inserting a New Record

```
1 <%
2 Set Con = Server.CreateObject( "ADODB.Connection" )
3 Con.Open "accessDSN"
4
5 sqlString = "INSERT INTO Products ( product_name, product_price ) " &_
6    "values ( 'Gift Basket', 34.54 )"
7 Con.Execute sqlString
8 Con.Close
9 %>
```

ANALYSIS This script inserts a new product into the Products table. Lines 2 and 3 are used to open a connection to the database. In line 5, a string that contains the SQL INSERT INTO statement is assigned to a variable named sqlString. The SQL statement is executed in line 7. Finally, in line 8, the database connection is closed.

The basic syntax of the SQL INSERT INTO statement is very simple:

```
INSERT INTO table_name ( column_list ) VALUES ( value_list )
```

5

You indicate the table in which you want the new record inserted with `table_name`. You list one or more columns from the table with `column_list`, and you provide the values you want assigned to each of these columns with `value_list`. The columns and the values must be listed in the same order in a comma-separated list.

When inserting string or date and time values, you must enclose the value in a pair of single quotes. When inserting numeric values, you do not include the quotes.

If you execute the script in Listing 5.2, you can prove to yourself that the new product was added to the Products table within Microsoft Access. Launch Microsoft Access, open the storeDB database, and double-click on the Products table. You should see the screen in Figure 5.4.

FIGURE 5.4

Updated Products table.

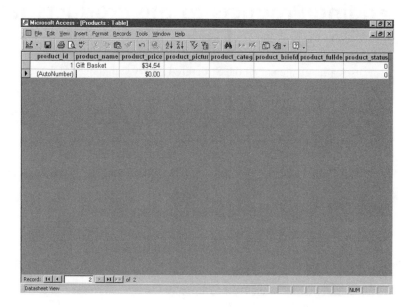

Because the `sqlString` variable has a string as its value, you can create the string dynamically. The script in Listing 5.3 does exactly the same thing as the previous script. However, the string is created by using the values of variables for the column values.

INPUT **LISTING 5.3** Inserting a New Record Using Variables

```
1 <%
2 Set Con = Server.CreateObject( "ADODB.Connection" )
3 Con.Open "accessDSN"
4
5 productName = "Gift Basket"
```

```
6 productPrice = 34.54
7 sqlString = "INSERT INTO Products ( product_name, product_price ) " &_
8    "values ( '" & productName & "', " & productPrice & " )"
9 Con.Execute sqlString
10 Con.Close
11 %>
```

ANALYSIS This script, like the previous script, inserts a new product into the Products table. However, two variables named productName and productPrice are assigned to the two new values that will be inserted into the database. In lines 5 and 6, the productName and productPrice variables are assigned a value. In line 7, the sqlString variable is assigned a string that is built from the productName and productPrice variables. Finally, in line 9, the sqlString is executed, and a new product is added to the database.

You might have noticed that whenever a value is assigned to the product_name column, the value is surrounded by single quotes. However, when a value is assigned to the product_price column, no quotes are used. Microsoft Access uses the single quote character in the same way as VBScript or HTML uses double quotes. They are used to indicate the start and end of a string. Because product_name is a text column, you must use single quotes when assigning a value to the column.

Creating the AddProducts Form

In this section, you'll learn how to create a form that you can use to easily add multiple products to your online store. We'll create the following two pages:

- addProduct.asp—This page will contain an HTML form that enables you to enter the product information.

- manageProducts.asp—When you submit the form contained in addProduct.asp, this page will actually add the new product information to the database.

The addProduct.asp page includes a normal HTML form with fields that correspond to columns of the Products table. The addProduct.asp page is contained in Listing 5.4. (The page is also included on the CD that accompanies this book.) Figure 5.5 shows what the form looks like.

5

FIGURE 5.5

The addProduct form.

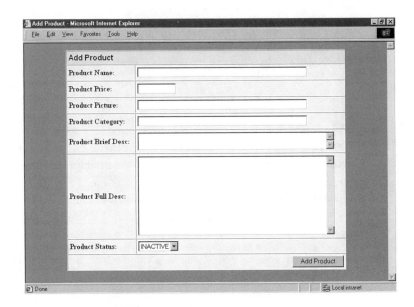

LISTING 5.4   The addProduct.asp Page

```
1 <html>
2 <head><title>Add Product </title></head>
3 <body bgcolor="gray">
4
5 <form method="post" action="manageproducts.asp">
6
7 <center>
8 <table width="600" border=1 bgcolor="lightyellow"
9  cellpadding="4" cellspacing="0">
10 <tr>
11    <td colspan="2" bgcolor="yellow">
12    <font face="Arial" size="3"><b>
13    Add Product
14    </b></font>
15    </td>
16 </tr>
17 <tr>
18    <td>
19    <b> Product Name:</b>
20    </td>
21    <td>
22    <input name="productName"
23      size="50" maxlength="50">
24    </td>
25 </tr>
26 <tr>
27    <td>
```

```
28    <b>Product Price:</b>
29    </td>
30    <td>
31    <input name="productPrice" size="10">
32    </td>
33 </tr>
34 <tr>
35    <td>
36    <b>Product Picture:</b>
37    </td>
38    <td>
39    <input name="productPicture"
40       size="50" maxlength="50">
41    </td>
42 </tr>
43 <tr>
44    <td>
45    <b>Product Category:</b>
46    </td>
47    <td>
48    <input name="productCategory"
49       size="50" maxlength="50">
50    </td>
51 </tr>
52 <tr>
53    <td>
54    <b>Product Brief Desc:</b>
55    </td>
56    <td>
57    <textarea name="productBriefDesc"
58       cols="50" rows="2" wrap="virtual"></textarea>
59    </td>
60 </tr>
61 <tr>
62    <td>
63    <b>Product Full Desc:</b>
64    </td>
65    <td>
66    <textarea name="productFullDesc"
67       cols="50" rows="10" wrap="virtual"></textarea>
68    </td>
69 </tr>
70 <tr>
71    <td>
72    <b>Product Status:</b>
73    </td>
74    <td>
75    <select name="productStatus">
76    <option value="0">INACTIVE
77    <option value="1">ACTIVE
```

5

continues

LISTING 5.4   continued

```
78    </select>
79    </td>
80 </tr>
81 <tr>
82    <td colspan=2 align="right">
83    <input type="submit" value="Add Product">
84    </td>
85 </tr>
86 </table>
87 </center>
88
89 <input name="addProduct" type="1"
90  value="1">
91 </form>
92
93 </body>
94 </html>
```

Listing 5.4 doesn't contain any ASP scripts. Its sole purpose is to gather the product information through an HTML form. The product information isn't added to the database until the form is submitted, and the second page—manageproducts.asp—is requested.

You should notice that line 89 creates a hidden form variable named addProduct. When the form is submitted, this hidden form variable is posted with the rest of the form information. The manageproducts.asp page uses this hidden form variable to know whether a new product should be added.

All the real work happens in the manageproducts.asp page. The manageproducts.asp page grabs all the form fields submitted in addProduct.asp, builds a SQL string, and executes the SQL string that results in a new product being added to the database. The manageproducts.asp page is contained in Listing 5.5. (It's also included on the CD that accompanies this book.)

INPUT   **LISTING 5.5**   The manageproducts.asp Page

```
1 <%
2 ' Get the Form Variables
3 addProduct          = TRIM( Request( "addProduct" ) )
4
5 productName       = TRIM( Request( "productName" ) )
6 productPrice      = TRIM( Request( "productPrice" ) )
7 productPicture    = TRIM( Request( "productPicture" ) )
8 productCategory   = TRIM( Request( "productCategory" ) )
9 productBriefDesc = TRIM( Request( "productBriefDesc" ) )
```

```
10 productFullDesc = TRIM( Request( "productFullDesc" ) )
11 productStatus   = TRIM( Request( "productStatus" ) )
12
13 ' Assign Default Values
14 IF productName = "" THEN
15   productName = "?????"
16 END IF
17 IF productPrice = "" THEN
18   productPrice = 0
19 END IF
20 IF productPicture = "" THEN
21  productPicture = "?????"
22 END IF
23 IF productCategory = "" THEN
24  productCategory = "?????"
25 END IF
26 IF productBriefDesc = "" THEN
27   productBriefDesc = "?????"
28 END IF
29 IF productFullDesc = "" THEN
30   productFullDesc = "?????"
31 END IF
32
33 ' Open the Database Connection
34 Set Con = Server.CreateObject( "ADODB.Connection" )
35 Con.Open "accessDSN"
36 %>
37 <html>
38 <head><title>Manage Products</title></head>
39 <body bgcolor="gray">
40 <%
41 ' Add New Product
42 IF addProduct <> "" THEN
43
44 sqlString = "INSERT INTO Products " &_
45   "( product_name, product_price, product_picture, " &_
46   "product_category, product_briefdesc, product_fulldesc, " &_
47   "product_status ) VALUES ( " &_
48   " '" & productName & "', " &_
49   cCUR( productPrice ) & ", " &_
50   " '" & productPicture & "', " &_
51   " '" & productCategory & "', " &_
52   " '" & productBriefDesc & "', " &_
53   " '" & productFullDesc & "', " &_
54   productStatus & "  )"
55
56 Con.Execute sqlString
57 %>
58 <center>
59 <table width="600" cellpadding="4"
```

5

continues

LISTING 5.5   continued

```
60   cellspacing="0" bgcolor="lightyellow">
61 <tr>
62     <td>
63     <%=productName%> was added to the database
64     </td>
65 </tr>
66 </table>                        .
67 </center>
68 <p>
69 <%
70 END IF
71 %>
72 <a href="addproduct.asp">Add Product</a>
72 </body>
73 </html>
```

ANALYSIS   Lines 2–11 are used to retrieve the form variables submitted from the
addProduct.asp page. Notice that the VBScript TRIM() function is used to
remove any leading and trailing spaces.

Lines 13–31 assigns a default value to each of the variables. If a variable doesn't have a
value, it is assigned the value ?????.

Lines 33–35 opens a database connection. The database connection is opened using the
accessDSN DSN.

The new product is actually added to the Products table in lines 41–56. First, a very long
SQL string is created by building it up out of the product information submitted in the
HTML form. Next, in line 56, the SQL string is executed and the new record is added.

Lines 58–67 display a message that the new product was successfully added. See Figure
5.6 to see what the page looks like after adding a new product named Holiday Gift
Basket.

A Problem with Databases and Quotation Marks

In the previous section, you learned how to add a new record to a database table. The
manageproducts.asp page adds new records to the Products table. However, as it stands,
the page has an important problem. This problem results from the use of single quotation
marks.

Microsoft Access uses a single quotation mark to mark the beginning and end of a string.
If the string itself contains a single quotation mark, however, problems will result when
you attempt to add the value to the database.

FIGURE 5.6

Results of adding a new product.

For example, suppose that you wanted to add a new product entitled `Gregory's Chocolate Gift Basket` to the Products table. This product name includes a single quotation mark—the apostrophe in `Gregory's`. If you attempted to execute the following SQL `INSERT INTO` statement, an error would result:

```
INSERT INTO Products ( product_name )
  VALUES ( 'Gregory's Chocolate Gift Basket' )
```

Microsoft Access will see the first quotation mark, the one immediately before the `G` in `Gregory`, and correctly interpret the quotation mark as indicating the beginning of a text string. However, Microsoft Access will interpret the next quotation mark, the single quotation mark that occurs in `Gregory's`, and interpret it as marking the end of the string. This would be the wrong interpretation. The end of the string is correctly marked by the single quote that occurs after the word `Basket`.

To fix this problem, you must make every single quotation mark into two quotation marks. Microsoft Access treats two quotation marks in a row as a single quotation mark when they occur in a text string. For example, the following `INSERT INTO` statement will correctly insert `Gregory's Chocolate Gift Basket` into the Products table:

```
INSERT INTO Products ( product_name )
  VALUES ( 'Gregory''s Chocolate Gift Basket' )
```

Whenever you add a new record or update a record that contains a quotation mark, you must double them up. The easiest way to do this is to create a VBScript function that does this automatically. Listing 5.6 contains a function named `fixQuotes()` that doubles all the single quotation marks in a string.

INPUT   **LISTING 5.6**   The fixQuotes() Function

```
1 FUNCTION fixQuotes( theString )
2   fixQuotes = REPLACE( theString, "'", "''" )
3 END FUNCTION
```

ANALYSIS   The fixQuotes() function uses the VBScript REPLACE() function to replace every single quotation mark (') with two single quotation marks ('').

To fix the manageproducts.asp page so that it can correctly handle single quotation marks submitted in the addProduct.asp page, you need to use the fixQuotes() function. You can add the function to the top of the manageproducts.asp page. Then, you will need to modify lines 44–54 to use the function. Here is what the modified lines look like:

```
44 sqlString = "INSERT INTO Products " &_
45   "( product_name, product_price, product_picture, " &_
46   "product_category, product_briefdesc, product_fulldesc, " &_
47   "product_status ) VALUES ( " &_
48   " '" & fixQuotes( productName ) & "', " &_
49    productPrice  & ", " &_
50   " '" & fixQuotes( productPicture ) & "', " &_
51   " '" & fixQuotes( productCategory ) & "', " &_
52   " '" & fixQuotes( productBriefDesc ) & "', " &_
53   " '" & fixQuotes( productFullDesc ) & "', " &_
54   productStatus & "  )"
```

The fixQuotes() function is used here to double any quotation marks that might occur in the product information variables. To see the final version of the manageproducts.asp page, you can open the page from the CD that accompanies this book.

Updating Product Information in the Products Table

If any of your product information changes, you'll need a way to update this information in the Products table. You can update a database record by using the SQL UPDATE statement. Here's the syntax for this statement:

```
UPDATE table_name SET column_name = expression
WHERE column_name = expression
```

The UPDATE statement updates a table row by setting one or more of its columns to a new value. It updates only those rows in which a certain column has a certain value.

For example, suppose that you want to change the price of the `Holiday Gift Basket`. You want to raise the price from $34.54 to $45.00. To do this, you can use the following SQL `UPDATE` statement:

```
UPDATE Products SET product_price = 45.00
WHERE product_name = 'Holiday Gift Basket'
```

This statement changes the price of the `Holiday Gift Basket` to $45.00 by updating the `product_price` column. The statement updates only those products that have the name `Holiday Gift Basket`.

You can use the SQL `UPDATE` statement within an ASP script in the same way as you can use the SQL `INSERT INTO` statement. To update a record, open a connection to the database, build a SQL string, and execute it. Listing 5.7 demonstrates how to change the price of the `Holiday Gift Basket` to $45.00 within an ASP page.

INPUT **LISTING 5.7** Update a Table Row

```
1 <%
2 Set Con = Server.CreateObject( "ADODB.Connection" )
3 Con.Open "accessDSN"
4
5 sqlString = "UPDATE Products " &_
6   "SET product_price = 45.00 " &_
7   "WHERE product_name = 'Holiday Gift Basket' "
8
9 Con.Execute sqlString
10 %>
```

ANALYSIS Lines 2 and 3 open a database connection. A SQL string is created in lines 5–7. Finally, the SQL string is executed in line 9.

Instead of using a product name to identify the row to be updated, you can use the product ID. The Products table contains a column named `product_id` that uniquely identifies each product with a number. For example, if the value of the `product_id` column for the `Holiday Gift Basket` is 17, you could update the price of the `Holiday Gift Basket` with the following statement:

```
UPDATE Products SET product_price = 45.00
WHERE product_id = 17
```

The advantage of using the `product_id` column instead of the `product_name` column to update a record is you know that every product has a distinct `product_id`. Two products, on the other hand, might have the same name.

5

Displaying the List of Products to Update

In this section, you will learn how to create a form that you can use to update the records in the Products table. We will modify the manageproducts.asp page to enable you to select a product to update. We'll also create a new page named updateProduct.asp that will enable you to modify the information for a particular product.

In order to update a product, you need a method of selecting a product to update. We'll provide a method for selecting an existing product by modifying the manageproducts.asp page so that it will list the current set of products in the database.

To retrieve a set of records from a database table, you must use the ADO Recordset object. In Day 6, "Displaying Your Products," you will learn how to use this object in detail. For the purpose of the current discussion, however, you only need to know that the Recordset object can be used to represent a set of records that result from a database query.

To retrieve and display the list of product names from the Products table, you can use the script in Listing 5.8.

INPUT   **LISTING 5.8**   Retrieve Product Names

```
1 <%
2 Set Con = Server.CreateObject( "ADODB.Connection" )
3 Con.Open "accessDSN"
4
5 sqlString = "SELECT product_name FROM Products"
6 SET RS = Con.Execute( sqlString )
7 WHILE NOT RS.EOF
8 %>
9   <%=RS( "product_name" )%> <p>
10 <%
11 RS.MoveNext
12 WEND
13 %>
```

ANALYSIS   This script opens a connection to the storeDB database in lines 2 and 3. Next, an SQL string is created that selects the name of each product from the Products table. In line 6, an instance of the ADO Recordset object is created and opened by executing the SQL string. When the Recordset is opened, it contains all the product names. Finally, in lines 7—12, a VBScript WHILE...WEND loop is used to loop through the Recordset, displaying all the product names.

We want the list of product names to work as links. When you click on a product name, you should be brought to the updateProduct.asp page with the correct product selected. For example, if you click on Holiday Gift Basket, you should be brought to a form that displays all the current information for the Holiday Gift Basket product.

We can make the list of product names act as hypertext links by using the HTML <A> tag. Listing 5.9 retrieves the list of product names from the Products table and displays each name as a hypertext link to the updateProduct.asp page.

INPUT   **LISTING 5.9**   Retrieve Product Names as Links

```
1 <%
2 Set Con = Server.CreateObject( "ADODB.Connection" )
3 Con.Open "accessDSN"
4
5 sqlString = "SELECT product_name FROM Products"
6 SET RS = Con.Execute( sqlString )
7 WHILE NOT RS.EOF
8 %>
9   <a href="updateProduct.asp">
10 <%=RS( "product_name" )%>
11 </a>
12 <%
13 RS.MoveNext
14 WEND
15 %>
```

ANALYSIS   This script is exactly the same as the previous one, except each product name is displayed as a hypertext link. The links are displayed in lines 9–11.

Finally, we want the correct product selected when you link to the updateProduct.asp page. For example, if you click on the Holiday Gift Basket, you should see the current information for the Holiday Gift Basket and not the information for some other product. To do this, we need to pass the product ID to the updateProduct.asp page, so the right product will be selected.

We can pass the product ID to the updateProduct.asp page by using a query string variable. We'll use a variable named pid that has the product ID as its value. Listing 5.10 demonstrates how this query string variable can be added to each of the hypertext links.

5

INPUT **LISTING 5.10** Display Links with Product IDs

```
1 <%
2 Set Con = Server.CreateObject( "ADODB.Connection" )
3 Con.Open "accessDSN"
4
5 sqlString = "SELECT product_id, product_name FROM Products"
6 SET RS = Con.Execute( sqlString )
7 WHILE NOT RS.EOF
8 %>
9   <a href="updateProduct.asp?pid=<%=RS( "product_id" )%>">
10 <%=RS( "product_name" )%>
11 </a>
12 <%
13 RS.MoveNext
14 WEND
15 %>
```

ANALYSIS This script displays the names of each product in the database as a hypertext link. Each link has a query string variable named `pid` that passes the product ID to the `updateProduct.asp` page. The query string variable is added to the hyperlinks in line 9.

After the script in Listing 5.10 has been added to the `manageproducts.asp` page, the page displays all the existing products in the Products table (see Figure 5.7). To see the final version of the `manageproducts.asp` page, open the `manageproducts.asp` page from the CD that accompanies this book.

FIGURE 5.7

Final version of `manageproducts.asp`.

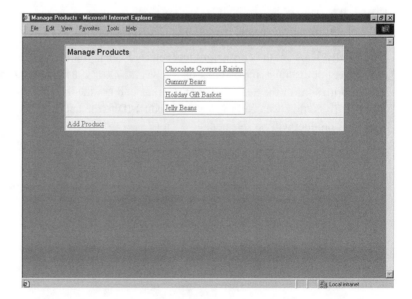

Creating the updateProduct Form

The updateProduct.asp page enables you to update the information for a particular product. When you click on the name of a particular product on the manageproduct.asp page, you are brought to this page (see Figure 5.8).

FIGURE 5.8

The updateProduct.asp page.

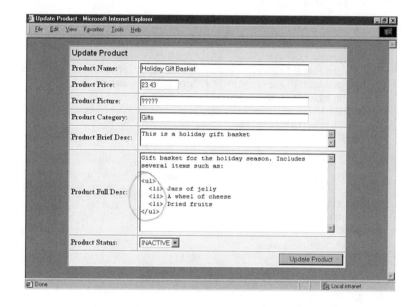

The updateProduct.asp page is similar to the addProduct.asp. It has an HTML form containing fields that correspond to the columns in the Products table. Unlike the addProduct.asp page, however, the form fields are automatically filled with the existing product information.

The updateProduct.asp page is contained in Listing 5.11. (It's also included on the CD that accompanies this book.)

INPUT   **LISTING 5.11**   The updateProduct.asp Page ✓

```
1 <%
2 ' Get the Product ID
3 productID = Request( "pid" )
4
5 ' Open the Database Connection
6 Set Con = Server.CreateObject( "ADODB.Connection" )
7 Con.Open "accessDSN"
8
9 ' Open the Recordset
```

continues

LISTING 5.11   continued

```
10 Set RS = Server.CreateObject( "ADODB.Recordset" )
11 RS.ActiveConnection = Con
12 RS.CursorType = 3
13 RS.Open "SELECT * FROM Products WHERE product_id=" & productID
14 IF NOT RS.EOF THEN
15   productName      = RS( "product_name" )
16   productPrice     = RS( "product_price" )
17   productPicture   = RS( "product_picture" )
18   productCategory  = RS( "product_category" )
19   productBriefDesc = RS( "product_briefDesc" )
20   productFullDesc  = RS( "product_fullDesc" )
21   productStatus    = RS( "product_status" )
22 END IF
23 ' Close the Recordset
24 RS.Close
25
26 FUNCTION SELECTED( firstVal, secondVal )
27   IF cSTR( firstVal ) = cSTR( secondVAL ) THEN
28     SELECTED = " SELECTED "
29   END IF
30 END FUNCTION
31
32 %>
33 <html>
34 <head><title>Update Product </title></head>
35 <body bgcolor="gray">
36
37 <form method="post" action="manageproducts.asp">
38
39 <center>
40 <table width="600" border=1 bgcolor="lightyellow"
41   cellpadding="4" cellspacing="0">
42 <tr>
43    <td colspan="2" bgcolor="yellow">
44    <font face="Arial" size="3"><b>
45    Update Product
46    </b></font>
47    </td>
48 </tr>
49 <tr>
50    <td>
51    <b> Product Name:</b>
52    </td>
53    <td>
54    <input name="productName"
55      size="50" maxlength="50"
56      value="<%=Server.HTMLEncode( productName )%>">
57    </td>
58 </tr>
```

Returning value (handwritten annotation)

```
59 <tr>
60    <td>
61    <b>Product Price:</b>
62    </td>
63    <td>
64    <input name="productPrice" size="10"
65      value="<%=productPrice%>">
66    </td>
67 </tr>
68 <tr>
69    <td>
70    <b>Product Picture:</b>
71    </td>
72    <td>
73    <input name="productPicture"
74      size="50" maxlength="50"
75      value="<%=Server.HTMLEncode( productPicture )%>">
76    </td>
77 </tr>
78 <tr>
79     <td>
80    <b>Product Category:</b>
81    </td>
82    <td>
83    <input name="productCategory"
84      size="50" maxlength="50"
85      value="<%=Server.HTMLEncode( productCategory )%>">
86    </td>
87 </tr>
88 <tr>
89    <td>
90    <b>Product Brief Desc:</b>
91    </td>
92    <td>
93    <textarea name="productBriefDesc"
94      cols="50" rows="2"
95      wrap="virtual"><%=Server.HTMLEncode( productBriefDesc )%>
96    </textarea>
97    </td>
98 </tr>
99 <tr>
100    <td>
101    <b>Product Full Desc:</b>
102    </td>
103    <td>
104    <textarea name="productFullDesc"
105      cols="50" rows="10"
106      wrap="virtual"><%=Server.HTMLEncode( productFullDesc )%>
107    </textarea>
108    </td>
```

continues

LISTING 5.11   continued

```
109 </tr>
110 <tr>
111   <td>
112   <b>Product Status:</b>
113   </td>
114   <td>
115   <select name="productStatus">
116   <option value="0" <%=SELECTED( "0", productStatus )%>>INACTIVE
117   <option value="1" <%=SELECTED( "1", productStatus )%>>ACTIVE
118   </select>
119   </td>
120 </tr>
121 <tr>
122   <td colspan=2 align="right">
123   <input type="submit" value="Update Product">
124   </td>
125 </tr>
126 </table>
127 </center>
128
129 <input name="productID" type="hidden" value="<%=productID%>">
130 <input name="updateProduct" type="hidden" value="1">
131 </form>
132
133 </body>
134 </html>
```

ANALYSIS   The product ID is grabbed from the query string variable in line 3. The script uses the product ID to show the information for the correct product in the form.

In lines 6 and 7, a connection to the storeDB database is opened. In lines 10–24, the product information is retrieved from the Products table and assigned to local variables.

The majority of Listing 5.11, lines 37–131, is used to display the HTML form. Each of the text form fields is given a default value by using the VALUE attribute of the <INPUT> tag.

A Problem with HTML Forms and Quotation Marks

In Listing 5.11, the text input fields are given default values by using the VALUE attribute of the <INPUT> tag. Each product variable is displayed as the value of this attribute. You should notice that each variable is HTML encoded with the HTMLEncode method of the Server object before being displayed. Why is this necessary?

HTML uses quotation marks (") to mark the beginning and end of a string. If one of the product variables itself includes a quotation mark, it will not be properly displayed. For example, if the brief description of a product were Our customers are saying, "This is a great gift!", the quotation marks that surround "This is a great gift!" would prematurely mark the end of the string.

The HTMLEncode method of the Server object automatically replaces each quotation mark with the special HTML code ". The special " character correctly displays a quotation mark within an HTML document.

Updating a Database Record

The final step in creating our updateProduct.asp form is to modify the manageproducts.asp page so that it will update the information for a product in the database.

When the updateProduct.asp page is submitted, the information is sent to the manageproducts.asp page. We need to add an additional section to this page to change the product information. Listing 5.12 contains the final version of the manageproducts.asp page. (The manageproducts.asp is also included on the CD that accompanies this book.)

INPUT   **LISTING 5.12**   Final Version of the manageproducts.asp Page

```
<%
1 FUNCTION fixQuotes( theString )
2   fixQuotes = REPLACE( theString, "'", "''" )
3 END FUNCTION
4
5 ' Get the Form Variables
6 addProduct        = TRIM( Request( "addProduct" ) )
7 updateProduct     = TRIM( Request( "updateProduct" ) )
8
9  productID        = TRIM( Request( "productID" ) )
10 productName      = TRIM( Request( "productName" ) )
11 productPrice     = TRIM( Request( "productPrice" ) )
12 productPicture   = TRIM( Request( "productPicture" ) )
13 productCategory  = TRIM( Request( "productCategory" ) )
14 productBriefDesc = TRIM( Request( "productBriefDesc" ) )
15 productFullDesc  = TRIM( Request( "productFullDesc" ) )
16 productStatus    = TRIM( Request( "productStatus" ) )
17
18 ' Assign Default Values
19 IF productName = "" THEN
20   productName = "?????"
21 END IF
22 IF productPrice = "" THEN
```

5

continues

LISTING **5.12**   continued

```
23  productPrice = 0
24 END IF
25 IF productPicture = "" THEN
26   productPicture = "?????"
27 END IF
28 IF productCategory = "" THEN
29   productCategory = "?????"
30 END IF
31 IF productBriefDesc = "" THEN
32   productBriefDesc = "?????"
33 END IF
34 IF productFullDesc = "" THEN
35   productFullDesc = "?????"
36 END IF
37
38 ' Open the Database Connection
39 Set Con = Server.CreateObject( "ADODB.Connection" )
40 Con.Open "accessDSN"
41 %>
42 <html>
43 <head><title>Manage Products</title></head>
44 <body bgcolor="gray">
45 <%
46 ' Add New Product
47 IF addProduct <> "" THEN
48
49 sqlString = "INSERT INTO Products " &_
50   "( product_name, product_price, product_picture, " &_
51 "product_category, product_briefdesc, product_fulldesc, " &_
52 "product_status ) VALUES ( " &_
53 " '" & productName & "', " &_
54 cCUR( productPrice ) & ", " &_
55 " '" & productPicture & "', " &_
56 " '" & productCategory & "', " &_
57 " '" & productBriefDesc & "', " &_
58 " '" & productFullDesc & "', " &_
59 productStatus & "  )"
60
61 Con.Execute sqlString
62
63 %>
64 <center>
65 <table width="600" cellpadding="4"
66  cellspacing="0" bgcolor="lightyellow">
67 <tr>
68    <td>
69    <%=productName%> was added to the database
70    </td>
71 </tr>
```

```
72 </table>
73 </center>
74 <p>
75 <%
76 END IF
77
78 ' Update Product
79 IF updateProduct <> "" THEN
80
81 sqlString = "UPDATE Products SET " &_
82   "product_name=' " & fixQuotes( productName ) & "'," &_
83   "product_price=" & productPrice & "," &_
84   "product_picture='" & fixQuotes( productPicture ) & "'," &_
85   "product_category='" & fixQuotes( productCategory ) & "'," &_
86   "product_briefdesc='" & fixQuotes( productBriefDesc ) & "'," &_
87   "product_fulldesc='" &  fixQuotes( productFullDesc ) & "'," &_
88   "product_status=" & productStatus & " WHERE " &_
89   "product_id=" & productID
90
91 Con.Execute sqlString
92
93 %>
94 <center>
95 <table width="600" cellpadding="4"
96  cellspacing="0" bgcolor="lightyellow">
97  <tr>
98    <td>
99    <%=productName%> was updated in the database
100   </td>
101 </tr>
102 </table>
103 </center>
104 <p>
105 <%
106 END IF
107 %>
108
109 <center>
110 <table width="600" border=1 bgcolor="lightyellow"
111  cellpadding="4" cellspacing="0">
112 <tr>
113   <td colspan="2" bgcolor="yellow">
114   <font face="Arial" size="3"><b>
115   Manage Products
116   </b></font>
117   </td>
118 </tr>
119 <tr>
120   <td align="center">
121
```

5

continues

LISTING 5.12 continued

```
122 <table border="1" size="400" cellpadding="3"
123  cellspacing=0 bgcolor="white">
124 <%
125 sqlString = "SELECT product_id, product_name FROM Products " &_
126  "ORDER BY product_name"
127 SET RS = Con.Execute( sqlString )
128 WHILE NOT RS.EOF
129 %>
130 <tr>
131    <td>
132    <a href="updateproduct.asp?pid=<%=RS( "product_id")%>">
133    <%=RS( "product_name" )%></a>
134    </td>
135 </tr>
136 <%
137 RS.MoveNext
138 WEND
139 %>
140 </table>
141    </td>
142 </tr>
143 <tr>
144    <td>
145    <a href="addProduct.asp">Add Product</a>
146    </td>
147 </tr>
148 </table>
149 </center>
150
151 </body>
152 </html>
```

ANALYSIS Lines 78—107 contain the section of code that updates a product's information in the database. The SQL UPDATE string is built in lines 81—89. Notice that the fixQuotes() function is used when building the SQL string to replace single quotes with double quotes. Next, the SQL string is executed in line 91.

Note

Notice that when you update product information, you need to use both the HTMLEncode() method, to fix potential problems with double quotes in HTML strings, and the fixQuotes() function, to handle potential problems with single quotes in the SQL UPDATE string. Using the HTMLEncode() method and the fixQuotes() function in sequence doesn't create a problem. When the HTML form is submitted, the special " character is automatically translated back into a normal quotation mark (").

After the product has been updated, a message appears confirming the product update. This message is displayed in lines 94–104. When a product is updated, the page in Figure 5.9 is displayed.

FIGURE 5.9

Results of updating a product.

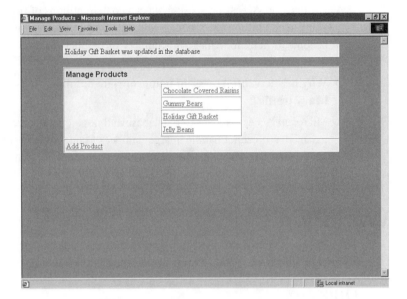

Summary

In this chapter, you were introduced to the methods of working with a Microsoft Access database in your ASP scripts. First, you learned how to create a new Microsoft Access database and open a connection to it using the ADO Connection object and a System DSN. Next, you learned how to add products to your online store with Active Server Pages by using the SQL INSERT INTO statement to add new rows to a database table. Finally, you created Active Server Pages that enable you to update existing product information by using the SQL UPDATE statement. In the course of this chapter, you also learned how to handle problems presented by both single and double quotation marks.

Q&A

Q When attempting to connect to a Microsoft Access Database within an ASP page, I receive the error "Data source name not found and no default driver specified." What could cause this error?

A You'll receive this error when your DSN isn't configured correctly. First, open the ODBC Data Sources applet from your computer's Control Panel to check whether you have created a DSN. Next, make sure that you have spelled the name of your DSN correctly within your ASP script.

Q Is there any limit to the number of products that I can list at my online store?

A A Microsoft Access database table can contain billions of rows. In theory, at least, you can add billions of products to the Products table. However, it would quickly become difficult to manage this number of products using the `manageproducts.asp` page discussed in this chapter.

Q Why is Microsoft Access an inappropriate database to use for a Web site with heavy traffic?

A Microsoft Access is a desktop database and not a client-server database. This means that it cannot handle a large number of concurrent users. If you expect to have more than 30 people simultaneously connecting to your database, you should seriously consider upgrading to Microsoft SQL Server.

Workshop

The Quiz and Exercise questions are designed to test your knowledge of the material covered in this chapter. The answers are in Appendix A, "Quiz Answers."

Quiz

1. If you move your Microsoft Access database, what do you need to do to allow your ASP scripts to find the database at its new location?

2. What's wrong with the following SQL `INSERT INTO` statement?

```
INSERT INTO Products ( product_name ) VALUES ( Holiday Gift Basket )
```

3. Why do single quotation marks cause problems when inserting or updating records in a database?

4. Why do quotation marks cause problems when displaying a variable with the `VALUE` attribute of an HTML form?

Exercises

How can you add additional product information to your online store? For example, suppose that you want to add a field named `product_sku` to track a product's sku. How would you modify the database table and Active Server Pages discussed in this chapter to include the new field?

DAY 6

Displaying Your Products

In today's lesson, you will learn how to display the products in your online store. You will learn how to create the customer interface to your list of products. Today, you will learn the following:

- How to retrieve database records with the Recordset object
- How to create Active Server Pages to display your list of products
- How to enable your customers to browse multiple pages of product listings
- How to optimize your Active Server Pages to display a list of products more efficiently

Using Recordsets

In yesterday's lesson, you were introduced to the Recordset object. The Recordset object represents a set of records retrieved from a database. In this section, you will learn how to use the Recordset object in more detail.

Whenever you use a Recordset to display database records within an ASP page, you must follow these steps:

1. Open a database connection with the `Connection` object.

2. Open a `Recordset` by using the SQL `SELECT` statement.

3. Display the records in the `Recordset` by looping through the `Recordset`.

For example, suppose that you want to display the names of all the products from the Products database table. You can display the names of all the products using the ASP script in Listing 6.1.

LISTING 6.1 Display Product Names

```
1  <%
2  ' Open Database Connection
3  Set Con = Server.CreateObject( "ADODB.Connection" )
4  Con.Open "accessDSN"
5  ' Open Recordset
6  Set RS = Server.CreateObject( "ADODB.Recordset" )
7  RS.ActiveConnection = Con
8  RS.Open "SELECT * FROM Products"
9  ' Loop through Recordset
10 WHILE NOT RS.EOF
11   Response.Write RS( "product_name" )
12 RS.MoveNext
13 WEND
14 %>
```

ANALYSIS Lines 2 and 3 are used to open the connection to the database. The connection is opened using the System DSN named `accessDSN` that you created in yesterday's lesson.

The records are retrieved from the Products table in lines 6–9. In line 6, an instance of the `Recordset` object is created. In line 7, the Recordset is associated with the open connection to the database. In line 8, a set of records is retrieved from the database by using the SQL `SELECT` statement.

The records are displayed in lines 10–13. A VBScript `WHILE...WEND` loop is used to move to each record in the Recordset and display it. Within the `WHILE...WEND` loop, the `MoveNext` method of the `Recordset` object is used to move to the next record in the Recordset. The loop continues until the EOF property of the `Recordset` object has the value `TRUE`.

EOF stands for End of File. One way to think of a `Recordset` is by using the analogy of a text file. Each row in a Recordset is like a separate row in a text file. When you open a Recordset, you begin at the first row in the text file. Whenever you call the `MoveNext` method, you are moved to the next line. When you reach the end of the `Recordset` (the end of the file), the EOF property is `TRUE`.

In Listing 6.1, the name of each product is outputted by using RS(product_name). If you wanted to show other columns from the Recordset, you could replace product_name with the name of the column that you want to display. For example, to display the product price, use RS(product_price).

You'll discover that you will use scripts like the one in Listing 6.1 over and over again in your Active Server Pages when working with databases. Whenever you need to display a set of records from a database, you will use a similar script.

Using the SQL SELECT Statement

You open a Recordset by using the SQL SELECT statement. The SQL SELECT statement is like most SQL statements. Although the complete syntax of the SELECT statement is quite complicated, the basic version is easy to understand. To select all the columns and all the rows from a table, use the following statement:

```
SELECT * FROM table_name
```

The asterisk (*) is used as a wildcard character to indicate that all the columns in a table should be retrieved. Typically, however, retrieving all the columns from a table with the SELECT statement is a bad idea. You shouldn't burden the database server by retrieving data that you don't really need. If you plan to show only certain columns from a table, you should limit the columns retrieved by listing the columns in the SELECT statement like this:

```
SELECT column1, column2, ... FROM table_name
```

For example, to select only the product_name and product_price columns from the Products table, use the following SELECT statement:

```
SELECT product_name, product_price FROM Products
```

You can also use the SQL SELECT statement to retrieve only certain rows in a database table. You do this by extending the SELECT statement with the WHERE clause. For example, if you want to select only those rows from the Products table in which the product_category column has the value Chocolates, you would use the following statement:

```
SELECT product_name FROM Products
WHERE product_category = "Chocolates"
```

The WHERE clause is very flexible. You can use Boolean and mathematical expressions within a WHERE clause to retrieve records that meet very precise conditions. For example, the following SQL statement retrieves only those products that have a price between $20.00 and $30.00:

```
SELECT product_name FROM Products
WHERE product_price > 20.00 AND product_price < 30.00
```

You can extend the SELECT statement even further by using the ORDER BY clause. An ORDER BY clause allows you to retrieve the records from a database table in a certain order. For example, the following statement retrieves the products from the Chocolates category in alphabetical order by the product name:

```
SELECT product_name FROM Products
WHERE product_category = "Chocolates"
ORDER BY product_name
```

You must use the ORDER BY clause if you want records returned from a database table in a certain order. By default, records are retrieved in no particular order.

Finally, you can use the SELECT statement to retrieve only distinct records in a table. For example, if you wanted to list all the distinct categories in the Products table, you could use the following SQL statement:

```
SELECT DISTINCT product_category
FROM Products
```

Imagine that the Products table contained 50 products in the Chocolates category and 34 products in the Hard Candy category. If you use the previous statement to select the distinct product categories, only two records would be returned: Chocolate and Hard Candy.

Recordset Cursor Types

When you open a Recordset, the Recordset is opened with a particular cursor type. You can open a Recordset with any of the following four types of cursors: forward-only, static, keyset, and dynamic.

The cursor type of a Recordset determines the methods and properties that the Recordset will support. By default, when a Recordset is opened, it is opened with a forward-only cursor. However, a forward-only cursor is the most limited type of cursor.

For example, using the RecordCount property of the Recordset object, you can determine the number of records contained in a Recordset. This property is not available when opening a Recordset with a forward-only cursor. To use the RecordCount property, you must open the cursor with a richer cursor type.

The script in Listing 6.2 demonstrates how you can open a Recordset with a static cursor and display a count of records.

LISTING 6.2   Using a Static Cursor

```
1   <!-- #INCLUDE VIRTUAL="adovbs.inc" -->
2   <%
3   ' Open Database Connection
```

```
 4  Set Con = Server.CreateObject( "ADODB.Connection" )
 5  Con.Open "accessDSN"
 6  ' Open Recordset with Static Cursor
 7  Set RS = Server.CreateObject( "ADODB.Recordset" )
 8  RS.CursorType = adOpenStatic
 9  RS.ActiveConnection = Con
10  RS.Open "SELECT * FROM Products"
11  ' Display Count of Products
12  Response.Write "Number of products: "
13  Response.Write RS.RecordCount
14  %>
```

ANALYSIS Line 1 uses the #INCLUDE directive to include the ADOVBS.inc file. This file contains a list of constants for the ActiveX Data Objects, including constants for the different cursor types. Without the ADOVBS.inc file, the constant adOpenStatic could not be used in line 8.

> **Note**
>
> The ADOVBS.inc file was installed on your hard drive when you installed Active Server Pages. The easiest way to find the file is to select Start, Find, Files or Folders and do a search for "ADOVBS.inc".

The Recordset is created and opened in lines 6–10. In line 8, the CursorType property of the Recordset is assigned a Static cursor. Notice that the cursor type is set before the Recordset is opened.

In lines 11–13, the number of products contained in the Products table is outputted. The RecordCount property is used to return a count of products.

If the Recordset had been opened with the default forward-only cursor, the RecordCount property would not have returned the correct result. It would have returned the value –1, indicating that the cursor doesn't support the property.

The RecordCount property is only one example of the properties and methods that require a non forward-only cursor type. Later in today's lesson in "Paging Through a Recordset", you will come across several other Recordset properties that depend on using a richer cursor type.

6

Displaying Products

In this section, you will learn how to create the customer interface to your online store. You will learn how to create the pages that enable your customers to browse your list of products.

Four files need to be created:

CatList.asp   This file contains a script that displays each
                              of the product categories. Customers can click
                              on a particular product category to view a list
                              of products in that category.

ProductList.asp   This file contains a script that lists all the
                              products in a particular category.

Default.asp   This file is the main ASP page for your online
                              store. This page displays the list of products.
                              It uses both Navbar.asp and
                              ProductList.asp.

Product.asp   This file displays the details for a particular
                              product. When a customer clicks on the name
                              of a product within the Default.asp page, the
                              details of the product are shown in this page.

Figure 6.1 shows what the finished version of your online store will look like. You can
also view the online store by visiting http://www.superexpert.com/candystore.

FIGURE 6.1

The online store.

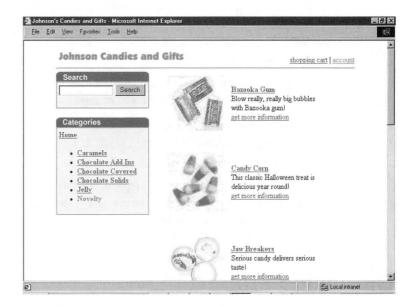

Selecting Product Categories

When you added the products to your online store, you entered a category for each of your products. When customers browse your store, they can select a particular product category and view only those products in that category.

Listing 6.3 contains the script that will display the list of categories.

LISTING 6.3 CatList.asp—Displaying Categories

```
1  <%
2  Set catRS = Server.CreateObject( "ADODB.Recordset" )
3  catRS.ActiveConnection = Con
4  sqlString = "SELECT DISTINCT product_category FROM Products "
5  sqlString = sqlString & "WHERE product_status=1 "
6  sqlString = sqlString & "ORDER BY product_category"
7  catRS.Open sqlString
8  %>
9  <% If cat = "Home" THEN %>
10  <font color="red"><b>Home</b></font>
11 <UL>
12 <% ELSE %>
13 <a href="default.asp?cat=home">Home</a>
14 <UL>
15 <% END IF %>
16 <% WHILE NOT catRS.EOF %>
17 <% IF catRS( "product_category" ) = cat THEN %>
18 <li><font color="red"><b>
19 <%=catRS( "product_category" )%>
20 </b></font>
21 <% ELSE %>
22 <li><a href="default.asp?cat=<%=Server.URLEncode(
23  catRS( "product_category" ) )%>">
24 <%=catRS( "product_category" )%></a>
25 <% END IF %>
26 <%
27 catRS.MoveNext
28 WEND
29 %>
20 </UL>
31 <% catRS.Close %>
```

ANALYSIS This script creates an instance of the ADO Recordset object named catRS. After catRS is opened, each of the product categories is displayed one by one by looping through the Recordset. If a product category isn't the current category, it is displayed as a hypertext link.

6

In lines 2 and 3, the `catRS` Recordset is created and associated with an already opened database connection. This connection isn't opened in this script. It will be opened in `Default.asp`.

Next, in lines 4–7, the `catRS` Recordset is opened with a SQL `SELECT` statement. The `SELECT` statement retrieves the name of each distinct product category from the Products table. The `SELECT` statement places the records in alphabetical order.

In lines 9–15, a link to the home page (`Default.asp`) is created. If a customer is browsing a particular category of products, the customer can click this link to return to the store's home page.

The list of product categories is displayed in lines 16–28. The list is formatted by using the HTML unordered list tag `<UL>`. This tag is used to create a bulleted list of category names.

If a category isn't the current category, it is displayed as a hypertext link. Each link passes a query string variable named `cat`. This query string variable contains the name of the category. Notice that the name of the category is URL encoded. You must URL Encode a string if the string might contain special characters (such as spaces or & or ") that cannot be passed in a query string.

Displaying the List of Products

The `ProductList.asp` script is used to display a list of all the products for a particular category. When a customer clicks a category, the name of the category is passed within the `cat` query string variable. The `ProductList.asp` script uses the `cat` variable to select only those products in the currently selected category.

Listing 6.4 contains the `ProductList.asp` script.

LISTING 6.4   `ProductList.asp`—Displaying Products

```
1  <%
2  Set prodRS = Server.CreateObject( "ADODB.Recordset" )
3  prodRS.ActiveConnection = Con
4
5  sqlString = "SELECT product_id, product_picture, product_name,
   ➥product_briefDesc " &_
6    "FROM Products WHERE product_category='" & cat & "' " &_
7    "AND product_status=1 " &_
8    "ORDER BY product_name "
9  prodRS.Open sqlString
10 %>
11 <table width="350" border=0
12 cellpadding=5 cellspacing=0>
```

```
13 <%
14 WHILE NOT prodRS.EOF
15 %>
16 <tr>
17  <td>
18  <% IF prodRS( "product_picture" ) <> "?????" THEN %>
19  <IMG SRC="<%=prodRS( "product_picture" )%>"
20   HSPACE=4 VSPACE=4 BORDER=0 align="center">
21  <% END IF %>
22  </td>
23  <td>
24  <a href="product.asp?pid=<%=prodRS( "product_id" )%>">
25  <b><%=prodRS( "product_name" )%></b></a>
26  <br><%=prodRS( "product_briefDesc" )%>
27  <br><a href="product.asp?pid=<%=prodRS( "product_id" )%>">
28  get more information</a>
29  </td>
30 </tr>
31 <tr>
32  <td colspan=2 align="center">
33   
34  </td>
35 </tr>
36 <%
37 prodRS.MoveNext
38 WEND
39 %>
40 </table>
```

ANALYSIS This script creates an instance of the ADO Recordset object named prodRS. The prodRS Recordset contains all the products from a certain category. A description of each product is displayed one by one.

The instance of the prodRS Recordset is created and associated with an open database connection in lines 2 and 3. The database connection is not created in this script. It will be created in Default.asp.

Next, an SQL SELECT statement is created in lines 5–8. This SELECT statement retrieves the records from Products table where the product has a status of 1 and the product belongs to the current category. The records are returned in alphabetical order of the product name.

The prodRS Recordset is opened in line 9. A description of each product is displayed in lines 11–40. The product descriptions are displayed within an HTML table. If a product has a picture, the picture is displayed in the left cell. The product name and brief description are displayed in the right cell.

6

The product names are displayed as hypertext links to the `Product.asp` page. If a customer clicks a product, he will be brought to the `Product.asp` page to view the product details. Each link to the `Product.asp` page contains a query string variable named `pid`. This variable is passed to the `Product.asp` page when the link is clicked. The `Product.asp` page uses this variable to display the information for the correct product.

Creating the Main Store Page

In the previous two sections, you learned how to create the `CatList.asp` script to display the list of product categories and the `ProductList.asp` scripts to display the list of products for a category. These scripts are brought together in the `Default.asp` page.

The `Default.asp` page is the main ASP page for your online store. Customers browse your products by requesting this page.

The `Default.asp` page is contained in Listing 6.5.

LISTING 6.5   Default.asp—The Main Store Page

```
1   <!-- #INCLUDE FILE="adovbs.inc" -->
2   <%
3   ' Get Current Category
4   cat = TRIM( Request( "cat" ) )
5   IF cat = "" THEN cat = "Home"
6
7   ' Open Database Connection
8   Set Con = Server.CreateObject( "ADODB.Connection" )
9   Con.Open "accessDSN"
10  %>
11  <html>
12  <head>
13  <title>Johnson's Candies and Gifts</title>
14  </head>
15  <body link="#ff4040" vtext="lightred">
16  <center>
17
18  <table width=640 border=0
19    cellspacing=0 cellpadding=0>
20  <tr>
21      <td>
22      <img src="logo.gif">
23      </td>
24      <td align=right valign="bottom">
25      <a href="cart.asp">shopping cart</a>
26      |
27      <a href="account.asp">account</a>
28      </td>
29  </tr>
30  <tr>
```

```
31      <td colspan=2>
32      <hr width="640">
33      </td>
34   </tr>
35   </table>
36
37
38   <table width=640 border=0
39    cellpadding=0 cellspacing=0>
40   <tr><td valign="top">
41
42   <table cellpadding=0 cellspacing=0 border=0>
43   <tr>
44       <td valign="bottom" bgcolor="pink">
45       <img src="search.gif" vspace=0 border=0></td>
46   </tr>
47   <tr>
48       <td>
49       <table width="200" cellpadding=4 cellspacing=0
50        bgcolor="lightyellow" border=1>
51       <tr>
52          <td>
53          <form method="post" action="search.asp">
54          <input name="searchfor" size="15">
55          <input type="submit" value="Search">
56          </form>
57          </td>
58       </tr>
59       </table>
60       </td>
61   </tr>
62   <tr>
63       <td>
64        
65       </td>
66   </tr>
67   <tr>
68       <td valign="bottom">
69       <img src="Categories.gif" vspace=0 border=0></td>
70   </tr>
71   <tr>
72       <td>
73       <table width="200" cellpadding=4 cellspacing=0
74        bgcolor="lightyellow" border=1>
75       <tr>
76          <td>
77          <font size="3"><b>
78          <!-- #INCLUDE FILE="CatList.asp" -->
79          </b></font>
80          </td>
81       </tr>
```

6

continues

LISTING 6.5   continued

```
82      </table>
83      </td>
84  </tr>
85  </table>
86
87  </td><td valign="top">
88  <% IF cat = "Home" THEN %>
89
90  <% ELSE %>
91  <!-- #INCLUDE FILE="ProductList.asp" -->
92  <% END IF %>
93
94
95  </td></tr>
96  </table>
97
98  <hr width=640>
99  Copyright &copy; 2000 the Johnson Gift Company
100
101
102  </center>
103  </body>
104  </hmtl>
```

ANALYSIS   The listing for Default.asp might appear to be very long. However, the majority of the page is devoted to plain old HTML.

In lines 3–5, the cat query string variable is retrieved and assigned to a variable named cat. If no category is currently selected, cat will equal home.

In lines 7–9, a database connection is opened. This connection is used within both the CatList.asp script and the ProductList.asp script. It is normally a good idea to open only one database connection within an ASP page and use it for all your database operations.

The CatList.asp script is included in line 78. This script displays the list of the product categories.

The ProductList.asp script is included in line 91. If there is no current category (the cat variable has the value home), no products are displayed.

Displaying Product Details

When a customer clicks the name of a product, or clicks Get More Information, she is brought to the Product.asp page. This page shows more detailed information on a product. A customer can also use this page to add a product to the customer's shopping cart (see Figure 6.2).

The Product.asp page is contained in Listing 6.6.

FIGURE 6.2

The Product Detail Page.

LISTING 6.6   Product.asp—Display Product Details

```
1   <%
2   ' Get the Product ID
3   productID = TRIM( Request( "pid" ) )
4
5   ' Open the Database Connection
6   Set Con = Server.CreateObject( "ADODB.Connection" )
7   Con.Open "accessDSN"
8
9   ' Get the Product Information
10  sqlString = "SELECT * FROM Products "
11  sqlString = sqlString & "WHERE product_id=" & productID
12  Set RS = Server.CreateObject( "ADODB.Recordset" )
13  RS.ActiveConnection = Con
14  RS.Open sqlString
15
16  ' Get Current Category
17  cat = RS( "product_category" )
18  %>
19  <html>
20  <head>
21  <title>Johnson's Candies and Gifts</title>
22  </head>
23  <body link="#ff4040" vtext="lightred">
```

continues

6

LISTING **6.6**   continued

```
24  <center>
25
26  <table width=640 border=0
27   cellspacing=0 cellpadding=0>
28  <tr>
29      <td>
30      <img src="logo.gif">
31      </td>
32      <td align=right valign="bottom">
33      <a href="cart.asp">shopping cart</a>
34      |
35      <a href="account.asp">account</a>
36      </td>
37  </tr>
38  <tr>
39      <td colspan=2>
40      <hr width="640">
41      </td>
42  </tr>
43  </table>
44
45
46  <table width=640 border=0
47   cellpadding=0 cellspacing=0>
48  <tr><td valign="top">
49
50  <table cellpadding=0 cellspacing=0 border=0>
51  <tr>
52      <td valign="bottom" bgcolor="pink">
53      <img src="search.gif" vspace=0 border=0></td>
54  </tr>
55  <tr>
56      <td>
57      <table width="200" cellpadding=4 cellspacing=0
58       bgcolor="lightyellow" border=1>
59      <tr>
60          <td>
61          <form method="post" action="search.asp">
62          <input name="searchfor" size="15">
63          <input type="submit" value="Search">
64          </form>
65          </td>
66      </tr>
67      </table>
68      </td>
69  </tr>
70  <tr>
71      <td>
```

```
72       
73      </td>
74   </tr>
75   <tr>
76      <td valign="bottom">
77      <img src="Categories.gif" vspace=0 border=0></td>
78   </tr>
79   <tr>
80      <td>
81      <table width="200" cellpadding=4 cellspacing=0
82       bgcolor="lightyellow" border=1>
83      <tr>
84         <td>
85         <font size="3"><b>
86         <!-- #INCLUDE FILE="CatList.asp" -->
87         </b></font>
88         </td>
89      </tr>
90      </table>
91      </td>
92   </tr>
93   </table>
94
95   </td><td valign="top">
96
97   <table cellpadding=10 cellspacing=0
98    border=0>
99   <tr>
100     <td>
101
102     <% IF RS( "product_picture" ) <> "?????" THEN %>
103     <img src="<%=RS( "product_picture" )%>">
104     <% END IF %>
105     <p>
106     <font size="3" face="Arial"><b>
107     <%=RS( "product_name" )%>
108     </b></font>
109     <p><%=RS( "product_briefDesc" )%>
110     <form method="post" action="cart.asp">
111     <input name="pid" type="hidden" value="<%=RS( "product_id" )%>">
112     <input type="submit" value="Add To Cart">
113     </form>
114
115     <%=RS( "product_fullDesc" )%>
116
117     <form method="post" action="cart.asp">
118     <input name="pid" type="hidden" value="<%=RS( "product_id" )%>">
119     <input type="submit" value="Add To Cart">
120     </form>
121     </td>
```

6

continues

LISTING 6.6   continued

```
122  </tr>
123  </table>
124
125  </td></tr>
126  </table>
127
128  <hr width=640>
129  Copyright &copy; 2000 the Johnson Gift Company
130
131
132  </center>
133  </body>
134  </hmtl>
```

ANALYSIS   This page displays detailed information for a particular product. The product ID is retrieved from the `pid` query string variable in line 3. This product ID is used to retrieve the information for the product in lines 10–14.

The product information is displayed in lines 97–126. Notice that two HTML forms are created. These forms are used to create the Add To Cart buttons. When a customer clicks either one of these buttons, the product is added to the customer's shopping cart.

Paging Through A Recordset

If you have listed a number of products under a single category, you might not want all the products to be displayed on a single page. For example, you might want no more than five product descriptions to be listed on a single page. In this section, you will learn how to divide your product listings into multiple pages.

The `Recordset` object has three properties that enable you to divide the results from a database query into multiple pages:

`AbsolutePage`—Sets or returns the current page of records.

`PageCount`—Returns the number of pages in a RecordSet.

`PageSize`—Sets or returns the number of records contained in a single page (the default is 10).

We are going to modify the `ProductList.asp` page so that it will display the product listings in multiple pages. Listing 6.7 contains the new version of `ProductList.asp`.

LISTING 6.7 `MPProduct.asp`—Display Pages of Products

```
1   <%
2   ' Get the Current Page
3   pg = TRIM( Request( "pg" ) )
4   IF pg = "" THEN pg = 1
5
6   ' Open the Recordset
7   Set prodRS = Server.CreateObject( "ADODB.Recordset" )
8   prodRS.ActiveConnection = Con
9   prodRS.CursorType = adOpenStatic
10  prodRS.PageSize = 5
11  sqlString = "SELECT product_id, product_picture, product_name,
    ➥ product_briefDesc " &_
12    "FROM Products WHERE product_category='" & cat & "' " &_
13    "AND product_status=1 " &_
14    "ORDER BY product_name "
15  prodRS.Open sqlString
16  prodRS.AbsolutePage = pg
17  %>
18  <table width="350" border=0
19   cellpadding=5 cellspacing=0>
20  <%
21  WHILE NOT prodRS.EOF AND rowCount < prodRS.PageSize
22  rowCount = rowCount + 1
23  %>
24  <tr>
25    <td>
26    <% IF prodRS( "product_picture" ) <> "?????" THEN %>
27    <IMG SRC="<%=prodRS( "product_picture" )%>"
28     HSPACE=4 VSPACE=4 BORDER=0 align="center">
29    <% END IF %>
30    </td>
31    <td>
32    <a href="product.asp?pid=<%=prodRS( "product_id" )%>">
33    <b><%=prodRS( "product_name" )%></b></a>
34    <br><%=prodRS( "product_briefDesc" )%>
35    <br><a href="product.asp?pid=<%=prodRS( "product_id" )%>">
36    get more information</a>
37    </td>
38  </tr>
39  <tr>
40    <td colspan=2 align="center">
41     
42    </td>
43  </tr>
44  <%
45  prodRS.MoveNext
46  WEND
47  %>
```

6

continues

LISTING 6.7 continued

```
48  </table>
49  <%
50  IF prodRS.PageCount > 1 THEN
51  %>
52  <font color="darkgreen">
53  <b>Go to page: </b>
54  <%
55    FOR i = 1 to prodRS.PageCount
56    IF i <> cINT( pg ) THEN
57  %>
58  <a href="default.asp?cat=<%=Server.URLEncode( cat )%>&pg=<%=i%>">
59  <%=i%></a> 
60  <% ELSE %>
61  <b><%=i%></b> 
62  <% END IF %>
63  <%
64    NEXT
65  %>
66  </font>
67  <%
68  END IF
69  %>
70
```

 The current page number is retrieved in lines 2–4. The query string variable named pg contains the current page number. If pg has no value, the page number is set to equal 1.

In lines 6–16, the prodRS Recordset is opened. Notice that the Recordset is opened with a Static cursor. You must use a Static cursor to use the Recordset paging properties.

> **Note**
>
> If you are using a version of Microsoft Access prior to Microsoft Access 2000, you will need to open the Recordset using a client-side cursor in order to use the Recordset paging properties. To use a client-side cursor, add the following line after line 8:
>
> ```
> prodRS.CursorLocation = adUSEClient
> ```

In line 10, the PageSize property is used to set the number of records contained in a single page. Because we want to show no more than five products on a page, the property is set to equal 5. If you want to show more products on a page, you can change this number to any value you prefer.

In line 16, the current page is set with the `AbsolutePage` property. For example, if `AbsolutePage` is set to the value 2, and there are 5 records to a page, the first record displayed by the Recordset will be record number 6.

The records are displayed in lines 21–46. Notice that the `PageSize` property is used in line 21 to limit the number of records shown. Contrary to what you might expect, you can continue to loop through a Recordset beyond the records in the current page.

Lines 50–68 are used to display a list of links to other pages. A `FOR...NEXT` loop is used to display a link for each of the page numbers. If you click on a link, the query string named `pg` is passed back to `Default.asp`, resulting in a different page being displayed.

Making Your Store More Scalable

Connecting and retrieving records from a database is expensive in terms of computer resources. If you want to create a Web site that scales to support hundreds of concurrent users, you should avoid selecting records from a database whenever possible.

The online store described in today's lesson retrieves records from a database whenever the product categories are displayed and whenever a list of products is displayed. The product categories are retrieved on every page.

Most likely, your product categories won't change very frequently. When working with data that is relatively static, you should attempt to find ways to avoid using the database.

One way to avoid retrieving the product categories from the database would be to simply list the product categories as static HTML links. In other words, you can make the `CatList.asp` file into a static HTML page.

The drawback to this approach is that you will need to update the `CatList.asp` file by hand whenever you add a product that belongs to a new category or you remove or deactivate all the products in a category. Web site maintenance also has significant costs.

Fortunately, there is a better solution. Instead of retrieving the list of product categories whenever you display a page, you can retrieve the product categories only once and store them in memory. If you store the categories in memory, you can avoid accessing the database whenever the product categories are displayed.

The advantage of this approach is that it makes your online store more scalable while not making it more difficult to maintain. The list of product categories is still generated automatically from the database. However, the list isn't generated every time a page is requested.

6

To store the list of product categories in memory, we will use an Application variable. The Application variable will be named `productCategories`. It will contain an array in which each element contains the name of a product category.

The modified version of `CatList.asp` is contained in Listing 6.8.

LISTING 6.8 `FastCatList.asp`—Fast Product Category List

```
1   <%
2   IF NOT isArray( Application( "productCategories" ) ) THEN
3     Set catRS = Server.CreateObject( "ADODB.Recordset" )
4     catRS.ActiveConnection = Con
5     sqlString = "SELECT DISTINCT product_category FROM Products "
6     sqlString = sqlString & "WHERE product_status=1 "
7     sqlString = sqlString & "ORDER BY product_category"
8     catRS.Open sqlString
9     productCategories = catRS.GetRows()
10    Application.Lock
11    Application( "productCategories" ) = productCategories
12    Application.UnLock
13    catRS.Close
14  END IF
15  %>
16  <% If cat = "Home" THEN %>
17  <font color="red"><b>Home</b></font>
18  <UL>
19  <% ELSE %>
20  <a href="default.asp?cat=Home">Home</a>
21  <UL>
22  <% END IF %>
23  <%
24  FOR i = 0 TO UBOUND( Application( "productCategories" ), 2 )
25  prodCat = Application( "productCategories" )( 0, i )
26  %>
27  <% IF prodCat = cat THEN %>
28  <li><font color="red"><b>
29  <%=prodCat%>
30  </b></font>
31  <% ELSE %>
32  <li><a href="default.asp?cat=<%=Server.URLEncode
    ➥( prodCat )%>"><%=prodCat%></a>
33  <% END IF %>
34  <%
35  NEXT
36  %>
37  </UL>
```

ANALYSIS The script in Listing 6.8 displays a list of all the product categories. The first time the script is executed, the list of product categories is retrieved from the database and assigned to the Application variable named `productCategories`. After the script has run once, the list of product categories is retrieved from the Application array.

The Application array is created in lines 2–16. The `GetRows()` method of the Recordset object is used to transfer the list of product categories from the Recordset to an array named `productCategories`. The `GetRows()` method returns a two-dimensional array. The first index of the array represents the database column, and the second index of the array represents the database record.

In line 11, the `productCategories` array is assigned to the Application variable with the same name. Assigning the list of product categories to the Application variable places the list in memory.

The list of product categories is displayed in lines 16–37. Notice that the categories are retrieved from the `productCategories` Application variable and not from the database.

Because the list of product categories is stored in memory, it won't be updated automatically if you change a product in the database. The product categories will be refreshed only when your computer is rebooted or the Web service is stopped and started. If you want to force the list of product categories to be refreshed, you can use the script in Listing 6.9.

LISTING 6.9 Reset.asp—Reset Product Categories

```
1  <%
2  Application.Lock
3    Application( "productCategories" ) = ""
4  Application.UnLock
5  %>
6  <html>
7  <head><title>Reset</title></head>
8  <body>
9  Product Categories have been reset!
10 </body>
11 </html>
```

ANALYSIS This script simply sets the Application variable named `productCategories` to a zero length string. This clears the array from the Application variable, causing the list of product categories to be retrieved from the database the next time a page is requested.

6

Summary

In today's lesson, you learned how to display the list of products in your online store. You learned how to work with the Recordset object and how to open different sets of records with the SELECT statement. You also learned how to divide a Recordset into different pages of records. Finally, you learned how to optimize your online store by transferring a Recordset into memory.

Q&A

Q When the list of products is displayed in the online store, the products are displayed alphabetically. Can I display the list of products in a different order? For example, can I list the products in order of price?

A You can order the list of products using any column in the Products table. To order the products using a different column, simply change the ORDER BY clause in the SELECT statement used in ProductList.asp. To order the products by price, use the database column product_price. To order the products in the same order that they were entered into the database, use the product_id column.

Q What's the best way to add pictures to my online store? How can I transfer a picture of a product to my computer?

A You can transfer a picture to your computer by using a flatbed scanner, a digital camera, or having your pictures transferred to a CD when they are developed. Check with your local Kinko's to rent a flatbed scanner. Most drugstores that develop film can transfer your film to a CD.

Workshop

The Quiz and Exercise questions are designed to test your knowledge of the material covered in this chapter. The answers are in Appendix A, "Quiz Answers."

Quiz

1. What is the correct SQL SELECT statement for retrieving the name of every product from the Products table that costs more than $20.25?
2. What method do you use to move to the next row in a Recordset?
3. What do you need to include in a script before you can use ADO constants such as adOpenStatic?
4. Which default property of a Recordset do you need to change before you can use Recordset properties such as RecordCount and PageSize?

Exercise

In today's lesson, you learned how to modify the CatList.asp page so that the list of product categories is retrieved from memory rather than the database. Modify the ProductList.asp page so that the list of products is retrieved from memory rather than the database.

6

DAY 7

Searching for Products

In yesterday's lesson, you learned how to create the main pages for your online store. You learned how to create the Active Server Pages that display your products. In today's lesson, you will learn how to add several additional features to your store. Today, you will learn the following:

- How to randomly display a list of featured products on your store's home page
- How to create a product search page for your store
- How to set up a special directory to enable your products to be indexed by Search Engines such as AltaVista

Displaying a Rotating List of Featured Products

In yesterday's lesson, you created the home page for your online store. The home page displays a list of product categories. However, unless you click on a particular product category, the home page is mostly blank.

Today, we are going to add some content to the home page. We are going to add a rotating list of featured products (see Figure 7.1). This list of featured products will enable you to promote particular products in your store on your home page.

FIGURE 7.1

*Displaying Featured
Products.*

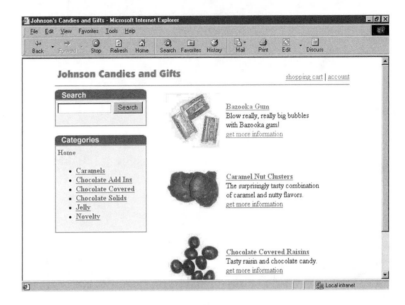

To create the list of featured products, we will need to modify the files discussed in Days 5, "Building Your Product Catalog," and 6, "Displaying Your Products." We will need to modify the manageproducts.asp and updateproduct.asp files discussed in Day 5 to enable you to select the products that you want to list as featured. We will also need to modify the home page file, default.asp, discussed in Day 6 so that it will display the list of featured products.

Selecting the List of Featured Products

In this section, you will learn how to add an additional field to the Products table to track featured products. You will also learn how to change the updateProduct.asp file and the manageproducts.asp file, so you can select the products that you want to list as featured.

Note

The steps for adding a featured field to the Products table described in this section are the same as you would use to add any other field to the Products table. For example, you could follow the same steps to add a product_saleprice field or a product_sku field.

First, you will need to add an additional field to the Microsoft Access table named Products. Launch Microsoft Access, and open the Products table in Design View. Next, go to the end of the list of fields and add a field named product_featured. Create this field as a Number field. It can be an integer field (see Figure 7.2).

FIGURE 7.2

Adding the product_featured field.

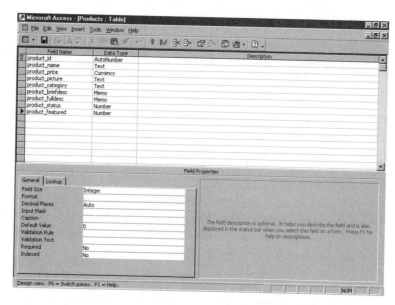

To enable you to select which products to list as featured, you will need to modify both the updateProduct.asp file and the manageproducts.asp file. You created these files in Day 5.

Open the updateProduct.asp file and add the following line to the Open the Recordset section:

```
1  productFeatured = RS( "product_featured" )
2  IF isNULL( productFeatured ) THEN productFeatured =
```

The first line assigns the value of the table column product_featured to the local variable named productFeatured. The second line takes care of the situation in which the product_featured table column is NULL. When the product_featured is NULL, the productfeatured variable is assigned the value 0.

Next, add the following HTML code within the HTML form in updateProduct.asp:

```
<tr>
    <td>
    <b>Product Featured:</b>
    </td>
```

7

```
<td>
<select name="productFeatured">
<option value="0" <%=SELECTED( "0", productFeatured )%>>Normal
<option value="1" <%=SELECTED( "1", productFeatured )%>>Featured
</select>
</td>
</tr>
```

This code fragment adds an HTML select list to the updateProduct.asp HTML form that enables you to select whether a product should be displayed on the home page as featured. The final version of updateProduct.asp is included on the CD-ROM that accompanies this book.

Finally, you will need to modify the manageproducts.asp page to update the database with information about whether a product is featured. Open the manageproducts.asp file and add the following line to the section labeled Get the Form Variables:

```
productFeatured = TRIM( Request( "productFeatured" ) )
```

This line retrieves the form field named productFeatured and assigns it to the productFeatured variable. Next, modify the SQL String created in the section labeled Update Product to include the productFeatured variable. The modified update string should resemble the following string:

```
sqlString = "UPDATE Products SET " &_
  "product_name='" & fixQuotes( productName ) & "'," &_
  "product_price=" & cCUR( productPrice ) & "," &_
  "product_picture='" & fixQuotes( productPicture ) & "'," &_
  "product_category='" & fixQuotes( productCategory ) & "'," &_
  "product_briefdesc='" & fixQuotes( productBriefDesc ) & "'," &_
  "product_fulldesc='" & fixQuotes( productFullDesc ) & "'," &_
  "product_featured=" & productFeatured & "," &_
  "product_status=" & productStatus & " WHERE " &_
  "product_id=" & productID
```

The final version of manageproducts.asp is included on the CD-ROM that accompanies this book.

After you perform these modifications to both updateProduct.asp and manageproducts.asp, you will be able to use these pages to select the products that you want listed as featured. Before reading the next section, open manageproducts.asp in your Web browser and select four or five products that you want featured on the home page of your store.

Retrieving the List of Featured Products

Now that you've selected the featured products for your online store, you will need a method of displaying the featured products on your home page. We will display the list of featured products with the help of an #INCLUDE file named `Featured.asp`. This #INCLUDE file will be displayed when no category is selected. It will be included in the following section of `default.asp`:

```
<% IF cat = "Home" THEN %>
<!-- #INCLUDE FILE="Featured.asp" -->
<% ELSE %>
<!-- #INCLUDE FILE="ProductList.asp" -->
<% END IF %>
```

This code fragment displays a list of products, generated within `ProductList.asp`, if a category is selected. Otherwise, if no category is selected, the `Featured.asp` page is displayed. The modified version of `default.asp` is included on the CD-ROM that accompanies this book.

The file named `Featured.asp` contains the code that displays the featured products. The complete listing for `Featured.asp` is contained in Listing 7.1.

INPUT   **LISTING 7.1**   Displaying Featured Products

```
1   <%
2   Randomize
3   CONST numFeatured = 3
4
5   ' Retrieve Featured Products
6   sqlString = "SELECT product_id, product_picture, product_name,
    product_briefDesc " &_
7     "FROM Products WHERE product_featured = 1 " &_
8     "AND product_status=1 " &_
9     "ORDER BY product_name "
10
11  SET Featured = Con.Execute( sqlString )
12  IF NOT Featured.EOF THEN
13    featuredArray = Featured.GetRows()
14  Featured.Close
15
16  ' Display Featured Products
17  topFeatured =  UBOUND( featuredArray, 2 ) + 1
18  skip =  topFeatured  / numFeatured
19  IF topFeatured <= numFeatured THEN skip = 1
20  %>
21  <table width="350" border=0
22    cellpadding=5 cellspacing=0>
23  <%
24  FOR i = 0 TO topFeatured - 1 STEP skip
25    offset = RND * ( skip - 1 )
26    productID = featuredArray( 0, i + offset )
27    productPicture = featuredArray( 1, i + offset )
```

continues

7

LISTING 7.1   continued

```
28   productName = featuredArray( 2, i + offset )
29   productBriefDesc = featuredArray( 3, i + offset )
30 %>
31 <tr>
32   <td>
33   <% IF productPicture <> "?????" THEN %>
34   <IMG SRC="<%=productPicture%>"
35    HSPACE=4 VSPACE=4 BORDER=0 align="center">
36   <% END IF %>
37   </td>
38   <td>
39   <a href="product.asp?pid=<%=productID%>">
40   <b><%=productName%></b></a>
41   <br><%=productBriefDesc%>
42   <br><a href="product.asp?pid=<%=productID%>">
43   get more information</a>
44   </td>
45 </tr>
46 <tr>
47   <td colspan=2 align="center">
48    
49   </td>
50 </tr>
51 <%
52 NEXT
53 %>
54 </table>
55 <%
56 END IF
57 %>
```

ANALYSIS   The script in Listing 7.1 randomly displays a predetermined number of featured products from the Products table. The constant in line 3, numfeatured, specifies the number of featured products to display. This script will display only three featured products, but you can change this constant to any value you want.

In lines 6–9, a SQL SELECT string is constructed that retrieves all the featured products from the database. This SQL string is executed in line 11, and the results of the database query are assigned to a Recordset named Featured.

In line 13, the contents of the Featured Recordset are transferred to an array named featuredArray. This transfer is accomplished with the GetRows() method of the Recordset object. The GetRows() method simply creates a two-dimensional array from any Recordset.

Note

> **The GetRows() Method**
>
> The GetRows() method copies the contents of a Recordset into a two-dimensional array. The first index of the array represents the table column: The second index of the array represents the table row.

In lines 17–19, two variables are assigned values: topFeatured and skip. The variable named topFeatured contains the index number of the top element of the Featured array. The variable named skip is used to indicate the number of elements to skip within the array when displaying the featured products.

For example, assume that 12 featured products are in the Products table. Assume that you want to display only three featured products on the home page and, therefore, the constant numFeatured has the value 3. In that case, the skip variable will have the value 4. This guarantees that exactly three products are shown.

Finally, in lines 21–54, the featured products are displayed by looping through the featuredArray Recordset. Notice, in particular, the FOR...NEXT loop in line 21. This loop uses the skip variable to step through the array.

In line 25, a variable named offset is used to randomly select a featured product to display. If the script in Listing 7.1 is executed multiple times, and there are more than three products marked as featured in the Products table, different featured products will be randomly displayed each time the script is executed.

Optimizing the Display of Featured Products

The script in Listing 7.1 does a good job of displaying the list of featured products. However, as it stands, the script isn't particularly efficient. Every time someone visits the store's home page, the script queries the Products database table to retrieve the list of featured products. Because, most likely, the list of featured products will change infrequently, this constant querying of the database is a waste of precious database resources.

If you remember yesterday's lesson, a solution should leap readily to mind: Application variables. Instead of querying the database every time the home page is displayed, the list of featured products can be stored in an Application variable within the server's memory. Listing 7.2 is the same as Listing 7.1; except the list of featured products is placed in an Application variable named Featured.

7

INPUT   **LISTING 7.2**   Displaying Featured Products from Memory

```
1  <%
2  Randomize
3  CONST numFeatured = 3
4
5  ' Retrieve Featured Products
6  IF NOT isArray( Application( "Featured" ) ) THEN
7
8  sqlString = "SELECT product_id, product_picture, product_name,
   ➥product_briefDesc " &_
9    "FROM Products WHERE product_featured = 1 " &_
10   "AND product_status=1 " &_
11   "ORDER BY product_name "
12
13 SET Featured = Con.Execute( sqlString )
14 IF NOT Featured.EOF THEN
15   featuredArray = Featured.GetRows()
16 Featured.Close
17 END IF
18
19 ' Add the Array To Application Variable
20 Application.Lock
21 Application( "Featured" ) = featuredArray
22 Application.UnLock
23
24 ELSE
25   featuredArray = Application( "Featured" )
26 END IF
27
28 ' Display Featured Products
29 topFeatured =  UBOUND( featuredArray, 2 ) + 1
30 skip =  topFeatured  / numFeatured
31 IF topFeatured <= numFeatured THEN skip = 1
32 %>
33 <table width="350" border=0
34  cellpadding=5 cellspacing=0>
35 <%
36 FOR i = 0 TO topFeatured - 1 STEP skip
37   offset = RND * ( skip - 1 )
38   productID = featuredArray( 0, i + offset )
39   productPicture = featuredArray( 1, i + offset )
40   productName = featuredArray( 2, i + offset )
41   productBriefDesc = featuredArray( 3, i + offset )
42 %>
43 <tr>
44   <td>
45   <% IF productPicture <> "?????" THEN %>
46   <IMG SRC="<%=productPicture%>"
47    HSPACE=4 VSPACE=4 BORDER=0 align="center">
```

```
48   <% END IF %>
49   </td>
50   <td>
51   <a href="product.asp?pid=<%=productID%>">
52   <b><%=productName%></b></a>
53   <br><%=productBriefDesc%>
54   <br><a href="product.asp?pid=<%=productID%>">
55   get more information</a>
56   </td>
57 </tr>
58 <tr>
59   <td colspan=2 align="center">
60    
61   </td>
62 </tr>
63 <%
64 NEXT
65 %>
66 </table>
```

ANALYSIS The conditional in line 6 is used to detect whether the list of featured products is already stored in memory within an `Application` variable. If the featured products list isn't in memory, the database is queried and the results are assigned to an `Application` variable named `Featured`. Otherwise, the list of featured products is retrieved directly from the `Application` variable named `Featured`.

After the first time this script is executed, the featured list will continue to be stored in memory until your computer is shut down (or it crashes). If you modify your store's list of featured products, you will need a way to clear the `Application` variable so that the list of featured products can be retrieved from the database once again. The script in Listing 7.3 clears the `Application` variable named `Featured`.

INPUT   **LISTING 7.3**   Reset Featured Products

```
1  <html>
2  <head><title>Reset Featured</title></head>
3  <body>
4  <%
5  Application( "Featured" ) = ""
6  %>
7  <big>Featured Products Reset!</big>
8
9  </body>
10 </html>
```

7

ANALYSIS   The script in Listing 7.3 sets the Application variable named Featured equal to a zero length string. This is accomplished in line 5. After running this script, the home page will retrieve the list of featured products from the database.

Creating a Search Page

In this section, you will learn how to add a page to your online store that will enable your customers to search for products. Customers will be able to enter search terms into the search box that appears on the store's home page and retrieve a list of matching products (see Figure 7.3).

FIGURE 7.3

The Search Page.

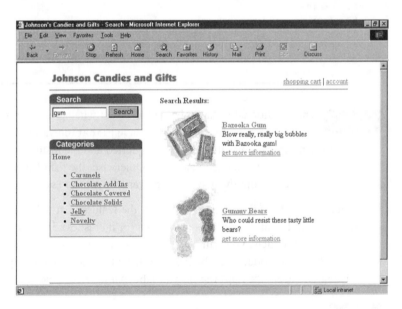

To create the search page, we will be using the SQL LIKE operator. The SQL LIKE operator performs matches that include wildcard characters. Here is an example of how the SQL LIKE operator can be used in a SQL statement:

```
SELECT * FROM Products
  WHERE product_name LIKE 'c%'
```

This SQL statement retrieves all the rows from the database table named Products in which the product_name field starts with the letter c. For example, it retrieves the rows where the product name is Caramel Nut Clusters or Chocolate Drops.

This SELECT statement is not case sensitive. It retrieves product names that start with either a lowercase c or uppercase C.

Notice how the wildcard character % is used in the SQL statement. The character % is a placeholder that represents one or more characters. In the search page, we will use the % character to retrieve all the products that contain a search phrase within the product's name or brief description.

> **Note**
>
> The % wildcard can only be used when using the Microsoft OLE DB Provider for Jet or Microsoft Jet version 4.0 or above. Otherwise, you must use the * character instead of the % character.s

For example, suppose that someone enters the search term Chocolate. In that case, the search page will use the following SQL SELECT statement to retrieve matching products:

```
SELECT product_id, product_picture, product_name, product_briefDesc
FROM Products
WHERE product_status = 1
AND ( product_name LIKE '%chocolate%'
OR product_briefDesc LIKE '%chocolate%' )
ORDER BY product_name
```

The SELECT statement uses the % wildcard character to match any product_name field or product_briefdesc field no matter where the search term chocolate appears within the field.

The complete script for the search page is contained in Listing 7.4. (It's also included on the CD-ROM as Search.asp.)

INPUT **LISTING 7.4** Searching for Products

```
1  <!-- #INCLUDE FILE="adovbs.inc" -->
2  <%
3  ' Get Current Category
4  cat = TRIM( Request( "cat" ) )
5  IF cat = "" THEN cat = "Home"
6
7  ' Get Search Phrase
8  searchFor = TRIM( Request( "searchFor" ) )
9
10  ' Open Database Connection
11  Set Con = Server.CreateObject( "ADODB.Connection" )
12  Con.Open "accessDSN"
13  %>
14  <html>
15  <head>
16  <title>Johnson's Candies and Gifts - Search</title>
```

7

continues

LISTING **7.4**   continued

```
17  </head>
18  <body link="#ff4040" vtext="lightred" bgcolor="#ffffff">
19  <center>
20
21  <table width=640 border=0 bgcolor="#ffffff"
22   cellspacing=0 cellpadding=0>
23  <tr>
24      <td>
25      <img src="logo.gif">
26      </td>
27      <td align=right valign="bottom">
28      <a href="cart.asp">shopping cart</a>
29      |
30      <a href="account.asp">account</a>
31      </td>
32  </tr>
33  <tr>
34      <td colspan=2>
35      <hr width="640">
36      </td>
37  </tr>
38  </table>
39
40
41  <table width=640 border=0 bgcolor="#ffffff"
42   cellpadding=0 cellspacing=0>
43  <tr><td valign="top">
44
45  <table cellpadding=0 cellspacing=0 border=0>
46  <tr>
47      <td valign="bottom" bgcolor="pink">
48      <img src="search.gif" vspace=0 border=0></td>
49  </tr>
50  <tr>
51      <td>
52      <table width="200" cellpadding=4 cellspacing=0
53       bgcolor="lightyellow" border=1>
54      <tr>
55          <td>
56          <form method="post" action="search.asp">
57          <input name="searchfor" size="15">
58          <input type="submit" value="Search">
59          </form>
60          </td>
61      </tr>
62      </table>
63      </td>
64  </tr>
65  <tr>
```

```
66       <td>
67        
68       </td>
69   </tr>
70   <tr>
71       <td valign="bottom">
72       <img src="Categories.gif" vspace=0 border=0></td>
73   </tr>
74   <tr>
75       <td>
76       <table width="200" cellpadding=4 cellspacing=0
77        bgcolor="lightyellow" border=1>
78       <tr>
79          <td>
80          <font size="3"><b>
81          <!-- #INCLUDE FILE="CatList.asp" -->
82          </b></font>
83          </td>
84       </tr>
85       </table>
86       </td>
87   </tr>
88   </table>
89
90   </td><td valign="top">
91
92   <%
93   sqlString = "SELECT product_id, product_picture, product_name,
     ➥product_briefDesc " &_
94     "FROM Products " &_
95     "WHERE product_status = 1 " &_
96     "AND ( product_name LIKE '%" & searchFor & "%' " &_
97     "OR product_briefDesc LIKE '%" & searchFor & "%' ) " &_
98     "ORDER BY product_name "
99
100  SET RS = Con.Execute( sqlString )
101  IF NOT RS.EOF AND searchFor <> "" THEN
102  %>
103  <table width="350" border=0
104    cellpadding=5 cellspacing=0>
105  <tr>
106    <td colspan=2>
107    <font color="darkblue" size="3">
108    <b>Search Results:</b>
109    </font>
110    </td>
111  </tr>
112  <%
113  WHILE NOT RS.EOF
```

7

continues

LISTING **7.4**   continued

```
114  %>
115  <tr>
116    <td>
117    <% IF RS( "product_Picture" ) <> "?????" THEN %>
118    <IMG SRC="<%=RS( "product_Picture" )%>"
119     HSPACE=4 VSPACE=4 BORDER=0 align="center">
120    <% END IF %>
121    </td>
122    <td>
123    <a href="product.asp?pid=<%=RS( "product_ID" )%>">
124    <b><%=RS( "product_Name" )%></b></a>
125    <br><%=RS( "product_BriefDesc" )%>
126    <br><a href="product.asp?pid=<%=RS( "product_ID" )%>">
127    get more information</a>
128    </td>
129  </tr>
130  <tr>
131    <td colspan=2 align="center">
132     
133    </td>
134  </tr>
135  <%
136  RS.MoveNext
137  WEND
138  %>
139  </table>
140  <%
141  ELSE
142  %>
143  <table width="350" border=0
144    cellpadding=5 cellspacing=0>
145  <tr>
146    <td>
147    <font face="Arial" color="darkblue">
148    <b>No products matched your search terms.</b>
149    </font>
150    </td>
151  </tr>
152  </table>
153  <%
154  END IF
155  %>
156
157  </td></tr>
158  </table>
159
160  <hr width=640>
161  Copyright &copy; 2000 the Johnson Gift Company
162
```

```
163
164   </center>
165   </body>
166   </hmtl>
```

ANALYSIS The search terms that the user entered into the search box on the home page are retrieved in line 8 and assigned to a variable named searchFor. Next, in lines 11–12, a database connection is created and opened.

The real work in the script happens in lines 93–98 where the SQL string is created. The string is built using the searchFor variable to retrieve all the products that contain the value of searchFor in their name or brief description.

If no matching products are retrieved, a message is displayed reporting this fact. Otherwise, the matching products are displayed. This is accomplished in lines 101–139.

Note To see a live, working sample of the search page, visit http://asp.superexpert.com/candystore/.

Optimizing the Search Page

Using the SQL LIKE operator to match search terms is hard on your database. If you have too many people attempting to perform searches at the same time, or you have thousands of products to search through, you should investigate an alternative method of enabling users to search for products at your Web site.

Microsoft has two products that you can use to add a more scalable search page to your Web site. If you need the ability to search through static files, you can use Microsoft Index Server. If you need to perform searches against database tables, you can use the Microsoft Full-text Search Service included with Microsoft SQL Server.

Microsoft Index Server is included with the NT Option Pack and can be downloaded from the Microsoft Web site at http://www.microsoft.com/downloads/. Index Server can be used to perform searches against static files on your computer's hard drive, but it cannot be used to search through database tables. For example, you couldn't use this product to search through the products in the Products table.

The Full-text Search Service included with Microsoft SQL 7.0, on the other hand, enables you to perform searches against SQL Server database tables. You can use it to perform either simple searches or complex Boolean queries. To use the Full-text Search Service, you must buy Microsoft SQL 7.0.

7

Creating Indexable Web Pages

Previously, you learned how to add a search page to your online store that enables users to search through the products at your Web site. In this section, you will learn how to enable Internet search engines such as Altavista, Lycos, Inktomi, and Google to index the pages on your Web site.

Getting your Web pages into the Internet search engines is extremely important if you want to attract customers to your store. If you don't get your pages indexed, most people will never find your store or buy your products.

Internet search engines have problems with indexing pages generated from a database. If a page displays different content depending on the values of the query string variables passed to it, an Internet search engine will fail to correctly index the page's content.

For example, the `Product.asp` page displays information about different products depending on the value of the product ID passed to the page. If you attempt to submit this page to a search engine, such as Altavista, the search engine wouldn't be able to index the page because it would attempt to index it without passing a product ID.

Fortunately, there is a way to get around this problem. The trick is to convince the search engine that it is getting a static page when, in fact, it is retrieving a page generated from the database. One easy way to do this is to take advantage of the Custom Errors feature of Internet Information Server. (This trick won't work with the Personal Web Server because it doesn't support Custom Errors.)

First, we need to create a special directory named `Products`. Follow these steps:

1. Create a new directory on your computer's hard drive named `Products` as a subdi-rectory of your Web site's root directory (for example, `c:\inetput\wwwroot\products`).

2. Next, launch the Internet Service Manager and open the property sheet for this directory by right-clicking the `Products` folder and selecting Properties.

3. Choose the tab labeled `Custom Errors`.

4. We are going to create a custom error for error `404 File Not Found`. Click the button labeled `Edit Properties` after selecting this error.

5. For `Message Type`, select `URL`. In the text box labeled `URL`, enter `/Product.asp`. These entries will redirect to the ASP page named `Product.asp` when a file is not found in the `Products` directory.

6. Click `OK` to save all your changes.

After you have completed the steps above, any time someone requests a page from the Products directory, he will be redirected automatically to the Products.asp page. For example, if someone requests the page at the address http://yourdomain/Products/Product12.htm, the Product.asp page will be returned instead.

We aren't finished yet. When someone requests the page Product12.htm, we want to show the product information for the product with the ID of 12. To do this, we need to modify the Product.asp page. Add the code in Listing 7.5 to the Product.asp page beneath the section labeled Get the Product ID. (The final version of Product.asp is included on the CD-ROM that accompanies this book.)

INPUT **LISTING 7.5** Retrieving the Product ID

```
1 IF productID = "" THEN
2 workString = Request.QueryString
3  workString = RIGHT( workString, LEN( workString ) -
  ➥ INSTRrev( workString, "/" ) )
4   FOR i = 1 TO LEN( workString )
5     IF isNumeric( MID( workString, i, 1 ) ) THEN
6       productID = productID & MID( workString, i, 1 )
7     END IF
8   NEXT
9 END IF
```

ANALYSIS When you request a page from the Products directory, you are automatically redirected to the Product.asp page. However, the query string includes the path of the page that was originally requested. The script in Listing 7.5 retrieves the query string (by using Request.QueryString) and assigns it to a variable named workString. Next, workString is stripped of all non-numeric content. What's left should be the product ID.

When you submit the product pages from your online store to the Internet search engines, you can submit them by using addresses like the following:

http://yourdomain/Products/product1.htm

http://yourdomain/Products/product2.htm

When an Internet search engine indexes these pages, it will correctly index the information for each product. In this case, the search engine will index the products with the product IDs of 1 and 2.

7

Summary

In today's lesson, you learned how to add some important additional features to your store. First, you learned how to add a randomly generated list of featured products to your store's home page. You also learned how to create a search page for your store using the SQL LIKE operator. Finally, you learned how to trick Internet search engines into indexing the database generated content at your Web site.

Q&A

Q When using the search page, I noticed that when searching for the word car, a search for "car" would return records that contain the word caramel or the word carpet. In other words, whole word matches aren't being performed. Is there any way to change this behavior?

A You could surround the search terms with single spaces. For example, instead of searching for "%car%", you would use the search expression "% car %". The problem with this approach is that it would cause problems if the search terms appeared at the end of a sentence (for example, followed by a period or exclamation mark). The best solution is not to use the SQL LIKE operator but use the SQL Server Full-text Search Service instead.

Q I believe I have an edge over my competition because I carry a wide range of products within a given category. Is submitting multiple product pages to an Internet search engine considered a form of spamming?

A You'll have to look at the particular submission guidelines for each search engine. However, in general, submitting multiple pages to a search engine is not the same as spamming. It wouldn't be considered spamming because you aren't attempting to trick the search engine into indexing content that doesn't actually appear on the page.

Workshop

The Quiz and Exercise questions are designed to test your knowledge of the material covered in this chapter. The answers are in Appendix A, "Quiz Answers."

Quiz

1. How do I transfer the contents of a Recordset into an array?
2. The following SQL SELECT statement is intended to retrieve all the records from the Products table where the product_name column contains the word "candy".

What's wrong with this statement?

```
SELECT * FROM Products WHERE product_name = '%candy%'
```

3. When using the Internet Information Server's Custom Errors feature to automatically redirect to a new page, how do I determine the name of the original page requested?

Exercise

The search page described in this chapter matches search terms in either the `product_name` or the `product_briefDesc` database fields. How would you modify the search page (`Search.asp`) so that it would also match terms appearing in the `product_fulldesc` field?

7

In Review

This week, you created the first pages for your online store. You started the week by completing a crash course in Active Server Pages programming. You learned how to use the Active Server Pages Request and Response objects to interact with a customer. You also learned how to track customer information with cookies and Session variables. Finally, you learned how to work with files in your E-Commerce application.

Later in the week, in the lessons on Days 5 through 7, you learned how to create Active Server Pages to manage the product catalog for your online store. You learned how to store product information in a database table and how to display the product information to customers with Active Server Pages. You also learned how to enable customers to search your catalog of products through your Web site.

Bonus Project

Creating a Customer Feedback Form

In this week's lessons, you learned how to work with a database in an ASP page. You learned how to use the SQL INSERT INTO statement to add information to a database table and how to use the SQL SELECT statement to retrieve it.

In this bonus lesson, you'll apply this knowledge by creating a customer feedback form. Your customers can use this form whenever they need to leave a message for the store administrator. For example, the form can be used by a customer to request support or to report errors at your Web site. When a customer leaves feedback, his feedback is stored in a database table.

To create the customer feedback form, you'll need to create a new database table and two additional Active Server Pages. The new database table is named feedback and it contains the following four fields:

- feedback_id—an AutoNumber field that uniquely identifies each row in the table.
- feedback_email—a Text field that contains the customer's email address.
- feedback_comment—a Memo field that contains the text of the customer's feedback.
- feedback_entrydate—a Date/Time field that automatically contains the date the feedback is entered. This field should have a default value of NOW().

You can create the feedback table in the storeDB database (The same Access database that you used in this week's lessons).

Next, you'll need to create an ASP page, named feedback.asp, that contains the HTML form for customer feedback. The customer feedback form is contained in Listing BP1.1.

LISTING BP1.1   The Customer Feedback Form

```
1   <HTML>
2   <HEAD><TITLE>Customer Feedback</TITLE></HEAD>
3   <BODY>
4
5   Thank you for leaving customer feedback on our Web site.
6   <br>Please enter your feedback in the form below:
7
8
9   <FORM METHOD="post" ACTION="saveFeedback.asp">
10  <P><B>Your Email Address:</B>
11  <BR><INPUT NAME="email" size="50" maxlength="255">
12  <P><B>Your Feedback:</B>
13  <BR><TEXTAREA NAME="comment" COLS=50 ROWS=4
14     WRAP="Virtual"></TEXTAREA>
15  <P><INPUT TYPE="submit" VALUE="Submit Feedback">
16  </FORM>
17
18  </BODY>
19  </HTML>
```

ANALYSIS The customer feedback form consists of a standard HTML form. It has an Email field and a Comments field. When a customer submits the form, the data is submitted to the `savefeedback.asp` page.

The `savefeedback.asp` page is contained in Listing BP1.2.

LISTING BP1.2 The Save Feedback Page

```
1  <%
2  FUNCTION fixQuotes( theString )
3    fixQuotes = REPLACE( theString, "'", "''" )
4  END FUNCTION
5
6  email = TRIM( Request( "email" ) )
7  comment = TRIM( Request( "comment" ) )
8  IF email <> "" AND comment <> "" THEN
9    Set Con = Server.CreateObject( "ADODB.Connection" )
10   Con.Open "accessDSN"
11   sqlString = "INSERT INTO feedback ( feedback_email, feedback_comment ) " &_
12     "VALUES ('" & fixQuotes( email ) & "','" & fixQuotes( comment ) & "')"
13   Con.Execute sqlString
14 END IF
15 %>
16 <HTML>
17 <HEAD><TITLE>Save Feedback</TITLE></HEAD>
18 <BODY>
19
20 <B>Thank you for submitting your feedback!</B>
21
22 </BODY>
23 </HTML>
```

ANALYSIS The `savefeedback.asp` page contained in Listing BP1.2 saves the information that the customer entered in the customer feedback form into the database table named feedback. You should find the Active Server Pages script that appears in this page easy to understand.

In lines 6 and 7, the customer's email address and comments are retrieved from the `Request` object. Next, in lines 9 and 10, a database connection is created and opened. A SQL `INSERT INTO` statement is constructed in lines 11 and 12, and executed in line 13. After the SQL `INSERT INTO` statement is executed, the customer feedback should appear in the database table.

Feel free to modify this customer feedback form by adding additional fields. For example, you might want to ask the customer for his name and telephone number. In next week's bonus lesson, we'll add some new features to the customer feedback form.

WEEK 2

At A Glance

This week, you'll finish building your online store. The first lesson contains an overview of the database tables used in your store. Next, on Days 9 and 10, you'll learn two methods of creating a virtual shopping cart. You'll learn how to create a shopping cart by using both Session variables and a database table.

On Day 11, the very important topic of processing credit card transactions is addressed. You'll be provided with an overview of the different options for processing credit cards. One method of processing credit cards will be discussed in detail. You'll learn how to build ASP scripts to authorize and settle credit card transactions with CyberCash.

On Day 12, you'll learn how to enable customers to track their product orders. You'll create a Web page that provides customers with a means to view the status of their orders. You'll also learn how to enable customers to track their orders as the orders are being shipped from your store to their homes.

Finally, you'll learn how to build a subscription Web site. On Day 13, you'll learn how to create a user registration system. You can use this registration system to create password-protected Web pages that can be viewed only by paying customers.

8

9

10

11

12

13

14

DAY 8

Building the Transaction Databases

In today's lesson, we will continue building our online store. First, you will get an overview of the database tables that we will need to create in this and the following chapter to receive and process customer orders. Next, you will learn how to create a user registration system that will enable you to track such information as user credit card numbers and shipping addresses. Finally, you will learn how to securely accept credit card information over the Internet. Today, you will learn the following:

- How to create a registration form and login page that requests user registration information
- How to validate the information that a user enters into a form, including credit card numbers
- How to create an error page that enables users to easily correct mistakes made when completing an online form
- How to use the Secure Sockets Layer to securely transmit information across the Internet

The Transaction Database Tables

Before we get into the details of how to process customer orders, it might be helpful to have an overview of the tables that we will need to create in order to complete our online store. You have already created one table, the Products table, that you have used in previous lessons to store product information. You will also need to create the following tables:

- The Users Table—This table will be used to store user information, such as usernames and passwords, address information, and credit card information. You will learn the details of creating this table in this chapter.

- The Cart Table—This table will be used to store customer shopping carts. When customers add items to their virtual shopping cart while browsing your store, the items will be added to this table. You will learn how to create the Cart table in tomorrow's lesson.

- The Orders Table—When a customer checks out and completes an order, all the products in the customer's shopping cart are transferred to this table. The orders table contains information about all the products that have been ordered in addition to information about the status of an order. You will learn how to create this table in the lesson on Day 10.

When customers add items to their shopping carts, a registration page appears requesting that the customer log in. If this is the first time a customer has used your store, they are required to enter registration information including their username and password. After customers have registered once, they can access their shopping cart in the future by simply entering their username and password, or automatically if their browser supports cookies.

 Note　To get a better sense of how all the pages in the online store interact, visit the live version of the store discussed in this book at superexpert. Go to http://www.superexpert.com/candystore.

After a user logs in, the item that the customer selected to add to the shopping cart is added to the Cart database table. Items remain in the shopping cart permanently. The customer can leave your site for a year and return to add and remove items from the shopping cart.

Finally, when customers are ready to complete their orders, they can click the Checkout button on their shopping cart. When the customer clicks Checkout, all the items are transferred to the Orders database table from the Cart table and the customers' items in the Cart table are deleted.

Notice that the Users table, the Cart table, and the Orders table are used in sequence. A customer selects an item, and then he must login. The Users table is employed to validate the login information. Next, the item selected is added to the Cart table. Finally, when a customer clicks Checkout, the items are transferred from the Cart table to the Orders table.

Creating the Users Database Table

All the customer registration information is contained in the Users table. This table has the following fields:

user_id—This field is an autonumber field. It contains an automatically generated unique number for each customer.

user_username—This field contains the name that the customer uses to login to your online store. Each user has a unique username.

user_password—This field contains the secret password that a customer uses to access her shopping cart.

user_email—The email address of the customer. We don't really use this field, but it is always good information to have in case you need to contact the customer.

user_street—The street address of the customer. For example, 775 Evergreen Road.

user_city—The city where the customer lives. For example, San Francisco.

user_zip—The customer's zip code. For example, 94108.

user_state—The two letter state code. For example, CA.

user_cctype—The type of credit card that the customer wants to use to make purchases. For example, VISA or MasterCard.

user_ccnumber—The customer's credit card number.

user_ccexpires—The expiration date of the customer's credit card.

user_ccname—The customer's name as it appears on the customer's credit card.

You can create the Users table by launching Microsoft Access and creating a new table called Users in the storeDB database with all the fields just described. Alternatively, you can copy the storeDB.mdb file from the CD that accompanies this book. This database already contains the Users table.

Registering Users

Before customers can add items to their shopping cart, they must first register.
Registration creates a better shopping experience for the customer. Instead of entering
address and payment information every time a new item is bought, the customer can
enter this information once. After the information has been entered once, it can be automatically retrieved from the database whenever the customer purchases additional items.

Another benefit to requiring customers to register is that it enables customers to retain a
shopping cart over many visits to your Web site. For example, a customer might add two
items to the shopping cart, but might wait a couple of days to consider purchasing the
items before clicking the Checkout button. It would not be possible to create a persistent
shopping cart without requiring the customer to enter registration information so that a
shopping cart can be matched with a user over time.

In this section, you'll learn how to create the Active Server Pages that enable a customer
to enter her register information and login to password protected pages.

Creating the `cart.asp` Page

When a customer clicks the Add to Cart button on a product page, he is brought to the
`cart.asp` page. In tomorrow's lesson, you'll learn how to create the shopping cart itself.
In today's lesson, you'll learn how to force the customer to register and login before
accessing the shopping cart.

The `cart.asp` page is contained in Listing 8.1. (You can also open `cart.asp` from the
CD-ROM that accompanies this book.)

LISTING 8.1   The `cart.asp` Page

```
1  <!-- #INCLUDE FILE="adovbs.inc" -->
2  <!-- #INCLUDE FILE="storefuncs.asp" -->
3  <%
4  ' Get Product ID
5  productID = TRIM( Request( "pid" ) )
6
7  ' Get Login Information
8  username = TRIM( Request( "username" ) )
9  password = TRIM( Request( "password" ) )
10 register = TRIM( Request( "register" ) )
11 error = TRIM( Request( "error" ) )
12
13 ' Open Database Connection
14  Set Con = Server.CreateObject( "ADODB.Connection" )
15  Con.Open "accessDSN"
16
```

```
17  ' Check For New Registration
18  IF register <> "" AND error = "" THEN
19    addUser
20  END IF
21
22  '  Get User ID
23  userID =  checkpassword( username, password, Con )
24
25  IF userID > 0 THEN
26    %>
27  <!-- #INCLUDE FILE="addCart.asp" -->
28  <% ELSE %>
29    <!-- #INCLUDE FILE="register.asp" -->
30    <%
31  END IF
32  %>
```

ANALYSIS When a customer arrives at the cart.asp page, one of two things will happen. If the customer's username and password can be retrieved from the Request collection, the addCart.asp page will be displayed. Otherwise, the registration page will be displayed. In other words, the customer can view the addCart.asp page only if the customer has already entered registration information.

Lines 1 and 2 include two files named adovbs.inc and storefuncs.asp. You should already be familiar with the adovbs.inc file. It's the file that contains all the constants for the ActiveX Data Objects. The storefuncs.asp file is used to contain all the common functions used in the pages of your online store. You'll learn how to create this file later in this chapter.

In line 5, the product ID is retrieved. This product ID will be used to identity the product that is added to the shopping cart.

In lines 7–11, the customer's username and password are retrieved. There are two ways that a customer's username and password might be passed to this page through the Request collection. If the customer has logged in, the username and password will be included in the Request collection as form fields. Alternatively, the username and password might be contained in the Request collection as cookies if the customer's browser supports cookies.

In lines 13–15, a database connection is opened by using the Data Source Name that you created in Day 5, "Building Your Product Catalog."

In lines 17–20, the customer's registration information is added to the database. This is accomplished with the addUser subroutine. You'll learn how to create this subroutine when you create the storefuncs.asp file later in this chapter.

In lines 22–23, the customer's username and password are checked against the Users table. If the username and password combination exist in this table, the user ID is returned. Otherwise, a negative number is returned indicating that the username and password entered by the customer is invalid. The function that checks the username and password, checkpassword(), is included in the storefuncs.asp file.

Finally, in lines 25–31, either the register.asp page or the addCart.asp page is displayed. If the customer hasn't entered valid login information, the registration page is displayed. Otherwise, the customer can access the shopping cart.

Notice how the pages are conditionally displayed by using #INCLUDE files. Both the addCart.asp and register.asp page are included in the cart.asp page. However, only one of the two pages will be displayed at any time.

> **Note**
>
> You might be tempted to conditionally display alternative pages by assigning a variable as the value of the #INCLUDE directive. For example, you might be tempted to use a script like this:
>
> ```
> <%
> IF userID > 0 THEN
>   showFile = "cart.asp"
> ELSE
>   showFile = "register.asp"
> END IF
> %>
> <!-- #INCLUDE FILE=<%=showFile%> -->
> ```
>
> Regrettably, however, this script won't work. The problem is that any #INCLUDE directives contained in an ASP page are processed before any scripts. This means that the above script will attempt to include a file named <%=showFile%>.
>
> You'll be happy to know that the new version of Active Server Pages (included with Windows 2000) supports a better method of including files.

Creating the register.asp Page

The register.asp page contains two HTML forms that enable a customer to either login with an existing username and password or register as a new customer (see Figure 8.1). The listing for register.asp is quite long, so it isn't included in this chapter. However, you can open the register.asp file from the CD-ROM that accompanies this book.

FIGURE 8.1

The register.asp
page.

8

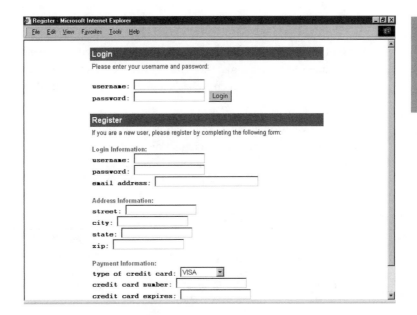

After a customer completes either of the two HTML forms, the customer is sent back to the page that includes register.asp. For example, if the register.asp page was displayed because the customer was attempting to access the shopping cart, the login information or registration information is sent to cart.asp. The register.asp page uses the following code to determine the page in which it is included:

```
submitpage = Request.ServerVariables( "SCRIPT_NAME" )
```

This statement uses the server variable named SCRIPT_NAME to retrieve the name of the current page. Because the register.asp page is contained in cart.asp, the value returned will be cart.asp rather than register.asp. The HTML forms are submitted to the correct containing page by using the following HTML code:

```
<form method="post" action="<%=submitpage%>">
```

This is a normal HTML <FORM> tag. However, it has the submitpage variable as the value of its ACTION attribute.

You might wonder why the ACTION attribute wasn't simply given the value cart.asp rather than the value of the submitpage variable. The reason is that the register.asp page will be contained in a number of pages in the store. For example, the register.asp page is also contained in the account.asp page. By not hard-coding the value of the ACTION attribute in the register.asp page, the register.asp page can be reused in multiple pages.

The Registration Functions

Most of the work of registering and validating the login information of customers happens in the `storefuncs.asp` file. The `storefuncs.asp` file contains the functions and subroutines that validate a customer's login information and adds the new registration information to the database.

When a new customer enters registration information, the `addUser` subroutine is called. This subroutine retrieves all the registration form fields, validates the field data, adds the information to the `Users` table, and adds cookies to the customer's browser that contains the username and password. The `addUser` subroutine is included in Listing 8.2.

LISTING 8.2   The addUser Subroutine

```
1   SUB addUser
2   ' Get Registration Fields
3     newusername = TRIM( Request( "newusername" ) )
4     newpassword = TRIM( Request( "newpassword" ) )
5     email = TRIM( Request( "email" ) )
6     street = TRIM( Request( "street" ) )
7     city = TRIM( Request( "city" ) )
8     state = TRIM( Request( "state" ) )
9     zip = TRIM( Request( "zip" ) )
10  cctype = Request( "cctype" )
11  ccnumber = TRIM( Request( "ccnumber" ) )
12  ccexpires = TRIM( Request( "ccexpires" ) )
13  ccname = TRIM( Request( "ccname" ) )
14
15  ' Check For Required Fields
16  backpage = Request.ServerVariables( "SCRIPT_NAME" )
17  IF newusername = "" THEN
18    errorForm "You must enter a username.", backpage
19  END IF
20  IF newpassword = "" THEN
21    errorForm "You must enter a password.", backpage
22  END IF
23  IF email = "" THEN
24    errorForm "You must enter your email address.", backpage
25  END IF
26  IF street = "" THEN
27    errorForm "You must enter your street address.", backpage
28  END IF
29  IF city = "" THEN
30    errorForm "You must enter your city.", backpage
31  END IF
32  IF state = "" THEN
33    errorForm "You must enter your state.", backpage
34  END IF
```

8

```
35  IF zip = "" THEN
36    errorForm "You must enter your zip code.", backpage
37  END IF
38  IF ccnumber = "" THEN
39    errorForm "You must enter your credit card number.", backpage
40  END IF
41  IF ccexpires = "" THEN
42    errorForm "You must enter your credit card expiration date.", backpage
43  END IF
44  IF ccname = "" THEN
45    errorForm "You must enter the name that appears on your credit card.",
      ↦backpage
46  END IF
47
48  ' Check for Necessary Field Values
49  IF invalidEmail( email ) THEN
50    errorForm "You did not enter a valid email address", backpage
51  END IF
52  IF NOT validCCNumber( ccnumber ) THEN
53    errorForm "You did not enter a valid credit card number", backpage
54  END IF
55  IF NOT isDATE( ccexpires ) THEN
56    errorForm "You did not enter a valid credit card expiration date",
      ↦backpage
57  END IF
58
59  ' Check whether username already registered
60  IF alreadyUser( newusername ) THEN
61    errorForm "Please choose a different username.", backpage
62  END IF
63
64  ' Add New User to Database
65  sqlString = "INSERT INTO users ( " &_
66    "user_username, " &_
67    "user_password, " &_
68    "user_email," &_
69    "user_street, " &_
70    "user_city," &_
71    "user_state," &_
72    "user_zip," &_
73    "user_ccnumber, " &_
74    "user_cctype, " &_
75    "user_ccexpires," &_
76    "user_ccname" &_
77    ") VALUES ( " &_
78    " '" & fixQuotes( newusername ) & "', " &_
79    " '" & fixQuotes( newpassword ) & "', " &_
80    " '" & fixQuotes( email ) & "', " &_
81    " '" & fixQuotes( street ) & "', " &_
```

continues

LISTING 8.2   continued

```
82     " '" & fixQuotes( city ) & "', " &_
83     " '" & fixQuotes( state ) & "', " &_
84     " '" & fixQuotes( zip ) & "', " &_
85     " '" & fixQuotes( ccnumber ) & "', " &_
86     " '" & cctype & "', " &_
87     " '" & ccexpires & "', " &_
88     " '" & fixQuotes( ccname ) & "' " &_
89     ")"
90
91  Con.Execute sqlString
92
93  ' Use the new username and password
94  username = newusername
95  password = newpassword
96
97  ' Add Cookies
98  addCookie "username", username
99  addCookie "password", password
100 END SUB
```

ANALYSIS   As you can see, Listing 8.2 is very long. However, the addUser subroutine performs a number of important functions, so it is worthwhile to examine how it
works in detail.

Lines 2–13 are used to retrieve all the registration form fields that the customer completed in register.asp. Next, in lines 15–46, all the fields are checked to make sure that
they aren't empty. We don't want to let a customer get away with entering an empty
email address or password, for instance. If a form field is, in fact, empty, the errorForm
subroutine is called. This subroutine displays a page to the customer reporting the error
and invites the customer to return to the form to make corrections. (The errorForm subroutine is described in detail in the next section of this chapter.)

Next, in lines 48–57, the data that the customer entered into the email address, credit
card number, and credit card expiration date form fields is validated. The email address
is validated by using a function named invalidEmail(). This function simply checks
whether the email address that the customer entered contains both a period and the @
sign. This function is contained in Listing 8.3.

LISTING 8.3   The invalidEmail() Function

```
1  FUNCTION invalidEmail( email )
2    IF INSTR( email, "@" ) = 0 OR INSTR( email, "." ) = 0 THEN
3      invalidEmail = TRUE
4    ELSE
```

```
5      invalidEmail = FALSE
6    END IF
7  END FUNCTION
```

The credit card expiration date that the customer entered is also validated. If the customer didn't enter a valid date, the errorForm subroutine is called so that the customer can fix the problem.

The credit card number that the customer entered is validated by using a Luhn check. All the major credit cards, such as VISA, MasterCard, American Express, and Discover cards, include a check digit that enables you to check whether a credit card number is valid. Of course, a Luhn check cannot be used to determine whether a customer actually has any credit left in their credit card account, or whether the credit card was actually issued to anyone. However, using a Luhn check is a good way to discard clearly bad credit card numbers. The Luhn check is performed in the validCCNumber() function contained in Listing 8.4.

LISTING 8.4   The validCCNumer() Function

```
1  FUNCTION validCCNumber( ccnumber )
2    ccnumber = cleanCCNum( ccnumber )
3    IF ccnumber = "" THEN
4      validCCNumber = FALSE
5    ELSE
6    isEven = False
7    digits = ""
8    for i = Len( ccnumber ) To 1 Step -1
9    if isEven Then
10     digits = digits & CINT( MID( ccnumber, i, 1) ) * 2
11   Else
12     digits = digits & CINT( MID( ccnumber, i, 1) )
13   End If
14   isEven = (Not isEven)
15   Next
16   checkSum = 0
17   For i = 1 To Len( digits) Step 1
18     checkSum = checkSum + CINT( MID( digits, i, 1 ) )
19   Next
20   validCCNumber = ( ( checkSum Mod 10) = 0 )
21   END IF
22 End Function
```

The validCCNumber() function checks whether a credit card number is valid by doubling every other digit, starting from the last digit, and adding the resulting numbers together. If the result can be divided by 10 without a remainder, the credit card number passes the check.

Notice that the first thing the `validCCNumber()` function does is to call another function named `cleanCCNum()`. The `cleanCCNum()` function removes any non-numeric characters from a credit card number. It's common for users to enter a credit card number including dashes and spaces. To validate the number, we must first strip these characters away. The `cleanCCNum()` function is contained in Listing 8.5.

LISTING 8.5   The `cleanCCNum()` Function

```
1   FUNCTION cleanCCNum( ccnumber )
2   FOR i = 1 TO LEN( ccnumber )
3     IF isNumeric( MID( ccnumber, i, 1 ) ) THEN
4         cleanCCNum = cleanCCNum & MID( ccnumber, i, 1 )
5     END IF
6   NEXT
7 END FUNCTION
```

The `cleanCCNumber()` function simply walks through all the characters in the credit card number one by one by using the `MID()` function. If a character is not numeric, the character is skipped. Otherwise, it is added back to the credit card number.

After the form fields have been validated in the `addUser` subroutine, the `alreadyUser()` function is called to check whether someone has already registered using the username the customer entered. The function is called in line 60. We need to check whether the username already exists so that we can guarantee that all the usernames in the Users table are unique. The `alreadyUser()` function is contained in Listing 8.6.

LISTING 8.6   The `alreadyUser()` Function

```
1   FUNCTION alreadyUser( theUsername )
2     sqlString = "SELECT user_username FROM users " &_
3       "WHERE user_username='" & fixQuotes( theUsername ) & "'"
4     SET RS = Con.Execute( sqlString )
5     IF RS.EOF THEN
6       alreadyUser = FALSE
7     ELSE
8       alreadyUser = TRUE
9     END IF
10    RS.Close
11 END FUNCTION
```

The `alreadyUser()` function constructs a SQL SELECT statement to check whether the username exists in the database. This SQL statement is used to open a Recordset named RS. If RS is empty (which is tested with the EOF property of the Recordset property), we know that the user doesn't already exist in the Users database table.

Next, returning to the addUser subroutine once again, a SQL INSERT INTO statement is constructed out of the form fields that the customer submitted. This statement is created in lines 65–89 and executed in line 91. After the statement is executed, the customer's registration information is added to the Users database table.

Finally, in lines 98 and 99, two cookies are added to the customer's browser that contain the username and password. This is done so that the customer doesn't have to log in every time the customer wants to access the shopping cart or view account information. The cookies are added with a subroutine named, appropriately enough, addCookie. The addCookie subroutine is contained in Listing 8.7.

LISTING 8.7   The addCookie Subroutine

```
1  SUB addCookie( theName, theValue )
2    Response.Cookies( theName ) = theValue
3    Response.Cookies( theName ).Expires = "July 31, 2001"
4    Response.Cookies( theName ).Path = "/"
5    Response.Cookies( theName ).Secure = FALSE
6  END SUB
```

The addCookie subroutine adds a cookie to a customer's browser by using the Cookies collection of the Response object. The cookie is set to expire on July 31, 2001 in line 3. If you don't set the Expires property, the cookie will automatically expire after the customer leaves your Web site (or closes the browser).

Note that there is no guarantee the cookie will persist until the year 2001. A cookie file can contain only a limited amount of information, so the username and password might be removed from the cookie file much earlier. If the cookies are lost from the customer's browser, it really doesn't matter. The user will merely need to login once again, and the cookies will be automatically re-added.

Gracefully Handling Form Errors

The addUser subroutine discussed in the previous sections makes extensive use of another subroutine named errorForm. The errorForm subroutine displays an error message and asks the user to return to the previous page to correct the mistake (see Figure 8.2).

The errorForm page has a nice feature. When the user clicks the button labeled Return, all the original data that the user entered into the HTML form is passed back to the form. Because the information is passed back to the form, the user doesn't need to start filling out the form again.

FIGURE 8.2

The errorForm *page.*

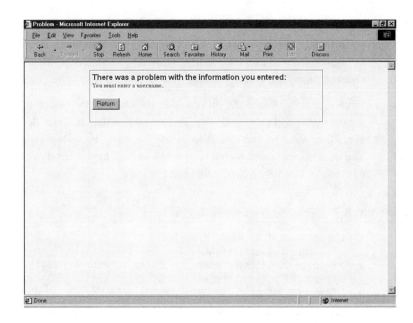

The errorForm subroutine is contained in Listing 8.8.

LISTING 8.8   The errorForm Subroutine

```
1   SUB errorForm( errorMSG, backpage )
2   %>
3   <html>
4   <head><title>Problem</title></head>
5   <body bgcolor="lightyellow">
6
7   <center>
8   <table width="500" border=1
9     cellpadding=5 cellspacing=0>
10  <tr>
11    <td>
12    <font face="Arial" size="3" color="darkblue"><b>
13    There was a problem with the information you entered:
14    </b></font>
15    <font size="2" color="red"><b>
16    <br><%=errorMSG%>
17    </b></font>
18    <br>
19    <form method="post" action="<%=backpage%>">
20    <input name="error" type="hidden" value="1">
21    <% formFields %>
22    <input type="submit" value="Return">
23    </form>
24    </td>
```

```
25    </tr>
26    </table>
27    </center>
28
29    </body>
30    </html>
31    <%
32    Response.End
33 END SUB
```

ANALYSIS The errorForm subroutine accepts two parameters: errorMSG and backpage. The errorMSG parameter contains the text of the error message to be displayed. The backpage parameter contains the path of the original form.

Lines 19–23 contain the form that passes the original values of the form fields back to the original page. The form fields are all hidden. The only thing the user sees is a submit button labeled Return.

The hidden form fields are created with the formFields subroutine. The formFields subroutine is contained in Listing 8.9.

LISTING 8.9 The formFields Subroutine

```
1 SUB formFields
2   FOR each item in Request.Form
3   %>
4   <input name="<%=item%>" type="hidden"
5     value="<%=Server.HTMLEncode( Request( item ) )%>">
6   <%
7   NEXT
8 END SUB
```

ANALYSIS The formFields subroutine loops through all the items contained in the Form collection of the Request object. Each item in the Form collection is made into a hidden form field. When the user clicks return, these hidden form fields are passed back to the original HTML form so that they can be displayed again.

Using the Secure Sockets Layer

When a customer fills out the registration form, he must enter credit card information. When the registration form is submitted, the credit card information is transmitted across the Internet in plain text form. This is very dangerous.

Whenever information travels across the Internet, it must pass through several intermediate connections. In theory, an individual with impure intentions could steal the information while it is en route to its destination.

To protect your customers' credit cart information, you must use the Secure Sockets Layer (SSL). SSL is a technology originally developed by Netscape that enables you to transfer information securely across the Internet. SSL provides a technical solution to three distinct security problems: encryption, authentication, and data integrity.

When information is transmitted using SSL, the information is encrypted. Even if someone manages to steal data off the wire as it travels from a customer's browser to your Web server, the data wouldn't be useable.

SSL encrypts information as it passes back and forth between a Web server and Web browser by encoding the information with a publicly known encryption algorithm and a secret session encryption key. The number of bits in the session key determines the strength of the encryption. There are currently two standard key sizes: 40-bit and 128-bit. Although there have been cases when messages encrypted with the 40-bit key have been hacked, the 128-bit key is considered unbreakable with current technology.

SSL can also be used to authenticate a Web server. In theory, a malicious individual could trick a customer into believing that another Web site is your Web site. The malicious individual could then steal credit card numbers when customers submit information to the fraudulent Web site.

Note

> SSL version 3.0 also supports client certificates. Client certificates work in exactly the same way as server certificates except that they are used to authenticate Web browser rather than Web servers. Both Microsoft Internet Explorer (version 3.0 and higher) and Netscape Navigator (version 3.0 and higher) support client certificates.

However, when you enable SSL on your Web server, you are required to install a server certificate. This server certificate prevents other Web sites from pretending to be your Web site. A server certificate verifies your Web site's identity in much the same way as your driver's license verifies your personal identity. A server certificate contains information about your Web site, your organization, and the issuer of the certificate.

Finally, SSL protects the integrity of the data as it is transmitted across the Internet. In theory, a person with questionable intentions could tamper with data as it is transmitted back and forth from a Web browser to a Web server. SSL protects the integrity of the data by including a message authentication code (MAC) with the data as it is transmitted. In other words, when you use SSL, you know that the message received is the same as the message sent.

Again, if you request confidential information such as credit card numbers from your customers, you have a responsibility to protect this information. The only generally available solution to this problem is to use SSL.

Enabling SSL on Your Web Server

You cannot use SSL with the Personal Web Server. You can only use SSL with Internet Information Server. This makes sense because the Personal Web Server was designed for prototyping Web sites and hosting small intranet Web sites and not for hosting commercial Web sites.

You should be warned that enabling SSL can be time-consuming and expensive. The time and expense results from the requirement that you obtain a server certificate from a certificate authority. VeriSign, for example, currently charges $349.00 for a 40-bit SSL key and $895.00 for the 128-bit key. I've personally experienced waits of six weeks for a server certificate to be processed.

To enable SSL with the Internet Information Server, you will need to complete the following three steps (each of these steps will be described in detail in the following sections):

1. Generate a Certificate Request File and an encryption key pair file using Microsoft Key Manager.
2. Apply for a server certificate from a certificate authority by providing your Certificate Request File.
3. Install your server certificate by using Microsoft Key Manager.

Generating the Certificate Request File

To create a Certificate Request File—also called a Certificate Signing Request (CSR)—you must use the Microsoft Key Manager. To access the Microsoft Key Manager, launch the Internet Service Manager and click the Key Manager icon that appears on the toolbar. Within the Key Manager, select Key, Create New Key. This starts a wizard that will guide you through the task of creating the Certificate Request File (see Figure 8.3).

To create the Certificate Request File, you will need to supply the following information:

- Request File—When you complete the wizard, your Certificate Request File will be stored on your hard drive with this name.
- Key Name—You can supply any name here. The name is used to identify the key.
- Password—You will need this password when you install your signed server certificate after you receive it from the certificate authority.

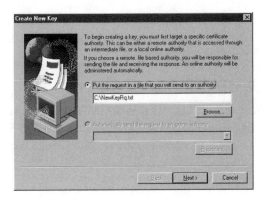

FIGURE 8.3

Creating a Certificate Request File.

- Key Size—By default, the Key Size will be 512 bits long. The key size refers to the strength of the server certificate, not the strength of the session key used to encrypt messages.
- Organization—The name of the owner of your domain name. Typically, the organization is the name of your company.
- Organizational Unit—The name of your department or business unit.
- Common Name—Your fully qualified domain name. For example, asp.superexpert.com. You shouldn't include the protocol (HTTP://).
- Country/Region—The two-letter ISO country code for your country. For example, US for the United States or CA for Canada. The wizard provides a link to a list of these country codes.
- State/Province—The full name of your state or province. For example, California.
- Locality—The name of your city or town. For example, San Francisco.
- Your Name—Your full name.
- Email Address—Your email address.
- Phone Number—Your phone number.

When you have completed the wizard, a Certificate Request File will be saved to your hard drive. A broken key will appear in Key Manager signifying that a Certificate Request File has been generated, but the server certificate hasn't been installed.

Applying for a Server Certificate

After you create your Certificate Request File, you must send it to a certificate authority in order to get your server certificate. Here is a list of three of the more popular certificate authorities:

- VeriSign Inc. (http://www.verisign.com)

- Thawte Consulting (`http://www.thawte.com`)
- GTE CyberTrust Solutions (`http://www.cybertrust.gte.com`)

For example, to apply for a VeriSign server certificate, go to `http://www.verisign.com` and choose Secure Server ID. You will need to provide VeriSign with identifying information about your organization such as your Dun and Bradstreet DUNS number, your articles of incorporation, or your business license. After you have provided this information, you can submit your certificate request file through an online form. After your information is verified, you will receive an email message that contains instructions for downloading your new server certificate.

Installing Your Server Certificate

The last step in configuring your server to use SSL is to actually install the server certificate after you receive it from the certificate authority. To install the server certificate, launch the Internet Service Manager and select the Microsoft Key Manager. Next, choose Key, Install Key Certificate. Open your new server certificate file from your hard drive and supply the same password as you used when you generated the Certificate Request File. Next, specify the IP address and port to use with SSL (You can change this information at any time in the future within the Internet Service Manager). When you have finished, an icon of a completed key should appear within Microsoft Key Manager.

A server certificate only lasts for a preset period of time. In the right frame of the Microsoft Key Manager, you can view the exact date when your certificate will expire. To continue using SSL, you must request a new server certificate before this date.

Note

> If you need to transfer your certificate to a new server, you can use Microsoft Key Manager to create a back-up copy of your certificate. Select Key, Export Key, Backup File. You can then load the certificate on the new server by selecting Key, Import Key, Backup File. The new server must have the same Internet domain name as the original server. (However, the IP address can be different.)

Using SSL in an ASP Page

After you have installed your server certificate, you can request any page from your Web site securely. To request a page using SSL, you must use an address that begins with the protocol https:// rather than the standard http://. For example, to request the `cart.asp` page using SSL, you would use `https://www.yourdomain.com/cart.asp`.

If you want to force a user to use SSL when requesting a page from your Web site, you can use the Internet Service Manager to configure a directory (or a particular file) to require SSL. To do this, launch the Internet Service Manager and open the property sheet for one of the directories within your Web site. Next, click the Edit button under Secure Communications and choose Require Secure Channel When Accessing This Resource.

Whenever we ask customers for registration information in the online store, we need to enable SSL to protect the customer's credit card information. For example, when a customer attempts to add an item to the shopping cart, the customer might be asked to register if the customer is using the shopping cart for the first time. The easiest way to enable SSL is to alter the address of the cart.asp page in the Product.asp page.

The HTML form that shows the Add To Cart button looks like this:

```
<form method="post" action="cart.asp">
<input name="pid" type="hidden" value="<%=RS( "product_id" )%>">
<input type="submit" value="Add To Cart">
</form>
```

To request the cart.asp page using SSL, you will need to modify the ACTION attribute of the <FORM> tag like this:

```
<form method="post" action="https://www.yourdomain.com/cart.asp">
<input name="pid" type="hidden" value="<%=RS( "product_id" )%>">
<input type="submit" value="Add To Cart">
</form>
```

After you have requested a page using SSL, all subsequent pages requested will also use SSL until you specify otherwise. To stop using SSL, use a link that uses http:// rather than https:// like this:

```
http://www.yourdomain.com/default.asp
```

Summary

In today's lesson, you were provided with an overview of the database tables that you will need in order to process customer orders. You learned how to create one of these database tables in detail. You learned how to create the Users table to store user registration information. You also learned how to create Active Server Pages that enable you to request registration information and store the information in the Users table. Next, you learned how to use a Luhn check to validate credit card numbers. Finally, you learned how to securely request confidential information, such as credit card numbers, from customers by using the Secure Sockets Layer.

Q&A

Q **How accurate is the Luhn check? Are there any credit card numbers that will pass the Luhn check but are not valid?**

A Because the Luhn check is nothing more than an algorithm, you cannot use it to test whether a credit card account with a certain number actually exists, or whether the credit card account has sufficient credit to cover a purchase. For example, the credit card number 8888-8888-8888-888 will pass the Luhn check because it satisfies the formal conditions of the algorithm.

Q **Is there any way to experiment with the Secure Sockets Layer without buying a server certificate?**

A Yes, several of the certificate authorities offer trial certificates that you can download. For example, VeriSign is currently offering a free 14-day trial certificate (go to http://www.verisign.com).

Workshop

The Quiz and Exercise questions are designed to test your knowledge of the material covered in this chapter. The answers are in Appendix A, "Quiz Answers."

Quiz

1. The following script was designed to conditionally display one of two pages depending on the value of the variable named showPage. What's wrong with this script?

```
<%
IF DATE() > "12/25/1999" THEN
   showPage = "page1.asp"
ELSE
   showPage = "page2.asp"
END IF
%>
<!-- #INCLUDE FILE="<%=showPage%>" -->
```

2. How can I add a cookie to a customer's browser named customerID that has the value 17?

3. What do I need to do in order to request a page named confidential.asp using the Secure Sockets Layer?

Exercise

The registration form described in this chapter has fields for login information, payment information, and address information. How would you add additional fields such as customer first and last name to this form?

WEEK 2

DAY 9

Building the Shopping Cart

In today's lesson, you will be presented with two methods of adding a shopping cart to your online store. You will also learn several additional methods of working with the ActiveX Data Objects (ADO). Today, you will learn the following:

- How to create a shopping cart using `Session` variables
- How to use the native methods of the ADO to add, delete, and update records in a Recordset
- How to create a shopping cart using a database table

Using `Session` Variables to Create a Shopping Cart

In this section, you'll learn how to create a shopping cart by storing product information in a `Session` variable. When a customer clicks the Add To Cart button on a product page, the product the customer selected will be added to an array contained in a `Session` variable named `cart`. As the customer continues to browse the store, new items can be added to the shopping cart or existing items can be removed. When the customer has finished shopping, the customer can click the Checkout button to actually purchase the items stored in the shopping cart.

Before discussing how to create a shopping cart using `Session` variables, you should be warned that this isn't the best method of creating a shopping cart. This is because the shopping cart relies on `Session` variables, and `Session` variables are notoriously unreliable.

When a visitor first arrives at a Web site that uses `Session` variables, the Web server adds a cookie to the visitor's browser that tracks the visitor as he moves from page to page. When a `Session` variable is created, this cookie is used to associate the variable with the proper user. If, for whatever reason, the cookie cannot be created on the user's browsers, the `Session` variables won't work.

What would prevent a cookie from being added to a user's browser? There are several possibilities. Some older browsers simply don't support cookies. Also, most recent browsers—including both Netscape Navigator and Internet Explorer—provide the user with the option to refuse to accept cookies. Finally, cookies might not work on a user's browser if the user's cookie file becomes corrupted.

Another significant problem with using `Session` variables is that they time out after a preset period of time. By default, a user session will end after 20 minutes of inactivity. After a session has timed out, all the `Session` variables associated with that user session are automatically removed from memory. This means that if you add some items to the shopping cart, the phone rings, and you have a pleasant 21-minute conversation, all the items that you added to your shopping cart will be gone when you return to shopping.

> **Note**
>
> By default, `Session` variables are deleted automatically after 20 minutes of activity. You can change this default behavior either by script or (if you are using Internet Information Server) by using the Internet Service Manager.
>
> To change the default session timeout period within an ASP script, modify the Timeout property of the `Session` object. For example, the following script changes the session timeout period to 40 minutes:
>
> ```
> <%
> Session.Timeout = 40
> %>
> ```
>
> To change the default session timeout period within the Internet Service Manager, open the property sheet for your default Web site, choose the Home Directory tab, click the Configuration button in the section labeled Application Settings, and select the App Options tab.

Later in this chapter, you will learn how to create a shopping cart by using a database table instead of `Session` variables. These problems with cookies can be completely avoided with this second method of creating a shopping cart. However, because creating a shopping cart with `Session` variables is a very popular method of creating a shopping cart, we will discuss this method first.

Creating the `SessionCart.asp` Page

One advantage to using `Session` variables to create a shopping cart is that you don't need to force customers to register or log in before adding items to the shopping cart. `Session` variables are associated with different users automatically. You can allow an anonymous customer to create a shopping cart, and register or log in only after deciding to buy the items in the shopping cart.

To use the shopping cart created with `Session` variables, we will need to modify the `Product.asp` page to link to the page with the shopping cart. Open the `Product.asp` page in a text editor and search for the two places in the code where the Add To Cart HTML form appears. The Add To Cart HTML form looks like this:

```
<form method="post" action="cart.asp">
<input name="pid" type="hidden" value="<%=RS( "product_id" )%>">
<input type="submit" value="Add To Cart">
</form>
```

Replace the previous code (in both places where it appears), with the following Add To Cart form:

```
<form method="post" action="sessionCart.asp">
<input name="pid" type="hidden" value="<%=RS( "product_id" )%>">
<input name="productName" type="hidden" value="<%=RS( "product_name" )%>">
<input name="productPrice" type="hidden" value="<%=RS( "product_price" )%>">
<input type="submit" value="Add To Cart">
</form>
```

This HTML form displays an Add To Cart button that submits the contents of the form to a page named `sessionCart.asp`. Notice that the form also passes the product ID, product name, and product price in hidden form fields to the `sessionCart.asp` page.

The `sessionCart.asp` page is where the shopping cart itself is displayed. The complete code for `sessionCart.asp` is contained in Listing 9.1. (You can also retrieve this page from the CD-ROM that accompanies this book.)

The `sessionCart.asp` Page

LISTING 9.1   The sessionCart.asp Page

```
1   <%
2   ' Define Constants
3   CONST CARTPID = 0
4   CONST CARTPNAME = 1
5   CONST CARTPPRICE = 2
6   CONST CARTPQUANTITY = 3
7
8   ' Get The Shopping Cart
9   IF NOT isArray( Session( "cart" ) ) THEN
10    DIM localCart( 4, 20 )
11  ELSE
12    localCart = Session( "cart" )
13  END IF
14
15  ' Get Product Information
16  productID = TRIM( Request( "pid" ) )
17  productName = TRIM( Request( "productName" ) )
18  productPrice = TRIM( Request( "productPrice" ) )
19
20  ' Add Item to cart
21  IF productID <> "" THEN
22    foundIT = FALSE
23    FOR i = 0 TO UBOUND( localCart )
24      IF localCart( CARTPID, i ) = productID THEN
25        localCart( CARTPQUANTITY, i ) = localCart( CARTPQUANTITY, i ) + 1
26        foundIT = TRUE
27        EXIT FOR
28      END IF
29    NEXT
30    IF NOT foundIT THEN
31      FOR i = 0 TO UBOUND( localCart, 2 )
32        IF localCart( CARTPID, i ) = "" THEN
33          localCart( CARTPID, i ) = productID
34          localCart( CARTPNAME, i ) = productName
35          localCart( CARTPPRICE, i ) = productPrice
36          localCart( CARTPQUANTITY, i ) = 1
37          EXIT FOR
38        END IF
39      NEXT
40    END IF
41  END IF
42
43  ' Update Shopping Cart Quantities
44  IF Request( "updateQ" ) <> "" THEN
45    FOR i = 0 TO UBOUND( localCart, 2 )
46      newQ = TRIM( Request( "pq" & localCart( CARTPID, i ) ) )
```

```
47      deleteProduct = TRIM( Request( "pd" & localCart( CARTPID, i ) ) )
48      IF newQ = "" or newQ = "0" or deleteProduct <> "" THEN
49        localCart( CARTPID, i ) = ""
50      ELSE
51        IF isNumeric( newQ ) THEN
52          localCart( CARTPQUANTITY, i ) = newQ
53        END IF
54      END IF
55    NEXT
56  END IF
57
58
59  ' Update Session variable with Array
60  Session( "cart" ) = localCart
61  %>
62  <html>
63  <head><title>Session Shopping Cart</title></head>
64  <body bgcolor="white">
65
66  <center>
67  <font face="Arial" size=3 color="darkgreen">
68  <b>Your shopping cart:</b>
69  </font>
70  <%
71  orderTotal = 0
72  %>
73  <form method="post" action="sessionCart.asp">
74  <input name="updateQ" type="hidden" value="1">
75  <table bgcolor="lightyellow" border=1
76    cellpadding=4 cellspacing=0>
77  <tr bgcolor="lightgreen">
78    <th>Product</th>
79    <th>Price</th>
80    <th>Quantity</th>
81  </tr>
82  <%
83  FOR i = 0 TO UBOUND( localCart, 2 )
84  IF localCart( CARTPID, i ) <> "" THEN
85  orderTotal = orderTotal + ( localCart( CARTPPRICE, i )
➥ * localCart( CARTPQUANTITY, i ) )
86  %>
87  <tr>
88    <td>
89    <%=Server.HTMLEncode( localCart( CARTPNAME, i ) )%>
90    </td>
91    <td>
92    <%=formatCurrency( localCart( CARTPPRICE, i ) )%>
93    </td>
```

continues

LISTING 9.1   continued

```
94    <td>
95    <input name="pq<%=localCart( CARTPID, i )%>" type="text" size=4
96     value="<%=localCart( CARTPQUANTITY, i )%>">
97    <input name="pd<%=localCart( CARTPID, i )%>" type="checkbox" value="1">
      ➥ Delete
98    </td>
99  </tr>
100 <%
101 END IF
102 NEXT
103 %>
104 <tr bgcolor="yellow">
105   <td colspan=2 align=right>
106   <b>Order Total:</b>
107   </td>
108   <td>
109   <%=formatCurrency( orderTotal )%>
110   </td>
111 </tr>
112 <tr>
113   <td colspan=3>
114   <table border=0>
115   <tr>
116    <td align="right">
117    <input type="submit" value="Update Cart">
118    </td>
119    </form>
120    <form method="post" action="checkout.asp">
121    <td>
122    <input type="submit" value="Checkout">
123    </td>
124    </form>
125    <form action="default.asp">
126    <td>
127    <input type="submit" value="Continue Shopping">
128    </td>
129    </form>
130   </tr>
131   </table>
132   </td>
133 </tr>
134 </table>
135
136
137 </center>
138
139 </body>
140 </html>
```

ANALYSIS   The `sessionCart.asp` page displays the shopping cart in Figure 9.1. For each product, it displays the name of the product, the quantity of the product being ordered, and the product price.

FIGURE 9.1

The Session virtual shopping cart.

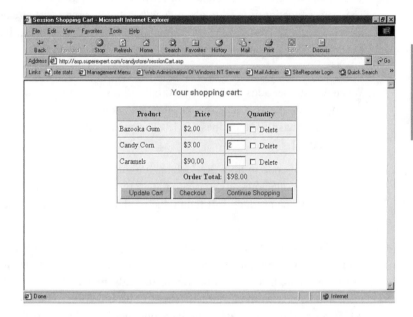

If a customer changes one or more of the product quantities and clicks Update Cart, the product quantities are updated in the shopping cart. If the customer changes any of the product quantities to either zero or nothing, the product is removed from the shopping cart. The customer can also remove a particular item by selecting the Delete check box.

If the customer clicks Checkout, she is brought to the `checkout.asp` page and the products in the shopping cart are ordered. We'll discuss the `checkout.asp` page in detail in tomorrow's lesson.

Finally, if the customer clicks Continue Shopping, she is brought back to the `default.asp` page of the store. If the customer leaves the `sessionCart.asp` page, the items in the shopping cart aren't lost. As long as the customer doesn't leave the Web site, all the items will remain in the shopping cart.

The `sessionCart.asp` page has three main sections of code. First, it has a section of code that adds a new item to a customer's shopping cart. Next, it has a code section that updates the quantities of the items in the shopping cart (after a customer clicks Update Cart). Finally, it has a section of code that displays all the items in the shopping cart.

The shopping cart is either created or retrieved in lines 8–13. In line 9, the VBScript isArray() function is used to check whether the shopping cart already exists in a Session variable named cart. If the shopping cart doesn't exist, it is created in line 10. Otherwise, if the shopping cart already exists, it is retrieved from the Session variable in line 12.

When a customer adds a new product to the shopping cart by clicking the Add To Cart button on the product page, information about the product is passed to the sessionCart.asp page in lines 15–18. The product information is added to the cart in lines 20–41.

The section of code in lines 20–41 loops through all the current items in the localCart array. If the product already exists in the array, its quantity is incremented by one. Otherwise, if the product isn't found, the product information is added to the localCart array.

Lines 43–56 contain the section of code that updates the quantity of each product in the shopping cart or completely removes a product from the shopping cart. When the customer clicks the Update Cart button, form fields are passed back to the sessionCart.asp page that represents the quantity desired for each product. The FOR...NEXT loop in lines 43–56 loops through the items in the shopping cart and updates the quantity value for each product.

The FOR...NEXT loop in lines 43–56 also checks whether a customer has clicked the Delete checkbox next to any item in the shopping cart. In line 47, the Delete check box form field is retrieved. If the check box is checked, the product is removed.

In line 60, the localCart array is saved in a Session variable named cart. It is necessary to create a local copy of the Session array because you cannot change the values of the items in a Session array directly. You must first copy the contents of a Session array to a local variable, modify the elements of the array contained in the local variable, and then reassign the local variable to the Session variable.

Note

It's worth emphasizing that although you can read the values of the elements of an array in an Application or Session variable directly, you cannot change the values directly. For example, the following script creates a Session array named myarray, assigns a value to one of its elements, assigns the array to a Session variable, and then displays the element:

```
<%
DIM myarray( 20, 20 )
myarray( 1, 3 ) = "Hello World!"
Session( "myarray" ) = myarray
Response.Write Session( "myarray" )( 1, 3 )
%>
```

This script works perfectly fine. However, the following script won't work. It won't work because it tries to modify an element in the Session array directly:

```
<%
DIM myarray( 20, 20 )
myarray( 1, 3 ) = "Hello World!"
Session( "myarray" ) = myarray
Session( "myarray" )( 1, 3 ) = "Hello Again!"
%>
```

If you need to modify the value of an element in a Session or Application array, you will need to copy the array to a local array first, make the modification, and then assign the array back to the Session or Application variable.

Finally, in lines 66–137, the shopping cart is displayed on the page. The shopping cart is displayed by looping through the items in the localCart array. If an array element has a value, it is displayed. Otherwise, the element is simply skipped.

The shopping cart contained in the sessionCart.asp page is limited to containing no more than 20 distinct products. This limitation is imposed in line 10 where the localCart array is declared. If you attempt to add more than 20 products to the shopping cart, the last product you attempt to add will be ignored. You can change the dimensions of the localCart array to any value you please. Remember, however, that a separate copy of this array will be created for each visitor to your Web site.

Using Native ADO Methods

In previous lessons, you learned how to pass SQL strings through the ADO to make changes to a database. For example, to insert a new record in a database, you used a script like the following:

```
<%
Set Con = Server.CreateObject( "ADODB.Connection" )
Con.Open "accessDSN"
sqlString = "INSERT myTable ( mycol ) VALUES ( 'somevalue' )"
Con.Execute sqlString
%>
```

This script creates an instance of the ADO Connection object and opens the database connection by using a Data Source Name named accessDSN. Next, a SQL string is constructed that inserts a new record into a database table. Finally, the SQL string is executed and the new record is inserted by calling the Execute method of the Connection object.

In this section, you'll learn a second method of using the ADO to work with a database. Instead of using the ADO to pass SQL strings to a database, you will learn how to use the native methods of the ADO to modify database records.

Why do you need an alternative method of using the ADO with a database? Although, strictly speaking, you never need to use the native ADO methods, in certain situations, it is much more convenient. For example, in the next section, you will learn how to create a shopping cart by using a database table. When the shopping cart is modified, multiple records in the database table need to be updated as a group. Although you could modify multiple records in a database table by executing multiple SQL strings, it's easier to make the modifications by using the native methods of the ADO.

Note

Be aware that there are some disadvantages to using the native ADO methods. In general, the native ADO methods are less efficient than using SQL strings (in other words, slower). Furthermore, it is more difficult to debug scripts that use the native ADO methods. When using the native ADO methods, it is quite likely that you will encounter the unhelpful error message "errors occurred". When using SQL strings to modify a database, on the other hand, you will receive more detailed error messages.

Creating Updateable Recordsets

Before you can use the native ADO methods to modify the records in a Recordset, you must open the Recordset in such a way that it is updateable. By default, when you open a Recordset, the Recordset is read-only. You can open a modifiable Recordset by changing

9

the Recordset's `LockType` property. For example, the following statement opens a Recordset using Optimistic Locking:

```
RS.LockType = adOpenOptimistic
```

This statement opens the Recordset using Optimistic Locking. The `LockType` property can accept any of the four values listed in Table 9.1.

TABLE 9.1   The LockType Property Values

`adLockReadOnly`	This is the default value. When a read-only Recordset is opened, you cannot modify any of the records contained in the Recordset.
`adLockPessimistic`	When a Recordset is opened with pessimistic locking, other users are prevented from accessing the records in the Recordset as soon as you begin editing a record.
`adLockOptimistic`	When a Recordset is opened with Optimistic locking, other users can access the record until the changes are actually committed.
`adLockBatchOptimistic`	This locking type is used when performing batch updates (modifying multiple records in the Recordset at once).

In general, you should use Optimistic Locking when you need to open a Recordset that can be modified because it results in the least interference with other users and it is least likely to cause database deadlock.

Note

> When you use ADO constants, such as `adLockOptimistic`, remember to include the ADOVBS.inc file in your ASP page by using the #INCLUDE directive.

Adding New Records with AddNew

After you have opened an updateable Recordset, you can modify the records that it contains. The script in Listing 9.2 adds a new record to a Recordset by using the native ADO AddNew method.

LISTING 9.2   The AddNew Method

```
1  <!-- #INCLUDE FILE="adovbs.inc" -->
2  <%
3  Set Con = Server.CreateObject( "ADODB.Connection" )
4  Con.Open "accessDSN"
```

continues

LISTING 9.2   continued

```
 5  Set RS = Server.CreateObject( "ADODB.Recordset" )
 6  sqlString = "SELECT * FROM cart WHERE 1<>1"
 7  RS.ActiveConnection = Con
 8  RS.lockType = adLockOptimistic
 9  RS.Open sqlString
10  RS.AddNew
11  RS( "cart_userID" ) = 1
12  RS( "cart_productID" ) = 34
13  RS( "cart_quantity" ) = 2
14  RS.Update
15  RS.Close
16  %>
```

ANALYSIS   The script in Listing 9.2 adds a new record to a database table named cart. (This table will be used for our shopping cart later in this chapter.) The script assigns the values 1, 34, and 2 to the table columns named cart_userID, cart_productID, and cart_quantity.

In line 1, the ADOVBS.inc file is included in the page by using the #INCLUDE directive. You need to include this file in order to use the adLockOptimistic constant in the script.

Next, in lines 5–8, an instance of an ADO Recordset object is created. In line 8, the Recordset is opened with Optimistic Locking. This allows a new record to be added to the Recordset.

In line 9, the Recordset is opened. Notice the syntax of the SQL string used to open the Recordset. The SQL string is defined in line 6. This string selects every record from the database table named cart in which 1 is not equal to 1. Because the case doesn't exist in which 1 is not equal to itself, no records are returned. This is what we want because we don't want to actually retrieve any records. We are only interested in opening the Recordset so that we can add a new record.

In line 10, the AddNew method of the Recordset object is called. This prepares the Recordset to accept a new record. The contents of the new record are created in lines 11–13. Finally, in line 14, the Update method of the Recordset is called. After the Update method is called, the new record is actually added to the database table.

The script in Listing 9.2 does exactly the same thing as the following SQL statement:

```
INSERT INTO cart (cart_userID, cart_productID, cart_quantity )
VALUES ( 1, 34, 2 )
```

Updating Existing Records

After you have created an updateable Recordset, you also can update existing records. Doing this is very simple. You merely need to assign a new value to a Recordset field.

The script in Listing 9.3 demonstrates how you can modify a record in the database table named cart.

LISTING 9.3   Updating a Recordset

```
1  <!-- #INCLUDE FILE="adovbs.inc" -->
2  <%
3  Set Con = Server.CreateObject( "ADODB.Connection" )
4  Con.Open "accessDSN"
5  Set RS = Server.CreateObject( "ADODB.Recordset" )
6  sqlString = "SELECT * FROM cart WHERE cart_productID=34"
7  RS.ActiveConnection = Con
8  RS.lockType = adLockOptimistic
9  RS.Open sqlString
10 RS( "cart_userID" ) = 3
11 RS( "cart_quantity" ) = 12
12 RS.Update
13 RS.Close
14 %>
```

ANALYSIS   The script in Listing 9.3 updates two columns in the database table named cart. In line 5–9, an instance of the Recordset object is created and opened that contains all the records from the cart table in which the value of the cart_productID column equals 34. Next, in lines 10–11, the table columns named cart_userID and cart_quantity are assigned the values 3 and 12. Finally, in line 12, the Update method of the Recordset object is called, which causes the cart database table to be updated with the new column values.

The script in Listing 9.3 has almost, but not quite, the same effect as executing the following SQL statement:

```
UPDATE cart SET cart_userID=3, cart_quantity=12
WHERE cart_productID=34
```

The script in Listing 9.3 will cause the same changes to a database table as this SQL statement when there is only one row in which the value of the cart_productID column is 34. The SQL UPDATE statement will update all rows in which the value of the cart_productID column is 34. The script, on the other hand, will update only the first row retrieved in which the value of the cart_productID column is 34.

Deleting Records with Delete

To remove a record from an updateable Recordset, you can use the DELETE method of the Recordset object. The script in Listing 9.4 demonstrates how the DELETE method is used.

LISTING 9.4   The `Delete` Method

```
1  <!-- #INCLUDE FILE="adovbs.inc" -->
2  <%
3  Set Con = Server.CreateObject( "ADODB.Connection" )
4  Con.Open "accessDSN"
5  Set RS = Server.CreateObject( "ADODB.Recordset" )
6  sqlString = "SELECT * FROM cart WHERE cart_productID=34"
7  RS.ActiveConnection = Con
8  RS.lockType = adLockOptimistic
9  RS.Open sqlString
10 RS.Delete
11 RS.Update
12 RS.Close
13 %>
```

ANALYSIS   The script in Listing 9.4 retrieves all the records from the cart table in which the `cart_productID` column has the value 34. In line 10, the first record retrieved in the `Recordset` is deleted by calling the ADO `DELETE` method. Finally, in line 11, the changes to the `Recordset` are updated in the underlying table by calling the Recordset `UPDATE` method.

If you attempt to run this script when there are no records in the cart table and in which the value of the `cart_productID` column has the value 34, you will receive the following error:

```
ADODB.Recordset error '800a0bcd'
Either BOF or EOF is True, or the current record has been deleted; the
operation requested by the application requires a current record.
/deleteRecord.asp, line 10
```

Using the ADO `DELETE` method is almost, but not quite, the same as executing the following SQL statement:

```
DELETE FROM cart
WHERE cart_productID = 34
```

Although this SQL `DELETE` statement will delete every record in which the `cart_productID` column has the value 34 from the cart table, the script in Listing 9.4 will delete only the first record retrieved into the `Recordset` in which the column has this value.

Using a Database Table to Create a Shopping Cart

Earlier in this chapter, you learned how to create a shopping cart using `Session` variables. There was one major drawback to this method of creating a shopping cart.

Session variables depend on cookies, and not all browsers reliably support cookies. In the section, you'll learn a better method of creating a shopping cart.

We are going to create a shopping cart by creating a database table named cart. To create this table, launch Microsoft Access, open the storeDB database, and create a new table named cart with the columns contained in Table 9.2 (You can also copy this database from the CD-ROM that accompanies this book).

9

TABLE 9.2   The Cart Database Table

cart_id	An autonumber field that contains a unique number for each item in the shopping cart.
cart_userID	A number field that associates an item in the shopping cart with a particular customer.
cart_productID	A number field that contains the product ID of the product contained in the shopping cart.
cart_quantity	A number field that contains the quantity of the item that the customer selected.

Next, if you modified the Product.asp page when creating the Session version of the shopping cart earlier in this chapter, you will need to replace the Add To Cart HTML forms with the original code. Find the two places in the Product.asp page where the following code appears.

```
<form method="post" action="sessionCart.asp">
<input name="pid" type="hidden" value="<%=RS( "product_id" )%>">
<input name="productName" type="hidden" value="<%=RS( "product_name" )%>">
<input name="productPrice" type="hidden" value="<%=RS( "product_price" )%>">
<input type="submit" value="Add To Cart">
</form>
```

Replace this HTML form (in both places where it appears in the Product.asp page) with the following HTML form:

```
<form method="post" action="cart.asp">
<input name="pid" type="hidden" value="<%=RS( "product_id" )%>">
<input type="submit" value="Add To Cart">
</form>
```

This HTML form submits the form to a page named cart.asp. You created this page in yesterday's lesson. The cart.asp page does one of two things. If a customer hasn't registered or logged in, the page displays a registration/login screen. Otherwise, the page shows another page called addCart.asp. The code for the shopping cart is contained in the addCart.asp page.

eating the addCart.asp Page

The addCart.asp page displays a shopping cart retrieved from the database table named cart. The complete code for the addCart.asp page is contained in Listing 9.5. (The addCart.asp is also included on the CD-ROM that accompanies this book.)

The addCart.asp Page

LISTING 9.5   The addCart.asp Page

```
1   <%
2   ' Get Product ID
3   productID = TRIM( Request( "pid" ) )
4
5
6   ' Add Item to cart
7   IF productID <> "" THEN
8     sqlString = "SELECT cart_id FROM cart " &_
9       "WHERE cart_userID=" & userID & " " &_
10      "AND cart_productID=" & productID
11    SET RS = Con.Execute( sqlString )
12    IF RS.EOF THEN
13    sqlString = "INSERT INTO cart ( " &_
14      "cart_userID, " &_
15      "cart_productID, " &_
16      "cart_quantity " &_
17      ") VALUES ( " &_
18      userID & ", " &_
19      productID & ", 1 )"
20    ELSE
21    sqlString = "UPDATE cart SET " &_
22      "cart_quantity=cart_quantity+1 " &_
23      "WHERE cart_id=" & RS( "cart_id" )
24    END IF
25    RS.Close
26    SET RS = Nothing
27    Con.Execute sqlString
28  END IF
29
30
31  ' Update Shopping Cart Quantities
32  IF Request( "updateQ" ) <> "" THEN
33  SET RS = Server.CreateObject( "ADODB.Recordset" )
34  RS.ActiveConnection = Con
35  RS.CursorType = adOpenDynamic
36  RS.LockType = adLockOptimistic
37  sqlString = "SELECT cart_id, cart_quantity FROM cart " &_
38    "WHERE cart_userID=" & userID
39  RS.Open sqlString
```

```
40  WHILE NOT RS.EOF
41  newQ = TRIM( Request( "pq" & RS( "cart_id" ) ) )
42  deleteProduct = TRIM( Request( "pd" & RS( "cart_id" ) ) )
43  IF newQ = "" OR newQ = "0" OR deleteProduct <> "" THEN
44    RS.Delete
45  ELSE
46    IF isNumeric( newQ ) THEN
47      RS( "cart_quantity" ) = newQ
48    END IF
49  END IF
50  RS.MoveNext
51  WEND
52  RS.Close
53  SET RS = Nothing
54  END IF
55
56
57
58
59  %>
60  <html>
61  <head><title>Shopping Cart</title></head>
62  <body bgcolor="white">
63
64  <center>
65  <font face="Arial" size=3 color="darkgreen">
66  <b><%=username%>'s shopping cart:</b>
67  </font>
68
69  <%
70  ' Get the shopping cart
71  sqlString = "SELECT cart_id, product_name, " &_
72    "product_price, cart_quantity " &_
73    "FROM cart, products " &_
74    "WHERE cart_userID=" & userID & " " &_
75    "AND cart_productID = product_id " &_
76    "ORDER BY cart_id DESC"
77  SET RS = Con.Execute( sqlString )
78
79  IF RS.EOF THEN
80  %>
81  <p><b>You do not have any items in your shopping cart</b>
82  <p>
83  <form action="default.asp">
84  <input type="submit" value="Continue Shopping">
85  </form>
86  <%
87  ELSE
88  orderTotal = 0
89  %>
```

continues

LISTING 9.5   continued

```
90   <form method="post" action="cart.asp">
91   <input name="updateQ" type="hidden" value="1">
92   <input name="username" type="hidden" value="<%=username%>">
93   <input name="password" type="hidden" value="<%=password%>">
94   <table bgcolor="lightyellow" border=1
95     cellpadding=4 cellspacing=0>
96   <tr bgcolor="lightgreen">
97     <th>Product</th>
98     <th>Price</th>
99     <th>Quantity</th>
100  </tr>
101  <%
102  WHILE NOT RS.EOF
103  orderTotal = orderTotal + ( RS( "product_price" ) * RS( "cart_quantity" ) )
104  %>
105  <tr>
106    <td>
107    <%=Server.HTMLEncode( RS( "product_name" ) )%>
108    </td>
109    <td>
110    <%=formatCurrency( RS( "product_price" ) )%>
111    </td>
112    <td>
113    <input name="pq<%=RS( "cart_id" )%>" type="text" size=4
114     value="<%=RS( "cart_quantity" )%>">
115    <input name="pd<%=RS( "cart_id" )%>"
116     type="checkbox" value="1"> Delete
117    </td>
118  </tr>
119  <%
120  RS.MoveNext
121  WEND
122  %>
123  <tr bgcolor="yellow">
124    <td colspan=2 align=right>
125    <b>Order Total:</b>
126    </td>
127    <td>
128    <%=formatCurrency( orderTotal )%>
129    </td>
130  </tr>
131  <tr>
132    <td colspan=3>
133    <table border=0>
134    <tr>
135      <td align="right">
136      <input type="submit" value="Update Cart">
137      </td>
```

```
138        </form>
139        <form method="post" action="checkout.asp">
140        <input name="username" type="hidden" value="<%=username%>">
141        <input name="password" type="hidden" value="<%=password%>">
142        <td>
143        <input type="submit" value="Checkout">
144        </td>
145        </form>
146        <form action="default.asp">
147        <td>
148        <input type="submit" value="Continue Shopping">
149        </td>
150        </form>
151    </tr>
152    </table>
153    </td>
154  </tr>
155  </table>
156  <% END IF %>
157
158
159  </center>
160
161  </body>
162  </html>
```

ANALYSIS   The script in Listing 9.5 displays the shopping cart shown in Figure 9.2. The addCart.asp page has three main sections of code. Lines 2–28 contain the code to add a new item to the shopping cart. This section of code is executed after the customer clicks the Add To Cart button on the Product.asp page. Next, lines 31–54 contain the code to update the product quantities in the shopping cart. This section of code is executed after the customer clicks the Update Cart button on the shopping cart. Finally, the majority of the script, lines 64–159, is used to actually display the shopping cart.

Lines 2–28 contain the script that adds a new item to the shopping cart. This script will do one of two things. If the item is already contained in the shopping cart, the quantity of the item in the shopping cart is incremented by one. Otherwise, the new item is added. This prevents duplicate items from being displayed in the shopping cart.

Lines 31–54 contain the code to update the quantity of each item in the shopping cart. A customer can change the quantity of each item ordered by entering new values in the HTML form that represent the shopping cart and clicking Update Cart. Also, a customer can completely remove an item by setting its quantity to zero or nothing in the shopping cart form. The code in lines 31–54 is executed after the customer clicks the Update Cart button.

FIGURE 9.2

*The Database virtual
shopping cart.*

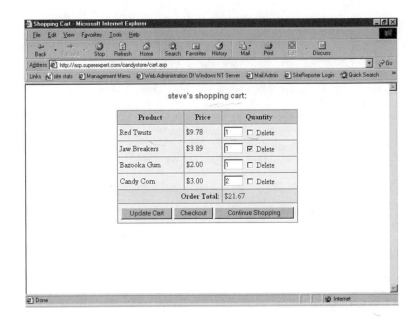

The script for updating the shopping cart item quantities makes heavy use of the native ADO methods discussed in the second part of this chapter: "Using Native ADO Methods." In lines 33–39, an instance of a Recordset is created and opened. Notice that in line 36, the LockType property of the Recordset is assigned the value adLockOptimistic. By opening the Recordset with an Optimistic LockType, the records in the Recordset can be modified.

In lines 40–51, a WHILE...WEND loop is used to loop through all the records in the Recordset. Each record in the Recordset is compared against the quantity value that the customer submitted in the shopping cart form. If the quantity of an item submitted by the customer in the shopping cart form doesn't match the quantity of the item in the database, the database record is updated.

Lines 40–51 also contain the code to check whether a customer has selected a product to delete. In line 42, the value of the Delete check box field is retrieved. If this field has a value, the item is removed from the customer's shopping cart.

Finally, in lines 64–159, the contents of the shopping cart are displayed. This is accomplished by retrieving all the records contained in the cart database table for a particular customer. Each of the items in the shopping cart is displayed one by one.

Unlike the shopping cart created with Session variables discussed in the first part of this chapter, the shopping cart created in this section is permanent. In theory, a customer can add some items to the shopping cart, go on an extended vacation to Borneo, return to the online store, and the items will still be in the shopping cart. Furthermore, this shopping cart doesn't rely on the properties of a user's browser. Not a single cookie is used.

Summary

In today's lesson, you learned two methods of creating a shopping cart. First, you learned how to create a shopping cart by using `Session` variables. In particular, you learned how to store the items in a shopping cart in an array stored in a `Session` variable. You also learned how to create a shopping cart using a database table. The advantages of this second method of creating a shopping cart were discussed. Finally, you were introduced to the native ADO methods of adding, updating, and deleting records in a Recordset. You learned how to create an updateable Recordset by modifying a Recordset's `LockType` property.

In tomorrow's lesson, you'll learn how to create the Checkout page that enables a customer to place an order for the items contained in the customer's shopping cart. You will also learn how to create the Active Server Pages that you will need to manage customer orders after they have been placed.

Q&A

Q Two methods of creating a shopping cart were discussed in this chapter. Which method should I use?

A If the warnings about `Session` variables and cookies in today's lesson don't concern you, there is a significant advantage to creating a shopping cart with `Session` variables. When you create a shopping cart with session variables, customers don't need to log in before using the shopping cart. Because registration forms have a tendency to prematurely scare customers away, not requiring a customer to register before using the shopping cart might result in more business.

Q When using the native ADO methods to add a new record, I receive the error `"errors occurred"`. What could cause this error?

A The current version of the ADO doesn't provide very descriptive error messages for the native ADO methods. The message `"errors occurred"` could result from a number of different problems. For example, you might receive this error when attempting to insert a `NULL` value in a table column that doesn't accept `NULL` values. Or, you might receive this error when attempting to insert a value of the wrong data type.

9

Workshop

The Quiz and Exercise questions are designed to test your knowledge of the material covered in this chapter. The answers are in Appendix A, "Quiz Answers."

Quiz

1. The following script assigns the value `"Hello World"` to an element in an array stored in a `Session` variable. What's wrong this script?

```
Session( "myarray" )( 2 ) = "hello world!"
```

2. Before you can add new records or update existing records in a Recordset, you must modify a property of the `Recordset` object. What is the name of this property?

Exercise

Assume that you wanted to add a new button to the shopping cart labeled Clear Cart that enables customers to remove all the existing items from their shopping cart. How would you add this button to both of the shopping carts described in this chapter?

DAY 10

Checking Out

In today's lesson, you will finish building the shopping cart that was introduced in yesterday's lesson. You will learn how to enable customers to order the items contained in their shopping carts. You will also learn how to create a page that will allow you to process these orders. Today, you will learn the following:

- How to create transactional Active Server Pages and transactional database connections
- How to create a Checkout page
- How to create a page that enables you to process customer orders

Understanding Transactions

When a customer clicks the Checkout button on the shopping cart, two things must happen. First, all the items in the shopping cart must be transferred to the Orders table. Second, the items must be deleted from the shopping cart. This is a perfect example of a transaction.

In a transaction, a series of steps either succeeds or fails as a whole. A transaction strictly abides by the slogan:

If it's worth doing at all, it's worth doing it right.

The standard example of a transaction is transferring money from one account to another (for instance, transferring money using an ATM machine). If you transfer money from your checking account to your savings account, two things must happen. Your checking account must be debited a certain amount and your savings account must be credited the same amount. However, if the first step completes and the second step doesn't complete, a certain amount of money will disappear never to be found again.

Note

> Ideally, every transaction should satisfy a set of properties collectively known as the ACID properties. ACID stands for
>
> Atomic—A transaction is atomic if it either succeeds or fails as a single unit.
>
> Consistent—A transaction is consistent if it preserves the consistency of the data that it transforms.
>
> Isolated—A transaction is isolated if no other concurrent transaction can access partial results of the uncompleted transaction.
>
> Durable—A transaction is durable when changes made by the transaction are guaranteed to persist if the transaction succeeds.

Using transactions solves this problem. If any step in a transaction fails, all the other steps are rolled back. So, if your ATM machine is hit by lightning the moment after it debits your checking account, your money won't be lost. All the steps in the transaction will be rolled back, and the money will be credited to your checking account once again.

There are three different methods of using transactions within an ASP page. You can create transactional Active Server Pages, create ADO transactions, or use database transactions.

ASP Page Transactions

In a transactional ASP page, changes made within the page are automatically rolled back if an error occurs or the transaction is explicitly aborted. Both the Internet Information Server and the Personal Web Server use Microsoft Transaction Server to manage transactions in an ASP page.

> **Note** Because transactional Active Server Pages depend on Microsoft Transaction Server, you must have this program installed before you can use the scripts discussed in this section. Microsoft Transaction Server is included with the NT Option Pack. It's compatible with Windows 95 (with DCOM installed), Windows 98, and Windows NT.

It is important to understand that Microsoft Transaction Server only supports rolling-back certain types of transactions. For example, Microsoft Transaction Server cannot roll back changes made to Application or Session variables, the file system, or components that weren't designed to support transactions. Generally, you will use a transactional ASP page to roll back only database changes. In particular, changes made to a Microsoft SQL Server database.

You create a transactional ASP page, by including the @TRANSACTION directive at the top of the page. The @TRANSACTION directive must appear as the very first line in the page. For example, the following page (as shown in Listing 10.1) correctly uses the directive.

LISTING 10.1 A Transactional ASP page

```
1  <%@ TRANSACTION=REQUIRED %>
2  <html>
3  <head><title>Transaction</title></head>
4  <body>
5  <%
6  blah.blah
7  %>
8  </body>
9  </html>
```

If you open this page in your Web browser, you will receive the following error:

```
Microsoft VBScript runtime error '800a01a8'
Object required: ''
/transaction.asp, line 6
```

This error results from calling the blah method of the blah object within the ASP script. Because, as a matter of fact, there is no such thing as the blah object, an error occurs. However, because the script is contained within a transactional ASP page, you can trap this error. You do this by using the ObjectContext object.

The ObjectContext object is a built-in ASP object like the Server or Request objects. However, it has one feature that makes it unique. Unlike any of the other ASP objects, the ObjectContext object supports events. The object supports the OnTransactionAbort and the OnTransactionCommit events.

The `OnTransactionAbort` event occurs whenever there is an error in a page. For example, an `OnTransactionAbort` event would occur if a script included a call to the `blah` object. Listing 10.2 demonstrates how you would use this event in an ASP page.

LISTING 10.2   The `OnTransactionAbort` Event

```
1  <%@ TRANSACTION=REQUIRED %>
2  <%
3  SUB OnTransactionAbort
4    Response.Write "<p>Uh oh! An error has occurred!"
5  END SUB
6  %>
7  <html>
8  <head><title>Transaction</title></head>
9  <body>
10 <%
11 blah.blah
12 %>
13 </body>
14 </html>
```

ANALYSIS   The ASP page contained in Listing 10.2 is the same as the page in Listing 10.1, except that it includes a new subroutine that handles the `OnTransactionAbort` event. When the error is encountered in the script, the `OnTransactionAbort` subroutine is called, and a message is displayed on the screen.

The `OnTransactionAbort` event is useful in two situations. You can use this event to roll back changes made by your script that aren't handled by Microsoft Transaction Server. For example, if the script changes the value of a `Session` variable, you can change the value back to its original value within the `OnTransactionAbort` subroutine if an error occurs.

You can also use the `OnTransactionAbort` event to trap and gracefully report errors. For example, imagine that your store is receiving heavy traffic. Every once in a while, no matter how well you design your database queries, you will receive database errors that result from database deadlocks, connection timeouts, and so on. Listing 10.3 shows how you can use the `OnTransactionAbort` event to display better error messages. (This ASP page is included on the book's CD-ROM with the name `transaction.asp`.)

LISTING 10.3   Better Error Handling

```
1 <%@ TRANSACTION=REQUIRED %>
2 <%
3 Response.Buffer = TRUE
```

```
4 SUB OnTransactionAbort
5   Response.Clear
6   %>
7   <html>
8   <head><title>Error</title></head>
9   An error has occurred.
10  <a href="<%=Request.ServerVariables( "script_name" )%>">
11    Click Here</a>
12    to try this page again.
13  <%
14 END SUB
15 %>
16 <html>
17 <head><title>Transaction</title></head>
18 <body>
19 <%
20 blah.blah
21 %>
22 </body>
23 </html>
```

ANALYSIS The ASP page in Listing 10.3 displays the message `"Click Here to try this page again."` if an error is encountered while processing the page (see Figure 10.1). Notice that page buffering is enabled for the page. This is necessary to hide the default error message. The `Clear` method is called in line 5 to prevent the script error from being sent to the browser.

FIGURE 10.1

A transactional ASP page.

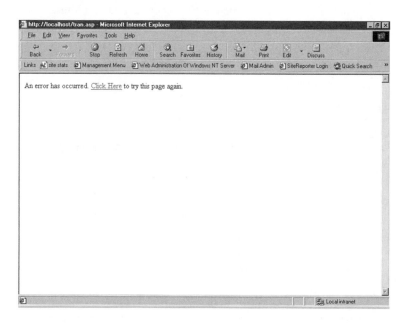

The `ObjectContext` object also supports an additional event called the `OnTransactionCommit` event. This event is called when a page completes successfully. When you use a transactional ASP page, either the `OnTransactionAbort` or the `OnTransactionCommit` event will always be called.

Finally, the `ObjectContext` has two methods for working with transactions. You can use the `SetAbort()` method to manually cause the `OnTransactionAbort` method to be called. You can use this method to prevent a transaction from completing even if the transaction doesn't encounter any errors.

The `SetComplete()` method forces the `OnTransactionCommit` event to occur. This method can be used to override any calls to the `SetAbort()` method.

When you need to ensure that an ASP page either fails or succeeds as a whole, it is a good idea to use transactions. You can use transactions to automatically respond to failure by providing a customer a chance to try a page again or by cleaning up partially completed steps in a transaction.

ADO Transactions

ASP transactions apply to a whole ASP page. If you want to process only database operations within a transaction, you can use ADO transactions.

The ADO `Connection` object has three methods—`BeginTrans()`, `CommitTrans()`, and `RollbackTrans()`—that enable you to manage transactions. To begin a new transaction, call the `BeginTrans()` method. To mark the end of a transaction, call the `CommitTrans()` method. Finally, to abort a transaction and start over, call the `RollbackTrans()` method.

The script in Listing 10.4 demonstrates how you can use these methods when updating two database tables.

LISTING 10.4   ADO Transaction

```
1  <%
2  Set Con = Server.CreateObject( "ADODB.Connection" )
3  Con.Open "accessDSN"
4  Con.BeginTrans
5  ' Debit Checking Account
6  sqlString = "UPDATE checking SET checking_balance = " &_
7    "checking_balance - 15 WHERE checking_userID = 3"
8    Con.Execute sqlString
9  ' Credit Savings Account
10 sqlString = "UPDATE savings SET savings_balance = " &_
11   "savings_balance + 15 WHERE savings_userID = 3"
12 Con.Execute sqlString
13 Con.CommitTrans
14 %>
```

ANALYSIS   The script in Listing 10.4 updates two database tables named checking and savings. It removes $15.00 from a customer's checking account and adds $15.00 to the customer's savings account. This is accomplished by executing two SQL UPDATE statements in a row.

The beginning of the transaction is marked by calling the `BeginTrans()` method in line 4. The end of the transaction is marked by calling the `CommitTrans()` method in line 13. All the database operations that are executed between lines 4 and 13 will either succeed or fail as a unit.

You can test this by adding the following statement immediately after line 8:

```
blah.blah
```

Adding a call to the `blah` object will generate an error. However, the error will cause both SQL UPDATE statements to be rolled back, so no changes will be made to either the checking or savings table.

If the `BeginTrans()` and `CommitTrans()` methods weren't used in this script and an error occurred, the customer's checking account would be debited, but the customer's savings account would not be credited. In other words, the ADO transaction has prevented the potential of angry customers.

Database Transactions

Although this topic is beyond the scope of this book, it is worth mentioning yet a third method of working with transactions. The Microsoft SQL Server database uses a transaction log to record almost every change made to the database. This allows changes to be rolled back in case of trouble.

The Transact-SQL language, the language used to interact with SQL Server, has several statements for controlling transactions. You can use these statements within SQL stored procedures to mark the beginning and end of transactions. For more information on programming with the Transact-SQL language, see *Microsoft SQL 7 Programming Unleashed* by John Papa, et al (ISBN: 067231293X).

Completing the Order

When a customer has finished shopping and clicks the button labeled Checkout on the shopping cart, he is presented with two pages. First, he is presented with a form that enables him to update address and payment information. For example, he can change the shipping address or the credit card number used for the order.

10

Next, the customer is presented with a page that thanks him for placing the order. Within this page, his order is actually completed. The items are transferred from the shopping cart to the Orders table.

In the next two sections, you will learn how to create the Active Server Pages necessary to complete a customer's order. You'll also learn how to complete the order using an ADO transaction.

Retrieving Address and Payment Information

Immediately after a customer clicks the Checkout button, he will see the page shown in Figure 10.2. This ASP page is named doCheckout.asp. It contains a normal HTML form that displays the customer's address and payment information. This data is retrieved from the Users database table with the script in Listing 10.5.

FIGURE 10.2

Updating customer information.

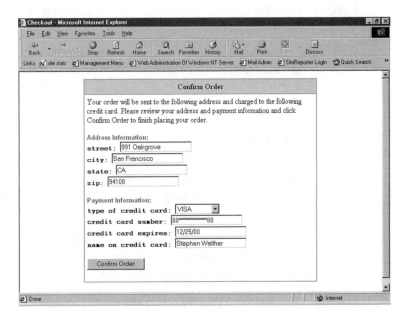

LISTING 10.5   Retrieving Customer Data

```
1   sqlString = "SELECT * FROM users " &_
2     "WHERE user_id=" & userID
3   SET RS = Con.Execute( sqlString )
4   IF NOT RS.EOF THEN
5     street = RS( "user_street" )
6     city = RS( "user_city" )
7     state = RS( "user_state" )
```

```
8    zip = RS( "user_zip" )
9    cctype = RS( "user_cctype" )
10   ccnumber = RS( "user_ccnumber" )
11   ccexpires = RS( "user_ccexpires" )
12   ccname = RS( "user_ccname" )
13 END IF
14
15 ' Hide Credit Card Number
16 ccnumber = LEFT( ccnumber, 2 ) &_
17    "************" &_
18    RIGHT( ccnumber, 2 )
```

ANALYSIS The script in Listing 10.5 uses a SQL SELECT statement to retrieve all the fields from the Users database table in which the user has the current customer's user ID. Next, in lines 4–13, local variables are assigned the values of the database fields.

The customer's current information is displayed in the HTML form by assigning the local variables to the VALUE attribute of each form field. For example, to display the customer's current street address in the HTML form, the following HTML <INPUT> tag is used:

```
<br><b>street:</b>
<input name="street" size=20 maxlength=50
value="<%=Server.HTMLEncode( street )%>">
```

The credit card number is treated different from the other variables. You should notice that the credit card number is hidden in lines 15–18. Only the first two digits and the last two digits of the credit card number are shown. This is done for security reasons. If someone manages to guess a customer's username and password, the thief wouldn't be able to steal the customer's credit card number. The worst thing the thief could do would be to buy quite a lot of candy.

Updating Address and Payment Information

When the form in the doCheckout.asp page is submitted, the customer is brought to the doCheckout2.asp page. This page does two things. First, it takes the address and payment information just submitted within the HTML form and updates the Users table. Second, it contains a script that transfers the items from the shopping cart to the Orders table.

The customer information is updated with the updateUser subroutine contained in Listing 10.6. This subroutine is included in the storefuncs.asp file contained on the CD-ROM that accompanies this book.

LISTING 10.6   The updateUser Subroutine

```
1   SUB updateUser
2     ' Get Registration Fields
3     street = TRIM( Request( "street" ) )
4     city = TRIM( Request( "city" ) )
5     state = TRIM( Request( "state" ) )
6     zip = TRIM( Request( "zip" ) )
7     cctype = Request( "cctype" )
8     ccnumber = TRIM( Request( "ccnumber" ) )
9     ccexpires = TRIM( Request( "ccexpires" ) )
10    ccname = TRIM( Request( "ccname" ) )
11
12    ' Check For Required Fields
13    backpage = "checkout.asp"
14    IF street = "" THEN
15      errorForm "You must enter your street address.", backpage
16    END IF
17    IF city = "" THEN
18      errorForm "You must enter your city.", backpage
19    END IF
20    IF state = "" THEN
21      errorForm "You must enter your state.", backpage
22    END IF
23    IF zip = "" THEN
24      errorForm "You must enter your zip code.", backpage
25    END IF
26    IF ccnumber = "" THEN
27      errorForm "You must enter your credit card number.", backpage
28    END IF
29    IF ccexpires = "" THEN
30      errorForm "You must enter your credit
➥ card expiration date.", backpage
31    END IF
32    IF ccname = "" THEN
33      errorForm "You must enter the name that appears on your
➥ credit card.", backpage
34    END IF
35
36    ' Check for Necessary Field Values
37    IF INSTR( ccnumber, "*" ) = 0 THEN
38      IF NOT validCCNumber( ccnumber ) THEN
39        errorForm "You did not enter a valid credit
➥ card number", backpage
40      ELSE
41        ccnumber = "'" & ccnumber & "'"
42      END IF
43    ELSE
44      ccnumber = "user_ccnumber"
45    END IF
```

```
46   IF NOT isDATE( ccexpires ) THEN
47     errorForm "You did not enter a valid credit card
➥ expiration date", backpage
48   END IF
49
50   ' Update user information in the database
51   sqlString = "UPDATE users SET " &_
52     "user_street='" & fixQuotes( street ) & "', " &_
53     "user_city='" & fixQuotes( city ) & "'," &_
54     "user_state='" & fixQuotes( state ) & "'," &_
55     "user_zip='" & fixQuotes( zip ) & "'," &_
56     "user_ccnumber=" & ccnumber & ", " &_
57     "user_cctype=" & cctype & ", " &_
58     "user_ccexpires='" & ccexpires & "'," &_
59     "user_ccname='" & fixQuotes( ccname ) & "' " &_
60     "WHERE user_id=" & userID
61
62   Con.Execute sqlString
63 END SUB
```

ANALYSIS The first lines of this subroutine, lines 2–10, retrieve the HTML form fields into local variables. Next, in lines 12–34, each field is checked to see whether it contains any data. If someone submits an empty form field, the errorForm subroutine is called. This subroutine displays an error page and invites the user to return to the HTML form to correct any problems.

Lines 36–38 are used to validate the field values. For example, if someone hasn't entered a real date for the credit card expiration date, an error page is displayed by calling the errorForm subroutine.

Lines 37–45 checks the value of the credit card number. This section is a bit complicated because the credit card number displayed within the HTML form is partially hidden for security reasons.

If the customer doesn't alter the credit card number within the HTML form, the credit card number submitted will contain * characters (the * is used to hide numbers). The statement in line 37 checks whether the credit card number contains an * by using the VBScript INSTR() function. If the credit card number submitted does, in fact, contain an *, the user_ccnumber database field isn't altered. This is accomplished by setting the value of the database field equal to itself (user_ccnumber=user_ccnumber).

On the other hand, if the customer enters a new credit card number, the database field is updated. The user_ccnumber database field is assigned the value of the ccnumber form field.

In lines 50–60, the SQL UPDATE string that updates the Users database table is constructed. The string is built from each of the values of the form variables. Notice that the fixQuotes() function is used to construct the sqlString. The fixQuotes() function replaces single quotes (') with two consecutive single quotes (''). You'll remember that this is necessary to prevent Microsoft Access from getting confused about the beginning and end of strings when the sqlString is executed.

Finally, in line 62, the sqlString is executed and the customer's payment and address information is updated.

Transferring the Shopping Cart

After the customer's address and payment information has been updated in the doCheckout2.asp page, the order must be completed. This is accomplished by transferring all the customer's items from the Cart database table (which represents the customer's shopping cart) to the Orders database table (which represents completed orders). The Orders database table contains the following columns:

order_id—A number field that uniquely identifies each product order

order_productID—A number field that represents the product ID of the item

order_quantity—A number field that represents the number of items ordered

order_userID—A number field that contains the unique ID of the user placing the order

order_entrydate—A Date/Time field that represents the date and time the order was placed

order_status—A number field that represents the status of the order

order_shipdate—The date and time the product was shipped

To transfer the items from one table to another, we can use a variant of the SQL INSERT INTO statement. By combining the INSERT INTO statement with the SELECT statement, we can select a certain row of data from one table to insert into another table. Here is the syntax of this variant of the INSERT INTO statement:

```
INSERT INTO table_name ( column_list )
SELECT column_list
FROM table_name
WHERE condition
```

To move the items from the Cart database table to the Orders database table, we will use the script in Listing 10.7.

LISTING 10.7   Transferring Between Cart and Orders

```
1  <%
2  ' Begin A Transaction
3  Con.BeginTrans
4
5  ' Transfer cart to orders table
6  sqlString = "INSERT INTO orders (" &_
7    "order_id, " &_
8    "order_productID, " &_
9    "order_quantity, " &_
10   "order_userID, " &_
11   "order_entrydate, " &_
12   "order_status " &_
13   ") SELECT " &_
14   "cart_id, " &_
15   "cart_productID, " &_
16   "cart_quantity, " &_
17   "cart_userID, " &_
18   "NOW(), " &_
19   "0 " &_
20   "FROM cart WHERE " &_
21   "cart_userID =" & userID
22
23 Con.Execute sqlString
24
25 ' Empty shopping cart
26 sqlString = "DELETE FROM cart " &_
27   "WHERE cart_userID=" & userID
28
29 Con.Execute sqlString
30
31
32 ' End the transaction
33 Con.CommitTrans
34
35 %>
```

ANALYSIS   The script in Listing 10.7 does five things. First, in line 3, a new transaction is created by calling the `BeginTrans()` method of the ADO Connection object. Next, in lines 5–23, the items in the Cart database table are transferred to the Orders database table. In lines 25–29, the items are deleted from the customer's shopping cart. Finally, in line 33, the transaction is completed.

An ADO transaction is used in this script to guarantee that if the items are copied from the Cart table to the Orders table, the items will also be deleted from the Cart table. The transaction prevents one step from happening without the other step.

10

After the customer has finished checking out, the page in Figure 10.3 is displayed. This page thanks the customer for purchasing the products and invites the customer to return to the list of products to continue shopping.

FIGURE 10.3

A completed order.

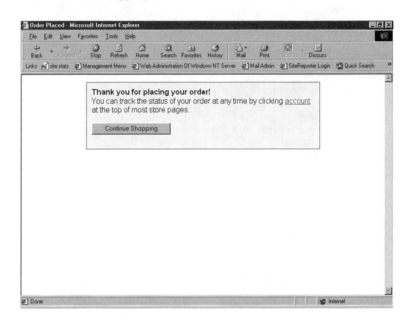

Processing Orders

In this section, you will learn how to create an ASP page that will enable you to process orders after they have been placed by a customer. This page is used by the administrator of your store and not the customer. It provides you with a method of viewing and updating the status of each order. Each order can have one of the following status values:

Pending—This is the default value of an order. An order has this status immediately after it has been placed.

Credit Card Declined—An order has this status when the customer's credit card account couldn't be charged and the product couldn't be shipped.

Not in Stock—An order has this status when the product requested isn't in stock and, therefore, won't be shipped.

Shipped—An order has this status when the credit card was successfully charged and the product was shipped.

We are going to create a page named processOrders.asp that provides you with a method of updating the status of each order. (The processOrders.asp page is included

on the CD-ROM that accompanies this book.) Figure 10.4 shows the final version of
`processOrders.asp`.

FIGURE 10.4

Processing customer orders.

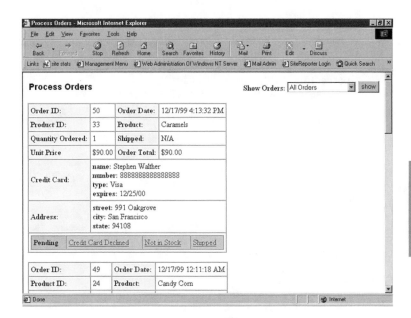

The `processOrders.asp` page displays all the information for each order. Each order
appears within its own HTML table. For each order, you can view the order ID, the product ID, the customer's payment and address information, and the current status of the
order.

When viewing orders, by default, you only see pending orders. Typically, this is what
you will want because you will want to update only the new orders that have been
placed. However, you can use an HTML pick list to show only pending orders, only
credit card declined orders, only not in stock orders, only shipped orders, or all orders.

Orders are displayed five on a page. A list of page numbers that act as links to other
pages appears at the bottom of the page. If business is good, you don't want to display
too many orders on a single page.

Finally, you can update the status of any order by clicking a hypertext link. The current
status of an order is highlighted in a blue table cell. The other status options appear in
gray table cells as hypertext links.

The `processOrders.asp` page is quite long. However, because it illustrates several
important programming techniques, it is worth looking at the page in detail. The complete code for the `processOrders.asp` page is contained in Listing 10.8.

LISTING 10.8   processOrders.asp

```
1  <!-- #INCLUDE FILE="adovbs.inc" -->
2  <%
3  ' Get Form Variables
4  showOrders = TRIM( Request( "showOrders" ) )
5  showPage = TRIM( Request( "showPage" ) )
6  orderStatus = TRIM( Request( "os" ) )
7  orderId = TRIM( Request( "oid" ) )
8  allPages = TRIM( Request( "allpages" ) )
9
10  ' Assign Default Values
11  IF showOrders = "" THEN
12     showOrders = 0
13  END IF
14  IF showPage = "" THEN
15     showPage = 1
16  END IF
17
18  ' Open the Database Connection
19  Set Con = Server.CreateObject( "ADODB.Connection" )
20  Con.Open "accessDSN"
21
22  ' Update Order Status
23  IF orderID <> "" THEN
24     IF orderStatus = 3 THEN
25     sqlString = "UPDATE Orders " &_
26      "SET order_status=" & orderStatus & ", " &_
27      "order_shipdate=NOW() " &_
28      "WHERE order_id=" & orderID
29     ELSE
30     sqlString = "UPDATE Orders " &_
31      "SET order_status=" & orderStatus & ", " &_
32      "order_shipdate=NULL " &_
33      "WHERE order_id=" & orderID
34     END IF
35
36     Con.Execute sqlString
37  END IF
38
39
40  ' Retrieve Orders
41  sqlString = "SELECT * " &_
42     "FROM Orders, Users, Products " &_
43     "WHERE order_userID = user_id " &_
44     "AND order_productID = product_id "
45  IF showOrders < 99 THEN
46     sqlString = sqlString & "AND order_status=" & showOrders
47  END IF
48  sqlString = sqlString & " ORDER BY order_entrydate DESC"
```

```
49
50  SET RS = Server.CreateObject( "ADODB.Recordset" )
51  RS.CursorType = adOpenStatic
52  IF allPages = "" THEN
53    RS.PageSize = 5
54  ELSE
55    RS.PageSize = 99999
56  END IF
57  RS.ActiveConnection = Con
58  RS.Open sqlString
59  IF NOT RS.EOF THEN
60    RS.AbsolutePage = cINT( showPage )
61  END IF
62
63  FUNCTION SELECTED( val1, val2 )
64    IF cSTR( val1 ) = cSTR( val2 ) THEN
65      SELECTED = " selected "
66    END IF
67  END FUNCTION
68
69  %>
70  <html>
71  <head><title>Process Orders</title></head>
72  <body>
73
74  <form action="processOrders.asp">
75  <table width="100%" border=0>
76  <tr>
77    <td>
78    <font face="Arial" size="4">
79    <b>Process Orders</b>
80    </font>
81    </td>
82    <td align="right">
83    <b>Show Orders:</b>
84    <select name="showOrders">
85    <option value="0" <%=SELECTED( "0", showOrders )%>>
➥ Pending
86    <option value="1" <%=SELECTED( "1", showOrders )%>>
➥ Credit Card Declined
87    <option value="2" <%=SELECTED( "2", showOrders )%>>
➥ Not in Stock
88    <option value="3" <%=SELECTED( "3", showOrders )%>>
➥ Shipped
89    <option value="99" <%=SELECTED( "99", showOrders )%>>
➥ All Orders
90    </select>
91    <input type="submit" value="show">
92    </td>
```

10

continues

LISTING 10.8 continued

```
93   </tr>
94   </table>
95   </form>
96
97   <%
98   WHILE NOT RS.EOF AND rowCount < RS.PageSize
99     rowCount = rowCount + 1
100    %>
101    <p>
102    <table border=1
103     cellpadding=4 cellspacing=0>
104    <tr>
105      <td bgcolor="lightyellow"><b>Order ID:</b></td>
106      <td><%=RS( "order_id" )%></td>
107      <td bgcolor="lightyellow"><b>Order Date:</b></td>
108      <td><%=RS( "order_entrydate" )%></td>
109    </tr>
110    <tr>
111      <td bgcolor="lightyellow"><b>Product ID:</b></td>
112      <td><%=RS( "product_id" )%></td>
113      <td bgcolor="lightyellow"><b>Product:</b></td>
114      <td><%=RS( "product_name" )%></td>
115    </tr>
116    <tr>
117      <td bgcolor="lightyellow"><b>Quantity Ordered:</b></td>
118      <td><%=RS( "order_quantity" )%></td>
119      <td bgcolor="lightyellow"><b>Shipped:</b></td>
120      <td>
121      <% IF isDATE( RS( "order_shipdate" ) ) THEN %>
122        <%=RS( "order_shipdate" )%>
123      <% ELSE %>
124      N/A
125      <% END IF %>
126      </td>
127    </tr>
128    <tr>
129      <td bgcolor="lightyellow"><b>Unit Price</b></td>
130      <td><%=FormatCurrency( RS( "product_price" ) )%></td>
131      <td bgcolor="lightyellow"><b>Order Total:</b></td>
132      <td>
133      <%=FormatCurrency( RS( "order_quantity" ) *
➥ RS( "product_price" ) )%>
134      </td>
135    <tr>
136      <td bgcolor="lightyellow"><b>Credit Card:</b></td>
137      <td colspan=3>
138      <b>name:</b> <%=RS( "user_ccname" )%>
139      <br><b>number:</b> <%=RS( "user_ccnumber" )%>
```

```
140     <br><b>type:</b>
141     <%
142     SELECT CASE RS( "user_cctype" )
143       CASE "1" Response.Write "Visa"
144       CASE "2" Response.Write "MasterCard"
145     END SELECT
146     %>
147     <br><b>expires:</b> <%=RS( "user_ccexpires" )%>
148     </td>
149   </tr>
150   <tr>
151     <td bgcolor="lightyellow"><b>Address:</b></td>
152     <td colspan=3>
153     <b>street:</b> <%=RS( "user_street" )%>
154     <br><b>city:</b> <%=RS( "user_city" )%>
155     <br><b>state:</b> <%=RS( "user_zip" )%>
156     </td>
157   </tr>
158   <tr>
159     <td colspan=4>
160     <table border=1 width="100%"
161      cellpadding=4 cellspacing=0>
162     <tr bgcolor="lightgrey">
163       <% IF RS( "order_status" ) = 0 THEN %>
164       <td bgcolor="lightblue">
165       <b>Pending</b>
166       </td>
167       <% ELSE %>
168       <td>
169       <a href="processOrders.asp?showpage=<%=showPage%>&
➡ oid=<%=RS( "order_id" )%>&os=0&showOrders=<%=showOrders%>">
170       Pending</a>
171       </td>
172       <% END IF %>
173       <% IF RS( "order_status" ) = 1 THEN %>
174       <td bgcolor="lightblue">
175       <b>Credit Card Declined</b>
176       </td>
177       <% ELSE %>
178       <td>
179       <a href="processOrders.asp?showpage=<%=showPage%>&
➡ oid=<%=RS( "order_id" )%>&os=1&showOrders=<%=showOrders%>">
180       Credit Card Declined</a>
181       </td>
182       <% END IF %>
183       <% IF RS( "order_status" ) = 2 THEN %>
184       <td bgcolor="lightblue">
185       <b>Not in Stock</b>
186       </td>
187       <% ELSE %>
```

10

continues

LISTING 10.8   continued

```
188          <td>
189          <a href="processOrders.asp?showpage=<%=showPage%>&
➥ oid=<%=RS( "order_id" )%>&os=2&showOrders=<%=showOrders%>">
190          Not in Stock</a>
191          </td>
192          <% END IF %>
193          <% IF RS( "order_status" ) = 3 THEN %>
194          <td bgcolor="lightblue">
195          <b>Shipped</b>
196          </td>
197          <% ELSE %>
198          <td>
199          <a href="processOrders.asp?showpage=<%=showPage%>&
➥ oid=<%=RS( "order_id" )%>&os=3&showOrders=<%=showOrders%>">
200          Shipped</a>
201          </td>
202          <% END IF %>
203        </tr>
204        </table>
205      </tr>
206      </table>
207      <%
208      RS.MoveNext
209    WEND
210    %>
211    <hr>
212    <% IF RS.PageCount > 1 THEN %>
213    Page:
214    <%
215    FOR i = 1 TO RS.PageCount
216    IF cINT( showPage ) = i THEN
217      %>
218      <b><%=i%></b> |
219      <% ELSE %>
220      <a href="processOrders.asp?showpage=<%=i%>&
➥ showorders=<%=showOrders%>">
221      <%=i%>
222      </a> |
223      <%
224    END IF
225    NEXT
226    IF allPages <> "" THEN
227    %>
228      <b>All</b>
229    <% ELSE %>
230      <a href="processOrders.asp?showorders=<%=showOrders%>&
➥allPages=1">
231      All
```

```
232    </a>
233    <%
234    END IF
235    END IF
236    %>
237
238    </body>
239    </html>
```

ANALYSIS The first line in processOrders.asp includes the adovbs.inc file. You must include this file because the processOrders.asp page makes use of the ADO constant adOpenStatic.

In lines 3–8, all the form and URL variables are retrieved. These variables represent such things as the current page, the ID of the order being updated, and the new order status.

Lines 10–16 assign default values to variables that don't have a value. For example, if no page of orders has been selected, the page defaults to the first page.

In lines 18–20, a connection to the Microsoft Access database is opened. The System DSN named "accessDSN" is used to open the connection.

Lines 22–37 are used to update the status of a particular order. This is accomplished with a SQL UPDATE statement. The UPDATE statement changes the value of the order_status column for the database record with a certain order ID.

When an order's status is changed to shipped, the order_shipdate column is also updated to reflect the current date. Otherwise, if any other status is selected, the order_shipdate column is assigned the value NULL.

In lines 40–61, the order information is retrieved from the database. The information is drawn from three tables: the Orders table, the Products table, and the Users table. A SQL ORDER BY clause is used to retrieve the last orders placed first.

Line 46 is used to restrict the orders retrieved. For example, you can use the HTML pick list to view only shipped orders. Line 46 adds a clause to the SQL SELECT statement that retrieves only the orders with a certain order status. This statement is skipped if the All Orders option is selected.

The PageSize and AbsolutePage properties of the Recordset object are used to display only a certain page of orders at a time. The PageSize property sets the number of records to show on a single page. The AbsolutePage property sets the page to display.

The HTML pick list is created in lines 74–95. This pick list enables you to view only those orders with a certain status (for example, shipped) or all orders.

The bulk of processOrders.asp, lines 97–210, are used to display the details of a particular order. A WHILE...WEND loop is used to loop through all the orders for a certain page. The information for each order is formatted and displayed.

An HTML table is displayed in lines 160–204. This table contains a list of possible order status values in each of the table cells. The current status of an order is highlighted with a blue background.

Finally, in lines 212–236, a list of page numbers is displayed. By clicking on any one of these page numbers, you can navigate to a particular page of orders. The list of page numbers is created with a FOR...NEXT loop. The PageCount property of the Recordset object is used to retrieve the number of pages.

Summary

In today's lesson, you learned how to work with transactions. You learned how to create both transactional Active Server Pages and ADO transactions. You learned how to use a transaction to guarantee that a series of steps either succeeds or fails as a whole.

Next, you learned how to create a checkout page for the shopping cart. You learned how to update a customer's address and payment information. You also learned how to transfer a customer's shopping cart to the Orders table.

Finally, you learned how to process completed orders. You learned how to create a page that enables you to view and update the status of customer orders.

Q&A

Q ADO transactions seem really great. When shouldn't I use them?

A You should avoid using transactions whenever possible. You must be particularly careful with using transactions when you have a large number of concurrent users. Long running transactions can lock up the records in your database, preventing other users from accessing the records.

Q When attempting to use the @TRANSACTION directive, I receive the following error:

```
error 'ASP 0216'
MSDTC Service not running
/tran.asp
Transactional web pages cannot be run if the MSDTC service is not running.
```

A ASP transactions rely on the Microsoft Distributed Transaction Coordinator. The Microsoft Distributed Transaction Coordinator is included with both Microsoft

Transaction Server and Microsoft SQL Server. On both Windows 98 and Windows NT computers, the MSDTC service should start automatically when you start your computer.

You can manually start MSDTC on either a Windows 98 or Windows NT computer by using the Microsoft Transaction Server Explorer. Launch this program, select the name of your computer, and then choose Action, Start MS DTC.

If you have SQL Server installed, you can also enable the Microsoft Distributed Transaction Coordinator from either the SQL Server Service Manager or the MSDTC Administrative Console. (Both programs are located in the SQL Server program group.)

Workshop

10

The Quiz and Exercise questions are designed to test your knowledge of the material covered in this chapter. The answers are in Appendix A, "Quiz Answers."

Quiz

1. What's wrong with the following script?

```
<%
Set Con = Server.CreateObject( "ADODB.Connection" )
Con.Open "accessDSN"
SET RS = Server.CreateObject( "ADODB.Recordset" )
RS.ActiveConnection = Con
RS.BeginTrans
RS.Open "select * FROM Orders"
RS.CommitTrans
%>
```

2. Suppose that you want to copy a particular row from the Orders table to a second table named Orders_bak. The Orders_bak table is used to back up the data in the Orders table. How can you copy the row from the Orders table in which the value of the order_id column is 17 to the Orders_bak table?

Exercise

The processOrders.asp page discussed in today's lesson enables you to assign one of four status values to an order: Pending, Credit Card Declined, Not in Stock, or Shipped. How would you modify the processOrders.asp page (contained in Listing 10.8) to enable a fifth status value, Back Ordered, to be selected?

DAY **11**

Working with Credit Cards

In today's lesson, you'll learn how to implement the most important function for your online store: how to process customer credit cards. The lesson begins with a brief overview of the different options available for credit card processing. Next, you'll be provided with detailed information on implementing one credit card processing system: CyberCash. In today's lesson, you'll learn the following:

- How to set up and configure CyberCash
- How to use CyberCash to authorize credit cards transactions
- How to use CyberCash to settle credit card transactions

Methods of Processing Credit Cards

There is a wide variety of options for processing the credit cards accepted at your Web site, too many to be discussed in a single chapter. However, the various credit card processing systems can be somewhat arbitrarily divided into three different types: offsite payment processors, payment terminals, and component-based solutions.

Offsite Payment Processors

Severalcompanies enable you to link to their Web sites and they will process the credit card transactions for you. They host the payment page that prompts the customer to enter credit card information. After the customer has completed the payment transaction, the customer is sent back to your Web site.

The advantage of this type of system is that it is very easy to set up. You don't need to configure and use the Secure Sockets Layer, and you don't need to take special precautions to maintain the privacy of the customer's credit card information. All this is done for you at another Web site.

The disadvantage of these offsite payment processors is that you lose some control over the appearance of your payment page. You also never collect credit card information directly from your customers. Finally, if something goes wrong with the offsite payment processor—for example, its Web site goes down—the problem is out of your hands and you can do nothing about it.

One example of a company that offers offsite payment processing is Authorize.Net (www.authorizenet.com). To use the Authorize.Net WebLink service, you include the following HTML form in your ASP page:

```
<form method="POST" action="https://secure.authorize.net/gateway/transact.dll">
<input type="hidden" name="x_Version" value="3.0">
<input type="hidden" name="x_Login" value="your login here">
<input type="hidden" name="x_Amount" value="total amount here">

<input type="hidden" name="x_Show_Form" value="Payment_Form">
<input type="hidden" name="x_Invoice_Num" value="your invoice number here">
<input type="hidden" name="x_Description" value="order description here">
<input type="hidden" name="x_Cust_ID" value="customer id here">
<input type="submit" value="Click Here for Secure Payment Form">
</form>
```

This HTML form creates a button labeled Click Here for Secure Payment Form that links to the Authorize.Net Web site. You can substitute variables for the value attributes of the HTML form to enable customers to purchase different products. For example, the value of the x_Amount field is the amount that you want to charge the customer's credit card.

Another company that offers offsite payment processing is iBill. Currently, iBill offers a service called the Resellers Subscription Sales service. This service cannot be used to sell tangible goods. You can use this service only to sell Web site subscriptions and informational content. The iBill service is worth mentioning, however, because it is the only payment system discussed in this chapter that does not require you to have a credit card merchant account. The only requirement to use this service is that you have a credit card.

Payment Terminal Solutions

A different approach to processing credit cards is represented by payment terminal solutions. A prime example of this type of software is ICVerify (`www.icverify.com`).

ICVerify is a software product that contains an easy-to-use interface for authorizing and settling credit card transactions. You can launch the program, type in a customer's credit card information, click a button, and the program authorizes a credit card transaction.

ICVerify does not work over the Internet. You must use this program with a modem. When you authorize or settle a credit card transaction, the program connects to your processor over the phone line and completes the transaction.

Although it is possible to use ICVerify to perform real-time credit card authorizations, I do not recommend doing this. ICVerify is better suited for processing credit card transactions in batches. For example, you can manually run ICVerify once a night and run all the credit card transactions for that day in a single batch.

ICVerify allows you to import CSV files (comma-separated value files). So, to process the credit cards from your online store, you would need to export the credit card transactions from your database to a flat file in CSV format. You can generate CSV files from SQL Server by using the Data Transformation Services (DTS). With Microsoft Access, you can use the Microsoft Access Export option to convert a database table to a delimited text file.

The main advantage of using ICVerify is that it is one of the cheapest solutions for processing credit cards. Because ICVerify uses normal phone lines and not the Internet, the banks do not need to configure special gateways to accept credit card transactions performed with ICVerify. The end result is that banks typically charge you much lower fees.

Component-Based Solutions

The third and final method of processing credit cards is to use a component-based solution. This approach provides you with the greatest flexibility over processing credit cards. You can write Active Server Pages scripts to do such things as authorize, capture, and refund credit card transactions.

Two examples of this approach are CyberCash (`www.cybercash.com`) and VeriFone's vPos software (`www.verifone.com`). We'll discuss CyberCash in detail for the remainder of this chapter.

11

The advantage of a component-based solution to payment processing is that it gives you complete control over credit card transactions from your Active Server Pages scripts. Unlike offsite payment solutions, the customer never needs to leave your Web site. Unlike terminal-based solutions, the credit card transactions can be processed in real-time over the Internet.

Component-based solutions have two main disadvantages. First, they are typically more expensive than terminal solutions because they require the bank to set up a custom Internet gateway. Second, setting up a component-based solution requires you to write custom scripts. Writing the scripts can be time-consuming.

Choosing a Method of Processing Credit Cards

So, you might ask, what is the best method of processing credit cards? Which of the credit card processing systems discussed should I implement at my Web site?

If you want a quick and easy method of processing credit cards from your Web site, I recommend using an offsite payment processing method such as Authorize.Net (www.authorizenet.com). If you want to implement the method with the lowest fees, seriously consider using ICVerify (www.icverify.com). Finally, if you want the greatest flexibility, CyberCash might be the best solution (www.cybercash.com).

To make it easier to research the various options for processing credit cards, here is a list of some of the more popular solutions:

- Authorize.Net (www.authorizenet.com)
- CyberCash (www.cybercash.com)
- CyberSource (www.cybersource.com)
- iBill (www.ibill.com)
- ICVerify (www.icverify.com)
- OpenMarket (www.openmarket.com)
- Signio (www.signio.com)

Preparing for CyberCash

In this section, you'll learn how to complete the three requirements for using CyberCash. You'll learn how to open a credit card merchant account. You will also learn how to register as a merchant at the CyberCash Web site. Finally, you'll learn how to download and install the necessary software for communicating with CyberCash.

Note

Unless you plan to use a wallet (see Day 20, "Working with Wallets"), you must install a server certificate and enable the Secure Sockets Layer (SSL) before you can use the CyberCash service. You must use SSL to protect the privacy of customer credit card information when the information is entered at your Web site. For more information on configuring SSL, see Day 8, "Building the Transaction Databases."

Opening a Credit Card Merchant Account

Before you can use a credit card processing system such as CyberCash, you must open a credit card merchant account with an acquiring financial institution. Typically, your acquiring financial institution will be a bank such as Wells Fargo, Bank of America, or BankBoston. Your acquiring financial institution works with a third-party processor to process credit card transactions and deposit money into your merchant account.

Before opening a credit card merchant account, you need to check whether the bank supports CyberCash because not all banks support it. Most banks select and promote only a handful of credit card processing systems.

When choosing a bank to act as your acquiring financial institution, don't be afraid to comparison shop. Banks might charge any of the following fees:

- Application fee—This is a fee that a bank charges you just for applying for a merchant account. Not all banks charge this fee, so you should avoid it if possible.

- Setup fee—This is a one-time fee that a bank charges you for opening a new merchant account. Again, not all banks charge this fee, so try to avoid it.

- Transaction fee—Almost all banks charge you a transaction fee. The transaction fee is the amount the bank charges you every time you process a credit card. Transaction fees can range anywhere from 10 cents to 50 cents a transaction.

- Monthly minimum fee—Some banks, but not all, charge you a monthly minimum fee. If your sales do not meet a certain threshold, you are charged this fee.

- A discount rate—Most banks retain a percentage of each transaction. This percentage is called the *discount rate*. Discount rates typically fall in the range of 2.00% to 3.00% per transaction.

When researching the fees a bank charges, it is important to separate the bank's fees from the fees charged by CyberCash. CyberCash charges additional setup, transaction, and monthly fees over and above the bank's fees.

Depending on your credit history, opening a credit card merchant account can be very easy, difficult and time-consuming, or impossible. If you already have an established

11

brick-and-mortar business, opening a merchant account might take only the time and effort necessary to complete a one-page application.

If there are problems with your credit history, you might be forced to pay higher fees. Again, don't be afraid to comparison shop. CyberCash maintains a valuable list of acquiring financial institutions at its Web site. To see this list, go to

```
http://www.cybercash.com/fi_display/home.html
```

Registering at CyberCash

After you have opened a credit card merchant account, you are ready to register at CyberCash. CyberCash will lead you through the registration process in a series of HTML forms (see Figure 11.1). To register at CyberCash, go to the following URL:

```
https://amps.cybercash.com/
```

You will be asked for the following information:

- The legal name of your business
- Your Doing Business As name (DBA name)
- Your business address
- Contact information, including phone number and email address

FIGURE 11.1

CyberCash registration.

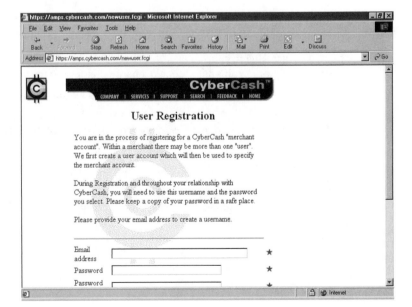

After you have registered, you will be given a CyberCash ID (CCID), hash secret, and merchant key. You will need this information when you install the CyberCash software, so record this information and keep it in a safe place.

After you have registered, you can download the CyberCash Merchant Connection Kit (MCK) and the CyberCash documentation. The MCK contains the components you will need to communicate with CyberCash to process credit card transactions. It also contains several sample scripts. (Sadly, most of these sample scripts are written using PERL instead of ASP.) At the time of this writing, the current version of the MCK is version 3.2.0.4.

Immediately after you register at CyberCash, your CyberCash account is not "live." All the transactions are performed in test mode. This is good because you want to test your scripts before you actually start charging credit cards. When you are ready to go live, log in to the CyberCash Merchant Control Panel and select the Going Live option (see Figure 11.2). You can access the Merchant Control Panel at the following URL:

```
https://amps.cybercash.com/
```

FIGURE 11.2

The Merchant Control Panel.

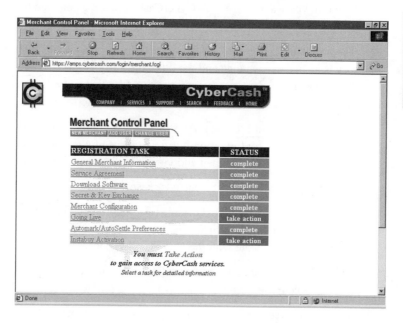

11

Installing the CyberCash Software

After you download the MCK from CyberCash, you need to install it. The installation procedure for the MCK is a little confusing because you need to run two installation programs. First, you must install the MCK itself. Next, you need to execute the build-merchant installation program from Start, Programs, CyberCash Merchant Connection Kit.

You must enter the following information to complete the installation program:

- The fully qualified domain name of your computer—For example, www.yourdomain.com.
- Your CyberCash ID (CCID) and hash secret—You receive this information from CyberCash after you register.
- The name of your store and a customer service phone number.
- Your merchant key—You receive your merchant key from CyberCash after you register.
- The URL of your secure server—For example, https://www.yourdomain.com. You must have the Secure Sockets Layer configured on your server to use CyberCash.

When you run the build-merchant installation program, you must specify the computer language you want to use with CyberCash. You are given the choice of using PERL, C, or ASP. Because this book is on Active Server Pages, I assume you want to choose ASP.

The installation programs add two virtual directories to your Web site. One virtual directory is named mck-shared and the other directory is given the same name as your store. These directories contain the configuration files that CyberCash needs to process credit card transactions. They also contain some sample Active Server Pages scripts.

The most important file that the installation program installs is named merchant_conf. This file contains configuration information specific to your CyberCash account. It's a normal text file. You can open and view it with Notepad. Typically, this file is located at

 c:\inetpub\wwwroot\yourstorename\mck-cgi\conf\merchant_conf

The installation program also installs two important components: the MessageBlock and the Socket components. You will use these components in your Active Server Pages scripts to communicate with the CyberCash service.

 After you finish installing the CyberCash software, you can test your installation by launching your Web browser and opening the following URL:

https://www.yourdomain.com/yourstorename/mck-htdocs/test-mck.html

Opening this page in your Web browser will open a test page that enables you to test various functions of CyberCash. For example, you can test the process of charging a credit card (select the script named Direct Connect Credit Sale).

Authorizing a Credit Card Transaction

Two steps are involved in transferring money from a customer's credit card account to your merchant account. First, you must authorize the transaction. Next, you must capture the transaction. Capturing a transaction submits a transaction for financial settlement. Both steps—authorization and capture—must be completed for the money to be transferred into your account.

In this section, you will learn how to create Active Server Pages scripts that enable you to authorize credit card transactions with the CyberCash service. Remember, however, that the transaction is not complete until you capture and settle the transaction. This second step will be covered in the next section.

To authorize a credit card transaction, you use the CyberCash MessageBlock and Socket components. These are ActiveX components you can use in your Active Server Pages in the same way as you would use the Ad Rotator and Browser Capabilities components.

The MessageBlock component represents a message that you either send or receive from the CyberCash service. Before you authorize a transaction, you load the MessageBlock component with a list of values. For example, you add the customer's credit card number and credit card expiration date to the MessageBlock before you send it.

The CyberCash Socket component is responsible for sending the message to the CyberCash service. It's a standard WinSock component. It imitates the process of posting an HTML form.

The script in Listing 11.1 uses the MessageBlock and Socket components to authorize a credit card transaction. (This file is included on the CD-ROM that accompanies this book with the name `Authorize.asp`.)

INPUT   **LISTING 11.1** Authorizing a Credit Card Transaction

```
1  <%
2  FUNCTION addForm( theFormData, theName, theValue )
3    IF theFormData <> "" THEN
4      theFormData = theFormData & "&"
5    END IF
6    theFormData = theFormData & Server.URLEncode( theName )
7    theFormData = theFormData & "="
8    theFormData = theFormData & Server.URLEncode( theValue )
9    addForm = theFormData
10 END FUNCTION
11
12 ' Set the location of Cash Register and Configuration File
13 paymentURL = "http://cr.cybercash.com/cgi-bin/directcardpayment.cgi"
```

continues

LISTING 11.1   continued

```
14 configLoc = "C:\\inetpub\\wwwroot\\yourstore\\mck-cgi\\conf\\merchant_conf"
15
16 ' Create MessageBlock Object
17 Set Args = CreateObject( "CyberCashMCK.MessageBlock" )
18
19 ' Create the Merchant Offer Form Fields
20 formData = addForm( formData, "mo.cybercash-id", "test-mck" )
21 formData = addForm( formData, "mo.version", "3.2.0.4" )
22 formData = addForm( formData, "mo.order-id", "11111111" )
23 formData = addForm( formData, "mo.price", "usd 1.50" )
24 Args.Add "MO", formData
25
26 ' Create the Credit Payment Information Fields
27 formData = ""
28 formData = addForm( formData, "cpi.card-number", "4111111111111111" )
29 formData = addForm( formData, "cpi.card-exp", "02/00" )
30 formData = addForm( formData, "cpi.card-name", "Stephen Walther" )
31 formData = addForm( formData, "cpi.card-address", "877 Oakgrove" )
32 formData = addForm( formData, "cpi.card-city", "Berkeley" )
33 formData = addForm( formData, "cpi.card-state", "CA" )
34 formData = addForm( formData, "cpi.card-zip", "94108" )
35 formData = addForm( formData, "cpi.card-country", "USA" )
36 Args.Add "CPI", formData
37
38 ' Send the Fields to CyberCash
39 set SockObj = Server.CreateObject("CyberCashMCK.socket.1")
40 set Result = SockObj.SendCCServer( paymentURL, configLoc, Args)
41
42 ' Display Status and any Error Message
43 Response.Write "<hr>Status=" & Result.Lookup( "MStatus" )
44 Response.Write "<br> " & Result.Lookup( "MErrMsg" )
45 %>
```

ANALYSIS   The script in Listing 11.1 contains the bare minimum of code necessary to per-form an authorization transaction with CyberCash. It charges Stephen Walther's credit card account the amount of $1.50. This information is hardcoded into the script.

Lines 12–14 define two variables named paymentURL and configLoc. The paymentURL variable contains the URL of the CyberCash program that performs the credit card autho-rization. The configLoc variable contains the path of the merchant configuration file (merchant_conf). Before you use this script, you must enter the correct path of the merchant_conf file on your server.

Next, in lines 16 and 17, an instance of the CyberCash MessageBlock component is cre-ated. In lines 19–36, a number of values are loaded into the MessageBlock component. This is accomplished with the Add method of the MessageBlock component.

In lines 19–24, the merchant offer fields are added to the MessageBlock. Here's an explanation of each of these fields:

- `mo.cybercash.id`—This field is used to determine your identity. You are given your CyberCash ID when you register. You can also look in your `merchant_conf` file to find your CyberCash ID.

- `mo.version`—The version of the Merchant Connection Kit.

- `mo.order-id`—A unique identifier that contains an order ID. The order ID must be 25 characters or fewer. It can contain letters, numbers, periods, underscores, and dashes. Every time you perform a transaction, you must use a new order ID.

- `mo.price`—The amount that the credit card should be charged. The first three characters represent the currency code. In Listing 11.1, `usd` is used to represent US dollars. When specifying the amount, you must trim any leading digits.

In lines 26–39, the credit information fields are added to the MessageBlock component. These fields should be self-explanatory. They represent such things as the customer's credit card number, credit card expiration date, and home address.

You should notice that a function named `addForm()` is used to add each of the fields to the MessageBlock object. This function is created in lines 2–10. The name and value of each field must be URL encoded before it is added to the MessageBlock. Also, all the fields must be joined together with an & character. The `addForm()` function performs both these tasks.

In lines 38–40, the MessageBlock is sent to CyberCash through the Socket component. The `SendCCServer()` method accepts three parameters: the URL of the CyberCash program that processes the transaction, the path of the merchant configuration file on your server, and the MessageBlock object. The `SendCCServer()` method returns a new MessageBlock object that represents the results of the transaction.

In lines 42–44, two fields are retrieved from the MessageBlock returned from CyberCash. The `MStatus` field contains a status code. It can have any one of the following values:

- `success`—Indicates the transaction completed successfully

- `success-duplicate`—Indicates the result of a previously successful transaction

- `partial-success`—Batch with failed transactions

- `failure-hard`—Failed transaction; trying again will not help

- `failure-q-or-cancel`, `failure-q-or-discard`—Failed transaction due to a communication failure; may be retried

11

- `failure-swversion`—Transaction failed because you are using an old (or nonexistent) software version
- `failure-badmoney`—Failed transaction because of a credit problem with the financial institution

In line 44, the `MErrMsg` field is displayed. This field contains a more verbose explanation of any error that occurred when attempting to process the transaction. If the credit card was successfully authorized, this field will be empty.

The first time you execute the script in Listing 11.1, you will see the screen shown in Figure 11.3. The next time you execute the script, you will receive the following error:

```
Status=failure-hard
CR message: MerchantAuth: Order ID '11111111' has been completed already
```

The error results from the fact that the same order ID was submitted more than once. Every time you perform a new credit card transaction, you must use a new order ID. The easiest way to generate a new order ID for each transaction is to use an autonumber field in an Access database table or an identity field in a SQL database table.

FIGURE 11.3

The Authorize *script.*

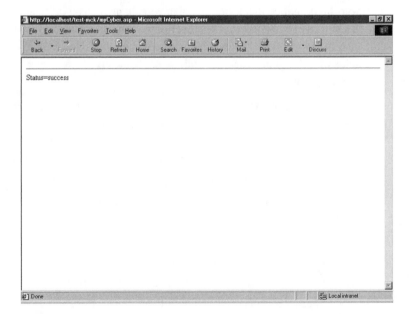

Integrating the Authorization Script into Your Store

The authorization script in Listing 11.1 is too simple to be useful. All the values, such as the credit card number and purchase amount, are hardcoded into the script. In this section, you will learn how to modify the script so that it can be integrated into the online store discussed in previous lessons.

The first thing we need to do is to convert the script in Listing 11.1 into a function. By making the script into a function, we can pass different values for the credit card number and purchase price. Listing 11.2 contains the modified script. (The `authorizeFunction.asp` script is included on the CD-ROM that accompanies this book.)

INPUT　**LISTING 11.2**　Authorize Function Script

```
1  <%
2  FUNCTION addForm( theFormData, theName, theValue )
3    IF theFormData <> "" THEN
4      theFormData = theFormData & "&"
5    END IF
6    theFormData = theFormData & Server.URLEncode( theName )
7    theFormData = theFormData & "="
8    theFormData = theFormData & Server.URLEncode( theValue )
9    addForm = theFormData
10 END FUNCTION
11
12 FUNCTION authorize( orderID, price, cardnumber, cardexp,
➥cardname, cardaddress,  cardcity, cardstate, cardzip, cardcountry )
13 ' Set the location of Cash Register and Configuration File
14 paymentURL = "http://cr.cybercash.com/cgi-bin/directcardpayment.cgi"
15 configLoc = "D:\\inetpub\\wwwroot\\test-mck\\mck-cgi\\conf\\merchant_conf"
16
17 ' Create MessageBlock Object
18 Set Args = CreateObject( "CyberCashMCK.MessageBlock" )
19
20 ' Create the Merchant Offer Form Fields
21 formData = addForm( formData, "mo.cybercash-id", "test-mck" )
22 formData = addForm( formData, "mo.version", "3.2.0.4" )
23 formData = addForm( formData, "mo.order-id", orderID )
24 formData = addForm( formData, "mo.price", "usd " & price )
25 Args.Add "MO", formData
26
27 ' Create the Credit Payment Information Fields
28 formData = ""
29 formData = addForm( formData, "cpi.card-number", cardnumber )
30 formData = addForm( formData, "cpi.card-exp", cardexp )
31 formData = addForm( formData, "cpi.card-name", cardname )
32 formData = addForm( formData, "cpi.card-address", cardaddress )
33 formData = addForm( formData, "cpi.card-city", cardcity )
34 formData = addForm( formData, "cpi.card-state", cardstate )
35 formData = addForm( formData, "cpi.card-zip", cardzip )
36 formData = addForm( formData, "cpi.card-country", cardcountry )
37 Args.Add "CPI", formData
```

11

continues

LISTING 11.2   continued

```
38
39 ' Send the Fields to CyberCash
40 set SockObj = Server.CreateObject("CyberCashMCK.socket.1")
41 set Result = SockObj.SendCCServer( paymentURL, configLoc, Args)
42
43 ' Return Status field
44 authorize = Result.Lookup( "MStatus" ) & Result.Lookup( "MErrMsg" )
45 END FUNCTION
46 %>
```

ANALYSIS   The script in Listing 11.2 is very similar to the script in Listing 11.1, except the
code for authorizing a credit card transaction has been converted into a function.
The `authorize()` function accepts 10 parameters that contain the credit card information. The function returns the result of the transaction.

For example, to authorize a charge of $2.00 on Stephen Walther's credit card, you would
use the following statement:

```
result = authorize( "111119", "2.00", "4111111111111111",
➥ "02/00", "Stephen Walther", "899 Oakgrove",  "Berkeley",
➥ "CA", "94108", "USA" )
```

There are three ways in which you can integrate the `authorize()` function into your
store. First, you might authorize the credit card transaction immediately after the customer clicks the Checkout button on the shopping cart and places an order. To do this,
you would need to modify the `doCheckout2.asp` page to include the `authorize()`
function.

The advantage of this approach is that if, for whatever reason, the credit card transaction
fails, the customer will immediately know it. In that case, the customer can attempt the
same transaction again or try a different credit card.

Instead of authorizing the credit card transaction immediately after a customer checks
out, you could integrate the `authorize()` function into the page where you process customer orders (`processOrders.asp`). The advantage of this approach is that you can
check whether items are in stock before performing the transaction.

Finally, you could create a standalone ASP page devoted to the task of processing credit
cards. The page in Listing 11.3 contains a standard HTML form that has all the fields
necessary to perform an authorization. (This page is named `processCards.asp` on the
CD-ROM that accompanies this book.) By completing the form fields and clicking
Authorize, you can authorize a credit card transaction (see Figure 11.4).

INPUT   **LISTING 11.3**   processCards.asp

```
1   <html>
2   <head><title>Process Cards</title></head>
3   <body>
4   <center>
5   <font face="Arial" size="3"><b>Process Cards</b></font>
6   <p>
7   <form method="post" action="processCards2.asp">
8   <table bgcolor="#cccccc" border=1>
9   <tr>
10    <td align=right><b>Order ID:</b></td>
11    <td><input name="orderID" size="20"></td>
12  </tr>
13    <td align=right><b>Amount:</b></td>
14    <td><input name="price" size="20"></td>
15  </tr>
16  <tr>
17    <td align=right><b>Card Number</b></td>
18    <td><input name="cardnumber" size="16"></td>
19  </tr>
20  <tr>
21    <td align=right><b>Card Expires</b></td>
22    <td>
23    <input name="monthExpires" size="2"> /
24    <input name="yearExpires" size="2">
25    </td>
26  </tr>
27  <tr>
28    <td align=right><b>Customer Name</b></td>
29    <td><input name="cardname" size="20"></td>
30  </tr>
31  <tr>
32    <td align=right><b>Customer Address</b></td>
33    <td><input name="cardaddress" size="20"></td>
34  </tr>
35  <tr>
36    <td align=right><b>Customer City</b></td>
37    <td><input name="cardcity" size="20"></td>
38  </tr>
39  <tr>
40    <td align=right><b>Customer State</b></td>
41    <td><input name="cardstate" size="20"></td>
42  </tr>
43  <tr>
44    <td align=right><b>Customer ZIP:</b></td>
45    <td><input name="cardzip" size="20"></td>
46  </tr>
47  <tr>
48    <td align=right><b>Customer Country:</b></td>
```

11

continues

LISTING 11.3   continued

```
49   <td><input name="cardcountry" size="20">
50  </tr>
51  <tr>
52   <td align=right colspan=2>
53   <input type="submit" value="Authorize">
54   </td>
55  </tr>
56  </table>
57  </form>
58  </center>
59  </body>
60  </html>
```

FIGURE 11.4

*Submitting an autho-
rization transaction.*

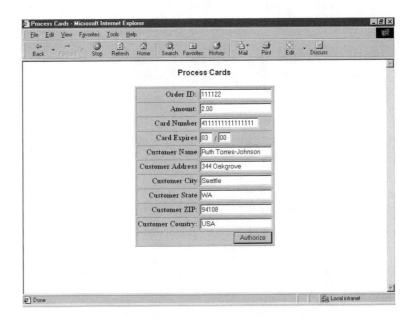

When the form in Listing 11.3 is submitted, the `authorize()` function is called in
`processCards2.asp`. The `processCards2.asp` page simply shows the result of the transaction (see Figure 11.5). The complete code for `processCards2.asp` is included in
Listing 11.4. (`processCards2.asp` is also included on the CD-ROM that accompanies
this book.)

INPUT **LISTING 11.4** processCards2.asp

```
1  <!-- #INCLUDE FILE="authorizeFunction.asp" -->
2  <%
3  ' Retrieve Form Fields
4  orderID = Request( "orderID" )
5  price = Request( "price" )
6  cardnumber = Request( "cardnumber" )
7  cardexp = Request( "monthExpires" ) & _
8    "/" & Request( "yearExpires" )
9  cardname = Request( "cardname" )
10 cardaddress = Request( "cardaddress" )
11 cardcity = Request( "cardcity" )
12 cardstate = Request( "cardstate" )
13 cardzip = Request( "cardzip" )
14 cardcountry = Request( "cardcountry" )
15
16 result = authorize( orderID, price, cardnumber, cardexp,
➥cardname, cardaddress, cardcity, cardstate, cardzip, cardcountry )
17 %>
18 <html>
19 <head><title>Result</title></head>
20 <body>
21
22 <center>
23 <% IF result = "success" THEN %>
24 <table bgcolor="lightgreen" border=1 cellpadding=15>
25 <tr>
26   <td>
27   <font face="Arial" size="4"><b>Success!</b></font>
28   </td>
29 </tr>
30 </table>
31 <% ELSE %>
32 <table bgcolor="yellow" border=1 cellpadding=15>
33 <tr>
34   <td>
35   <font face="Arial" size="2"><b><%=Result%></b></font>
36   </td>
37 </tr>
38 </table>
39 <% END IF %>
40 <a href="processCards.asp"><b>Continue</b></a>
41 </center>
42 </body>
43 </html>
```

11

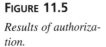

FIGURE 11.5

*Results of authoriza-
tion.*

Settling Credit Card Transactions

After you authorize a credit card transaction, you must capture and settle the transaction in order for the money to be transferred from the customer's account to your merchant account. Exactly how this second step is performed depends on the arrangement you made with your acquiring financial institute (your bank).

There are three different processing models for capturing and settling transactions. First, in the AuthCapture model, transactions are automatically captured when they are authorized. In other words, you do not need to do anything special to complete the transaction.

If your online store sells tangible goods, such as the candy store discussed in previous chapters, your merchant account will most likely *not* be set up to use AuthCapture. The AuthCapture model is intended for use when products or services can be delivered to a customer immediately. For example, your bank might set up your merchant account to use AuthCapture if you plan to sell subscriptions from your Web site.

A second processing model is the Auth/PostAuthCapture processing model. If your merchant account is set up to use this processing model, you must capture the transactions that have been authorized as a separate operation.

The Auth/PostAuthCapture model is intended for use when a product or service is not immediately delivered to the customer. For example, if your online store sells candy, you might not be able to ship the candy immediately after it has been ordered. In this case, you should not capture the transaction until you are actually ready to ship the merchandise. You authorize the transaction when an order is made, and you capture the transaction when the order ships.

If your merchant account has been set up to use the Auth/PostAuthCapture processing model, you must explicitly capture transactions after they have been authorized. The easiest way to do this is to use the CyberCash Merchant Administration Server. (After you register, you should receive instructions that enable you to access the Merchant Administration Server from your Web browser.) To capture authorized transactions, log in to the Merchant Administration Server at `http://cr.cybercash.com` and select the option Query Local Database and/or do PostAuths/Voids/Returns (see Figure 11.6).

FIGURE 11.6

Capturing transactions.

Finally, your merchant account may be set up to use the TerminalCapture processing model. In this processing model, there are two additional steps to completing a transaction after it has been authorized. First, the transactions must be marked to be included in a batch. Next, the batch must be sent to the processor for settlement.

When using the TerminalCapture processing model, you can configure the CyberCash service to automatically mark and settle transactions for you. To automatically mark transactions to be included in a batch, enable the Auto-Mark feature. To automatically submit transactions for settlement, enable the Auto-Settle feature. You can enable both of these features by going to the Merchant Control Panel (`http://amps.cybercash.com`) and clicking the Automark/AutoSettle Preferences link.

If you use the TerminalCapture processing model, you can also mark and settle transactions by using the CyberCash Merchant Administration Server. To mark a transaction for a batch, log in to the Merchant Administration Server at `http://cr.cybercash.com` and select the option Query Local Database and/or do Marking/Unmarking/Returns. To submit transactions for settlement, select the option Assemble and Submit a Batch.

Your credit card merchant account is set up to use one of these three types of processing models: AuthCapture, Auth/PostAuthCapture, or TerminalCapture. If you do not know which processing model you should use, you should contact your bank. Alternatively, you can log in to the Merchant Control Panel (`http://amps.cybercash.com`) and select the Merchant Configuration link. Your processing model will be listed on this page.

Summary

In today's lesson, you learned how to process credit cards. In the first section, you were provided with a brief overview of the various options for processing credit cards, such as Authorize.Net and ICVerify. The remainder of this chapter focused on one credit card processing service: CyberCash. You learned how to open a credit card merchant account that you can use with CyberCash, register at the CyberCash Web site, and install the CyberCash software. Next, you learned how to create Active Server Pages scripts to authorize credit card transactions with CyberCash. Finally, three different processing models for capturing and settling credit card transactions were discussed.

Q&A

Q What is the SET standard and how is it relevant to processing credit cards?

A SET stands for Secure Electronic Transaction. It is a standard for transmitting credit card information over the Internet that was developed by, among others, VISA and MasterCard. The SET standard has not been widely adopted, mainly because it requires customers to download and install special software on their Web browsers.

Q How does CyberCash protect the privacy of credit card information as it is passed across the Internet?

A All communication between your Web server and the CyberCash service is encrypted using triple DES encryption. This is done automatically when you use the CyberCash MessageBlock and Socket components.

However, you are responsible for protecting the security of customer information when it is entered into an HTML form at your Web site. You must use either the Secure Socket Layer (see Chapter 8) or a wallet (see Chapter 20) to protect a customer's payment information.

Workshop

The Quiz questions are designed to test your knowledge of the material covered in this chapter. The answers are in Appendix A, "Quiz Answers."

Quiz

1. Where is my merchant configuration information stored on my server when I use the CyberCash service?

2. What are the names of the two CyberCash components used when sending an authorization request to the CyberCash service?

3. After a transaction is authorized, what other steps must I take to transfer the money from the customer's credit card account to my merchant account?

11

DAY 12

Letting Customers Track Their Orders

After customers place orders at your store, it is important to provide them with a method of tracking their orders. Enabling customers to track their own orders has two major benefits.

First, providing customers with a method of tracking orders lowers customer service costs. If a customer becomes anxious about the status of an order, instead of telephoning you or your customer service department, the customer can check on the order at your Web site. Human time and effort is expensive. Whenever possible, you should automate customer service tasks.

A second benefit to enabling customers to track their orders is that it draws customers back to your Web site. If a customer knows that he can view the status of an order by opening a Web page at your site, the customer might return many times to check the status of an order. Every time a customer visits your Web site is a new opportunity to sell the customer another product.

In today's lesson, you'll learn:

- How to create a Web page that enables customers to view the status of each of their orders.
- How to automatically calculate the cost of shipping an order to a customer and display this information in a Web page.

Enabling Customers to Track Orders with a Web Page

In this section, you'll learn how to create an Account page. Customers can view the Account page by clicking the Account link from the store home page. The Account page displays status information for each order a customer has placed (see Figure 12.1) and the product price.

FIGURE 12.1

The Account page.

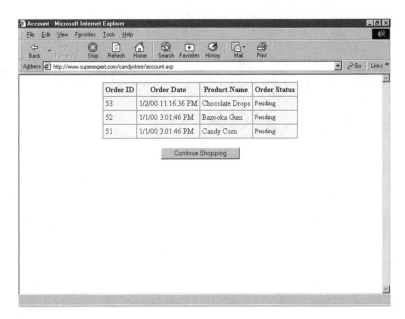

The Account page is created with the help of two ASP pages: `account.asp` and `showorders.asp`. The `account.asp` page contains a script that checks whether the customer can be identified by her username and password. If the customer's username and password cannot be retrieved, the customer is forced to log in.

The complete code for `account.asp` is contained in Listing 12.1. (`account.asp` is also included on the CD-ROM that accompanies this book.)

INPUT **LISTING 12.1** The Account Page

```
1  <!-- #INCLUDE FILE="adovbs.inc" -->
2  <!-- #INCLUDE FILE="storefuncs.asp" -->
3  <%
4
5  ' Get Login Information
6  username = TRIM( Request( "username" ) )
7  password = TRIM( Request( "password" ) )
8  register = TRIM( Request( "register" ) )
9  error = TRIM( Request( "error" ) )
10
11 ' Open Database Connection
12 Set Con = Server.CreateObject( "ADODB.Connection" )
13 Con.Open "accessDSN"
14
15 ' Check For New Registration
16 IF register <> "" AND error = "" THEN
17    addUser
18 END IF
19
20 '  Get User ID
21 userID = checkpassword( username, password, Con )
22
23 IF userID > 0 THEN
24    %>
25    <!-- #INCLUDE FILE="showorders.asp" -->
26    <% ELSE %>
27    <!-- #INCLUDE FILE="register.asp" -->
28    <%
29 END IF
30 %>
```

ANALYSIS In lines 6 and 7, the username and password items are retrieved from the Request object. All the collections of the Request object are searched, including the Form collection and the Cookies collection.

In line 21, the checkpassword() function is called. The checkpassword() function is contained in the storefuncs.asp file. If the username and password combination does not exist in the Users table, the checkpassword() function returns a negative number. Otherwise, the user ID of the customer with the username and password is returned.

Lines 23–29 contain a conditional that displays one or another of two #INCLUDE files. If the user ID is a negative number, the register.asp page is displayed. This page enables a customer to log in or register. Otherwise, if the user ID is not a negative number, the showorders.asp page is displayed.

12

The showorders.asp page displays all the orders that the current customer has placed. For each order, the page displays the order ID, the date of the order, the name of the product ordered, and the status of the order. The complete code for showorders.asp is included in Listing 12.2. (The showorders.asp is also included on the CD that accompanies this book.)

INPUT   **LISTING 12.2**   Display List of Orders

```
1 <%
2 ' Get List of Orders
3 sqlString = "Select orders.*, product_name " &_
4    "from orders, products " &_
5    "WHERE order_productID=product_id " &_
6    "AND order_userid=" & userID & " " &_
7    "ORDER BY order_entrydate DESC"
8
9 SET RS = Con.Execute( sqlString )
10 %>
11 <html>
12 <head><title>Account</title></head>
13 <body>
14
15 <center>
16 <%
17 IF RS.EOF THEN
18 %>
19 <b>You have not placed any orders</b>
20 <%
21 ELSE
22 %>
23 <table cellpadding=4 cellspacing=0
24    bgcolor="lightyellow" border=1>
25 <tr>
26    <th>Order ID</th>
27    <th>Order Date</th>
28    <th>Product Name</th>
29    <th>Order Status</th>
30 </tr>
31 <%
32 WHILE NOT RS.EOF
33 %>
34 <tr>
35    <td>
36    <%=RS( "order_id" )%>
37    </td>
38    <td>
39    <%=RS( "order_entrydate" )%>
40    </td>
```

```
41   <td>
42   <%=RS( "product_name" )%>
43   </td>
44   <td>
45   <small>
46   <%=showOrderStatus( RS( "order_status" ), RS( "order_shipdate" ) )%>
47   </small>
48   </td>
49 </tr>
50 <%
51 RS.MoveNext
52 WEND
53 %>
54 </table>
55 <%
56 END IF
57 %>
58 <p>
59 <form action="default.asp">
60 <input type="submit" value="Continue Shopping">
61 </form>
62
63 </center>
64
65 </body>
66 </html>
```

ANALYSIS   The showorders.asp page retrieves all the rows for a customer from the database table named Orders. The list of orders is retrieved in lines 2–9. In lines 3–7, the SQL string is constructed. In line 9, the SQL string is executed and the records are retrieved into a Recordset named RS.

The remainder of the script loops through each record in the Recordset. Each field of the Recordset is displayed within an HTML table.

Line 46 displays an order's status. This is accomplished with the showOrderStatus() function. This function is defined in the storefuncs.asp file. Listing 12.3 contains the showOrderStatus() function.

INPUT   **LISTING 12.3**   Showing an Order's Status

```
1   FUNCTION showOrderStatus( theStatus, theShipDate )
2     SELECT CASE theStatus
3     CASE 0
4       showOrderStatus = "Pending"
5     CASE 1
```

continues

LISTING 12.3 continued

```
6      showOrderStatus = "Problem with Credit Card"
7    CASE 2
8      showOrderStatus = "Product not in stock"
9    CASE 3
10     showOrderStatus = "Shipped on " & theShipDate
11   CASE ELSE
12     showOrderStatus = "Unknown"
13   END SELECT
14 END FUNCTION
```

The showOrderStatus() function takes the order status and order shipping date values as input, and outputs a string representing the status of the order. The proper string is selected by using a VBScript SELECT CASE statement.

The Account page is updated automatically when you use the processOrders.asp page to update the status of an order. By using the Account page, a customer can determine whether his credit card was declined, whether a product is out of stock, or the exact date and time a product was shipped.

Calculating Shipping Costs

In this section, you'll learn how to use the iisCARTship component. This component enables you to calculate the cost of shipping a package and enables you to display this information in an ASP page.

You'll discover that this component is very valuable for E-Commerce applications. For example, assume that customers can select products from your Web site by using a standard shopping cart. When a customer clicks the Checkout button to complete his order, you'll want to present a list of shipping options. You can use the iisCARTship component to automatically query each of the major shipping companies—United Parcel Service, Federal Express, and the United States Postal Service—and display the cost of shipping the order with each company.

When you use this component, you don't have to worry about displaying outdated shipping rates. Each time you use the component, it retrieves the latest rate information from each shipping company. The component retrieves the cost of shipping an order from each company in real-time.

We'll begin by discussing the procedure for installing the component. Next, you'll be provided with an overview of the component's methods and properties. Finally, we'll build an ASP page that demonstrates how you can use this component in a real-world application.

Installing the `iisCARTship` Component

The `iisCARTship` component isn't included with Active Server Pages. It's a commercial component that you must download and buy. You can purchase it by visiting the following Internet address: `http://www.iiscart.com`.

After you have downloaded and unzipped the component, you'll need to install it. Before you can use the component in an ASP page, you must add information about the component to your computer's registry. The component is bundled with two scripts that will automatically add the correct registry information.

If you are using the component with the Personal Web Server running on Windows 95 or Windows 98, you'll need to execute the script named win9x.bat. Otherwise, if you are using the component with Internet Information Server running on Windows NT or Windows 2000, execute the script named winNT.bat. If everything goes smoothly, a dialog box should pop up reporting that the DLLs were successfully installed.

`iisCARTship` Properties and Methods

Whenever you use the `iisCARTship` component, you must complete the following three steps:

1. Create an instance of the component.
2. Set certain required properties of the component such as the postal code for the origin and desination of the package.
3. Query the shipping companies.

To create an instance of the `iisCARTship` component, use the following statement:

```
Set myShip = Server.CreateObject( "iiscartship.ship" )
```

The previous statement creates an instance of the `iisCARTship` component named myShip. Before you can use the component to query the shipping companies, you must first set the following properties:

- `OrigPostal`—The postal code of the sender of the package (must be in the United States)
- `DestPostal`—The postal code of the recipeint of the package (can be outside the United States)
- `Weight`—The weight of the package (by default, in pounds)
- `DestCountry`—The country code for the destination of the package

The previous properties must be set when using any of the shipping companies. If you want to retrieve shipping rates from Federal Express, there are two additional required properties:

12

- FDXPack—The type of packaging used for the shipment.

- FDXPick—This property indicates whether the package will be dropped off by you or picked up by Federal Express.

The first property, FDXPack, can have any one of the five values Your Packaging, FedEx Letter, FedEx Pak, FedEx Box, or FedEx Tube. The second property, FDXPick can have any one of the three values Will drop-off at FedEx location, Will give to scheduled courier at my location, or Will request a courier pickup.

For example, the script in Listing 12.4 uses the two required Federal Express properties to indicate that the item being shipped will be packaged using a Federal Express letter envelope, and the item will be brought to a Federal Express drop-off location.

LISTING 12.4   Using Federal Express Properties

```
1  <%
2  Set myShip = Server.CreateObject( "iiscartship.ship" )
3  myShip.OrigPostal = "02138"
4  myShip.DestPostal = "94108"
5  myShip.DestCountry = "US"
6  myShip.Weight = "2"
7  myShip.FDXPack = "FedEx Letter"
8  myShip.FDXPick = "Will drop-off at FedEx location"
9  %>
```

After you have set all the required properties, you can query the shipping companies by calling the ShipCalc() method. When you call this method, you can pass the names of any of the three shipping companies ("UPS", "USPS", "FEDEX"). For example, the script in Listing 12.5 retrieves shipping rates from both Federal Express and the United Parcel Service.

LISTING 12.5   Retrieving Shipping Rates

```
1  <%
2  Set myShip = Server.CreateObject( "iiscartship.ship" )
3  myShip.OrigPostal = "02138"
4  myShip.DestPostal = "94108"
5  myShip.DestCountry = "US"
6  myShip.Weight = "2"
7  myShip.FDXPack = "FedEx Letter"
8  myShip.FDXPick = "Will drop-off at FedEx location"
9  myShip.ShipCalc "FEDEX, UPS"
10 FOR EACH item IN myShip.ShipInfo
11   Response.Write "Service: " & item.cSingleService & "<br>"
```

```
12    Response.Write "Company: " & item.cShipCompany & "<br>"
13    Response.Write "Charge: " & item.cTotalCharge & "<br>"
14    Response.Write "Commit Time: " & item.cShipTime & "<br>"
15 NEXT
16 %>
```

Calling the ShipCalc() method returns a collection named ShipInfo that contains the shipping rates. In the previous script, a VBScript FOR...EACH loop is used to loop through each item of the ShipInfo collection and display its properties.

All the interesting information is contained in the ShipInfo collection. Each item in this collection has the following properties:

- cError—Service specific error
- cSingleService—The name of the particular service being offered
- cShipCompany—The name of the company providing the service
- cTotalCharge—Total cost to ship the package (base + add charge)
- cBaseCharge—Base charge to ship the package
- cAddCharge—Any additional charges to ship the package
- cShipTime—When the package is guaranteed to arrive

The most useful properties are the cSingleService, cShipCompany, cTotalCharge, and cShipTime properties. The cSingleService property contains the name of a particular service such as Priority Mail or Express Mail. Each of the three companies have different names for their services.

The cShipCompany property contains the name of the company that offers the service. This property can have any of the three values FEDEX (Federal Express), UPS (United Parcel Service), or USPS (United States Postal Service).

The cTotalCharge property contains the actual cost of shipping the package using the service. Finally, the cShipTime property indicates when the package will arrive. This property can have values such as 7 DAY(S) or OVERNIGHT TO MOST AREAS. Again, the specific values depend on the shipping company.

The information that you get back from the United Parcel Service can be a little cryptic. UPS uses codes for its services like 2DA and GNDCOM. Fortunately, the iisCARTship component includes a method for converting these codes into a more understandable form: the UPSproductConversion() method. For example, the script in Listing 12.6 shows all the available UPS services using both the raw UPS code and the UPS code converted with the UPSproductConversion() method.

12

LISTING 12.6   Converting UPS Codes

```
1   <%
2   Set myShip = Server.CreateObject( "iiscartship.ship" )
3   myShip.OrigPostal = "02138"
4   myShip.DestPostal = "94108"
5   myShip.DestCountry = "US"
6   myShip.Weight = "2"
7   myShip.ShipCalc "UPS"
8   FOR EACH item IN myShip.ShipInfo
9     Response.Write "Service: "
10    Response.Write item.cSingleService & " = "
11    Response.Write myShip.UPSproductConversion( item.cSingleService )
12    Response.Write "<BR>"
13  NEXT
14  %>
```

When displaying shipping options, you might want to display information for only particular services. For example, you might want to display only the rates for shipping packages overnight. You can restrict the services retrieved by the iisCARTship using the LimitServices() method. The script in Listing 12.7 uses the LimitServices() method to show rates for the Express Mail and One Day Air Saver services.

LISTING 12.7   Limiting Services

```
1   <%
2   Set myShip = Server.CreateObject( "iiscartship.ship" )
3   myShip.OrigPostal = "02138"
4   myShip.DestPostal = "94108"
5   myShip.DestCountry = "US"
6   myShip.Weight = "2"
7   myShip.LimitServices = "1DP, EXPRESS MAIL"
8   myShip.ShipCalc "UPS, USPS"
9   FOR EACH item IN myShip.ShipInfo
10    Response.Write "Service: " & item.cSingleService & "<br>"
11    Response.Write "Company: " & item.cShipCompany & "<br>"
12    Response.Write "Charge: " & item.cTotalCharge & "<br>"
13    Response.Write "Commit Time: " & item.cShipTime & "<br>"
14  NEXT
15  %>
```

There's one final method of the iisCARTship component that you should know about. If you sell products through your Web site to customers outside of the United States, you'll need to provide customers with a method of specifying their country. You can use the iisCARTship component's CountryList() method to automatically generate an HTML combo box that contains a list of valid country codes.

The script in Listing 12.8 uses the `CountryList()` method to display a list of country codes.

LISTING 12.8   Displaying Country Codes

```
1  <%
2  Set myShip = Server.CreateObject( "iiscartship.ship" )
3  Response.Write myShip.CountryList( "country" )
4  %>
```

In the previous script, the `CountryList()` method is passed one parameter that is used for the name of the combo box. You can also include a second optional parameter that specifies the default country for the combo box. If you don't include this parameter, the United States is picked by default.

`iisCARTship` Component Sample Application

In this section, you'll learn how the `iisCARTship` component can be used in a real-world application. We'll build an ASP page that enables customers to compare the cost of shipping a product using the different shipping services offered by UPS. The ASP page contains an HTML form that enables a customer to enter the weight of the package, the origin of the package, and the destination of the package. When the Calculate Costs button is clicked, a list of package shipping options is displayed.

The page is called `compareShip.asp` and it is contained in Listing 12.9. (It's also included on the CD that accompanies this book.)

LISTING 12.9   Compare Shipping Rates

```
1  <%
2  ' Retrieve Form Variables
3  compareShip = TRIM( Request( "compareShip" ) )
4  weight      = TRIM( Request( "weight" ) )
5  origPostal  = TRIM( Request( "origPostal" ) )
6  destPostal  = TRIM( Request( "destPostal" ) )
7  destCountry = TRIM( Request( "destCountry" ) )
8
9  ' Set Default Values
10 IF weight = "" OR NOT isNumeric( weight ) THEN
11   weight = 5
12 END IF
13 IF origPostal = "" THEN
14   origPostal = "95350"
15 END IF
```

continues

12

LISTING **12.9**   continued

```
16 IF destPostal = "" THEN
17   destPostal = "95350"
18 END IF
19 IF destCountry = "" THEN
20  destCountry = "US"
21 END IF
22
23 ' Query UPS
24 Set myShip = Server.CreateObject( "iiscartship.ship" )
25 myShip.weight = weight
26 myShip.origPostal  = origPostal
27 myShip.destPostal  = destPostal
28 myShip.destCountry = destCountry
29 myShip.ShipCalc "UPS"
30 %>
31 <HTML>
32 <HEAD>
33 <TITLE>Comparing Shipping Costs</TITLE>
34 </HEAD>
35 <BODY>
36 <h3>Compare Shipping Costs:</h3>
37
38 <table border=1 cellspacing=0 cellpadding=4>
39 <tr bgcolor="lightyellow">
40   <td>UPS Service</td>
41   <td>Arrival Time</td>
42   <td>Cost</td>
43 </tr>
44 </tr>
45 <% FOR EACH item IN myShip.ShipInfo %>
46 <tr>
47   <td>
48   <%=myShip.UPSProductConversion( item.cSingleService )%>
49   (<%=item.cSingleService%>)
50   </td>
51   <td><%=item.cShipTime%></td>
52   <td><%=formatCurrency( item.cTotalCharge )%></td>
53 </tr>
54 <% NEXT %>
55 </table>
56
57 <FORM method="post" ACTION="compareShip.asp">
58 <input name="compareShip" type="hidden" value="1">
59
60 <p><b>Package Weight:</b>
61 <br>Pounds:
62 <input name="weight" size="10"
63   value="<%=Server.HTMLEncode( weight )%>">
64
```

```
65 <p><b>Package Origin:</b>
66 <br>Postal Code:
67 <input name="origPostal" size="20"
68   value="<%=Server.HTMLEncode( origPostal )%>">
69
70 <p><b>Package Destination:</b>
71 <br>Postal Code:
72 <input name="destPostal" size="20"
73  value="<%=Server.HTMLEncode( destPostal )%>">
74 <br>Country:
75 <%=myShip.CountryList( "destCountry", destCountry )%>
76
77 <p><input type="submit" value="Calculate Cost">
78 </FORM>
79
80 </BODY>
81 </HTML>
```

If you read the previous section, you should find the script in the listing easy to understand. In the first section, labeled "Retrieve Form Variables", several form variables are retrieved from the Form collection and assigned to local variables. The variables represent the weight, origin, and destination of the package.

Next, in the section labeled "Set Default Values", if any of the variables don't have a value, they are assigned default values. We do this to avoid having an error generated when the page is first opened or when a customer neglects to complete a form field.

In the section labeled "Query UPS", an instance of the iisCARTship component is used to retrieve a list of services and their costs from UPS. This information is retrieved into the ShipInfo collection. The contents of this collection is displayed within an HTML table using a VBScript FOR...EACH loop.

12

The remainder of the page contains a normal HTML form. The customer can enter information about a package into the form in order to calculate the shipping costs. When a customer submits the form, the form data is sent back to the same page (compareShip.asp).

Summary

In today's lesson, you learned how to enable customers to track their orders through a Web page. You learned how to create a Web page that displays the status of each order placed by a particular customer. You also learned how to use the iisCARTship component to display the cost of shipping a product order to a customer. You learned how to use the iisCARTship component to retrieve shipping rates from the United Parcel Service, the United States Postal Service, and Federal Express.

Q&A

Q In today's lesson, I learned how to use the `iisCARTship` component to retrieve shipping rates from the major shipping companies. Is there any way to retrieve package tracking information as well?

A Yes, the United Parcel Service (www.ups.com), the United States Postal Service (www.usps.com), and Federal Express (www.fedex.com) all offer tools that you can use with your Web site to enable customers to track packages as they are shipped from your store to their home. To find out more about these tools, visit the following Web sites:

United Parcel Service:
`http://www.ec.ups.com/ecommerce/ontools/index.html`

United States Postal Service:
`http://www.uspsprioritymail.com/et_tool.html`

Federal Express:
`http://www.fedex.com/us/software/ecommerce/shipapi.html`

Q I'm having trouble with the `iisCARTship` component. When I use it, I get an empty Web page. Is there any way to find out what is going wrong?

A You can diagnose errors with the `iisCARTship` component by using two properties. You can use the `iisCARTship` Error property to display general errors. For service specific errors, you can use the `cError` property of the `ShipInfo` collection. For example, to use the Error property, just add a line to your script like this:

```
Response.Write myShip.Error
```

Workshop

The following questions are designed to test your knowledge of the material covered in this chapter.

Quiz

1. Is the `iisCARTship` component included with Active Server Pages?

2. What four properties of the `iisCARTship` component must you set before you can query rate information from any of the shipping companies?

3. What is the name of the collection returned by the `ShipCalc()` method that contains the shipping rates?

DAY 13

Creating a Subscription-Based Site

In today's lesson, you'll learn how to create a subscription Web site. You'll learn how to password protect a private area of your Web site so that it is accessible only to registered customers.

There are many examples of successful subscription Web sites on the Internet. For example, Match.com (www.match.com) requires users to subscribe before they can browse their listings of potential romantic partners. Both the *Wall Street Journal* (www.wsj.com) and the *New York Times* (www.nyt.com), require visitors to subscribe before they can read news articles. Finally, the Internet is overflowing with pornography Web sites, like Playboy.com, that require visitors to subscribe before they can view images.

In this lesson, you'll learn several methods of password protecting your Web site's content. You'll learn

- How to password protect Active Server Pages using HTTP Authentication
- How to password protect Active Server Pages using a database.
- How to combine HTTP and database authentication

Using HTTP Authentication

The easiest, and least flexible, method of password protecting an ASP page is to use HTTP Authentication. When HTTP Authentication is enabled, a password dialog box appears when a visitor first attempts to retrieve a protected page (see Figure 13.1). In order to view the page, the user must enter a valid Windows username and password. If the user doesn't enter a valid username and password, the password dialog box is repeatedly displayed.

FIGURE 13.1

Standard password dialog box.

You cannot use HTTP Authentication with the Personal Web Server for Windows 95/98. It only works when you use Internet Information Server with Windows NT or Windows 2000.

The most recent release of Internet Information Server (version 5.0) supports three types of authentication:

- Basic Authentication—Basic Authentication is part of the HTTP specification, and it is compatible with all Web browsers. However, when this form of authentication is used, usernames and passwords are transmitted across the Internet in a lightly encrypted form. Usernames and passwords are simply base64 encoded. Because base64 encoded strings are easy to decode (you'll learn how later in this chapter), Basic Authentication doesn't offer a very high level of security.

- Integrated Authentication—Integrated authentication improves upon Basic Authentication by not sending usernames and passwords across the Internet. The major drawback of Integrated Authentication is that it works only with Microsoft Internet Explorer (version 2.0 or higher). Also, it doesn't work over proxy connections. In previous versions of Internet Information Server, Integrated Authentication was called Windows NT Challenge/Response Authentication or NTLM Authentication.

- Digest Authentication—This is a new form of authentication introduced with Internet Information Server 5.0. Like Basic Authentication, Digest Authentication is part of the public HTTP standard. However, because it is part of the relatively recent HTTP 1.1 specification, many browsers still don't support it. To use Digest

Authentication, your server must be a directory server in a Windows 2000 domain. You must also save a copy of the passwords being used in plain encrypted text (for more information, see the knowledge base article Q222028 at the Microsoft Web site).

Previous to Internet Information Server 5.0, you could choose only between Basic and Integrated Authentication. When you wanted to ensure compatibility with any browser, you would use Basic Authentication. When you needed stronger security—for example, when performing Web site administration functions—you would use Integrated Authentication.

Digest Authentication offers a useful alternative to Integrated Authentication. It offers the promise of a non-proprietary authentication mechanism that will be supported by all browsers. Regrettably, however, this promise hasn't yet been fulfilled because currently only Internet Explorer (version 5.0 or greater) supports it.

Enabling HTTP Authentication

You can use HTTP Authentication to password protect a particular file, directory, or a whole Web site. To enable HTTP Authentication, follow these steps:

1. Launch the Internet Service Manager (this is called the Internet Services Manager on Windows 2000).

2. Select the file, directory or Web site that you want to password protect.

3. Open the property sheet for the file, directory, or Web site.

4. Select the tab labeled File Security or Directory Security.

5. Click the button labeled Edit in the section entitled Anonymous Access and Authentication Control. Doing this will open the Authentication Methods dialog box (see Figure 13.2).

6. Select a form of authentication. To force a dialog box to appear, you will also need to disable anonymous access by deselecting the check box labeled Allow Anonymous Access.

FIGURE 13.2

Enabling Directory Authentication.

13

After you complete these steps, whenever you first attempt to retrieve a file that requires authentication, a password dialog box will appear. You won't be able to view the file until you enter a valid Windows username and password.

> **Note**
>
> If you are using Windows NT, you can add new Windows accounts by using the User Manager applet (or User Manager for Domains applet if the computer is a domain controller).
>
> If you are using Windows 2000, you can add new Windows accounts by using the Computer Management applet. If the computer is a Windows 2000 domain controller, use the Active Directory Users and Computers applet.

When You Should Use HTTP Authentication

HTTP Authentication is useful when you need to password protect a section of your Web site so that it can be accessed by a small number of authorized users. For example, if you have an administration area of your Web site that contains Active Server Pages that are used to maintain your site, you can use HTTP Authentication to prevent the public from accessing these pages.

However, it is difficult to setup HTTP Authentication to work with an automated user registration system. The problem results from the fact that you need to add a Windows NT account for each authorized user. If you have thousands of registered users at your Web site, you would need to set up thousands of Windows accounts. If you need to create an automated user registration system, it is much easier to use database authentication. You'll learn how to use database authentication, and create an automated user registration system, in the next section.

> **Note**
>
> There are third-party components that enable you to add a new Windows account from an ASP page. See, for example, the AspUser component at www.aspuser.com. To see an extensive list of third-party components, visit the software section of superexpert at http://asp.superexpert.com/software.

Using Database Authentication

In this section, you'll learn how to password protect pages at your Web site by comparing usernames and passwords against columns in a database table. You'll create a standard include file that you can include in all the pages that you want to password protect. When someone attempts to open a page that contains this include file, the person will be required to enter his registered username and password. If the person is a new user, he can register by using a registration page. This include file can be included in any page that you want to password protect.

You'll need to create one new database table and three new Active Server Pages:

- userlist—This table contains all the registered usernames and passwords.
- register.asp—This page contains a simple registration form.
- login.asp—This page contains a simple login form.
- checkpassword.asp—This is an Include file that you must include in every page that you want password protected.

First, you'll need to create a new access database named usersDB and add a new table named userlist. Follow these steps:

1. Launch Microsoft Access, select Blank Access database, and click OK. Enter the name **userDB** for the new database.

2. Click the Design icon, and create a new table that contains three fields: user_id, user_username, and user_password. The user_id field is a AutoNumber field. You'll use this field to uniquely identify every user. The user_username and user_password fields are text fields. They will contain the usernames and passwords.

3. Click Save, and save the new table with the name **userlist**.

After you create the new database and database table, you will need to configure a new System Data Source Name (DSN) so that you can connect to the database. Follow these steps:

 Note   Before you create a DSN or work with the new database in an ASP page, make sure that you close Microsoft Access—or you might receive errors.

13

1. Go to Start, Settings, Control Panel, and click the ODBC Data sources applet.
2. Choose the tab labeled System DSN.
3. Click the button labeled Add, choose the Microsoft Access Driver, and click Finish.
4. In the section labeled Databases, click the button labeled Select. Next, select the userDB database on your hard drive.
5. Enter the name **userDSN** for the Data Source Name and click OK.

After you complete these steps, you will have a new DSN named userDSN that you can use in your Active Server Pages. Remember, if you ever change the location of your database, you will need to create a new DSN.

The first ASP page that you need to create is named `register.asp`. This page contains a registration form for new users. The page is included in Listing 13.1 (it's also included on the CD that accompanies this book).

LISTING 13.1   The Registration Page

```
1  <%
2  nextPage = Request( "nextPage" )
3  newUsername = Request( "newUsername" )
4  newPassword = Request( "newPassword" )
5  %>
6  <HTML>
7  <HEAD><TITLE>Register</TITLE></HEAD>
8  <BODY>
9
10 Register at this Web site by selecting a username and password:
11 <FORM METHOD="post" ACTION="<%=nextPage%>">
12 <INPUT NAME="newUser" TYPE="hidden" VALUE="1">
13 <P><B>USERNAME:</B>
14 <INPUT NAME="newUsername" SIZE=20 MAXLENGTH="20"
15   VALUE="<%=Server.HTMLEncode( newUsername )%>">
16 <P><B>PASSWORD:</B>
17 <INPUT NAME="newPassword" SIZE=20 MAXLENGTH="20"
18   VALUE="<%=Server.HTMLEncode( newPassword )%>">
19 <P><INPUT TYPE="submit" VALUE="Register!">
20 </FORM>
21
22 </BODY>
23 </HTML>
```

ANALYSIS   There's nothing tricky going on with this page. This page is used by a new customer to register (see Figure 13.3). It contains a simple HTML form that has two form fields named newUsername and newPassword. The form also contains a hidden form field named newUser. The `register.asp` page is never opened directly. A new user links to the page from the `login.asp` page.

Next, you need to create a page named `login.asp`. This page appears when a user attempts to access a password protected page without the proper authentication information. It's contained in Listing 13.2, and it is also available on the CD that accompanies this book.

FIGURE 13.3

The Registration Form.

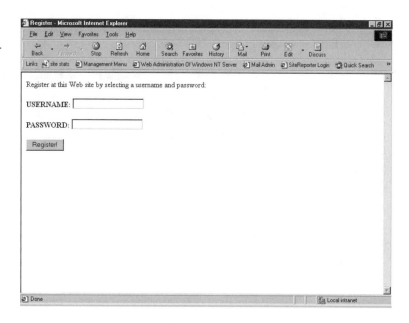

LISTING 13.2 The Login Page

```
 1  <HTML>
 2  <HEAD><TITLE>Login</TITLE></HEAD>
 3  <BODY>
 4
 5  <%=loginMessage%>
 6  <FORM METHOD="post" ACTION="<%=nextPage%>">
 7  <P><B>USERNAME:</B>
 8  <INPUT NAME="username" SIZE=20 MAXLENGTH="20"
 9    VALUE="<%=Server.HTMLEncode( username )%>">
10  <P><B>PASSWORD:</B>
11  <INPUT NAME="password" SIZE=20 MAXLENGTH="20"
12    VALUE="<%=Server.HTMLEncode( password )%>">
13  <p><INPUT NAME="addCookie" TYPE="Checkbox"
14    VALUE="1"> Remember me with a cookie
15  <P><INPUT TYPE="submit" VALUE="Login">
16  </FORM>
17  <p>
18  <a href="register.asp?nextpage=<%=Server.URLEncode( nextpage )%>">
19  Click here to register</a>
20
21  </BODY>
22</HTML>
```

13

ANALYSIS This page also contains a simple HTML form. The form has three fields named username, password, and addCookie. The addCookie field is a check box. If the

customer wants his username and password added to his browser with a cookie, he can
check the box (see Figure 13.4).

FIGURE 13.4

The Login Page.

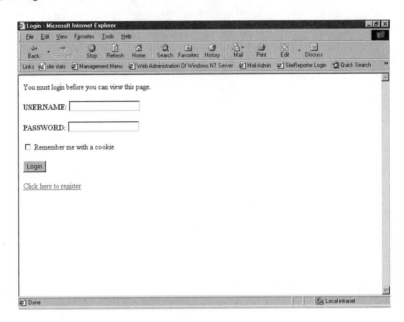

All the interesting stuff happens in the file named `checkpassword.asp`. This file is
included at the top of every page that you want to password protect. You can include the
page by using the ASP `#INCLUDE` directive like this:

```
<!-- #INCLUDE FILE="checkpassword.asp" -->
```

The `checkpassword.asp` page is too long to list in this chapter, but you can open the
page from the CD that accompanies this book. We'll go through the `checkpassword.asp`
section by section.

First, the `checkpassword.asp` page retrieves several variables from the `Request` collection:

```
' Retrieve Form Variables
username = TRIM( Request( "username" ) )
password = TRIM( Request( "password" ) )
newUser = TRIM( Request( "newUser" ) )
newUsername = TRIM( Request( "newUsername" ) )
newPassword = TRIM( Request( "newPassword" ) )
addCookie = TRIM( Request( "addCookie" ) )
```

If a visitor arrives at this page from the login page, the username and password variables
will have values. If a visitor has just completed the `register.asp` page, the `newUser`,
`newUsername`, and `newPassword` variables will have values. Finally, if a user checks the

check box named addCookie in the `login.asp` page, then the `addCookie` variable will have a value.

Next, the full virtual path of the current page is retrieved from the `ServerVariables` collection of the `Request` object and assigned to a variable named `nextpage`:

```
' Retrieve Current Page
nextPage = Request.ServerVariables( "SCRIPT_NAME" )
```

Next, a database connection is opened to the userDB database. The connection is opened with the userDSN Data Source Name.

```
' Ready Database Connection
Set Con = Server.CreateObject( "ADODB.Connection" )
Con.Open "userDSN"
```

Next, if the `newUser` form variable has a value, the script attempts to add the username and password of the new user to the database (see Listing 13.3). The `newUser` form variable is passed by the `register.asp` page when the registration form is submitted.

LISTING 13.3 The Add User Script

```
1  ' Add New User
2  IF newUser <> "" THEN
3    IF newUsername = "" THEN
4      showError "You must enter a username"
5    END IF
6    IF newPassword = "" THEN
7      showError "You must enter a password"
8    END IF
9    IF usernameTaken( newUsername ) THEN
10     showError "The username you entered has already " &_
11       "been chosen by a previous user. Please select " &_
12       "a new username"
13   END IF
14   sqlString = "INSERT INTO userlist ( user_username, user_password ) " &_
15     "VALUES ('" & newUsername & "','" & newPassword & "')"
16   Con.Execute sqlString
17   username = newUsername
18   password = newPassword
19   IF useSession THEN Session( "loggedIn" ) = "Yes"
20 END IF
```

13

ANALYSIS In lines 3–8, the script checks whether either one of the username or password variables were submitted without values. If a customer registers without entering a username or a password, an error page is displayed.

Next, in lines 9–13, a function named usernameTaken() is used to check whether the username the customer entered has already been claimed by a previous customer. Because we need to guarantee that each customer is registered with a unique username, an error page is displayed if the username was, in fact, already taken.

In lines 14–16, the new username and password are added to the userlist database table. In lines 14–15, the SQL string is constructed. In line 16, the SQL string is executed.

After the new username and password are added to the database, they are assigned to new variables in lines 17–18. Finally, in line 19, a Session variable named LoggedIn is given the value 1. The LoggedIn variable indicates that the customer has already logged in and can access future pages without entering her username and password.

The next section of code in checkpassword.asp is used to authenticate a user who arrives at the page through the login.asp page. The authentication script is contained in Listing 13.4.

LISTING 13.4   Authenticating a User

```
1  ' Authenticate User
2  IF Session( "loggedIn" ) = "" THEN
3  IF username = "" OR password = "" THEN
4    loginMessage = "You must login before you can view this page."
5    showLogin
6  END IF
7  result = validateLogin( username, password )
8  IF result = 1 THEN
9    loginMessage = "You entered an unregistered username."
10   showLogin
11 END IF
12 IF result = 2 THEN
13   loginMessage = "You did not enter a valid password."
14   showLogin
15 END IF
16 IF useSession THEN Session( "loggedIn" ) = "Yes"
17 END IF
```

ANALYSIS   The authentication script starts by checking whether the LoggedIn Session variable has a value. If this variable has a value, the customer has already logged in and the rest of the authentication script is skipped.

Next, in lines 3–6, if either one of the username or password variables do not have a value, the login.asp page is displayed and the script ends. Otherwise, the username and password are checked against the userlist database table with the validatelogin() function. This function returns three possible values:

0	If the username and password exist in the userlist database table.
1	If the username doesn't exist in the userlist database table.
2	If the username exists in the table, but the password is invalid.

If the `validatelogin()` function returns the value 0, the customer has successfully logged in. In this case, the `Session` variable named `LoggedIn` is given the value 1.

The `valiatelogin()` function is contained in Listing 13.5.

LISTING 13.5   Validate Username and Password

```
1   ' Check Username and Password
2   FUNCTION validateLogin( theUsername, thePassword )
3     sqlString = "SELECT user_password FROM userlist " &_
4       "WHERE user_username='" & fixQuotes( username ) & "'"
5     Set RS = Con.Execute( sqlString )
6     IF RS.EOF THEN
7       validateLogin = 1
8     ELSE
9       IF RS( "user_password" ) <> thePassword THEN
10        validateLogin = 2
11      ELSE
12        validateLogin = 0
13      END IF
14    END IF
15  END FUNCTION
```

ANALYSIS   The `validatelogin()` function returns three possible values. First, in lines 3–4, a SQL query string is constructed, which retrieves the password from the userlist database table that matches the username the customer entered into the `login.asp` page. If no rows are retrieved from the table, you know that the username doesn't exist, and the value 1 is returned (line 7). Next, if the username exists in the table, but the password the customer entered into the `login.asp` page doesn't match the password in the database, the value 2 is returned (line 10). Finally, if both the username and password entered by the customer exist in the userlist table, the value 0 is returned (line 12).

13

After a customer's username and password have been validated against the userlist table, the `checkpassword.asp` script performs three more tasks. First, if the customer indicated that he wants his username and password added to his browser with a cookie, this is accomplished with the following script:

```
' Add a Cookie
IF addCookie <> "" THEN
  Response.Cookies( "username" ) = username
  Response.Cookies( "username" ).Expires = "12/25/2002"
```

```
  Response.Cookies( "password" ) = password
  Response.Cookies( "password" ).Expires = "12/25/2002"
END IF
```

Next, a variable named `sq` is constructed. This variable is used to pass security information (the customer's username and password in a query string variable). Here is the script that creates the `sq` variable:

```
' Create Security Query String Variable
sq = "username=" & Server.HTMLEncode( username ) & "&"
sq = sq & "password=" & Server.HTMLEncode( password )
```

Finally, a variable named `sf` is constructed. The `sf` variable is used to pass a customer's security information in a hidden form field. Here is the script that creates the `sf` variable:

```
' Create Security Form Variable
sf = "<input name=""username"" type=""hidden"" "
sf = sf & "value=""" & Server.HTMLEncode( username ) & """>"
sf = sf & "<input name=""password"" type=""hidden"" "
sf = sf & "value=""" & Server.HTMLEncode( password ) & """>"
```

It's easy to lose track of how the `login.asp`, `register.asp`, and `checkpassword.asp` pages interact, so we'll walk through an example of how a new customer would encounter each of these pages. Assume that the `checkpassword.asp` page is included at the top of a page named `test.asp`:

1. A customer requests the page named `test.asp`.

2. The `checkpassword.asp` script included in `test.asp` attempts to retrieve the customer's username and password from the `Request` collection. Because these variables cannot be retrieved, the `login.asp` page is displayed.

3. Because the customer has never registered at this Web site, he clicks the link on the `login.asp` page to go to the `register.asp` page.

4. The customer enters a username and password into the `register.asp` page and clicks Register.

5. The data in the `register.asp` page is submitted back to the `test.asp` page. The form is submitted with a hidden form field named addUser that has the value 1.

6. In the `checkpassword.asp` script included in the `test.asp` page, the addUser hidden form field is detected, and the customer's username and password are added to the userlist database table.

7. The customer is authenticated, and can view the contents of the `test.asp` page.

8. The customer is called away from his computer by a strange noise just outside his window. Investigating, he leaves his house.

9. Three hours later, after many adventures, the customer decides to return to your Web site. He requests the `test.asp` page once again.

10. Because the customer's username and password cannot be retrieved from the `Request` collection, the `login.asp` page is displayed.

11. This time, the customer enters his username and password. He submits the `login.asp` page and the data is submitted to the `test.asp` page.

12. Within the `checkpassword.asp` script included in `test.asp`, the customer's username and password are retrieved from the `Request` collection.

13. The customer's username and password are checked against the userlist database table; the customer is authenticated; and the content of the `test.asp` page is displayed.

Passing Security Information From Page to Page

When a customer has logged in to one page at your Web site, he shouldn't be bothered with logging in to each additional page he requests. Entering a username and password to view each and every page would quickly become tedious. The information should be passed to each new page automatically.

There are five general mechanisms that you can use to pass information, including security information, from one ASP page to another:

- Browser cookies
- `Session` variables
- `Form` variables
- `Query String` variables
- Browser headers

The `checkpassword.asp` page uses the first four methods to track customer security information. Why are all these mechanisms of passing authentication information from page to page necessary?

Note

> You'll learn how to use the last method of passing information from page to page, browser headers, in the next section.

13

Each method of passing information has its advantages and disadvantages. The advantage of browser cookies is that they provide a method of storing customer information over many visits to a Web site. So, if a user enters her username and password once, she never needs to enter the information again. In theory, the user can be automatically authenticated every time she requests a page.

The disadvantage of cookies is that not all browsers support them. For one reason or another, cookies tend to fail. So, you should not rely on cookies to authenticate a customer across multiple pages.

Because Session variables rely on cookies, they have the same disadvantage as cookies. However, Session variables have one advantage that cookie lack. Because Session variables are stored on the server rather than the browser, you can store a username and password more securely using Session variables. If a username and password are stored in a Session variable, they won't be passed back and forth across the Internet every time a page is requested.

Using Query String and Form variables is more reliable than using either cookies or Session variables. If you want your Web site to work with any browser, no matter how old or obscure, you should seriously consider using Query String and Form variables to pass security information from page to page.

Using Query String or Form variables has a couple of major disadvantages. First, when you use Query String variables, the variables are clearly visible in the address bar of your browser. If you are worried about strangers looking over your shoulder and learning your password, Query String variables present a risk.

More importantly, it takes a lot of work to pass Query String and Form variables from page to page. You must include the variables within every hypertext link and every form in a page to pass the variables to other pages.

The checkpassword.asp Include file makes the task of passing Query String and Form variables slightly easier. The script automatically constructs two variables, named sq and sf, which contain the username and password. The sq variable contains a Query String variable and the sf variable contains a hidden Form variable.

For example, suppose that you have a page named page1.asp that contains a hypertext link to a page named page2.asp. If you want to pass the customer's username and password to page2.asp, you would use the sf Query String variable in the way it is used in Listing 13.6.

LISTING 13.6   Passing Security Information with a Query String

```
1   <!-- #INCLUDE FILE="checkpassword.asp" -->
2   <HTML>
3   <HEAD><TITLE>Password Protected</TITLE></HEAD>
4   <BODY>
5
6   This page is password protected!
7   <p>
8   <a href="test2.asp?<%=sq%>">Next Page</a>
```

```
9
10 </BODY>
11 </HTML>
```

ANALYSIS The `checkpassword.asp` Include file is added to the page in line 1. The `sq` variable is constructed in this file. The `sq` variable is used in line 8 to add the username and password to the hypertext link.

Now, suppose that you have a page that contains an HTML form. In that case, you would need to add hidden fields to the form that contain the username and password. You can do this by using the `sf` variable (see Listing 13.7).

LISTING 13.7 Passing Security Information with Hidden Form Fields

```
1  <!-- #INCLUDE FILE="checkpassword.asp" -->
2  <HTML>
3  <HEAD><TITLE>Password Protected</TITLE></HEAD>
4  <BODY>
5
6  This page is password protected!
7  <p>
8  <form method="post" action="test2.asp">
9  <%=sf%>
10 <input type="submit" value="Next Page with Hidden Field">
11 </form>
12
13 </BODY>
14 </HTML>
```

ANALYSIS The `sf` variable is used in the page contained in Listing 13.7 to add two hidden form fields named username and password. When the form is submitted, these two form fields are automatically passed with the form data.

When using `Query String` and `Form` variables to pass usernames and passwords from page to page, you must be careful to add the variables to every form and every link. If a user clicks on a link that doesn't contain the `Query String`, the username and password won't be passed, and the user will need to login again.

Using Hybrid Authentication

In this section, you'll learn how to combine both HTTP Authentication and database authentication to password protect a Web page. You'll learn how to force a standard password dialog box to appear in a Web page and how to check the username and password that a user enters into the dialog box against a database table.

13

Understanding How Basic Authentication Works

Before going any further, you need to understand how Basic Authentication works in more detail. Here's an overview of what happens when a user requests a page that has been protected with Basic Authentication.

1. You request a page protected with Basic Authentication.
2. The Web server responds with the status code `401 Not Authorized`.
3. The 401 status code forces a password dialog box to appear on your browser. Enter your username and password and click OK.
4. Your browser sends your username and password in a browser header (a request header) named AUTHORIZATION. The AUTHORIZATION header contains your username and password encoded using base64 encoding.
5. The Web server decodes the username and password passed in the AUTHORIZATION header and checks whether they correspond to a valid Windows account.
6. If the username and password are valid, the page is displayed. Otherwise, the Web server sends a 401 status code and the process starts over again.

After a browser has been authenticated at a Web site, the browser will continue to send the AUTHORIZATION header with the username and password every time a page is requested. This is great. This means that you don't have to worry about passing the username and password from page to page.

As you learned in the first part of this chapter, the major drawback of Basic Authentication is that Internet Information Server will only validate the usernames and passwords against Windows accounts. This means that you cannot easily use Basic Authentication when creating an automated registration system.

In this section, you'll learn how to work around this problem. You'll learn how to grab the username and password from the AUTHORIZATION header and validate the username and password against a database table. In order to do this, you will need to learn the following:

- How to force a password dialog box to appear on a browser
- How to grab the AUTHORIZATION header from the browser
- How to decode the AUTHORIATION header so that you can extract the username and password

Forcing a Password Dialog to Appear

You can force a password dialog box to appear by sending a `401 Not Authorized` status code to a browser. The `Response` object has a property named `Status` that provides you with a method of sending a status code. The ASP page in Listing 13.18 forces a password dialog box to appear (This page is included on the book's CD with the name `forcepassword.asp`).

LISTING 13.8   Forcing a Password Dialog Box

```
1  <%
2  auth = TRIM( Request.ServerVariables( "HTTP_AUTHORIZATION" ) )
3  IF auth = ""  THEN
4     Response.Status = "401 Not Authorized"
5     Response.AddHeader "WWW-Authenticate", "Basic realm=""localhost"""
6     Response.End
7  END IF
8  %>
9  <HTML>
10 <HEAD><TITLE>Protected Page</TITLE></HEAD>
11 <BODY>
12
13 The AUTHORIZATION header contains: <%=auth%>
14
15 </BODY>
16 </HTML>
```

ANALYSIS   In line 2, the AUTHORIZATION browser header is retrieved from the `ServerVariables` collection. If the AUTHORIZATION header doesn't have a value, the status code `401 Not Authorized` is sent to the browser. This status code forces a password dialog box to appear. The status code is set in line 4.

In line 5, the `AddHeader` method of the `Response` object is used to add a header named WWW-Authenticate. A browser uses this header to detect what type of authentication to use. In Listing 13.8, a header is sent that causes the browser to use Basic Authentication.

After a user enters a username and password into the password dialog box, the browser will send back the AUTHORIZATION header. If the script above can retrieve the AUTHORIZATION header, it will display the value of the header. For example, if you enter `Bob` for the username and `yellow` for the password, the AUTHORIZATION header will contain the following value:

`Basic Qm9iOnllbGxvdw==`

The first part of the header indicates the authentication method being used. The strange characters that constitute the remainder of the header contain the username and password in base64 encoded form. You'll learn how to decode this header and extract the username and password in the next section.

13

> Do not use Internet Information Server to enable Basic Authentication for the directory that contains the page in Listing 13.8. We are forcing the password dialog box to appear.

Decoding the AUTHORIZATION Header

When a browser sends an AUTHORIZATION header, it sends the header in base64 encoded form. Base64 is an old method of encoding text. It was originally created as part of the MIME standard for sending email attachments with messages.

To extract the username and password from the header, we'll need to write a script to decode base64 encoded text.

> Instead of using a script to decode base64 encoded text, you can use a commercial component. See the AspConv component at www.serverobjects.com. For an extensive list of third-party Active Server Pages components, visit the software section at superexpert at http://asp.superexpert.com/software.

The first step in decoding base64 encoded text is to convert the characters from the ANSI character set to a base 0 character set. We need to map each character to a code from 0 to 65:

- A–Z maps to 0 to 25
- a–z maps to 26 to 51
- 0–9 maps to 52 to 61
- + maps to 62
- / maps to 63

We'll use a `Dictionary` object to create a mapping from the ANSI character set to a base 0 character set. See Listing 13.9.

> The `Dictionary` object is an installable component. You can use it to create a mapping between keys and values. You can enter any type of data that you please for the keys and values including both strings and integers. For example, the keys might be words and the values might be definitions. Or, the keys might be country codes and the values might be full country names.

LISTING 13.9   UUEncoding

```
1  SET UUEncode = Server.CreateObject( "Scripting.Dictionary" )
2  FOR i=0 TO 63
3    SELECT CASE i
4      CASE 0 offset = 65
5      CASE 26 offset = 71
6      CASE 52 offset = -4
7    END SELECT
8    UUEncode( CHR( i + offset) ) = i
9  NEXT
```

ANALYSIS   The script in Listing 13.9 creates an instance of the `Dictionary` object in line 1. A `FOR...NEXT` loop is used to loop through the numbers 0 to 63. The `SELECT...CASE` statement assigns the proper offsets for ANSI character. The `Dictionary` object has ANSI characters for keys and the codes of a base 0 character set as values.

Next, we'll need to unpack each of the characters. When text is base64 encoded, characters that are normally represented in four bytes are compressed into three bytes. For example, the four bytes

```
00aaaaaa 00bbbbbb 00cccccc 00dddddd
```

are compressed into

```
aaaaaabb bbbbcccc ccdddd
```

To decode the text, we need to unpack each group of three bytes back into four bytes. This is accomplished with the `Decode()` function contained in Listing 13.10.

LISTING 13.10   The `Decode()` Function

```
1  Function Decode( theString )
2    For byteGroup = 1 To Len( theString ) Step 4
3      numBytes = 3
4      groupBytes = 0
5      For CharCounter = 0 To 3
6        thisChar = Mid( theString, byteGroup + CharCounter, 1)
7        If thisChar = "=" Then
8          numBytes = numBytes - 1
9          thisByte = 0
10       Else
11         thisByte = UUEncode( thisChar )
12       End If
13       groupBytes = 64 * groupBytes + thisByte
14     Next
15     For k = 1 To numBytes
```

continues

13

LISTING **13.10**   continued

```
16        Select Case k
17          Case 1: thisChar = groupBytes \ 65536
18          Case 2: thisChar = (groupBytes And 65535) \ 256
19          Case 3: thisChar = (groupBytes And 255)
20        End Select
21        Decode = Decode & Chr( thisChar)
22     Next
23   Next
24 End Function
```

> **Note**
>
> I wouldn't have been able to create the scripts in this section without the help of two very valuable articles available on the Internet. For a very elegant implementation of a base64 decoding script, visit the PSTRUH Web site at http://www.pstruh.cz/tips/detpg_Base64.htm.
>
> For general background information on the mechanism of Basic Authentication, see Kevin Flick's article on Self-Authenticating Scripts at http://www.learnasp.com/learn/authenticateself.asp.

Finally, we are ready to extract the username and password from the AUTHORIZATION header. The script in Listing 13.11 retrieves the username and password from a standard password dialog box and compares them against the userlist database table (This page is included on the CD with the name hybrid.asp).

LISTING **13.11**   Hybrid Authentication

```
1   <%
2   SET UUEncode = Server.CreateObject( "Scripting.Dictionary" )
3   FOR i=0 TO 63
4     SELECT CASE i
5       CASE 0 offset = 65
6       CASE 26 offset = 71
7       CASE 52 offset = -4
8     END SELECT
9     UUEncode( CHR( i + offset) ) = i
10  NEXT
11
12  Function Decode( theString )
13    For byteGroup = 1 To Len( theString ) Step 4
14      numBytes = 3
15      groupBytes = 0
16      For CharCounter = 0 To 3
17        thisChar = Mid( theString, byteGroup + CharCounter, 1)
18        If thisChar = "=" Then
19          numBytes = numBytes - 1
```

```
20          thisByte = 0
21        Else
22          thisByte = UUEncode( thisChar )
23        End If
24        groupBytes = 64 * groupBytes + thisByte
25      Next
26
27      For k = 1 To numBytes
28        Select Case k
29          Case 1: thisChar = groupBytes \ 65536
30          Case 2: thisChar = (groupBytes And 65535) \ 256
31          Case 3: thisChar = (groupBytes And 255)
32        End Select
33        Decode = Decode & Chr( thisChar)
34      Next
35    Next
36  End Function
37
38  auth = Request( "HTTP_AUTHORIZATION" )
39  IF auth = "" THEN
40      Response.Status = "401 Not Authorized"
41      Response.AddHeader "WWW-Authenticate", "Basic realm=""localhost"""
42      Response.End
43  END IF
44
45  auth = TRIM( MID( auth, 6 ) )
46  auth = Decode( auth )
47  authSplit = SPLIT( auth, ":" )
48  username = authSplit( 0 )
49  password = authSplit( 1 )
50
51  sqlString = "SELECT user_id FROM userlist " &_
52      "WHERE user_username='" & username & "'" &_
53      "AND user_password='" & password & "'"
54  Set Con = Server.CreateObject( "ADODB.Connection" )
55  Con.Open "userDSN"
56  Set RS = Con.Execute( sqlString )
57  IF RS.EOF THEN
58      Response.Status = "401 Not Authorized"
59      Response.AddHeader "WWW-Authenticate", "Basic realm=""localhost"""
60      Response.End
61  END IF
62  %>
63  <HTML>
64  <HEAD><TITLE>Welcome</TITLE></HEAD>
65  <BODY>
66
67  Welcome <%=username%>!
68
69  </BODY>
70  </HTML>
```

13

> **Note**
>
> Do not enable any form of authentication for the directory that contains hybrid.asp. We are forcing Basic Authentication manually. Only Allow Anonymous Access should be enabled.

ANALYSIS The bulk of Listing 13.11, lines 2–36, is devoted to decoding the username and password contained in the AUTHORIZATION header. In line 38, the AUTHORIZATION header is retrieved from the Request collection. If the AUTHORIZATION header contains no information, the status code 401 is sent to the browser to force a password dialog.

In line 45, the first six characters are stripped from the AUTHORIZATION header. These first six characters contain the plaintext characters BASIC, which indicate the authorization scheme. We already know this, so we get rid of the characters.

In line 46, the AUTHORIZATION header is base64 decoded with the help of the Decode() function. The decoded header will contain the username and password separated by a colon. In lines 47–49, the VBScript SPLIT() function is used to extract the username and password from the header.

In lines 51–56, the username and password are compared against the usernames and passwords contained in the userlist database table. If there are no matches, the status code 401 is sent to the browser to force the password dialog box to appear. Otherwise, the user can view the page.

Summary

In today's lesson, you learned how to create a subscription Web site by implementing three different types of authentication. In the first section, you learned how to use HTTP Authentication. You were given an overview of the three types of authentication supported by Internet Information Server and you learned how to enable authentication for a file, directory, or Web site.

In the next section, you learned how to use database authentication to password protect areas of your Web site. You created a database table named userlist that contains a list of usernames and passwords. You also created an Include file that checks usernames and passwords against the database table.

In the final section, you learned how to create a hybrid authentication system. You learned how to force a password dialog box to appear from within an ASP script. You also learned how to retrieve a username and password entered into the dialog box and compare them against a database table.

Q&A

Q **Three different methods of authentication were discussed in today's lesson. Which method of authentication should I use for my Web site?**

A If you need to create an automated registration system, you should use either database authentication or hybrid authentication. By using a database to store usernames and passwords, you can easily create a system that supports hundreds of thousands of registered users. Storing usernames and passwords in a database also makes it easier to backup the data.

Because you need to setup individual Windows accounts to use HTTP Authentication, this form of authentication is more appropriate for password protecting administrative areas of your Web site. Normally, you will use HTTP Authentication only when you need to setup a small number of user accounts.

Q **Doesn't database authentication place a heavy load on my database server?**

A If every user must be authenticated against the database whenever a page is requested, database authentication can place a heavy load on your database server. However, in the database authentication script you created in today's lesson (checkpassword.asp), Session variables were also used to authenticate users. When a user is authenticated against the database after requesting a password protected page for the first time, a Session variable named LoggedIn is assigned the value Yes. If the user requests additional pages, the Session variable can be checked instead of the database. Of course, if someone is using a browser that doesn't support Session variables, the database must be accessed every time the user requests a new page.

Workshop

The Quiz questions are designed to test your knowledge of the material covered in this chapter. The answers are in Appendix A, "Quiz Answers."

Quiz

1. Can you use HTTP Authentication with the Netscape Navigator browser?
2. Why is it considered a security risk to use Basic Authentication?
3. How can I force a password dialog box to appear on a Web browser?
4. When using Basic Authentication, how is a username and password passed from page to page?

13

DAY **14**

Customizing the Shopping Experience

Today we will customize our customers' shopping experience based on their preferences and buying patterns. To make this project more interesting, we also will allow our customers to review their purchase history with our storefront. Today, you will learn the following:

- Presenting the user with the choice to change his existing registration settings
- Storing those new registration settings in the user database
- Displaying previous purchases
- Determining layout based on customer preferences
- Advertising items your customers would like

Retrieving the Existing User Settings

A user needs to see his settings before he can modify them. Therefore, you need to create a new file, `mypage.asp` to go into the user's database and retrieve that information. In order to continue, we must create a file to display settings, mypage.asp.

Creating mypage.asp

The mypage.asp file is relatively unique among the files you've created thus far. It can both read from the database (to display existing settings) and write to the database (to store the new settings). Generally, the structure thus far has been one file to read and one file to write. To better understand each of the functions performed by mypage.asp, the code will be broken into two different listings. The first bit of relevant code deals with controlling the flow of the site, and is contained in Listing 14.1.

LISTING 14.1   Retrieve Existing User Info

```
1 <!-- #INCLUDE FILE="adovbs.inc" -->
2 <!-- #INCLUDE FILE="storefuncs.asp" -->
3 <%
4 ' Get Product ID
5 productID = TRIM( Request( "pid" ) )
6   ' Get Login Information
7   login = TRIM( Request( "login" ) )
8   IF login <> "" THEN
9       username = TRIM( Request( "username" ) )
10      password = TRIM( Request( "password" ) )
11  ELSE
12      username = TRIM( Request( "newusername" ) )
13      password = TRIM( Request( "newpassword" ) )
14  END IF
15  mypage = TRIM( Request( "mypage" ) )
16  error = TRIM( Request( "error" ) )
17  register = TRIM( Request( "register" ) )
18   If username = "" then
19     username = request.cookies("username")
20     password = request.cookies("password")
21   End If
22 ' Open Database Connection
23  Set Con = Server.CreateObject( "ADODB.Connection" )
24  Con.Open "accessDSN"
25
26   ' Check For Update code
27  IF mypage <> "" AND error = "" THEN
28    updateUser
29  END IF
30  IF register <> "" AND error = "" THEN
31      addUser
32  END IF
33' Get User ID
34 userID =  checkpassword( username, password, Con )
```

```
35 'See if user exists in db, or if user info was ever passed
36 IF userID > 0 THEN
37  SET RS = Con.Execute("SELECT * FROM users WHERE user_ID = "&userid)
38  'Populate string values with existing settings
39     newusername = RS("user_username")
40     newpassword = RS("user_password")
41     email = RS("user_email")
42     street = RS("user_street")
43     city = RS("user_city")
44     state = RS("user_state")
45     zip = RS("user_zip")
46     cctype = RS("user_cctype")
47     ccnumber = RS("user_ccnumber")
48     ccexpires = RS("user_ccexpires")
49     ccname = RS("user_ccname")
50 %>
```

ANALYSIS   This first page is basically the traffic cop of the mypage.asp file. First of all, the page determines if the user has just logged in, created a new user, or updated his settings. Each of these options has a monitor value set in the form that passes the information. For example, if the user had just registered as a new account, the register monitor variable would not be NULL. If the user had just logged in, the login monitor variable would not be NULL. By checking these monitor values, we can determine which data fields we need to plunder in order to get the updated information. If the username is already in memory, or the user just logged in, the page will display the user's current settings with the option to update them. If there is no username available, the page will display the login/register screen. Finally, if the monitor value indicates that the user had updated his settings, the page stores the new settings in the database.

The code in lines 7–16 traps the login monitor value. When login is not NULL, it means we can retrieve the user's settings information and put it in the form for editing.

Next in lines 18–21, we check to see if the username is still empty after trying to get info from the form. If it is, we try and pull the username value from the cookie, just in case it got missed somewhere.

Lines 22–24 are the familiar ADO object instantiations we've seen several times before. Moving on to lines 27–28 we encounter another monitor value check. If mypage is not NULL, that means the user has submitted the update form, and wants his changes added to the database. To accomplish this, the page calls the updateUser subroutine from the storefuncs.asp file.

Lines 26–32 contain the last monitor value check, which tests for new account requests. If register is not NULL, it means that the user has completed the new user form and wants to be added to the database. The page then calls the addUser subroutine from the storefuncs.asp file.

14

Note   For more information on the addUser subroutine, investigate Day 8, "Building the Transaction Databases." updateUser is identical to addUser except that it updates an existing record instead of creating a new one.

Lines 33–35 compare the username and password against entries in the user's table. When both columns match, the query returns the userid of the selected row.

Lines 36–49 do two things. The first two lines check to see if the userid variable is a valid one (that is, greater than 0). If the userid is valid, the page loads all the current user's settings into accessible variable and then loads them into a form, so the user can modify them. If the userid is invalid, we assume that it is for a new or non-logged in user and go straight to the register.asp page.

The actual HTML surrounding the user settings form is identical to that found in register.asp and various other parts of the site, so I won't repeat it here. However, you should take a look at Listing 14.2 and see how the form displays the current settings by inserting variables into the VALUE field of the input tag.

LISTING 14.2   Displaying Current User Information

```
1  <form method="post" action="<%= submitpage%>">
2    <input name="mypage" type="hidden" value="1">
3  <input name="pid" type="hidden" value="<%=productID%>">
5  <font face="Arial" size="2">
6  Change the values below and hit 'Update' to change your personal settings:
7  </font>
8  <font face="Arial" size="2" color="darkgreen">
9  <p><b>Login Information:</b>
10  </font>
11  <font face="Courier" size="2">
12  <br><b>username:</b>
13  <input name="newusername" size=20 maxlength=20
14    value="<%=newusername%>">
15  <br><b>password:</b>
16  <input name="newpassword" size=20 maxlength=20
17    value="<%=newpassword%>">
18  <br><b>email address:</b>
19  <input name="email" size=30 maxlength=75
20    value="<%=email%>">
21  </font>
22  <font face="Arial" size="2" color="darkgreen">
23  <p><b>Address Information:</b>
24  </font>
```

```
25  <font face="Courier" size="2">
26  <br><b>street:</b>
27  <input name="street" size=20 maxlength=50
28   value="<%=street%>">
29  <br><b>city:</b>
30  <input name="city" size=20 maxlength=50
31   value="<%=city %>">
32  <br><b>state:</b>
33  <input name="state" size=20 maxlength=2
34   value="<%=state %>">
35  <br><b>zip:</b>
36  <input name="zip" size=20 maxlength=20
37   value="<%= zip %>">
38  </font>
39  <font face="Arial" size="2" color="darkgreen">
40  <p><b>Payment Information:</b>
41  </font>
42  <font face="Courier" size="2">
43  <br><b>type of credit card:</b>
44  <select name="cctype">
45  <option value="1"
46   <%=SELECTED( cctype, "1" )%> > VISA
47  <option value="2"
48    <%=SELECTED( cctype, "2" )%> >MasterCard
49  </select>
50  <br><b>credit card number:</b>
51  <input name="ccnumber" size=20 maxlength=20
52    value="<%=ccnumber%>">
53  <br><b>credit card expires:</b>
54  <input name="ccexpires" size=20 maxlength=20
55    value="<%=ccexpires%>">
56  <br><b>name on credit card:</b>
57  <input name="ccname" size=20 maxlength=20
58   value="<%=ccname%>">
59  <BR><BR><input type="submit" value="Update">
60  </font>
61  </form>
```

This code takes the variables you assigned at the very beginning of the file and then drops them into input tags. You'll only see this information when you've logged into the site and want to change your settings (see Figure 14.1 to see how mypage.asp appears in a Web browser).

14

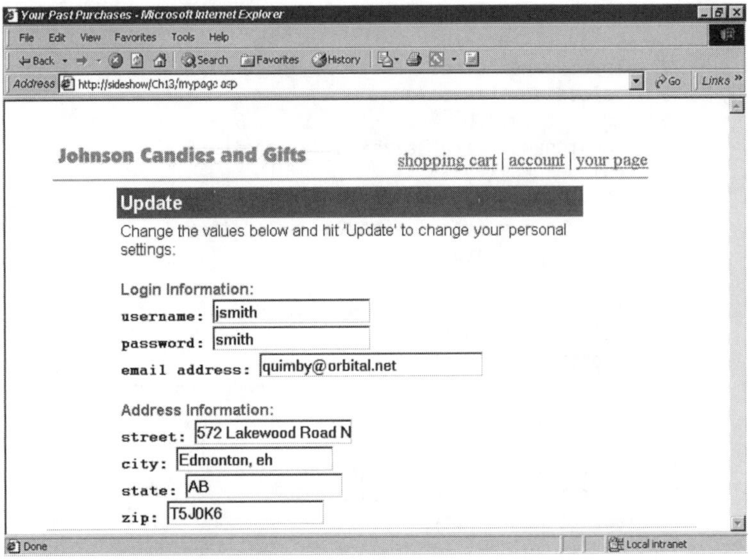

FIGURE 14.1

Changing your user information— `mypage.asp`.

Showing Past Purchases

In the last few weeks, you have built the basic storefront for your E-Commerce Web site. You built the Product Catalog in Day 5, "Building Your Product Catalog," and extended it with the ability for customers to purchase items from our catalog in Day 8. You also have built the ability for customers to view their purchase status, such as whether their item had shipped, for example. Today you will add the ability for your customers to review their past purchases. This facility will be straightforward and will focus only on successful purchases that the customer has made.

The purchases that a customer makes are recorded, as you should remember, in the Orders table of our database. The Orders table is structured as follows:

- `order_id`—The unique numeric identifier for each order recorded.
- `order_productID`—The numeric product identifier for the item purchased by the customer. This identifier is based on a value in the Products table.
- `order_quantity`—The total number of items (as identified by the previous column) purchased by the customer.
- `order_userID`—The numeric identifier that represents the customer, as determined from the Users table.
- `order_entrydate`—The date and time that the purchase order was made on our Web site.

- order_status—A numeric status identifier that indicates the state of the customer's order.

- order_shipdate—the date and time that the customer's purchase order was shipped.

To review, the numeric status codes found in the order_status column are

- 0—Pending

- 1—Credit Card Declined

- 2—Not in Stock

- 3—Shipped

When looking to display previous purchases to our customers, we can assume that any item identified as Shipped and has a date and time specified in the order_shipdate column as a complete order. (After all, we're not going to charge someone for something that isn't in stock, are we?) Creating a page to display only items that have been shipped to the customer will prove to be very easy, by adapting the code we created in Day 11, "Working with Credit Cards," to allow customers to view their order's status. Listing 14.3 contains the code for a new page that we will add to our site, pastpurchases.asp. We will link to this page from the showorders.asp page.

LISTING 14.3 Display List of Previous Orders

```
1 <!-- #INCLUDE FILE="adovbs.inc" -->
2 <!-- #INCLUDE FILE="storefuncs.asp" -->
3 <%
4 ' Get Login Information
5 username = TRIM( Request( "username" ) )
6 password = TRIM( Request( "password" ) )
7 ' Open Database Connection
8 Set Con = Server.CreateObject( "ADODB.Connection" )
9 Con.Open "accessDSN"
10 ' Get User ID
11 userID = checkpassword( username, password, Con )
12 sqlString = "Select orders.*, product_name, product_price " &_
13   "from orders, products " &_
14   "WHERE order_productid=product_id " &_
15   "AND order_userid=" & userID & " " &_
16   "AND order_status=3 " &_
17   "ORDER BY order_entrydate DESC"
18 SET RS = Con.Execute( sqlString )
19 %>
20 <html>
21 <head><title>Your Past Purchases</title></head>
```

14

continues

LISTING 14.3   continued

```
22 <body>
23 <center>
24 <font face="Arial" size=3 color="darkgreen">
25 <b><%= username %>'s past purchases:</b>
26 </font>
27 <br> 
28 <%
29 IF RS.EOF THEN
30 %>
31 <b>You have not placed any orders</b>
32 <%
33 ELSE
34 %>
35 <table cellpadding=4 cellspacing=0
36  bgcolor="lightyellow" border=1>
37 <tr>
38   <th>Order ID</th>
39   <th>Order Date</th>
40   <th>Product Name</th>
41   <th>Order Total</th>
42   <th>Order Shipped Date</th>
43 </tr>
44 <%
45 WHILE NOT RS.EOF
46 %>
47 <tr>
48   <td>
49   <%=RS( "order_id" )%>
50   </td>
51   <td>
52   <%=RS( "order_entrydate" )%>
53   </td>
54   <td>
55   <%=RS( "product_name" )%>
56   </td>
57   <td>
58    $ <%= (RS( "order_quantity" ) * RS( "product_price" ) )%>
59   </td>
60   <td>
61   <small>
62   <%=showOrderStatus( RS( "order_status" ), RS( "order_shipdate" ) )%>
63   </small>
64   </td>
65 </tr>
66 <%
67 RS.MoveNext
68 WEND
69 %>
70 </table>
71 <%
```

```
72 END IF
73 %>
74 <p>
75 <form action="account.asp" id=form1 name=form1>
76 <input type="submit" value="View Current Order Status"
   ➥ id=submit1 name=submit1>
77 </form>
78 <form action="default.asp" id=form1 name=form1>
79 <input type="submit" value="Continue Shopping" id=submit1 name=submit1>
80 </form>
81 </center>
82 </body>
83 </html>
```

ANALYSIS This page operates almost identically to the showorders.asp page. On lines 1 and 2, we use the #INCLUDE directive to insert the adovbs.inc file (which contains the standard ADO constants) and the storefuncs.asp file (which contains the standard functions that we have been using throughout our site). On lines 5 and 6, we retrieve the customer's username and password. Next, we ensure that we are retrieving information for the correct user by executing the checkpassword function on line 11.

On lines 12–17, we build the SQL query to retrieve any records from the Orders table where the order_status is equal to 3 (indicating a Shipped Order) and the order_userid is equal to the current user. We also query the Products table for the product_name and product_price for each item that the customer has purchased. To ensure that the list makes chronological sense to the customer, we set an ORDER BY clause on line 16 stipulating that we want the records displayed in a descending fashion based on the order_entrydate column.

After executing the query on line 18, we're ready to determine if any records were returned by the query on line 29. Testing to see if the EOF property of the recordset is TRUE, indicating no results, line 29 starts an IF..THEN statement. The possible actions are

- If no results are returned (EOF returns TRUE), a message is displayed to the customer indicating that he hasn't placed any orders (line 31).
- If records are returned, a table is built containing rows that represent each order (lines 35–70)

On line 45, we open a WHILE..WEND statement that will loop through each record in the recordset and build a table row. Of note in building the rows are lines 58 and 62. On line 58, we calculate the total cost of the order to the customer by multiplying the order_quantity column value found in the Orders table against the product_price column value found in the Products table. On Line 62, just as we did with the showorders.asp page, we call upon the showOrderStatus subroutine to display the order's status (which should always be "Shipped on ...") with the shipping date.

14

Finally, on lines 75–77, we build a new form button that allows our customers to switch from viewing their shipped orders to their current order's status, via the `account.asp` page.

Now that we have built the `pastpurchases.asp` page, we need to provide a link for customers to view it. In this example, we will provide a link on the `showorders.asp` page, allowing customers to switch between their previously shipped orders and their current pending orders. To do so, follow these steps:

1. Open the `showorders.asp` page in your editor.

2. In the `showorders.asp` page, locate the following lines:

```
<form action="default.asp">
<input type="submit" value="Continue Shopping">
</form>
```

3. Insert the following code above the indicated lines:

```
<form action="pastpurchases.asp">
<input name="username" type="hidden" value="<%=username%>">
<input name="password" type="hidden" value="<%=password%>">
<input type="submit" value="View Past Purchases">
</form>
```

4. Save your changes to this page.

Your customers can now alternate back and forth between their current orders status and their past purchases. The `pastpurchases.asp` page is illustrated in Figure 14.2.

FIGURE 14.2

The `pastpurchases.asp` *page.*

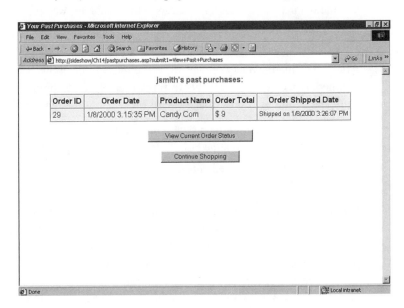

Advertising Items Your Customers Would Like

The next step in souping up our site is to advertise products that are of interest to our customers. Targeted advertising is of immense value to your business because items of interest to your customers will be displayed when they visit your site. You can also build an advertising system that displays certain products based on the customer's purchase history; however, today we're going to allow the customers to select what categories are of interest to them from our catalog, and we will use that information to determine what will be advertised to them.

Our method of determining what to feature to our customers requires the completion of following tasks:

- Update the Users table to store the customer's favorite categories.

- Build a new page, `favorites.asp`, that will be used for customers to select what types of products they are interested in (Novelties versus Chocolate Solids, for example).

- Build a second page, `savefavorites.asp`, that will store the favorites for the customer after they are submitted from the `favorites.asp` page.

- Update the `features.asp` inclusion file that will be used to target what products are featured for the customers based on their selected favorite categories.

- Update the `default.asp` page to personalize its content according to who is visiting.

Updating the Users Table for Favorites

Before we can build any pages for our customers, we need to update the Users table to store their favorites. To store the customer's preferences, we will add one new column to the Users table:

- `user_favorites`—a text column that will store a comma separated list of categories that the customer has identified as her favorites. You should provide this column with a default value of `"NONE"`. (Remember to add this default value for all the existing rows in the users database table.) You will also need to assign the field size of this column the value `255`.

Using Microsoft Access, add this new column to the User table. The `user_favorites` column will store the full-text name of the category, as it is found in the Products table. This allows us to quickly retrieve the categories for our products without converting from a numeric identifier. This structure also allows us to add new categories without adverse effect to our code.

14

Building the `favorites.asp` Page

Our next step is to build the page that customers will use to alter their favorite categories of products. This page will query the Products table to determine the available product categories and present them to the customer as selectable checkboxes. The customer will be able to select (or deselect) each category as they prefer. The `favorites.asp` page will also retrieve the customer's current favorites each time it is loaded to improve usability. The code that comprises the `favorites.asp` page can be found in Listing 14.4 (It's also included with the CD that accompanies this book.)

LISTING 14.4   The `favorites.asp` Page

```
1  <!-- #INCLUDE FILE="adovbs.inc" -->
2  <!-- #INCLUDE FILE="storefuncs.asp" -->
3  <%
4  ' Get Login Information
5  username = TRIM( Request( "username" ) )
6  password = TRIM( Request( "password" ) )
7  ' Open Database Connection
8  Set Con = Server.CreateObject( "ADODB.Connection" )
9  Con.Open "accessDSN"
10 '  Get User ID
11 userID =  checkpassword( username, password, Con )
12 ' Retrieve the existing user favorites and split them into an array
13 arrFavorites = retrieveFavorites
14 arrFavorites = split(arrFavorites, ",")
15 %>
16 <html>
17 <head><title>Pick Your Favorites</title></head>
18 <body>
19 <center>
20 <font face="Arial" size=3 color="darkgreen">
21 <b><%= username %>, pick your favorites:</b>
22 </font>
23 <br> 
24 <table cellpadding=4 cellspacing=0
25   bgcolor="lightyellow" border=1>
26 <tr>
27    <td>
28     
29    </td>
30    <td>
31    <B>Category</B>
32    </td>
33 </tr>
34 <form action="savefavorites.asp" name=frmFavorites method=Post>
35 <input name="username" type="hidden" value="<%=username%>">
36 <input name="password" type="hidden" value="<%=password%>">
```

```
37 <%
38 Set catRS = Server.CreateObject( "ADODB.Recordset" )
39 catRS.ActiveConnection = Con
40 sqlString = "SELECT DISTINCT product_category FROM Products "
41 sqlString = sqlString & "WHERE product_status=1 "
42 sqlString = sqlString & "ORDER BY product_category"
43 catRS.Open sqlString
44 %>
45 <% WHILE NOT catRS.EOF %>
46 <tr>
47    <td>
48    <INPUT type="checkbox"
49    <%
50    ' Check to see if the current item is already a favorite
51    ' If so, set the checkbox to CHECKED
52    If UBound(arrFavorites) > 0 Then
53       For i = 0 to (UBound(arrFavorites) - 1)
54          If arrFavorites(i) = catRS( "product_category" ) Then
55             Response.Write(" CHECKED ")
56          End If
57       Next
58    End If
59    %>
60    name="<%=catRS( "product_category" )%>">
61    </td>
62    <td>
63    <%=catRS( "product_category" )%>
64    </td>
65 </tr>
66 <%
67 catRS.MoveNext
68 WEND
69 %>
70 </table>
71 <% catRS.Close %>
72 <p>
73 <input type="submit" value="Save Your Favorites" name=submit1>
74 </form>
75 </center>
76 </body>
77 </html>
```

ANALYSIS Lines 1–9 should look familiar from our other pages in the site. As usual, we are including our standard function include files and then retrieving the current customer's username and password for validation on line 11. On line 13, we call a new function that we will build in just a moment, retrieveFavorites. This function will retrieve the current customer's favorites from the database as a comma separated list of categories (that is, "category1, category2, category3"). We then use the Split function on line 14 to turn the comma separated string into an array named arrFavorites.

14

Lines 38–43 execute a SQL query against the Products table to retrieve a distinct list of the product categories available. This recordset will be used to build our form elements. On line 45 we test to see if any results were returned using the EOF property. If results are returned from the query (as they should), we then begin to build the rows for each product category on lines 46–65.

Each row is comprised of two cells—the first is an INPUT field for the check box. Using the arrFavorites array, lines 52–58 loop through each element in the array to see if the category in the array element matches the current category in the recordset. If they match, we use the Response.Write method on line 55 to add a CHECKED attribute to the checkbox field, indicating that the customer has previously identified this category as a favorite category. The name attribute of the check box is set to the category name, on line 60, and will be used by the savefavorites.asp page to determine which check boxes the user selected.

This process repeats itself for each category returned by the query, providing the customer with a real-time list of categories within the Products table. On line 73, we provide a Submit button that will submit the form to the savefavorites.asp page that was specified by the <FORM> tag on line 34.

Before we move on to the savefavorites.asp page, we need to add the retrieveFavorites function used on line 13. Without doing so, any attempt to open this page will result in an error. The retrieveFavorites function is a simple set of code that you should add to the storefuncs.asp file. The code for this function is shown in Listing 14.5.

LISTING 14.5   The retrieveFavorites Function

```
1 FUNCTION retrieveFavorites
2    sqlString = "SELECT user_Favorites FROM users " &_
3      "WHERE user_username='" & Request( "username" ) & "'"
4    SET RS = Con.Execute( sqlString )
5  IF RS.EOF THEN
6    strFavorites = "NONE"
7  ELSE
8    strFavorites = RS("user_favorites")
9  END IF
10     retrieveFavorites = strFavorites
11 END FUNCTION
```

ANALYSIS   This 11 line function executes a simple SELECT query against the User table to retrieve the user_favorites column for the current user. The value is stored to a temporary variable (strFavorites) and is returned to the originating statement (in this case, line 13 of Listing 14.4). Notice that if the username of the current user cannot be retrieved from the Request collection (which includes the Cookies collection), the SQL statement will not retrieve any rows. In that case, the `strFavorites` variable will have the value NONE. The `favorites.asp` page is shown in Figure 14.3.

FIGURE 14.3

The favorites.asp *page.*

Building the `savefavorites.asp` Page

The second step in allowing our customers to assign their preference to our product categories is to store their selections. After completing the form provided in the `favorites.asp` page, the `savefavorites.asp` page is called to deal with the checkboxes that were selected. The code for `savefavorites.asp` can be found in Listing 14.6.

LISTING 14.6 The savefavorites.asp Page

```
1 <!-- #INCLUDE FILE="adovbs.inc" -->
2 <!-- #INCLUDE FILE="storefuncs.asp" -->
3 <%
4     ' Retrieve the selected items
5     For i = 3 to (Request.Form.Count - 1)
6         arrItems = arrItems & Request.Form.Key(i) & ","
7     Next
8
9     ' Provide Default Value
10    IF TRIM( arrItems ) = "" THEN arrItems = "NONE"
11
```

14

continues

LISTING 14.6   continued

```
12    ' Get Login Information
13    username = TRIM( Request( "username" ) )
14    password = TRIM( Request( "password" ) )
15     ' Open Database Connection
16     Set Con = Server.CreateObject( "ADODB.Connection" )
17     Con.Open "accessDSN"
18     ' Get User ID
19     userID = checkpassword( username, password, Con )
20     ' Update the user's favorites
21    updateFavorites(arrItems)
22     Response.Redirect("default.asp")
23 %>
```

ANALYSIS   On line 5 of Listing 14.6, we begin a For..Next loop through the number of form items (checkboxes) returned from the previous page. The Request.Form.Count method returns the total number of form elements passed from the favorites.asp page. However, this also includes the Submit button, the username, and password fields as part of the form, thus we remove 3 from the count to only include the checkboxes from the form. The For..Next statement builds a comma separated list for the selected categories, which are then stored into the database using the updateFavorites subroutine on line 21. We will create this subroutine in just a moment. Finally, on line 22 we redirect the customer back to the default.asp page after storing the values, thereby never displaying the savefavorites.asp page to the customer's browser.

The updateFavorites subroutine needs to be added to the storefuncs.asp function file before the savefavorites.asp page will function. The code for the updateFavorites subroutine can be found in Listing 14.7.

LISTING 14.7   The updateFavorites Subroutine

```
1 SUB updateFavorites( strFavorites )
2    ' Update user information in the database
3    sqlString = "UPDATE users SET " &_
4    "user_favorites='" & fixQuotes( strFavorites ) & "' " &_
5    "WHERE user_id=" & userID
6    Con.Execute sqlString
7 END SUB
```

ANALYSIS   On lines 3–5, we build the UPDATE SQL query that is used to update the current user's Users table record with an up-to-date user_favorites column that represents their selections on the previous page. The SQL query is then executed on line 6, and the subroutine returns to line 22 of Listing 14.6.

Updating the `featured.asp` Page

In our existing `default.asp` page, we call on the `featured.asp` page to randomly display featured items on our site's main page. To personalize this for the customer's favorite product categories, we need to update the `featured.asp` page to display random items from the customer's selected categories. If the customer hasn't selected any categories, however, we still want to use the existing method of a random selection of products.

Open the `featured.asp` page in your editor and locate the following line of code:

```
SET Featured = Con.Execute( sqlString )
```

We'll replace every line of code above the indicted line. The complete code for the modified version of `featured.asp` is contained in Listing 14.8.

LISTING 14.8 The Updated `featured.asp` Code

```
1 <%
2 Randomize
3 CONST numFeatured = 3
4 ' Retrieve the customer's favorites and split them into an array
5 arrFavorites = retrieveFavorites
6 arrFavorites = Left(arrFavorites, Len(arrFavorites) - 1)
7 arrFavorites = split(arrFavorites, ",")
8
9 ' If the customer has favorites, randomly choose one category
10 ' to feature from
11 If UBound(arrFavorites) > 0 Then
12     intCategory = Int((((UBound(arrFavorites)) * Rnd) + 1)
13     strCategory = arrFavorites(intCategory)
14     Response.Write("Now featured from our <I>" & strCategory &
➡ "</I> selection:</p>")
15     ' Build the featured products query with the category
16     sqlString = "SELECT product_id, product_picture, product_name,
➡ product_briefDesc " &_
17     "FROM Products WHERE product_featured = 1 " &_
18     "AND product_status=1 " &_
19     "AND product_category='" & Trim(strCategory) & "' " & _
20     "ORDER BY product_name "
21 Else
22     ' Build the featured products query to query all categories
23     sqlString = "SELECT product_id, product_picture, product_name,
➡product_briefDesc " &_
24     "FROM Products WHERE product_featured = 1 " &_
25     "AND product_status=1 " &_
26     "ORDER BY product_name "
27 End If
28 SET Featured = Con.Execute( sqlString )
```

14

continues

LISTING 14.8   continued

```
29 IF NOT Featured.EOF THEN
30  featuredArray = Featured.GetRows()
31 Featured.Close
32
33 ' Display Featured Products
34 topFeatured =  UBOUND( featuredArray, 2 ) + 1
35 skip =  topFeatured  / numFeatured
36 IF topFeatured <= numFeatured THEN skip = 1
37 %>
38 <table width="350" border=0
39  cellpadding=5 cellspacing=0>
40 <%
41 FOR i = 0 TO topFeatured - 1 STEP skip
42   offset = RND * ( skip - 1 )
43   productID = featuredArray( 0, i + offset )
44   productPicture = featuredArray( 1, i + offset )
45   productName = featuredArray( 2, i + offset )
46   productBriefDesc = featuredArray( 3, i + offset )
47 %>
48 <tr>
49   <td>
50   <% IF productPicture <> "?????" THEN %>
51 <IMG SRC="<%=productPicture%>"
52   HSPACE=4 VSPACE=4 BORDER=0 align="center">
53 <% END IF %>
54 </td>
55 <td>
56 <a href="product.asp?pid=<%=productID%>">
57 <b><%=productName%></b></a>
58 <br><%=productBriefDesc%>
59 <br><a href="product.asp?pid=<%=productID%>">
60 get more information</a>
61 </td>
62 </tr>
63 <tr>
64  <td colspan=2 align="center">
65   
66  </td>
67 </tr>
68 <%
69 NEXT
70 %>
71 </table>
72 <%
73 END IF
74 %>
```

ANALYSIS This code is not all that dissimilar from the original `featured.asp` page. The new additions all pertain to retrieving and acting on the current user's favorite categories. On line 5, we use our `retrieveFavorites` function again to determine the current user's favorite categories. We store the categories as a comma separated list in the database, so on line 6 we remove the trailing comma from the string. The string is then converted into an array (`arrFavorites`) on line 7 using the VBScript `Split` function.

On line 11 we test to see if the current user has selected any favorites by determining the size of the `arrFavorites` array. If the array contains at least one value, a random category is selected from the array on lines 12–13. The category is then displayed on line 14, and then used to populate the SQL `SELECT` query that will retrieve items from the Products table on lines 16–20.

If the customer hasn't specified any favorites, a separate SQL query is generated on lines 23–26 that carries out a general query against the Products table for featured items, just as with our original `featured.asp` page.

The rest of our `featured.asp` page is untouched, lines 28–74, leaving the functionality the same as before.

Updating the `default.asp` Page

Before we can put our updated `featured.asp` to use, we need to update the `default.asp` page to set the stage for our changes in the `featured.asp` file. Our changes to the `default.asp` page will be minor cosmetic changes, such as a greeting to our customer, and the current date and time. Locate the following line in the `default.asp` page:

```
<% IF cat = "Home" THEN %>
```

Just above the identified line, insert the following line of code:

```
<b><%= formatDateTime( now(), vbLongDate ) %> - Welcome Back <%= username
➥%>!</b><br>
```

This displays the current date and time and welcomes the customer back by name just above the featured items.

The next step is for us to provide a link to the `favorites.asp` page, allowing customers to select their favorite categories. Locate the following lines in the `default.asp` page:

```
<!-- #INCLUDE FILE="ProductList.asp" -->
<% END IF %>
```

Just below that line, add the following code:

```
<% IF Request.Cookies( "username" ) <> "" THEN %>
<a href="favorites.asp">Pick your favorite kind of candies!</a>
<% END IF %>
```

14

Finally, you'll need to check whether the `storefuncs.asp` file is included in the `default.asp` page. If not, add the following line to the top of the `default.asp` file:

```
<!-- #INCLUDE FILE="storefuncs.asp" -->
```

The new `default.asp` page can be seen in Figure 14.4.

FIGURE 14.4

The updated main page—default.asp.

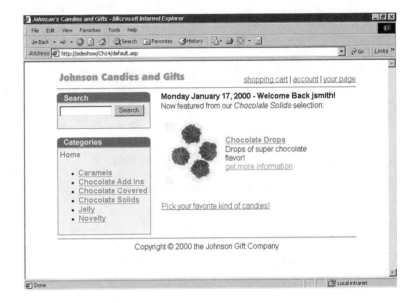

Summary

Today we outlined how to enhance the Web site with some useful features to improve its usability for your customers. First, we created a page that allows customers to review their past purchases. This page built off of the functionality that was created to allow customers to check on the status of their existing orders. Secondly, we added the ability to target the advertisement of items based on a customer's preferences. Using these preferences, the site can then determine what is of interest to the customer and ensure that the items that are most likely to sell to that customer are displayed first.

Q&A

Q Why does the `default.asp` page sometimes not display any featured items?

A This is based on the `product_featured` column in the Products table and the `featured.asp` file. By default, the `featured.asp` file only queries for items in the Products table that have been identified as items that you want to promote or feature. This is done by specifying a value of 1 in the `product_featured` column. You need to be sure that there are featured items for each product category, or you potentially won't be displaying anything to the customer.

Another option is to assume that you want to promote any item that is of interest to a customer based on the favorite categories. To do so, you could remove the `product_featured=1` qualification in the SQL query.

Q What happens if I remove a product category from the Products table, but a customer has marked it as a favorite?

A Nothing, really. When the customer visits the site, he might attempt to query for products in a category that doesn't exist. In that case, no items would be returned and nothing would be displayed to the customer. If the customer returns to the `favorites.asp` page, the category will be gone as well.

Workshop

The Quiz and Exercise questions are designed to test your knowledge of the material covered in this chapter. The answers are in Appendix A, "Quiz Answers."

Quiz

1. What purpose does the `retrieveFavorites` function serve?
2. Why don't we store product categories as numeric identifiers in our example?

Exercise

Currently, our site only features items that are of interest to a customer based on their favorite selections. Try adding to our site a display of favorites based on the past purchases of our customer.

14

WEEK 2

In Review

This week, you finished building your online store. In the beginning of the week, on Days 8 and 9, you learned two methods of creating a virtual shopping cart. Next, on Day 10, you learned how to enable a customer to check out the products in their shopping cart and complete an order.

Later in the week, on Day 11, you learned how to process credit card transactions with ASP scripts. You learned how to use CyberCash to authorize and settle credit card transactions.

Next, you learned how to enable customers to track their orders. You created a Web page that customers can use to check the status of their orders. You also learned how to enable customers to compare shipping rates for shipping packages from your store to their home.

Finally, at the end of the week, you learned how to create a subscription Web site. You learned how to create a user registration system and password protect pages on your Web site so that the pages can be viewed only by paying customers.

Bonus Project

Creating a Transactional Customer Feedback Form

In this week's bonus project, you'll modify the customer feedback form that you created in last week's bonus project so that it uses an Active Server Pages transaction. In the lesson on Day 10, "Checking Out", you learned about the advantages of using an Active Server Pages transaction. By using a transaction, you can create a subroutine that automatically executes if any errors are encountered in an ASP page.

If a customer submits his feedback through the customer feedback form and an error is encountered, an emergency customer support phone number will be displayed. The idea is that if your Web server is in such a sorry state that a customer cannot even leave feedback, you'll want to know this as quickly as possible. The emergency customer support phone number is displayed only if something goes seriously wrong.

You'll remember from last week's bonus project that the customer feedback pages rely on the following database table (named feedback):

- feedback_id—an AutoNumber field that uniquely identifies each row in the table.
- feedback_email—a Text field that contains the customer's email address.
- feedback_comment—a Memo field that contains the text of the customer's feedback.
- feedback_entrydate—a Date/Time field that automatically contains the date the feedback is entered. This field should have a default value of NOW().

A customer submits his feedback through an ASP page named feedback.asp. This page contains a simple HTML form with no ASP scripts. The customer feedback form is contained in Listing BP2.1 (It's the same page as used in last week's bonus project).

LISTING BP2.1   The Customer Feedback Form

```
1  <HTML>
2  <HEAD><TITLE>Customer Feedback</TITLE></HEAD>
3  <BODY>
4
5  Thank you for leaving customer feedback on our Web site.
6  <br>Please enter your feedback in the form below:
7
8
9  <FORM METHOD="post" ACTION="saveFeedback.asp">
10 <P><B>Your Email Address:</B>
11 <BR><INPUT NAME="email" size="50" maxlength="255">
12 <P><B>Your Feedback:</B>
```

```
13 <BR><TEXTAREA NAME="comment" COLS=50 ROWS=4
14   WRAP="Virtual"></TEXTAREA>
15 <P><INPUT TYPE="submit" VALUE="Submit Feedback">
16 </FORM>
17
18 </BODY>
19 </HTML>
```

When a customer submits the customer feedback form, the data is submitted to the save-feedback.asp page. The savefeedback.asp page has been modified in this bonus project to use an Active Server Pages transaction. The new version of the savefeedback.asp page is contained in Listing BP2.2.

LISTING BP2.2 The Transactional Save Feedback Page

```
1  <%@ TRANSACTION=REQUIRED %>
2  <%
3  Response.Buffer = TRUE
4
5  SUB OnTransactionAbort
6    Response.Clear
7    %>
8    <HTML>
9    <HEAD><TITLE>Problem</TITLE></HEAD>
10   <BODY>
11
12   <B>An error was encountered while submitting your feedback.</B>
13   <BR>Please call our customer support number at:
14   <BLOCKQUOTE>
15     (555) 555-8989
16   </BLOCKQUOTE>
17
18   </BODY>
19   </HTML>
20   <%
21 END SUB
22
23 FUNCTION fixQuotes( theString )
24 fixQuotes = REPLACE( theString, "'", "''" )
25 END FUNCTION
26
27 email = TRIM( Request( "email" ) )
28 comment = TRIM( Request( "comment" ) )
29 IF email <> "" AND comment <> "" THEN
30   Set Con = Server.CreateObject( "ADODB.Connection" )
31   Con.Open "accessDSN"
32   sqlString = "INSERT INTO feedback ( feedback_email, feedback_comment ) " &_
```

continues

LISTING BP2.2 continued

```
33    "VALUES ('" & fixQuotes( email ) & "','" & fixQuotes( comment ) & "')"
34  Con.Execute sqlString
35 END IF
36 %>
36 <HTML>
37 <HEAD><TITLE>Save Feedback</TITLE></HEAD>
38 <BODY>
39
40 <B>Thank you for submitting your feedback!</B>
41
42 </BODY>
43 </HTML>
```

ANALYSIS Several changes have been made to the savefeedback.asp page to support a transaction. In line 1, the @TRANSACTION directive has been added to the script. Next, in line 3, page buffering is enabled. Buffering the page is necessary because we don't want an error message displayed if an error is encountered. Instead, the contents of the page will be cleared, and the customer support phone number will be displayed.

Lines 5–21 contain the subroutine that is triggered if an error occurs. The OnTransactionAbort subroutine clears the error message with the Clear method of the Response object and displays the customer support phone number.

You can test the savefeedback.asp by introducing an error into the script. Just stick blah.blah within a script in the page and attempt to submit the customer feedback form. The customer support phone number should be displayed.

WEEK 3

At A Glance

In this final week, you'll learn several methods of maintaining and promoting your commercial Web site. You'll begin by learning how to safeguard your Web site from malicious users. You'll learn how to use the security features of the Web server and operating system to secure your Web site from anonymous hackers.

16

Next, you'll learn how to maintain your Web site by taking advantage of several debugging techniques. You'll learn how to use Microsoft Visual InterDev's integrated debugger. You'll also learn how to create a standard library of debugging functions that you can use to monitor and maintain your Active Server Pages.

Later in the week, you'll learn how to administer your Web site over the Internet. You'll learn how to use a Web browser to administer your Web server. You'll also learn how to use the FTP service to manage your Web site's files remotely.

Next, you'll learn how to promote your Web site through email marketing. You'll learn how to use the Collaboration Data Objects for Windows NT Server (CDO for NTS) to send email from an ASP script. You'll learn how to use the CDO for NTS to send batches of personalized email to promote your site.

You'll also learn how to maintain your Web site by analyzing your Web server's log files. An overview of the different log file formats will be presented. You'll learn how to extract and analyze the information from the log files to monitor the performance of your Web site.

Finally, you'll learn how to display banner advertisements at your Web site and generate revenue. You'll learn how to promote your Web site and use the Ad Rotator component to display advertisements.

DAY **15**

Securing Your Store

With a physical store, gaining a customer's trust is a primary step to a successful business, and one key way to earn this is by showing your customer that you have maximized store security. You do that by establishing your business in fixed locations, hiring trustworthy people, posting (and honoring) store hours, and keeping private information locked up. Businesses that don't demonstrate their store security might find that people trust them less—for example, consumers typically don't buy expensive diamond rings from traveling vendors at flea markets.

When you visit other E-Commerce Web sites, claims about security often figure prominently. You can use similar security cues to help give your customers confidence in you and your site. Without that confidence, customers cannot submit personal information, such as their credit card number, address, or telephone number. Today you will learn the following ways to add security features and security cues to your Web site:

- Registering your own domain
- Making your server more secure
- Protecting your users' private information with SSL

- Protecting your database
- Registering with the Better Business Bureau Reliability program
- Establishing a privacy policy and joining a privacy seal program
- Reviewing the Better Business Bureau's Children's Advertising Review Unit guidelines

Registering Your Own Domain

Many companies offer free Web hosting with a complicated domain name like `http://www.hostingservice.com/Neighborhood/WallaWalla/~yourplace`. Just as a physical store has its own address, your Web store should have its own Web address. As you most likely know by now, you can choose the part of your address that's to the left of the `.com` by *registering a domain*.

Domain Names and Marketing

When you open a retail business, you usually try to put it on a heavily trafficked street. The cyberspace equivalent of a good retail location is a domain name that clearly describes your business. You've probably read a lot lately about the land rush for domain names. Unlike the physical world, regardless of the quality of the location, registering a domain name for the first time is the same, inexpensive price. So in the last few years, folks have been registering as many domain names as they can think of. Because of this, you might find that all the domain names you prefer are taken.

One solution to this problem is to register your Web site in another country. The domain that ends in `.com` belongs to the United States; other countries have their own domains that end in their two-letter country abbreviation (for example, domains registered in Canada end in `.ca`, and those registered in Great Britain end in `.uk`). Larger countries usually require companies registering in their country domains to have an office in their country; however, many smaller, poorer countries have made their domains available for companies located anywhere in the world.

Technically, these foreign domain names are just as good as the domains that end in `.com`; unfortunately, they often aren't considered as prestigious. If you can't get your first choice of domain name, you'll have to decide for yourself whether it's better to have a `.com` domain name that's harder to remember, or a foreign domain name that's easier to remember. If you decide that you want to use a foreign domain name, you can register it by visiting international Web registrars like one of the following:

```
http://www.alldomains.com
```

```
http://www.register.com
```

If you decide you'd rather have one of your first choices in .com, and it's registered to someone else, you can try to buy your domain name of choice. You can do this by sending an email directly to the owner of the domain or by going through a domain name brokerage. Finding the email address of a domain name owner can be a bit complicated. A good place to start is http://www.internic.net/whois.html. Remember, though—just like good real estate, good domain names vary widely in price on the secondary market. Prices for domain names in the secondary market have recently ranged from hundreds to millions of dollars.

You can register your domain name directly through most good Internet service providers. You will want to ask your ISP to point at least two domain names to your Web server's IP address: *yourdomain.com* and www.yourdomain.com.

Note   We are using *yourdomain.com* as a placeholder for the domain name you actually choose for your Web site.

Registering Your Domain Name Yourself

If you're a committed do-it-yourselfer, you can register a domain name by visiting a *domain name registrar*, an organization that keeps track of which domain names go with which Web addresses. Recent changes to the domain naming policy have deregulated the price of domain names, so it can pay to shop around. The current list of domain name registrars is available at http://www.internic.net/alpha.html. The steps involved in registering and implementing a domain name are quite complicated, and beyond the scope of this book.

Caution   When asking your ISP to register your domain, ask them to point the DNS for the email for your new domain to your email server. If you don't already have an email server, a good ISP can forward all the email sent to any address in your domain to a single email address.

Your domain name will become your company's identity, so you want to make sure that when people send mail to you@yourdomain.com, it can be delivered and answered.

After your ISP has registered your DNS entries, you will want to change the name of your Web server to match by following these steps:

1. Bring up the Control Panel by selecting Start, Settings, Control Panel.

2. The system will open the Control Panel. Double-click the icon labeled Network.

3. Click the Protocols tab (see Figure 15.1).

FIGURE 15.1

The Network Protocols control panel.

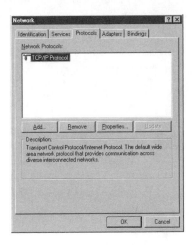

4. Double-click the line labeled TCP/IP Protocol.

5. Click the DNS tab.

6. Change the Host Name to www and the Domain to yourdomain.com (see Figure 15.2).

FIGURE 15.2

Changing the host name and domain.

Making Your Server More Secure

Operating system security is an extremely complex and detailed subject that is, for the most part, beyond the scope of this book. There are, however, a few simple things you can do to help make your Web server more resilient.

Outsourcing Your Operations

A much easier way to make keeping your Web server secure and reliable is to outsource your Web server operations to your ISP. Many ISPs are now offering complete, all-inclusive Web server hosting packages. When shopping for a Web server hosting service, look for the following services as a minimum:

1. Use of name-brand hardware with extensive fault-tolerance. Fault-tolerance features can keep your server from going down even if a single piece of hardware inside of it fails.

2. Hardware and software maintenance.

3. Facility security, network security, and firewall services.

4. Continuous (24x7) monitoring.

5. Guaranteed service level agreements. Remember to insist on the highest level of service available—99% availability might seem great, but it means that your server might be down for more than three days a year.

6. Battery and generator power.

7. Tape backups. Your ISP should be offering to back up your entire server every week, and it should be performing a differential backup every day.

ISPs are competing furiously in this market, and are offering many additional value-added services on top of the ones previously mentioned. Choose your outsourced operations partner as carefully as you'd choose any other vendor. They will be responsible for making sure that your E-Commerce site is always available.

Use NT Server or Windows 2000 Server, not NT Workstation or Windows 2000 Professional

There are many reasons to use the server versions of Microsoft's advanced operating systems for your Web site, but one of the most important reasons is security. When you install Windows NT Server or Windows 2000 Server, the default security levels that it chooses are much higher than the default levels of Windows NT Workstation or Windows 2000 Professional. Even though the workstation versions of these operating systems are cheaper, resist the urge to run an E-Commerce site on one of them.

> **Caution**
>
> When you install Windows NT Server, the installation program will ask you whether you want your computer to be a Primary Domain Controller, Backup Domain Controller, or Stand-alone Server. Web servers should always be installed as Stand-alone servers. For security reasons, *under no circumstances* should you make your Web server a Primary Domain Controller or Backup Domain Controller.
>
> When you install Windows 2000 Server, the installation program will ask you various questions about Active Directory. Active Directory is an extremely powerful and complex way to manage system resources and permissions; needless to say, a detailed discussion of Active Directory is beyond the scope of this book. In most cases, it will be OK to accept the default settings for Active Directory.

Make Sure That the Latest Service Packs and Hotfixes Are Applied to Your System

In general, Windows NT and Windows 2000 are very secure operating systems; however, Microsoft and computer hackers are in a constant battle. As a result, Microsoft constantly releases fixes that cure security problems discovered by hackers. These fixes are released as service packs and hotfixes.

You can download or order the latest NT Service Packs and hotfixes from Microsoft's NT Server Web site, http://www.microsoft.com/NTServer/all/downloads.asp. The corresponding files for Windows 2000 are available from http://www.microsoft.com/windows2000/downloads/. If you are in the United States or Canada, when downloading or ordering a Service Pack or hotfix, you should choose the high encryption version whenever one is available.

Whether you download an NT Service Pack or receive it on CD, it comes as a program named MSNT128.EXE. To install the service pack, simply run the program, choose to Accept the License Agreement and Backup files, and then press Install. The Service Pack installer will spend the next few minutes installing new files, and then it will prompt you to reboot your server. The installation process for NT hotfixes is similar. As of the writing of this book, Microsoft had not released any service packs for Windows 2000; however, it is likely that the installation process for that operating system will be similar.

Caution Before and after installing any service pack or hotfix on Windows NT, you should make sure to create a before and after Emergency Recovery Disk by running RDISK.EXE. These disks can be used to reconstruct your Windows NT system files in the unlikely event that something goes wrong during the Service Pack or hotfix installation process.

15

Microsoft offers a free email service that will notify you when new security-related Service Packs and hotfixes are available. You can get more information by visiting http://www.microsoft.com/security/services/subscribe.asp.

Change the Name and Password of Your System's Administrator Account

The Administrator account on Windows NT and Windows 2000 is the most powerful account on the machine. To prevent hackers from trying to guess the password on that account, change the name of the account.

In order to change the name of the Administrator account on your Windows NT Server, perform the following steps:

1. Log in as a user who has Administrative rights on your NT Server.

2. Run User Manager for Domains by selecting Start, Programs, Administrative Tools (Common), User Manager for Domains.

3. Select User, Domain. Enter the NT name of your Web server into the box labeled Domain (see Figure 15.3).

   You should see the title bar of the User Manager change to User Manager—\\COMPUTERNAME.

FIGURE 15.3

Changing the domain to the Web server computer.

Note
We are using *COMPUTERNAME* as a placeholder for the actual NT name of your Web server.

4. Click on the User named Administrator.

5. Select User, Rename. Enter a name for the Administrator account that will be hard for someone else to guess but easy for you to remember (see Figure 15.4).

FIGURE 15.4

Changing the adminis-trator account.

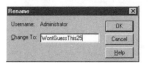

Caution
Make sure that you write down the new name of the Administrator account and keep it in a safe place. If you can't remember the Administrator account name, you won't be able to administer your system in the future.

In Windows 2000, there is a similar process for changing the name of the Administrator account. It is as follows:

1. Log in as a user who has Administrative rights on your NT Server.

2. Run Computer Management by selecting Start, Settings, Control Panel.

3. Double-click Administrative Tools, and then double-click Computer Management.

4. In the console tree, in Local Users and Groups, click Users.

5. Click on the Administrator account, and then click Action and select Rename.

Use NTFS

NTFS stands for NT File System, Microsoft's more advanced file system for NT and Windows 2000. NTFS allows you to restrict access to specific files on your Web server. If you aren't sure whether your system uses NTFS, you can check by running Disk Administrator in Windows NT, or Disk Management in Windows 2000 to check. Each of these tools displays each disk graphically (see Figure 15.5).

FIGURE 15.5

Examining your drives with Disk Administrator.

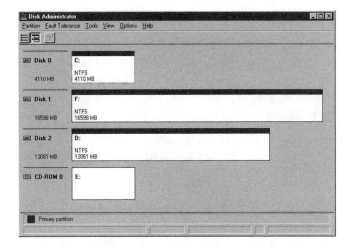

All the disk graphics should read NTFS. If any of them read FAT, you should convert each of them by selecting Start, Run and typing **CONVERT drive /FS:NTFS** into the Open dialog box (see Figure 15.6).

Note

Converting a file system from FAT to NTFS might require you to reboot your server.

FIGURE 15.6

Converting the C: drive to NTFS.

After your drives are converted, you can change the level of security on individual directories and files by using the Permissions dialog in the File Manager. To access the Permissions dialog, perform the following steps:

1. Navigate to the file or folder you want to protect, right-click on it, and select Properties.

2. Select the Security tab.

3. Click the Permissions button.

See the section "Protecting your Database" for more information on using NTFS to protect your store's database.

Use a Firewall

Although running IIS on Windows NT or Windows 2000 Server can make for a very secure Web server, Microsoft doesn't recommend placing machines running Windows NT directly on the Internet. Instead, it's far safer to use a device called a *firewall* that will sit between your Web server and your Internet connection and block malicious Internet traffic from reaching your Web server.

Detailed evaluations of firewall strategies are beyond the scope of this book; however, you can implement one of the following two ways to protect your Web server:

- Purchase a firewall appliance.
- Outsource your firewall protection to your ISP as described earlier in "Outsourcing Your Operations."

Assuming that your ISP can assure you of the competence of its security staff, it's probably safer to outsource your operations. Questions to ask your ISP include

- What kind of firewall do they use? Some of the better brands are PIX, Checkpoint, and Nokia.
- What ports do they allow through the firewall? (Ports should be limited to only 80 and 443.)
- How often do they review the firewall logs? (Logs should be reviewed at least daily; monthly if they have automated intrusion detection.)

If you decide you would rather operate your own firewall appliance, SonicWALL (http://www.sonicwall.com) makes an inexpensive, highly regarded firewall device. It will probably be necessary for you to discuss installation of the device with your ISP, and they might be able to give you other equipment recommendations.

 Caution

> If you decide to operate your own firewall, be sure to update the firewall software and review the firewall logs on a regular basis. Information on how to do this will be in the documentation that comes with your firewall.

Keep Your Server Locked Up

Many people make their networks and operating systems secure but forget to restrict physical access to their servers. Think of your server as a filing cabinet that contains sensitive files. Make sure that it's in a room with a door that locks, and when you aren't using the server, make sure that you log off and lock the door to the room.

Keep Your Server Running

One of the worst impressions you can make on a potential customer is for them to visit your Web site and find it down. Now that you are operating an e-business, it's important for you to do your best to always keep your e-business open.

The easiest way to do this is to outsource your Web server operations to your ISP (see the previous section, "Outsourcing Your Operations"). If you decide not to do this, you can do the following simple things to make your Web server more reliable:

- Plug your Web server into an Uninterruptible Power Supply (UPS).
- Take regular (preferably daily) backups of your Web server.
- Make sure that your Web server is running on a machine with brand-name hardware and plenty of processor, memory, and disk space. Also, many manufacturers now offer somewhat more expensive server machines that have advanced high-availability features. These features are usually worth it.
- Choose an ISP with a reputation for high reliability.

As more people use your server, you should also consider the following:

- Using a client-server database (like Microsoft SQL Server) and installing the database server on a separate machine.
- Adding more machines to run your Web site, and using Windows Load Balancing Services or another load balancing product to distribute the user load between machines that run your Web site.

Protecting Your Users' Private Information with SSL

You already know that the power of the Internet is that it makes every computer connected to it *appear* to be connected to every other computer. If two computers aren't actually connected, software on those computers automatically exchanges information by forwarding the information through other computers. This is an extremely powerful, flexible, and easy-to-use system, but it leaves you and your customers open to risks when accessing your E-Commerce site. The major risks are Spoofing, Unauthorized Disclosure, and Data Alteration.

15

Note

Spoofing is when a hacker or con artist copies your Web site in order to convince your customers to enter private information like credit card numbers.

Unauthorized Disclosure and Data Alteration can occur when private information is sent unencrypted. A hacker might be able to intercept or change private information as it passes between a customer's computer and your own.

As described in Chapter 8, "Building the Transaction Databases," you can reduce these risks by installing a secure certificate on your Web server. The secure certificate prevents spoofing by identifying your Web site to your customers through a third party known as a *Certification Authority*. The certificate also prevents unauthorized disclosure and data alteration by activating the encryption feature of IIS.

Server certificates are available for purchase from a large variety of certification authorities around the world. Certificates from any certification authority will enable the encryption features of IIS; however, the procedures that each Certification Authority follows to ensure the identity of your company can vary. The prices also vary, so it can pay to shop around. The Certification Authorities that issue server certificates at the time this book was written are listed in Table 15.1. The largest Certification Authority is VeriSign, and the instructions in Chapter 8 cover purchasing a certificate from VeriSign. The procedures for obtaining certificates from other Certification Authorities are similar; however, be sure to contact the specific Certification Authority you plan to use for details.

TABLE 15.1 Certification Authorities

Certification Authority	Location	URL
Asociacion Nacional del Notariado Mexicano	Mexico	http://www.notariadomexicano.org.mx
Belgacom e-trust	Belgium	http://www.e-trust.be
Certiposte	France	http://www.laposte.fr
Certisign	Brazil	http://www.certisign.com.br
Certplus	France	http://www.certplus.fr
Correo	Uruguay	http://www.correo.com.uy
Deutsche Telekom	German	http://www.deutschetelekom.de
Digital Signature Trust	Washington, DC	http://www.digsigtrust.com
Entrust	Plano, TX	http://www.entrust.net
Equifax	Atlanta, GA	http://www.equifaxsecure.com

Certification Authority	Location	URL
FNMT	Spain	http://www.fnmt.es
Fundacion FESTE	Spain	http://www.feste.com
Hong Kong Telecom	Hong Kong	http://www.hkt.com
GlobalSign	Belgium	http://www.globalsign.com
GTE Cybertrust	Irving, TX	http://www.cybertrust.com
Internet Publishing Services	Spain	http://seguridad.ips.es
Netlock	Hungary	http://www.netlock.net
PTT Post	Netherlands	http://www.ptt-post.nl
Saunalahti.fi	Finland	http://saunalahti.fi
SIA	Italy	http://www.sia.it
Swisskey	Switzerland	http://www.swisskey.com
Thawte	South Africa	http://www.thawte.com
TrustCenter	Germany	http://www.trustcenter.de
Usertrust	Salt Lake City, UT	http://www.usertrust.com
ValiCert	Mountain View, CA	http://www.valicert.com
VeriSign	Mountain View, CA	http://www.verisign.com

Protecting Your Database

In contrast with securing your Windows NT Server and installing a server certificate, basic protection for your database is relatively simpler, especially if you've changed your server's file system to NTFS. To be sure that your database is secure, follow these guidelines:

1. Don't keep your Access databases (*.mdb) in the same directory as your Web site.

2. Make sure that you keep your server logged off and physically locked up when you aren't using it.

3. Keep your Access database in a directory that isn't shared on your network. You can use the Windows NT Explorer to specify that disks and directories are not shared by clicking on any directory with a hand icon (see Figure 15.12), selecting File, Properties, going to the Sharing tab, and specifying Not Shared.

Caution

If a directory is shared, all its sub-directories will also be shared. If your Access .mdb file is in a subdirectory, make sure that you have specified Not Shared for all directories above it.

FIGURE 15.7

Shared directories.

4. Use NTFS security to further restrict access to your database.

You can use the NTFS Permissions dialog (see the section "Use NTFS") to further protect your users' sensitive information by changing the protections on the folder that contains your store's Microsoft Access database, or by changing the protections on the Access database itself. By default, anyone who has login access to the Web server will have access to the store's Access database. You can safely limit access to your own account and the Internet Guest Account. The name of the Guest Account begins with IUSR_.

 Caution

Unfortunately, because Microsoft Access is a file-based database, it is difficult to provide adequate protection for information stored in the database. For increased security, consider using a client-server database like Microsoft SQL Server. Client-server databases like SQL Server provide finer-grained permissions mechanisms that allow you to protect particular database tables and columns. Detailed descriptions of these security features are beyond the scope of this book.

Registering with the Better Business Bureau Reliability Program

The Better Business Bureau offers two programs to help online businesses reassure their customers—a reliability program and a privacy program. The BBBOnLine Reliability Program requires that you

• Become a member of your local Better Business Bureau.

- Allow the local BBB to verify information about your physical business, including your street address, telephone number, and names of owners and managers.

- Be in business for at least one year.

- Agree to respond promptly to consumer complaints, and have a satisfactory complaint record with the BBB.

- Agree to participate in binding arbitration for unresolved disputes involving the products and services you offer online.

- Agree to conform to the BBB's guidelines for online advertising, and to change your advertising when necessary to conform to those guidelines.

You can apply for this program by visiting the BBBOnLine Web site at `http://www.bbbonline.org`. Participating businesses can display the Better Business Bureau's Reliability Program graphic on their home page (see Figure 15.8).

FIGURE 15.8

The BBBOnLine Reliability Program logo.

Establishing a Privacy Policy and Joining a Privacy Seal Program

A 1998 BusinessWeek/Harris Poll identified Web privacy as the number one concern of Web users. A way to allay that concern and promote trust in your Web site and your company is to assure your users that the information they disclose to you will remain private. The best way to do this is to develop and articulate a strong *privacy policy* and to join and publicize participation in a *privacy seal* program.

Similar to the Underwriters' Laboratories and Good Housekeeping seals, Internet privacy seal programs are administered by third-party organizations to provide a trustworthy means of communication between consumers and businesses. These organizations

- Guide online businesses in developing comprehensive privacy policies.

- Monitor business compliance with these policies.

- Educate consumers on the Internet privacy.

- Provide recourse for consumers who feel their privacy has been violated.

As of the writing of this book, there were three major online privacy programs: TRUSTe, CPA WebTrust, and the BBBOnLine Privacy Program. Each program is similar in that it requires members to establish, publicize, and adhere to a privacy policy. Each provides a graphic that participants display on their home pages (see Figure 15.9), but each varies in cost and level of oversight.

FIGURE 15.9

Various privacy seal graphics.

Sample Privacy Policy

The following sample privacy policy is provided as a starting point for you in building your own site privacy policy.

Privacy statement for www.yoursite.com

Yoursite Industries has created this privacy statement in order to demonstrate our strong commitment to privacy. This statement discloses how we collect and disseminate information on www.yoursite.com.

We use your IP address to help diagnose problems with our Web server and to administer our Web site. Your IP address can also be used to help identify you and keep track of the items in your shopping cart.

This site contains links to other sites. www.yoursite.com isn't responsible for the privacy practices or the content of such Web sites.

Our site has an order form for customers to request information, products, and services. We collect contact information (like email addresses) and financial information (like credit card numbers). We use contact information to send orders and information about orders to our customers, as well as to communicate special offers from us or our partners. Users can opt not to receive these special offers by sending us email.

Our site has security measures in place to prevent the loss, misuse, and alteration of customer information. These include securing forms with SSL and digital certificates, physical security, network firewalls, and regular data backups.

If you have any questions about this privacy statement or the practices of this site, contact John Smith, 1 First Street, My Town, USA, or send email to jsmith@yourdomain.com.

The BBBOnLine is the simplest and lowest cost privacy program. First, you submit an online application, which includes a detailed questionnaire about how you collect, use, and store data; your privacy policy; and whether your site is directed toward children. Next, you pay the first year of an annual fee (scaled by the annual revenues of your business), which covers a Compliance Analyst's review of your site. Third, you submit a signed copy of the BBBOnLine license agreement. Finally, the BBB will send you some

HTML that will allow you to post the BBBOnLine Privacy Seal on your home page. More information about this program is available at `http://www.bbbonline.org`.

The TRUSTe program is intermediate in cost and oversight. TRUSTe allows you to build a privacy statement by completing a privacy statement wizard. You then sign and submit a license agreement, a self-assessment form, and the first year of an annual fee (which is scaled by the annual revenues of your business). Next, a TRUSTe account executive reviews the policy with you and sends you HTML that allows you to post the TRUSTe trustmark on your site. Periodically thereafter, representatives review your site and seed your site with user information. *Seeding* is the process of entering traceable user information in order to verify that you are conforming with your stated privacy policy. What this means is that periodically a TRUSTe representative will pretend to be a user of your site, enter information about themselves, and then verify that you aren't using that information in a way that conflicts with your privacy statement. Information about the TRUSTe program is available at `http://www.truste.org`.

The CPA WebTrust program is the most expensive and most thorough. The program requires you to enlist a specially licensed and trained CPA who helps you build a privacy policy; then quarterly privacy and security audits of your site are conducted. As with the other programs, after you meet the CPA WebTrust requirements, you will be given HTML to allow you to post the CPA WebTrust Seal on your Web site. More information is available at `http://www.cpawebtrust.org`.

The Better Business Bureau's Children's Advertising Review Unit Guidelines

As more children have been gaining unsupervised access to the Internet through their schools, libraries, and home computers, some of the same social forces that changed television advertising have come to bear on the Web. The Better Business Bureau's Children's Advertising Review Unit was originally formed to allow television broadcasters and advertisers to regulate themselves; the unit has recently become involved in writing guidelines for Web sites directed toward children thirteen years old or younger.

The CARU guidelines ask Web site designers to

1. Take into account the limited sophistication and maturity of their audience. Young children are often unable to evaluate the credibility of information they read or hear, and advertisers and web site designers shouldn't try to exploit children's limitations.

2. Not foster unreasonable expectations of product quality or performance through the use of imagination or make-believe.

3. Communicate information in a truthful and accurate manner.

4. Promote positive and beneficial social behavior.

5. Provide positive minority role models and avoid stereotyping and appeals to prejudice.

6. Contribute to the parent-child relationship in a constructive manner.

In designing an E-Commerce site for children, it's important to avoid encouraging the child to ask his parents to buy products for him, and not to create a sense of urgency or exclusivity around products. Auctions are especially inappropriate for children. Also, whenever you have to present a disclosure or disclaimer to a child, make sure that it's worded in a way that the child can understand. In addition, if your site mixes content and commerce, it's important to provide a clear separation between these sections. Finally, when you give children an opportunity to enter into a transaction, you must make it clear to them that they need a parent or guardian's permission before proceeding, and there should be a clear way for the child or the parent to cancel the order. This last item is also for your own protection—under existing laws, parents usually aren't obligated to fulfill sales contracts that their children enter into.

Another concern of the CARU, and indeed of the U.S. government, is the collection and use of Web site data about children. The *Children's Online Privacy Protection Act of 1998* requires parental permission before collecting personal data from children under thirteen. In order to conform to the law and the CARU guidelines, be sure to remind children that they need their parents' permission before providing any personal data. **If you intend to collect any real-world information about a child** (such as an address or phone number)**, you must first have verifiable consent from the child's parent or guardian.**

Summary

In this chapter, we discussed how to foster confidence in your company and your E-Commerce site. You learned how to registering your own domain, request and install a server certificate, and protect your users' private information with SSL. You also learned how to make your servers and databases more secure. Finally, you learned about privacy issues, how to write a privacy statement, and how to register with third-party privacy and reliability monitoring organizations.

Q&A

Q **When I try to install my server certificate, I get an error message. What can I do?**

A Installing a server certificate can be tricky. Make sure that you are entering the password for your certificate signing request correctly, and that the certificate file you are installing matches the certificate signing request you created. If all else fails, VeriSign technical support often is helpful in diagnosing these sorts of problems.

Q **Is NT secure and reliable enough to run a commerce site?**

A Security and reliability are usually more a matter of how well your site is put together and maintained than what operating system you use. There are many secure, reliable commerce sites running NT. Following the guidelines in this chapter is a good start at keeping your E-Commerce site secure and reliable.

Workshop

The Quiz and Exercise questions are designed to test your knowledge of the material covered in this chapter. The answers are in Appendix A, "Quiz Answers."

Quiz

1. What version of Windows NT should you be using for your E-Commerce Web server?
2. What ports need to be allowed through your firewall?
3. What is Spoofing?
4. How large of a key should you use for a certificate signing request?
5. What are three ways to improve the security of your web site's Access database?

Exercise

Write a privacy statement for your E-Commerce site. Be sure to take into account whether your site will target children.

DAY 16

Debugging Your E-Commerce Applications

Active Server Pages is now a few years old, and is certainly more robust than they were in the days of IIS 3.0; however, like any newer computer technology, diagnostics and debugging in Active Server Pages is still much less mature than it is in the more mature Visual C++ and Visual Basic. Finding problems in Active Server Pages is made more difficult by the transactional nature of the Web—programming errors on the server are revealed only by actions on a client, and it is sometimes difficult to relate the client action to the server error. Further complicating the problem is the fact that some errors aren't encountered unless the server is under a large amount of load or unless many clients are submitting particular requests in a particular order.

Today, you will learn the following:

- How to keep a development system that's separate from your production system (and why that's important)
- How to debug your application using Visual InterDev's integrated debugger

- How to debug your application on a production server
- How to capture errors into a log file
- Testing for scalability

Keeping Your Development and Production Systems Separate

An old axiom of software development is that every piece of software has bugs. When you develop your system for the first time, you will be the only person using it, which will make finding and fixing problems easier. After you put your site up for business, however, your customers will expect it to run 24 hours a day, 7 days a week. Making changes to a Web site as it is running isn't compatible with the goal of 24x7 operations—any change you make on a production system runs the risk of interrupting the service for anyone currently using the system.

 Note

> Web programmers use the term *production system* to refer to the Web site that their customers actually use.
>
> A Web site used only by a company's Web programmers for development and testing is referred to as a *development system*.

One example of a change that could interrupt service is altering a database schema. Changing the structure of a database often "breaks" your SQL queries; if you do this on your production system, your users will see the error, and it might take some time for you to restore the database, during which time your site might seem to have stopped working to your customers. Similarly, when you place a breakpoint in Visual InterDev (see the following section, "Debugging Your Application Using Visual InterDev's Integrated Debugger"), the breakpoint is *global*, meaning that any user of the system who causes a script to hit your breakpoint will bring up the debugger and wait for you to start debugging.

To prevent conflicts like these, professional developers work around this problem by keeping two Web servers—one for debugging, and a second one for actual operations. Now that PCs are so cheap, this is practical for even the smallest installations. A low-end Celeron (running Windows NT Server, of course) should be adequate for developing and testing most E-Commerce applications. An added bonus of using a lower powered system is that you'll be able to recreate scalability problems more easily on a system with a slower processor and a slower, smaller hard disk. If you decide to pursue a separate development system, get your new system ready and skip to the section "Creating a Second Web Site."

 Caution | Although you can use Windows NT Workstation or even Windows 95 or Windows 98 to run a Web server and Visual InterDev, running Windows NT Server will provide a more realistic environment for testing.

16

Should you choose not to keep a separate development machine, you can "fake it" by using *multihoming* to create a second IP address for your machine, and then creating a separate Web site for development that uses the same IP address.

Note | Before you start, you should be sure that your NT username has Administrator privileges on your production server. If you choose to keep a separate development server, your NT username will need to have Administrator privileges on the development server.

Creating a Second IP Address

You can create a second IP address for your computer via the Network control panel by implementing the following steps:

1. Go to the Start menu and select Settings, Control Panel.
2. Double-click the Network icon.
3. After the Network dialog comes up, click the Protocols tab.
4. Select TCP/IP Protocol, and then click Properties.
5. When the Microsoft TCP/IP Properties dialog appears (see Figure 16.1), click the Advanced button.
6. When the Advanced IP Addressing dialog appears (see Figure 16.2), click the Add button.
7. When the TCP/IP Address dialog appears, enter another IP address, and then click the Add button to dismiss the dialog.

FIGURE 16.1

Microsoft TCP/IP Properties.

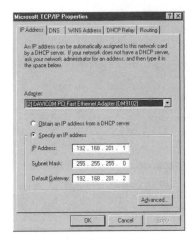

FIGURE 16.2

Advanced IP Addressing.

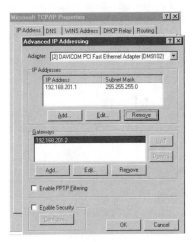

Caution

Be sure that the IP address you enter isn't being used already by another machine on your network.

8. Observe that your new IP address now appears in the IP Addresses list of the Advanced IP Addressing dialog. Click OK in this dialog, and OK in the TCP/IP Properties dialog. Click Close in the Network dialog.

9. You will be prompted to reboot your machine.

After you have created your second IP address, you can create a new Web site to correspond to it.

Creating a Second Web Site

Now that you've either created a second home IP address for your Web server, or installed Windows NT Server and IIS on a new machine, you are ready to create your development Web site. To do this, implement the following steps:

1. Copy your production Web site to a new directory on the machine you will be using for development (for example, `C:\Dev_Store`).

2. Go to the Start menu and select Programs, Windows NT 4.0 Option Pack, Microsoft Internet Information Server, Internet Service Manager.

3. When the management console appears, in the left panel, select the folder labeled Internet Information Server. In the right panel, select your computer (see Figure 16.3).

FIGURE 16.3

The IIS Management Console.

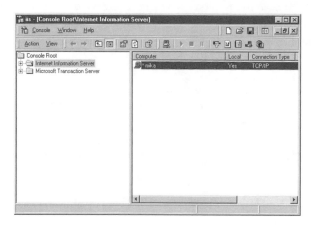

4. Select Action, New, Web Site. You will see the New Web Site Wizard.

5. In the Web Site Description box, type **Dev_store**. Click Next.

6. The next page prompts you to select the IP address and TCP ports to use for this Web server. If you are using a single machine for development and production, select the IP address you created in Advanced IP Addressing (see Figure 16.4). If you are using separate machines for development or deployment, don't change the IP address. In either case, leave the other settings the same and click Next.

7. The next page prompts you to enter a directory for your new Web site. Enter the directory from step 1 and click Next. When the next page appears, click Finish.

FIGURE 16.4

Selecting a new IP address.

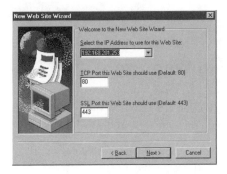

You can now make changes to your development Web site without affecting your production site. When you want to test, point your browser to the IP address of the development site (for a single machine, the IP address you created previously; for separate machines, the IP address of your development machine). When you are satisfied with the changes you make, you can use Explorer to copy the pages from the development directory to the production directory in order to deploy them, or you can use the deployment feature of Visual InterDev.

 Note   The word *deploy* refers to the process of moving software from a development and testing system to a production system.

Deploying Your Application Using Visual InterDev

Visual InterDev includes a deployment feature that makes moving Web pages from a development system to a production system simpler. To use the feature, implement the following:

1. If you haven't already, install either the Microsoft Posting Acceptor or the FrontPage server extensions on your development and production servers.
2. Set write permissions on your development and production deployment directories.
3. Confirm that your IIS Scripts folders have their permissions set to Execute (including script).
4. Create a Visual InterDev Project for your development Web site.

You can install Posting Acceptor from the Visual Studio installation program, or by running `pasetup.exe`, which is located in the Deploy directory. You can then set the write permissions on your development and production deployment directories by implementing the following:

1. Returning to the IIS Management Console on your development machine.

2. Opening the node for your production Web server, and clicking your development Web site.

3. Selecting Action, Properties.

4. Selecting the Home Directory tab, and then checking the Write check box (under Access Permissions—see Figure 16.5).

16

FIGURE 16.5

Allowing Write permissions for your deployment directory.

5. Repeating this process for your production Web server.

To confirm that your Scripts folder has its permissions set to Execute (including script),

1. Return to the IIS Management Console on your development machine.

2. In the left pane, open the node for your development Web server and select the Default Web Site.

3. In the right pane, select SCRIPTS.

4. Select Action, Properties.

5. When the SCRIPTS Properties dialog appears, select the Virtual Directory tab.

6. Toward the bottom of the page, select the Execute (including script) radio button (see Figure 16.6).

7. Repeat the previous process for your production Web site.

FIGURE 16.6

Allowing Execute permissions for your SCRIPTS *directory.*

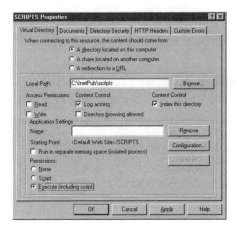

Now that your development and production systems are ready, you should create a Visual InterDev project for your development Web site, and a separate deployment target for your production server. To do this, implement the following:

1. Return to your development system and copy your Web site to a work directory.

> **Note**
>
> Yes, it's true: You now have *three* copies of your Web site floating around. This is how most professional Web developers develop, test, and deploy their systems.

2. Run Visual InterDev. By default, the New Project dialog will appear; if it doesn't, you can bring it up by selecting File, New Project.

3. In the Name box, enter **Store**, and in the Location box, enter the location of the work copy of your Web server made in step 1. The Web Project Wizard then appears.

4. Select your development Web server as the server you want to use, and select Master Mode as the mode you would like to work in. Click Next.

5. Select Connect to an existing Web application, and select the directory of your production store application (probably the Root Web). Click Finish.

6. The Wizard might ask if you would like to install the Visual InterDev script library. You should choose No.

7. In the upper right corner of Visual InterDev, you will see a small window labeled Project Explorer (see Figure 16.7). Go to Project and select New Deployment Target.

FIGURE 16.7

Project Explorer.

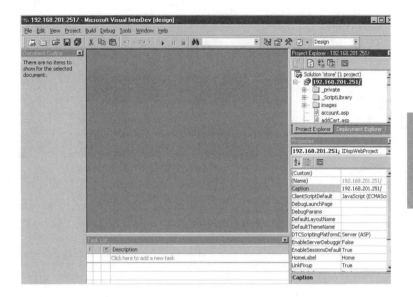

16

> **Caution**
>
> You must enter the complete URL to your production server, including
> `http:`; for example, `http://www.yourdomain.com`.

8. In the window that appears, enter the URL for your Production server. The window in the upper right corner will have a new section labeled Deployment Explorer.

Your Web site is now set up for three levels of deployment: development, testing, and production. When you want to edit a file, you'll double-click the file's name in the Project Explorer window. You might be prompted to copy the file locally, and will then see a small pencil icon appear to the left of the filename (see Figure 16.8). When you are finished editing files, place them on your testing site by selecting Project, Web Project, Synchronize Files.

When you are satisfied that your E-Commerce application works correctly on your testing site, you can copy it to your production server by selecting Project, Deploy, Deploy to `http://www.yourdomain.com`.

FIGURE 16.8

A file copied locally.

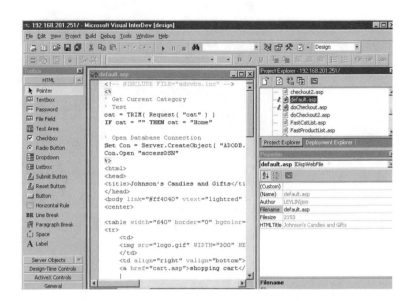

Debugging Your Application Using Visual InterDev's Integrated Debugger

A great advantage to using Visual InterDev for ASP development is the InterDev debugger. If you are running Visual InterDev on Windows NT, you can perform sophisticated debugging of both server-side ASP and client-side Dynamic HTML. You can set server-side breakpoints, and while your script is stopped at a breakpoint, you can examine the contents of variables, step through your scripts line-by-line, and step into functions. In fact, if your database is running on Microsoft SQL Server, you can even step into database stored procedures.

Note

A *breakpoint* is an instruction to the server to stop execution at a specific line of code so that the programmer can examine the state of the scripts variables.

Caution

The debugging features of Visual InterDev only work when Visual InterDev is installed on Windows NT, not on Windows 95 or Windows 98.

Getting Ready to Debug

In order to start debugging your server-side ASP, you will need to install Remote Machine Debugging and Visual InterDev Server on your development server. The Remote Machine Debugging component is available on your Visual Studio disks in a directory called Scrpt_ss. The Visual InterDev Server components are in a directory called Vid_ss. Run the setup.exe program from each directory and, after the setup programs finish, reapply the latest service pack and reboot your server.

Now that Remote Machine Debugging is installed, you must enable debugging on your development site. To do this, implement the following:

1. Go to the IIS Management Console and select your development Web site.

2. Select Action, Properties.

3. Go to the Home Directory tab. On the bottom right part of the tab, click Configuration (see Figure 16.9).

FIGURE 16.9

The Configuration button.

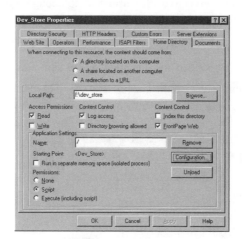

4. From the Application Configuration page, click the App Debugging tab and select both debugging flags (see Figure 16.10). Select OK for both dialogs.

Caution

Installing and enabling the debugger on a production Web site is a significant security risk. Only enable the debugger on your development Web site.

FIGURE 16.10

The App Debugging tab of Application Configuration.

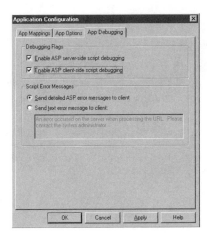

Now that you have installed Remote Machine Debugging and enabled debugging on your development site, you must give yourself permission to debug on the development server. You can do this as follows:

1. From the Start button, click Run.

2. In the small box that appears, type **Dcomcnfg.exe** and click OK.

3. On the Applications tab, find the Catalog class (see Figure 16.11) and click the Properties button. This will bring up a dialog called Catalog Class Properties.

FIGURE 16.11

The Applications tab.

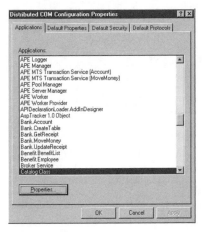

4. Click the Security tab (see Figure 16.12). In each of the three permissions sections, use the Edit button to bring up a dialog that will allow you to give yourself access permission for the resource. Click OK.

FIGURE 16.12

The Security tab.

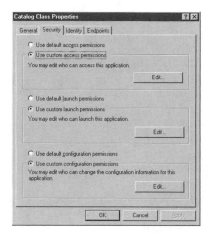

16

5. You will return to the Applications tab of the previous dialog. Find the Machine Debug Manager and repeat step 4.

Debugging a Site

You are now ready to debug the development Web site. Re-open Visual InterDev, and open the project you created in the previous section, "Deploying Your Application Using Visual InterDev." Go to the Project Explorer, and select `default.asp`, and then from the menu select Project, Web Files, Set as Start Page.

To try debugging out, double-click `default.asp` to open it. The file will open in the center area of the Visual InterDev IDE, and you will notice a gray strip running down the left side of the window. You can set a breakpoint by clicking the gray strip next to the line you'd like to stop on. To try out debugging, click to the left of the first executable line of the file, `cat = TRIM ( Request( "cat" ) )`. You will see a red circle appear next to the line as shown in Figure 16.13. (In the figure, the red circle is black.) Press the F5 button to start debugging, and you will be prompted for your Windows NT username and password. Enter it to continue.

Internet Explorer will now launch, and the Visual InterDev IDE will change from editing view to debugging view. The line broken on will appear highlighted in yellow, and there will be a yellow arrow pointing to the highlighted line (see Figure 16.14).

FIGURE 16.13

A breakpoint set in `default.asp.`

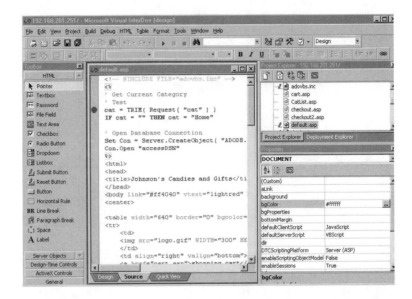

FIGURE 16.14

Stopped at a break-point set in `default.asp.`

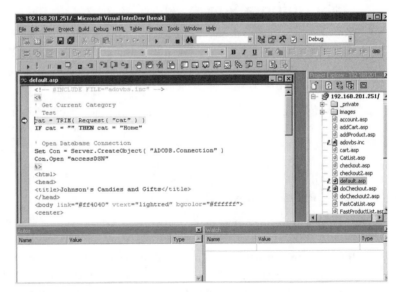

You can now watch the .asp script execute line-by-line and, as the script executes, you can monitor the contents of VBScript variables in the watch window in the lower right side of the IDE. Try it now by clicking on the blank cell in the Name column of the watch window, entering `cat` and pressing return. You will observe `Variable is`

undefined: 'cat' in the Value column, and Error in the Type column (see Figure 16.15). Press the F10 key once, and you will see several things happen:

- The yellow arrow moves to the next line of VBScript

  `IF cat = "" THEN cat = "Home".`

- The yellow highlight moves to the next line of VBScript.
- The Value column in the watch window changes to `""`.
- The Type column in the watch window changes to String.

FIGURE 16.15

The watch window.

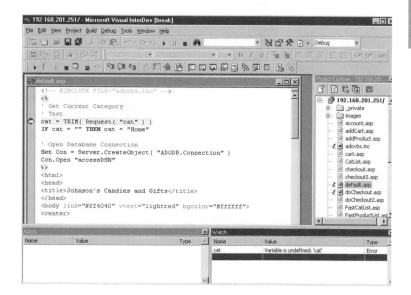

According to the current line, because the value of the variable cat is `""`, it should be set to `"Home"`. Try it by pressing F10 again. You will observe that the Value column in the watch window changes to `"Home"`. The color of the string is red to signify that the value changed as a result of executing the previous statement (see Figure 16.16).

The watch window can also look inside COM objects that your ASP script instantiates. The line of ASP script currently highlighted creates an ADO Connection. Try looking into it by clicking the watch window on the empty cell in the Name column (underneath cat) and typing **Con**. Press F10 again, and you will see a plus sign inside a box next to the variable name Con. Click the plus sign to expand the object, and you will see the members of the new Connection object (see Figure 16.17).

FIGURE **16.16**

The watch window changes as a result of the single statement executed.

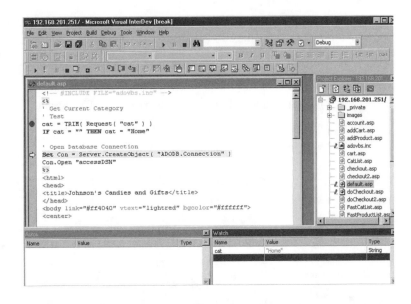

FIGURE **16.17**

Examining an ADO Connection object in the watch window.

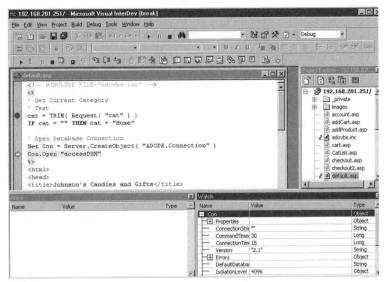

The Visual InterDev IDE can also show you all the variables and objects defined for the current script. Go to the View menu and select Debug Windows, Locals. The Locals window will appear on the lower left side of the IDE, and will include all the objects that ASP defines for your page (like Request, Response, Session, Application) as well as the variables defined in adovbs.inc and the variables defined in default.asp as of the current line (see Figure 16.18). You can exit the debugger by going to the Debug menu and selecting End, or by pressing Shift+F5.

FIGURE 16.18

The Locals window.

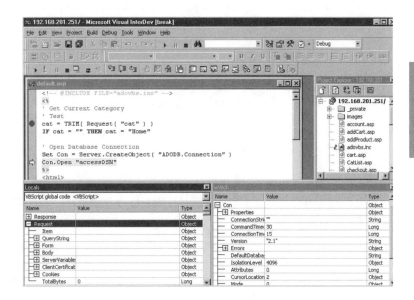

As you can imagine, this is an extremely powerful way to examine potential errors in your ASP code. Many bugs result from unanticipated data or typing errors; these kinds of bugs are easy to diagnose and fix with the Visual InterDev IDE. Single-step debugging isn't appropriate for diagnosing every problem; for example, bugs that relate to multiple users accessing your Web site simultaneously. This is because when the debugger is stopped at a breakpoint, the Web server isn't able to respond to requests from other Web clients. To debug problems related to multiple requests, you will need to use techniques like those described in the next two sections.

Debugging Your Application on a Production Server

Although you might test your application thoroughly on your development site, a few bugs will almost always slip into your production system. The best way to diagnose these problems is to try to reproduce the bug on your development system while watching ASP execution in the Visual Studio debugger; however, as discussed in the previous section, this isn't always possible. In those cases, you will need a way to have the production Web site output additional information to you while your customers continue to use the

Web site normally. The ASP Session object offers a straightforward way to do this by allowing you to set a per-session debugging level and adding a hidden administrative page to allow you to set the debugging level. You can then use that debugging variable in your code to decide how much debugging information to add to the output of your ASP.

Note

This technique takes advantage of ASP Sessions. Although Sessions have many advantages, keeping per-session information in an ASP-driven Web site will degrade performance when your site is under high levels of load. You will need to explore the specific performance characteristics of your own Web site to decide whether using this technique is worth the potential performance impact.

Creating and Maintaining a Session Variable for Debugging

To create the debugging variable, you will first need to create a global.asa file if it isn't already created. To create an instance of the Global.asa file using Visual InterDev, go to the Project Explorer window and right-click your Web project. In the context menu that appears, select Add, Active Server Page. Change the name of the file in the Add Item page from ASPPage1.asp to global.asa. The new global.asa file will open in a new window in the center of the IDE. Delete all the text from the window and add the lines of code in Listing 16.1. If you aren't using the Visual InterDev IDE, you can simply create the global.asa file in Notepad or another text editor.

INPUT   **LISTING 16.1**   Setting iDebugLevel to 0 for Each Session

```
1 <SCRIPT LANGUAGE="VBScript" RUNAT="Server">
2
3 Sub Session_OnStart
4     Session("iDebugLevel") = 0
5 End Sub
6 </SCRIPT>
```

ANALYSIS   Whenever a new user comes to your Web site, line 4 of this script initializes a session variable called iDebugLevel and sets it to 0. In the future, you will use values of iDebugLevel that are greater than 0 as a signal to emit additional information on your Web pages.

You will need to add a hidden, administrative page that allows you to reset the value of iDebugLevel. For additional flexibility, we will do this by adding a subfolder called Admin, and a page in the Admin folder called adminPage.asp. You can do this in the Visual InterDev IDE by going to the Project Explorer and right-clicking your Web project. In the context menu that appears, select New Folder. In the dialog that appears, enter Admin. A new Admin folder will appear in the Project Explorer. Right-click that folder and select Add, Active Server Page. Change the name of the file in the Add Item page from ASPPage1.asp to **adminPage.asp**. A template for the new page will appear in the center of the IDE. If you aren't using the Visual InterDev IDE, you can create the folder and adminPage.asp file using Notepad or another text editor. In either case, the ultimate contents of adminPage.asp are in Listing 16.2. Although there is not a link to adminPage.asp on your Web site, you can access it directly by going to http://www.yoursite.com/Admin/adminPage.asp, changing the debug level, and clicking Submit.

16

INPUT **LISTING 16.2** Resetting iDebugLevel in adminPage.asp

```
1 <%@ Language="VBScript" %>
2 <%
3    If Request.Form("ProcForm") = "Process" Then
4       Session("iDebugLevel") = Request.Form("debugLevel")
5        If Session("iDebugLevel") = "" Then
6           Session("iDebugLevel") = 0
7        End If
8    End If
9 %>
10 <HTML>
11 <HEAD>
12 <META NAME="GENERATOR" Content="Microsoft Visual Studio 6.0">
13 <title>Johnson's Candies and Gifts Administration Page</title>
14 </head>
15 <body link="#ff4040" vtext="lightred" bgcolor="#ffffff">
16 <center>
17
18 <table width="640" border="0" bgcolor="#ffffff" cellspacing="0"
   ➥cellpadding="0">
19 <tr>
20    <td>
21       <img src="logo.gif" WIDTH="300" HEIGHT="30">
22    </td>
23 </tr>
24 <tr>
25    <td colspan="2">
```

continues

LISTING 16.2   continued

```
26      <hr width="640">
27      </td>
28 </tr>
29 </table>
30
31 <H2>Administration Page<H2>
32 <FORM method="POST" action="adminPage.asp">
33 <input type="hidden" name="ProcForm" value="Process">
34 <table>
35 <tr>
36      <td> Debug Level </td>
37      <td> <input name="debugLevel" value="<%=Session.Value
   ➥("iDebugLevel")%>"></td>
38 </tr><tr>
39      <td> <input type="submit" value="Submit"> </td>
40 </tr>
41 </table>
42 </FORM>
43 </BODY>
44 </HTML>
```

ANALYSIS   When the page is first executed, the value of the hidden variable `ProcForm` is not
defined, so the page ignores the script between lines 4 and 7. On line 37, the current value of `iDebugLevel` is placed into an input textbox. When the user clicks the Submit button, the hidden variable `ProcForm` has been defined as `"Process"` on line 33, so the script between lines 4 and 7 sets the value of the session variable `iDebugLevel` to whatever the user entered. The form is now regenerated with the new value of `iDebugLevel` placed into the input textbox (line 37).

Using the Session-level Debugging Variable

A second axiom of programming is that errors most frequently occur when two different pieces of software interact. As you've seen, in building an E-Commerce site, the external software interacted with the most is the database, which is accessed via SQL and ADO. Using the `iDebugLevel` variable defined previously, you can now add code that displays extra debugging information in your Web pages—an especially useful technique for production debugging when your ASP is interacting with the database. For example, you might want to display SQL statements before they are executed if `iDebugLevel` is 1, and then display both SQL statements and their results if `iDebugLevel` is 2, and so on. In these examples, we will only take advantage of setting `iDebugLevel` to 1.

To show the power of this technique, we will take, as an example, a page we created on Day 5, "Building Your Product Catalog," called `updateProducts.asp`, and add session-level debugging output to that script to allow us to diagnose our SQL queries. (This file is included with the CD-ROM that accompanies this book with the name debugUpdateProducts.asp.)

First, we'll add a subroutine to the top of the page that will capture the logic of deciding whether to display extra information. We'll insert the code in Listing 16.3 between lines 1 and 2 of updateProducts.asp so that the routine is available to the entire script.

16

INPUT **LISTING 16.3** Adding a Debug Routine to updateProducts.asp

```
1.1 Sub DebugWrite(sDebugText, iDebugLevel)
1.2   If CInt(Session("iDebugLevel")) >= CInt(iDebugLevel) Then
1.3     Response.Write(vbNewLine & "<COMMENT>" & vbNewLine &
        ➥"Debugging output level " & iDebugLevel & vbNewLine)
1.4     Response.Write(sDebugText)
1.5     Response.Write(vbNewLine & "</COMMENT>" & vbNewLine)
1.6   End If
1.7 End Sub
```

ANALYSIS When the DebugWrite subroutine is called, if the current value of the session debugging level is greater than or equal to the value passed in as iDebugLevel (line 1.1), the information passed in as sDebugText is emitted in an HTML comment (lines 1.3–1.5).

Now that the DebugWrite subroutine is available, we can place it in strategic places in updateProducts.asp. As we're concerned about our SQL statements, we will insert code that emits the SQL statements when iDebugLevel is 1. The code we add is in Listing 16.4.

INPUT **LISTING 16.4** Adding Strategic DebugWrite Calls to updateProducts.asp

```
6 Set Con = Server.CreateObject( "ADODB.Connection" )
6.1 DebugWrite "Opening accessDSN", 1
7 Con.Open "accessDSN"

13 RS.CursorType = 3
13.1 selectStr = "SELECT * FROM Products WHERE product_id=" & productID
13.2 DebugWrite selectStr, 1
14 RS.Open selectStr
```

Now, go to admin/adminPage.asp and change the Debug Level to 1. Next, go to manageProducts.asp, and click one of the product links to bring you to an updateProduct.asp generated page. Although the output of the page looks the same in the browser, if you select View, Source, you will observe that the first four lines of HTML

```
<COMMENT>
Debugging output level 1
Opening accessDSN
</COMMENT>
<COMMENT>
Debugging output level 1
SELECT * FROM Products WHERE product_id=26
</COMMENT>
```

are comments generated by our `DebugWrite` routine.

Creating a Debug Library

Before writing any more debugging functions and subroutines, now is a good time to create an .asp page that can serve as a debugging library. (This file is included on the CD-ROM that accompanies this book with the name `debug.asp`.) Keeping all the debugging routines in a single file (in this site, we will call it `debug.asp`) makes the routines much easier to use and maintain. Rather than having to copy and paste the same functions into multiple files, it will be much easier to `INCLUDE="/debug.asp"` at the top of each page. This technique also gives each of your pages access to new functions (or fixes to existing functions) without having to make the same changes to many pages. The first routine to add to `debug.asp` is `DebugWrite`, which we will move from the top of `updateProduct.asp` to the top of `debug.asp`.

Recovering from and Capturing Errors

When your ASP calls ADO and encounters an error in the database, the VBScript interpreter stops processing your Web page and emits text like this:

```
Microsoft OLE DB Provider for ODBC Drivers error 80004005
 [Microsoft][ODBC Driver Manager] Data source name not found and no default
 driver specified
 /updateProduct.asp, line 7
```

and the currently executing script stops. This can make it difficult to diagnose problems because the error messages are often cryptic and, although there is sometimes more information available in various error state objects, because execution stops immediately, there is no opportunity to examine that information. Also, some errors are recoverable but, again, because execution stops immediately, there is no opportunity to examine the error and decide whether to continue or to present a friendlier error. Adding the `On Error Resume Next` statement to the top of a script gives the programmer the opportunity to do both.

When a script contains `On Error Resume Next`, it becomes the programmer's responsibility to handle runtime errors. To help handle these errors, we will add the `CheckError` subroutine to our debugging library, which will be called after each ADO operation (see Listing 16.5). The CheckError subroutine checks for errors and, if encountered, emits extended error information.

> **Note**
>
> The ADO diagnostics in CheckError assume that all ADO connections are named Con. If you decide to add pages that use ADO to the sample site, make sure to name your ADO connections Con.

INPUT   **LISTING 16.5**   CheckError

```
1   Sub CheckError
2
3     If Err.Number > 0 Then
4       Response.Write vbNewLine & "<COMMENT>" & vbNewLine & "ASP Error! " &
      ➥vbNewLine
5       Response.Write "      Number: " & err.number & vbNewLine
6       Response.Write "      Description: " & err.description & vbNewLine
7       Response.Write "      Source: " & err.source & vbNewLine
8       Response.Write "</COMMENT> " & vbNewLine
9     End If
10
11    If Not IsEmpty(Con) Then
12      If Con.Errors.Count > 0 Then
13        '
14        ' First count the real errors
15        '
16        Dim i, j
17        j = 0
18        For i = 1 to Con.Errors.Count
19          if Con.Errors(i-1).number <> 0 Then
20            j = j + 1
21          End if
22        Next
23        '
24        ' Now output them if necessary
25        '
26        If j > 0 Then
27          j = 1
28          Response.Write (vbNewLine & "<COMMENT>" & vbNewLine & "ADO Errors! "
        ➥ & vbNewLine)
29          For i = 1 to Con.Errors.Count
30            If Con.Errors(i-1).number <> 0 Then
31              Response.Write " ADO Error " & j & vbNewLine
32              Response.Write "      Number: " & Con.Errors(i-1).number &
            ➥vbNewLine
```

continues

LISTING 16.5   continued

```
33              Response.Write "    Description: " & Con.Errors(i-1).description
                ➥ & vbNewLine
34              Response.Write "    Source: " & Con.Errors(i-1).source &
                ➥vbNewLine
35              If Con.Errors(i-1).nativeerror <> "" Then
36                Response.Write "    Native Error: " &
                  ➥Con.Errors(i-1).nativeerror & vbNewLine
37              End If
38              If Con.Errors(i-1).sqlstate <> "" Then
39                Response.Write "    SQL State: " & Con.Errors(i-1).sqlstate &
                  ➥ vbNewLine
40              End If
41            End If
42          Next
43          Response.Write ("</COMMENT> " & vbNewLine)
44        End If
45      End If
46    End If
47
48 End Sub
```

ANALYSIS   The CheckError subroutine has two parts. The first part (lines 2–10) checks for a VBScript error. Line 2 checks the VBScript intrinsic object Err to see if an unhandled error occurred. If one did, lines 4–8 emit an HTML comment with information about the error.

The second part (lines 11–47) checks the ADO connection object, if any, for errors. This code is more complicated than the code that checks the Err intrinsic object because a single ADO call can cause more than one error, and because some ADO errors are simply informational. Line 12 checks to see if there are any errors or informational messages. Lines 18–22 loop through each of the ADO errors. Line 19 checks to see if each error is an actual error (informational messages have Error.Number = 0) and, if it is, line 20 counts them in j. Line 26 checks j to see if there were any actual errors. If there were, lines 29–42 loop through the errors again and output detailed information about each of them, if available, in an HTML comment.

To demonstrate CheckError in action, we will introduce a common error into manageProducts.asp. We'll change the manageProducts.asp as shown in Listing 16.6 so that debug.asp is included and product names with single quotes are no longer escaped.

INPUT   **LISTING 16.6**   Changes to managePvoducts.asp

```
1 <!-- #INCLUDE FILE="debug.asp" -->
2 <%
3 On Error Resume Next
4
5 FUNCTION fixQuotes( theString )
6 '   fixQuotes = REPLACE( theString, "'", "''" )
7     fixQuotes = theString
8 END FUNCTION
```

To check for errors, we will need to call the CheckError subroutine after each SQL operation. You should add the CheckError subroutine after every Con.Execute statement in the managePvoducts.asp file.

Now, go to managePvoducts.asp in your browser and try to update the entry for Hershey's Chocolate Bar. Although the page reports that the update was successful, go to View, Source in the browser. You will see the following comment in your HTML:

```
<COMMENT>
ADO Errors!
 ADO Error 1
    Number: -2147217900
    Description: [Microsoft][ODBC Microsoft Access Driver] Syntax error
    (missing operator) in query expression ''Hershey's Chocolate
Bar',product_price=9,product_picture='hersheys.jpg',product_category='Chocolate
Solids',product_briefdesc='A solid bar of delicious chocolate.
',product_fulldesc='Everybody loves this classic candy!
',product_status=1 WHERE produ'.
    Source: Microsoft OLE DB Provider for ODBC Drivers
    Native Error: -3100
    SQL State: 37000
</COMMENT>
```

This illustrates the importance of capturing and reporting errors in a user-friendly manner after On Error Resume Next has been specified. In many cases, error checking is easy; for example, here you can just add a check for errors before displaying the user message about data being updated; for example,

```
<%=productName%> was <% if Con.Errors.Count > 0 Then %> <B>not</B>
➥<% end if %> updated in the database
```

Capturing Errors into a Log File

Writing errors to comments in an HTML page is very powerful; however, you might encounter errors that only happen to your customers and that you can't reproduce. In these cases, you might find it helpful to capture errors into a log file. VBScript provides a straightforward way to do this with the `FileSystemObject` object. (To learn more about using the `FileSystemObject`, see Day 4, "Working with Files in Your E-Commerce Application.") You can write the errors by making the changes in Listing 16.7 to `debug.asp`.

INPUT   **LISTING 16.7**   Changes to `debug.asp` to Capture Errors into a File

```
1    Sub WriteToFileAndHtml(fFileStream, sString)
2      Response.Write sString
3      If Not IsEmpty(fFileStream) Then
4        fFileStream.Write sString
5      End If
6    End Sub
7
8    Sub CheckError
9      Dim fs
10     Dim f
11
12     If Err.Number > 0 Then
13       Set fs = CreateObject("Scripting.FileSystemObject")
14       Set f = fs.CreateTextFile(fs.GetTempName())
15
16       WriteToFileAndHtml f, vbNewLine & "<COMMENT>" & vbNewLine & "ASP Error!
     ➥ " & vbNewLing
17       WriteToFileAndHtml f, "      Number: " & err.number & vbNewLine
18       WriteToFileAndHtml f, "      Description: " & err.description & vbNewLine
19       WriteToFileAndHtml f, "      Source: " & err.source & vbNewLine
20       WriteToFileAndHtml f, "</COMMENT> " & vbNewLine
21
22     End If
23     If Not IsEmpty(Con) Then
24       If Con.Errors.Count > 0 Then
25         '
26         ' First count the real errors
27         '
28         Dim i, j
29         j = 0
30         For i = 1 to Con.Errors.Count
31           if Con.Errors(i-1).number <> 0 Then
32             j = j + 1
33           End if
34         Next
35         '
36         ' Now output them if necessary
37         '
38         If j > 0 Then
39           j = 1
```

```
40          If IsEmpty(fs) Then
42
41             Set fs = CreateObject("Scripting.FileSystemObject")
43             Set f = fs.CreateTextFile(fs.GetTempName())
44          End If
45
46          WriteToFileAndHtml f, vbNewLine & "<COMMENT>" & vbNewLine &
            ➥"ADO Errors!" & vbNewLine
47          For i = 1 to Con.Errors.Count
48            If Con.Errors(i-1).number <> 0 Then
49              WriteToFileAndHtml f, " ADO Error " & j & vbNewLine
50              WriteToFileAndHtml f, "     Number: " & Con.Errors(i-1).number &
                ➥ vbNewLine
51              WriteToFileAndHtml f, "     Description: "
                ➥ & Con.Errors(i-1).description & vbNewLine
52              WriteToFileAndHtml f, "     Source: " & Con.Errors(i-1).source &
                ➥ vbNewLine
53              If Con.Errors(i-1).nativeerror <> "" Then
54                WriteToFileAndHtml f, "     Native Error: "
                  ➥ & Con.Errors(i-1).nativeerror & vbNewLine
55              End If
56              If Con.Errors(i-1).sqlstate <> "" Then
57                WriteToFileAndHtml f, "     SQL State: "
                  ➥ & Con.Errors(i-1).sqlstate & vbNewLine
58              End If
59            End If
60          Next
61          WriteToFileAndHtml f, "</COMMENT> " & vbNewLine
62
63        End If
64      End If
65    End If
66
67    If Not IsEmpty(fs) Then
68      f.Close
69    End If
70 End Sub
```

ANALYSIS The modified version of debug.asp is included on the CD-ROM that accompanies this book with the name debug2.asp. The first change to debug.asp is to add a new function (lines 1–6) that echoes strings to both the ASP page and a file that is passed in as fFileStream. Next, new objects are created in CheckError (lines 9–10) that can keep track of a file. The temporary file is potentially created in two places, lines 13–14 and lines 40–44, because if there's no ASP error, lines 13–14 won't be executed. The temporary file is then closed, if necessary, in lines 67–69. Finally, each of the calls to Response.Write is changed to WriteToFileAndHtml (lines 16–20 and 46–61).

Note

> The temporary files created in this manner are, by default, placed in the
> \winnt\system32 directory, and are named with strange looking filenames—
> three letters, followed by five numbers, with a .tmp extension. The exercises
> will give you an opportunity to change the location and filenames, if you
> want.

The new version of CheckError writes a separate log file for each error that your users
might encounter as they navigate your site. As previously mentioned in the section
"Creating a Debug Library," because CheckError is in debug.asp, any of the ASP
pages that call it to log errors take advantage of this new functionality. Of course, you
will need to proactively check the temporary files periodically to look for these sorts of
errors. In a later chapter, we will discuss how to have the Web server automatically email
these logs to you.

Testing for Scalability

Before you decide to open your E-Commerce site, imagine how much traffic you would
need to have to feel really successful; then multiply that traffic by 10. This algorithm for
calculating traffic is a standard metric that commercial Web sites use. The reason for this
is that if you do exceed your own expectations, you want to make sure that you provide
all your customers a good experience.

If you are expecting a small number of customers (a few hundred per day), testing for
scalability isn't so important. On the other hand, if you are expecting thousands of customers, you owe it to yourself and to them to measure how well the site responds to that
kind of load. To do so, you will either need a lot of friends and a lot of computers, or you
will need a tool that can create simulated load, like WebLoad, LoadRunner, or the
Microsoft Web Capacity Analysis Tool.

Microsoft's WCAT is available for free from Microsoft's Web site at http://
msdn.microsoft.com/workshop/server/toolbox/wcat.asp. Using WCAT requires you
to have at least three computers: a server, a controller, and one or more clients. The server is your production Web server; the controller and clients are Windows NT Workstation
or Windows NT Server machines. Run the WCAT setup program on all these machines.
On the server machine, run the Extract Server Content program.

WCAT also requires you to know the IP addresses of your client and controller
machines. If you don't know these addresses, you can use the command-line utility ping
to find them out. Go to the Start menu and select Programs, Command Prompt. When the
Command Prompt appears, type **ping <machine name>**. The machine's IP address will

appear within square brackets. In the example in Figure 16.19, the IP address of the machine named MIKA is 192.168.201.1. Repeat this process for the server and the controller.

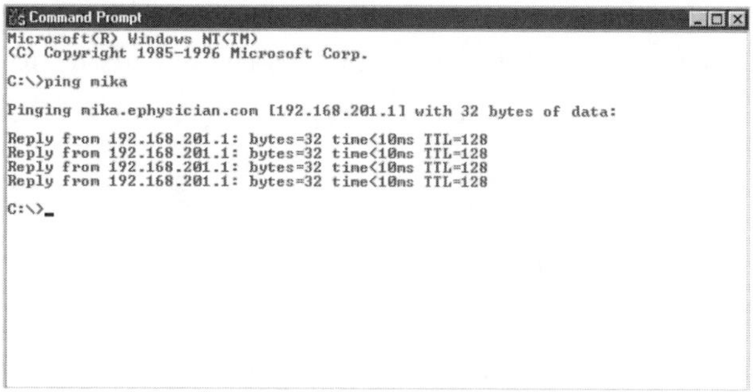

FIGURE 16.19

Pinging MIKA.

```
Command Prompt                                                    _ □ X
Microsoft(R) Windows NT(TM)
(C) Copyright 1985-1996 Microsoft Corp.

C:\>ping mika

Pinging mika.ephysician.com [192.168.201.1] with 32 bytes of data:

Reply from 192.168.201.1: bytes=32 time<10ms TTL=128
Reply from 192.168.201.1: bytes=32 time<10ms TTL=128
Reply from 192.168.201.1: bytes=32 time<10ms TTL=128
Reply from 192.168.201.1: bytes=32 time<10ms TTL=128

C:\>_
```

16

To configure the controller and each client, you will need to bring up a Command Prompt. On the controller, change to the directory that contains the controller (by default c:\webctrl, so type **cd \webctrl**); then type **config <Server-IP-Address>**. For example, if MIKA is the controller, you would type **config 192.168.201.1**. On each client, change to the directory for the WCAT client and type **config <controller-name> <controller-IP>**. You can now start your clients by typing **client** at a command prompt on each client; then start the controller by typing **run <testname>**.

A simple way to test your customers' experience is to run the asp75 test that comes with the WCAT utility; then, from an unused machine, try using your Web site. This will give you the user experience of using a loaded server. As you get more adventurous, the WCAT documentation explains how to script your own tests and capture a wide variety of statistics. Should you want to, you might also explore using commercial tools to script your testing, or using commercial firms to monitor your E-Commerce site's performance from various parts of the country.

Summary

This chapter introduces deployment, debugging, and testing. You learned how and why to keep your development system separate from your production system. You also learned how to install and use Visual InterDev's integrated debugger on a development system, and how to debug your application on a production system using HTML comments and temporary files. Finally, you learned about Microsoft's WCAT tool.

Q&A

Q **My debugger is no longer breaking at breakpoints. Instead of a red circle, I see a red circle with a question mark in it. What do I do?**

A This is a very common problem. First, make sure that you have installed the latest NT Service Pack. If this doesn't fix the problem, try the following:

1. Go to Control Panel, Services and stop the World Wide Web Publishing Service.
2. Open a command prompt. Type `cd \winnt\system32\inetsrv`.
3. Type `regsvr32 asp.dll`.
4. Restart the World Wide Web Publishing Service.

For more information, see the article "Microsoft Visual InterDev 6.0 Debugging" at the Microsoft MSDN Web site at the following URL:

`http://msdn.microsoft.com/library/techart/msdn_videbugging.htm`

Q **I've done scalability testing and am disappointed with the results—or—my customers are complaining about the speed of my site. What do I do?**

A Congratulations! This is a great problem to have.

Performance on Web servers can be influenced by a variety of factors—amount of memory in the machine, processor speed, network speed, or disk drive (or disk controller) speed.

The first thing to do is isolate which of these factors is causing your problem. NT comes with a tool called Performance Monitor that allows you to measure how much of each resource your system is using. If your processor utilization is maximized, try running with a faster machine. If your hard drive keeps spinning, try increasing memory. If neither of these is the problem, you might need faster disk drives, or you might need to talk with your ISP about getting more bandwidth.

Q **I have a bug that I can't figure out. What do I do?**

A Even the best programmers run into problems that at first look unsolvable. Relax, get a cup of coffee, and think about something else for awhile. If the answer still doesn't come to you, visit Microsoft's Web site or some of the sites listed in the inside back cover of this book for helpful troubleshooting tips. So many people are writing ASP these days that chances are someone else has run into your problem.

Workshop

The Quiz and Exercise questions are designed to test your knowledge of the material covered in this chapter. The answers are in Appendix A, "Quiz Answers."

Quiz

1. Why is it important to keep separate development and production Web sites?
2. What is a breakpoint?
3. Can I install the debugger on my production server?
4. Why should I keep all my debugging routines in a single script?
5. How much load should I plan to handle?

16

Exercise

Update the CheckError function so that it writes log files into a directory on your Web site.

DAY 17

Administering Your Store Remotely with ASPs

After your E-Commerce site is up and debugged, if unchanged, it will normally keep running without intervention. Of course, you will want to make changes to your store as it runs. The changes you make might be administrative, they might be additions to, changes to, or deletions from the catalog, or they might be structural changes. These changes are simple when you make them from your system's console; however, they are also easy to perform remotely.

IIS comes with a built-in Web site that allows you to administrate your Web site through an HTML based interface. In addition, you can use a combination of your own Web pages and the FTP server, or Microsoft Posting Acceptor to modify your store's catalog.

Today, you will learn

- How to install and secure the IIS administration pages
- How to administer your Web server with the IIS administration pages
- How to install and administer the IIS FTP service

- How to upload files to your site using FTP
- How to perform advanced, Web-based catalog maintenance

The IIS Administration Pages

In previous chapters, you have learned to use the Internet Service Manager to administer your E-Commerce site's Web server. The Internet Service Manager for the Microsoft Management Console is a powerful and useful tool, but it can only be used from a computer that is part of the same Windows domain as your Web server. You might find yourself in a situation in which you don't have access to such a machine but need to administer your site. The IIS Internet Service Manager Web pages give you the ability to perform many site administration tasks from any machine with Internet access and a Web browser.

Installing the Administration Pages

If you are using Windows 2000, the Internet Service Manager Web pages should already be installed on your machine. If you are using Windows NT, you can install the Internet Service Manager Web pages by doing the following:

1. Go to the Start menu and select Programs, Windows NT 4.0 Option Pack, Windows NT 4.0 Option Pack Setup.

2. When the Setup program appears, press the Next button, and then press the Add/Remove button.

3. Select Internet Information Server (IIS) and press the Show Subcomponents button.

4. Check the box beside Internet Service Manager (HTML) (see Figure 17.1) and press OK. Press the Next button. The setup program will then install the additional components and might prompt you to reboot your computer. Do so.

FIGURE 17.1

Installing IIS sub-components.

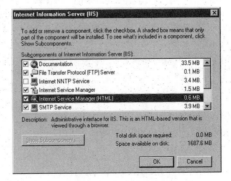

5. Re-install the latest Windows NT Service Pack.

The Internet Service Manager (HTML) is now installed into a virtual directory called IISADMIN. It is ready to use, but only from a browser running on the server on which it was installed. Navigate to http://localhost/IISADMIN to explore its features (see Figure 17.2).

FIGURE 17.2

The home page of the Internet Service Manager (HTML).

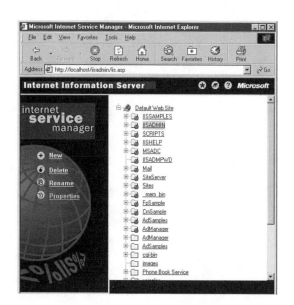

Securing the Administration Pages

At this point, if you try to access the Internet Service Manager (HTML) with a browser running on a machine other than the Web server that runs your E-Commerce site, you will observe the following messages:

```
HTTP Error 403 - Access to Internet Service Manager (HTML) is
restricted to Localhost

403.6 Forbidden: IP address rejected
```

Note

Every machine that runs TCP/IP can refer to itself by using either its assigned IP address (or, in the case of a multi-homed machine, assigned IP addresses) or the special IP address *127.0.0.1*. Similarly, all machines that run TCP/IP can refer to themselves with the special name *localhost*, which always refers to 127.0.0.1.

You'll receive this error message because, as a security precaution, the setup program uses the IP address restriction feature of IIS to limit access to the Internet Service Manager (HTML) to browsers running on the server on which it was installed. To enable access to the Internet Service Manager (HTML) for browsers running on other machines, you will need to use the Internet Service Manager to broaden these restrictions.

To update the IP address restrictions for the Internet Service Manager (HTML), you can use either the Internet Service Manager for MMC or the Internet Service Manager (HTML) from the Web server machine. To use the Internet Service Manager (HTML), go to the Web server machine and follow these steps:

1. Open a browser and navigate to `http://localhost/IISADMIN`.

2. If it isn't already expanded, expand the default Web site by clicking the plus symbol next to the text Default Web Site (see Figure 17.3).

FIGURE 17.3

Expanding the Default Web Site.

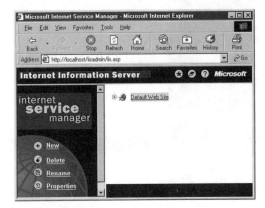

3. Click on the virtual directory `IISADMIN`.

4. Select Properties, Security link in the left hand navigation bar (see Figure 17.4).

5. Click the Edit button in the IP Address and Domain Name Restrictions section of the security page (see Figure 17.5).

6. Change the IP Address Access Restrictions to Grant Access to All Computers by default (see Figure 17.6) and click the OK link.

Caution

At this point, anyone with access to the Internet can administer your Web site by visiting `http://www.yoursite.com/iisadmin`. So don't stop here. Continue through steps 7–10.

FIGURE 17.4

The WWW Properties page for IISADMIN.

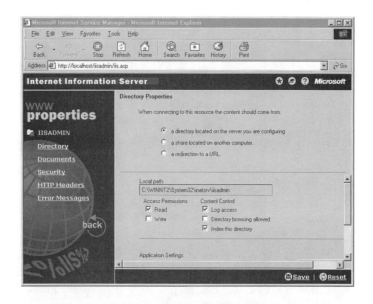

FIGURE 17.5

The security administration page.

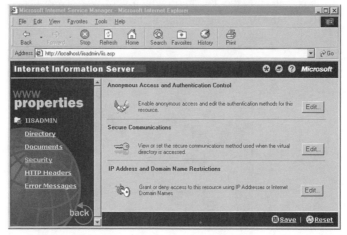

7. Click the Edit button in the Anonymous Access and Authentication Control section of the security page (see Figure 17.5).

8. In the Access methods page that appears (see Figure 17.7), verify that the Allow Anonymous check box is **not** checked and the Windows NT Challenge/Response check box is checked. (This is called Integrated Windows Authentication in the case of Windows 2000.)

FIGURE 17.6

Granting access to the admin pages to all computers.

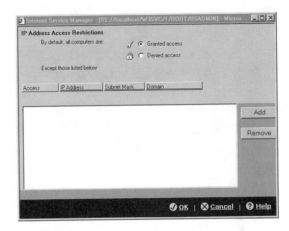

If you plan to administer your Web site from machines running browsers other than Internet Explorer such as Netscape Navigator, you can check the Basic Authentication box. Click the Edit button in the Basic Authentication section of the dialog box, and enter the domain in which your Web server is a member. Otherwise, verify that the Basic Authentication check box is **not** checked. Finally, click the OK link.

FIGURE 17.7

The Access Methods page.

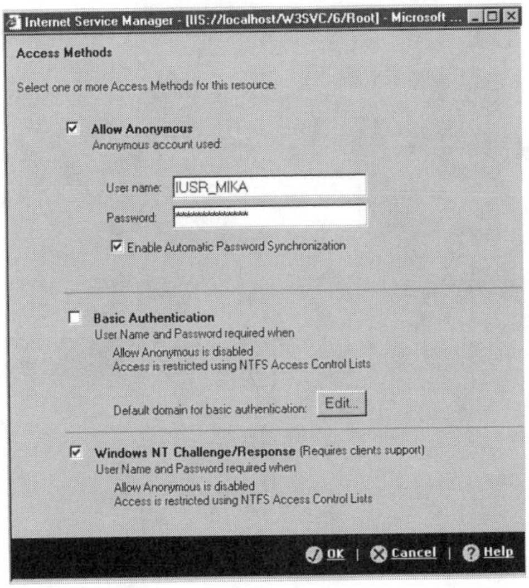

> **Caution**
>
> Basic Authentication is less secure than other forms of authentication. Only enable Basic Authentication if you are sure that you will need to administer your site from a machine that doesn't have Internet Explorer installed.

If you have installed a server certificate on your Web server and enabled the Secure Sockets Layer (see Days 8, "Building the Transaction Databases," and 15, "Securing Your Store"), you should require secure communications with the administration pages by following steps 9 and 10.

9. Click the Edit button in the Secure Communications section of the security page (see Figure 17.5). This button will appear only if you have a server certificate installed.

10. Check the box labeled Require Secure Channel when accessing this resource (see Figure 17.8). Click the OK link.

17

FIGURE 17.8

*The Secure
Communications page.*

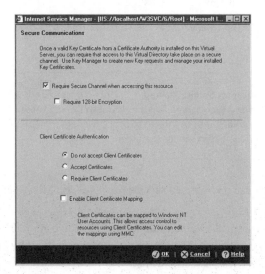

> **Note**
>
> If you know that you will always be accessing the administration pages with a browser that has 128-bit security (Netscape Navigator or Internet Explorer 128-bit, US/Canada versions), you should check the box labeled Require 128-bit Encryption for additional security.

After completing step 10, the access methods page will refresh, and you will observe the following messages:

```
HTTP Error 403

403.4 Forbidden: SSL Required.
```

Don't worry—this is to be expected, as you just reconfigured your Web server to require SSL to access the administration pages. Close the page with the error, go back to the Web browser you are using to configure your Web server and change the beginning of the URL from http to https. You can now administer your E-Commerce site from anywhere by pointing a browser to https://www.yoursite.com/iisadmin.

Using the Administration Pages

You can use the Internet Service Manager (HTML) to remotely perform many of the administrative functions for which you would normally use the Internet Service Manager for MMC. The most obvious differences are

- You cannot use the Internet Service Manager (HTML) to start or stop a Web service.

> **Note** The Internet Service Manager (HTML) is Web-based, which means that it requires a Web server. As such, it doesn't make sense to be able to stop the Web server that the Internet Service Manager (HTML) is running on from the HTML-based service manager.

- You can only use the Internet Service Manager (HTML) to administer the Default Web Site.
- Although you can add new virtual directories, you cannot change the physical (NT) directories they point to. The physical directories will all be contained within the physical directories for their parents.

Other than these exceptions, you will find the Internet Service Manager (HTML) a useful tool for performing emergency maintenance on your E-Commerce site.

Installing and Administering the IIS FTP Service

One of the more common remote tasks you might need to perform on your E-Commerce site will be to add and remove content—for example, directories, Web pages, and images. Using the *File Transport Protocol (FTP)* Service is one way to do just that.

Note

The FTP service implements one of the oldest Internet technologies, the File Transport Protocol, which dates back to 1971.

By default, the FTP service is installed on Windows 2000. If you are using Windows NT, the FTP service might not be installed. To check whether it is, go to the Start Menu and select Windows NT 4.0 Option Pack, Microsoft Internet Information Server, Internet Service Manager. Go to the left panel, open the Internet Information Server node, and select your server. In the right panel, you should observe an icon for an FTP Site (often called *Default FTP Site*—see Figure 17.9).

17

FIGURE 17.9

The Default FTP Site.

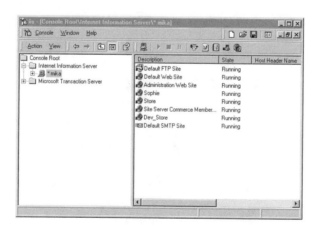

If the FTP server is not installed, you can install it by doing the following:

1. Go to the Start menu and select Programs, Windows NT 4.0 Option Pack, Windows NT 4.0 Option Pack Setup.

2. When the Setup program appears, press the Next button, and then press the Add/Remove button.

3. Select Internet Information Server (IIS) and press the Show Subcomponents button.

4. Check the box beside File Transport Protocol(FTP) (see Figure 17.1) and press OK. Press the Next button. The setup program will then install the additional components and might prompt you to reboot your computer. Do so.

5. Re-install the latest Windows NT Service Pack.

After the FTP service is installed on your Web server, you can examine its configuration by right-clicking the FTP site in Internet Service Manager and choosing Properties. You will want to make several changes to the default configuration to improve security. First, you will want to restrict *anonymous access* to your FTP server; then you will want to add a *virtual FTP directory* for your Web site.

| Caution | Anonymous access to an FTP server dates back to the early days of the Internet, when FTP servers were used to share data. Enabling anonymous access is useful for Web sites that, like Download.com, are primarily intended to distribute files. It is generally not appropriate for E-Commerce sites. |

To configure your FTP server, follow these steps:

1. To turn off anonymous access to your FTP server, select the Security Accounts tab of the FTP Site Properties dialog box (see Figure 17.10) and uncheck the Allow Anonymous Connections box. Press the OK button.

FIGURE 17.10

The Security Accounts tab of the FTP Site Properties dialog box.

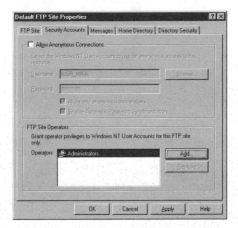

2. To add a virtual FTP directory for your Web site, select Actions, New, Virtual Directory from the Internet Service Manager. The New Virtual Directory wizard will appear and prompt you to enter a directory name. Enter a name (for example, **Site**) and press the Next button.

3. The next page will prompt you to enter the physical path for your new directory. Enter the path to your Web server (for example, `C:\InetPub\wwwroot\candystore`).

4. The next page will prompt you for the kinds of access permissions you want to provide for the directory. Check both boxes to allow read and write access.

The new directory will appear in the Internet Service Manager (see Figure 17.11). You are now ready to use the FTP service to upload and download files to and from your Web site.

FIGURE 17.11

The new virtual FTP directory appears in the Internet Service Manager.

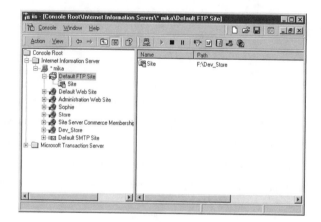

17

Uploading Files to Your Site Using FTP

Like the Web, FTP is a client-server protocol. Whereas the Web uses a Web server as the server and a browser as the client, FTP uses an FTP server as the server and an FTP client as the client. By installing and configuring the FTP Service as described in the previous section, you have set up your Web server to also function as an FTP server and to communicate with FTP clients. You can now use an FTP client to connect to the FTP service.

Note

A *client-server* protocol is a standardized method for allowing client processes and server processes to communicate. A *client process* interacts with users, allowing the users to request services from server processes. A *server process* waits for a request to arrive from the client process and then responds to those requests. The standardization of protocols allows a wide variety of client processes that might run on a wide variety of machines to request the same set of services from a wide variety of server processes that also might run on a wide variety of machines.

Windows 95, Windows 98, Windows NT, and Windows 2000 come with a simple, text-oriented FTP client. Figure 17.12 illustrates the steps involved in using the simple Windows FTP client to transfer a file to the Web site:

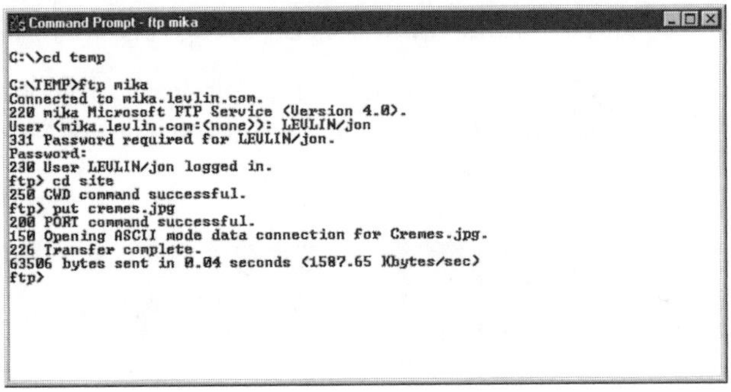

FIGURE 17.12

A transcript of uploading a file to a Web server.

```
C:\>cd temp

C:\TEMP>ftp mika
Connected to mika.leulin.com.
220 mika Microsoft FTP Service (Version 4.0).
User (mika.leulin.com:(none)): LEULIN/jon
331 Password required for LEULIN/jon.
Password:
230 User LEULIN/jon logged in.
ftp> cd site
250 CWD command successful.
ftp> put cremes.jpg
200 PORT command successful.
150 Opening ASCII mode data connection for Cremes.jpg.
226 Transfer complete.
63506 bytes sent in 0.04 seconds (1587.65 Kbytes/sec)
ftp>
```

1. Open an MS-DOS (Windows 95 or Windows 98) or Command Prompt.
2. Change the directory to the directory that contains the file you want to transfer; for example, cd temp.
3. Run the FTP program by typing **ftp yourhost.com**.
4. The FTP program will prompt you for a username. Enter **DOMAIN/username**.

> **Note**
>
> We are using *DOMAIN* as a placeholder for the Windows NT domain of your Web server, and *username* as a placeholder for your Windows NT username. Note that, unlike many Windows applications, we use the forward slash to separate domain and username.

5. The program will then prompt you for a password. Enter your Windows account password.
6. Change the directory to the virtual directory you created above by typing **cd site**.

> **Note**
>
> Subdirectories of the Web server appear as subdirectories of the virtual directory, so in order to upload files to a subdirectory named dir, you would type **cd site/dir** instead of **cd site**.

7. Upload the file by typing **put filename**.

The file will now be available on your Web server.

> **Note**
>
> More modern, easier to use FTP client software is available as shareware or freeware from sources like download.com. One of my favorites is CuteFTP. CuteFTP allows you to perform FTP transfers with an interface that appears more like the Windows Explorer.

In addition to sending a file from a client computer to the FTP server, the FTP client can also be used to download files (the `get` command) and delete files (the `del` command). To get a list of commands, type **?** at the ftp prompt. To get help on a specific command, type **Help command**.

You will find that FTP is an invaluable tool for site maintenance, especially if you are on the road. For example, before installing the FTP service, adding or updating a product's picture with the `addproduct.asp` and `updateproduct.asp` requires physical access to the server. With the installation of the FTP service, you can now add and update product images using a combination of FTP and the catalog maintenance pages.

Advanced Web-Based Product Catalog Maintenance

In Chapter 5, we introduced the `addproduct.asp`, `updateProduct.asp`, and `manageproducts.asp` pages, which allow you to add, update, and manage the products in your catalog. In this section, we will integrate these pages into the administration pages created in Day 16, "Debugging Your E-Commerce Applications," making `adminPage.asp` the home page of an administrative Web site. To prepare for these changes, move the following files to the admin directory:

- `addProduct.asp`
- `updateProduct.asp`
- `manageProducts.asp`

We will then extend each of these pages to add functionality that will allow easier, more secure, remote catalog maintenance. The maintenance is made easier by using the Microsoft Posting Acceptor (installed in Chapter 16) to extend these pages to add or update all a product's attributes, including images, from a browser page. After you move these files, you must secure the admin directory by setting a password on the administrative pages (see sidebar).

17

Setting a Password on Your Administrative Pages Directory

The interfaces described in this section make it quick and easy to modify your catalog. This is convenient, but it presents a significant security risk. In general, any pages that can perform powerful operations should be protected.

IIS makes it easy to require a user to enter a password when he accesses a directory. As we will place all these pages into the admin directory, protecting that directory is the most obvious way to protect the pages. You can require a Windows NT username and password for any access to files in the admin directory in the following manner:

1. Launch the Internet Service Manager (called the Internet Services Manger on Windows 2000).

2. Choose Action, Properties and go to the Directory Security tab. Press the Anonymous Access and Authentication Control button.

3. In the Authentication Methods dialog that appears (see Figure 17.13), deselect the Allow Anonymous Access button.

The next time a user attempts to access any of the pages in the admin directory, he will be prompted for a username and password (see Figure 17.14).

FIGURE 17.13

The Authentication Methods dialog box.

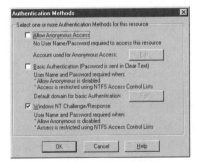

FIGURE 17.14

The Enter Network Password dialog box.

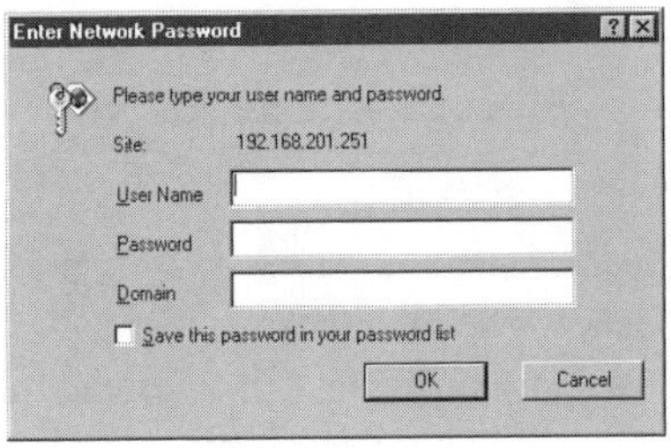

The way the addProduct.asp and updateProduct.asp pages were originally written assumes that, when the store administrator wants to add or modify a product's picture, the file that contains the image is already in the root directory of the store's Web site. This requires the administrator to use an FTP client to upload the image file, and then switch to a browser to change the product database. The Posting Acceptor makes it possible to add or update all a product's attributes, including images, from the same Web page, as long as the store administrator has a relatively recent browser (Netscape Navigator version 3.0 and above or Internet Explorer version 4.0 or above).

How the Posting Acceptor Makes it Easier for the User and the Programmer

We'll need to modify the HTML forms in the addproduct.asp and updateproduct.asp pages to enable the store administrator to upload product pictures. You can upload a file through a standard HTML form by using the FILE attribute of the HTML <INPUT> tag. When you use the FILE attribute in an HTML form, the HTML form will include a Browse button that enables you to select a file from your local hard drive to upload to the Web site (see Figure 17.15). You can use this form element to upload any type of file including documents and images.

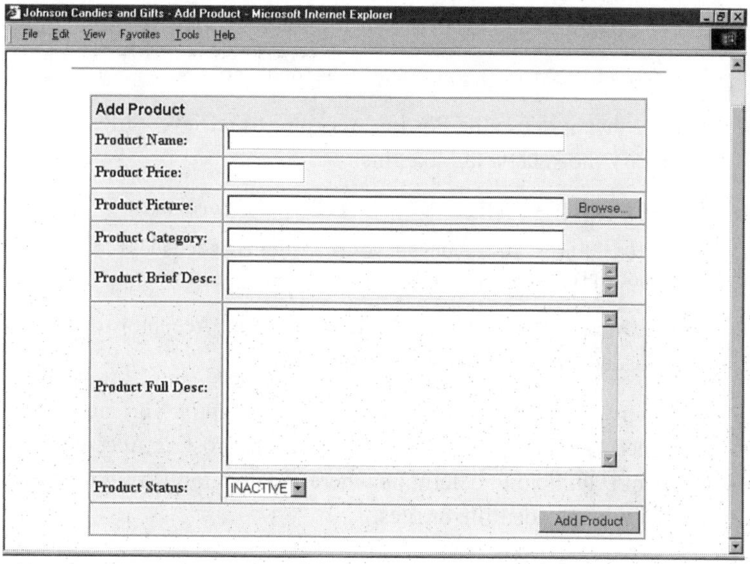

17

FIGURE 17.15

A new Add Product page that supports image file upload, including a Browse button to help users find the file.

Using the FILE attribute has a serious drawback. If you accept file uploads in an HTML form, you can no longer use the Form collection of the Request object to retrieve the form variables. You must use an alternative method of retrieving the form variables. In this section, you will learn how to use the Microsoft Posting Acceptor to accept files uploads.

Note	There are several third-party upload components that you can use instead of the Microsoft Posting Acceptor to accept file uploads. Although these components can be expensive, they are typically much easier to use. To see a list of these components, visit the software section of superexpert at http://asp.superexpert.com/software.

Before you can use an HTML form with the Posting Acceptor, you must make several modifications to the form. First, you must add an ENCTYPE attribute to the <FORM> tag. The ENCTYPE attribute must have the value multipart/form-data. This value enables the form to upload binary files.

Next, you must modify the ACTION attribute of the <FORM> tag. Instead of submitting the form directly to another ASP page, you must submit the form to the Posting Acceptor. For example, suppose that your <FORM> tag looks like this:

```
<FORM METHOD="POST" ACTION="saveform.asp">
```

If you want to use the Posting Acceptor to retrieve a file uploaded in the form, you must modify the <FORM> tag like this:

```
<FORM METHOD="POST" ENCTYPE="multipart/form-data"

ACTION="http://www.yourserver.com/Scripts/cpshost.dll?
➥PUBLISH?saveform.asp">
```

This modified <FORM> tag allows the Posting Acceptor to submit the form data, minus the uploaded file, to the saveform.asp page.

Finally, before you can use the Posting Acceptor, you must add a hidden form field named TargetURL to the HTML form. The Posting Acceptor uses the value of the TargetURL field to determine where, relative to the root directory of the Web server, to post the uploaded file or files.

> **Caution**
>
> By default, the Posting Acceptor cannot be used to enable anonymous visitors to your Web site to upload files. You must place all the pages discussed in this section in a password-protected directory of your Web site.
>
> To enable anonymous visitors to use the Posting Acceptor, you can change a setting in your server's registry. For more information, see Knowledge Base Article Q179566 at the Microsoft Web site.

One significant problem with the Posting Acceptor results when a user doesn't specify a file to be uploaded. If a file isn't uploaded, the Posting Acceptor will simply return an error message. We'll solve this problem by modifying storeFuncs.asp (see Listing 17.1) and by creating a special client-side upload subroutine in upload.asp (see Listing 17.2).

INPUT   **LISTING 17.1**   Additions to storeFuncs.asp

```
1   ' ==========================
2   ' Upload variables
3   ' ==========================
4
5   Dim strServerURL
6   Dim strTargetURL
7   Dim strRepostURL
8   Dim strPathToPA
9   Dim strPostingURL
10
11  strServerURL = "http://" & Request.ServerVariables("SERVER_NAME")
12  strTargetURL = "/Images"
13  strRepostURL = strServerURL & "/donePost.asp"
14  strPathToPA =  strServerURL & "/Scripts/cpshost.dll"
15  strPostingURL = strPathToPA & "?PUBLISH?" + strRepostURL
```

ANALYSIS   Line 11 specifies strServerURL as the default URL to the server and is used as a base to construct other URLs. Line 12 sets strTargetURL, which is used in addProduct.asp (see Listing 17.3) and updateProduct.asp (see Listing 17.4) to inform the Posting Acceptor of the destination directory for uploaded files. In line 13, the variable named strRepostURL is assigned the URL of an ASP page that is used in two situations. When the user doesn't specify a file to be uploaded, it is the URL to which we post directly; when the user specifies a file, it is the URL to which the Posting Acceptor passes control after placing the uploaded file in the strTargetURL directory. In either case, the script in question is named donePost.asp (see Listing 17.5). Line 14 specifies the URL to the Posting Acceptor, and line 15 specifies the actual URL that we use as the value for the FORM tag's ACTION attribute in addProduct.asp and updateProduct.asp.

17

INPUT   **LISTING 17.2**   The upload Subroutine in `upload.asp`

```
1  <script language="VBScript">
2  SUB upload(BYREF frm)
3    DIM numFiles, i
4
5    numFiles = 0
6    FOR i = 0 TO frm.elements.length - 1
7      IF frm.elements(i).type = "file" AND LEN(frm.elements(i).value) > 0 THEN
8        numFiles = numFiles + 1
9      END IF
10   NEXT
11
12   IF numFiles = 0 THEN
13     frm.action = "<%=strRepostURL%>"
14     frm.encoding = "application/x-www-form-urlencoded"
15   END IF
16
17   frm.submit()
18 END SUB
19 </script>
```

Note

The upload subroutine contained in `upload.asp` is a client-side script that uses VBScript. This means that it won't work on browsers such as Netscape Navigator that do not support VBScript. To use the `upload.asp` file, you must use Microsoft Internet Explorer.

ANALYSIS   Line 1 declares that the script inside the `<script></script>` tags is for execution on the client. Line 2 declares the `upload` subroutine, which takes the form to be submitted as an argument. Lines 6–10 count the number of files the user specified for upload. Lines 12–15 handle the case in which the user hasn't specified any files for upload by changing the URL in which the form is submitted (line 13) and the type of the form to the default (line 14). Line 14 assumes that `storeFuncs.asp` has been included so that `strRepostURL` is set to the form processing URL. The subroutine assumes that the form passed in has its attributes set to upload to the Posting Acceptor by default, so if the user has specified at least one file, it submits the form according to its defaults (line 17).

> **Note**
>
> `upload.asp` should be placed in the admin directory where the other product management pages, such as `manageproducts.asp` and `updateproduct.asp`, are stored.

With the common code above, we are almost ready to change the existing product catalog maintenance pages to use the Posting Acceptor and to integrate them into our administration site. The last few steps before making these changes are

1. Verify that the Posting Acceptor is installed. Look for a file called cpshost.dll in your site's script directory.

2. Create a new images directory and move all the image files (*.jpg) there.

3. Go to the Internet Service Manager and right-click the images directory. Set the Access permissions to Read and Write and the Execution permissions to None as shown in Figure 17.16.

> **Caution**
>
> These permission changes are necessary to prevent unauthorized users from uploading and running scripts on your site.

FIGURE 17.16

Permissions set for the new images directory.

4. Change the <IMG> tags in `search.asp`, `productlist.asp`, `product.asp`, `featured.asp`, and `fastproductlist.asp` that refer to the pictures of products so that they refer to the new images directory (for example, change `<IMG SRC="<%=RS ( "product_Picture)%>>` to `<IMG SRC="images/<%=RS("product_Picture)%>>`).

Uploading Pictures from `addProduct.asp` and `updateProduct.asp`

Now that the Posting Acceptor is installed, the images directory created, the directories protected, and the common code written, you are ready to change `addProduct.asp` (see Figure 17.15 and Listing 17.3) and `updateProduct.asp` (see Figure 17.17 and Listing 17.4) so that users can submit pictures. The new pages feature a more consistent look-and-feel and use the common code written in the previous section along with an `<INPUT TYPE="FILE">` tag to allow users to upload new or changed product pictures.

INPUT   **LISTING 17.3**   New `addProduct.asp` that Can Upload Images

```
1   <!-- #include file="../storeFuncs.asp" -->
2
3   <html>
4   <head><title>Johnson Candies and Gifts - Add Product </title></head>
5   <body link="#ff4040" vtext="lightred" bgcolor="#ffffff">
6
7   <!-- #include file="upload.asp" -->
8
9   <center>
10  <table width="640" border="0" bgcolor="#ffffff" cellspacing="0"
    ➥ cellpadding="0">
11  <tr>
12      <td>
13      <img src="../logo.gif" WIDTH="300" HEIGHT="30">
14      </td>
15  </tr>
16  <tr>
17      <td colspan="2">
18      <hr width="640">
19      </td>
20  </tr>
21  </table>
22  <form method="post" enctype="multipart/form-data" name="form"
    ➥action="<%=strPostingURL%>">
23  <input type="hidden" name="TargetURL" value="<%=strTargetURL%>">
24  <table width="600" border=1 bgcolor="lightyellow" cellpadding="4"
    ➥cellspacing="0">
25  <tr>
26      <td colspan="2" bgcolor="yellow">
27      <font face="Arial" size="3"><b>Add Product</b></font>
28      </td>
29  </tr>
30  <tr>
31      <td><b> Product Name:</b></td>
32      <td><input name="productName" size="50" maxlength="50"></td>
```

```
33 </tr>
34 <tr>
35    <td><b>Product Price:</b></td>
36    <td><input name="productPrice" size="10"></td>
37 </tr>
38 <tr>
39    <td><b>Product Picture:</b></td>
40    <td><input name="productPicture" type="file"
      ➥size="50" maxlength="50"></td>
41 </tr>
42 <tr>
43    <td><b>Product Category:</b></td>
44    <td><input name="productCategory" size="50" maxlength="50"></td>
45 </tr>
46 <tr>
47    <td><b>Product Brief Desc:</b></td>
48    <td><textarea name="productBriefDesc" cols="50"
      ➥rows="2" wrap="virtual"></textarea></td>
49 </tr>
50 <tr>
51    <td><b>Product Full Desc:</b></td>
52    <td><textarea name="productFullDesc" cols="50"
      ➥rows="10" wrap="virtual"></textarea></td>
53 </tr>
54 <tr>
55    <td><b>Product Status:</b></td>
56    <td><select name="productStatus"><option value="0">INACTIVE
57    <option value="1">ACTIVE</select></td>
58 </tr>
59 <tr>
60    <td colspan=2 align="right"><input type="button" value="Add Product"
      ➥ onclick="upload(form)"> </td>
61 </tr>
62 </table>
63
64 <input name="addProduct" type="hidden" value="1">
65 </form>
66 </center>
67 </body>
68 </html>
```

17

ANALYSIS Lines 1 and 7 include the common code from the previous section. Line 22 gives the form the name "form" so that it can be passed to the upload subroutine (see line 60) and sets it to be submitted by default to strPostingURL (defined in storeFuncs.asp, Listing 17.1) as a multipart/form-data, which allows the image file to be submitted in binary form. Line 23 defines the hidden TargetURL input to tell the Posting Acceptor where to place the uploaded file. Line 40 is the <INPUT TYPE="FILE"> tag, in which the user can specify where to find the new item's picture on his computer.

Line 60 changes the Add Product button from a TYPE="submit" (which just submits the form as specified in the <FORM> tag) to a TYPE="button", and calls the upload subroutine (see Listing 17.2) with the form when the button is clicked. Finally, line 64 is a hidden INPUT field that informs the form processor that the data is coming from addProduct.asp.

INPUT **LISTING 17.4**   Changes to updateProduct.asp to Allow Images to Be Uploaded

```
1  <!--#include file='../storefuncs.asp'-->
2  <%
3  Response.Buffer = TRUE
4
5  ' Get the Product ID
6  productID = Request( "pid" )
7
8  ' Open the Database Connection
9  Set Con = Server.CreateObject( "ADODB.Connection" )
10 Con.Open "accessDSN"
11
12 ' Open the Recordset
13 Set RS = Server.CreateObject( "ADODB.Recordset" )
14 RS.ActiveConnection = Con
15 RS.CursorType = 3
16 RS.Open "SELECT * FROM Products WHERE product_id=" & productID
17 IF NOT RS.EOF THEN
18   productName      = RS( "product_name" )
19   productPrice      = RS( "product_price" )
20   productPicture    = RS( "product_picture" )
21   productCategory  = RS( "product_category" )
22   productBriefDesc = RS( "product_briefDesc" )
23   productFullDesc   = RS( "product_fullDesc" )
24   productStatus      = RS( "product_status" )
25 END IF
26 ' Close the Recordset
27 RS.Close
28
29 ' Assign Default Values
30 IF productName = "?????" THEN
31   productName = ""
32 END IF
33
34 IF productCategory = "?????" THEN
35   productCategory = ""
36 END IF
37 IF (productBriefDesc = "?????") OR (productBriefDesc = ("?????" & vbCrLf))
   ➥THEN
38   productBriefDesc = ""
39 END IF
```

```
40 IF (productFullDesc = "?????") OR (productFullDesc = ("?????" & vbCrLf)) THEN
41   productFullDesc = ""
42 END IF
43
44 FUNCTION SELECTED( firstVal, secondVal )
45   IF cSTR( firstVal ) = cSTR( secondVAL ) THEN
46     SELECTED = " SELECTED "
47   END IF
48 END FUNCTION
49
50 %>
51 <html>
52 <head><title>Johnson Candies and Gifts - Update Product </title></head>
53 <body link="#ff4040" vtext="lightred" bgcolor="#ffffff">
54
55 <!-- #include file="upload.asp" -->
56
57 <center>
58 <table width="640" border="0" bgcolor="#ffffff" cellspacing="0"
   ➥cellpadding="0">
59 <tr><td><img src="../logo.gif" WIDTH="300" HEIGHT="30"></td></tr>
60 <tr><td colspan="2"><hr width="640"></td></tr>
61 </table>
62 <form method="post" enctype="multipart/form-data"
   ➥name="form" action="<%=strPostingURL%>">
63 <input type="hidden" name="TargetURL" value="<%=strTargetURL%>">
64     <table width="600" border=1 bgcolor="lightyellow"
      ➥cellpadding="4" cellspacing="0">
65     <tr>
66       <td colspan="2" bgcolor="yellow"><font face="Arial" size="3">
        ➥<b>Update Product</b></font></td>
67     </tr>
68     <tr>
69       <td><b>Product Name:</b></td>
70       <td><input name="productName" size="50" maxlength="50"
        ➥value="<%=Server.HTMLEncode(productName)%>"></td>
71     </tr>
72     <tr>
73       <td><b>Product Price:</b></td>
74       <td><input name="productPrice" size="10"
        ➥value="<%=productPrice%>"></td>
75     </tr>
76     <tr>
77       <td> <b>Current Product Picture:</b> </td>
78       <td>
79       <% IF productPicture <> "?????" THEN %>
80         <img src="/images/<%=productPicture%>">
81         <input type="hidden" name="currentPicture"
          ➥value="<%=productPicture%>">
82       <% ELSE %>
```

continues

17

LISTING 17.4   continued

```
83           No picture currently specified.
84          <% END IF %>
85         </td>
86       </tr>
87       <tr>
88         <td><b>New Product Picture:</b></td>
89         <td><input name="productPicture" type="file" size="50" maxlength="50">
           ➥</td>
90       </tr>
91       <tr>
92         <td><b>Product Category:</b></td>
93         <td><input name="productCategory" size="50" maxlength="50"
           ➥value="<%=Server.HTMLEncode(productCategory)%>"></td>
94       </tr>
95       <tr>
96         <td><b>Product Brief Desc:</b></td>
97         <td><textarea name="productBriefDesc" cols="50" rows="2"
           ➥wrap="virtual"><%=Server.HTMLEncode(productBriefDesc)%></textarea></td>
98
99       </tr>
100      <tr>
101        <td><b>Product Full Desc:</b></td>
102        <td><textarea name="productFullDesc" cols="50" rows="10"
           ➥wrap="virtual"><%=Server.HTMLEncode(productFullDesc)%></textarea></td>
103      </tr>
104      <tr>
105        <td><b>Product Status:</b></td>
106        <td><select name="productStatus">
107          <option value="0" <%=SELECTED( "0", productStatus )%>>INACTIVE
108            <option value="1" <%=SELECTED( "1", productStatus )%>>ACTIVE
109        </select></td>
110      </tr>
111      <tr>
112        <td colspan=2 align="right"><input type="button" value="Update Product"
           ➥onclick="upload(form)"></td>
113      </tr>
114    </table>
115
116    <input name="productID" type="hidden" value="<%=productID%>">
117    <input name="updateProduct" type="hidden" value="1">
118  </form>
119
120  </center>
121  </body>
122  </html>
```

ANALYSIS   The new updateproduct.asp page is shown in Figure 17.17. Lines 1 and 55 include the common code from the previous section. Lines 6–27 get information about the selected product from the database: the product's ID is passed in as the Request item `pid` (line 6), the record is selected from the database (lines 13–16), and the information about the product is stored in script variables (lines 18–24). If a user doesn't specify information for a specific product property, five question marks are stored in the database; lines 29–42 detect the question marks and convert them to blanks for display to the user.

Line 62 gives the form the name `"form"` so that it can be passed to the upload subroutine (see line 112), and sets it to be submitted by default to `strPostingURL` (defined in `storeFuncs.asp`, Listing 17.1) as a `multipart/form-data`, which allows the image file to be submitted in binary. Line 63 defines the hidden `TargetURL` input to tell the Posting Acceptor where to place the uploaded file.

Lines 76–86 display the product's current picture, if in the database; if no product picture is available, a message is displayed (line 83). Line 89 is the `<INPUT TYPE="FILE">` tag, in which the user can specify where to find the item's new picture on his computer. Along with the function `SELECTED` (lines 44–48), lines 106–109 display whether the product is currently set to be available in the database. Line 112 changes the Update Product button from a `TYPE="submit"` (which just submits the form as specified in the `<FORM>` tag) to a `TYPE="button"`, and calls the upload subroutine (Listing 17.2) with the form when the button is clicked. Line 116 identifies the existing product's ID to the processing form. Finally, line 117 is a hidden `INPUT` field that informs the form processor that the data is coming from `updateProduct.asp`.

Note

Identifying the form as we do in lines 64 (see Listing 17.3) and 117 (see Listing 17.4) allows us to place the form processing code for both `addProduct.asp` and `updateProduct.asp`, most of which is shared, in the same place (`donePost.asp`, Listing 17.5).

Moving Form Processing Logic from `manageProducts.asp` to the New `donePost.asp`

The old versions of `addProduct.asp` and `updateProduct.asp` always submit directly to `manageProducts.asp`. Because of limitations of the Posting Acceptor, the new versions of these files submit to the new file `donePost.asp` (see Listing 17.5), either via the Posting Acceptor or directly. The scripts in this new file perform the database processing that was previously done by scripts in `manageProducts.asp`. The changes to `manageProducts.asp` are primarily deletions and are available on the CD-ROM that accompanies this book.

FIGURE **17.17**

A new Update Product
page that supports
image file upload.

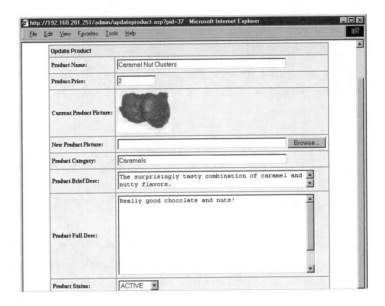

INPUT   **LISTING 17.5**   The New File donePost.asp

```
1    <%@ Language=VBScript %>
2    <!--#include file='storefuncs.asp'-->
3    <%
4    Response.Buffer = TRUE
5
6    Dim addProduct
7    Dim updateProduct
8    Dim productID
9    Dim productName
10   Dim productPrice
11   Dim productPicture
12   Dim currentPicture
13   Dim productCategory
14   Dim productBriefDesc
15   Dim productFullDesc
16   Dim productStatus
17
18   ' Get the Form Variables
19   addProduct        = TRIM( Request.Form( "addProduct" ) )
20   updateProduct     = TRIM( Request.Form( "updateProduct" ) )
21
22   productID         = TRIM( Request.Form( "productID" ) )
23   productName       = TRIM( Request.Form( "productName" ) )
24   productPrice      = TRIM( Request.Form( "productPrice" ) )
25   productPicture    = Request.Form( "fileName" ) &
     ➥Request.Form("fileExtention")
26   currentPicture    = TRIM( Request.Form ( "currentPicture" ) )
27   productCategory   = TRIM( Request.Form( "productCategory" ) )
```

```
28  productBriefDesc  = TRIM( Request.Form( "productBriefDesc" ) )
29  productFullDesc   = TRIM( Request.Form( "productFullDesc" ) )
30  productStatus     = TRIM( Request.Form( "productStatus" ) )
31
32  ' Assign Default Values
33  IF productName = "" THEN
34     productName = "?????"
35  END IF
36  IF productPrice = "" or NOT isNUMERIC( productPrice ) THEN
37     productPrice = 0
38  END IF
39
40  IF productPicture = "" THEN
41     IF currentPicture = "" THEN
42        productPicture = "?????"
43     ELSE
44        productPicture = currentPicture
45     END IF
46  END IF
47
48  IF productCategory = "" THEN
49     productCategory = "?????"
50  END IF
51  IF productBriefDesc = "" THEN
52     productBriefDesc = "?????"
53  END IF
54  IF productFullDesc = "" THEN
55     productFullDesc = "?????"
56  END IF
57
58  ' Open the Database Connection
59  Set Con = Server.CreateObject( "ADODB.Connection" )
60  Con.Open "accessDSN"
61  %>
62  <html>
63  <head><title>Johnson's Candies and Gifts</title></head>
64  <META NAME="GENERATOR" Content="Microsoft Visual Studio 6.0">
65  <body link="#ff4040" bgcolor="#ffffff" vtext="lightred">
66  <center>
67  <table width="640" border="0" bgcolor="#ffffff" cellspacing="0"
    ➥cellpadding="0">
68  <tr><td><IMG height=30 src="logo.gif" width=300></td></tr>
69  <tr><td colspan="2"><hr width="640"><P> </P></td></tr>
70  </table>
71  </center>
72
73  <%
74  ' Add New Product
75  IF addProduct <> "" THEN
76
```

continues

LISTING 17.5   continued

```
77  sqlString = "INSERT INTO Products " &_
78    "( product_name, product_price, product_picture, " &_
79    "product_category, product_briefdesc, product_fulldesc, " &_
80    "product_status ) VALUES ( " &_
81    " '" & productName & "', " &_
82    productPrice & ", " &_
83    " '" & productPicture & "', " &_
84    " '" & productCategory & "', " &_
85    " '" & productBriefDesc & "', " &_
86    " '" & productFullDesc & "', " &_
87    productStatus & "  )"
88
89  Con.Execute sqlString
90
91  %>
92  <CENTER>
93  <table width="600" cellpadding="4" cellspacing="0">
94    <tr>
95      <td><%=productName%> was added to the database</td>
96    </tr>
97    <tr>
98      <td><P align=center><A href="/admin/addProduct.asp">
          ➥Add Another Product</A></P></td>
99      <td><P align=center><A href="/admin/manageproducts.asp">
          ➥Manage Products</A></P></td>
100     <td><P align=center><A href="/admin/adminPage.asp">
          ➥Administration Page</A></P></td>
101   </tr>
102 </table>
103 </CENTER>
104 <p>
105 <%
106 END IF
107
108 ' Update Product
109 IF updateProduct <> "" THEN
110
111 sqlString = "UPDATE Products SET " &_
112   "product_name='" & fixQuotes( productName ) & "'," &_
113   "product_price=" & cCUR( productPrice ) & "," &_
114   "product_picture='" & fixQuotes( productPicture ) & "'," &_
115   "product_category='" & fixQuotes( productCategory ) & "'," &_
116   "product_briefdesc='" & fixQuotes( productBriefDesc ) & "'," &_
117   "product_fulldesc='" &  fixQuotes( productFullDesc ) & "'," &_
118   "product_status=" & productStatus & " WHERE " &_
119   "product_id=" & productID
120
121 Con.Execute sqlString
122
```

```
123 %>
124 <center>
125 <table width="600" cellpadding="4" cellspacing="0">
126   <tr>
127     <td><%=productName%> was updated in the database</td>
128   </tr>
129   <tr>
130     <td><P align=center><A href="/admin/manageproducts.asp">
        ⇥Manage Products</A></P></td>
131     <td><P align=center><A href="/admin/adminPage.asp">
        ⇥Administration Page</A></P></td>
132   </tr>
133 </table>
134 </center>
135 <p align="left"> <%
136 END IF
137 %></p>
138
139 </body>
140 </HTML>
```

ANALYSIS Lines 18–30 retrieve the product data that the user entered in his form. With the exception of productPicture (line 25), this data is taken direct from <INPUT> fields. As for productPicture, if the Posting Acceptor calls the script, the Posting Acceptor will provide the uploaded file's name and extension in two fields called fileName and fileExtension; if addProduct.asp or updateProduct.asp calls the script directly, there will be no uploaded file, and the fields will be blank. Lines 33–56 check whether the fields have not been filled in and, if not, assign them default values. Lines 59–60 open a database connection that is used for either inserting or updating, depending on whether donePost.asp is invoked to add or update a product. If donePost.asp is invoked because of an operation in addProduct.asp, lines 75–89 insert the new product into the database, and lines 92–104 display a confirmation message. Otherwise, if donePost.asp is invoked because of an operation in updateProduct.asp, lines 109–121 update the appropriate record in the database, and lines 124–137 display a confirmation message.

Integrating the Pages into the Administration Web

Now that the scripts are written, we are ready to integrate addProduct.asp and manageProducts.asp into the home page of our administration Web, adminPage.asp. These changes comprise of simply adding links to the two pages (see Listing 17.6) and, *voilá!*—a rudimentary, but very functional administration Web site. The adminPage.asp is shown in Figure 17.18.

LISTING 17.6   Updated adminPage.asp

```
1   <%@ Language="VBScript" %>
2   <%
3     If Request.Form("ProcForm") = "Process" Then
4        Session("iDebugLevel") = Request.Form("debugLevel")
5        If Session("iDebugLevel") = "" Then
6           Session("iDebugLevel") = 0
7        End If
8     End If
9   %>
10  <HTML>
11  <HEAD>
12  <META NAME="GENERATOR" Content="Microsoft Visual Studio 6.0">
13  <title>Johnson's Candies and Gifts Administration Page</title>
14  </head>
15  <body link="#ff4040" vtext="lightred" bgcolor="#ffffff">
16  <center>
17
18  <table width="640" border="0" bgcolor="#ffffff" cellspacing="0"
    ➥cellpadding="0">
19    <tr><td><img src="../logo.gif" WIDTH="300" HEIGHT="30"></td></tr>
20    <tr><td colspan="2"><hr width="640"></td></tr>
21  </table>
22
23  <H2>Administration Page</H2>
24    <H4 align="left">Maintain Catalog</H4>
25    <p><a href="addproduct.asp">Add product</a> </p>
26    <p><a href="manageProducts.asp">Manage Products</a></p>
27  <FORM method="POST" action="adminPage.asp">
28    <h4 align="left">Set Debug Level <input type="hidden" name="ProcForm"
      ➥value="Process"></h4>
29    <table>
30      <tr>
31        <td><div align="right">Debug Level: </div></td>
32        <td><input name="debugLevel" value="
        ➥<%=Session.Value("iDebugLevel")%>"></td>
33      </tr>
34      <tr><td colspan="2"><div align="center">
        ➥<input type="submit" value="Submit"></div></td></tr>
35    </table>
36    </FORM>
37  </center></BODY></HTML>
```

ANALYSIS   The links to addProduct.asp and manageProducts.asp are defined in lines 25 and 26, respectively.

FIGURE 17.18

The new
adminPage.asp.

Summary

In today's lesson, you learned how to administer your Web server from a remote location. In the first section, you learned how to configure your Web server with a standard Web browser by using the HTML interface to the Internet Service Manager. You learned methods of using the HTML version of the Internet Service Manager to perform standard administrative functions such as altering the security settings for a directory.

In the next section, you were introduced to the FTP service. You learned how to use the FTP service to upload and download files from a remote location. You were introduced to basic FTP commands such as the put command, which enables you to upload files from a remote location and the get command, which allows you to download files from a remote location.

Finally, you learned how to upload files to your Web site from a remote location by using the Microsoft Posting Acceptor. First, you learned how to configure the Posting Acceptor to work on your Web server. Next, you modified the store administration pages discussed in previous lessons to enable you to upload pictures of the products contained in your store.

Q&A

Q `upload.asp` **contains something called a** *client-side script*. **What's the difference between a client-side and server-side script?**

A Most of the scripts in this book are *server-side scripts*, which, as the name suggests, are scripts that execute on the server. Any script in an ASP file that appears between the `<%` and `%>` script delimiters is executed on the server. Scripts that are contained between `<SCRIPT></SCRIPT>` tags by default are interpreted and executed on the Web browser. Because these scripts run on the user's machine, they are called client-side scripts.

Server-side scripts are appropriate for most database applications, but in some cases you will need a page to take a different action based on user input. One example of this can be found in this chapter, where the `upload.asp` script submits a page to the Posting Acceptor when a user specifies a file and submits it to an ASP page when she doesn't. The only way this could work is if the browser can execute scripts.

Client-side scripts are also useful in cases in which you don't want the user to have to wait for the server to receive and respond to a message. Many E-Commerce sites use client-side scripts for input verification. This makes the verification faster because the user doesn't have to wait for the server to validate the data the user inputs. It also helps improve the scalability of these sites because the server only processes correct input. The `selectCust.asp` script in the next chapter illustrates the use of client-side script as a technique for improving response time and scalability.

Workshop

The Quiz questions are designed to test your knowledge of the material covered in this chapter. The answers are in Appendix A, "Quiz Answers."

Quiz

1. What are three administrative tasks that the Internet Service Manager (HTML) cannot perform?

2. What is FTP? Is it advisable to allow anonymous access to your FTP service?

3. What is the Posting Acceptor?

4. What happens if you submit a form to the Posting Acceptor that doesn't include a file for upload?

DAY 18

Using Email from Active Server Pages

A powerful, but hidden, feature of IIS is the ability to send email from within an ASP page. As alluded to in Day 16, "Debugging Your E-Commerce Applications," you can use this feature to send yourself email when something goes wrong (or when something goes right!). You can also use this to automatically send individual email messages to your customers. Finally, and perhaps most powerfully, you can use this feature for direct email marketing.

If you have ever had an email account, you already know about email-based direct marketing. Direct email marketing is very similar to the postal email marketing that many retailers use, but with one big advantage—it's free. In previous Days, you collected email addresses when your customers signed up for subscription-based services or submitted orders. With IIS and Active Server Pages, you now have an easy way to take advantage of those collected addresses.

Today, you will learn

- The basics of Internet mail
- How to configure the IIS SMTP server

- Information about the Collaboration Data Objects for NT Server (CDONTS)
- How to use CDONTS to send an email from an ASP page
- How to send batches of personalized email

The Basics of Internet Mail

Electronic messaging dates back to the 1970s. The original email systems were designed to enable people in a single organization to communicate. In those early systems, sending email to someone in a different organization was difficult, if not impossible. As more and more computers became connected, users wanted to access those connections to send email, and a variety of methods of transferring mail between email systems briefly flourished. Those methods are known as *mail protocols*, and all of them have two key features: They guarantee delivery or notification of delivery failure, and they perform format conversions. The protocol that eventually survived was the Simple Mail Transmission Protocol (SMTP), developed by David Crocker in 1982. SMTP was extended in 1992 to handle large messages with attachments in the Multipurpose Internet Mail Extensions (MIME).

If you have been using the Internet for even a brief period of time, you are familiar with sending email using SMTP and MIME. To a user, in fact, sending an email is quite simple: Specify a destination address in the format *user@domain*. To an SMTP server, the process of getting the message to its intended recipient is more complex.

If the destination domain is the same as your own, the server simply delivers the email to the user. If the destination domain is not the same as yours, the SMTP server at your domain stores the message in a queue, and then asks its DNS server for a server that knows how to deliver mail to the domain you have specified. This machine might be at the destination domain or at an intermediate domain. Your SMTP server then converts the mail, if necessary, and delivers it to the server specified by the DNS server. That destination machine stores the message in its own queue, and then acknowledges receipt to your SMTP server. Your SMTP server can then delete the message from its queue. If the destination machine doesn't acknowledge the message, your server keeps trying to send the message, and if it still cannot deliver the message, your server sends a message back to you. This process repeats until the message arrives at the recipient's SMTP server. This entire process is known as "store-and-forward" communication, and is depicted in Figure 18.1. The use of intermediate servers was much more common in earlier days of the Internet. It is now usual for email to pass through only two SMTP servers—the sender's server and the recipient's server—before being delivered.

FIGURE 18.1

An illustration of SMTP store-and-forward communication.

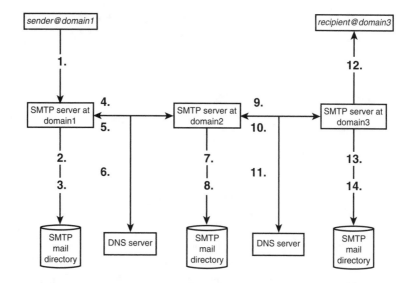

1. Sender addresses mail to recipient@domain3, submits message to local SMTP server.
2. SMTP server stores mail locally pending delivery.
3. After acknowledgement from SMTP server at domain2, SMTP server deletes message.
4. SMTP server at domain1 performs data conversions if necessary and transmits message to domain2.
5. SMTP server at domain2 acknowleges receipt.
6. SMTP server asks Domain Name Server (DNS) for the SMTP server that handles mail for domain3. DNS replies with a server name, perhaps at domain2.
7. SMTP server stores mail locally pending delivery.
8. After acknowledgement from SMTP server at domain3, SMTP server deletes message.
9. SMTP server at domain1 performs data conversions if necessary and transmits message to domain3.
10. SMTP server at domain3 acknowledges receipt.
11. SMTP server asks Domain Name Server (DNS) for the SMTP server that handles mail for domain3. DNS replies with a server name.
12. SMTP server delivers mail to recipient, performing formatting conversion if necessary.
13. SMTP server stores mail locally pending delivery.
14. After verification of delivery, SMTP server deletes message.

Configuring the SMTP Service

If you are using Windows 2000, then the SMTP Service is installed by default. If you are using Windows NT, then you can verify that the SMTP Service is installed by launching the Internet Service Manager. Go to the left panel, open the Internet Information Server node, and select your server. In the right panel, you should see an icon for an SMTP site, often called *Default SMTP Site* (see Figure 18.2).

18

FIGURE 18.2

Verifying that the SMTP service is installed on your server.

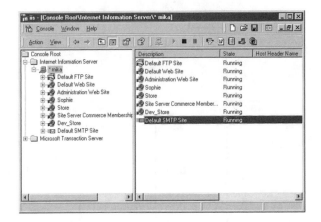

If you are using Windows NT Server and the SMTP service is not installed, you can install it by going to the Start Menu and selecting Windows NT 4.0 Option Pack, Windows NT 4.0 Option Pack Setup. The SMTP server is a subcomponent of Internet Information Server. After installing the SMTP service, be sure to reapply the latest Windows NT Service Pack.

After you have verified that the SMTP service is installed on your Web server, you should verify its configuration with your ISP. You can examine the SMTP service's configuration by double-clicking the SMTP site in Internet Service Manager. In general, the default configuration is correct. However, you should check that relaying is turned off. You can verify this by bringing up the SMTP site configuration and clicking the Directory Security tab (see Figure 18.3). In the Relay Restrictions box, click the Edit button and be sure that By Default, All Computers Are Not Allowed to Relay is selected (see Figure 18.4).

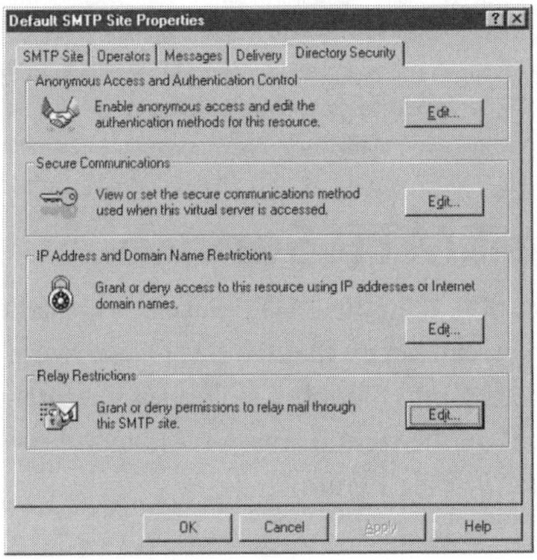

FIGURE 18.3

The Directory Security tab of the Default SMTP Site Properties dialog.

18

FIGURE 18.4

The Relay Restrictions dialog.

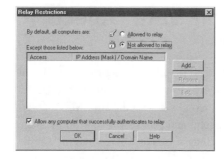

> **Caution**
>
> If relaying is not restricted, spammers will be able to exploit your Web server to send unsolicited bulk email through your site. You don't want to get blamed for the questionable activities of others.

The SMTP service performs the process discussed in the previous section ("The Basics of Internet Mail") by using four directories. When installed, it creates a set of directories beneath a root directory, MailRoot. The directories are Pickup, Queue, BadMail, and Drop. To send a message, an application (such as a mail client) places a properly formatted message into the Pickup directory. The SMTP service monitors this directory, and when it finds a file there, it tries to deliver the file to the destination SMTP server. If the service delivers the message successfully, it deletes the message. If it does not deliver the message successfully, it moves the message to the Queue directory.v

When a message is in the Queue directory, the SMTP service keeps trying to send the message to its destination. The number of times it tries and the interval between the tries are configurable in the Internet Service Manager. When messages cannot be delivered, the SMTP service writes transcript files (text files with the extensions LTR and RTR) to the Queue directory. You can use these transcript files to diagnose problems with mail delivery.

After a message is successfully delivered, it is deleted from the Queue directory. If the number of delivery tries exceeds the configured value in the Internet Service Manager, the service returns the mail to the sender. If the message cannot be returned to the sender and cannot be delivered to its recipient, the SMTP service moves the message to the BadMail directory.

The last directory is the Drop directory. If any other SMTP server tries to deliver mail to a recipient of the SMTP service, the service stores the message in the Drop directory. The SMTP service in IIS concentrates on sending and relaying mail; to use the SMTP service to receive mail, you must write some ASP pages to move the incoming mail into individual user mailboxes.

The Collaboration Data Objects for NT Server (CDONTS)

It is possible to use ASP to send mail by writing message files into the SMTP server's `MailRoot\Pickup` directory. However, Collaboration Data Objects for NT Server (CDONTS), which are installed along with the IIS SMTP server, provide a convenient, easy-to-use, server-independent, and robust way to send messages from within ASP. The CDONTS are the latest in a long series of Microsoft's messaging technologies. CDONTS are similar to the ActiveX Data Objects (ADO) you learned about in Day 5, "Building Your Product Catalog." They give users of any programming or scripting language access to a complex, robust set of operating system features. Where ADO is specific to databases, CDONTS enables ASP programmers to send and receive email by wrapping the Windows native messaging services with ActiveX. Sending email using CDONTS is a simple matter of creating a mail object and setting a few of its properties.

> **Note**
>
> The Collaboration Data Objects for NT Server also work with Windows 2000 Server.

> **Caution**
>
> Early versions of CDONTS have some serious bugs. If you are using Windows NT Server, before continuing, check to see that you are using the correct version of CDONTS by using Windows Explorer to go to your `WINNT\SYSTEM32` directory. Right-click `CDONTS.DLL`, and select the Properties menu item. In the Properties dialog, select the Version tab (see Figure 18.5). The version number should be equal to or greater than 5.5.1877.28.
>
> If your `CDONTS.DLL` is earlier than version 5.5.1877.28, you can obtain a newer version by downloading the latest Microsoft Exchange 5.5 Service Pack from Microsoft's Web site.

FIGURE 18.5

The Version tab of the
CDONTS.DLL *Properties*
dialog.

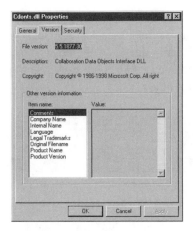

Sending Email from an ASP Page

The code in Listing 18.1 demonstrates just how easy it is to send an email from an ASP page. Simply create a CDONTS.Newmail object and call its Send method with four parameters: sender address, recipient address, subject, and body. Whenever the page is executed, mail is sent. (See Figures 18.6 and 18.7.)

18

INPUT   **LISTING 18.1**   Sending a Simple Email Message from ASP

```
1  <%@ Language=VBScript %>
2  <%
3  Set NewMailObj = CreateObject("CDONTS.NewMail")
4  recipStr = "asprecipient@yahoo.com"
5  NewMailObj.Send "jon@levlin.com", recipStr, "Check it out!", "Here's some
   ➥email for you"
6  Set NewMailObj = Nothing
7  %>
8
9  <HTML>
10 <HEAD>
11 <META NAME="GENERATOR" Content="Microsoft Visual Studio 6.0">
12 </HEAD>
13 <BODY>
14
15 <P>Sent mail to <%=recipStr%>.</P>
16
17 </BODY>
18 </HTML>
```

ANALYSIS Line 3 of the script creates a `CDONTS.NewMail` object, and line 5 sends the mail specified to the recipient specified. Line 4 stores recipient name in a variable so that it can be echoed to the browser in line 15. After the `Send` method is called in line 5, the `CDONTS.NewMail` object is no longer usable; however, line 6 signals to the VBScript interpreter that it can clean up the object.

FIGURE 18.6

The output of the simple NewMail *script.*

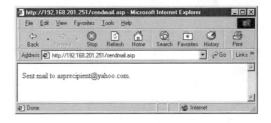

FIGURE 18.7

Checking out the mail sent from the script.

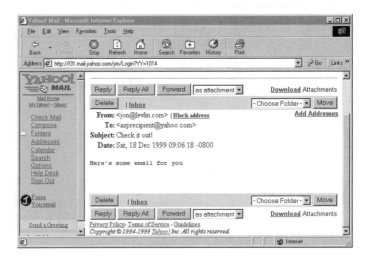

Using the `NewMail.Send` method with parameters is quite impressive. The entire process of sending a message is encapsulated in as few as two lines of ASP. The `CDONTS.NewMail` object also offers a more verbose way of addressing and setting the contents of a message (illustrated in Listing 18.2). This verbose way is a bit easier to debug should there be a logic error. Also, as you will see later in this lesson, using the object this way is somewhat more compatible with using a database and ASP to generate lists of message recipients and complex message bodies from the database.

> **Caution**
>
> Because the IIS SMTP server does not perform any address checking, you can theoretically specify whatever you like as a From address. It's *not* a good idea to take advantage of this feature.
>
> The actual IP address source of every message is stored as it passes through SMTP servers on the Internet. Should an SMTP administrator decide that your IP address is a source of email with forged return addresses, he can refuse to accept email from your server. Even worse, a group of mail administrators maintain something called the Realtime Blackhole List (RBL). The RBL is a list of IP addresses that are thought to be the sources of bad email, often known as *spam*. Thousands of mail administrators have programmed their SMTP servers to automatically reject email from any server on the RBL. You certainly do not want your server's IP address to end up on that list!

INPUT   **LISTING 18.2**   A More Verbose Way to Send the Same Message

```
1  <%
2  Set NewMailObj = CreateObject("CDONTS.NewMail")
3  NewMailObj.From = "jon@levlin.com"
4  NewMailObj.To = "asprecipient@yahoo.com"
5  NewMailObj.Subject = "Check it out!"
6  NewMailObj.Body = "Here's some email for you"
7  NewMailObj.Send
8  Set NewMailObj = Nothing
9  %>
```

ANALYSIS   Line 2 of the script creates a `CDONTS.NewMail` object. Lines 3–6 set each property (From, To, Subject, and Body) of a message separately, and line 7 sends the mail specified to the recipient specified. As in Listing 18.1, line 8 signals to the VBScript interpreter that it can clean up the object.

The CDONTS Constants

Before going any further, notice that there are a number of numeric constants that CDONTS use as flags. Although it's possible to specify these constants as numeric values, that makes the resulting code quite hard to read and maintain. Even worse, as you examine the documentation for the CDO for NTS Library, you might notice that some of the numeric values for flags aren't documented! To solve these issues, take the code from Listing 18.3 and place it in a file called `cdonts.inc`. If you include that file in any ASP page that uses CDONTS, you will be able to specify the flags textually.

INPUT   **LISTING 18.3**   Constants for CDONTS to Be Placed in `cdonts.inc`

```
1  <%
2  ' CDONTS Constants
3
4  ' CDONTS Attachment.Type values
5  Const CdoFileData = 1
6  Const CdoEmbeddedMessage = 4
7
8  ' CDONTS Message.Importance Values.  Also used in NewMail.Importance
9  Const CdoLow = 0
10 Const CdoNormal = 1
11 Const CdoHigh = 2
12
13 ' CDONTS Message.MessageFormat and Session.MessageFormat Values
14 Const CdoMime = 0
15 Const CdoText = 1
16
17 ' CDONTS NewMail.AttachFile and NewMail.AttachURL EncodingMethod Values
18 Const CdoEncodingUUencode = 0
19 Const CdoEncodingBase64 = 1
20
21 ' CDONTS NewMail.BodyFormat Values
22 Const CdoBodyFormatHTML = 0
23 Const CdoBodyFormatText = 1
24
25 ' CDONTS NewMail.MailFormat Values
26 Const CdoMailFormatMime = 0
27 Const CdoMailFormatText = 1
28
29 ' CDONTS Recipient.Type Values
30 Const CdoTo = 1
31 Const CdoCc = 2
32 Const CdoBcc = 3
33
34 ' CDONTS Session.GetDefaultFolder Values
35 Const CdoDefaultFolderInbox = 1
36 Const CdoDefaultFolderOutbox = 2
37
38 %>
```

ANALYSIS   The constants here are used to pass various numeric flags to CDONTS objects. The constants in lines 5–6 specify whether a particular attachment is a file or another message. Those constants in lines 9–11 specify whether a message has low, normal, or high priority. The constants in lines 14–15 and 26–27 signal whether a message is to be transferred as plain text or as MIME. In lines 18–19, the constants specify whether attachments should be transferred as UUEncoded (the standard format for text attachments) or Base64 (the standard format for MIME attachments). Lines 22–23 contain constants that specify whether the body of a message includes HTML or is exclusively text. The constants in lines 30–32 are used when examining the kinds of recipients of a message (for example, whether they are direct recipients or have received a CC or BCC copy of the message). Finally, the constants in lines 35–36 are used to specify which folder to open when using the Session object to open a folder.

> **Caution**
>
> You will find it useful to specify <% Option Explicit %> in ASP files where you use CDONTS.
>
> Because the default value of an unspecified VBScript variable is 0, it is easy to create bugs that are extremely difficult to find. The most common example of this is misspelling a constant. With Option Explicit, the VBScript interpreter will flag an error when you reference an unspecified variable.

Send Yourself Email on Errors

In Day 16, you learned how to write errors into a log file when your users encounter a problem with your Web site. This is very helpful to isolate hard-to-reproduce bugs, but it requires that you periodically check the error logs on your Web server. Finding these errors is even easier when you use CDONTS to automatically email you when your users encounter an error.

Listing 16.6 shows how to write a CheckError function that writes errors into log files. Listing 18.4 adds a SendErrorLog function to debug.asp, which attaches that log file to an email message. By calling SendErrorLog from CheckError whenever an error occurs, the Web server sends the error and error log to the Webmaster whenever a problem occurs. You can then delete the file from the server.

INPUT   **LISTING 18.4**   Changes to debug.asp to Send Error Logs in Email

```
1   <!-- #include file="cdonts.inc" -->
2
3   Sub SendErrorLog(sLogFileName)
4     Dim NewMailObj
5     Set NewMailObj = CreateObject("CDONTS.Newmail")
6     NewMailObj.From = "webServer@levlin.com"
7     NewMailObj.To = "asprecipient@yahoo.com"
8     NewMailObj.Subject = "Web Server Error Log"
9     NewMailObj.Body = "An error occurred on the webserver.  The error log
      ➥ is attached."
10    NewMailObj.AttachFile sLogFileName, "Error Log"
11    NewMailObj.Importance = CdoHigh
```

continues

LISTING 18.4   continued

```
12    NewMailObj.Send
13    Set NewMailObj = Nothing
14 End Sub
```

 First, the CDONTS constants are included in line 1. Then, lines 4–13 create and send a message as in previous listings in this lesson. The differences are that a filename is passed into the subroutine in line 3, and then that file is attached to the email message in line 10. Finally, the importance of the message is set to high in line 11.

The results are displayed in Figures 18.8 and 18.9. In Figure 18.8, you might notice that the attachment is called `Error Log`. You can specify this name in the `NewMailObj.AttachFile` method (refer to Listing 18.4, line 10). The value of the file-name is arbitrary; that is, you may specify any text for it that you like.

> **Note**
>
> The appearance of the attachments will vary from mail reader to mail reader. The relatively Spartan appearance of Figure 18.8 is due to use of the Yahoo! mail reader. Note that the Yahoo! mail reader does not display the high importance (line 11) of the message. Whether and how the `NewMail.Importance` property is displayed is up to the particular mail reader. (The Importance property is displayed in Microsoft Outlook and Microsoft Outlook Express.)

FIGURE 18.8

The text of the error email.

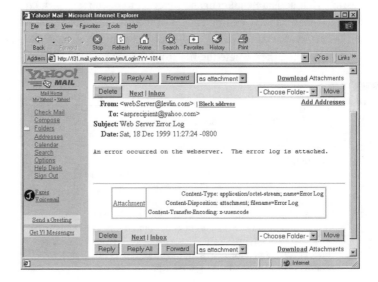

FIGURE 18.9
The error log attachment.

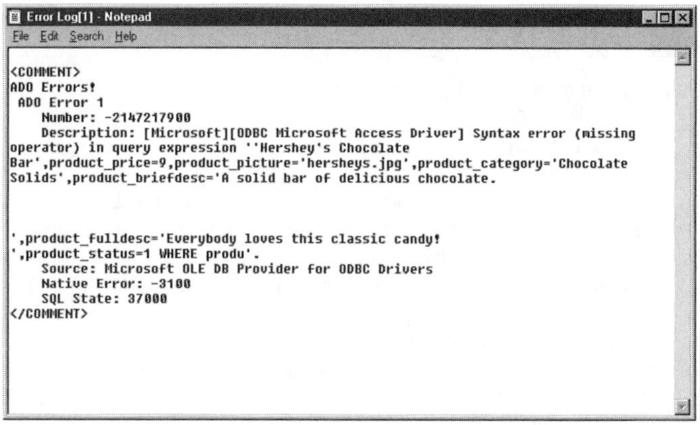
Error Log[1] - Notepad
File Edit Search Help

```
<COMMENT>
ADO Errors!
 ADO Error 1
    Number: -2147217900
    Description: [Microsoft][ODBC Microsoft Access Driver] Syntax error (missing
operator) in query expression ''Hershey's Chocolate
Bar',product_price=9,product_picture='hersheys.jpg',product_category='Chocolate
Solids',product_briefdesc='A solid bar of delicious chocolate.


',product_fulldesc='Everybody loves this classic candy!
',product_status=1 WHERE produ'.
    Source: Microsoft OLE DB Provider for ODBC Drivers
    Native Error: -3100
    SQL State: 37000
</COMMENT>
```

Sending New Users Email

Many E-Commerce sites send their users email after registration. This allows the site to reconnect with its customers, and provides an opportunity to encourage the customers to revisit the Web site—perhaps by sending them a coupon or other special offer. Using the techniques we have learned so far today, this feature is simple to add to the Candy Store Web site.

18

First, we will add the `sendNewUserMail` function in Listing 18.5 to the `storeFuncs.asp` file. Then, as the last line of the `addUser` function, call the `sendNewUserMail` function with the user's name and email address. When a user successfully completes the registration form, the `sendNewUserMail` function will automatically send that user an email (as shown in Figure 18.10).

Note

This function requires adding <!-- #include file="cdonts.inc" --> to the top of `storeFuncs.asp` in order to give the function access to the CDONTS constants.

LISTING 18.5   The sendNewUserMail Function

```
1   SUB sendNewUserMail(sUserName, sUserMail)
2     Dim NewMailObj
3     Dim sMailBody
4
5     Set NewMailObj = CreateObject("CDONTS.Newmail")
6     NewMailObj.From = "customer-service@JohnsonGifts.com"
7     NewMailObj.To = sUserMail
8     NewMailObj.Subject = "Welcome to Johnson Candy and Gifts"
9     NewMailObj.MailFormat = CdoMailFormatMime
10    NewMailObj.BodyFormat = CdoBodyFormatText
11    sMailBody = "Dear " & sUserName & "," & vbNewLine & vbNewLine
12    sMailBody = sMailBody & "   Thank you for registering at our site!" &
      ➥vbNewLine & vbNewLine
13    sMailBody = sMailBody & "   We look forward to serving you in the
      ➥future.   "
14    sMailBody = sMailBody & "Visit us again soon at
      ➥http://www.johnsongifts.com" & vbNewLine & vbNewLine
15    sMailBody = sMailBody & "Sincerely yours," & vbNewLine & vbNewLine
16    sMailBody = sMailBody & "David Johnson," & vbNewLine
17    sMailBody = sMailBody & "CEO, Johnson Candy and Gifts."
18    NewMailObj.Body = sMailBody
19
20    NewMailObj.Send
21    Set NewMailObj = Nothing
22 END SUB
```

ANALYSIS   The sendNewUserMail function (line 1) takes two strings: the new user's name
and his email address. Lines 5–20 create and send a message as we have in previous listings in this lesson. The passed-in mail address is used to set the destination address of the email in line 7, and the passed-in name is used to personalize the email in line 11. Finally, line 14 sends a URL back to the store Web site so that the user can easily return to the store after reading the message.

Note   Lines 9 and 10 work around a known issue with CDONTS. Unless the
MailFormat property of the NewMail object is set to CdoMailFormatMime, the line length of messages is limited to 74 characters or fewer. If the MailFormat property is set to CdoMailFormatMime, however, the default body format will be HTML; therefore, you must also set the BodyFormat property to CdoBodyFormatText.

Figure 18.10

The automatic email sent to a new user.

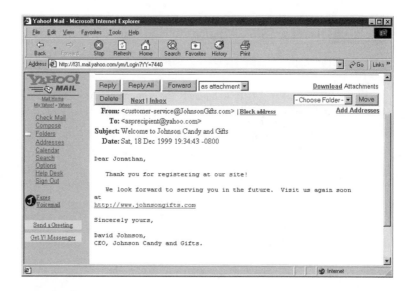

Sending HTML Mail

So far, we have used only CDONTS to send text email. Most of your customers, however, are probably using email viewers that enable them to read HTML email. If you are not familiar with it, HTML email is exactly what its name implies: email messages formatted with HTML tags. This presents you with the opportunity to send your customers eye-catching promotional material through email.

When read with an HTML-enabled mail reader such as Outlook, Outlook Express, or Hotmail, HTML messages are more attractive and easier to read than their text equivalents. When read with an old-fashioned mail reader such as Pine or elm, these messages look like... well... like HTML tags. Therefore, it's important to make sure that any customer to whom you send HTML mail can actually read it.

Most sites that send HTML mail ask customers during user registration whether they can read HTML mail. We can easily add this question to the Candy Store site. First, add a Boolean field called user_HTML to the Users table in the database. Then, add the lines in bold in Listing 18.6 to register.asp and to the addUser function in storeFuncs.asp. When a new customer registers, he will now be asked whether he can read HTML-formatted email and the response will be stored in the Users table of the database.

Note

The user_HTML field is already part of the storeDB.mdb file on the CD-ROM that accompanies this book.

INPUT   **LISTING 18.6**   Changes to `register.asp` and to `storeFuncs.asp`

`register.asp`

```
1   <%
2   newusername = TRIM( Request( "newusername" ) )
3   newpassword = TRIM( Request( "newpassword" ) )
4   email = TRIM( Request( "email" ) )
5   street = TRIM( Request( "street" ) )
6   city = TRIM( Request( "city" ) )
7   state = TRIM( Request( "state" ) )
8   zip = TRIM( Request( "zip" ) )
9   cctype = Request( "cctype" )
10  ccnumber = TRIM( Request( "ccnumber" ) )
11  ccexpires = TRIM( Request( "ccexpires" ) )
12  ccname = TRIM( Request( "ccname" ) )
12.1 html = TRIM( Request ( "html" ) )
13
14  submitpage = Request.ServerVariables( "SCRIPT_NAME" )
15  %>
...
70    <font face="Courier" size="2">
71    <br><b>username:</b>
72    <input name="newusername" size=20 maxlength=20
73      value="<%=Server.HTMLEncode( newusername )%>">
74    <br><b>password:</b>
75    <input name="newpassword" size=20 maxlength=20
76      value="<%=server.HTMLEncode( newpassword )%>">
77    <br><b>email address:</b>
78    <input name="email" size=30 maxlength=75
79      value="<%=Server.HTMLEncode( email )%>">
79.1  <br><input name="html" type="checkbox" value="Yes" <% if
      ➥Server.HTMLEncode( html ) = "Yes" then %>CHECKED<% end if %>>
79.2  <b>I can read E-Mail formatted in HTML.</b>
80    </font>
```

`storeFuncs.asp`

```
115 SUB addUser
116   ' Get Registration Fields
117   newusername = TRIM( Request( "newusername" ) )
118   newpassword = TRIM( Request( "newpassword" ) )
119   email = TRIM( Request( "email" ) )
120   street = TRIM( Request( "street" ) )
121   city = TRIM( Request( "city" ) )
122   state = TRIM( Request( "state" ) )
123   zip = TRIM( Request( "zip" ) )
124   cctype = Request( "cctype" )
125   ccnumber = TRIM( Request( "ccnumber" ) )
126   ccexpires = TRIM( Request( "ccexpires" ) )
```

```
127   ccname = TRIM( Request( "ccname" ) )
127.1 if html <> "Yes" then
127.2     html = "1"
127.3 else
127.4     html = "0"
127.5 end if
...
179   sqlString = "INSERT INTO users ( " &_
180     "user_username, " &_
181     "user_password, " &_
182     "user_email," &_
183     "user_street, " &_
184     "user_city," &_
185     "user_state," &_
186     "user_zip," &_
187     "user_ccnumber, " &_
188     "user_cctype, " &_
189     "user_ccexpires," &_
190     "user_ccname," &_
190.1     "user_HTML" &_
191     ") VALUES ( " &_
192     " '" & fixQuotes( newusername ) & "', " &_
193     " '" & fixQuotes( newpassword ) & "', " &_
194     " '" & fixQuotes( email ) & "', " &_
195     " '" & fixQuotes( street ) & "', " &_
196     " '" & fixQuotes( city ) & "', " &_
197     " '" & fixQuotes( state ) & "', " &_
198     " '" & fixQuotes( zip ) & "', " &_
199     " '" & fixQuotes( ccnumber ) & "', " &_
200     " '" & cctype & "', " &_
201     " '" & ccexpires & "', " &_
202     " '" & fixQuotes( ccname ) & "', " &_
202.1     " " & html & " " &_
203     ")"
```

ANALYSIS Lines 79.1 and 79.2 of register.asp add a check box to the registration form asking the new customer whether he can read HTML mail. When the customer clicks submit, and if his entries pass the validation in the addUser function, lines 127.1–127.5 of storeFuncs.asp set the value of the variable html to something that can be inserted into an SQL database. Lines 190.1 and 202.1 of storeFuncs.asp insert that value into the database along with other information about the new user.

If the customer's entries do not pass the validation in the addUser function, addUser displays an error page that allows the customer to return to the registration form. If this occurs, lines 12.1 and 79.1 of register.asp make sure that the value of the new check box is reset to the value originally set by the user.

18

Now that we know whether each user can receive HTML-formatted email, we can
change the code that sends welcoming email to send formatted email to appropriate
users. Listing 18.7 demonstrates a new `sendNewUserMail` function that sends messages
in HTML format to new users who check the I Can Read HTML box on the registration
form. A sample HTML-formatted message is illustrated in Figure 18.11.

INPUT   **LISTING 18.7**   A `sendNewUserMail` Function That Sends HTML

```
1    SUB sendNewUserMail(sUserName, sUserMail, fHtml)
2      Dim NewMailObj
3      Dim sMailBody
4
5      Set NewMailObj = CreateObject("CDONTS.Newmail")
6      NewMailObj.From = "customer-service@JohnsonGifts.com"
7      NewMailObj.To = sUserMail
8      NewMailObj.Subject = "Welcome to Johnson Candy and Gifts"
9
10     if fHtml = "0" then
11       NewMailObj.BodyFormat = CdoBodyFormatText
12       NewMailObj.MailFormat = CdoMailFormatMime
13       sMailBody = "Dear " & sUserName & "," & vbNewLine & vbNewLine
14       sMailBody = sMailBody & "   Thank you for registering at our site!" &
       ➥ vbNewLine & vbNewLine
15       sMailBody = sMailBody & "   We look forward to serving you in the
       ➥future.  "
16       sMailBody = sMailBody & "Visit us again soon at
       ➥http://www.johnsongifts.com." & vbNewLine & vbNewLine
17       sMailBody = sMailBody & "Sincerely yours," & vbNewLine & vbNewLine
18       sMailBody = sMailBody & "David Johnson," & vbNewLine
19       sMailBody = sMailBody & "CEO, Johnson Candy and Gifts."
20       NewMailObj.Body = sMailBody
21     else
22       NewMailObj.BodyFormat = CdoBodyFormatHTML
23       NewMailObj.MailFormat = CdoMailFormatMime
24       NewMailObj.ContentBase = "http://www.superexpert.com/"
25       NewMailObj.ContentLocation = "candystore/"
26       sMailBody = "<HTML><HEAD><TITLE>Thanks from Johnson's Candy and
       ➥Gifts</TITLE></HEAD>"
27       sMailBody = sMailBody & "<BODY><table width=""640"" border=""0""
       ➥bgcolor=""#ffffff"" cellspacing=""0"" cellpadding=""0"">"
28       sMailBody = sMailBody & "<tr><td><img src=""http://www.superexpert.com/
       ➥candystore/logo.gif"" WIDTH=""300"" HEIGHT=""30""></td></tr>"
29       sMailBody = sMailBody & "<tr><td colspan=""2""><hr width=""640""></td>
       ➥</tr></table>"
30       sMailBody = sMailBody & "<font face=""Arial"" size=""2""><p>Dear "
       ➥& sUserName & ", "
31       sMailBody = sMailBody & "<p>Thank you for registering at our site!
       ➥<p>We look forward to serving you in the future. "
```

```
32     sMailBody = sMailBody & "Visit us again soon at
       ➥<a href=""http://www.superexpert.com/candystore"">"
33     sMailBody = sMailBody & "http://www.johnsongifts.com</a>.<br>
       ➥<br>Sincerely yours,<br><br>David Johnson"
34     sMailBody = sMailBody & "<br>CEO, Johnson Candy and Gifts</font>
       ➥</BODY></HTML>"
35     NewMailObj.Body = sMailBody
36   end if
37   NewMailObj.Send
38   Set NewMailObj = Nothing
39 END SUB
```

ANALYSIS Line 22 sets the format of the message body to HTML. Lines 24 and 25 set the `ContentBase` and `ContentLocation` properties, which provide a default root URL and directory for images and other embedded objects. Lines 26–34 actually set the contents of the body to essentially the same contents as the text version of the message, but with HTML formatting that includes tables (lines 27–29), embedded images (line 28), and links (line 33). The mail is personalized for the recipient in line 30.

 Note

Not all mail readers support the `ContentBase` and `ContentLocation` properties. To be safe, fully qualify all the references to images and other embedded objects in your HTML-formatted email by using an absolute address rather than a relative address.

18

FIGURE 18.11

A new user email in HTML format.

Sending email in HTML enables you to give your sent messages the graphical punch of Web pages. In fact, you can use an HTML editor such as FrontPage or HomeSite to compose very sophisticated, formatted email and save the format to a file. VBScript can then read the file by using the `FileSystemObject` you learned about in Day 16 or by using the `<INPUT type=file>` tag discussed later in this lesson. The results can be extremely powerful, indeed.

Sending Batches of Email

Automatically sending a single email message is certainly useful, but even more useful is sending batches of email. With CDONTS, it is possible to write ASP scripts that send large volumes of personalized email. With your database of email addresses and names, you can use these scripts to quickly and easily send newsletters, promotions, or other messages to some of or all your customers.

In order to demonstrate this, we will add three scripts to the admin directory we created in Day 16. The first script enables the sender to select which customers will receive the email message, the second to compose a message, and the third to send the message. These scripts enable a hypothetical marketing director to send messages to his company's customer base.

 Caution

> If you haven't already protected your admin directory (as described in Day 17, "Administering Your Store Remotely with ASPs") by requiring a username and password for access, you should do so now. The ASP pages that follow allow anyone with access to the admin directory to send email to all your customers!

Increasing the Granularity of Security on ASP Scripts

You might want to restrict access to ASP scripts on a user-by-user basis. For example, you might want only the marketing director to be able to send mail to your customers, but anyone in the marketing department to be able to add or change product information.

Windows NT and Windows 2000 provide a sophisticated set of access controls through the security features of the NTFS file system. By assigning each of your employees his own Windows NT username and password and setting file access permissions on specific ASP scripts for specific users, IIS can limit access to those scripts to users who enter one of a specific set of usernames.

A detailed description of Windows NT and Windows 2000 security features is beyond the scope of this book, but you can begin your exploration of the NTFS file system security features by going to Windows NT Explorer, right-clicking one of your ASP scripts, and selecting Properties. Go to the Security tab of the Properties dialog and click the Permissions button. The File Permissions dialog enables you to control access to ASP scripts on a file-by-file and basis (see Figure 18.12).

FIGURE 18.12

The File Permissions dialog.

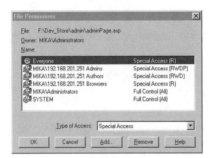

Selecting Customers

18

First, to enable the marketing director to select the customers who will receive this message, the `selectCust.asp` page lists the registered customers next to check boxes that allow their selection (see Listing 18.8). A simple server-side script generates a table of each registered customer and his email address along with a selection check box in a single page. A client-side script provides a quick shortcut for the marketing director to select and deselect all the customers at one time (see Figure 18.13). All the check boxes in the table have the same name: `sendEMail`; each check box's value is the email address of the corresponding customer. As you will see in the next page, this technique makes it easier for the script writer to find the email addresses and usernames of each customer once the form is submitted.

INPUT   **LISTING 18.8**   The `selectCust.asp` Page That Allows Selection of Customers

```
1   <%@ Language=VBScript %>
2   <!-- #include file="../adovbs.inc" -->
3   <%
4
5   Dim Con
6   Dim rs
7
8   Set Con = Server.CreateObject( "ADODB.Connection" )
9   Con.Open "accessDSN"
```

continues

LISTING 18.8   continued

```
10 Set rs = Server.CreateObject( "ADODB.Recordset" )
11 rs.Open "users", Con, adOpenForwardOnly, adLockReadOnly
12
13 %>
14 <HTML>
15 <HEAD>
16 <META NAME="GENERATOR" Content="Microsoft Visual Studio 6.0">
17 <title>Johnson's Candies and Gifts - Send Mail To Customers Pages
   ➥(Step 1)</title>
18 </head>
19 <body link="#ff4040" vtext="lightred" bgcolor="#ffffff">
20 <center>
21
22 <table width="640" border="0" bgcolor="#ffffff" cellspacing="0"
   ➥ cellpadding="0">
23 <tr>
24     <td>
25     <img src="../logo.gif" WIDTH="300" HEIGHT="30">
26     </td>
27 </tr>
28 <tr>
29     <td colspan="2">
30     <hr width="640">
31     </td>
32 </tr>
33 </table>
34
35 <H2>Send Mail to Customers<H2>
36 </center>
37
38 <SCRIPT Language="VBScript">
39 <!--
40 SUB CheckAll
41
42     For Each cb in document.custlist.elements
43         If cb.name <> "allbox" Then
44             cb.checked = document.custlist.allbox.checked
45         End If
46     Next
47 END SUB
48 -->
49 </SCRIPT>
50 <H3> Step 1: </H3>
51 <H4> Check the boxes next to the customers to whom you wish to send E-Mail
       ➥ and press the Next button. </H4>
52
53 <FORM name="custlist" method="POST" action="composeMsg.asp">
```

```
54
55 <TABLE cellpadding="2" cellspacing="0" bordercolor="#cccccc" bgcolor="Gray"
   ➥ border="1" cols="3" rules="ALL">
56 <TR bgcolor="#003468" align="Left">
57    <TH></TH>
58    <TH WIDTH="136"><Font face="Arial" size="4" color="White">
      ➥<b>Customer</TH>
59    <TH WIDTH="136"><Font face="Arial" size="4" color="White">
      ➥<b>E-Mail Address</TH>
60 </TR>
61
62 <%
63
64 rs.MoveFirst()
65 WHILE rs.EOF <> true
66 %>
67    <TR bgcolor = "White" align="Left" bordercolor="#cccccc">
68        <TD><Font Size="2" Face="Arial" Color="Black"><input type="checkbox"
          ➥ name="sendEMail" value="<%=rs("user_email")%>"> </TD>
69        <TD WIDTH="136"><Font Size="2" Face="Arial" Color="Black">
          ➥<% =rs("user_username") %></TD>
70        <TD WIDTH="136"><Font Size="2" Face="Arial" Color="Black">
          ➥<% =rs("user_email") %></TD>
71    </TR>
72 <%    rs.MoveNext()
73 WEND
74 %>
75 </TABLE>
76 <TABLE>
77    <TR bgcolor = "White" bordercolor = "White">
78        <td valign="top"><input name="allbox" type="checkbox"
          ➥value="Check All" onClick="CheckAll"></td>
79        <td colspan="2">Select all customers</td>
80    </tr>
81
82 </TABLE>
83 <BR><BR>
84 <INPUT type="submit" value="Next >" id="submit1" name="submit1">
85 </FORM>
86 </BODY>
87 <%
88 rs.Close()
89 Con.Close()
90 Set rs = Nothing
91 Set Con = Nothing
92 %>
93 </HTML>
```

18

ANALYSIS Lines 8–11 open a `Recordset` for a database table that contains each customer's name and email address.

Lines 53–85 define a form named `custlist` that is used to select the customers to whom the message will be sent. Within that form, lines 55–76 define a table that is used to view each user. Lines 56–60 define the header of that table. Lines 64–74 loop through the customers in the database table and create a row in the table for each. Line 68 defines a table cell that contains a check box with the name `sendEMail` and the value of the particular customer's email address, line 69 defines a cell that includes the customer's name, and line 70 defines a cell that includes the email address.

Lines 76–82 define an additional check box named `allbox` that enables the user to select or deselect all users at the same time. The `onClick` attribute of the check box defined in line 78 causes a call to the client-side script subroutine named `CheckAll` when the additional check box is clicked.

Note   The `selectCust.asp` page uses client-side VBScript. This means that it will work with Microsoft Internet Explorer but not Netscape Navigator. This limitation should not present a problem since the page is intended to be accessed only by authorized administrators and not the general public.

Lines 38–49 define the client-side script subroutine named `CheckAll`. Lines 38 and 49 are the `SCRIPT` tags that define a client-side script. Lines 42–46 iterate through each named item in the `custlist` form and set the state of each item that is not `allbox` to match `allbox`'s state.

The technique of listing all customers on the same page is adequate for a site that has up to a thousand or so registrants. When the number of customers is too large, you will find that the `selectCust.asp` page takes a long time to generate, even longer to transfer, and makes navigation difficult for users. Handling large numbers of customers requires limiting the number of customers displayed on a single page. The "Webbiest" way to solve this problem is to split the generation of the table over multiple pages, similar to the way that products are displayed over multiple pages in Day 6, "Displaying Your Products."

Composing the Message

After customers are selected, the marketing director presses the Next button. Control passes to the `composeMsg.asp` page, which provides a simple interface for writing an email (see Figure 18.14). The user enters a subject and the text of a message and presses `Send`. The source code for `composeMsg.asp` is shown in Listing 18.9.

FIGURE **18.13**

*The list of customers
with selection check
boxes.*

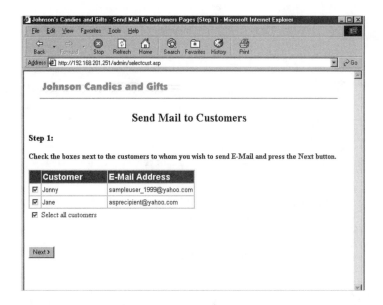

FIGURE **18.14**

The composeMsg.asp
*interface to enter a
message for customers.*

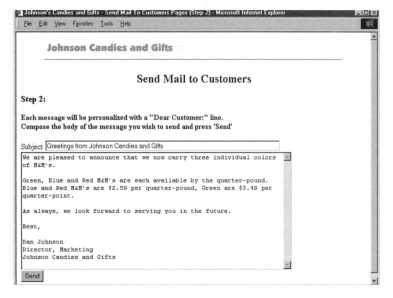

18

LISTING 18.9   The composeMsg.asp Page That Allows Entering the Message

```
1  <%@ Language=VBScript %>
2  <HTML>
3  <HEAD>
4  <META NAME="GENERATOR" Content="Microsoft Visual Studio 6.0">
5
6  <title>Johnson's Candies and Gifts - Send Mail To Customers Pages
   ➥(Step 2)</title>
7  </head>
8  <body link="#ff4040" vtext="lightred" bgcolor="#ffffff">
9  <center>
10
11 <table width="640" border="0" bgcolor="#ffffff" cellspacing="0"
   ➥cellpadding="0">
12<tr>
13    <td>
14    <img src="../logo.gif" WIDTH="300" HEIGHT="30">
15    </td>
16 </tr>
17 <tr>
18    <td colspan="2">
19    <hr width="640">
20    </td>
21 </tr>
22 </table>
23
24 <H2>Send Mail to Customers</H2>
25 </center>
26 <H3>Step 2:</H3>
27 <H4>Each message will be personalized with a "Dear Customer:" line.<br>
28 Compose the body of the message you wish to send and press 'Send'</H4>
29
30 <FORM name="composemsg" method="POST" action="sendMsg.asp">
31 Subject: <INPUT type="text" name="subject" size="70">
32 <textarea name="messageText" rows=15 cols=70 wrap="soft">
33 </textarea>
34 <br>
35 <INPUT type="submit" value="Send" id="submit1" name="submit1">
36 <%
37 For i = 1 to Request.Form("sendEmail").Count %>
38    <INPUT type="hidden" value="<%=Request.Form("sendEmail")(i)%>"
   ➥name="sendEmail"> <%
39 Next %>
40 </FORM>
41 </BODY>
42 </HTML>
```

ANALYSIS Lines 30–40 define the form used to compose the customer message. Line 31 accepts the subject of the message. The <TEXTAREA> tag in lines 32 and 33 allows the user to enter multiple lines of text. Finally, lines 37–39 create a hidden input field named sendEmail for each box in the selectCust.asp page.

When ASP scripts execute as the result of a form POST, the value of each <INPUT> or <TEXTAREA> tag appears in the Request.Form collection, and is referenced by using the name attribute of the tag. For example, Request.Form("messageText") refers to the message the user enters in the TEXTAREA named messageText. When multiple <INPUT> tags share the same name, such as the customer selection check boxes in selectCust.asp, their contents appear as a subcollection referred to by their shared name, whereas their individual values are referred to within the subcollection by numbers. For example, the second customer selected from the table in selectCust.asp is referred to as Request.Form("sendEmail")(2). This makes it easy to iterate through each value. Because we will need individual email addresses when sending the personalized email messages in the sendMsg.asp page, a separate hidden <INPUT> tag with the same name is inserted for each selected customer address.

Sending the Messages

After the message is entered and the Send button is pressed, control passes to the sendMsg.asp script (see Listing 18.10). Just as composeMsg.asp iterates through the list of customer email addresses, sendMsg.asp enumerates each address, this time creating a message for each address. Because the customer names are not directly available, in order to personalize the message, we must go back into the database and recover each customer's name given his email address. An example of the results of the personalizations is shown in Figure 18.15.

INPUT   **LISTING 18.10**   The sendMsg.asp Page That Sends the Composed Message

```
1  <%@ Language=VBScript %>
2  <!-- #include file="../adovbs.inc" -->
3  <%
4
5  Dim Con
6  Dim rs
7
8  Set Con = Server.CreateObject( "ADODB.Connection" )
9  Con.Open "accessDSN"
10 Set rs = Server.CreateObject( "ADODB.Recordset" )
11
12 Dim NewMailObj
13 Dim sMailBody
```

continues

LISTING **18.10**   continued

```
14 Dim sSql
15
16 For i = 1 to Request.Form("sendEMail").Count
17    sSql = "select user_username from users where user_email='"&
➥Request.Form("sendEMail")(i) &"'"
18    rs.Open sSql, Con, adOpenForwardOnly, adLockReadOnly
19
20    Set NewMailObj = CreateObject("CDONTS.Newmail")
21    NewMailObj.From = "marketing@JohnsonGifts.com"
22    NewMailObj.To = Request.Form("sendEMail")(i)
23    NewMailObj.Subject = Request.Form("subject")
24
25    NewMailObj.BodyFormat = CdoBodyFormatText
26    sMailBody = "Dear " & rs.Fields("user_username") & "," & vbNewLine
       ➥& vbNewLine
27    sMailBody = sMailBody & Request.Form("messageText")
28    NewMailObj.Body = sMailBody
29    NewMailObj.Send
30    Set NewMailObj = Nothing
31    rs.Close()
32 next
33
34 Con.Close()
35 Set rs = Nothing
36 Set Con = Nothing
37
38 %>
39
40 <HTML>
41 <HEAD>
42 <META NAME="GENERATOR" Content="Microsoft Visual Studio 6.0">
43 <title>Johnson's Candies and Gifts - Send Mail To Customers Pages
    ➥(Step 3)</title>
44 </head>
45 <body link="#ff4040" vtext="lightred" bgcolor="#ffffff">
46 <center>
47
48 <table width="640" border="0" bgcolor="#ffffff" cellspacing="0"
    ➥ cellpadding="0">
49 <tr>
50    <td>
51    <img src="../logo.gif" WIDTH="300" HEIGHT="30">
52    </td>
53 </tr>
54 <tr>
55    <td colspan="2">
56    <hr width="640">
57    </td>
```

```
58 </tr>
59 </table>
60
61 <H2>Send Mail to Customers</H2>
62 </center>
63 <H3>Step 3:</H3>
64 <H4>Your message has been sent!</H4>
65 </BODY>
66 </HTML>
```

ANALYSIS Lines 8–14 create objects that are used in the loop in lines 16–32. That loop actually does the work of selecting the customer's name into a Recordset given his email address (lines 17–18), creating a message for the user (line 20), addressing (line 22) and personalizing (line 26) the message, and then sending it (line 29). Line 34–36 closes the ADO connection. Closing ADO connections when they are not being used helps increase database scalability.

> **Caution**
>
> The Recordset is closed at the end of each loop because reopening a Recordset before closing it generates an ADO exception.

18

FIGURE 18.15

A personalized message for Jane.

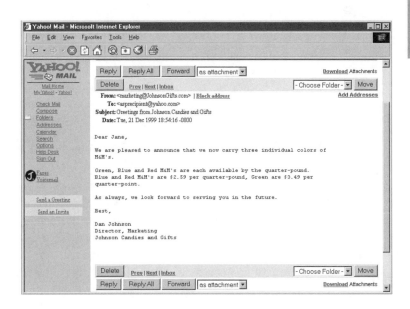

Doing Email Marketing

Your historical orders database is one of the most valuable assets you have, and just like the big boys in the e-tailing businesses, you can easily mine it for sales. With a few SELECT statements, you can extend the techniques discussed in this lesson for sending bulk email to promote repeat orders. With a little more effort, you can cross-promote slower-selling items based on customers' buying patterns. The techniques for doing this are beyond the scope of this book, but it certainly behooves the serious, aspiring e-commerce site owner to learn more about databases!

Summary

In today's lesson, you learned the basics of Internet mail and how to configure the IIS SMTP service. You then learned the basics of sending email from an ASP page, first sending an error log to yourself when the CheckError function detects a problem, and then sending mail to new customers as they register. Finally, you modified user registration to capture whether a user can receive HTML email and learned to send formatted HTML mail and bulk email to groups of your users.

Q&A

Q When I configure my SMTP service, how many times should I have it try to deliver a message before giving up? How much time should I wait between delivery attempts?

A The default settings for the SMTP service are adequate for nearly all servers. If many of your customers have ISPs with unreliable Internet connections, you might want to increase the length of time between delivery attempts.

Q The interfaces of composeMsg.asp and sendMsg.asp are pretty inconvenient and don't seem to provide much flexibility in the way of formatting. How can I change these pages to have a better interface?

A You can use the techniques described in Day 17 for uploading pictures with the Posting Acceptor to upload HTML files created in FrontPage, HomeSite, or Word. Start by changing the <TEXTAREA> tag in composeMsg.asp to the <INPUT TYPE="file"> tag we used in Day 17, having the <FORM> in composeMsg.asp submit to the Posting Acceptor and from there to sendMsg.asp, and then changing the loop in the sendMsg.asp script to send MIME HTML messages.

Workshop

The following Quiz and Exercise questions are designed to test your knowledge of the material covered in this lesson. The answers are provided in Appendix A, "Quiz Answers."

Quiz

1. What is an SMTP server?

2. Why is it important to restrict relaying on your SMTP server?

3. What is the difference between text and MIME mail messages? How do you send one or the other?

4. What happens if more than one <INPUT> tag in a form has the same name attribute?

18

DAY **19**

Generating Store Reports

Now that you've gotten your store up and working, you will want to manage it.
Bill Hewlett, co-founder of Hewlett-Packard, was reputed to say, "You can't
manage what you can't measure." If you haven't already, you will soon find
yourself wanting to measure your store's effectiveness: how many people are
accessing it, and what pages are they looking at. As with reports on other
aspects of your business, these measurements will help you evaluate your past
investments and plan for future ones.

Today, you will learn the following:

- How IIS logs usage
- What you can learn about your customers by analyzing these usage logs

Reporting on Site Usage

One of the first things the operator of a new E-Commerce site wants to know is
how many people are visiting his site. This impulse might originate from an
emotional source—wanting to know for certain that all the hard work that has
gone into developing the store hasn't been wasted—but learning about site

traffic has a business utility that goes far beyond feeling better. It helps an E-Commerce company in at least three areas: technical development, marketing, and business strategy.

On the technical front, the more detailed knowledge you can gather about your site's usage, the better you can plan your future capital and operating expenditures. More usage certainly means that you will need to buy more Internet bandwidth, and it might also mean that you will need to upgrade your Web site hardware, your database software, or maybe even hire a professional operations staff. In addition to raw information about Web site "hits" (see the sidebar, "The Vocabulary of Web Usage"), knowing the time it takes to answer a request, the number of requests that are answered with errors, and the geographic and ISP distribution of your users can help you make better decisions about where to invest technical resources. For example, if the customers connecting via a specific ISP are experiencing longer download times than your other customers, you might want to buy bandwidth directly from that ISP.

As the prime directive of marketing professionals is to "know your customer," you will also find usage information critical to your marketing effort. Raw information is more useful than no information when you evaluate the success of your marketing campaigns, but the more specific information you can gather about your users and their interests, the more targeted and efficient your marketing can be. Taking the Candy Store example, if you find that most of your customers are children, you might want to advertise on Web sites children frequent. If you find that many of your customers come from a specific geographic location, you might choose to advertise on radio stations in that area.

Specific user and usage information is even more critical when you evaluate your Web-specific business strategy. To extend the Candy Store example, suppose that you operate a physical Candy Store in which chocolate candies are very popular. When you open an Internet store, your initial impulse might be to focus on chocolates; however, customers might come to your Internet store for entirely different products. Your Internet customers might visit your store to buy specialty regional candies they cannot easily purchase in their home area. Just as you would do for your physical store, examining your Internet store's purchase data separately will help you know how much of what products to stock, and with what other sites to partner.

The Vocabulary of Web Usage

By now, you have noticed that the Web seems to have established its own argot. Some important Web terms to know with respect to Internet site usage are

CPM—*Cost per mille*, or one thousand impressions (*mille* is French for thousand). CPM comes directly from the print world, and it is the standard unit for Web advertising charges. (See *impressions* in a later paragraph.)

Hits—A *hit* is a browser's request for a file from a Web server. Web pages typically comprise several elements, each of which is typically contained in its own file. The main text of the page—its graphic elements, Java applets, and ActiveX controls, for example—are almost always each contained in a separate file. Because Web servers count each request for a file as a hit, on average, each complete Web page download causes about six hits. Hits are the most useful measurement for estimating the technical requirements of a site.

Impressions—An *impression* is a browser request for an advertising element (like a banner or button). It is another term that comes from the print advertising world.

Page views—By contrast with a hit, a *page view* is the delivery to the user of an entire Web page, including graphics elements. Because they measure user activity rather than server activity, page views are a more useful measurement than hits for marketing and strategic planning purposes. Content Web sites typically report their traffic in term of page views.

Unique users—*Unique users* are the number of different people who visit a site within a specific period, usually a day or week. Unique users also offer a useful measurement for marketing and strategic planning purposes.

Site Usage Logs

19

As users browse the pages of your store, their browsers are requesting files from your Web server. Like most Web servers, IIS records each of these requests with an entry in a *log*, usually a file. The most obvious way to analyze your store's usage is to examine these Web site logs. Unfortunately, because of the nature of *HTTP*, the protocol that underlies the Web, these logs are somewhat limited in what they can show. Knowing the information that IIS records when a browser requests a file can help you understand exactly what sort of information you can extract from the IIS logs.

Note

Log and *log file* are standard computer jargon for records that operating systems, programs, and services keep about their operations. For example, Windows NT keeps records of its operation using a program called *Event Log*. Event Log isn't related to the IIS logging feature.

IIS records logs on a site-by-site basis and can store its logs in one of four different formats: NCSA Common Log File Format, ODBC Logging Format, Microsoft IIS Log File Format, or W3C Extended Log File Format. The log file format can be configured from the Internet Service Manager (called the Internet Services Manager on Windows 2000). Select your store's Web site and choose Action, Properties. The Web Site tab (see Figure 19.1) allows you to turn on or off logging and to adjust the log file format. By clicking the Properties button, you can use the Logging Properties dialog (see Figures 19.2, 19.3, and 19.4) to control various logging settings. The IIS default for file-based logs is to store the log files for service subdirectories of \LOGFILES—each service getting its own subdirectory—and to create a new log file for each service every day. This helps keep the size of each log file under control.

FIGURE 19.1

The Web Site Properties page, with the logging properties at the bottom of the page.

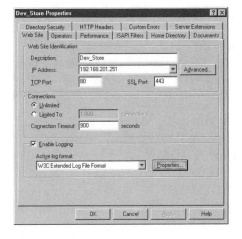

> **Note**
>
> As discussed in Chapter 16, "Debugging Your E-Commerce Applications," IIS allows a single computer to provide multiple services. For example, one Windows NT Server could host three Web sites, two SMTP servers, and one FTP site. The computer would be hosting six different sites and would record information about each site in a separate log file.

The NCSA Common Log File Format

The NCSA Common Log File Format is the oldest and simplest Web server log file format. It dates back to the original Web servers, which were written in the early 1990s at the National Center for Supercomputing Applications. You might want to set your Web server to use this format if you are trying to maintain compatibility with log files from a legacy Web server. When your server is set to log in NCSA Common Log File Format and you click the Properties button in the Web Site tab of the Internet Service Manager site properties dialog, you will see the NCSA Logging Properties page (see Figure 19.2). You can use this page to configure where the log files will be stored and how often a new file will be created. The names of the log files depend on how often a new file is created, as shown in Table 19.1.

FIGURE 19.2

The NCSA Logging Properties page.

TABLE 19.1   Naming Conventions for NCSA Common Log File Format Files

How Often a New File Is Created	File Name Format
Daily	ncyymmdd.log
Weekly	ncyymmww.log
Monthly	ncyymm.log
When log file exceeds specified size *or* Unlimited file size	ncsann.log

Where

- *yy* is the last two digits of the year.
- *mm* is the number of the month.
- *ww* is the number of the week in the month.
- *dd* is the date.
- *nn* is a sequence number.

An NCSA Common Log File Format log file contains the following information about each request to a Web server:

- The IP address of the computer requesting the file.
- The username of the user requesting the file, if available, or a - if the name isn't available.

19

- Date and time of request in server local time, including the offset of server local time from Greenwich Mean Time (GMT). It is stored in the format [*DD*/*MMM*/*YYYY*:*HH*:*MM*:*SS* *TAABB*], where *DD* is the date, *MMM* is the three-letter abbreviation for the month, *YYYY* is the year, *HH* is the hour in 24-hour time, *MM* is the minute, *SS* is the second, *T* is + if the server's local time is ahead of GMT or - if the local time is behind GMT, *AA* is the number of hours ahead or behind of GMT and *BB* is the number of minutes ahead or behind GMT.
- The request made.
- The status code of the request.
- Bytes sent.

Elements in NCSA Common Log File Format log files are separated by spaces so that when a log file in this format is opened in NOTEPAD or another text editor, its entries look like this:

```
192.168.201.3 LEVLIN\jon [06/Jan/2000:13:39:04 -0800]
➡"GET /admin/adminPage.asp, HTTP/1.0" 200 1503
```

This sample log file entry is for a request to download the adminPage.asp file made from a computer at IP address 192.168.201.3 by the user jon in the LEVLIN domain at 1:39:04 p.m. Pacific Time. The server processed the request without an error (status code 200) and sent 1503 bytes in response to the request (see Table 19.2 for detailed, element-by-element interpretation).

TABLE 19.2   Interpreting the Sample NCSA Common Log File Format Log File Entry

Information Element	Value
IP address of requestor	192.168.201.3
Username of requestor	LEVLIN/jon
Date and time of request	06/Jan/2000:13:39:04 -0800
Actual request	GET /admin/adminPage.asp, HTTP/1.0
Status code	200
Number of bytes sent	1503

The ODBC Logging Format

The ODBC Logging Format is interesting because it allows you to store Web server logs directly in a table in an ODBC-compliant database like Access, SQL Server, or Oracle. The format also makes it convenient to aggregate log file information from several servers in a single place. Finally, it allows you to use the database to report on Web server activity in real-time. When set to ODBC Logging, the Web server stores the following information about each Web server request:

- The IP address of the computer making the request
- The username of the user making the request, if available
- Date and time of request in server local time
- The name of the service that fielded the request (W3SVC for a Web service)
- The name of the machine that fielded the request
- The IP address of the machine that fielded the request
- The amount of time the server spent processing the request, in milliseconds
- The length of the request, in bytes
- The number of bytes sent in response to the request
- The HTTP status code returned to the browser (200 means no error)
- The Windows status code of the request (0 means no error)
- The operation (typically GET to retrieve a file or POST to submit data for a form)
- The target (usually the name of a file to be retrieved or ASP page to be run)
- Any parameters sent or returned (parameters sent are the text that follows the ? symbol in the URL)

Information about each Web server request is stored in a separate database row.

Before setting your Web server to use the ODBC Logging Format, you must create the table that will contain the log entries and create an ODBC System DSN (Data Source Name) for the table. The new table must contain columns as specified in Table 19.3. The process you use to create the table will vary from database to database, although the default installation of IIS includes a template that creates the appropriate columns in a SQL database. This template is in a file named Logtemp.sql, which is located in the \WINNT\SYSTEM32\INETSRV directory by default. To create the ODBC System DSN, follow the same steps listed in Chapter 5, "Building Your Product Catalog," (see the section "Connecting to a Database"), but name your data source logDSN.

19

TABLE 19.3 Column Names and Data Types for ODBC Logging

Column Name	Data Type
ClientHost	Varchar(255)
Username	Varchar(255)
LogTime	Datetime

continues

TABLE 19.3   continued

Column Name	Data Type
Service	Varchar(255)
Machine	Varchar(255)
ServerIP	Varchar(50)
ProcessingTime	Int
BytesRecvd	Int
BytesSent	Int
ServiceStatus	Int
Win32Status	Int
Operation	Varchar(255)
Target	Varchar(255)
Parameters	Varchar(255)

You are now ready to use the Web Site properties page of the Internet Service Manager site properties dialog to configure the Web server to store log file entries in the database table.

1. Set the server to log in ODBC Logging format.

2. Click the Properties button. The ODBC Logging Properties page (see Figure 19.3) will appear.

FIGURE 19.3

The ODBC Logging Properties page.

3. Enter **logDSN** as the ODBC Data Source Name, the name of the table you created (**inetlog** if you used the template file), and any username and password information if appropriate.

4. Click OK or Apply.

The IIS log file entries will now be stored in the newly created database table.

The Microsoft IIS Log File Format

TheMicrosoft IIS Log File Format is the original log file format for IIS versions 3.0 and earlier. It records more information than the NCSA Common Log File Format and a similar amount of information as the ODBC Logging Format. As with the NCSA Common Log File Format, you might want to set your Web server to use this format if you are trying to maintain compatibility with log files from an older Web server. When your server is set to log in Microsoft IIS Log File Format and you click the Properties button in the Web Site tab of the Internet Service Manager site properties dialog, you will see the Microsoft Logging Properties page, which is essentially the same as the NCSA Logging Properties page in Figure 19.2. As with the NCSA Logging Properties page, you can use this page to configure where the log files will be stored and how often a new file will be created. The names of the log files depend on how often a new file is created, as shown in Table 19.4.

TABLE 19.4 Naming Conventions for Microsoft IIS Log File Format Files

How Often a New File Is Created	File Name Format
Daily	`inyymmdd.log`
Weekly	`inyymmww.log`
Monthly	`Inyymm.log`
When log file exceeds specified size *or* Unlimited file size	`inetsvnn.log`

Where

- *yy* is the last two digits of the year.
- *mm* is the number of the month.
- *ww* is the number of the week in the month.
- *dd* is the date.
- *nn* is a sequence number.

A Microsoft IIS Log File records the following information about each request to a Web server, replacing missing items with a hyphen:

- The IP address of the computer requesting the file
- The username of the user requesting the file, if available

19

- Date of request in server local time, in the format *MM*/*DD*/*YY*, where *MM* is the month number, *DD* is the date, and *YY* is the last two digits of the year
- The time of the request, in server local time, in the format *HH*:*MM*:*SS*, where *HH* is the hour in 24-hour time, *MM* is the minute, and *SS* is the second
- The name of the service that fielded the request
- The name of the machine that fielded the request
- The IP address of the machine that fielded the request

 Note

> It might seem silly to collect the IP address of the server answering the request; however, this information can be useful when your Web server is multi-homed.

- The amount of time the server spent fielding the request, in milliseconds
- The number of bytes in the request
- The number of bytes the server returned in response to the request
- The HTTP status code returned to the browser (200 means no error)
- The Windows status code of the request (0 means no error)
- The operation (typically GET to retrieve a file or POST to submit data for a form)
- The target (usually the name of a file to be retrieved or ASP page to be run)
- Any parameters sent or returned (parameters sent are the text that follows the ? symbol in the URL)

Commas separate elements in the Microsoft IIS Log File Format. When a log file in this format is opened in NOTEPAD or another text editor, its entries look like this:

```
192.168.200.3, levlin\jon, 1/7/00, 14:43:55, W3SVC6,
➡MIKA, 192.168.201.251, 100, 578, 3607, 200, 0,
➡GET, /admin/updateproduct.asp, pid=35,
```

This sample log file entry is for a request to download the updateProduct.asp file for product 35 made from a computer at IP address 192.168.200.3 by the user jon in the levlin domain on January 7, 2000 at 2:43:55 p.m. server local time. The request was made of service W3SVC6 running on server MIKA at IP address 192.168.201.251. The server spent 100 milliseconds processing the request, which was 578 bytes long. The server processed the request without an error (status code 200) and sent 3607 bytes in response to the request (see Table 19.5 for detailed, element-by-element interpretation).

TABLE 19.5   Interpreting the Sample Microsoft IIS Log File Entry

Information Element	Value
IP address of requestor	192.168.201.3
Username of requestor	levlin/jon
Date of request	1/7/00
Time of request	14:43:55
Service Name	W3SVC6
Server Name	MIKA
Server IP address	192.168.201.251
Time spent processing (ms)	100
Bytes in request	578
Bytes returned to client	3607
HTTP status code	200
Windows NT return code	0
HTTP operation	GET
Target file	/admin/updateproduct.asp
Parameters	pid=35

The W3C Extended Log File Format

The W3C Extended Log File Format is the most extensive logging format available, and it is probably the format you will choose for your log files. The format is customizable, meaning that you can select the information you would like to record in your log file. When your server is set to log in W3C Extended Log File Format and you click the Properties button in the Web Site tab of the Internet Service Manager site Properties dialog, you will see the General Properties page of the Extended Logging Properties dialog, which is essentially the same as the NCSA Logging Properties page in Figure 19.2. As with the NCSA Logging Properties page, you can use this page to configure where the log files will be stored and how often a new file will be created. The names of the log files depend on how often a new file is created, as shown in Table 19.6. If you switch to the Extended Properties tab (see Figure 19.4), you can select the information you would like to collect in the log file from among the possibilities enumerated in Table 19.7.

19

TABLE 19.6 Naming Conventions for W3C Extended Log File Format Files

How Often a New File Is Created	File Name Format
Daily	exyymmdd.log
Weekly	exyymmww.log
Monthly	Exyymm.log
When log file exceeds specified size *or* Unlimited file size	extendnn.log

Where

- *yy* is the last two digits of the year.
- *mm* is the number of the month.
- *ww* is the number of the week in the month.
- *dd* is the date.
- *nn* is a sequence number.

FIGURE 19.4

The W3C Logging Extended Properties page.

TABLE 19.7 Information Recordable in W3C Extended Log File Format Files

Element Name (As It Appears in the Log File Header)	Properties Dialog Choice	Meaning
date	Date	The Greenwich mean date that the request was made, in the format YYYY-MM-DD, where YYYY is the year, MM is the number of the month, and DD is the date

Element Name (As It Appears in the Log File Header)	Properties Dialog Choice	Meaning
Time	Time	The Greenwich mean time that the request was made, in the format *HH:MM:SS*, where *HH* is the hour in 24-hour time, *MM* is the minute, and *SS* the second
c-ip	Client IP Address	The IP address of the computer requesting the file
cs-username	User Name	The username of the user requesting the file, if available
s-sitename	Service Name	The name of the service that fielded the request (usually W3SVC)
s-computername	Server Name	The name of the machine that fielded the request
s-ip	Server IP	The IP address of the machine that fielded the request
s-port	Server Port	The TCP port that the request was submitted on (usually 80, or 443 for secure HTTP)
cs-method	Method	The request operation (typically GET to retrieve a file or POST to submit data for a form)
cs-uri-stem	URI Stem	The file to be retrieved or ASP page to be run
Cs-uri-query		Any parameters to the URI Stem (text that follows the ? symbol in the URL)
sc-status	Http Status	The HTTP status code returned to the browser (200 means no error)
sc-win32-status	Win32 Status	The Windows status code for the request (0 means no error)
sc-bytes	Bytes sent	The number of bytes the server returned in response to the request
cs-bytes	Bytes Received	The number of bytes in the request
time-taken	Time Taken	The amount of time the server spent processing the request, in milliseconds
cs-version	Protocol Version	The version of HTTP used for the request, usually either HTTP/1.0 or HTTP/1.1

19

continues

TABLE 19.7 continued

Element Name (As It Appears in the Log File Header)	Properties Dialog Choice	Meaning
cs(User-Agent)	User Agent	The string the browser sends to identify itself, which includes browser name and version
cs(Cookie)	Cookie	The value of any cookie that this site previously stored on the browser
cs(Referer)	Referer	The last page the user was browsing, if the request is the result of the user clicking on a link

If IIS is set to log in W3C Extended Log File Format, whenever the Web server starts or creates a new log file, it writes four comment lines into the log file that look like this:

```
#Software: Microsoft Internet Information Server 4.0
#Version: 1.0
#Date: 2000-01-07 23:12:20
#Fields: date time c-ip cs-username s-sitename s-computername s-ip cs-method
➡ cs-uri-stem cs-uri-query sc-status sc-win32-status sc-bytes cs-bytes
➡time-taken s-port cs-version cs(User-Agent) cs(Cookie) cs(Referer)
```

These comments identify the version of the Web server, the version of the log file format, and the date the log started. Most important, because the format is customizable, the last comment details which of the fields from Table 19.7 are going to be present in the log file, and in what order the fields will appear. When the server starts logging, it records a line for each request, separating fields with spaces and replacing unavailable information with hyphens; for example:

```
2000-01-07 23:12:20 192.168.200.3 levlin\jon W3SVC6 MIKA 192.168.201.251
➡GET /admin/updateproduct.asp pid=35 200 0 3607 573 110 80 HTTP/1.1
➡ Mozilla/4.0+(compatible;+MSIE+5.01;+Windows+98)
➡ASPSESSIONIDQQGGQGVY=LLEDNABABDDBONADGFBJBAMM
➡http://192.168.201.251/admin/manageProducts.asp
```

This sample log file entry is for a request to GET the updateProduct.asp file for product 35 made from a computer at IP address 192.168.200.3 by the user jon in the levlin domain on January 7, 2000 at 11:12:20 p.m. GMT. The user was running IE 5.01 on Windows 98. The request was the result of the user clicking on a link from manageProducts.asp, and an existing cookie was uploaded. The request was made of service W3SVC6 running on server MIKA on port 80 at IP address 192.168.201.251. The server spent 110 milliseconds processing the request, which was 573 bytes long. The server processed the request without an error (HTTP status code 200, Windows status code 0) and sent 3607 bytes in response to the request (see Table 19.8 for detailed, element-by-element interpretation).

TABLE 19.8   Interpreting the Sample W3C Extended Log File Entry

Information Element	Value
date	2000-01-07
time	23:12:20
c-ip	192.168.200.3
cs-username	levlin\jon
s-sitename	W3SVC6
s-computername	MIKA
s-ip	192.168.201.251
cs-method	GET
cs-uri-stem	/admin/updateproduct.asp
cs-uri-query	pid=35
sc-status	200
sc-win32-status	0
sc-bytes	3607
cs-bytes	573
time-taken	110
s-port	80
cs-version	HTTP/1.1
cs(User-Agent)	Mozilla/4.0+(compatible;+MSIE+5.01;+Windows+98)
cs(Cookie)	ASPSESSIONIDQQGGQGVY=LLEDNABABDDBONADGFBJBAMM
cs(Referer)	http://192.168.201.251/admin/manageProducts.asp

19

Analyzing Your Logs

Because of the design of the HTTP protocol, there is no reliable way to identify confidently and completely your site's users (see the sidebar, "The Limitations of Logging"). Even so, you can still use your logs to gain some insight into the people using your site and how they are using it. You can study your Web server's logs by viewing them in a text editor such as NOTEPAD, but you will find analyzing log files this way to be extremely difficult and tedious. It is better to use the ODBC Logging Format to log directly into a database, or to periodically load log files into a database. After the logs are in a database, you can use any number of tools to analyze them.

The Limitations of Logging

You might have noticed that the even the information collected by the most detailed server log format, the W3C Extended Log File Format, is quite limited. Even worse, as you analyze your logs, you will find that log information seems inaccurate—particularly that the number of hits, page views, and unique users seems low. This is because the Internet, and specifically the HTTP protocol, are designed for efficient operation rather than accurate logging. In other words, the HTTP protocol's primary function is to get information to its destination, not to track that information's delivery. In between your store and your customer, there are many tricks that browsers and ISPs use to increase response time and minimize traffic, and each of these tricks distorts the view of your users that you are attempting to tease out of your logs.

To start with, most browsers store each page, graphic, applet, and ActiveX control in a *cache* in order to reduce the time it takes to present them to users. When a user requests a page or when a page references another file, the browser first checks its cache before asking for the item from a server. This means that if a customer requests the same page twice, the second access might never actually make it to your server, which means that it won't show up in your server log.

In addition to the browser cache, ISPs and corporations reduce the number of entries in your server log by implementing *proxy servers*. Proxy servers are like browser caches, except that they are shared between users. When proxy server users request pages or other objects from Web servers, the proxy server first checks its cache before passing the request on to the server. If the page isn't in the cache, the proxy server requests it from the site, presents it to the user, and stores it in its cache for the next user request. This means that if Kathy and Ken are both using the same ISP and they both request the same page from your store, only one visit will appear in your server's log.

Although there is a tag that you can add to any of your pages that asks browsers and proxy servers not to cache them, many proxy servers purposefully ignore this tag. Even if a proxy server honors the `<META HTTP-EQUIV="Expires" CONTENT="0">` tag, requests made through proxy servers often all appear to be from the same IP address, and so appear to be from the same person. To further confuse your tracking mechanisms, many ISPs and corporations use firewalls, which in part protect by obscuring. Even if a firewall doesn't cache, users accessing your server from a network protected by a firewall will appear to be using the same IP address, and so will appear to be the same person.

Finally, Web spiders, or *bots*, from search engines and other automated information gathering services will confuse your user accounting by inflating your server logs. When a service like Alta Vista visits your site to index your pages, it retrieves the page the same way that a browser does, by performing an HTTP GET. This means that, to your Web server, indexing requests appear to be user requests, even though there is no one actually looking at the retrieved pages.

There is a lot of commercial software available that tries to work around these difficulties, but Web privacy advocates are implementing workarounds to the workarounds in a kind of privacy versus commerce arms race. In the final analysis, as with nearly anything else, you will have to decide whether imperfect data is better than no data.

Loading Text Logs into a Database with ASP

If you aren't using ODBC logging and own Microsoft Access or Microsoft Excel, you can use their Import Text feature to load log files into your database. Many other database and spreadsheet programs also include an Import Text feature. You can also use an ASP script to load your data into a Microsoft Access database.

> **Caution**
>
> If you decide to use the Import Text feature of a database or spreadsheet to load information from a W3C Extended Log File into a database, first be sure to delete the comment lines from the top of the file. The comment lines are the lines that begin with the # character.

If you want to roll your own log file import support, you need to allow the administrator to select the log file or files to be imported, and then pass the selected files to a script that actually imports the files into the database. The code in Listing 19.1 allows an administrator to select log files to load in a manner similar to the code in Listing 18.8 that selects email recipients. The `fs.inc` file that is included on line 2 of the following code can be found on the CD.

> **Caution**
>
> As with other Administration functions, it is important to keep the pages that maintain the logging database in a password-protected database.

19

INPUT   **LISTING 19.1**   ListLogs.asp, Which Uses ASP to Enumerate the Log Files

```
1  <%@ Language="VBScript" %>
2  <!-- #include file="../fs.inc" -->
3  <%
4    Dim fs, folder
5    Set fs = CreateObject("Scripting.FileSystemObject")
6
7    ' Replace with logic that opens the logging folder for your store
8    Set folder = fs.GetSpecialFolder(SystemFolder)
9    Set folder = folder.SubFolders.Item("LogFiles")
10   Set folder = folder.SubFolders.Item("w3svc6")
11 %>
12
13 <html>
14 <head><title>Johnson's Candies and Gifts - Log File List</title></head>
15 <body link="#ff4040" vtext="lightred" bgcolor="#ffffff">
```

continues

LISTING 19.1 continued

```
16 <center>
17 <table width="640" border="0" bgcolor="#ffffff"
   ➥cellspacing="0" cellpadding="0">
18  <tr><td><img src="../logo.gif" WIDTH="300" HEIGHT="30"></td></tr>
19  <tr><td colspan="2"><hr width="640"></td></tr>
20 </table>
21 </center>
22 <SCRIPT Language="VBScript">
23 <!--
24 SUB CheckAll
25   Dim cb
26
27   For Each cb in document.loglist.elements
28     If cb.name = "logFileName" Then
29       cb.checked = document.loglist.allbox.checked
30     End If
31   Next
32 END SUB
33 -->
34 </SCRIPT>
35 <center>
36 <H4>Check the boxes next to the log files you wish to load.</H4>
37
38 <FORM name="loglist" method="POST" action="LoadLog.asp">
39 <table width="600" border="1" bgcolor="white" cellpadding="4"
   ➥cellspacing="0">
40  <TR border="0" bgcolor="yellow" align="Left">
41    <TH>
42    <table border="0" width="550" cellspacing="0"><tr>
43     <td><Font face="Arial"><b>Log File Name</b></td>
44     <td align="right"><a href="adminPage.asp">
       ➥Return to Administration Page</a></td>
45    </tr></table></TH>
46  </TR>
47 <%
48   Dim fileList, logFile
49   Set fileList = folder.Files
50   For Each logFile in fileList
51 %>
52  <TR bgcolor = "White" align="Left" bordercolor="#cccccc">
53    <TD WIDTH="1"><Font Size="2" Face="Arial" Color="Black">
54     <input type="checkbox" name="logFileName" value="<%=logFile.Path%>">
       ➥</TD>
55    <TD><Font Size="2" Face="Arial" Color="Black"><% =logFile.Name %></TD>
56  </TR>
57 <%
58     Set logFile = Nothing
59   Next
```

```
60   Set fileList = Nothing
61 %>
62 </table>
63 <table width="600" border="0" bgcolor="white" cellpadding="4"
   ➥cellspacing="0">
64  <TR bgcolor = "White" bordercolor = "White">
65    <td width="1" valign="top">
66      <input name="allbox" type="checkbox"
        ➥value="Check All" onClick="CheckAll"></td>
67    <td>Select all files</td>
68  </tr>
69 </TABLE>
70 <INPUT type="submit" value="Next >" id="submit1" name="submit1">
71 </form>
72 </center>
73 </body>
74 </html>
75 <%
76  Set fs = Nothing
77  Set folder = Nothing
78 %>
```

ANALYSIS Line 2 of the script includes some VBScript constants for use with the GetSpecialFolder function below. Lines 8–10 sets the folder variable to the logging folder for the store—you should change lines 8–10 so that they locate the appropriate folder. Lines 38–71 define a form named loglist that is used to select the log files to be imported. Within that form, Lines 39–62 define a table that is used to view each user. Lines 41–45 define the header of that table. Lines 48–60 loop through each of the files in the log file directory pointed to by the folder variable and create a row in the table for each. Lines 53–55 define a table cell that contains a check box with the name logFileName and the value of the fully-qualified path name of the log file, and line 55 defines a cell that includes the file's short name. Lines 66–72 define an additional check box named allbox that allows the user to select or deselect all users at the same time. The onClick attribute of the check box defined in line 66 causes a call to the client-side script subroutine named CheckAll when the additional check box is clicked. As with the homonymous function in selectCust.asp (see Listing 18.8), lines 22–34 define a client-side script subroutine named CheckAll, and it is intended to be called when the state of the allbox check box changes. Lines 22 and 34 are the SCRIPT tags that define a client-side script. Lines 27–31 iterate through each named item in the loglist form and line 29 sets the state of each item named logFileName to match allbox's state.

19

Note

> A fully-qualified pathname is the entire name of a file, including the disk
> drive letter and path.

After the user selects the log files and clicks the Next button, control passes to the code
in Listing 19.2, which is an ASP script that loads the selected W3C Extended Log Files
into a database. This script can be easily modified to load files in the other IIS logging
formats. Integrating these scripts into the Administration Web site is a matter of simply
adding a few links to the adminPage.asp file. An updated version of adminPage.asp and
the fs.inc file included on line 3 is included on the CD-ROM that accompanies this
book.

INPUT   LISTING 19.2   Loading a W3C Extended Log File with ASP

```
1  <%@ Language=VBScript %>
2  <!-- #include file="../adovbs.inc" -->
3  <!-- #include file="../fs.inc" -->
4  <%
5    Response.Buffer = TRUE
6  %>
7  <HTML>
8  <HEAD>
9  <META NAME="GENERATOR" Content="Microsoft Visual Studio 6.0">
10 <title>Johnson's Candies and Gifts - Load Log Files</title>
11 </head>
12 <body link="#ff4040" vtext="lightred" bgcolor="#ffffff">
13 <center>
14 <table width="640" border="0" bgcolor="#ffffff"
   ➥cellspacing="0" cellpadding="0">
15 <tr><td><img src="../logo.gif" WIDTH="300" HEIGHT="30"></td></tr>
16 <tr><td colspan="2"><hr width="640"></td></tr>
17 </table>
18 </center>
19 <%
20
21 Dim Con, rs, fs, file, fileName, fileString, fieldNameArray
22
23 Set Con = Server.CreateObject( "ADODB.Connection" )
24 Con.Open "logDSN"
25 Set rs = Server.CreateObject( "ADODB.Recordset" )
26 rs.Open "logTable", Con, adOpenDynamic, adLockOptimistic
27 Set fs = CreateObject("Scripting.FileSystemObject")
28
29 For Each fileName in Request.Form("logFileName")
30   Set file = fs.OpenTextFile(fileName, ForReading)
31
```

```
32    While file.AtEndOfStream <> True
33      fileString = file.ReadLine
34      If Left(fileString, 8) = "#Fields:" Then
35        fieldNameArray = Split(Mid(fileString, 10))
36      Elseif Left(fileString, 1) <> "#" Then
37        rs.AddNew fieldNameArray, Split(fileString)
38      End If
39    Wend
40
41    rs.Update
42    file.Close
43    Set file = Nothing
44  Next
45  rs.Close
46  Set rs = Nothing
47  Con.Close
48  Set Con = Nothing
49
50 %>
51
52 <H4>Log files loaded!</H4>
53 </BODY>
54 </HTML>
```

ANALYSIS Lines 2 and 3 include some VBScript constants for use with the file and database calls contained later in the script. Lines 23–26 create a Database Connection to the logging database, and open a `Recordset` to the logging table. You can modify lines 24 and 26 if you have named your logging DSN or table name differently. Line 27 creates a file system object that allows you to manipulate the actual log files. The outer loop (lines 29–44) iterates through each file submitted to the form from `ListLogs.asp` the same way that `sendMsg.asp` (see Listing 18.10) iterates through the email addresses selected from `selectCust.asp` (see Listing 18.8). Line 30 opens each file for reading, and the inner loop (lines 32–39) iterates through each line of the opened file. Line 33 reads a line and line 34 checks to see if the line is a field comment. If it is, line 35 parses the comment into fields and stores them as the column headers into the `fieldNameArray`. If it's another kind of comment, line 36 simply skips over it; otherwise, line 37 parses the line into fields and inserts the fields into the logging database. After the entire file is processed, line 42 closes the file and line 43 sets the file object to be reclaimed. Finally, when the program reaches the end of the list of files to be uploaded, lines 45–48 close and mark the `Recordset` and Database Connection for reclaiming.

19

Note

> The #Fields: comment appears in a W3C Extended Log File before any records are logged, but might appear more than once if the Web server is restarted. Each time the #Fields: comment is encountered, it is re-parsed because the logging parameters can be changed (see Figure 19.4) while the server is running. So a single W3C Extended Log File might include log entries in a variety of formats.

Analyzing the Logs with ASP

When your logs are in a database, you can also use ASP to perform usage analysis. As an example, Listing 19.3 shows the contents of `DailyHits.asp`, an ASP script that shows the number of hits a site handles each day. The results of running this script are illustrated in Figure 19.5. If you want to perform different sorts of analysis, you can start by modifying the SQL query in line 26. For example, changing the query to

```
SELECT logTable.date, logTable.[c-ip],
➥ Count(*) FROM logTable GROUP BY logTable.date, logTable.[c-ip]
```

displays the number of hits from each unique customer IP address on each day.

INPUT   **LISTING 19.3**   Displaying the Daily Hits Computed from the Database

```
1   <%@ Language=VBScript %>
2   <!-- #include file="../adovbs.inc" -->
3   <%
4      Response.Buffer = TRUE
5   %>
6   <HTML>
7   <HEAD>
8   <META NAME="GENERATOR" Content="Microsoft Visual Studio 6.0">
9   <title>Johnson's Candies and Gifts - Display Daily Hits</title>
10  </head>
11  <body link="#ff4040" vtext="lightred" bgcolor="#ffffff">
12  <center>
13
14  <table width="640" border="0" bgcolor="#ffffff" cellspacing="0"
    ➥cellpadding="0">
15    <tr><td><img src="../logo.gif" WIDTH="300" HEIGHT="30"> </td></tr>
16    <tr><td colspan="2"><hr width="640"></td></tr>
17  </table>
18  </center>
19
20  <%
21  Dim Con, rs, record
22
23  Set Con = Server.CreateObject( "ADODB.Connection" )
```

```
24 Con.Open "logDSN"
25 Set rs = Server.CreateObject( "ADODB.Recordset" )
26 rs.Open "SELECT date, count(*) FROM logTable Group by date", Con
27
28 rs.MoveFirst
29 %>
30
31 <table border="1" bgcolor="white" cellpadding="4" cellspacing="0">
32   <TR border="0" bgcolor="yellow" align="Left">
33     <TH>Date</TH>
34     <TH>Number of Hits</TH>
35   </TR>
36
37 <%
38 While rs.EOF <> true
39 %>
40   <TR>
41     <TD><%=rs.Fields(0)%></TD>
42     <TD><%=rs.Fields(1)%></TD>
43   </TR>
44 <%
45   rs.MoveNext
46 Wend
47
48 rs.Close
49 Set rs = Nothing
50 Con.Close
51 Set Con = Nothing
52 %>
53 </table>
54 <H4><a href="adminPage.asp">Return to Administration Page</a></H4>
55 </BODY>
56 </HTML>
```

19

ANALYSIS Line 2 of the script includes some VBScript constants for use with the database functions used in later lines of the script. Lines 23–25 create a Database Connection to the logging database and a Recordset for use with the Database Connection. Line 26 is where the analysis work is actually done—it queries the logging table with an SQL statement that counts the number of records (count(*)) collected on each date (Group by date). As with the code in Listing 19.2, you can modify lines 24 and 26 if you have named your logging DSN or table name differently. When the Recordset is open, line 28 moves to its first record, and lines 31–53 create a table to display its results. Lines 32–35 define the header of the table; lines 38–46 loop through each record in the recordset (each of which represents the summary results for a single day) and creates table row entries for the date (line 41) and the number of hits (line 42).

Finally, lines 48–51 clean up the Recordset and Database Connection. Figure 19.5 shows the output of the DailyHits.asp page.

FIGURE 19.5

Usage analysis results.

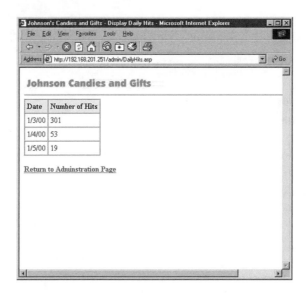

Other Ways to Analyze Logs

Depending on the statistics you are collecting in your logs, the SQL used in the script in Listing 19.3 can be modified to show many other site statistics. However, you might not have the time, or the knowledge of SQL, to write your own analyses. Instead, when your logs are in a database, you might find it faster and easier to use other tools to analyze your store usage. If you choose this route, you will find Crystal Reports, Microsoft Access, and Microsoft Excel to be quite helpful.

In addition to this "do-it-yourself" log file analysis, many products are available to help you analyze your logs. Site Server Express 3.0, which is available in a free download from Microsoft's Web site, includes a surprisingly robust set of usage analysis tools. Other products are available for purchase and range in price from hundreds to tens of thousands of dollars. These products include workarounds for the kinds of problems described earlier in the sidebar, "The Limitations of Logging." You will certainly find one of the products useful as your customer base grows.

Summary

In today's lesson, you learned the information that IIS stores as it logs Web site usage, and the differing methods for logging that IIS provides. You were presented with an overview of the NCSA Common Log File Format, the ODBC Logging Format, the Microsoft IIS Log File Format, and the W3C Extended Log File Format. You learned what can and cannot be learned from analysis of those logs. Also, you learned how to use ASP to load IIS logs into an ODBC database. Finally, you learned how to use ASP to analyze and report on the logs in those databases.

Q&A

Q What happens if log files fill my server's disk space?

A If your Web server fills up a disk with log files, it will stop.

Q What if I load the same log file twice?

A If you load the same log file into your logging database twice, you will double-count visits to your Web site for the period of time covered by that log file. You might want to add functionality to your log processing scripts that tracks the log files that have been loaded so you can prevent any double-counting.

Q How can I measure how much my customers are buying from my store?

A Because you are storing your customers' orders in a database, you can use the techniques we reviewed for log file analysis to generate sales and inventory reports. You can also use tools like Crystal Reports or Microsoft Excel to generate more sophisticated reports.

19

Workshop

The Quiz questions are designed to test your knowledge of the material covered in this chapter. The answers are in Appendix A, "Quiz Answers."

Quiz

1. What is the difference between a hit, a page view, and a unique user? For what is each useful?

2. What are the different log file formats that IIS supports? Which ones are you likely to want to use? Why?

3. Why is log file analysis an unreliable way to measure site traffic?

DAY **20**

Working with Wallets

After running your store for even a short period of time, you might discover E-Commerce's dirty little secret: abandoned transactions. Just like it sounds, an abandoned transaction happens when a user gets part of the way through an order but leaves the Web site before completing the purchase. Most sites find that a surprisingly large number of their transactions are left uncompleted.

Why does this happen? It might be that the customer has subsequently decided not to purchase a particular set of items, but in many cases, it has something to do with the store that he or she is visiting. The new customer registration form might be too long, the customer might not remember his previously used registration name, or the customer might not be sufficiently convinced of the site's trustworthiness to enter a credit card number.

Many companies have been working hard to improve the abandoned transaction situation by developing software and technologies that have become known as *electronic wallets*. In today's lesson, you will learn

- What electronic wallets are and why they are being developed
- The different kinds of wallets
- Wallet standards and why they are important

- How to create your own single-store wallet with wallet standards in mind
- How your store can accept information from one or more wallets

Physical Commerce Versus Electronic Commerce

Everyone knows about the biggest hassle of physical commerce: You have to visit a store in order to know for certain what is there and how much it costs. After you have found what you want, however, buying things at physical stores is simple. You take the item up to the front of the store, pull out some cash or a credit card, and you are done. If there is a long line, you might decide to try again some other time, but because the checkout lines are visible at the front of the store, you can know how long your wait will be ahead of time. On the whole, this means that most of the time, if a customer picks something out at a physical store, the chances are high that he will buy it.

Contrast this with electronic commerce. You can quickly and easily visit lots of stores and add items to your electronic "shopping basket." When you are finished picking out your items, though, the check-out process is harder than it is in a physical store. This is because every electronic store requires a user to enter information in a way that is unnecessary in most physical stores.

Even when purchasing from an Internet store that offers excellent performance, if it is your first visit, completing a transaction can seem interminable. Electronic stores often require a new customer to fill out a lengthy, intrusive form, enter a credit card number, and select a username that is not already being used. Customers are used to this sort of work when buying cars or houses, but, at best, it seems, like overkill—and, at worst, like a security risk—when buying a book or even a television. All in all, even a cursory analysis of the electronic shopping process suggests that getting people through a virtual checkout line can be as difficult or more difficult than getting them to visit an electronic commerce site in the first place.

Recent Web studies seem to bear this hypothesis out. A February 1999 study performed by Jupiter Communications, a New York-based information technology research firm, found that more than a quarter of users surveyed have abandoned a transaction because order forms are too long or complicated. Other studies suggest that the number of abandoned transactions could be as high as *two-thirds of all transaction attempts.*

Two-thirds of transactions abandoned is a staggering number. If two out of every three customers left a shopping cart in the aisles of a supermarket, a huge number of employees would be needed just to reshelf unwanted items! Although restocking is not a problem in the electronic world, the loss still means that most of the potential revenue of E-Commerce sites is being left on the table. It is no wonder, then, that electronic commerce companies are working so assiduously to make completing electronic transactions simpler and more efficient.

Electronic Wallets

As mentioned previously, the biggest hassle in purchasing on the Web is filling in the order form. This hassle is multiplied by the number of transactions an online customer makes. In other words, it is bad enough that in order to buy a book, one has to enter name, address, phone number, and so on, but when buying a book from a second merchant, one has to enter all that information anew. The credit card industry made purchasing easier by centralizing the credit application so that a customer only had to fill out one application in order to receive credit at thousands of stores. Similarly, the big E-Commerce players are trying to make Web purchasing easier with electronic wallets.

An *electronic wallet* is software that holds credit card numbers and other personal information such as name, shipping addresses, and telephone numbers. When a customer visits a site that uses electronic wallets, he or she doesn't need to fill out an entire order form. Instead, the wallet automatically adds the necessary information for the user into the appropriate fields on the merchant's order form.

This doesn't just make E-Commerce faster and more convenient; it also has the potential to make it safer. A well-implemented wallet encrypts customer information to keep it private. Also, like a valid credit card, a well-implemented wallet provides some extra assurance of a customer's legitimacy to a merchant. In some cases, electronic wallet vendors are even offering merchants and customers additional anti-fraud assurances along with their wallet implementations.

Client-Side Wallets

The first software to be called "wallets" was the so-called "client-side" wallet. These wallets are called client-side because they store user information on a customer's computer. Aside from the merchant-specific wallets (see the section "Single-Site Wallets" later in the chapter), client-side wallets are the most widely used commerce software. Table 20.1 lists a selected set of client-side wallets.

20

TABLE 20.1   Some Client-Side Wallets

Product Name	Company Name	Product URL
Ascendent Wallet	Hypercom	`http://www.hypercom.com/web/` `products/software/wallet/wallet.htm`
Consumer Wallet	IBM	`http://www-4.ibm.com/software/` `commerce/payment/wallet.html`
Element Wallet	Element	`http://www.element.be/` `products/productsSETWallet1.html`
eWallet	EntryPoint	`http://www.entrypoint.com/` `help/ewhelp02.html#FormFiller`
EzCard	Trintech	`http://www.trintech.com`
Gator	Gator.com	`http://www.gator.com`
ITP Wallet	Compaq	`http://www.tandem.com/prod_des/` `walletpd/walletpd.htm`
Java Wallet	Sun	`java.sun.com/products/` `commerce/docs/`
Jotter	JTI	`http://www.jotter.com`
NetPay Wallet	Maithean	`http://www.maithean.com/` `products/wallet.html`
NetWallet	Trintech	`http://www.trintech.com/` `products/netwallet/index.html`
Q*Wallet	Qwallet.com	`http://www.qwallet.com`
SecureLynx	SaskTel	`http://www.securelynx.com/` `digital_wallet/`
v-Go	Passlogix	`http://www.passlogix.com/` `welcome.html#center`
WebFormFill	Micro Systems Designs	`http://www.maxlock.com`

From a consumer's perspective, client-side wallets have a distinct privacy advantage—her personal information cannot be inadvertently disclosed by an employee of the wallet company because the company doesn't have access to the information. Instead, the user's private data is all stored and encrypted on the user's computer. Unfortunately, the same thing that gives these wallets this privacy advantage gives them two big disadvantages. First, most of them require a download. Second, after the product is downloaded and the personal information entered, the wallet is only available on a single computer.

The download disadvantage is a problem that has killed many otherwise promising ideas on the Internet. Downloads take extra time, and the slower a user's connection, the longer downloads take. Also, wallets are typically offered for free, and software that has been offered for free download has often been buggy, hard to install, and even harder to configure. These disadvantages mean that, unless a user sees a compelling, immediate utility for a piece of software, typically she will be unwilling to try it out.

The single computer disadvantage seems slight at first, but it is as significant as the download disadvantage, if not more so. Most customers are using the Internet from computers in at least two places: home and work. Some are using the Internet from several different computers in each location. In order to effectively use a client-side wallet, a customer would have to first download the wallet software to each computer that he uses, and then reenter personal information on each computer. It seems nearly as inconvenient as the pre-wallet situation.

Client-side wallet vendors are caught in a bind. Merchants will not take the time to adapt their Web sites to client-side wallets because there are too many wallets, not one of which has a significant number of users. Customers will not adopt client-side wallets because the stores that they frequent do not support them. As a result, some vendors (like Microsoft) have abandoned their client-side wallets, whereas others (like EntryPoint) have tried to integrate their wallets with software that is otherwise useful. (EntryPoint bundles their wallet with other utilities such as stock tickers and news headlines.) It is too early to tell for certain, but many E-Commerce analysts have already written off client-side wallets. This does not mean implementation support for client-side wallets on your E-Commerce site is a waste; however, it suggests that, if you have limited resources, you might be better advised to allocate them somewhere else.

Server-Side Wallets

The alternative to a client-side wallet is a server-side wallet, which, as the name implies, stores customer information on a server at a financial institution or wallet vendor. These wallets can be divided into two categories: *single-site wallets* and *general-site wallets*.

Single-Site Wallets

Single-site wallets store a customer's private information to make his next transaction at a particular store faster and more convenient. Well-designed sites have been implementing this functionality without calling it a "wallet" almost since the beginning of the Internet. The Candy Store sample application, as written, implements a rudimentary single-site, server-side wallet through its Registration feature.

Unfortunately, taking advantage of single-site wallets requires a customer to remember usernames and passwords—lots of them. In the single-site world, these usernames and passwords are usually specific to each store; thus a customer is likely to accumulate a large number of different identities. Larger Internet companies are trying to work around

20

this problem by creating electronic "malls" bringing together several E-Commerce businesses where the mall's single-site wallets can be used (see Table 20.2 for examples).

TABLE 20.2 Some Larger Site-Specific Wallets

Company Name	Description
Amazon.com	Available for all Amazon.com products, as well as selected zShops and Auctions vendors.
BillPoint	Only available for eBay auctions.
Yahoo! Wallet	Can be used for any store on Yahoo! Shopping. Username and password are the same as the username and password for other Yahoo! features such as Yahoo! mail.

Joining one of these malls is an easy, albeit potentially expensive, way to take advantage of server-side wallets. It is easy for your customers because it limits the number of usernames and passwords to remember, and it is easy for you because you don't have to handle any programming or charge clearing. It is potentially expensive because, if you already have a credit-card clearing account for a physical store, you might find that these vendors charge more per month and per transaction than your current merchant bank does.

General Server-Side Wallets

At first glance, client-side wallets seem to be the best answer to commerce in the electronic world because they leave all the information on the customer's computer, much like a physical wallet exists only in a customer's pocket. This analogy is misleading. On closer examination, it becomes clear that general server-side wallets are really the most similar to the current general-purpose credit card system.

In the physical world, information about a customer—such as billing address, account balance, and credit history—is not kept in his wallet, but at his financial institution. Plastic credit cards are simply devices that enable quick and convenient, but also extremely limited, merchant access to that information. When a consumer uses a credit card at a store, the store delegates the handling of the financial part of the transaction to the credit card network and the card-issuing bank. The customer's financial information remains private between himself and the issuing bank.

General server-side wallets replace the physical token of the credit card with a common username and password; otherwise, the scheme is remarkably similar to the credit card system. During a customer's first purchase at a general server-side-wallet–enabled E-Commerce site, the customer completes payment and shipping information on the merchant's Web form. The difference is that at the end of the transaction, the merchant asks the customer to sign up for a free digital wallet. If the customer accepts, he or she selects a username and password, and a financial institution or other third-party securely stores the entered payment and shipping information under that username. Alternatively, the customer can sign up for a general server-side wallet by visiting a wallet provider's site (see Table 20.3 for some general server-side wallets).

TABLE 20.3   Some General Server-Side Wallets

Product Name	Company Name	Product URL
AOL Quick Checkout	AOL	Quickcheckout.aol.com
Arzoo	Arzoo	http://www.arzoo.com
Brodia.com	Brodia.com	http://www.brodia.com
Doughnet	Doughnet	http://www.doughnet.com
InstaBuy	CyberCash	http://www.instabuy.com
MBNAWallet	MBNA	http://www.mbnawallet.com
MyOneWallet	Capital One	http://www.myonewallet.com
NetHost	Trintech	http://www.trintech.com/products/ payware/payware_nethost.html
Network Wallet	BlueMoney	http://www.bluemoney.com/comprod/ products/network_wallet.html
Companion	Obongo	http://www.obongo.com
Passport	Microsoft	http://www.passport.com/business/ wallet_services.asp
PowerWallet	Qpass.com	http://www.qpass.com
ServerWallet	Netlife	http://www.netlife.de
ZixWallet	ZixIt	http://www.zixcharge.com

It does not matter whether a customer sets up a wallet through a merchant's site or directly with the wallet vendor. When that customer visits any merchant that participates in the same server-side wallet program, she can use the wallet username and password instead of manually entering the payment and shipping information. The shipping information is transferred securely to the merchant site. Depending on the specific server-side wallet provider, either the provider handles charging the user's credit card or the payment information is transferred securely to the merchant along with the shipping information.

20

Other Kinds of Wallets

There are several emerging E-Commerce technologies based on *SmartCards*, plastic cards the same size as a credit card which have a small computer embedded within. Although SmartCards are not very common now, they are beginning to gain popularity with credit card issuers and are contained in certain types of cellular phones and satellite dishes. SmartCards' increasing availability has encouraged technology vendors and banks to develop E-Commerce applications that take advantage of their embedded microprocessors.

Perhaps the most interesting SmartCard-based applications from an E-Commerce point of view are the so-called "electronic purses." An electronic purse enables a user to download cash into his or her SmartCard, and then transfer the downloaded cash directly to another SmartCard, without having to make a round-trip transaction to a bank or other server computer. Because transactions can be completed without the use of a central clearing computer, these transactions should be much less expensive to complete, and should therefore facilitate electronic payment for low-cost items. Some of the vendors of E-Commerce SmartCard technologies are listed in Table 20.4.

TABLE 20.4   Information Sources on E-Commerce Applications for SmartCards

Company Name	Product Description	Product URL
ActivCard	SmartCard, plus PC or modem reader	http://www.activcard.com/solutions/ewallet.html
GemPlus	SmartCard, plus PC reader	http://www.gemplus.com/products/software/wallet
Hitachi	Electronic Mondex wallet device, interfaces with Mondex SmartCard	http://www.hitachi.co.jp/Div/nfs/products/wallet-E.html
Mondex	MasterCard-backed ePurse	http://www.mondexusa.com
Schlumberger	Mondex, Proton, and Visa Cash cards	http://www.slb.com/smartcards/products/banking
Sun	JavaCard	http://www.javasoft.com/products/javacard/index.html
VISA	Visa Cash	http://www.visa.com/nt/cash/main.html

Wallet Standards

Internet analysts are predicting that customers will adopt wallets in greater numbers between now and 2003, with a fairly large number of customers using them by 2001. At publication of this book, it is unclear which wallet will be successful, in large part because it is unclear how the general server-side wallet vendors plan to make money. All vendors plan to make their wallets free to customers. Some vendors plan to charge merchants a flat rate per month or per transaction; others plan to charge merchants a percentage of each transaction. Some plan to do both, and a fourth group plans to offer the payment information for free in the hope of selling other services to merchants and customers.

If you plan to take advantage of wallets, it is best to evaluate wallet companies as you would any other financial services vendor and make a selection based on more than simply price. Ultimately, you will get the most value from participation in a wallet scheme that has a large number of members. The best strategy is to start early, while vendors are aggressively recruiting vendors in order to establish a critical mass of merchant partners. Seek out a wallet that seems likely to be successful in attracting your store's target customers. Wallet vendors will try to attract customers by offering a wide variety of added benefits, so look for a vendor offering the kinds of added benefits that seem attractive to your target customers.

> **Note**
>
> Remember that the wallet vendors need to demonstrate their wallets' utility to consumers. In the early stages of wallet adoption, wallet utility will be determined in large part by the number of merchant partners the vendors successfully recruit. These early times offer merchants the greatest amount of negotiating leverage with wallet vendors.

Merchants will likely be able to align with more than one wallet vendor. If you choose to participate in wallet programs that follow similar operating standards, you should be able to successfully sell to customers of multiple wallet services with a minimum of additional programming effort. There are a number of wallet standards, including Secure Electronic Transactions (SET). But in October 1999, a group of major Internet and E-Commerce vendors announced their endorsement of the E-Commerce Modeling Language (ECML) standard for shipping, billing, and payment data interchange (see Table 20.5). This standard is extremely simple to implement, and E-Commerce sites that adhere to these standards will be able to receive customer data from any ECML-compatible wallet, whether it is a client-side or server-side one.

20

TABLE 20.5   Participants in E-Commerce Modeling Language as of January 2000

Company Name	URL
American Express	http://www.americanexpress.com
AOL	http://www.aol.com
Beyond.com	http://www.beyond.com
Brodia	http://www.brodia.com
Compaq	http://www.compaq.com
CyberCash	http://www.cybercash.com
Dell	http://www.dell.com
Discover	http://www.discovercard.com
Fashionmall.com	http://www.fashionmall.com
FSTC	http://www.fstc.org
IBM	http://www.ibm.com
MasterCard	http://www.mastercard.com
Microsoft	http://www.microsoft.com
Nordstrom	http://www.nordstrom.com
Novell	http://www.novell.com
Reel.com	http://www.reel.com
SETCo	http://www.setco.org
Sun Microsystems	http://www.sun.com
Trintech	http://www.trintech.com
VISA	http://www.visa.com

The steps to implement ECML support on your store's Web site are discussed later in this chapter.

Your Own Store Wallet

As mentioned previously in the section "Single-Site Wallets," the Candy Store Registration page already implements a rudimentary single-site wallet that allows a customer to identify himself with a username, to store shipping and payment information, and to select a password to protect this information. The first version of ECML is simply a prescription for how to name the input fields of your store's forms. To enable your registration page to accept input from any ECML-compliant wallet, simply update the registration form implemented by `register.asp` and the checkout form implemented by `doCheckout.asp`.

The changes to `register.asp` (see Listing 20.1) and `doCheckout.asp` (see Listing 20.2) are, for the most part, changes to `<INPUT>` field names and values. These changes are mandated by the ECML standard, the details of which are described in Table 20.6. The standard also requires minor changes to the store database's `user` table, the most significant of which include modifying the type of the credit card type column (`user_cctype`) from number to text, adding the fields `user_street2` and `user_street3`, and changing the representation of the expiration date from one Date/Time field (`user_expires`) to three number fields (`user_ccexpiredate`, `user_ccexpiremonth` and `user_ccexpireyear`). It also requires changes to the `addUser` and `updateUser` functions of `storeFuncs.asp` (see Listings 20.3 and 20.4).

The changes to `register.asp` (see Listing 20.1) are, for the most part, changes to `<INPUT>` field names and values.

INPUT **LISTING 20.1** `Register.asp` Changes for Wallets

```
1   <%
2   Dim newusername, newpassword, email, street, street2, street3, city,
    ➥state, zip, cctype
3   Dim ccnumber, ccexpiremonth, ccexpiredate, ccexpireyear, ccname, html
4
5   newusername = TRIM( Request( "newusername" ) )
6   newpassword = TRIM( Request( "newpassword" ) )
7   email = TRIM( Request( "Ecom_BillTo_Online_Email" ) )
8   street = TRIM( Request( "Ecom_BillTo_Postal_Street_Line1" ) )
9   street2 = TRIM( Request( "Ecom_BillTo_Postal_Street_Line2" ) )
10  street3 = TRIM( Request( "Ecom_BillTo_Postal_Street_Line3" ) )
11  city = TRIM( Request( "Ecom_BillTo_Postal_City" ) )
12  state = TRIM( Request( "Ecom_BillTo_Postal_StateProv" ) )
13  zip = TRIM( Request( "Ecom_BillTo_Postal_PostCode" ) )
14  cctype = TRIM( Request( "Ecom_Payment_Card_Type" ) )
15  ccnumber = TRIM( Request( "Ecom_Payment_Card_Number" ) )
16  ccexpiremonth = Request( "Ecom_Payment_Card_ExpDate_Month" )
17  ccexpireyear = Request( "Ecom_Payment_Card_ExpDate_Year" )
18  ccexpiredate = Request( "Ecom_Payment_Card_ExpDate_Day" )
19  ccname = TRIM( Request( "Ecom_Payment_Card_Name" ) )
20  html = TRIM( Request ( "html" ) )
21
22  submitpage = Request.ServerVariables( "SCRIPT_NAME" )
23  %>
24
25  <html>
26  <head><title>Register</title></head>
27  <body bgcolor="white">
28
```

20

continues

LISTING 20.1   continued

```
29   <center>
30   <table width="500" border=0 cellpadding=4 cellspacing=0>
31     <tr><td bgcolor="darkgreen"><font color="white" face="Arial"><b>Login
       ➥</b></font></td></tr>
32     <tr>
33       <td><form method="post" action="<%=submitpage%>">
34         <input name="login" type="hidden" value="1">
35         <input name="pid" type="hidden" value="<%=productID%>">
36         <font face="Arial" size="2">Please enter your username and
         ➥password:</font>
37         <font face="Courier" size="2"><p><b>username:</b><input
         ➥name="username" size="20">
38         <br><b>password:</b><input name="password" size="20">
39         <input type="submit" value="Login">
40         </font>
41       </form></td>
42     </tr>
43     <tr>
44       <td bgcolor="darkgreen"><font color="white" face="Arial">
       ➥<b>Register</b></font></td>
45     </tr>
46     <tr>
47       <td><form method="post" action="<%=submitpage%>">
48         <input name="register" type="hidden" value="1">
49         <input name="pid" type="hidden" value="<%=productID%>">
50         <font face="Arial" size="2">
51           If you are a new user, please register by completing the
           ➥following form:
52         </font>
53       <p><font face="Arial" size="2" color="darkgreen"><b>Login Information:
       ➥</b></font>
54       <font face="Courier" size="2"><br><b>username:</b>
55         <input name="newusername" size=20 maxlength=20 value="<%
       ➥=Server.HTMLEncode( newusername )%>">
56       <br><b>password:</b>
57         <input name="newpassword" size=20 maxlength=20 value="
       ➥<%=server.HTMLEncode( newpassword )%>">
58       <br><b>email address:</b>
59         <input name="Ecom_BillTo_Online_Email" size=30 maxlength=75 value
       ➥="<%=Server.HTMLEncode( email )%>">
60       <br><input name="html" type="checkbox" value="Yes"
61         <% if Server.HTMLEncode( html ) = "Yes" then %>checked<% end if %>>
62         <b>I can read E-Mail formatted in HTML.</b>
63       </font>
64       <p><font face="Arial" size="2" color="darkgreen"><b>Address Information:
       ➥</b></font>
65       <font face="Courier" size="2"><br><b>street:</b>
66         <input name="Ecom_BillTo_Postal_Street_Line1" size=20 maxlength=50
       ➥value="<%=Server.HTMLEncode( street )%>">
```

```
67     <br><b>street:</b>
68      <input name="Ecom_BillTo_Postal_Street_Line2" size=20 maxlength=50
       ➥value="<%=Server.HTMLEncode( street2 )%>">
69     <br><b>street:</b>
70      <input name="Ecom_BillTo_Postal_Street_Line3" size=20 maxlength=50
       ➥value="<%=Server.HTMLEncode( street3 )%>">
71     <br><b>city:</b>
72      <input name="Ecom_BillTo_Postal_City" size=20 maxlength=50 value="<%
       ➥=Server.HTMLEncode( city )%>">
73     <br><b>state:</b>
74      <input name="Ecom_BillTo_Postal_StateProv" size=20 maxlength=2
       ➥value="<%=Server.HTMLEncode( state )%>">
75     <br><b>zip:</b>
76      <input name="Ecom_BillTo_Postal_PostCode" size=20 maxlength=20 value
       ➥="<%=Server.HTMLEncode( zip )%>">
77     </font>
78     <p><font face="Arial" size="2" color="darkgreen"><b>Payment
       ➥Information:</b></font>
79     <font face="Courier" size="2"><br><b>type of credit card:</b>
80     <select name="Ecom_Payment_Card_Type">
81      <option value="VISA" <%=SELECTED( cctype, "VISA" )%> > VISA
82      <option value="MAST" <%=SELECTED( cctype, "MAST" )%> >MasterCard
83     </select>
84     <br><b>credit card number:</b>
85     <input name="Ecom_Payment_Card_Number" size=20 maxlength=20 value
       ➥="<%=Server.HTMLEncode( ccnumber )%>">
86     <br><b>credit card expires:</b>
87     <select name="Ecom_Payment_Card_ExpDate_Month">
88      <option value=1 <%=SELECTED( ccexpiremonth, 1)%>>01
89      <option value=2 <%=SELECTED( ccexpiremonth, 2)%>>02
90      <option value=3 <%=SELECTED( ccexpiremonth, 3)%>>03
91      <option value=4 <%=SELECTED( ccexpiremonth, 4)%>>04
92      <option value=5 <%=SELECTED( ccexpiremonth, 5)%>>05
93      <option value=6 <%=SELECTED( ccexpiremonth, 6)%>>06
94      <option value=7 <%=SELECTED( ccexpiremonth, 7)%>>07
95      <option value=8 <%=SELECTED( ccexpiremonth, 8)%>>08
96      <option value=9 <%=SELECTED( ccexpiremonth, 9)%>>09
97      <option value=10 <%=SELECTED( ccexpiremonth, 10)%>>10
98      <option value=11 <%=SELECTED( ccexpiremonth, 11)%>>11
99      <option value=12 <%=SELECTED( ccexpiremonth, 12)%>>12
100    </select>
101    <select name="Ecom_Payment_Card_ExpDate_Year">
102     <option value=2000 <%=SELECTED( ccexpiremonth, 2000)%>>2000
103     <option value=2001 <%=SELECTED( ccexpiremonth, 2001)%>>2001
104     <option value=2002 <%=SELECTED( ccexpiremonth, 2002)%>>2002
105     <option value=2003 <%=SELECTED( ccexpiremonth, 2003)%>>2003
106     <option value=2004 <%=SELECTED( ccexpiremonth, 2004)%>>2004
107     <option value=2005 <%=SELECTED( ccexpiremonth, 2005)%>>2005
108    </select>
```

20

continues

LISTING 20.1   continued

```
109     <br><b>name on credit card:</b>
110     <input name="Ecom_Payment_Card_Name" size=20 maxlength=30 value
        ➥="<%=Server.HTMLEncode( ccname )%>">
111     <input type="submit" value="Register">
112     <input type="hidden" name="Ecom_SchemaVersion" value
        ➥="http://www.ecml.org/version/1.0">
113     <input type="hidden" name="Ecom_TransactionComplete">
114     </font>
115   </form></td>
116   </tr>
117 </table>
118 </center>
119 </body>
120 </html>
```

 ANALYSIS   register.asp is included by four files: account.asp, cart.asp, checkout2.asp, and sometimes checkout.asp. When register.asp is included, it handles most of the display and submission processing for these files. When the file is handling a POST, lines 2–20 read the information submitted from the form in Listing 20.1. Line 22 reads the context of the running page, so that when the user submits the form it is submitted to the correct page (line 33 and line 47).

> **Note**
> register.asp is included by checkout.asp when the customer tries to buy something but has not yet logged in.

Lines 33–41 define a form that enables users to log in. Line 34 is a hidden field that indicates that the form is being used to login customers. Line 35 is a hidden field that remembers the product ID if the registration page is displayed because the user is trying to buy a product but has not yet logged in.

Lines 47–115 define the registration form. Line 48 is a hidden field that identifies that the action to be performed on the post is a registration, and if the user is registering as the result of an attempted product purchase, line 49 remembers the product ID selected. Lines 55–113 define input fields using ECML standard field names. Lines 80–83 define a selection field that enables the customer to choose between VISA and MasterCard as a credit card type, and submits the result using the ECML standard values. Lines 87–100 define a selection field that enables a customer to specify the month of expiration of his or her credit card, and lines 101–108 define a selection field that enables specification of the year of expiration. Note that the month and year are both specified as numbers, and that the year is specified with four digits. Lines 112 and 113 define hidden fields that are required by the ECML standard.

You will also change `<INPUT>` field names and values in doCheckout.asp (see Listing 20.2).

INPUT   **LISTING 20.2**   doCheckout.asp Changes for Wallets

```
1   <%
2   ' Retrieve Registration Information
3   sqlString = "SELECT * FROM users WHERE user_id=" & userID
4   SET RS = Con.Execute( sqlString )
5   IF NOT RS.EOF THEN
6     street = RS( "user_street" )
7     street2 = RS( "user_street2" )
8     street3 = RS( "user_street3" )
9    city = RS( "user_city" )
10    state = RS( "user_state" )
11    zip = RS( "user_zip" )
12    cctype = RS( "user_cctype" )
13    ccnumber = RS( "user_ccnumber" )
14    ccexpiremonth = RS( "user_ccexpiremonth" )
15    ccexpireyear = RS( "user_ccexpireyear" )
16    ccname = RS( "user_ccname" )
17  END IF
18
19  ' Hide Credit Card Number
20  ccnumber = LEFT( ccnumber, 2 ) & "************" & RIGHT( ccnumber, 2 )
21  %>
22  <html>
23  <head><title>Checkout</title></head>
24  <body>
25  <center>
26  <table border=1 width=500 cellpadding=5 cellspacing=0>
27    <tr><td align="center" bgcolor="lightgreen"><b>Confirm Order</b></td></tr>
28    <tr><td>
29      Your order will be sent to the following address and charged to the
         ➥following credit card.
30      Please review your address and payment information
31      and click Confirm Order to finish placing your order.
32      <form method="post" action="checkout2.asp">
33        <input name="username" type="hidden" value="<%=username%>">
34        <input name="password" type="hidden" value="<%=password%>">
35        <p><font face="Arial" size="2" color="darkgreen"><b>Address
           ➥Information:</b></font>
36        <p><font face="Courier" size="2"><br><b>street:</b>
37        <input name="Ecom_BillTo_Postal_Street_Line1" size=20 maxlength=50
           ➥value="<%=Server.HTMLEncode( street )%>">
38        <br><b>street:</b>
39        <input name="Ecom_BillTo_Postal_Street_Line2" size=20 maxlength=50
40        <% IF street2 <> "" THEN %>
41          value="<%=Server.HTMLEncode( street2 )%>"
```

continues

20

LISTING 20.2   continued

```
42      <% END IF %>  >
43      <br>
44      <b>street:</b>
45      <input name="Ecom_BillTo_Postal_Street_Line3" size=20 maxlength=50
46      <% IF street3 <> "" THEN %>
47        value="<%=Server.HTMLEncode( street3 )%>"
48      <% END IF %>  >
49      <br><b>city:</b>
50       <input name="Ecom_BillTo_Postal_City" size=20 maxlength=50 value
        ➥="<%=Server.HTMLEncode( city )%>">
51      <br><b></b><b>state:</b>
52      <input name="Ecom_BillTo_Postal_StateProv" size=20 maxlength
        ➥=2 value="<%=Server.HTMLEncode( state )%>">
53      <br><b>zip:</b>
54      <input name="Ecom_BillTo_Postal_PostCode" size=20 maxlength
        ➥=20 value="<%=Server.HTMLEncode( zip )%>">
55      </font>
56      <p><font face="Arial" size="2" color="darkgreen"><b>Payment
        ➥Information:</b></font>
57      <font face="Courier" size="2"><br><b>type of credit card:</b>
58      <select name="Ecom_Payment_Card_Type">
59        <option value="VISA"<%=SELECTED( cctype, "VISA" )%>> VISA
60        <option value="MAST"<%=SELECTED( cctype, "MAST" )%> >MasterCard
61      </select>
62      <br><b>credit card number:</b>
63      <input name="Ecom_Payment_Card_Number" size=20 maxlength=20 value
        ➥="<%=Server.HTMLEncode( ccnumber )%>">
64      <br><b>credit card expires:</b>
65      <select name="Ecom_Payment_Card_ExpDate_Month">
66        <option value=1 <%=SELECTED( ccexpiremonth, 1)%>>01
67        <option value=2 <%=SELECTED( ccexpiremonth, 2)%>>02
68        <option value=3 <%=SELECTED( ccexpiremonth, 3)%>>03
69        <option value=4 <%=SELECTED( ccexpiremonth, 4)%>>04
70        <option value=5 <%=SELECTED( ccexpiremonth, 5)%>>05
71        <option value=6 <%=SELECTED( ccexpiremonth, 6)%>>06
72        <option value=7 <%=SELECTED( ccexpiremonth, 7)%>>07
73        <option value=8 <%=SELECTED( ccexpiremonth, 8)%>>08
74        <option value=9 <%=SELECTED( ccexpiremonth, 9)%>>09
75        <option value=10 <%=SELECTED( ccexpiremonth, 10)%>>10
76        <option value=11 <%=SELECTED( ccexpiremonth, 11)%>>11
77        <option value=12 <%=SELECTED( ccexpiremonth, 12)%>>12
78      </select>
79      <select name="Ecom_Payment_Card_ExpDate_Year">
80        <option value=2000 <%=SELECTED( ccexpireyear, 2000)%>>2000
81        <option value=2001 <%=SELECTED( ccexpireyear, 2001)%>>2001
82        <option value=2002 <%=SELECTED( ccexpireyear, 2002)%>>2002
83        <option value=2003 <%=SELECTED( ccexpireyear, 2003)%>>2003
84        <option value=2004 <%=SELECTED( ccexpireyear, 2004)%>>2004
85        <option value=2005 <%=SELECTED( ccexpireyear, 2005)%>>2005
```

```
86          </select>
87          <br><b>name on credit card:</b>
88          <input name="Ecom_Payment_Card_Name" size=20 maxlength=20 value
            ➥="<%=Server.HTMLEncode( ccname )%>">
89          <p><input type="submit" value="Confirm Order">
90          <input type="hidden" name="Ecom_SchemaVersion" value=
            ➥"http://www.ecml.org/version/1.0">
91          <input type="hidden" name="Ecom_TransactionComplete">
92          </font>
93        </form>
94      </td></tr>
95   </table>
96   </center>
97   </body>
98   </html>
```

ANALYSIS   doCheckout.asp is included by checkout.asp when a customer buys something and has already logged in. When included, it handles the display processing for that checkout.asp. It assumes that the customer's user ID is set into the variable userID. Lines 3–17 read the customer's wallet information from the users table of the store database for later display and use. Before displaying the credit card number, line 20 obscures it.

Lines 32–93 define a form that enables the customer to verify his payment and shipping information before completing an order. The fields in the form are named according to the ECML standard. Because the second and third lines of the address are optional, lines 40–42 and 46–48 handle the case when they are not specified in the database. Lines 58–61 define a selection field that enables the customer to verify or change the choice of VISA or MasterCard as the purchase credit card type, and submits the result using the ECML standard values. Lines 65–78 define a selection field that enables a customer to verify or change the month of expiration of his or her credit card, and lines 79–86 define a selection field that enables verification or change of the year of expiration. Note that the month and year are both specified as numbers, and that the year is specified with four digits. Lines 90 and 91 define hidden fields that are required by the ECML standard.

These changes are mandated by the ECML standard, the details of which are described in Table 20.6. The standard also requires minor changes to the store database's user table, the most significant of which include

- Modifying the type of the credit card type column (user_cctype) from number to text

- Adding the fields user_street2 and user_street3

- Changing the representation of the expiration date from one Date/Time field (user_expires) to three number fields (user_ccexpiredate, user_ccepxiremonth, and user_ccexpireyear)

20

TABLE 20.6   ECML Fields

Field Name	Explanation	Minimum Size1
Ecom_ShipTo_Postal_Name_Prefix	Title (Mr., Mrs., and so on) for Ship To address.	4
Ecom_ShipTo_Postal_Name_First	First name for Ship To address.	15
Ecom_ShipTo_Postal_Name_Middle	Middle name or initial for Ship To address.	15
Ecom_ShipTo_Postal_Name_Last	Last name for Ship To address.	15
Ecom_ShipTo_Postal_Name_Suffix	Suffix (PhD, III, and so on) for Ship To address.	4
Ecom_ShipTo_Postal_Street_Line1	First line of Ship To address.	20
Ecom_ShipTo_Postal_Street_Line2	Second line of Ship To address.	20
Ecom_ShipTo_Postal_Street_Line3	Third line of Ship To address.	20
Ecom_ShipTo_Postal_City	City for Ship To address.	22
Ecom_ShipTo_Postal_StateProv	State or province abbreviation for Ship To address.	2
Ecom_ShipTo_Postal_PostCode	Postal or zip code for Ship To address.	14
Ecom_ShipTo_Postal_CountryCode	Two letter country code for Ship To address (for example, US, CA, MX).	2
Ecom_ShipTo_Telecom_Phone_Number	Telephone number for Ship To address.	10
Ecom_ShipTo_Online_Email	Email address for Ship To address.	40
Ecom_BillTo_Postal_Name_Prefix	Title (Mr., Mrs., and so on) for Bill To address.	4

Field Name	Explanation	Minimum Size1
Ecom_BillTo_Postal_Name_First	First name for Bill To address.	15
Ecom_BillTo_Postal_Name_Middle	Middle name or initial for Bill To address.	15
Ecom_BillTo_Postal_Name_Last	Last name for Bill To address.	15
Ecom_BillTo_Postal_Name_Suffix	Suffix (PhD, III, and so on) for Bill To address.	4
Ecom_BillTo_Postal_Street_Line1	First line of Bill To address.	20
Ecom_BillTo_Postal_Street_Line2	Second line of Bill To address.	20
Ecom_BillTo_Postal_Street_Line3	Third line of Bill To address.	20
Ecom_BillTo_Postal_City	City for Bill To address.	22
Ecom_BillTo_Postal_StateProv	State or province abbreviation for Bill To address.	2
Ecom_BillTo_Postal_PostCode	Postal or zip code for Bill To address.	14
Ecom_BillTo_Postal_CountryCode	Two letter country code for Bill To address (for example, US, CA, MX).	2
Ecom_BillTo_Telecom_Phone_Number	Telephone number for Bill To address.	10
Ecom_BillTo_Online_Email	Email address for Bill To address.	40
Ecom_ReceiptTo_Postal_Name_Prefix	Title (Mr., Mrs., and so on) for Receipt To address.	4
Ecom_ReceiptTo_Postal_Name_First	First name for Receipt To address.	15
Ecom_ReceiptTo_Postal_Name_Middle	Middle name or initial for Receipt To address.	15

20

continues

TABLE 20.6   continued

Field Name	Explanation	Minimum Size1
Ecom_ReceiptTo_Postal_Name_Last	Last name for Receipt To address.	15
Ecom_ReceiptTo_Postal_Name_Suffix	Suffix (PhD, III, and so on) for Receipt To address.	4
Ecom_ReceiptTo_Postal_Street_Line1	First line of Receipt To address.	20
Ecom_ReceiptTo_Postal_Street_Line2	Second line of Receipt To address.	20
Ecom_ReceiptTo_Postal_Street_Line3	Third line of Receipt To address.	20
Ecom_ReceiptTo_Postal_City	City for Receipt To address.	22
Ecom_ReceiptTo_Postal_StateProv	State or province abbreviation for Receipt To address.	2
Ecom_ReceiptTo_Postal_PostCode	Postal or zip code for Receipt To address.	14
Ecom_ReceiptTo_Postal_CountryCode	Two letter country code for Receipt To address (for example, US, CA, MX).	2
Ecom_ReceiptTo_Telecom_Phone_Number	Telephone number for Receipt To address.	10
Ecom_ReceiptTo_Online_Email	Email address for Receipt To address.	40
Ecom_Payment_Card_Name	Name on credit card used for payment.	30
Ecom_Payment_Card_Type	First four letters of the card association name (for example, AMER, JCB, MAST).	4
Ecom_Payment_Card_Number	The number on the credit card.	19

`Ecom_Payment_Card_Verification`	Any verification number defined by the card issuing organization.	4
`Ecom_Payment_Card_ExpDate_Day`	Expiration date (day of month).	2
`Ecom_Payment_Card_ExpDate_Month`	Expiration month.	2
`Ecom_Payment_Card_ExpDate_Year`	Expiration year (always four digits).	4
`Ecom_Payment_Card_Protocol`	The transmission protocols available. Currently defined protocols are none (field fill only), set (using a set client-side wallet), and setcert (using a set client-side wallet with a certificate).	20
`Ecom_ConsumerOrderID`	A number the merchant assigned to the order.	20
`Ecom_SchemaVersion`	Should be `http://www.ecml.org/version/1.0`. Usually contained in a hidden field, and must appear after the `<INPUT>` tags for any `Ecom_field` except `Ecom_Transaction Complete`.	30
`Ecom_TransactionComplete`	Valueless `<INPUT>` tag that indicates the last page of a multi-page form set. Usually hidden. If on a page, must be the last `<Ecom>` tag on that page.	

20

1. *Minimum Size is not the minimum database size, but simply the minimum field size. You should be able to handle larger fields in your databases.*

ECML standard requires changes to the addUser functions of storeFuncs.asp (see Listing 20.3).

 LISTING 20.3   New addUser Function for storeFuncs.asp

```
1   SUB addUser
2     ' Get Registration Fields
3     newusername = TRIM( Request( "newusername" ) )
4     newpassword = TRIM( Request( "newpassword" ) )
5     email = TRIM( Request( "Ecom_BillTo_Online_Email" ) )
6     street = TRIM( Request( "Ecom_BillTo_Postal_Street_Line1" ) )
7     street2 = TRIM( Request( "Ecom_BillTo_Postal_Street_Line2" ) )
8     street3 = TRIM( Request( "Ecom_BillTo_Postal_Street_Line3" ) )
9     city = TRIM( Request( "Ecom_BillTo_Postal_City" ) )
10    state = TRIM( Request( "Ecom_BillTo_Postal_StateProv" ) )
11    zip = TRIM( Request( "Ecom_BillTo_Postal_PostCode" ) )
12    cctype = TRIM( Request( "Ecom_Payment_Card_Type" ) )
13    ccnumber = TRIM( Request( "Ecom_Payment_Card_Number" ) )
14    ccexpiremonth = Request( "Ecom_Payment_Card_ExpDate_Month" )
15    ccexpireyear = Request( "Ecom_Payment_Card_ExpDate_Year" )
16    ccname = TRIM( Request( "Ecom_Payment_Card_Name" ) )
17    html = TRIM( Request ( "html" ) )
18
19    if html = "Yes" then
20       html = "1"
21    else
22       html = "0"
23    end if
24
25    ' Check For Required Fields
26    backpage = Request.ServerVariables( "SCRIPT_NAME" )
27    IF newusername = "" THEN
28      errorForm "You must enter a username.", backpage
29    END IF
30    IF newpassword = "" THEN
31      errorForm "You must enter a password.", backpage
32    END IF
33    IF email = "" THEN
34      errorForm "You must enter your email address.", backpage
35    END IF
36    IF street = "" THEN
37      errorForm "You must enter your street address.", backpage
38    END IF
39    IF city = "" THEN
40      errorForm "You must enter your city.", backpage
41    END IF
42    IF state = "" THEN
43      errorForm "You must enter your state.", backpage
44    END IF
45    IF zip = "" THEN
46      errorForm "You must enter your zip code.", backpage
47    END IF
```

```
48    IF ccnumber = "" THEN
49      errorForm "You must enter your credit card number.", backpage
50    END IF
51    IF ccname = "" THEN
52      errorForm "You must enter the name that appears on your credit card.",
➥ backpage
53    END IF
54
55    ' Check for Necessary Field Values
56    IF invalidEmail( email ) THEN
57      errorForm "You did not enter a valid email address", backpage
58    END IF
59    IF NOT validCCNumber( ccnumber ) THEN
60      errorForm "You did not enter a valid credit card number", backpage
61    END IF
62
63    ' Check whether username already registered
64    IF alreadyUser( newusername ) THEN
65      errorForm "Please choose a different username.", backpage
66    END IF
67
68    ' Add New User to Database
69    sqlString = "INSERT INTO users ( "user_username, user_password,
➥ user_email, user_street, " &_
70      "user_city, user_state, user_zip, user_ccnumber, user_cctype,
➥ user_ccexpiremonth," &_
71      "user_ccexpireyear, user_ccname, user_HTML") VALUES ( " &_
72      " '" & fixQuotes( newusername ) & "', " &_
73      " '" & fixQuotes( newpassword ) & "', " &_
74      " '" & fixQuotes( email ) & "', " &_
75      " '" & fixQuotes( street ) & "', " &_
76      " '" & fixQuotes( city ) & "', " &_
77      " '" & fixQuotes( state ) & "', " &_
78      " '" & fixQuotes( zip ) & "', " &_
79      " '" & fixQuotes( ccnumber ) & "', " &_
80      " '" & cctype & "', " &_
81      " '" & ccexpiremonth & "', " &_
82      " '" & ccexpireyear & "', " &_
83      " '" & fixQuotes( ccname ) & "', " &_
84      " " & html & ")"
85
86    Con.Execute sqlString
87    CheckError
88
89    ' Use the new username and password
90    username = newusername
91    password = newpassword
92
93    ' Add Cookies
94    addCookie "username", username
95    addCookie "password", password
96  END SUB
```

20

ANALYSIS The addUser function assumes that it is being called as part of POST processing
for a register.asp submission. The function reads the new customer's information, most of which is submitted with ECML-compliant field names, into local variables,
trimming leading and trailing spaces and performing type conversions where appropriate
(lines 3–23). Line 26 stores the name of the file that included register.asp so that, in
case of an error in the following lines, the page can be redisplayed. Lines 27–61 verify
that all required information is filled in, and lines 64–66 verify that someone else hasn't
registered with the same username. When the checks are complete, lines 69–86 insert the
new user into the database, and lines 90–95 set a cookie so that the user doesn't have to
log in again.

The ECML standards also require changes to the updateUser functions of
storeFuncs.asp (see Listing 20.4).

INPUT   **LISTING 20.4**   New updateUser Function for storeFuncs.asp

```
1   SUB updateUser
2     ' Get Registration Fields
3     street = TRIM( Request( "Ecom_BillTo_Postal_Street_Line1" ) )
4     street2 = TRIM( Request( "Ecom_BillTo_Postal_Street_Line2" ) )
5     street3 = TRIM( Request( "Ecom_BillTo_Postal_Street_Line3" ) )
6     city = TRIM( Request( "Ecom_BillTo_Postal_City" ) )
7     state = TRIM( Request( "Ecom_BillTo_Postal_StateProv" ) )
8     zip = TRIM( Request( "Ecom_BillTo_Postal_PostCode" ) )
9     cctype = TRIM( Request( "Ecom_Payment_Card_Type" ) )
10    ccnumber = TRIM( Request( "Ecom_Payment_Card_Number" ) )
11    ccexpiremonth = Request( "Ecom_Payment_Card_ExpDate_Month" )
12    ccexpireyear = Request( "Ecom_Payment_Card_ExpDate_Year" )
13    ccname = TRIM( Request( "Ecom_Payment_Card_Name" ) )
14
15    ' Check For Required Fields
16    backpage = "checkout.asp"
17    IF street = "" THEN
18      errorForm "You must enter your street address.", backpage
19    END IF
20    IF city = "" THEN
21      errorForm "You must enter your city.", backpage
22    END IF
23    IF state = "" THEN
24      errorForm "You must enter your state.", backpage
25    END IF
26    IF zip = "" THEN
27      errorForm "You must enter your zip code.", backpage
28    END IF
29    IF ccnumber = "" THEN
30      errorForm "You must enter your credit card number.", backpage
31    END IF
```

```
32   IF ccname = "" THEN
33     errorForm "You must enter the name that appears on your credit card.",
       ➥backpage
34   END IF
35
36   ' Check for Necessary Field Values
37   IF INSTR( ccnumber, "*" ) = 0 THEN
38     IF NOT validCCNumber( ccnumber ) THEN
39       errorForm "You did not enter a valid credit card number", backpage
40     ELSE
41       ccnumber = "'" & ccnumber & "'"
42     END IF
43   ELSE
44     ccnumber = "user_ccnumber"
45   END IF
46
47   ' Update user information in the database
48   sqlString = "UPDATE users SET " &_
49     "user_street='" & fixQuotes( street ) & "', " &_
50     "user_city='" & fixQuotes( city ) & "'," &_
51     "user_state='" & fixQuotes( state ) & "'," &_
52     "user_zip='" & fixQuotes( zip ) & "'," &_
53     "user_ccnumber=" & ccnumber & ", " &_
54     "user_cctype='" & cctype & "', " &_
55     "user_ccexpiremonth='" & ccexpiremonth & "'," &_
56     "user_ccexpireyear='" & ccexpireyear & "'," &_
57     "user_ccname='" & fixQuotes( ccname ) & "' " &_
58     "WHERE user_id=" & userID
59
60   Con.Execute sqlString
61 END SUB
```

ANALYSIS　The updateUser function assumes that it is being called as part of POST processing for a doCheckout.asp submission. The function reads the customer's information, which is submitted with ECML-compliant field names, into local variables, trimming leading and trailing spaces and performing type conversions where appropriate (lines 3–13). Line 16 assumes that doCheckout.asp has been included by checkout.asp, and stores that page's name so that, in case of an error in the following lines, it can be redisplayed. Lines 17–45 verify that all required information is filled in. If the customer changed the obscured credit card number (line 37), the function validates the entered number (line 38), and, if the number is valid, sets ccnumber to a SQL fragment that will be used later to update the database with the new credit card number (line 41). If the customer didn't change the credit card number, then the function sets ccnumber to a SQL fragment that leaves the contents of the credit card column unchanged when the rest of the customer's data is updated (line 44). Once the checks are complete, lines 48–60 update the customer's wallet information in the database. Of special note is line 53, which updates the customer's credit card number using the SQL fragment from either line 41 or line 44.

20

> The other customer information is safe to update "as-is," but because
> `doCheckout.asp` obscures the customer's credit card number, if lines 37–45
> didn't check the credit card number, the customer's credit card number
> would be corrupted after any transaction in which the customer used the
> credit card in her wallet!

> To maximize database scalability for a production system, you wouldn't
> want to perform a database update unless the customer had actually
> changed some wallet information.

Accepting Information from Wallets

In principle, the changes you made in the previous section to your own store wallet
would be enough to enable users to start using wallets on your site. Unfortunately,
although ECML seems like a simple standard, invariably there are slight differences in
standards implementation between vendors. Describing the details of specific wallet
implementations is beyond the scope of this book (and, indeed, many wallet vendors
treat their wallet implementations as confidential information). However, you should plan
to create a separate page, similar to the `register.asp` and `doCheckout.asp`, for each
wallet that you intend to support. You should contact your preferred wallet vendor or
vendors for other implementation details after you have made your selection.

> Except for the `Ecom_SchemaVersion` and `Ecom_TransactionComplete` tags, the
> ECML specification does not require the presence of any `<INPUT>` tags, nor
> does it specify an order for tag presentation. This means that wallet soft-
> ware might not provide information about a customer that you require. In
> addition, wallet customers might come from countries that you cannot ship
> to or might hold a credit card that you cannot process. Therefore, you
> should be sure to carefully validate all information presented to your sub-
> mission forms by a wallet.

Summary

In today's lesson, you learned about the difficulties consumers have had with online purchasing, and the kinds of electronic wallets that are being developed in an attempt to
make Web stores easier and more enjoyable for Internet consumers to use. You also

learned about the differences between client-side and server-side wallets, and about the ECML standard that facilitates Web site interoperability with multiple wallets. Finally, you learned how to modify the Candy Store example's rudimentary wallet to be ready for interaction with ECML-compliant wallets.

Q&A

Q **The code in this chapter stores the customer's credit card number in plain text. Is this safe?**

A It is never safe to store sensitive information like credit card numbers and passwords in plain-text databases. If your store database is ever compromised, you might find your customers' credit card numbers posted on a Web site. This actually happened to at least one electronic commerce site in early 2000.

One possible solution is to use encryption to scramble each customer's sensitive information. Another is to work with a preferred wallet vendor and depend on the vendor to store the credit card information. By delegating credit card number storage to the wallet vendor, you can destroy the credit card number after the customer's order has been processed, and therefore mitigate some of your security risk.

Workshop

The Quiz and Exercise questions are designed to test your knowledge of the material covered in this chapter. The answers are in Appendix A, "Quiz Answers."

Quiz

1. What is the difference between a client-side wallet and a server-side wallet?
2. What is the difference between a SmartCard and a wallet?
3. What is the ECML standard?

Exercises

1. Some credit cards specify an expiration day as well as a month and year. Other cards don't specify any expiration date. Extend the code in Listings 20.1–20.4 to handle all these cases.
2. Enhance updateUser in Listing 20.4 so that it only performs a database transaction when a piece of information about the user has changed. (Hint: You might have to change more files than just updateUser.)

20

DAY 21

Promoting Your Site and Managing Banner Advertising

"My store is open. Now, how do I make money?"

If you have ever run a physical store, you will have asked yourself that question dozens of times before. When you open a store—after all the hard work of renovating, painting, ordering, stocking, and managing the thousands of other details that come with a store—you nearly invariably have the same, opening day experience: No customers, no cash flow.

As you have been learning all this week, there is much about Web commerce that is like physical commerce, and this is another similarity. What makes Web commerce appear more difficult is that on the Web, there is no sidewalk traffic. What does a small Web business owner do? First, drive traffic. Second, maximize revenue.

Today, you will learn

- Ways to make yourself attractive to search engines
- How to join a Web ring
- How to market your site with free banner ads
- How to buy banner ads
- How to encourage your customers to return with reward programs
- How to sell banner ads, and other ways to bring in revenues that aren't sales

Search Engines

When you think about how you find information on the Web, you probably think about search engines. According to the Georgia Tech Graphic, Visualization, and Usability Center, search engines are one of the most common ways people find information on the Web, second only to links from other Web pages. This means that, if you want people to find your E-Commerce site, you need to get it into search engines.

How Do They Work?

Search engines are actually the product of a combination of two tasks: "spidering" and "indexing." First, the search engine must try to find every page on the Web. This is no mean feat, as the Web grows and changes dramatically every month, and there is no central list of all the pages. A search engine's Web spider tries to build that central list by periodically requesting every Web page with every URL it has ever seen. If there is no longer a Web page at a URL, the spider deletes the URL from its list. If there is a Web page, the spider scans the page for links to other pages and, if it finds any, adds those URLs to its central list.

When the spider finds a URL, the search engine's indexer goes to work. The indexer scans each page for key words and stores them along with the page's URL and a summary or abstract of the page. Thus, after a page has been spidered and indexed, it can be found.

Nearly all the search engines automate the spidering process to some degree. Two major kinds of search engines handle the indexing process: Web directories and Web indices. Web directories, such as Yahoo! and the Open Directory Project, use people to place Web sites into a search structure. Web indices use software to perform the same function.

What's the Best Way to Get Listed?

Now that you know, in general, how the search engines work, it probably seems that getting a site listed on a search engine should be very straightforward—just get your store's main URL onto the Web spider's central list. Because search engines actually *want* to index as many sites as they can, each of them makes it easy to do just that by providing an Add URL link. Problem solved, right?

Unfortunately, no. Getting your URL onto a search engine spider's central list is necessary, but not sufficient, to meet your E-Commerce goals. To see why, try searching for "Candy Store" using a search engine. As of the date this book was written, searching for "Candy Store" on Google matched 107,000 pages (see Figure 21.1)! Imagine if your candy store wound up as site number 105,523. Would anyone ever find it?

FIGURE 21.1

The results of searching for "Candy Store" on Google.

> **Note**
>
> Not only were there 107,000 pages that matched "Candy Store" on Google, but site number two, "Mark's Candy Store," does not actually have anything to do with candy (The site lists DOS programming utilities).

Suffice it to say that getting into a search engine's results for appropriate search phrases is only the smallest part of the battle to attract customers through search engines. If you want to have any hope of customers actually finding your store by searching for the products or services you sell, your page must not simply appear in the results list—it must appear as close to the top of the results list as possible. Getting your site to appear at the top of a search engine's results page is part science, part art, and part plain hard work. In general, there are three things to remember:

21

- Shorter is better than longer.
- More is better than fewer.
- A few search engines handle most of the searches.

The Search Engine Arms Race

In this section of the chapter, most of the discussion centers on the "more honest" things you can do to get your site noticed. There's a strong temptation to do even more to get one's site noticed, and an entire industry has developed around that temptation. Consultants who specialize in getting Web sites ranked higher in search engine results pages call themselves "optimization specialists."

Optimization specialists spend countless hours designing pages that appear higher in search engines result pages. The result is that pages "tuned" by optimization consultants sometimes appear higher in a search engine result page than untuned pages, even though the tuned pages are less relevant to the search phrase, and less useful to the user. The most egregious examples of this are the "adult" sites, which usually try to get their pages indexed toward the top of any search, whether or not it is adult-oriented.

You might have already experienced the results of an optimization consultant's work when performing one of your own searches. If you have, you know how frustrating that can be to a search engine's user, and how much less useful search engines seem as a result. It is for this reason that the search engine companies have a less flattering term for optimization consultants—"spammers"—and that companies like Inktomi and Lycos have engineering teams dedicated to countering the work of the consultants. These engineers perform search after search, examine the results, and adjust the indexing and searching programs to return more useful results and to work around spammer tricks.

All of this probably seems a lot like an arms race, and in a lot of ways, it is. Each side spends money and time trying to defeat the other. Before choosing to join this arms race, it is important for the small business owner to learn the lesson of the Cold War—only a true superpower can afford to spend its resources on an arms race. For the rest of us, it is best to concentrate on getting sites noticed without the kinds of tricks that the search engine companies will eventually learn to defeat.

Shorter Is Better Than Longer

If all a search engine did was index the words on a page, it wouldn't be able to order the results of a search in a meaningful way. In addition to indexing, search engines calculate scores, or *relevance metrics,* for each page. These scores are computed with respect to common search phrases. When you search for one of these phrases, the search results are sorted by relevance metrics.

Search engine companies think of the formulas that they use to compute these relevance metrics as the real value they add to searches, and so they guard the formulas carefully.

In general, though, search engines first try to determine whether *any* part of a page is relevant to a particular search phrase. Search engines consider a page to be relevant to a search phrase if some or all of the phrase appears in the title, the keywords, the description, or, of course, the body, of the page.

> **Note**
>
> As you already know, the title of a Web page is the text between the `<TITLE>` and `</TITLE>` tags. Most browsers place the text inside these tags in the browser title bar window when displaying a page.
>
> In addition to the `<TITLE>` tag, there are two `<META>`tags that exist primarily for indexers: the *description* tag and the *keywords* tag. These tags take the formats
>
> ```
> <META NAME="description" content="this is the description of the page">
> ```
>
> and
>
> ```
> <META NAME="keywords" content="these are keywords for this page">
> ```
>
> In addition to using the text marked by these tags for indexing, nearly every search engine uses the text inside the `<TITLE></TITLE>` tags as the text for the link to your site. The search engines also commonly uses the text in the `content` property of the meta `description` tag as the *abstract*—that is, the short description of the site presented below the title in a search results page (see the abstracts in Figure 21.1).
>
> The moral? Keep your marketing hat on when you write your page titles and descriptions.

When a search engine determines that a page is relevant to a search phrase, it uses its relevance formulas to determine how much of the page is on the topic and, conversely, how much of the page is not on the topic. Pages get a higher relevance metric with respect to a search phrase when:

- The search phrase appears in one or more of the *hot areas* of the page.

> **Note**
>
> Most search engines consider the *hot areas* to be the page title, the page description and keywords, and the first few paragraphs of the body of the page.

21

- The search phrase appears in the document more than once. Up to a point, more phrase appearances mean a higher score.
- There is less overall text in the document, especially in the *hot areas* of the page.

Note

Because the relevance metric is an attempt to compute a ratio of how much of the page is "on-topic" versus how much is "off-topic", it is just as important to make a document appear less off-topic as it is to make it seem more on-topic.

More Is Better Than Fewer

If it is important to reduce the amount of off-topic text in a page in order to make it score higher in a search, you might wonder how to make your site appear in more than one search result set. The optimization consultants get around this by creating a separate page that is optimized for each search phrase. For example, if you want your site to come up high on the search results for "candy store", "chocolate bar", and "bubble gum", make three separate pages. Give each page a title and meta tags that are optimized to score high for one of these phrases.

A Few Search Engines Handle Most of the Searches

After the pages are created, you need to let the search engines know about them. Services exist that will submit your site to hundreds of search engines for a fee, but most of the searches are done on a small number of search engines. In fact, according to MediaMetrix, a ratings service for Web pages, the most popular search engine handles more than 10 times as many searches as 15th most popular search engine. It is easy enough for you to submit your site to the few engines that really matter. A list of popular search engines, along with the URLs to their respective "Add a URL" pages, are listed in Table 21.1.

TABLE 21.1 Twenty-five Popular Search Engines and Their "Add a URL" Pages

Search Engine	Add a URL Page
About.com	Find the appropriate category for your site at www.about.com and email the page's guide
AltaVista	www.altavista.com/cgi-bin/query?pg=addurl
Britannica	www.britannica.com/bcom/recommend/
DirectHit	www.directhit.com/util/addurl.html
Excite	www.excite.com/info/add_url
Go Network	www.go.com/AddUrl?pg=SubmitUrl.html
Google	www.google.com/addurl.html
Goto.com	goto.com/d/about/advertisers/
HotBot	hotbot.lycos.com/addurl.asp
Jump City	www.jumpcity.com/start.shtml

Search Engine	Add a URL Page
LookSmart	www.looksmart.com/aboutus/partners/ subsite2.html
Lycos	www.lycos.com/addasite.html
Magellan	magellan.excite.com/info/add_url
MSN Search	search.msn.com/addurl.asp
National Directory	www.nationaldirectory.com/addurl.html
Netscape	home.netscape.com/netcenter/smallbusiness/ onlineessentials/addsite.html
Northern Light	www.northernlight.com/docs/regurl_help.html
Open Directory (also AOL)	dmoz.org/add.html
SearchIt	www.searchit.com/addurl.htm
Snap	home.snap.com/LMOID/resource/0,566,-1077,00.html
WebCrawler	www.webcrawler.com/info/add_url
WhatsNu	www.whatsnu.com/cgi-bin/addlink.cgi
Whatuseek	www.whatuseek.com/addurl-tableset.shtml
Worldlight	www.worldlight.com/addsite.html *or* worldlight.com/freesubmit
Yahoo!	docs.yahoo.com/info/suggest

Figure 21.2 shows Excite's version of this sort of page.

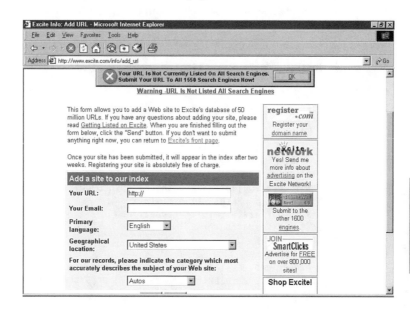

FIGURE 21.2

Adding a URL to Excite.

21

Although you can individually add each page on your site to the search engines to ensure that your entire site gets spidered, it is easier to build your own *spider page*, that is, a page that lists the URLs of all the pages on your site. You can then just submit the URL to that spider page to the search engines. When a search engine's spider retrieves your spider page, it will follow the URLs in the page and grab the rest of the pages from your site for later indexing. This will ensure that the spider retrieves all your site's pages before exiting the site by following an external link.

One complication to getting the complete Candy Store site spidered is that much of it is built dynamically. You could easily use VBScript to dynamically generate a spider page like the one in Listing 21.1, which contains a URL for each product. Unfortunately, these URLs contain a question mark (?), and many search engines will not index URLs with question marks because the question mark signifies that the page is a CGI script.

INPUT   **LISTING 21.1**   A Sample Spider Page That Won't Work

```
1   <a href="/product.asp?pid=22">Kisses</a>
2   <br>
3   <a href="/product.asp?pid=23">Jaw Breakers</a>
4   <br>
...
```

To work around this problem, you can use ASP to generate a static search page for each of your products. Listing 21.2 shows how to add a function to storeFuncs.asp that creates a crawler-optimized static page from added or updated product information, and then stores that page in the search subdirectory. The function will be called from donePost.asp.

LISTING 21.2   CreateStaticPage Function That Generates Static Pages for
INPUT   Spidering

```
1    SUB createStaticPage (productID, productName, productPrice,_
2                  productPicture, productCategory, productBriefDesc,
                   ➥productFullDesc,_
3                  productStatus)
4
5    Dim fs, file, path
6    Set fs = CreateObject("Scripting.FileSystemObject")
7    path = Server.MapPath("/") & "\static"
8    IF (fs.FolderExists(path) <> true) THEN
9       fs.CreateFolder(path)
10   END IF
11
12   ' Create or replace the static asp file for the product.
13   Set file = fs.CreateTextFile(path & "\pid" & productID & ".asp", true)
```

```
14
15   file.WriteLine("<html>")
16   file.WriteLine("<head>")
17   file.WriteLine("<title>" & productName & " Candy</title>")
18   file.WriteLine("<meta name=""description"" content=""Purchase " &
    ➥productName & " Candy from Johnson's Candy and Gifts " & productBriefDesc &
    ➥" " & productFullDesc & """>")
19   file.WriteLine("<meta name=""keywords"" content=""Candy " & productName &
    ➥" " & productBriefDesc & " " & productFullDesc & """>")
20   file.WriteLine("</head>")
21   file.WriteLine("<body link=""#ff4040"" vtext=""lightred"">")
22   file.WriteLine("<center>")
23
24   file.WriteLine("<table width=""640"" border=""0"" cellspacing=""0""
    ➥cellpadding=""0"">")
25   file.WriteLine("<tr>")
26   file.WriteLine("    <td>")
27   file.WriteLine("    <img src=""../logo.gif"" WIDTH=""300"" HEIGHT=""30"">")
28   file.WriteLine("    </td>")
29   file.WriteLine("    <td align=""right"" valign=""bottom"">")
30   file.WriteLine("    <a href=""../cart.asp"">shopping cart</a>")
31   file.WriteLine("    | ")
32   file.WriteLine("    <a href=""../account.asp"">account</a>")
33   file.WriteLine("    </td>")
34   file.WriteLine("</tr>")
35   file.WriteLine("<tr>")
36   file.WriteLine("    <td colspan=""2"">")
37   file.WriteLine("    <hr width=""640"">")
38   file.WriteLine("    </td>")
39   file.WriteLine("</tr>")
40   file.WriteLine("</table>")
41
42   file.WriteLine("<table width=""640"" border=""0"" cellpadding=""0""
    ➥cellspacing=""0"">")
43   file.WriteLine("<tr><td valign=""top"">")
44
45   file.WriteLine("<table cellpadding=""0"" cellspacing=""0"" border=""0"">")
46   file.WriteLine("<tr>")
47   file.WriteLine("    <td valign=""bottom"" bgcolor=""pink"">")
48   file.WriteLine("    <img src=""../search.gif"" vspace=""0"" border=""0"">
    ➥</td>")
49   file.WriteLine("</tr>")
50   file.WriteLine("<tr>")
51   file.WriteLine("    <td>")
52   file.WriteLine("    <table width=""200"" cellpadding=""4""
    ➥cellspacing=""0"" bgcolor=""lightyellow"" border=""1"">")
53   file.WriteLine("    <tr>")
54   file.WriteLine("       <td>")
55   file.WriteLine("          <form method=""post"" action=""../search.asp""
    ➥id=form1 name=form1>")
```

continues

21

LISTING 21.2   continued

```
56  file.WriteLine("           <input name=""searchfor"" size=""15"">")
57  file.WriteLine("           <input type=""submit"" value=""Search""
    ➥id=submit1 name=submit1>")
58  file.WriteLine("         </form>")
59  file.WriteLine("         </td>")
60  file.WriteLine("       </tr>")
61  file.WriteLine("     </table>")
62  file.WriteLine("     </td>")
63  file.WriteLine("</tr>")
64  file.WriteLine("<tr>")
65  file.WriteLine("   <td> </td>")
66  file.WriteLine("</tr>")
67  file.WriteLine("<tr>")
68  file.WriteLine("   <td valign=""bottom"">")
69  file.WriteLine("     <img src=""../Categories.gif"" vspace=""0""
    ➥border=""0""></td>")
70  file.WriteLine("</tr>")
71  file.WriteLine("<tr>")
72  file.WriteLine("   <td>")
73  file.WriteLine("     <table width=""200"" cellpadding=""4""
    ➥cellspacing=""0"" bgcolor=""lightyellow"" border=""1"">")
74  file.WriteLine("     <tr>")
75  file.WriteLine("       <td>")
76  file.WriteLine("       <font size=""3""><b>")
77  file.WriteLine("<SCRIPT Language=""VBScript"" RunAt=""Server""> Dim cat")
78  file.WriteLine("cat = """ & productCategory & """")
79  file.WriteLine("</SCRIPT>")
80  file.WriteLine("         <!- #INCLUDE FILE=""../CatList.asp"" ->")
81  file.WriteLine("         </b></font>")
82  file.WriteLine("         </ul></td>")
83  file.WriteLine("     </tr>")
84  file.WriteLine("     </table>")
85  file.WriteLine("     </td>")
86  file.WriteLine("</tr>")
87  file.WriteLine("</table>")
88
89  file.WriteLine("</td><td valign=""top"">")
90
91  file.WriteLine("<table cellpadding=""10"" cellspacing=""0"" border=""0"">")
92  file.WriteLine("<tr>")
93  file.WriteLine("  <td>")
94
95  If productPicture <> "?????" THEN
96    file.WriteLine("  <img src=""../images/" & productPicture & """>")
97  END IF
98  file.WriteLine("  <p>")
99  file.WriteLine("  <font size=""3"" face=""Arial""><b>")
100 file.WriteLine(productName)
101 file.WriteLine("  </b></font><p>")
```

```
102 file.WriteLine(productBriefDesc)
103 file.WriteLine("  <form method=""post"" action=""../cart.asp"" id=form1
    ➥name=form1>")
104 file.WriteLine("  <input name=""pid"" type=""hidden"" value=" & productID
    ➥& ">")
105 file.WriteLine("  <input type=""submit"" value=""Add To Cart"" id=submit1
    ➥name=submit1>")
106 file.WriteLine("  </form>")
107 file.WriteLine(productFullDesc)
108 file.WriteLine("  <form method=""post"" action=""../cart.asp"" id=form2
    ➥name=form2>")
109 file.WriteLine("  <input name=""pid"" type=""hidden"" value=" & productID
    ➥& ">")
110 file.WriteLine("  <input type=""submit"" value=""Add To Cart"" id=submit2
    ➥name=submit2>")
111 file.WriteLine("  </form>")
112 file.WriteLine("  </td>")
113 file.WriteLine("</tr>")
114 file.WriteLine("</table>")
115 file.WriteLine("</td></tr>")
116 file.WriteLine("</table>")
117
118 file.WriteLine("<hr width=""640"">")
119 file.WriteLine("Copyright © 2000 the Johnson Gift Company")
120 file.WriteLine("</center>")
121 file.WriteLine("</body>")
122 file.WriteLine("</html>")
123 file.Close
124 Set file = Nothing
125 Set fs = Nothing
126 END SUB
```

ANALYSIS   The CreateStaticPage function first creates the static directory if it does not already exist (lines 6–10). Line 13 creates the static, indexable page if it doesn't already exist, replacing it if it does. Lines 15–122 actually write the static page. Line 17 writes a <TITLE> tag that includes the product name. Line 18 writes a <META name= "description"> tag that will provide a description of the page to a person using a search engine; Line 19 writes a <META name="keywords"> tag for searching that includes the product name and product descriptions. Lines 77–79 write script into the file that sets the product category into the cat variable; this is for code in the CatList.asp script that gets included by line 80.

Caution   Lines 77–79 use the <SCRIPT RunAt="Server"></SCRIPT> tags because the <% %> delimiters get interpreted before the WriteLine method; the <SCRIPT> and </SCRIPT> tags do exactly the same thing at the <% and %> script delimiters.

21

Line 96 writes an <IMG> tag that points to the appropriate image for the product.
Although the search engine will not look at the picture, it is necessary to write the tag, in
case a customer clicks through to the static page. Similarly, lines 104 and 109 write a
hidden product ID <INPUT> field, in case a customer decides to buy the product after
clicking through.

> **Caution**
>
> The current Candy Store site does not make use of frames. If you decide to
> implement your Web store using frames, you should be aware that many
> search engines do not index text inside an HTML frameset. To work around
> this, duplicate the text of the site, including <TITLE> and <META> tags inside
> a <noframes></noframes> tag set. Most search engines will index content
> between <noframes> tags.

After you have created your static pages, you need to make them visible to the search
engines. Listing 21.3, crawler.asp, is a simple ASP script that generates a spider file
from the current contents of the search subdirectory (The static directory). In addition to
your home page, you can submit crawler.asp to search engines as a URL to index.
When a crawler requests crawler.asp, it will get a file that contains links to each of the
static pages.

LISTING 21.3   crawler.asp, Which Generates Links to Each of the Static
INPUT   Pages Generated by CreateStaticPage

```
1  <%@ Language=VBScript %>
2  <%
3  Dim fs, folder, files, fileName, path
4
5  Set fs = CreateObject("Scripting.FileSystemObject")
6  path = Server.MapPath("/") & "\static"
7  If (fs.FolderExists(path) = true) Then
8    Set folder = fs.GetFolder(path)
9
10   Set files = folder.Files
11   For Each fileName in files
12 %>
13 <a href="/static/<%=fs.GetFileName(fileName)%>"><%=fs.GetFileName
   ➥(fileName)%></a>
14 <br>
15 <%
16   Next
17 End If
18 Set files = Nothing
19 Set folder = Nothing
```

```
20 Set fs = Nothing
21 %>
```

ANALYSIS The script first makes sure that the static page directory exists (Lines 5–7). If it does, it gets a Folder object (line 8) and retrieves the list of files from the object (line 10). It then iterates through the list of files, creating a link for each file (lines 11–16).

Indexable Pages Are Not Enough

After you've created your static pages and submitted your home page and your crawler page to the popular search engines, be patient. It can take weeks or even months to get spidered for the first time. Unfortunately, you might also need to be persistent.

The Web has been growing at a geometric pace, and search sites are struggling to maintain the amount of disk space needed to hold indexing info about the Web. This means that every time a search engine spiders and indexes a new page, it might have to throw out the index information about an old page to make room. Typically, search engines try to be smart about the pages that they throw away, throwing away pages that haven't changed or haven't been accessed for a long time. This underscores the importance of good <META name="description"> tags that encourage users to click.

> **Note** *Geometric growth* refers to growth rates that accelerate over time.

Another reason to have your marketing hat on when writing your <META name="description"> is the emergence of *popularity algorithms*. One of the ways that search engine developers try to defeat index spammers and improve relevance algorithms is by keeping track of the popularity of each link presented in a search result. For example, if you search for Candy Corn at a search engine, you can see results like those in Listing 21.4. On most search engines, the ordering in that list changes depending in part on how many users click through the title link. This might seem obvious, but many sites use their <META name="description"> tags the way the first site in the list does; that is, to deliver some sort of uniform corporate branding message. Resist the temptation to be lazy when composing descriptions: Better descriptions mean more click-throughs, and more click-throughs mean better placement.

21

INPUT   **LISTING 21.4**   Sample Search Results for "Candy Corn"

```
1. Candy Corn
        All items are and personalized. Home. Girls. Boys. Accessories. About
        the Company. Reasons for Ordering. FAQ. Contact Us. Phone:...

2. Candy Corn
        XXX pics jpg jpeg gif mp3 sex Candy Corn candyxxx.jpg ccorn001.jpg
        pirate software warez naked

3. Candy Corn
        If you love classic candy, your going to go crazy over this tasty
        treat!1/2 Pound. Please order in 1/2# units (one pound = 2 units)$2.25.
        the Goody...
```

Get Linked to Other Pages

A recent way that search engine developers have been trying to improve their search results is by taking a lead from academia. One way that academics decide which papers are important is to count how many other papers refer to them. The founders of Google applied that technique to search engines and call it *PageRank*.

PageRank applies the academic technique to the Web by ordering a search result set by link popularity. Pages with more links to them from other Web sites get listed higher than pages with fewer links to them. The technique has the advantage of being difficult to spam, and seems to be quite effective.

As search algorithms like PageRank become more popular on the Web, it will become more important to invest time in getting other Web sites to link to your E-Commerce store. Some ways to do this include cultivating relationships with people who operate enthusiast sites, developing sales affiliate programs, and simply trading links.

Web Rings

Many people use search engines almost exclusively to find sites; however, recreational Web surfers often use *Web rings* to find new sites that interest them. A Web ring, as its name suggests, is a collection of Web sites that have something in common. The home page of each of these sites is linked to two other sites on the same topic, so that it is possible to navigate among all the sites that belong to the ring. You can establish your own Web ring or join an existing ring by visiting www.webring.org.

Try It Out!

Here is a demonstration Web ring that you can use to walk through the Web ring signup process:

1. Fill out the demonstration Web ring sign up form located at
   `http://www.levlin.com/demoring.asp`.

2. Wait to receive an email message, which will include a site ID.

3. Add the HTML from Listing 21.5 to your site's home page.

> **Caution**
>
> Don't forget to substitute the site ID you received in email in the HTML in Listing 21.5

4. Reply to the email you received in step 2 to let the ring owner know your site is ready to participate in the ring.

5. In a day or so, the ring owner will approve your site.

INPUT

LISTING 21.5   The HTML to Add to a Page to Allow It to Participate in the Demonstration Web Ring

```
1  <!-- Begin HTML comment
2  This is an HTMLfragment to be pasted at the bottom
3  of your webpage for the Demonstration WebRing. It is what
4  links you to the rest of the ring. :)
5  End HTML comment -->
6
7  <P>
8  <CENTER>
9  This <a href="http://www.levlin.com/demoring.asp"> Demonstration WebRing</a>
   ➥ site owned by
10 <a href="mailto:jono@netcom.com">Jonathan Levine</a>.
11 <br>
12 [ <a href="http://nav.webring.org/cgi-bin/navcgi?ring=demoring;
   ➥id=Site_ID_Here;prev5">
13 Previous 5 Sites</a> |
14 <a href="http://nav.webring.org/cgi-bin/navcgi?ring=demoring;
   ➥id=Site ID Here;prev">
15 Previous</a> |
16 <a href="http://nav.webring.org/cgi-bin/navcgi?ring=demoring;
   ➥id=Site ID Here;next">Next</a> |
17 <a href="http://nav.webring.org/cgi-bin/navcgi?ring=demoring;
   ➥id=Site ID Here;next5">
18 Next 5 Sites</a> |
19 <a href="http://nav.webring.org/cgi-bin/navcgi?ring=demoring;random">
   ➥Random Site</a> |
20 <a href="http://nav.webring.org/cgi-bin/navcgi?ring=demoring;list">
   ➥List Sites</a> ]
21 </CENTER>
```

21

ANALYSIS   All Web rings are managed by servers at `webring.org`. Lines 8–20 produce the links you see in Figure 21.3. Lines 12–17 enable the user to navigate through the Web ring by passing the current site ID and an operation (`prev`, `next`, `prev5`, or `next5`) to the `webring.org` servers. Lines 19–20 enable the user to see all the sites or navigate to a random site; neither operation requires a site ID.

FIGURE 21.3

The Web Ring naviga-
tion bar for the demon-
stration Web ring.

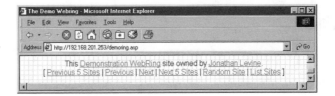

Banner Ads

Another way to increase the traffic to your Web store is to advertise. If you have used the Internet at all, you are familiar with the most common way to advertise on the Internet—the banner advertisement (see Figure 21.4). Banner ads are available for purchase, but are also available through advertising-sharing programs known as *link exchanges*.

FIGURE 21.4

A sample banner
advertisement.

Link Exchanges

As with other advertising, you can easily pay for Internet advertising; however, the Internet makes *cooperative advertising* available to everyone.

> **Note**
>
> *Cooperative advertising* is the practice of sharing advertising space and advertising costs. In the computer hardware industry, Intel is a ubiquitous example of a cooperative advertiser; in exchange for placing the "Intel inside" logo on computers and advertisements, Intel pays PC manufacturers to defray the cost of that advertising.

Note

The size and format standards for Internet advertising are developed by the Internet Advertising Bureau (www.iab.net).

Most banner advertisers limit the size of banners files to 10K or smaller in order to reduce the impact of the banner download on the user.

With Internet banner advertising, cooperative advertising manifests itself in *link exchanges*. Link exchanges provide an easy way for Web site operators to trade advertising impressions with each other. A Webmaster signs up with a link exchange, uploads a banner, and inserts some exchange-provided HTML on his Web site. The HTML that the exchange provides automatically downloads a banner from the exchange and records an impression on behalf of the site. For each banner impression on the Webmaster's site, the exchange credits the member Web site with some number of ad impressions. The exchange then shows the Webmaster's banner on another exchange member site once for each full credit.

Note

An *impression* is an industry standard term for the number of times a banner advertisement has been displayed. For example, if you display a banner advertisement five times, that counts as five impressions (even if the same person views the ad all five times).

Impressions are often contrasted with what are variously called transfers or click-throughs. Impressions measure the number of times that an ad has been displayed; *transfers* and *click-throughs* measure the number of times that an ad has been clicked.

Exchanges typically require that a Web site display more than one ad in order to earn a display credit. The exchange finances its operations by selling the resulting additional inventory. The ratio of impressions-required to impressions-granted is known as the *exchange rate*.

Note

As with everything on the Web, there are many, many link exchanges, each of which offers a variety of exchange rates. Some popular exchanges and their rates are shown in Table 21.2.

21

TABLE 21.2   Some Popular Banner Exchange Cooperatives

Company	Exchange Rate	URL
123Banners	2 for 1	www.123banners.com
1for1.com	About 1.7 for 1[1]	www.1for1.com
AdSwap	2 for 1[2]	www.adswap.com
Ad-Xchange	2 for 1[4]	www.ad-xchange.com
abe 1to1	1 for 1[5]	abe.com.au/121/index.html
BannerSwap	2 for 1[2]	www.bannerswap.com
BannerWomen	2 for 1	www.bannerwomen.com
CyberLink Exchange	2 for 1[3, 5, 6]	cyberlinkexchange.usww.com
Disney Banner Network	1 for 1[7]	www.disneybanner.net
Exchange-it	2 for 1	www.exchange-it.com
Free Banners	2 for 1	www.free-banners.com
EIS Banner Exchange	Varies, as high as 5 for 4	www.lycos.com/addasite.html
HyperBanner	2 for 1	www.hyperbanner.com
LinkBuddies	Varies depending on click-through rate	www.linkbuddies.com
LinkExchange	2 for 1	www.linkexchange.com
MS-Links Exchange	4 for 3	msbannerexchange.com
SmartAge	2 for 1	www.smartage.com
TradeBanners	2 for 1[8]	resource-marketing.com/banner.shtml
Web Resources	3 for 2	exchange.Web-resources.com
Webmaster Exchange	1 for 1[9]	www.webmasterexchange.com

1. Gives 2-for-1 exchange rate except for 5 days a month, when the exchange rate is 1 for 1. Also offers $0.10 advertising credit for each banner click-through.

2. Gives 1-for-1 exchange credit for each banner that is clicked.

3. Gives 500 free banner impressions for signing up.

4. Gives 1,000 free banner impressions for signing up.

5. Uses non–standard-sized banners.

6. Also offers "Premium Membership" with higher exchange rates and click-through bonuses.

7. Disney-related sites only.

8. Paid membership upgrades ratio to 4 for 3.

9. Webmaster-oriented sites only.

Paying for Banner Ads

One disadvantage to using a link exchange is that you have to show banner ads in order to earn banner ads. This makes link exchanges a poor choice if what you really want to do is jump start page views for a new E-Commerce site. Of course, it is easy enough to purchase banner advertisements. The banner exchanges all offer banner advertisements for low prices. There are also a large number of Internet advertising agencies, some of which are shown in Table 21.3.

TABLE 21.3 Internet Advertising Agencies

Company	URL
AdAuction.com	www.adauction.com
AdBase.net	www.adbase.net
AdForce	www.adforce.com
DoubleClick	www.doubleclick.net
Flycast	www.flycast.com
Microsoft bCentral	store.linkexchange.com
Pegasus Ad Network	www.pegasusads.com
ValueClick	www.valueclick.com

Each Internet advertising agency handles ad placements on its own exclusive sites, and each agency offers more or less sophisticated *ad targeting*. They also offer a very wide variety of pricing models and costs per unit of advertising. The most common pricing models are cost-per-click-through and cost-per-thousand-impressions (CPM), as described in Chapter 19, "Generating Store Reports".

Note

> *Ad targeting* is the practice of only displaying ads to a limited audience. Internet ad agencies target ads by placing cookies on a user's browser, and then tracking the user's Internet surfing patterns, click-through patterns, and any other information they can gather about the user.

Participating in Reward Programs

1999 was the year of the Internet loyalty program. In a loyalty program, customers are rewarded for visiting your site. Participating in a loyalty program is easy and relatively inexpensive. These programs are of two major types: Customers receive cash, and

21

customers receive points (points are typically exchanged for such things are gift certificates, CDs, and movie tickets). Some of them are listed in Table 21.4.

TABLE 21.4   Internet Loyalty Programs

Company	Program Reward	URL
Beenz	Points	www.beenz.com
CyberGold	Cash	www.cybergold.com
Dash	Cash	www.dash.com
FreeRide	Points	www.freeride.com
iPoints	Points	www.ipoints.co.uk
MyPoints	Points	www.mypointsinc.com
NetCentives	Points and Miles	www.netcentives.com

Other Ways to Increase Revenue

You will, of course, endeavor to earn most of your revenue by selling items or services on your Web site. However, if your Web site gains popularity, you might want to join another retailer's affiliate program, use some of your Web site's space to sell advertising, sell your customer email lists, or develop some other enterprise based at your site.

Affiliate Programs

Joining an affiliate program is probably the easiest way to add supplementary revenues to your site. Nearly every merchandiser offers a commission on referrals that result in sales; however, other companies are offering commissions on clicks, registrations, and more. Because of the dynamic nature of these programs, it is best to research them when you are ready to sign up and to monitor them closely. www.affiliatesdirectory.com is a useful place to learn about these programs.

Running Your Own Advertising

There are several ways that you can run advertising on your own Web site. Any of the advertising agencies listed in Table 21.3 will likely to be happy to help you, providing that your Web site generates enough traffic. Otherwise, you can use the Ad Rotator component that comes with IIS to schedule and deliver advertisements to your visitors.

> **Caution**   Although implementing and using the Ad Rotator component is easy enough, actually managing advertising traffic is exceedingly difficult. That can explain why there are so many successful public companies that out-source advertising management!

Using the Ad Rotator is simple: First, create a redirection file, which enables you to measure click-throughs. Then create a schedule file, which enables you to define the ads to show, the links for the ads, and the relative weight of each ad. Finally, on each page where you want to display an advertisement, you simply create an instance of the Ad Rotator object and call `AdRotator.GetAdvertisement`.

The Redirection File

When people click on an advertisement displayed through the Ad Rotator component, they are sent to the redirection file. You can place any content that you please in the redirection file. Typically, however, you include a script that records the number of times that an ad has been clicked. You can record this information in a database table.

Next, the redirection file will need to redirect the user to the Web site associated with the banner. When you click on an ad displayed by the Ad Rotator component, the path to the site associated with the ad is passed to the redirection file as a query string variable. This query string variable is named URL. Listing 21.6 illustrates how to create a simple redirection file, named `adredir.asp`, that transfers the user using the URL query string variable.

INPUT   **LISTING 21.5**   `adredir.asp`—The Simplest Redirection File

```
1  <%@ Language=VBScript %>
2  <%  Response.Redirect(Request.QueryString("url")) %>
```

The Schedule File

A schedule file (see Listing 21.6) contains information that the Ad Rotator component uses to manage and display advertisement images. It has two sections: One applies to all the advertisements in the schedule; the other defines each individual ad. The general section enables you to specify the URL for the redirection script and the width, height, and border width for each ad. The specific section specifies the image files to use, the pages to be linked to, and the relative percentage of time that each ad will be displayed.

21

INPUT **LISTING 21.6** A Sample Schedule File

```
1  REDIRECT /adredir.asp
2  WIDTH 468
3  HEIGHT 60
4  BORDER 0
5  *
6  http://www.levlin.com/images/yawn.gif
7  http://www.levlin.com/
8  Check out the most boring site on the Internet!
9  80
10 http://www.mcp.com/images/informit_ad/enman_blk.gif
11 -
12 InformIT from Macmillian
13 20
```

ANALYSIS Lines 1–4 define the common parameters for each ad: the redirection page (line 1), the width and height of each ad (lines 2–3), and the thickness of the border (line 4). The values of lines 2–4 are in pixels. The single asterisk in line 5 separates the general section from the per-ad section. Line 6–9 and lines 10–13 both define individual ads. Lines 6 and 10 are URLs to the banner advertisements. Lines 7 is the URL to a page that the line 6 banner links to. If the banner doesn't link , it shows a hyphen as in line 11. Lines 8 and 12 are text displayed for browsers that don't display graphics. Finally, lines 9 and 13 indicate the relative weights of each advertisement.

Note

The way that *relative weights* work is that the Ad Rotator takes the sum of all the relative weights and displays each ad in proportion to its relative weight. For example, if a Rotator Schedule file contains two ads with the impressions set to 80 and 20, the first ad is displayed 80 percent of the time and the second is displayed 20 percent of the time.

Caution

If the sum of the impressions parameters for all items exceeds 10,000, an error will be generated the first time the Rotator Schedule file is accessed by a call to the GetAdvertisement method.

The Ad Rotator

The last step to implementing the Ad Rotator is to add the code from Listing 21.7 to the body of each Web page in which you want to display an ad. The results look like this:

```
<AHREF="/adredir.asp?url=http://www.levlin.com/&image=http://www.levlin.com/
images/yawn.gif" ><IMG SRC="http://www.levlin.com/images/yawn.gif"
```

```
ALT="Check out the most boring site on the Internet!" WIDTH=468 HEIGHT=60
BORDER=1></A>.
```

INPUT **LISTING 21.7** Code to Implement the Ad Rotator on a Web Page

```
1  <%
2  Dim ad
3  Set ad = Server.CreateObject("MSWC.AdRotator")  %>
4  <%=ad.GetAdvertisement("/schedule.txt") %>
5  <% Set ad = Nothing %>
```

ANALYSIS Line 3 creates an instance of the Ad Rotator, and line 4 uses the schedule file from Listing 21.6 to display the advertisement. Finally, line 5 cleans up the Ad Rotator instance.

Summary

In today's lesson, you learned the basics of Internet marketing—both getting your site noticed, and getting people to pay you for exposure. You learned how to make your site attractive to search engines and how to join a Web ring. You then learned how to promote your site with free and paid-for advertising. Finally, you learned how to rotate ads, bring in revenue through affiliate programs, and how to encourage your customers to return with reward programs.

Q&A

Q How does (pick your favorite search engine) index its sites?

A Nearly every search engine guards its indexing algorithm as carefully as Coca-Cola guards its secret recipe. One exception is Google, whose founders presented an overview of their algorithms at the WWW7 conference. This overview is available on the Web at `http://www7.scu.edu.au/programme/fullpapers/1921/com1921.htm`.

Workshop

The Quiz and Exercise questions are designed to test your knowledge of the material covered in this chapter. The answers are in Appendix A, "Quiz Answers."

21

Quiz

1. What is a "spider"?

2. What is a relevance metric?

3. What is a Web ring?

4. What is a link exchange?

Exercises

1. The `CreateStaticPage` script is only called when a product is added or updated. Write a script that initializes the `static` directory by iterating through each product in the database and calling `CreateStaticPage`.

2. Write a Web-based interface that enables you to maintain the ad rotation schedule file `schedule.txt`.

WEEK 3

In Review

This week, you learned how to maintain and market your Web site. In the first lesson, you learned how to secure your Web site from malicious users. On the following day, you learned several valuable techniques for debugging your Web site with Microsoft Visual InterDev's integrated debugger and a library of standard Active Server Pages debugging subroutines.

Next, you learned how to promote your Web site through email marketing. You learned how to use the CDO for NTS to bulk email personalized messages to potential customers.

Later in the week, you were introduced to several methods for maintaining your Web site remotely. You learned how to administer your Web server from a remote location through a Web browser. You also learned how to use the FTP service to remotely manage your Web site files.

Next, you were given an overview of the different log file formats supported by your Web server. You learned how to extract and analyze information from your log files to monitor the performance of your site.

Finally, you learned how to display banner advertisements at your Web site. You learned how to rotate through different advertisements and track how often each advertisement is displayed.

Bonus Project

Sending Customer Feedback Acknowledgement Emails

In this week's bonus project, you'll modify the customer feedback form that you created in the two previous bonus projects to support sending email. In the lesson on Day 18, "Using Email with Active Server Pages", you learned how to use the CDO for NTS to send email from an Active Server Page. You'll apply this knowledge in this bonus project by incorporating the CDO for NTS into the customer feedback pages.

When customers submit feedback, they will automatically receive an email message informing them that the feedback was received. The purpose of this acknowledgement email is to reassure the customer that their feedback hasn't been lost. You could also include information in this message such as answers to frequently asked questions and additional support options.

You'll remember from last week's bonus project that the customer feedback pages rely on the following database table (named feedback):

- feedback_id—an AutoNumber field that uniquely identifies each row in the table.
- feedback_email—a Text field that contains the customer's email address.
- feedback_comment—a Memo field that contains the text of the customer's feedback.
- feedback_entrydate—a Date/Time field that automatically contains the date the feedback is entered. This field should have a default value of NOW().

A customer submits his feedback through an ASP page named feedback.asp. This page contains a simple HTML form with no ASP scripts. The customer feedback form is contained in Listing BP3.1 (It's the same page as used in the bonus projects for the previous two weeks).

LISTING **BP3.1**   The Customer Feedback Form

```
1   <HTML>
2   <HEAD><TITLE>Customer Feedback</TITLE></HEAD>
3   <BODY>
```

```
4
5  Thank you for leaving customer feedback on our Web site.
6  <br>Please enter your feedback in the form below:
7
8
9  <FORM METHOD="post" ACTION="saveFeedback.asp">
10 <P><B>Your Email Address:</B>
11 <BR><INPUT NAME="email" size="50" maxlength="255">
12 <P><B>Your Feedback:</B>
13 <BR><TEXTAREA NAME="comment" COLS=50 ROWS=4
14   WRAP="Virtual"></TEXTAREA>
15 <P><INPUT TYPE="submit" VALUE="Submit Feedback">
16 </FORM>
17
18 </BODY>
19 </HTML>
```

When a customer submits the customer feedback form, the data is submitted to the save-feedback.asp page. The savefeedback.asp page has been modified in this bonus project to send email. The new version of the savefeedback.asp page is contained in Listing BP3.2.

LISTING BP3.2 The Save Feedback Page with Email

```
1  <%@ TRANSACTION=REQUIRED %>
2  <%
3  Response.Buffer = TRUE
4
5  SUB OnTransactionAbort
6    Response.Clear
7  %>
8  <HTML>
9  <HEAD><TITLE>Problem</TITLE></HEAD>
10 <BODY>
11
12 <B>An error was encountered while submitting your feedback.</B>
13 <BR>Please call our customer support number at:
14 <BLOCKQUOTE>
15   (555) 555-8989
16 </BLOCKQUOTE>
17
18 </BODY>
19 </HTML>
20 <%
21 END SUB
22
23 FUNCTION fixQuotes( theString )
```

continues

LISTING **BP3.2**   continued

```
24   fixQuotes = REPLACE( theString, "'", "''" )
25 END FUNCTION
26
27 email = TRIM( Request( "email" ) )
28 comment = TRIM( Request( "comment" ) )
29 IF email <> "" AND comment <> "" THEN
30   Set Con = Server.CreateObject( "ADODB.Connection" )
31   Con.Open "accessDSN"
32   sqlString = "INSERT INTO feedback ( feedback_email, feedback_comment ) " &_
33     "VALUES ('" & fixQuotes( email ) & "','" & fixQuotes( comment ) & "')"
34   Con.Execute sqlString
35   Set myMail = Server.CreateObject( "CDONTS.NewMail" )
36   myMail.From = "feedback@yourdomain.com"
37   myMail.To = email
38   myMail.Subject = "Your feedback was received!"
39   myMail.Body = "Thank you for submitting feedback.  " &_
40     "Your feedback will be reviewed by our customer support department.  " &_
41     "You should expect an email response to your feedback with the next 2
       ➡business days."
42   myMail.Send
43 END IF
44 %>
45 <HTML>
46 <HEAD><TITLE>Save Feedback</TITLE></HEAD>
47 <BODY>
48
49 <B>Thank you for submitting your feedback!</B>
50
51 </BODY>
52 </HTML>
```

ANALYSIS   The CDO for NTS is used in this page in lines 35–42. In line 35, an instance of the NewMail object is created. Next, in line 36, the From property is assigned the sender's email address (This should be your store's email address). In line 37, the To property is assigned the customer's email address. In line 38–41, the Subject and Body properties of the NewMail object are assigned values. Finally, in line 42, the email message is sent.

You can modify the email message sent from the customer feedback form in any way you please. To change the body of the email message, simply modify the text in lines 39–41.

APPENDIX A

Quiz Answers

Answers for Day 1

Quiz

1. What are the three types of E-Commerce?

   Business-to-consumer, business-to-business, and consumer-to-consumer.

2. Can Microsoft Personal Web Server be used to create a commercial Web site that supports thousands of visitors a day?

   No. Microsoft Personal Web Server can only be used for prototyping a Web site or running a very lightly used Web site.

3. Can Microsoft Access be used in a commercial Web site that supports thousands of visitors a day?

   No. Microsoft Access is a desktop database and not a client/server database.

4. Do you need Visual InterDev to create Active Server Pages?

   No. Microsoft Visual InterDev is a development environment for creating Active Server Pages. You can create an ASP page using any standard text editor.

5. How does a Web server distinguish an ASP Page from a normal HTML page?

   Active Server Pages end with the extension .ASP whereas normal HTML files end with the extension .HTML or .HTM.

6. Are Active Server Pages compatible with all Web browsers?

   Yes. An ASP page is processed on the Web server and not the Web browser.

7. Can you create ASP scripts using any language other than VBScript?

   Yes, some other examples of scripting languages that you can use with Active Server Pages are JScript and PerlScript.

Answers for Day 2

Quiz

1. Is there any difference between using the `Write` method of the Response object to send output to the browser and using the `<%=` and `%>` output delimiters?

   No, there is no difference between outputting content to the browser using the `Write` method of the Response object and using the `<%=` and `%>` output delimiters.

2. The following ASP page passes a query string variable named `myvar` that has the value Active Server Pages. However, there is an error in this page that will prevent the query string variable from being passed. How would you fix this page?

   ```
   <html>
   <head><title>Fix Me!</title></head>
   <body>
   <%
   myvar = "Active Server Pages"
   %>
   <a href="page2.asp?myvar=<%=myvar%>">click here</a>
   </body>
   </html>
   ```

   The error results from the spaces that appear in the string `"Active Server Pages"`. Before you can pass this string, you must first URL-encode it using the `URLEncode()` method of the Server object. Here's how the script should be rewritten:

   ```
   <html>
   <head><title>Fix Me!</title></head>
   <body>
   <%
   myvar = "Active Server Pages"
   myvar = Server.URLEncode( myvar )
   %>
   ```

```
<a href="page2.asp?myvar=<%=myvar%>">click here</a>
</body>
</html>
```

3. How can you output the string "He said, "Hello World!" " using the Write method of the Response object?

   There are two solutions. First, you can use two quotation marks in a row:

```
Response.Write "He said, ""Hello World!"" "
```

   You can also output a quotation mark by using the CHR() function like this:

```
Response.Write "He said, " & CHR( 34 ) & "Hello World" & CHR( 34 )
```

4. How would you write a script that displays all the variables in the Form collection of the Request object?

   You can display all the variables in the form collection in a FOR...EACH loop like this:

```
<%
FOR EACH thing IN Request.Form
  Response.Write thing & Request( thing ) & "<br>"
NEXT
%>
```

Answers for Day 3

Quiz

1. Suppose that you want to create a cookie which lasts longer than a particular user session. What attribute of the Cookies collection must you set to cause the cookie to persist until a certain date?

   You must set the Expires attribute. For example, to create a cookie named password that doesn't expire until December 25, 2002, you would use:

```
<%
Response.Cookies( "password" ) = "secret"
Response.Cookies( "password" ).Expires = "12/25/2002"
%>
```

2. Suppose that Andrew requests an ASP page which assigns the value red to a Session variable named color. Now, suppose that Ruth requests an ASP page which assigns the value blue to the Session variable named color. If Andrew requests an ASP page which outputs the value of the color Session variable, what value will be displayed?

   The Session variable would have the value red. Session variables are created relative to a particular user.

3. How can you remove all the Session variables associated with a particular user from memory?

You can remove all Session variables associated with a particular user by calling the Abandon() method of the Session object.

4. Suppose that Andrew requests an ASP page which assigns the value red to an Application variable named color. Now, suppose that Ruth requests an ASP page which assigns the value blue to the Application variable named color. If Andrew requests an ASP page which outputs the value of the color Application variable, what value will be displayed?

The Application variable would have the value blue. Application variables can be shared among all the users of a Web site.

5. What's wrong with the following Global.asa file?

```
<%
Sub Session_OnStart
  Application.Lock
  Application( "customerCount" ) = Application( "customerCount" ) + 1
  Application.UnLock
End Sub

Sub Session_OnEnd
  Application.Lock
  Application( "customerCount" ) = Application( "customerCount" ) - 1
  Application.UnLock
End Sub

Sub Application_OnStart
  Application( "customerCount" ) = 0
End Sub
%>
```

You cannot use the script delimiters <% and %> within the Global.asa file. You must use the HTML <SCRIPT> tag instead.

Exercise

Create an ASP page that lists the SessionID and the entry time of all the customers who have visited your Web site. To do this, you will need to create a Global.asa file to detect when the customer arrives and an ASP page to display the list of SessionIDs and entry times.

Here's the Global.asa file:

```
<SCRIPT LANGUAGE="VBScript" RUNAT="SERVER">
Sub Session_OnStart
  Application.Lock
```

A

```
   Application( "customers" ) = Application( "customers" )
➥ & Session.SessionID & " (" & NOW() & ")<br>"
   Application.UnLock
End Sub
</SCRIPT>
```

Here's the ASP page that displays the customers:

```
<HTML>
<HEAD><TITLE>Customers</TITLE></HEAD>
<BODY>

Customers:
<p><%=Application( "customers" )%>

</BODY>
</HTML>
```

Answers for Day 4

Quiz

1. What's the difference, if any, between using the FILE attribute of the #INCLUDE
   directive and the VIRTUAL attribute of the #INCLUDE directive?

   You use the FILE attribute when you want to include a file that is located in the
   same directory or in a subdirectory of the directory that contains the ASP page that
   has the #INCLUDE directive. You use the VIRTUAL attribute when you want to
   include a file by specifying its full virtual path.

2. There is a problem with the following script. How can the script be rewritten so
   that it works as intended?

   ```
   <%
   answer = Request( "answer" )
   IF answer = "yes" THEN
     displayPage = "page1.asp"
   ELSE
     displayPage = "page2.asp"
   END IF
   %>
   <!-- #INCLUDE VIRTUAL="<%=displayPage%>" -->
   ```

   Because Active Server Pages doesn't support dynamic includes, you cannot use a
   variable as the value of the #INCLUDE directive. The script should be written like
   this:

   ```
   <%
   answer = Request( "answer" )
   IF answer = "yes" THEN
   ```

```
%>
<!-- #INCLUDE FILE="page1.asp" -->
<%
ELSE
%>
<!-- #INCLUDE FILE="page2.asp" -->
<%
END IF
%>
```

3. How would you rewrite the following script so that it does not use the `Redirect` method?

```
<%
username = TRIM( Request( "username" ) )
IF username = "" THEN
  Response.Redirect "/login.asp"
END IF
%>
```

Instead of using the `Redirect` method, you can use the `#INCLUDE` directive like this:

```
<%
username = TRIM( Request( "username" ) )
IF username = "" THEN
  %>
  <!-- #INCLUDE FILE="login.asp" -->
  <%
  Response.End
END IF
%>
```

4. What method of the `FileSystemObject` object do you use to detect whether a file exists?

You use the `FileExists()` method of the `FileSystemObject` object to detect whether a file exists.

Exercise

Create an ASP page that displays its own source code. Use the `FileSystemObject` and `TextStream` objects in the page.

The following ASP page, named `myself.asp`, displays its own source:

```
<HTML>
<HEAD><TITLE>MySelf</TITLE></HEAD>
<BODY>

<PRE>
<%
```

```
myPath = "c:\myself.asp"
Set fs = Server.CreateObject( "Scripting.FileSystemObject" )
Set mySource = fs.OpenTextFile( myPath )
WHILE NOT mySource.AtEndOfStream
  Response.Write Server.HTMLEncode( mySource.ReadLine ) & vbNewline
WEND
%>
</PRE>

</BODY>
</HTML>
```

Answers for Day 5

Quiz

1. If you move your Microsoft Access database, what do you need to do to allow your ASP scripts to find the database at its new location?

   If you move a Microsoft Access database, then you will need to update the System DSN by using the ODBC Data Sources applet in the Control Panel.

2. What's wrong with the following SQL INSERT INTO statement?

   ```
   INSERT INTO Products ( product_name ) VALUES ( Holiday Gift Basket )
   ```

   The text Holiday Gift Basket must be enclosed in single quotation marks. The INSERT INTO statement should be written like this:

   ```
   INSERT INTO Products ( product_name ) VALUES ( 'Holiday Gift Basket' )
   ```

3. Why do single quotation marks (') cause problems when inserting or updating records in a database?

   Microsoft Access uses a single quotation mark to mark the beginning and end of text. If the text itself contains a quotation mark, Microsoft Access will mistakenly interpret it as marking the end of the text. To get around this problem, you must double all the quotation marks that occur in the string.

4. Why do quotation marks (") cause problems when displaying a variable with the VALUE attribute of an HTML form?

   HTML uses quotation marks to mark the beginning and end of text. So, if the value of a variable includes a quotation mark, it will be incorrectly interpreted as marking the end of the text. To get around this problem, you need to HTML encode variables before you display them.

Exercise

How can you add additional product information to your online store? For example, suppose that you want to add a field named product_sku to track a product's SKU. How would you modify the database table and Active Server Pages discussed in this chapter to include the new field?

You can add one or more additional columns to the Products table by launching Microsoft Access and opening the Products table in Design View. After you have added a new column, you will need to make the following modifications to the Active Server Pages discussed in this chapter:

addProduct.asp—Add the new field to the HTML form.

updateProduct.asp—You'll need to add the new field to the list of fields retrieved from the database. Add this line:

```
productSKU = RS( "product_sku" )
```

Next, you'll need to add a new form field to the HTML form. The VALUE attribute of the new form field should have the productSKU variable as its value.

manageproducts.asp—Add the new field to the list of variables retrieved when an HTML form is submitted. Use the following statement:

```
productSKU  = TRIM( Request( "productSKU" ) )
```

Next, you'll need to create a default value for the productSKU variable if it doesn't have a value. Use the following statements:

```
IF productSKU = "" THEN
  productSKU = "?????"
END IF
```

Finally, you'll need to modify both the SQL string used to add a new product to the database and the SQL string used to update a product in the database. Both of these strings will need to be modified to include the productSKU variable.

Answers for Day 6

Quiz

1. What is the correct SQL SELECT statement for retrieving the name of every product from the Products table that costs more than $20.25?

```
SELECT product_name FROM Products
WHERE product_price > 20.25
```

2. What method do you use to move to the next row in a Recordset?

To move to the next row in a Recordset, you use the MoveNext method.

A

3. What do you need to include in a script before you can use ADO constants such as adOpenStatic?

Before you can use ADO constants, you must include the ADOVBS.inc file in your ASP script.

4. Which default property of a Recordset do you need to change before you can use Recordset properties such as RecordCount and PageSize?

You need to change the CursorType of the Recordset from a forward-only cursor to a richer type of cursor such as a Static cursor.

Exercise

In today's lesson, you learned how to modify the CatList.asp page so that the list of product categories is retrieved from memory rather than the database. Modify the ProductList.asp page so that the list of products is retrieved from memory rather than the database.

Storing the list of products in memory is more difficult than storing the list of product categories in memory because the products need to be divided into different categories. The trick is to create different Application arrays for each of the various categories. The following script correctly transfers the list of products to memory:

```
<%
IF NOT isArray( Application( cat ) ) THEN
  Set prodRS = Server.CreateObject( "ADODB.Recordset" )
  prodRS.ActiveConnection = Con

  sqlString = "SELECT product_id, product_picture, product_name,
➥product_briefDesc " &_
    "FROM Products WHERE product_category='" & cat & "' " &_
    "AND product_status=1 " &_
    "ORDER BY product_name "
  prodRS.Open sqlString

  prodList = prodRS.GetRows()
  Application( cat ) = prodList
  prodRS.Close
END IF
%>
<table width="350" border=0
 cellpadding=5 cellspacing=0>
<%
FOR i = 0 TO UBOUND( Application( cat ), 2 )
productID = Application( cat )( 0, i )
productPicture = Application( cat )( 1, i )
productName = Application( cat )( 2, i )
```

```
productBriefDesc = Application( cat )( 3, i )
%>
<tr>
  <td>
  <% IF productPicture <> "?????" THEN %>
  <IMG SRC="<%=productPicture %>"
   HSPACE=4 VSPACE=4 BORDER=0 align="center">
  <% END IF %>
  </td>
  <td>
  <a href="product.asp?pid=<%=productID %>">
  <b><%=productName %></b></a>
  <br><%=productBriefDesc %>
  <br><a href="product.asp?pid=<%=productID %>">
  get more information</a>
  </td>
</tr>
<tr>
  <td colspan=2 align="center">
   
  </td>
</tr>
<%
NEXT
%>
</table>
```

Answers for Day 7

Quiz

1. How do I transfer the contents of a Recordset into an array?

   You can transfer the contents of a Recordset into an array by using the `GetRows()` method of the Recordset object.

2. The following SQL `SELECT` statement is intended to retrieve all the records from the `Products` table where the `product_name` column contains the word "candy". What's wrong with this statement?

   `SELECT * FROM Products WHERE product_name = '%candy%'`

   This `SELECT` statement retrieves only those records where the product name *equals* %candy%. To retrieve the product names that contain the phrase candy, you need to use the SQL `LIKE` operator in the following manner:

   `SELECT * FROM Products WHERE product_name LIKE '%candy%'`

3. When using the Internet Information Server's Custom Errors feature to automatically redirect to a new page, how do I determine the name of the original page requested?

A

The path of the original page is passed to the new page within the page's query string. Therefore, you can determine the name of original page requested by accessing the QueryString collection of the Request object.

Exercise

The search page described in this chapter matches search terms in either the `product_name` or the `product_briefDesc` database fields. How would you modify the search page (`Search.asp`) so that it would also match terms appearing in the `product_fulldesc` field?

To match search terms in the `product_fulldesc` field, you would need to modify the SQL string used to perform the search in the following manner:

```
sqlString = "SELECT product_id, product_picture, product_name,
➥product_briefDesc " &_
  "FROM Products " &_
  "WHERE product_status = 1 " &_
  "AND ( product_name LIKE '%" & searchFor & "%' " &_
  "OR product_briefDesc LIKE '%" & searchFor & "%'  " &_
  "OR product_fullDesc LIKE '%" & searchFor & "%' ) " &_
  "ORDER BY product_name "
```

Answers for Day 8

Quiz

1. The following script was designed to conditionally display one of two pages depending on the value of the variable named showPage. What's wrong with this script?

```
<%
IF DATE() > "12/25/1999" THEN
  showPage = "page1.asp"
ELSE
  showPage = "page2.asp"
END IF
%>
<!-- #INCLUDE FILE="<%=showPage%>" -->
```

This script will attempt to include a file named <%=showPage%>. The #INCLUDE directive is processed before any Active Server Page scripts. Therefore, you cannot use a variable as the value of an #INCLUDE directive.

2. How can I add a cookie to a customer's browser named customerID that has the value 17?

You can add a new cookie by using the Cookies collection of the Response object.

The following script adds a cookie named customerID that has the value 17:

```
Response.Cookies( "customerID" ) = "17"
Response.Cookies( "customerID" ).Expires = "July 31, 2001"
Response.Cookies( "customerID" ).Path = "/"
Response.Cookies( "customerID" ).Secure = FALSE
```

3. What do I need to do in order to request a page named `confidential.asp` using the Secure Sockets Layer?

   After you have installed SSL, you can request the `confidential.asp` page using SSL like this:

   ```
   https://www.yourdomain.com/confidential.asp
   ```

Exercise

The registration form described in this chapter has fields for login information, payment information, and address information. How would you add additional fields such as customer first and last name to this form?

To add additional fields to the registration page, you will need to modify the Users database table, the `register.asp` page, and the `storefuncs.asp` file.

First, you will need to add two additional columns to the table named Users in the `storeDB` database. You'll need to add a column named user_firstname and a column named user_lastname.

Next, you must modify the `register.asp` form to include a form field named firstname and lastname. Both of the new fields will need to be added to the list of form fields retrieved at the top of the page. You'll also need to actually add the firstname and lastname form fields to the HTML form.

Finally, you will need to modify the `addUser` subroutine so that it will add the two new form fields to the Users database table.

Answers for Day 9

Quiz

1. The following script assigns the value `"Hello World"` to an element in an array stored in a `Session` variable. What's wrong this script?

   ```
   Session( "myarray" )( 2 ) = "hello world!"
   ```

   You cannot update an array stored in a `Session` array. Before you modify any of the elements of a `Session` array, you must copy the array to a local variable like this:

```
myarray = Session( "myarray" )
myarray( 2 ) = "hello world!"
Session( "myarray" ) = myarray
```

2. Before you can add new records or update existing records in a Recordset, you must modify a property of the Recordset object. What is the name of this property?

Before you can modify the records contained in a Recordset, you must modify the Recordset's LockType property. By default, the LockType property is read-only.

Exercise

Assume that you wanted to add a new button to the shopping cart labeled Clear Cart that enables customers to remove all the existing items from their shopping cart. Describe the script that needs to be executed to remove the items from both shopping carts.

In the case of the Session shopping cart, you simply need to erase the Session variable that contains the shopping cart (If a customer adds a new item to the shopping cart in the future, this Session variable is automatically re-created). Therefore, you can clear the shopping cart with the following statement:

```
Session( "cart" ) = ""
```

In the case of the database shopping cart, you will need to remove all the items associated with the customer in the cart database table. The following line of code will remove all the items associated with the current customer:

```
Con.Execute "DELETE FROM cart WHERE cart_userID=" & userID
```

Answers for Day 10

Quiz

1. What's wrong with the following script?
```
<%
Set Con = Server.CreateObject( "ADODB.Connection" )
Con.Open "accessDSN"
SET RS = Server.CreateObject( "ADODB.Recordset" )
RS.ActiveConnection = Con
RS.BeginTrans
RS.Open "select * FROM Orders"
RS.CommitTrans
%>
```

The BeginTrans() and CommitTrans() methods are methods of the Connection object and not the Recordset object.

2. Suppose that you want to copy a particular row from the Orders table to a second table named Orders_bak. The Orders_bak table is used to backup the data in the Orders table. How can you copy the row from the Orders table in which the value of the order_id column is 17 to the Orders_bak table?

The following SQL INSERT INTO statement selects the proper row from the Orders table and inserts it into the Orders_bak table.

```
INSERT INTO Orders_bak (
order_id,
order_userID,
order_quantity,
order_productID,
order_entrydate,
order_status
) SELECT
order_id,
order_userID,
order_quantity,
order_productID,
order_entrydate,
order_status
FROM Orders
WHERE order_id=17
```

Exercise

The processOrders.asp page discussed in today's lesson enables you to assign one of four status values to an order: Pending, Credit Card Declined, Not in Stock or Shipped. How would you modify the processOrders.asp page (contained in Listing 10.8) to enable a fifth status value, Back Ordered, to be selected?

To add an additional order status value, you'll need to make two changes. First, directly below line 202, you'll need to add the following statements:

```
<% IF RS( "order_status" ) = 4 THEN %>
<td bgcolor="lightblue">
<b>Back Ordered</b>
</td>
<% ELSE %>
<td>
<a href="processOrders.asp?showpage=<%=showPage%>&
➥ oid=<%=RS( "order_id" )%>&os=4&showOrders=<%=showOrders%>">
Back Ordered</a>
</td>
<% END IF %>
```

Next, you'll need to add the following line to the section that creates the HTML pick list (after line 88):

```
<option value="4" <%=SELECTED( "4", showOrders )%>>
➥ Back Ordered
```

Answers for Day 11

Quiz

1. Where is my merchant configuration information stored on my server when I use the CyberCash service?

   Your merchant configuration information is stored in a file named `merchant_conf`. The CyberCash Socket component loads this file when it sends messages to the CyberCash service.

2. What are the names of the two CyberCash components used when sending an authorization request to the CyberCash service?

   The CyberCash Merchant Connection Kit uses the MessageBlock and the Socket components.

3. After a transaction is authorized, what other steps must I take to transfer the money from the customer's credit card account to my merchant account?

   After you authorize a transaction, the transaction must be captured and settled. How this is done depends on your credit card processing model: AuthCapture, Auth/PostAuthCapture, or TerminalCapture.

Answers for Day 12

Quiz

1. Is the `iisCARTship` component included with Active Server Pages?

   No. The `iisCARTship` component is a third-party ASP component. You must purchase the component by visiting the following Internet address:

   `http://www.iisCart.com`

2. What four properties of the `iisCARTship` component must you set before you can query rate information from any of the shipping companies?

   Before you can query the shipping companies, you must set the following four components:

   `OrigPostal`—The postal code of the sender of the package (must be in United States).

   `DestPostal`—The postal code of the recipient of the package (may be outside United States).

   `Weight`—The weight of the package (by default, in pounds).

   `DestCountry`—The country code for the destination of the package.

3. What is the name of the collection returned by the `ShipCalc()` method that contains the shipping rates?

   The `ShipCalc()` method returns a collection named `ShipInfo` that contains the shipping rates.

Answers for Day 13

Quiz

1. Can you use HTTP Authentication with the Netscape Navigator browser?

   Yes. Basic Authentication is part of the HTTP specification and it is supported by almost every browser.

2. Why is it considered a security risk to use Basic Authentication?

   When usernames and passwords are transmitted across the Internet using Basic Authentication, they are simply base64 encoded. Because it is so easy to decode text that is base64 encoded, the usernames and passwords might as well be sent as plain text.

3. How can I force a password dialog box to appear on a Web browser?

   By sending a `401 Not Authorized` Status Code and adding a WWW-Authenticate header like this:
   ```
   Response.Status = "401 Not Authorized"
   Response.AddHeader "WWW-Authenticate", "Basic realm=""localhost"""
   Response.End
   ```

4. When using Basic Authentication, how is a username and password passed from page to page?

   Usernames and passwords are passed from page to page within the AUTHORIZA-TION browser header.

Answers for Day 14

Quiz

1. What purpose does the `retrieveFavorites` function serve?

   We use the `retrieveFavorites` function to query the `user` table of the database and retrieve the comma separated list of categories in the `user_favorites` column. We then use the returned value to determine what featured items to display to the customer.

2. Why don't we store product categories as numeric identifiers in our example?

In our example, our product database uses a full-text name for each category. In this case, we would need to add another column to the database representing columns and then carry out a query to convert the numeric category identifier into a readable string. For our small example, it proves more efficient to use a full-text name.

Answers for Day 15

Quiz

1. What version of Windows NT or Windows 2000 should you be using for your E-Commerce Web server?

Windows NT Server or Windows 2000 Server with the latest service pack and hotfixes. If you are in the United States or Canada, you should install the 128-bit version of the latest service pack.

2. What ports need to be allowed through your firewall?

Ports 80 and 443 are the only ports that should be allowed through your firewall.

3. What is Spoofing?

Spoofing is when a con artist or a hacker copies your Web site in order to fool your customers into entering private information like credit card numbers.

4. How large of a key should you use for a certificate signing request?

You should use the largest key size available. As of the writing of this book, that was 1024 bits.

5. What are three ways to improve the security of your Web site's Access database?

Don't keep your Access database in the same directory as your Web site, make sure to keep your server logged off and locked up when not using it, and keep your Access database in a directory that isn't shared.

Answers for Day 16

Quiz

1. Why is it important to keep separate development and production Web sites?

So that any development and testing you do doesn't impact your customers adversely.

2. What is a breakpoint?

An instruction to the debugger to stop at a particular line of script so that you can look at the contents of variables and watch the line-by-line execution of scripts.

3. Can I install the debugger on my production server?

No.

4. Why should I keep all my debugging routines in a single script?

So that changes to the debugging scripts are available to all the scripts that call them.

5. How much load should I plan to handle?

As a rule of thumb, imagine how much traffic you would need to have to feel really successful; then multiply that traffic by 10.

Exercise

Update the CheckError function so that it writes log files into a directory on your Web site.

To update the CheckError function to save error messages to a custom log directory, you'll need to replace the expression fs.GetTempName() in both places where it occurs in the CheckError function with the path to your log file.

Answers for Day 17

Quiz

1. What are three administrative tasks that the Internet Service Manager (HTML) cannot perform?

The Internet Service Manager (HTML) cannot manage Web sites other than the default Web site, cannot start or stop a Web service and cannot change the physical directories for Web site virtual directories.

2. What is FTP? Is it advisable to allow anonymous access to your FTP service?

FTP stands for *File Transfer Protocol*, which is a standard way to transfer files between two servers on the Internet. It is not advisable to allow anonymous access to an FTP service unless the service is being used to host a download site (something like download.com).

3. What is the Posting Acceptor?

The Posting Acceptor is a component of IIS that allows users to submit files via a standard HTML form.

A

4. What happens if a user submits a form to the Posting Acceptor that doesn't include one or more files for upload?

The Posting Acceptor sends back an error message if a user submits a form that doesn't include a file for upload. To work around this, use a script like that found in `upload.asp`, which checks to see if a file is specified and, if not, programmatically changes the attributes of the form.

Answers for Day 18

Quiz

1. What is an SMTP server?

An SMTP server is a server that stores and forwards messages using the Simple Mail Transport protocol.

2. Why is it important to restrict relaying on your SMTP server?

If relaying isn't restricted on your SMTP server, spammers will be able to exploit your server by using it as an origination point for bulk email. This ties up your bandwidth and leaves you open for the possibility of having your SMTP server black-holed by being added to the Realtime Blackhole List.

3. What is the difference between text and MIME mail messages? How do you send one or the other?

Text messages are simple, unformatted messages, whereas MIME mail can have attachments and formatted HTML text. You can use CDONTS to send text messages by setting the `BodyFormat` attribute of the new message to `CdoBodyFormatText`, and setting the `MailFormat` attribute to `CdoMailFormatMime`. You can use CDONTS to send formatted messages by setting the `BodyFormat` to `CdoBodyFormatHTML` and the `MailFormat` attribute to `CdoMailFormatMime`.

4. What happens if more than one <INPUT> tag in a form has the same name attribute?

If more than one <INPUT> tag in a form has the same name attribute, when the form is posted, the various values are added to a subcollection of the `Request.Form` item that has that name. For example, if the following two lines appear in an HTML form

```
<INPUT type="hidden" name="foo" value="bar">
<INPUT type="hidden" name="foo" value="baz">
```

`Request.Form("foo")` will contain a collection that has two members. `Request.Form("foo")(1)` will equal bar; `Request.Form("foo")(2)` will equal baz.

Answers for Day 19

Quiz

1. What is the difference between a hit, a page view and a unique user? For what is each useful?

   A hit is a browser's request for a file from a Web server. A page view is the delivery to the user of an entire Web page, including graphics elements. A unique user is a different person who visited a site within a specific period. Hits are the most useful measurement for estimating the technical requirements of a site, whereas page views and unique users are useful for marketing and strategic planning purposes.

2. What are the different log file formats that IIS 4.0 supports? Which ones are you likely to want to use? Why?

   IIS 4.0 can write log files in one of four different formats: NCSA Common Log File Format, ODBC Logging Format, Microsoft IIS Log File Format, or W3C Extended Log File Format. The most useful of these are ODBC Logging and W3C Extended Log File Format. ODBC Logging Format allows multiple Web sites to log information to the same database table, and allows you to report on Web site statistics in real-time. W3C Extended Log File Format allows you to record the most information, and allows you to save space by recording only the information that you are interested in.

3. Why is log file analysis an unreliable way to measure site traffic?

   Log files are an inexact way to measure site traffic because browsers, proxy servers, and firewalls tend to make traffic seem lower, whereas bots and Web spiders tend to make traffic seem higher. Still, log file analysis is more useful than not having any information at all.

Answers for Day 20

Quiz

1. What is the difference between a client-side wallet and a server-side wallet?

   A client-side wallet is a relatively large piece of software that must be downloaded onto a computer. The software stores a customer's credit card and other personal information in an encrypted file on that computer's hard disk, and submits the information to electronic stores upon the customer's request.

A server-side wallet has little or no software to be downloaded onto a computer. Instead, the wallet vendor provides a Web site where the customer can enter his information, which is then stored encrypted on the wallet vendor's servers. The wallet vendor submits the customer's information upon the customer's request.

2. What is the difference between a SmartCard and a wallet?

A SmartCard is a computer that is the size of a credit card, whereas a wallet is a piece of software. SmartCards can be used instead of (or in addition to) usernames and passwords to help secure client-side or server-side wallets. They can also run client-side wallets or "electronic purse" software. Electronic purse software enables consumers to download small amounts of electronic money directly into the SmartCard, and transfer the electronic money to merchants or other electronic purse users without involving a bank or other clearing company.

3. What is the ECML standard?

The ECML standard is a defined set of names for the `<INPUT>` fields on an electronic order form. It facilitates the compatibility of electronic wallets with E-Commerce sites.

Answers for Day 21

Quiz

1. What is a "spider"?

There is no central index to the Web. A spider is the part of a search engine that tries to finds as many Web sites as it can, by starting with a group of known Web pages and following all the links it can find.

2. What is a relevance metric?

A relevance metric computes how well a particular page answers a query string. It takes into account the structure and contents of the page, sometimes including `<TITLE>`, `<META name="keywords">`, and `<META name="description">` tags.

3. What is a Web ring?

A Web ring is an alternative to search engines and Web directories that makes browsing the Web on particular topics easier. A particular Web ring is an informal association of Web sites on a single topic that enables a surfer to navigate between all the sites in the ring.

4. What is a link exchange?

A link exchange enables Web site owners to cross-promote their sites with banner advertisements. For each banner ad the Web site owner displays, he gets a fractional credit toward displaying his own banner on another exchange member's Web site.

APPENDIX B

Frequently Asked Questions About Active Server Pages

This appendix addresses the questions that are most frequently posted on the Active Server Pages newsgroups and the ASPSite (the companion Web site to this book at www.aspsite.com). When appropriate, references are provided to specific chapters in this book where more information can be found. For updated information, please visit http://www.aspsite.com/answers.

Installation Questions

Which Operating Systems Support Active Server Pages?

Active Server Pages runs natively on Microsoft Windows NT Server 4.0, Microsoft Windows NT Workstation 4.0 with Peer Web Services, and Windows 95/98 with the Personal Web Server.

Using Chili!Soft's Chili!ASP (see `http://www.chilisoft.com`), you also can use Active Server Pages with SUN Solaris and IBM AIX. Chili!ASP enables Active Server Pages to run on Apache servers, Netscape Enterprise and FastTrack servers, the Lotus Domino Go Webserver, and O'Reilly Website Pro.

How Do I Get the Latest Version of Internet Information Server and Active Server Pages?

You can download the latest version of Active Server Pages and Internet Information Server at the Microsoft Web site. Go to `http://www.microsoft.com/iis` and select Downloads. Download the Windows NT Server 4.0 Option Pack. You will be provided with the option of downloading either the Windows NT or Windows 95/98 version of the Option Pack.

How Do I Get the Latest Version of the ActiveX Data Objects (ADO)?

The latest version of the ActiveX Data Objects (ADO) is available at the Microsoft Web site. Go to `http://www.microsoft.com/data` and download the Microsoft Data Access Components (MDAC).

General Scripting Questions

How Do I Add a Quotation Mark to a VBScript String?

There are two ways to add a quotation mark to a VBScript string:

```
myVar = "He said, ""Hello!"" "
myVar = "He said, " & CHR( 34 ) & "Hello!" & CHR( 34 )
```

The first method uses two quotation marks in a row to create a single quotation mark. The second method uses the ASCII value of the quotation mark character.

How Can I Break a Single VBScript Statement into Multiple Lines?

You can break a single VBScript statement into multiple lines by using the _ underscore character. For example, the string in the following statement is broken into several lines of code by using the &_ character combination:

```
myVar = "When in the Course of human events, " &_
    "it becomes necessary for one people to " &_
    "dissolve the political bands which have " &_
```

```
"connected them with another, and to assume " &_
"among the powers of the earth, the separate " &_
"and equal station to which the Laws of " &_
"Nature and of Nature's God entitle them, " &_
"a decent respect to the opinions of " &_
"mankind requires that they should declare " &_
"the causes which impel them to the separation. "
```

What Is the Proper Method of Comparing Strings in VBScript?

When you compare two strings with the identity operator, the comparison is case sensitive. For example, the following statement returns the value `false`:

```
<%= "apple" = "APPLE" %>
```

There are two methods of performing a case-insensitive comparison of two strings:

```
<%= StrComp( "apple", "APPLE", vbTextCompare )%>
<%= UCASE( "apple" ) = UCASE( "APPLE" ) %>
```

The first method uses the VBScript StrComp function with the `vbTextCompare` constant. The second method forces both strings into uppercase.

You should be aware that several other VBScript string functions, such as the `InStr` and `Replace` functions, are also case sensitive. To perform case-insensitive comparisons with these functions, you must use the `vbTextCompare` constant.

How Can I Re-enable Errors After Using ON ERROR RESUME NEXT?

The VBScript ON ERROR RESUME NEXT statement suppresses errors in your script. If you include the statement outside any functions or subroutines, the statement will apply to every statement that follows it (otherwise, it will apply only within the function or subroutine). To re-enable the reporting of errors, use the ON ERROR GOTO 0 statement like this:

```
<%
ON ERROR RESUME NEXT
' The following error is ignored
fakeOBJ.Blah
ON ERROR GOTO 0
' The following error is reported
fakeOBJ2.Blah
%>
```

How Can I Prevent My Script from Timing Out?

By default, an Active Server Page script will stop executing and time out after 90 seconds. If you have a long running script, the script may stop executing too early. You can extend the amount of time a script is allowed to run by using the `ScriptTimeout` property of the `Server` object. Here's an example:

```
<% Server.ScriptTimeout = 200 %>
```

This statement changes the timeout period to 200 seconds.

When Do I Need to Explicitly Convert a Variable to a Particular Data Type?

If you are comparing numbers or dates and times and there is a danger that VBScript might interpret the values as strings, you should use one of the VBScript conversion functions. For example, suppose an HTML form contains two input boxes for two numbers, and you execute the following script:

```
<%
firstNum = Request( "firstNum" )
secondNum = Request( "secondNum" )
%>
<%=firstNum > secondNum %>
```

If you enter 32 for the first number and 223 for the second number into the form, the script will output the wrong result. The script will return the value TRUE because the string 32 is greater than the string 223, even though the number is not. To force an integer comparison, rather than a string comparison, use a script like this:

```
<%
firstNum = CInt( Request( "firstNum" ) )
secondNum = CInt( Request( "secondNum" ) )
%>
<%=firstNum > secondNum %>
```

The CInt function converts a value to the Integer subtype (also see the CDate, CCur, IsNumeric, and IsDate functions).

When Should I Pass a Variable by Value and When by Reference?

When you pass a variable by value to a subroutine or function, a new instance of the variable is created. Any changes made to the value of the variable do not affect the value of the original variable. On the other hand, when you pass a variable by reference, changes made to the variable do affect the value of the original variable. Here's an example:

```
<%
SUB addOne( ByVal fvar, ByRef svar )
  fvar = fvar + 1
  svar = svar + 1
END SUB
firstvar = 0
secondvar = 0
addOne firstvar, secondvar
%>
```

B

After this script is executed, the variable named firstvar has the value 0 and the variable named secondvar has the value 1.

How Can I Add a Space Between the Output of Two Variables?

For some mysterious reason, when you output two variables in a row in an Active Server Page, any spaces that appear between the variables will disappear. For example, the following script outputs "AndrewJones" rather than "Andrew Jones":

```
<%
fname = "Andrew"
lname="Jones"
%>
<%=fname%> <%=lname%>
```

The easiest way to get around this problem is to use a script like the following:

```
<%
fname = "Andrew"
lname="Jones"
%>
<%=fname & " " & lname%>
```

Does Active Server Pages Support Dynamic Includes?

Some server-side scripting environments, such as Cold Fusion, support dynamic includes. A dynamic include enables you to use a variable for the name of the file to include in a page. Active Server Pages does not support dynamic includes. The following script will not work:

```
<%
myFile = "firstpage.asp"
%>
<!-- #INCLUDE FILE="<%=myFile%>" -->
```

This include directive will attempt to include a file named "<%=myFile%>", which probably does not exist. The problem is that all server-side directives, including the #INCLUDE directive, are processed before Active Server Page scripts. If you must dynamically include different pages within an Active Server Page, consider using a script like the following:

```
<%
myFile = "firstpage.asp"
if myFile = "firstpage.asp" then
%>
<!-- #INCLUDE FILE="firstpage.asp" -->
<%
end if
if myFile = "secondpage.asp" then
%>
<!-- #INCLUDE FILE="secondpage.asp" -->
<%
end if
if myFile = "thirdpage.asp" then
%>
<!-- #INCLUDE FILE="thirdpage.asp" -->
<%
end if
%>
```

This script conditionally displays one of three different pages. The version of Active Server Pages bundled with IIS 5.0 will include better methods for dynamically including files.

How Do I Use the `Option Explicit` Statement in an Active Server Page?

The `Option Explicit` statement forces you to declare all your variables. Using this statement can make it easier to program complicated Active Server Pages because misspelled variable names will generate errors.

You must use the `Option Explicit` statement before any other VBScript statement or HTML content in a script. If you don't, you'll receive an error like the following:

```
Microsoft VBScript compilation error '800a0400'
Expected statement
/test.asp, line 5
Option Explicit
^
```

Here's an example that uses the `Option Explicit` statement correctly:

```
<Option Explicit %>
<html>
<head><title>My Page</title></head>
<body>
<%
```

```
DIM myVar
myVar = "Hello!"
%>
</body>
<html>
```

Session and Application Variables Questions

Why Do Session Variables Sometimes Fail to Work?

Session variables depend on browser cookies. If a browser does not support cookies, or a user has turned off cookies or the user's cookie file is corrupted, Session variables will not work.

How Can I Remove an Application Variable?

The current version of Active Server Pages, included with IIS 4.0, does not contain a method for removing Application variables. After you create one, it remains in memory until the Internet Service is stopped, the Global.asa file is changed, or the current application is unloaded.

The version of Active Server Pages included with IIS 5.0, on the other hand, includes two new methods for removing Application variables: the Remove and RemoveAll methods.

File Questions

How Do I Detect Whether a File Exists?

You can check whether a file exists by using the FileExists method of the FileSystemObject. The following script detects whether a file named test.txt exists:

```
<%
Set fs = Server.CreateObject( "Scripting.FileSystemObject" )
if fs.FileExists( "c:\test.txt" ) then
  Response.Write "File Exists!"
else
  Response.Write "No File!"
end if
%>
```

How Can I Automatically Display a List of Files in a Directory?

You can display a list of files in a folder by using the `FileSystemObject` and the `Folder` object like this:

```
<%
Set fs = Server.CreateObject( "Scripting.FileSystemObject" )
Set folder = fs.GetFolder( "c:\myfolder" )
For Each thing In folder.Files
  Response.Write thing.name & "<br>"
Next
%>
```

This script lists the names of all the files in a folder named myfolder located on the c: drive.

Image Questions

How Can I Store an Image in a Database Table?

Although you can store an image in a SQL Server BLOB column, it is almost always better to store the URL of an image in a database table rather than the image itself. (Storing an image in a database table places unnecessary work on your database server.) For example, the following script displays several images in a row by retrieving the URL of each image from a database table named `myImages`:

```
<%
Set Con = Server.CreateObject( "ADODB.Connection" )
Con.Open "FILE NAME=c:\myDataLink.UDL"
mySQL = "SELECT image_URL from myImages"
Set RS = Con.Execute( mySQL )
While Not RS.EOF
%>
<img src="<%=RS( "image_URL" )%>">
<%
RS.MoveNext
Wend
%>
```

How Can I Dynamically Generate a Graph or Image in an Active Server Page?

Several third-party Active Server Pages components enable you to dynamically create custom images.

Browser Questions

How Do I Detect the Type of Browser a Person Is Using to Visit My Web Site?

The USER-AGENT header indicates the type of browser. The following script captures the value of the USER-AGENT header from the ServerVariables collection and displays it:

```
<%
browserType = Request.ServerVariables( "HTTP_USER_AGENT" )
Response.WRite browserType
%>
```

How Can I Detect the Page From Which a Person Originated?

The REFERER header contains the URL of the last page the person visited. This header can be retrieved from the ServerVariables collection. The following script displays the value of the REFERER header:

```
<%
browserType = Request.ServerVariables( "HTTP_REFERER" )
Response.WRite browserType
%>
```

ActiveX Data Objects Questions

Why Do I Sometimes Receive an Error When Using the Connection Object to Execute a SQL String?

Consider the following script. It retrieves a user's first name from an HTML form and inserts it into a database table:

```
<%
firstname = Request( "firstname" )
mySQL = "INSERT myTable ( firstname ) VALUES "
mySQL = mySQL & "('" & firstname & "')"
Set Con = Server.CreateObject( "ADODB.Connection" )
Con.Open "FILE NAME=c:\myDataLink.UDL"
Con.Execute mySQL
%>
```

Suppose, however, that the user entered a single quote when entering a first name. For example, the user entered the name O'Reilly. Because SQL uses a single quote to mark the beginning and end of a string value, the single quote would generate an error.

Before entering a string into a database table with the `Connection` object, you must first translate any single quotes into two quotes in a row. The following script avoids errors caused by a quotation mark:

```
<%
FUNCTION fixQuotes( theVar )
  fixQuotes = REPLACE( theVar, "'", "''" )
END FUNCTION
firstname = Request( "firstname" )
firstname = fixQuotes( firstname )
mySQL = "INSERT myTable ( firstname ) VALUES "
mySQL = mySQL & "('" & firstname & "')"
Set Con = Server.CreateObject( "ADODB.Connection" )
Con.Open "FILE NAME=c:\myDataLink.UDL"
Con.Execute mySQL
%>
```

In this example, the `fixQuotes` function replaces any single quote with two quotes. Doubling the quotes enables you to enter single quotes into a database table.

How Do I Retrieve a TEXT Field in an Active Server Page?

If you do not take special precautions when retrieving a TEXT field from a database table, the value of the TEXT field might be truncated. If you are using a forward-only cursor type, you should list the TEXT field as the very last field in your select list. Alternatively, consider using a richer cursor type when opening a Recordset that contains a TEXT field. The following script will correctly retrieve and display a TEXT field:

```
<!-- #INCLUDE VIRTUAL="/adovbs.inc" -->
<%
Set Con = Server.CreateObject( "ADODB.Connection" )
Con.Open "FILE NAME=c:\myDataLink.UDL"
Set RS = Server.CreateObject( "ADODB.RecordSet" )
RS.CursorType = adOpenDynamic
RS.Open "Select TextColumn FROM mytable", Con
%>
```

Why Does `RecordCount` Always Return the Value -1?

The `RecordCount` property returns the number of rows in a Recordset after it has been opened. You cannot use this property with a forward-only cursor when using SQL Server (it will always return -1). To use this property, open a Recordset with a richer cursor type like this:

```
<!-- #INCLUDE VIRTUAL="/adovbs.inc" -->
<%
mySQL = "SELECT * FROM WebUsers"
```

```
Set Con = Server.CreateObject( "ADODB.Connection" )
Con.Open "FILE NAME=c:\myDataLink.UDL"
Set RS = Server.CreateObject( "ADODB.Recordset" )
RS.CursorType = adOpenDynamic
RS.Open mySQL, Con
Response.Write RS.RecordCount
%>
```

Why Do I Receive an Error Whenever I Try to Update the Value of a Field in a Recordset?

By default, when you open a Recordset, it is opened with a forward-only cursor and read-only lock type. To update a Recordset, you must open a Recordset that is not read-only. Here is an example:

```
<!-- #INCLUDE VIRTUAL="/adovbs.inc" -->
<%
Set Con = Server.CreateObject( "ADODB.Connection" )
Con.Open "FILE NAME=c:\myDataLink.UDL"
Set RS = Server.CreateObject( "ADODB.Recordset" )
RS.LockType = adLockOptimistic
RS.Open "SELECT  * FROM Webusers WHERE 1<>1", Con
RS.AddNew
RS( "username" ) = "Andrew Jones"
RS( "password" ) = "won't say"
RS.Update
%>
```

This script opens a Recordset with an optimistic locking type and adds a new record to a table named Webusers.

How Can I Limit the Number of Rows Returned by a Database Query?

If you are using Microsoft SQL 7.0 or Microsoft Access, you can use the SQL TOP keyword to limit the number of records returned. Otherwise, if you are using Microsoft SQL 6.5, use the MaxRecords property of the Recordset object like this:

```
<%
Set Con = Server.CreateObject( "ADODB.Connection" )
Con.Open "FILE NAME=c:\myDataLink.UDL;DATABASE=pubs"
Set RS = Server.CreateObject( "ADODB.Recordset" )
RS.MaxRecords = 15
RS.Open "SELECT * FROM Authors ORDER BY au_lname", Con
While not RS.EOF
  Response.Write RS( "au_lname" ) & "<br>"
  RS.MoveNext
Wend
%>
```

How Do I Retrieve the Value from a SQL Statement That Uses COUNT(*), MAX, MIN, or @@IDENTITY?

There are two methods that you can use to retrieve the value from a SQL function or a SQL global variable. You can either use an alias for the value or refer to the value by its ordinal position in the Recordset. The following example displays the value returned from SQL COUNT(*) using both methods:

```
<%
mySQL = "SELECT COUNT(*) theCount from Authors"
Set Con = Server.CreateObject( "ADODB.Connection" )
Con.Open "FILE NAME=c:\myDataLink.UDL;DATABASE=pubs"
SET RS = Con.Execute( mySQL )
Response.Write RS( "theCount" )
Response.Write RS( 0 )
%>
```

The first Response.Write statement uses the alias theCount. The second Response.Write statement uses the ordinal position of the value.

How Do I Retrieve an Output Parameter from a SQL Stored Procedure Within an Active Server Page Script?

To retrieve an output parameter or a return code, you must use the ADO Command and Parameter objects.

Form and Query String Questions

What Causes the Value of a Form Field to Become Truncated?

HTML uses quotation marks to mark the beginning and end of a value. So, if a variable contains quotation marks in its value, the value of the variable will be truncated when displayed. For example, the HTML form in the following script will not display correctly:

```
<%
myVar = "He said, ""Hello!"""
%>
<form method="post" action="page.asp">
<input name="myfield" type="text"
  value="<%=myVar%>">
```

```
<input type="submit" value="Enter">
</form>
```

Instead of displaying the string He said, "Hello!" as the value of the form element, the value He said, appears. Every character after and including the " is cut off. To get around this problem, HTML encode the string before displaying it, like this:

```
<%
myVar = Server.HTMLEncode( "He said, ""Hello!""" )
%>
<form method="post" action="page.asp">
<input name="myfield" type="text"
  value="<%=myVar%>">
<input type="submit" value="Enter">
</form>
```

B

How Can I Include Spaces or Other Special Characters in a Query String?

To include spaces or other special characters—such as periods and quotation marks—in a query string, URL encode the query string. The following example correctly encodes a query string before displaying it:

```
<%
myVar = Server.URLEncode( "He said, ""Hello!""" )
%>
<a href="page.asp?qvar=<%=myVar%>">Go</a>
```

Questions About Active Server Pages Web Sites

Do Any Internet Service Providers Host Active Server Pages?

Several good Internet service providers host sites that use Active Server Pages and SQL Server. Two examples are Bitshop (www.bitshop.com) and Data Return (www.datareturn.com). Both companies enable you to administer an Active Server Page site remotely using Microsoft Visual InterDev and Microsoft SQL Server Enterprise Manager.

What Good Web Sites Have Information on Active Server Pages?

The number of good Web sites that have information on Active Server Pages is growing quickly. Here is a list of some of the Web sites that I visit on a weekly basis:

www.aspsite.com   The companion Web site to this book.

www.15seconds.com   This Web site has thousands of pages of information on Active Server Pages.

www.activeserverpages.com   This Web site has a great component section and several interesting articles.

www.asphole.com   This Web site contains lists of components and articles related to Active Server Pages.

www.swynk.com   Good site for information on Active Server Pages and SQL Server.

www.microsoft.com/iis   Microsoft's Internet Information Server site.

APPENDIX C

SQL Reference

This appendix provides a brief reference for the Microsoft SQL Server statements and stored procedures that you will find yourself using most often while programming Active Server Pages. However, SQL is a complicated language, and this appendix cannot even begin to cover all its nuances. The syntax of many of the SQL statements and functions has been simplified in this appendix. To learn everything you'd ever need to know about using SQL with Microsoft SQL Server, rush to your local bookstore and buy *Microsoft SQL Server 7.0 Unleashed* by Greg Mable, et al. (1999, Sams Publishing, ISBN 0-672-31227-1).

SQL Statements

The following SQL statements enable you to create and remove database tables and stored procedures, retrieve data from a database table, modify table data, and grant permissions on database objects.

SELECT

```
SELECT [TOP [PERCENT]] select_list
FROM table_source
WHERE search_condition
ORDER BY order_by_expression
```

The SELECT statement is used to retrieve one or more rows from a database table. Instead of listing particular column names in the *select_list*, you can also use * as a wildcard character to represent all columns.

Examples

- Using SELECT to retrieve all the columns and all the rows from the Authors table:

```
SELECT * FROM Authors
```

- Using SELECT to retrieve the last name of the author who has the first name Andrew:

```
SELECT au_lname
FROM Authors
WHERE au_fname = 'Andrew'
```

- Using SELECT to retrieve a list of publishers and book titles. The results are ordered by the name of the publisher:

```
SELECT pub_name, title
FROM publishers,titles
WHERE publishers.pub_id = titles.pub_id
ORDER BY pub_name
```

- Using SELECT to retrieve the names of the first 10 authors from the Authors table in order of the last name.

```
SELECT TOP 10 au_fname, au_lname
FROM Authors
ORDER BY au_lname
```

INSERT

```
INSERT table_name ( column_list )
VALUES ( value_list )
```

The INSERT statement is used to insert one or more rows into a database table (Microsoft Access uses INSERT INTO).

Examples

- Using INSERT to add a new username and password to a Passwords table.

```
INSERT Passwords ( username, password )
VALUES ( 'Andrew', 'Jones' )
```

- Using INSERT with SELECT to insert multiple rows into the newPasswords table from the oldPasswords table:

```
INSERT newPassword ( username, password )
SELECT username, password
FROM oldPasswords
```

UPDATE

```
UPDATE table_name
SET column_name = value
WHERE search_condition
```

The UPDATE statement is used to update one or more rows in a database table.

Examples

- Using UPDATE to change the password in every row in a table named Passwords where the username column has the value Andrew Jones:

```
UPDATE Passwords
SET password = 'secret'
WHERE username = 'Andrew Jones'
```

- Using UPDATE to change the values of multiple columns all at once:

```
UPDATE Passwords
SET username = 'Bill Gates',
    password = 'Billions'
WHERE username = 'Andrew Jones'
```

DELETE

```
DELETE table_name
WHERE search_condition
```

The DELETE statement is used to delete one or more rows from a database table.

Example

- Using DELETE to remove all the rows from the Passwords table in which the password column has the value secret:

```
DELETE Passwords
WHERE password = 'secret'
```

TRUNCATE TABLE

```
TRUNCATE TABLE table_name
```

This statement efficiently removes all the rows from a table.

Example

- Using TRUNCATE TABLE to remove all the rows from the Passwords table:

```
TRUNCATE TABLE Passwords
```

CREATE TABLE

```
CREATE TABLE table_name
( column_name data_type [,...n] )
```

The CREATE TABLE statement is used to create a new database table. See the later section, "SQL Server Data Types," for a list of data types that you can use when defining the columns for a table.

Examples

- Using CREATE TABLE to create a table named Passwords that contains usernames and passwords:

```
CREATE TABLE Passwords
( username VARCHAR( 50 ), password VARCHAR( 50 ) )
```

- Using CREATE TABLE to create a table with an IDENTITY column:

```
CREATE TABLE WebUsers
( user_id INT IDENTITY, username VARCHAR( 50 ) )
```

- Using CREATE TABLE to create a table with a column with a default value of the current data and time:

```
CREATE TABLE WebUsers
(
  username VARCHAR( 50 ),
  entrydate DATETIME DEFAULT GETDATE()
)
```

CREATE PROCEDURE

```
CREATE PROCEDURE procedure_name
[ @parameter_name data_type [OUTPUT] ]
[,...n]
AS
sql_statement [,...n]
```

The CREATE PROCEDURE statement is used to create a new SQL Server stored procedure.

Examples

- Using CREATE PROCEDURE to create a new stored procedure that retrieves all the rows from the Passwords table:

```
CREATE PROCEDURE getPasswords
AS
SELECT * FROM Passwords
```

- Using CREATE PROCEDURE to create a new stored procedure that accepts an input parameter and returns an output parameter:

```
CREATE PROCEDURE getUsername
(
  @password VARCHAR( 50 ),
  @username VARCHAR( 50 ) OUTPUT
)
AS
SELECT @username = username
FROM Passwords
WHERE password = @password
```

GRANT

```
GRANT ALL | permission
ON table | stored_procedure
TO security_account
```

The GRANT statement assigns permissions to use a database object to a database user or role.

Examples

- Using GRANT to give SELECT permission to the database user named WebUser for the table named Passwords:

  ```
  GRANT SELECT ON Passwords TO WebUser
  ```

- Granting all permissions on a table named Passwords to the public role.

  ```
  GRANT ALL ON Passwords TO public
  ```

DROP TABLE

```
DROP TABLE table_name
```

This statement permanently removes a database table.

Example

- Using DROP TABLE to permanently remove a table named Passwords:

  ```
  DROP TABLE Passwords
  ```

DROP PROCEDURE

```
DROP PROCEDURE procedure_name
```

This statement permanently removes a stored procedure.

Example

- Using DROP PROCEDURE to permanently remove a stored procedure named getPasswords:

  ```
  DROP PROCEDURE getPasswords
  ```

EXECUTE

```
EXECUTE
[@return_code = ] procedure_name
[@parameter = value | @variable [OUTPUT] ]
[,...n]
```

The EXECUTE statement is used to run a SQL stored procedure.

Examples

- Using EXECUTE to execute the getPasswords stored procedure:

  ```
  EXECUTE getPasswords
  ```

- Using EXECUTE to execute a stored procedure named getValue that returns a return code:

  ```
  DECLARE @returnCode INT
  EXECUTE @returnCode = getValue
  SELECT @returnCode
  ```

- Using EXECUTE to execute a stored procedure that has both an input parameter and an output parameter:

  ```
  DECLARE @password VARCHAR( 20 )
  EXECUTE getPassword 'Andrew Jones', @password OUTPUT
  SELECT @password
  ```

USE

```
USE database_name
```

The USE statement is used to specify the database in which subsequent SQL statements will be executed.

Example

- In this example, the USE statement switches the database to the master database. The sp_help statement is used to display all the objects in the database.

  ```
  USE Master
  sp_help
  ```

SQL Functions

All the following functions can be used with the SELECT statement. The majority of these functions can be used to retrieve summary information about the data stored in a table column.

GETDATE

GETDATE()

This function returns the current date and time.

Example

- Using GETDATE() to display the current date and time:

  SELECT GETDATE()

AVG

AVG(column_name)

The AVG function is used to retrieve the average value for a table column.

Example

- Using AVG to return the average number of times that all users have visited a Web site.

  SELECT AVG(user_numvisits)
  FROM WebUsers

COUNT

COUNT(* | column_name)

The COUNT function is used to retrieve either a count of the number of rows in a database table or a count of the number of rows in which a certain column has a value.

Examples

- Using COUNT to return the number of rows in a table named WebUsers:

  SELECT COUNT(*)
  FROM WebUsers

- Using COUNT to return the number of rows in a table named WebUsers where the username column does not have a NULL value:

  SELECT COUNT(username)
  FROM WebUsers

MAX

MAX(column_name)

The MAX function is used to retrieve the maximum value for a table column.

Example

- Using MAX to return the maximum number of times that any user has visited a Web site:

```
SELECT MAX( user_numvisits )
FROM WebUsers
```

MIN

```
MIN( column_name )
```

The MIN function is used to retrieve the minimum value for a table column.

Example

- Using MIN to return the minimum number of times that any user has visited a Web site:

```
SELECT MIN( user_numvisits )
FROM WebUsers
```

SUM

```
SUM( column_name )
```

The SUM function is used to add the values of a column.

Example

- Using SUM to return total number of times that a Web site has been visited:

```
SELECT SUM( user_numvisits )
FROM WebUsers
```

SQL Global Variables

The following two global variables can be used with the SELECT statement.

@@IDENTITY

The SQL Server global @@IDENTITY variable contains the value of an IDENTITY column after a row has been inserted.

Example

- This example assumes that the table named WebUsers has an IDENTITY column named user_id. After a row is inserted into the table, the value of the IDENTITY column for the new row is returned with the @@IDENTITY variable:

```
INSERT WebUsers ( username ) VALUES ( 'Andrew Jones' )
SELECT @@IDENTITY
```

@@ROWCOUNT

This variable contains a value representing the number of rows that the last statement affected.

Example

- This example displays the number of rows that were modified by an UPDATE statement using the @@ROWCOUNT variable:

```
UPDATE Passwords
SET username = 'Bill Gates'
WHERE password = 'Billions'
SELECT @@ROWCOUNT
```

SQL Server Stored Procedures

The following two system stored procedures can be used to retrieve information about the objects in a database.

sp_help

```
sp_help [table_name | procedure_name ]
```

The sp_help system stored procedure is used to display information on database objects. When used without a table or procedure name, it lists the properties of all the objects in the current database.

Examples

- Using sp_help to display information about the WebUsers table (Returns information including the table columns, indexes and constraints):

```
sp_help WebUsers
```

- Using sp_help to display information about the stored procedure named getAuthors (Returns information including the date and time the procedure was created):

```
sp_help getAuthors
```

sp_helptext

```
sp_helptext procedure_name
```

The sp_helptext system stored procedure can be used to display the SQL statements that constitute a SQL stored procedure.

Examples

- Using `sp_helptext` to display the contents of the `getAuthors` stored procedure:

```
sp_helptext getAuthors
```

- Using `sp_helptext` to display the contents of the `sp_helptext` system stored procedure:

```
USE master
sp_helptext sp_helptext
```

SQL Server Data Types

You can use any of the data types in Tables D.1–D.6 when defining table columns or local variables:

TABLE C.1 Character Data Types

Data Type	Description
CHAR	Fixed-length character data with a maximum size of 8,000 characters.
VARCHAR	Variable-length character data with a maximum size of 8,000 characters.
TEXT	Variable-length character data with a maximum size of 2,147,483,647 characters.
NCHAR	Unicode fixed-length character data with a maximum size of 4,000 characters.
NVARCHAR	Unicode variable-length character data with a maximum size of 4,000 characters.
NTEXT	Unicode Variable-length character data with a maximum size of 1,073,741,823 characters.

TABLE C.2 Numeric Data Types

Data Type	Description
BIT	Has the value 0 or 1.
INTEGER	Integer data between −2,147,483,648 and 2,147,483,647.
SMALLINT	Integer data between −32,768 and 32,767.
NUMERIC	Fixed precision and scale numeric data between $-10^{38}-1$ and $10^{38}-1$.
DECIMAL	Same as NUMERIC
FLOAT	Floating precision data type between $-1.79E+308$ through $1.79E+308$.
REAL	Floating precision data type between $-3.40E+38$ through $3.40E+38$.

TABLE C.3 Date and Time Data Types

Data Type	Description
DATETIME	Can have a value between January 1, 1753, and December 31, 9999 (accurate to 3.33 milliseconds)
SMALLDATETIME	Can have a value between January 1, 1900, through June 6, 2079 (accurate to one minute)

TABLE C.4 Money Data Types

Data Type	Description
MONEY	Can have a value between –922,337,203,685,477.5808 and 922,337,203,685,477.5807.
SMALLMONEY	Can have a value between –214,748.3648 and 214,748.3647.

TABLE C.5 Binary Data Types

Data Type	Description
BINARY	Fixed-length binary data with a maximum size of 8,000 bytes.
VARBINARY	Variable-length binary data with a maximum size of 8,000 bytes.
IMAGE	Variable-length binary data with a maximum size of 2,147,483,647 bytes.

TABLE C.6 Miscellaneous Data Types

Data Type	Description
CURSOR	Used with stored procedures that have a reference to a cursor as an OUTPUT parameter.
TIMESTAMP	Provides a database-wide unique identifier.
UNIQUEIDENTIFIER	Provides a Globally Unique Identifier (GUID).

C

INDEX

Symbols

#INCLUDE directive, 70
" (quotation marks), 24-25
Access databases and,
102-104
displaying, 24-25
HTML forms and,
112-113
<%=...%> output delim-
iters, 26
% (percent sign), 153
@TRANSACTION direc-
tive, 215, 234

A

Abandon method, 56-57
abandoned transactions,
467-468

AbsolutePage property
(Recordset object), 134
abstracts, 499
Access, 11
disadvantages, 118
product catalog databases
connecting to, 93-95
creating, 89-90
manageproducts.asp
page, 100-102,
113-117
Products table, 91-93
records, adding, 95-100
retrieving information
from, 106-108
updating, 104-105,
109-112
upgrading to SQL
Server, 90
quotation marks, 102-104
starting, 90
access control, Internet
Service Manager, 379-384

Account page (order track-
ing), 260
account.asp page, 260-261
showorders.asp page,
262-263
showOrderStatus method,
263-264
accounts
Administrator, 331-332
CyberCash, 241-242
ACID test, 214
acquiring financial institu-
tions (CyberCash), 241
active customers, display-
ing, 64-65
Active Data Objects. *See*
ADOs
Active Server Pages. *See*
ASPs
Ad Rotator component, 16,
514-515
implementing, 516-517
redirection files, 515
schedule files, 515-516

ad targeting, 513
Add User script (database authentication), 281-282
addCart.asp page, 206-211
addCookie method, 181
addForm method, 247
AddNew method, 201-202
addProduct.asp page, 97-100, 396-397
addresses (IP)
  retrieving, 41-42
  second IP addresses, 347-349
addUser method, 176-178, 488-489
administration
  Administrator accounts, 331-332
  ASP (Active Server Page) administrative pages, 389
    addProduct.asp, 396-397
    adminPage.asp, 405-406
    donePost.asp, 401-405
    passwords, 390
    Posting Acceptor, 391-395
    storeFuncs.asp, 393
    updateProduct.asp, 398-401
    upload.asp, 393-394
  FTP (File Transport Protocol) Service, 385
    anonymous access, 386
    configuring, 386-387
    CuteFTP, 389
    file uploads, 387-389
    installing, 385-386

Internet Service Manager (HTML), 377-378
  access restrictions, 379-384
  installing, 378-379
  remote administration tasks, 384
Administrator accounts, 331-332
adminPage.asp page, 405-406
ADO (Active Data Objects)
  database updates, 200
    adding records, 201-202
    deleting records, 203-204
    editing records, 202-203
  Recordset object, 119
    displaying records in, 119-121
    methods, 148-149, 201-203
    opening, 121-122
    properties, 122-123, 134, 200-201
  transactions, 218-219, 234
    example of, 218-219
    marking end of, 218
    stopping, 218
Advanced Server (Windows 2000), 11
advertising, 495-496
  Ad Rotator component, 514-515
    implementing, 516-517
    redirection files, 515
    schedule files, 515-516
  ad targeting, 513
  affiliate programs, 514

banner ads, 510
  link exchanges, 510-512
  purchasing, 513
  bulk mailings, 428
  marketing, 438
  message composition, 432-435
  recipients, 429-432
  sending messages, 435-437
  Children's Advertising Review Unit, 342-343
  favorite product categories (customized ads), 307
    default.asp page modifications, 315-316
    displaying featured products, 313-315
    retrieving, 310-311
    saving, 311-312
    selecting, 308-310
    storing, 307
    updating, 312
  reward/loyalty programs, 513-514
  search engines, 496
    listing sites with, 496-508
    spidering process, 496
  Web rings, 508-510
affiliate programs, 514
algorithms
  Luhn check, 189
  popularity algorithms, 507-508
alreadyUser method, 180
analyzing site usage logs, 455
  ASPs (Active Server Pages), 462-464
  commercial log-analysis tools, 464

anonymous access
FTP (File Transport
Protocol) Service, 386
Posting Acceptor, 393
appending text files, 81
Application arrays, 60
creating, 60
modifying elements in, 61
application fees (banks), 241
Application objects, 15
Application variables, 57
creating, 57-58
hit counter applications,
58-60
locking, 60
removing from memory
Remove method, 61
RemoveAll method, 62
storing arrays in, 60-61
**Application_OnEnd events,
63**
**Application_OnStart events,
63**
**applying for server certifi-
cates, 186-187**
arrays
Application arrays, 60
creating, 60
modifying elements in,
61
localCart, 198
Session arrays, 198-199
changing value of, 55
creating, 54-55
**asLockBatchOptimistic
value (Recordset
LockType property), 201**
**asLockOptimistic value
(Recordset LockType
property), 201**

**asLockPessimistic value
(Recordset LockType
property), 201**
**asLockReadOnly value
(Recordset LockType
property), 201**
asp filename extension, 71
ASPError objects, 15
**ASPs (Active Server Pages),
13-14.** *See also names of
specific pages*
administrative pages, 389
addProduct.asp,
396-397
adminPage.asp,
405-406
donePost.asp, 401-405
passwords, 390
Posting Acceptor,
391-395
storeFuncs.asp, 393
updateProduct.asp,
398-401
upload.asp, 393-394
components
Ad Rotator, 16,
514-517
Browser Capabilities,
16
Content Linking, 16
definition of, 15
File Access. *See* File
Access component
third-party compo-
nents, 17
current page name, retrieving, 39-40
customer survey form, 84
form data, saving,
85-86
marketing form, 84

database access, 17
definition of, 13
files
appending, 81
copying, 81-82
creating, 78-79
deleting, 82
including, 69-74
listing, 83-84
moving, 82
reading, 79-80
redirection, 75-76
verifying existance of,
83
writing to, 79
last page visited, retrieving, 41
limitations of, 18
objects. *See names of
specific objects*
operating system compata-
bility, 18
physical path, 40-41
scripting languages, 14
security, 428-429
sending email from, 415
CDONTS constants,
417-419
HTML mail, 423-428
Newmail.Send method,
415-416
on errors, 419-420
to new users, 421-422
verbose option,
416-417
SSL (Secure Sockets
Layer) and, 187-188
transactional pages, 214
error handling,
215-218
example of, 215

AtEndOfLine property (FileSystemObject object), 80

AtEndOfStream property (FileSystemObject object), 80

Auth/PostAuthCapture model (CyberCash), 254

AuthCapture model (CyberCash), 254

authentication

database authentication, 276-277

Add User scripts, 281-282

example of, 284-285

login pages, 278-280

login validation, 283-284

registration forms, 278

server load, 295

user authentication, 282

HTTP (Hypertext Transport Protocol), 274

basic authentication, 274, 288

digest authentication, 274

enabling, 275-276

integrated authentication, 274

when to use, 276

hybrid

decoding AUTHORIZATION headers, 290-292

forcing password dialogs, 288-289

hybrid.asp example, 292-294

security information, passing from page to page, 285

cookies, 286

hidden form fields, 287

query strings, 286-287

Session variables, 286

AUTHORIZATION headers, decoding, 290

Decode method, 291-292

UUEncoding, 290-291

authorize method, 250

Authorize.asp page, 245-248

Authorize.Net WebLink service, 238

authorizeFunction.asp page, 249-250

authorizing transactions (CyberCash), 245

Authorize.asp page, 245-248

authorizeFunction.asp page, 249-250

MessageBlock component, 245

processCards.asp page, 250-252

processCards2.asp page, 252-253

Socket component, 245

B

banks (CyberCash), 241

banner ads, 510

link exchanges, 510-512

purchasing, 513

base64 text, decoding, 290

Decode method, 291-292

UUEncoding, 290-291

basic authentication (HTTP), 274, 288

batches of email. *See* **bulk mailings**

BBBOnline privacy program, 341

beginning ADO (ActiveX Data Object) transactions, 218

BeginTrans method, 218

Better Business Bureau

Children's Advertising Review Unit, 342-343

Reliability Program, 338-339

bots, 456

breakpoints

definition of, 354

setting, 357

Browser Capabilities component, 16

browsers

cookies

adding, 50-51

displaying, 52

reading, 51-52

storing, 49

redirecting, 75

alternatives to, 76

disadvantages of, 75-76

example of, 75

retrieving type of, 42-43

built-in objects. *See* **names of specific objects**

bulk mailings, 428

marketing, 438

message composition, 432-435

recipients, 429-432

sending messages, 435-437

business transactions. *See* transactions
business-to-business E-Commerce, 8
buttons, radio, 33
buying banner ads, 513
Bytes Received property (W3C Extended Log File format), 453
Bytes sent property (W3C Extended Log File format), 453

C

c-ip element (W3C Extended Log Files), 453
calculating shipping costs
    iisCARTship component, 264-269, 272
    sample application, 269-271
capturing
    credit card transactions (CyberCash), 254-256
    errors, 366
        CheckError method, 367-368
        log files, 369-372
        manageProducts.asp page, 368-369
        On Error Resume Next statement, 366
Cart table, 170, 205
cart.asp page, 172-174, 205
cart_id column (Cart table), 205
cart_productID column (Cart table), 205

cart_quantity column (Cart table), 205
cart_userID column (Cart table), 205
CARU (Children's Advertising Review Unit), 342-343
catalogs
    administration. *See* administration
    product catalog databases, 89
        adding records to, 95-100
        connecting to, 93-95
        creating, 89-90
        manageproducts.asp page, 100-102, 113-117
        Products table, 91-93
        quotation marks, 102-104
        retrieving information from, 106-108
        updating, 104-105, 109-112
        upgrading to SQL Server, 90
categories of products, designing, 125-126
CatList.asp page, 124-126
CDONTS (Collaborative Data Objects for NT Server)
    bugs, 414
    constants, 417-419
certificate authorities, 186
Certificate Request Files, 185-186
Certificate Signing Requests (CSRs), 185-186

certificates (server certificates)
    applying for, 186-187
    installing, 187
Certification Authorities, 336-337
changing. *See* editing
charge cards. *See* credit card transactions
CheckError method, 367-368
checkout pages (shopping cart), 213
    address/payment information
        retrieving, 220-221
        updating, 221-224
    customer items, transferring to Orders table, 224-226
    order completion, 219-220
    order processing, 226
        order status values, 226
        processOrders.asp page, 227-234
checkpassword method, 174
Children's Advertising Review Unit, 342-343
Chili!Soft's ChiliASP, 18
ChiliASP, 18
clauses (SQL)
    ORDER BY, 122
    WHERE, 121
cleanCCNum method, 180
click-throughs, 511
Client IP Address property (W3C Extended Log File format), 453
client processes, 387
client-server protocols, 387
client-side scripts, 408

client-side wallets, 469
  advantages/disadvantages,
    470-471
  obtaining, 469-470
code listings. *See* **listings**
Collaborative Data Objects
  for NT Server. *See*
  CDONTS
collections
  Form, 31
  ServerVariables, 39
  ShipInfo, 267
Column property
  (FileSystemObject object),
  80
columns
  Cart table, 205
  Products table, 91
CommitTrans method, 218
compareShip.asp page,
  269-271
completing orders, 219-220
  address/payment informa-
    tion, 220-224
  Orders table, transferring
    information to, 224-226
component-based solutions
  (credit card processing),
  239-240. *See also*
  CyberCash
components
  Ad Rotator, 16, 514-515
    implementing, 516-517
    redirection files, 515
    schedule files, 515-516
  Browser Capabilities, 16
  Content Linking, 16
  definition of, 15
  File Access, 16, 77
    appending files, 81
    copying files, 81-82

  creating files, 78-79
  customer survey form,
    84
  marketing form, 84
  deleting files, 82
  Drive object, 78
  File object, 77
  FileSystemObject
    object, 77-83
  Folder object, 77
  listing files, 83-84
  moving files, 82
  permissions, 77
  reading files, 79-80
  saving form data,
    85-86
  TextStream object, 77,
    80
  verifying file existance,
    83
  writing to files, 79
iisCARTship, 264
  installing, 265
  instantiating, 265
  methods, 266-269
  properties, 265-266
  sample application,
    269-271
  ShipInfo collection,
    267
  troubleshooting, 272
third-party components,
  17
composeMsg.asp page, 434
configLoc variable
  (CyberCash), 246
configuring
  FTP (File Transport
    Protocol) Service,
    386-387
  SMTP Service , 411-413

connecting to databases,
  93-95
consumer-to-consumer
  E-Commerce, 8
contants (CDONTS),
  417-419
Content Linking compo-
  nent, 16
converting UPS shipping
  codes, 267
Cookie Central Web site, 48
Cookie property (W3C
  Extended Log File for-
  mat), 454
cookies, 48, 286. *See also*
  Session variables
  adding to customers'
    browsers, 50-51
  alternatives to, 66
  Cookie Central Web site,
    48
  displaying, 52
  persistent cookies, 49
  reading, 49-52
  session cookies, 48
  storing, 49
  support for, 50
cooperating with other
  e-businesses
  affiliate programs, 514
  cooperative advertising,
    510
  link exchanges, 510-512
  Web rings
    definition of, 508
    example of, 508-510
cooperative advertising,
  510-512
CopyFile method, 81
copying text files, 81-82

cost of shipping, calculating
 iisCARTship component,
 264-269, 272
 sample application,
 269-271
cost per mille (CPM), 443
**counter application (page
 hits), 58-60**
counting customers, 63-64
**country codes (shipping),
 269**
**CountryList method,
 268-269**
**CPA WebTrust privacy pro-
 gram, 341**
CPM (cost per mille), 443
crawler.asp page, 506-507
**Create parameter
 (OpenTextFile method), 81**
**CreateStaticPage method,
 502-505**
CreateTextFile method, 78
**Credit Card Declined status
 (order processing), 226**
**credit card merchant
 accounts (CyberCash),
 241-242**
credit card transactions, 237
 credit card form, 37
 CyberCash, 240
  acquiring financial
   institutions, 241
  authorizing transac-
   tions, 245-253
  capturing transactions,
   254-256
  credit card merchant
   accounts, 241-242
  installation, 243-244
  MCK (Merchant
   Connection Kit), 243
  MessageBlock compo-
   nent, 245

 registration, 242-243
 security, 256
 Socket component, 245
 processing systems, 237
  choosing, 240
  component-based
   solutions, 239-240
  offsite payment proces-
   sors, 238-239
  payment terminal
   solutions, 239
 security
  Luhn check, 189
  SSL (Secure Sockets
   Layer), 183-188
  SET (Secure Electronic
   Transaction) stan-
   dard, 256
 SmartCards, 474
 standards, 475-476
Crocker, David, 410
**cs-method element (W3C
 Extended Log Files), 453**
**cs-uri-query element
 (W3C Extended Log
 Files), 453**
**cs-uri-stem element (W3C
 Extended Log Files), 453**
**cs-username element
 (W3C Extended Log
 Files), 453**
**cs-version element (W3C
 Extended Log Files), 453**
**cShipCompany property
 (ShipInfo collection), 267**
**CSRs (Certificate Signing
 Requests), 185-186**
**cTotalCharge property
 (ShipInfo collection), 267**
**current ASP (Active Server
 Page) name, retrieving,
 39-40**

**current time, displaying,
 13-14**
cursors, 122-123
**CursorType property
 (Recordset object),
 122-123**
custom store wallets, 476
 addUser method, 488-489
 doCheckout.asp page,
  481-483
 ECML (E-Commerce
  Modeling Language)
  standards, 483-487
 register.asp page, 477-480
 updateUser method,
  490-491
customer interfaces
 dynamic content, 22
  date/time, 22
  long strings, 23
  output delimiters, 26
  quotation marks ("),
   24-25
  special characters,
   23-24
  Write method, 22-23
 favorite product categories
  (customized ads), 307
  default.asp page modi-
   fications, 315-316
  displaying featured
   products, 313-315
  retrieving, 310-311
  saving, 311-312
  selecting, 308-310
  storing, 307
  updating, 312
 forms, 31
  credit card form, 37
  customer registration
   forms. *See* registra-
   tion forms

customer survey forms, 84-86

empty fields, 33-35

redisplaying field data in, 35-37

radio buttons, 33

Rate Our Store form, 32-33

retrieving information from, 31-32

simple HTML form example, 31

variables, 38-39

multiple-page product listings, 134-137

order tracking, 260

account.asp page, 260-261

advantages, 259-260

showorders.asp page, 262-263

showOrderStatus method, 263-264

past purchases, displaying, 302-306

product displays, 123-124

lists of all products, 126-128, 137-139

main store page, 128-130

product categories, 125-126

product details, 130-134

product names, 1 20-121

shopping carts. See shopping carts

script execution, ending, 26-27

user settings, 297

displaying, 300-301

retrieving, 298-300

wallets, 469

accepting information from, 492

client-side, 469-471

customizing. See custom store wallets

definition of, 469

server-side, 471-473

SmartCards, 474

standards, 475-476

customer survey form, 84-86

customers

registering, 172

cart.asp page, 172-174

error handling, 181-183

register.asp page, 174-175

security (SSL), 183-188

storefuncs.asp page, 176-181

returning formation about

browser types, 42-43

Internet addresses, 41-42

selecting for bulk mailings, 429-432

tracking

Application variables, 57-62

cookies, 48-52

Global.asa files, 62-65

Session variables, 52-57

CuteFTP, 389

CyberCash, 240

acquiring financial institutions, 241

authorizing transactions, 245

Authorize.asp page, 245-248

authorizeFunction.asp page, 249-250

processCards.asp page, 250-252

processCards2.asp page, 252-253

capturing transactions, 254-256

credit card merchant accounts, 241-242

installation, 243-244

MCK (Merchant Connection Kit), 243

MessageBlock component, 245

registration, 242-243

security, 256

Socket component, 245

D

data alteration, 336

Data Source Names (DSNs), 93

configuring, 277

creating, 93

database authentication, 276-277

Add User scripts, 281-282

example of, 284-285

login pages, 278, 280

login validation, 283-284

registration forms, 278

server load, 295
user authentication, 282
databases
Access, 11
accessing with ADOs
(Active Data Objects),
17
product catalog databases,
89
adding records to,
95-100
connecting to, 93-95
creating, 89-90
manageproducts.asp
page, 100-102,
113-117
Products table, 91-93
rretrieving information
from, 106-108
updating, 104-105,
109-112
upgrading to SQL
Server, 90
quotation marks, 102-104
records
adding, 201-202
deleting, 203-204
updating, 202-203
recordsets, 119
cursors, 122-123
displaying records in,
119-121
opening, 121-122
paging through,
134-137
security, 337-338
shopping carts, creating
with, 204
addCart.asp page,
206-211
Cart table, 205
cart.asp page, 205
Product.asp page, 205

site usage logs, loading,
460-461
SQL Server, 11-12
transaction databases,
169-171, 219
**date element (W3C
Extended Log Files), 452**
**Date property (W3C
Extended Log File for-
mat), 452**
date/time, displaying, 22
debug libraries, 366
debug.asp page, 370-371
debugging, 345-346
development systems,
346-347
deploying applications
to, 350-353
IP (Internet Protocol)
addresses, 347-349
Web sites, 349-350
production servers, 361
capturing errors,
366-372
debug libraries, 366
session variables,
362-366
scalability, 372-374
Visual InterDev integrated
debugger, 354
breakpoints, 357
enabling, 355
Locals window,
360-361
permissions, 356-357
watch window,
358-359
Decode method, 291-292
**decoding AUTHORIZA-
TION headers, 290**
Decode method, 291-292
UUEncoding, 290-291

Default SMTP Sites, 411
default.asp page, 315-316
**Default.asp page, 124,
128-130**
Delete method, 203-204
DeleteFile method, 82
deleting
Application variables, 61
Remove method, 61
RemoveAll method, 62
Session variables, 192
text files, 82
deploying applications
definition of, 350
Visual InterDev, 350-353
**DestCountry property
(iisCARTship component),
265**
Destination parameter
CopyFile method, 82
MoveFile method, 82
**DestPostal property
(iisCARTship component),
265**
**development systems,
346-347**
definition of, 346
deploying applications to,
350-353
IP (Internet Protocol)
addresses, 347-349
Web sites, 349-350
**digest authentication
(HTTP), 274**
directives
#INCLUDE, 70
@TRANSACTION, 215,
234
**directories, Products direc-
tory, 158**
discount rates (banks), 241

Disk Administrator utility, 332

Disk Management utility, 332

displaying

active customers, 64-65

cookies, 52

dynamic content, 22

date/time, 22

long strings, 23

output delimiters, 26

quotation marks ("), 24-25

special characters, 23-24

Write method, 22-23

form fields, 35-37

lists of featured products, 146-149

password dialog boxes, 288-289

past purchases, 302-306

products, 123-124

lists of all products, 126-128

main store page, 128-130

multiple-page product listings, 134-137

product categories, 125-126

product details, 130-134

records, 119-121

Session variables, 53-54

SessionIDs, 56

time, 13-14

user settings, 300-301

doCheckout.asp page, 481-483

domain names, registering, 326

Control Panel settings, 327-328

domain name registrars, 327

foreign domains, 326-327

donePost.asp page, 401-405

downloading

Personal Web Server, 10

SQL Server, 12

Drive object, 78

DSNs (Data Source Names), 93

configuring, 277

creating, 93

dynamic content, 22

date/time, 22

long strings, 23

output delimiters, 26

quotation marks ("), 24-25

special characters, 23-24

Write method, 22-23

dynamically including files, 73-74

E

e-businesses, cooperation among

affiliate programs, 514

cooperative advertising, 510

link exchanges, 510-512

Web rings, 508-510

e-commerce

business-to-business transactions, 8

business-to-consumer transactions, 8

compared to physical commerce, 468-469

consumer-to-consumer transactions, 8

definition of, 8

overview of, 7-8

ECML (E-Commerce Modeling Language) standards

custom store wallet application, 483-487

participating companies, 475-476

Ecom_* fields (User table), 484-487

EDI (Electronic Data Interchange), 9

editing

address/payment information, 221-224

Administrator account name, 331-332

database records

UPDATE statement, 104-105

updateProduct.asp page, 109-112

favorite product list, 312

Electronic Commerce Policy Web site, 9

Electronic Data Interchange (EDI), 9

electronic mail. *See* **email**

electronic wallets. *See* **wallets**

email, 409-410

bulk mailings, 428

marketing , 438

message composition, 432-435

recipients, 429-432

sending messages, 435-437

sending from ASPs (Active Server Pages)

  CDONTS constants, 417-419

  on errors, 419-420

  HTML mail, 423-428

  Newmail.Send method, 415-416

  to new users, 421-422

  verbose option, 416-417

SMTP Service

  configuring, 411-413

  installing, 412

empty form fields, checking for, 33-35

enabling

HTTP authentication, 275-276

SSL (Secure Sockets Layer), 185

Visual InterDev debugging, 355

End of File (EOF), 120

ending user sessions, 56-57

enumerating site usage logs, 457-459

EOF (End of File), 120

error handling

ASP page transactions, 215

  OnTransactionAbort event, 216-218

  OnTransactionCommit event, 218

capturing errors, 366

  CheckError method, 367-368

  log files, 369-372

manageProducts.asp page, 368-369

On Error Resume Next statement, 366

customer registration forms, 181-183

sending email on errors, 419-420

errorForm method, 181-183

errors occurred (error message), 211

events

Application_OnEnd, 63

Application_OnStart, 63

OnTransactionAbort, 216-218

OnTransactionCommit, 218

Session_OnEnd, 63

Session_OnStart, 63

exchange rates, 511

Execute method, 77

F

failure-badmoney status code (CyberCash), 248

failure-hard status code (CyberCash), 247

failure-q-or-cancel status code (CyberCash), 247

failure-q-or-discard status code (CyberCash), 247

failure-swversion status code (CyberCash), 248

FalseSpecifier parameter (OpenTextFile method), 81

FastCatList.asp page, 138

favorite products

default.asp page modifications, 315-316

displaying featured products, 313-315

retrieving, 310-311

saving, 311-312

selecting, 308-310

upating, 312

favorites.asp page, 308-310

FDXpack property (iisCARTship component), 266

FDXPick property (iisCARTship component), 266

featured products lists, 143-144

displaying on Web page, 146-149

optimizing display, 149-152

selecting products for, 144-146

featured.asp page, 313-315

fees (banking), 241

fields (form)

credit card form, 37

empty fields, 33-35

Rate Our Store form, 32-33

redisplaying data in, 35-37

retrieving information from, 31-32

File Access component, 16, 77

appending files, 81

copying files, 81-82

creating files, 78-79

customer survey form, 84
  form data, saving,
    85-86
  marketing form, 84
deleting files, 82
Drive object, 78
File object, 77
FileSystemObject object,
  77
    methods, 78-83
    properties, 80
Folder object, 77
listing files, 83-84
moving files, 82
permissions, 77
reading files, 79-80
TextStream object, 77, 80
verifying file existance, 83
writing to files, 79
FILE attribute
  #INCLUDE directive), 70
  <INPUT> tag, 391
**File DSNs (Data Source
  Names), 93**
**File New Database dialog
  box (Access), 90**
File object, 77
**file systems, NTFS (NT File
  System), 332-333**
File Transport Protocol. *See*
  FTP Service
FileExists method, 83
files. *See also names of
  specific files*
  appending, 81
  Certificate Request Files,
    185-186
  copying, 81-82
  creating, 78-79
  deleting, 82

including in ASPs (Active
  Server Pages), 69
    #INCLUDE directive,
      70
    advantages, 70
    dynamic includsion,
      73-74
    examples, 70-73
  listing, 83-84
  logs. *See* log files
  moving, 82
  reading, 79-80
  redirection files, 75, 515
    alternatives to, 76
    disadvantages of, 75-76
    example of, 75
  schedule files, 515-516
  uploading
    ASPs (Active Server
      Pages), 396-401
    FTP (File Transport
      Protocol) Service,
      387-389
    Posting Acceptor,
      391-395
    third-party upload
      components, 392
  verifying existance of, 83
  writing to, 79
**FileSpecifier parameter
  (CreateTextFile method),
  78**
**FileSystemObject object, 77,
  370**
  methods
    CopyFile, 81
    CreateTextFile, 78
    DeleteFile, 82
    FileExists, 83
    MoveFile, 82
  properties, 80

firewalls, 334
fixQuotes method, 103-104
Folder object, 77
**FOR...NEXT loops (shop-
  ping cart application), 198**
**forcing password dialog
  boxes, 288-289**
Form collection, 31. *See also*
  forms
**Format parameter
  (OpenTextFile method), 81**
formats (log files)
  Microsoft IIS Log File
    format, 449-451
  NCSA Common Log File
    format, 444-446
  ODBC Logging format,
    446-449
  W3C Extended Log File
    format, 451-455
formFields method, 183
forms, 31. *See also* **ASPs
  (Active Server Pages)**
  credit card form, 37
  customer registration
    forms, 172
    cart.asp page, 172-174
    error handling,
      181-183
    register.asp page,
      174-175
    security (SSL),
      183-188
    storefuncs.asp page,
      176-181
  customer survey form,
    84-86
  empty fields, 33-35
  hidden fields, 287
  radio buttons, 33

Rate Our Store form, 32-33
redisplaying field data in, 35-37
retrieving information from, 31-32
simple HTML form example, 31
variables, 38-39
FrontPage, 12
FTP (File Transport Protocol) Service, 385
anonymous access, 386
configuring, 386-387
CuteFTP, 389
file uploads, 387-389
installing, 385-386
Full-text Search Service, 157
functions. *See* methods

G

general server-side wallets, 472-473
GetRows method (Recordset object), 148-149
Global.asa file, 62-63
counting customers, 63-64
displaying active customers, 64-65
GUIs (graphical user interfaces). *See* customer interfaces

H

header files
AUTHORIZATION headers, decoding, 290
Decode method, 291-292
UUEncoding, 290-291
including in ASPs (Active Server Pages)
header files with variables, 71-72
#INCLUDE directive, 70
standardheader.asp file, 71
Hello, World program, 16
hidden form fields, 287
hit counter application, 58-60
hits, 443
home pages, creating, 128-130
hot areas, 499
hot fixes, 330-331
HTML (Hypertext Markup Language)
HTML mail, sending, 423
register.asp, 423-425
sendNewUserMail method, 426-428
storeFuncs.asp, 423-425
tags
<INPUT>, 391
<META>, 72, 499
<TITLE>, 499
HTMLEncode method, 113, 116

I

HTTP (Hypertext Transport Protocol) authentication, 274
basic authentication, 274, 288
digest authentication, 274
enabling, 275-276
integrated authentication, 274
when to use, 276
Http Status property (W3C Extended Log File format), 453
hybrid.asp page (hybrid authentication), 292-294

I

iBill service, 238
ICVerify software, 239
iDebugLevel variable
resetting in adminPage.asp, 363-364
setting to 0, 362
IDs, SessionIDs, 56
IIS (Internet Information Server), 10
Internet Service Manager (HTML), 377-378
access restrictions, 379-384
installing, 378-379
remote administration tasks, 384
site usage logs, 441-444
analyzing, 455, 462-464
enumerating, 457-459
limitations of, 456

loading into databases, 460-461

Microsoft IIS Log File format, 449-451

NCSA Common Log File format, 444-446

ODBC Logging format, 446-449

W3C Extended Log File format, 451-455

iisCARTship component, 264

installing, 265

instantiating, 265

methods

CountryList, 268-269

LimitServices, 268

ShipCalc, 266-267

UPSproductConversion, 267

properties, 265-266

sample application, 269-271

ShipInfo collection, 267

troubleshooting, 272

impressions, 443, 511

#INCLUDE directive, 70

Index Server, 157

indexable Web pages, 158-159

indexing (search engines), 496

<INPUT> tag (HTML), 391

INSERT INTO statement (SQL), 95-96

installing

CyberCash, 243-244

FTP (File Transport Protocol) Service, 385-386

iisCARTship component, 265

Internet Service Manager (HTML), 378-379

server certificates, 187

SMTP Service , 412

Windows NT Server, 330

instantiating iisCARTship component, 265

integrated authentication (HTTP), 274

Internet Information Server. See IIS

Internet mail. See email

Internet Protocol. See IP addresses

Internet Service Manager (HTML), 377-378

access restrictions, 379-384

installing, 378-379

remote administration tasks, 384

invalidEmail method, 178

IOMode parameter (OpenTextFile method), 81

IP (Internet Protocol) addresses

retrieving, 41-42

second IP addresses, 347-349

isArray method, 198

ISPs (Internet Service Providers), outsourcing server operations to, 329, 335

J-L

legal issues

SQL Server licensing requirements, 12

United States Government Electronic Commerce Policy Web site, 9

LIKE operator (SQL), 152

LimitServices method, 268

Line property (FileSystemObject object), 80

link exchanges, 510-512

list of featured products, 143-144

displaying on Web page, 146-149

optimizing display, 149-152

selecting products for, 144-146

listing files, 83-84

listings

Abandon method, 56

Ad Rotator component, 16

implementing, 517

redirection file, 515

schedule file, 516

administrative pages

addProduct.asp, 396-397

adminPage.asp, 406

donePost.asp, 402-405

storeFuncs.asp, 393

updateProduct.asp, 398-400

upload.asp, 394

ADO (ActiveX Data Object) transactions, 218

Application arrays
  creating, 60
  modifying elements in,
    61
ASP page transactions
  example of, 215
  OnTransactionAbort
    event, 216
  transaction.asp,
    216-217
AUTHORIZATION head-
  ers, decoding
  Decode method,
    291-292
  UUEncoding, 291
bulk mailings
  message composition,
    434
  selecting recipients,
    429-431
  sending messages, 435,
    437
checkout page
  processOrders.asp,
    228-233
  retrieving customer
    data, 220-221
  transferring items to
    Orders table, 225
  updating customer
    data, 222-223
cookies, displaying, 52
customer registration form
  addCookie subroutine,
    181
  addUser subroutine,
    176-178
  alreadyUser subrou-
    tine, 180
  cart.asp page, 172-173

cleanCCNum subrou-
    tine, 180
  errorForm subroutine,
    182-183
  formFields subroutine,
    183
  invalidEmail subrou-
    tine, 178
  validCCNumber
    subroutine, 179
customer survey form
  marketing form, 84
  saving form data, 85
customized ads
  favorites.asp page,
    308-309
  featured.asp page,
    313-314
  retrieveFavorites
    method, 310
  savefavorites.asp page,
    311-312
  updateFavorites
    method, 312
CyberCash
  Authorize.asp page,
    245-246
  authorizeFunction.asp
    page, 249-250
  processCards.asp page,
    251-252
  processCards2.asp
    page, 253
DailyHits.asp, 462-463
database authentication
  Add User script, 281
  Login page, 279
  Registration page, 278
  user authentication,
    282
  username/password
    validation, 283

debugging
  CheckError method,
    367-368
  debug.asp page,
    370-371
  iDebugLevel, 362-364
  manageProducts.asp
    page, 369
  updateProducts.asp
    page, 365
dynamic content
  HTML-encoding
    strings, 24
  long strings, 23
  multiple values, 26
  output delimiters, 26
  quotation marks, 24-25
  time/date display, 22
  Write method, 23
email, sending from ASPs
  (Active Server Pages)
  CDONTS constants,
    418
  on errors, 419-420
  HTML mail, 424-427
  to new users, 422
  simple example, 415
  verbose option, 417
file redirection
  alternative to, 76
  example of, 75
files, including in ASPs
  (Active Server Pages)
  header file with vari-
    ables, 72
  header files, 70
  improper dynamic
    include, 73
  proper dynamic
    include, 74

standard functions, 73
standardfooter.asp
page, 71
standardfuncs.asp page,
73
standardheader.asp
page, 71
forms
Credit Card form, 34,
37
empty form fields,
34-35
HTML form and query
string, 38
radio buttons, 33
Rate Our Store from,
32-33
redisplaying field data,
36
retrieving information
from, 31
simple HTML form,
31
variables, retrieving, 38
Global.asa files
counting customers,
63-64
displaying count of
customers, 64
Hello, World program, 16
hybrid authentication,
292-293
iisCARTship component
compareShip.asp page,
269-271
CountryList method,
269
Federal Express prop-
erties, 266
LimitServices method,
268

ShipCalc method,
266-267
UPSproductConversion
method, 268
list of featured products
displaying, 147-148
optimizing display,
150-151
reset featured products,
151
ListLogs.asp, 457-459
log files, loading into
databases, 460-461
mypage.asp
displaying user set-
tings, 300-301
retrieving user settings,
298-299
order tracking (Account
page)
account.asp page,
261
showorders.asp page,
262-263
showOrderStatus
method, 263-264
page counters
better page counter, 59
simple page counter,
58
password dialogs, forcing,
289
pastpurchases.asp page,
303-305
product catalog database
addProduct.asp page,
98-100
adding records to,
95-96
connecting to, 94
displaying links, 108

fixQuotes method, 104
manageproducts.asp
page, 100-102,
113-116
retrieving product
names, 106
retrieving product
names as links, 107
table updates, 105
updateProduct.asp
page, 109-112
product IDs, retrieving,
159
products, displaying
fast product category
list, 138
lists of products,
126-127, 147-148,
150-151
main store pages,
128-130
multi-page product list-
ings, 135-136
product categories,
125
product details,
131-134
product names, 120
resetting product
categories, 139
query strings
example of, 28
multiple query string
variables, 29
query strings with
spaces, 30
retrieving, 28
URL-encoding a query
string, 30
variables, retrieving, 38

Recordset object
  AddNew method,
    201-202
  Delete method, 204
  Update method, 203
Remove method, 62
RemoveAll method, 62
script execution, ending,
  27
search engine results, 508
search pages, 153-157
security information,
  passing
    hidden form fields, 287
    query strings, 286-287
server variables
  REFERRER, 41
  REMOTE_ADDR, 42
  SCRIPT_NAME,
    39-40
  USER_AGENT, 42
Session arrays
  changing value of, 55
  creating, 55
Session variables
  creating, 53
  displaying, 54
SessionIDs, displaying, 56
shopping cart
  addCart.asp page,
    206-209
  sessionCart.asp page,
    194-196
showtime.asp
  content after process-
    ing, 14
  source code, 13
spider pages
  crawler.asp, 506-507
  CreateStaticPage
    method, 502-505
  example that won't
    work, 502

static cursors, 122
store wallet, creating
  addUser method,
    488-489
  doCheckout.asp page,
    481-483
  register.asp page,
    477-480
  updateUser method,
    490-491
text files
  appending to, 81
  copying, 82
  creating, 78
  deleting, 82
  listing, 83
  moving, 82
  reading, 79
  verifying existance of,
    83
Web rings, participating
  in, 509
lists of products
  catalog lists
    displaying, 126-128
    ordering, 140
    storing in memory,
      137-139
  featured products (cus-
    tomized ads), 143-144
    displaying on Web
      page, 146-149
    optimizing display,
      149-152
    selecting products for,
      144-146
loading site usage logs into
  databases, 460-461
localCart array, 198
Locals window (Visual
  InterDev debugger),
  360-361

locking
  Application variables, 60
  recordsets, 200-201
LockType property
  (Recordset object),
  200-201
log files
  capturing errors to,
    369-372
  definition of, 443
  site usage logs, 441-444
    analyzing, 455,
      462-464
    enumerating, 457-459
    limitations of, 456
    loading into databases,
      460-461
    Microsoft IIS Log File
      format, 449-451
    NCSA Common Log
      File format, 444-446
    ODBC Logging for-
      mat, 446-449
    W3C Extended Log
      File format,
      451-455
login pages (database
  authentication), 278-279
logs. *See* **log files**
loops
  FOR...NEXT, 198
  WHILE...WEND
    paging through record-
      sets, 120
    shopping cart applica-
      tion, 210
loyalty programs, 513-514
Luhn check, 189

M

MailFormat property (NewMail object), 422

main store pages, creating, 128-130

manageproducts.asp page, 100-102, 113-117, 368-369

MapPath method, 80

marketing form, 84

mass mailings. *See* **bulk mailings**

MCK (CyberCash), 243

memory

  Application variables, removing from, 61

    Remove method, 61

    RemoveAll method, 62

  lists of products, storing in, 137-139

merchandise. *See* **products**

Merchant Connection Kit (CyberCash), 243

MessageBlock component (CyberCash), 245

<META> tag (HTML), 72, 499

Method property (W3C Extended Log File format), 453

methods

  Abandon, 56-57

  addCookie, 181

  addForm, 247

  addUser, 176-178, 488-489

  AddNew, 201-202

  alreadyUser, 180

  authorize, 250

  BeginTrans, 218

  CheckError, 367-368

  checkpassword, 174

  cleanCCNum, 180

  CommitTrans, 218

  CopyFile, 81

  CountryList, 268-269

  CreateStaticPage, 502-505

  CreateTextFile, 78

  Decode, 291-292

  Delete, 203-204

  DeleteFile, 82

  errorForm, 181-183

  Execute, 77

  FileExists, 83

  fixQuotes, 103-104

  formFields, 183

  GetRows, 148-149

  HTMLEncode, 113, 116

  including in ASPs (Active Server Pages), 72-73

  invalidEmail, 178

  isArray, 198

  LimitServices, 268

  MapPath, 80

  MoveFile, 82

  OpenTextFile, 81

  Read, 80

  ReadAll, 80

  ReadLine, 80

  Redirect, 75

  Remove, 61

  RemoveAll, 62

  retrieveFavorites, 310-311

  RollbackTrans, 218

  Send, 415-416

  SendCCServer, 247

  sendNewUserMail, 421-422, 426-428

  SetAbort, 218

  SetComplete, 218

  ShipCalc, 266-267

  Skip, 80

  SkipLine, 80

  showOrderStatus, 263-264

  Transfer, 77

  Update, 202-203

  updateFavorites, 312

  updateUser, 222-223, 490-491

  UPSproductConversion, 267

  validatelogin, 282-283

  validCCNumber, 179

  Write, 22-23, 79

  WriteBlankLines, 79

  WriteLine, 78-79

Microsoft Access. *See* **Access**

Microsoft FrontPage, 12

Microsoft IIS Log File format, 449

  naming conventions, 449

  sample entry, 450-451

Microsoft Index Server, 157

Microsoft Internet Information Server. *See* **IIS**

Microsoft Personal Web Server. *See* **Personal Web Server**

Microsoft Posting Acceptor, 391-395

Microsoft SQL Server. *See* **SQL Server**

Microsoft Visual InterDev. *See* **Visual InterDev**

Microsoft WCAT (Web Capacity Analysis Tool), 372-373

Microsoft Web site

  Personal Web Server, 10

  Upsizing Tools, 90

mo.cybercash.id field (CyberCash MessageBlock component), 247

**mo.order-id field
(CyberCash MessageBlock
component), 247**
**mo.price field (CyberCash
MessageBlock compo-
nent), 247**
**mo.version field
(CyberCash MessageBlock
component), 247**
**monthly minimum fees
(banks), 241**
MoveFile method, 82
moving text files, 82
**MPProduct.asp page,
134-137**
multihoming, 347
mypage.asp page
displaying user settings,
300-301
retrieving user settings,
298-300

N

names
Administrator account
name, 331-332
domain names, 326-328
DSNs (Data Source
Names), 93
configuring, 277
creating, 93
product names, displaying,
120-121
**NCSA (National Center for
Supercomputing
Applications), 444**
**NCSA Common Log File
format, 444-446**

**new users, sending email to,
421-422**
Newmail object, 415-416
**Not in Stock status (order
processing), 226**
**NT File System (NTFS),
332-333**
**NTFS (NT File System),
332-333**

O

ObjectContect object, 15
OnTransactionAbort event,
216-218
OnTransactionCommit
event, 218
**ObjectContext objects
objects.** *See names of specific objects*
**ODBC Logging format,
446-449**
**offsite payment processors,
238-239**
**On Error Resume Next
statement, 366**
online stores, 7-8
administration. *See* administration
checkout pages, 213
order completion,
219-220
order processing, 226
processOrders.asp
page, 227-234
retrieving customer
information, 220-221
transferring items to
Orders table, 224-226

updating customer
information, 221-224
customer registration
forms, 172
cart.asp page, 172-174
error handling,
181-183
register.asp page,
174-175
security (SSL),
183-188
storefuncs.asp page,
176-181
indexable pages, 158-159
list of featured products,
143-144
displaying on Web
page, 146-149
optimizing display,
149-152
selecting products for,
144-146
monitoring use of. *See* site
usage logs
past purchases, displaying,
302-306
pictures, 140
product catalog databases,
89
adding records to,
95-100
connecting to, 93-95
creating, 89-90
manageproducts.asp
page, 100-102,
113-117
Products table, 91-93
quotation marks,
102-104
retrieving information
from, 106-108

updating, 104-105,
109-112
upgrading to SQL
Server, 90
product displays, 123-124
lists of all products,
126-128, 137-139
main store page,
128-130
multiple-page product
listings, 134-137
product categories,
125-126
product details,
130-134
product names,
120-121
scalability, 137-139
search pages, 152
creating, 152-157
optimizing, 157
security, 325-326
Administrator
accounts, 331-332
Children's Advertising
Review Unit (Better
Business Bureau),
342-343
databases, 337-338
domain name registra-
tion, 326-327
Control Panel settings,
327-328
foreign domains,
326-327
privacy policies,
340-341
privacy seal programs,
339-341
Reliability Program
(Better Business
Bureau), 338-339

servers, 329-334
SSL (Secure Sockets
Layer), 335-337
shopping carts, 191
creating with database
tables, 204-209, 211
creating with Session
variables, 191-199,
211
subscription-based sites,
273
database authentica-
tion, 276-285, 295
HTTP (Hypertext
Transport Protocol)
authentication,
274-276, 288
hybrid authentication,
288-294
security information,
passing from page to
page, 285-287
transactions. *See* transactions
**OnTransactionAbort event,
216, 218**
**OnTransactionCommit
event, 218**
opening recordsets, 121-122
OpenTextFile method, 81
operators, LIKE, 152
**Optimistic Locking (record-
sets), 201**
optimization specialists, 498
optimizing
display of featured prod-
ucts, 149-152
search pages, 157
**ORDER BY clause (SQL),
122**
ordering product lists, 140

orders
completing, 219-220
address/payment infor-
mation, 220-224
transferring to Orders
table, 224-226
package tracking, 272
past purchases, displaying,
302-306
processing, 226
order status values, 226
processOrders.asp
page, 227-234
shipping costs, calculating
iisCARTship compo-
nent, 264-269, 272
sample application,
269-271
ShipInfo collection,
267
tracking, 260
account.asp page,
260-261
advantages, 259-260
showorders.asp page,
262-263
showOrderStatus
method, 263-264
Orders table, 170, 224
**OrigPostal property
(iisCARTship component),
265**
output delimiters, 26
**outsourcing server opera-
tions, 329, 335**
Overwrite parameter
CopyFile method, 82
CreateTextFile method, 78

P

package tracking, 272

page counter application,
58-60

page views, 443

PageCount property
(Recordset object), 134

PageRank, 508

PageSize property
(Recordset object), 134

paging through recordsets,
134-137

partial-success status code
(CyberCash), 247

passing
query strings
special characters,
30-31
variables, 29-30
security information from
page to page, 285
cookies, 286
hidden form fields, 287
query strings, 286-287
Session variables, 286

password dialog boxes, forcing, 288-289

password-protecting sites,
273
database authentication,
276-277
Add User scripts,
281-282
example of, 284-285
login pages, 278, 280
login validation,
283-284
registration forms, 278
server load, 295
user authentication,
282

HTTP (Hypertext
Transport Protocol)
authentication, 274
basic authentication,
274, 288
digest authentication,
274
enabling, 275-276
integrated authentica-
tion, 274
when to use, 276
hybrid authentication
AUTHORIZATION
headers, 290-292
forcing password
dialogs, 288-289
hybrid.asp example,
292-294
security information, passing from page to page,
285
cookies, 286
hidden form fields, 287
query strings, 286-287
Session variables, 286

past purchases, displaying,
302-306

pastpurchases.asp page,
303-305

paths (ASPs), 40-41

PATH_TRANSLATED vari-
able, 40-41

payment terminal solutions,
239

paymentURL variable
(CyberCash), 246

Pending status (order processing), 226

percent sign (%), 153

permissions
File Access component, 77
Visual InterDev debug-
ging, 356-357

persistent cookies, 49

Personal Web Server, 10

physical commerce, 468-469

physical paths (ASPs), 40-41

physical security (servers),
334

pictures, adding to online
stores, 140. *See also* customer interfaces

policies (privacy), 340-341

popularity algorithms,
507-508

Posting Acceptor, 391-395

privacy policies, 340-341

privacy seal programs,
339-341
BBBOnline, 341
CPA WebTrust, 341
TRUSTe, 341

processCards.asp page,
250-252

processCards2.asp page,
252-253

processes, 387

processing credit cards, 237
choosing processing
systems, 240
component-based solu-
tions, 239-240
CyberCash, 240
acquiring financial
institutions, 241
authorizing transac-
tions, 245-253
capturing transactions,
254-256
credit card merchant
accounts, 241-242
installation, 243-244
MCK (Merchant
Connection Kit), 243

MessageBlock compo-
nent, 245
registration, 242-243
security, 256
Socket component, 245
offsite payment proces-
sors, 238-239
payment terminal solu-
tions, 239
SET (Secure Electronic
Transaction) standard,
256
processing orders, 226
order status values, 226
processOrders.asp page,
227-234
**processOrders.asp page,
227-234**
**product catalog database
(storeDB), 89**
adding records to, 95
addProduct.asp page,
97-100
INSERT INTO state-
ment, 95-96
variables, 96-97
connecting to, 93-95
creating, 89-90
manageproducts.asp page,
100-102, 113-117
Products table
columns, 91
creating, 92-93
quotation marks, 102-104
recordsets, paging
through, 134-137
retrieving information
from, 106-108
updating
UPDATE statement,
104-105
updateProduct.asp
page, 109-112

upgrading to SQL Server,
90
**Product.asp page, 124,
131-134**
production systems
debugging applications on
capturing errors,
366-372
debug libraries, 366
session variables,
362-366
definition of, 346
separating from develop-
ment systems, 346-347
deploying applications,
350-353
IP addresses, 347, 349
Web sites, 349-350
**ProductList.asp page,
124-128**
products
displaying, 123-124
details, 130-134
lists of all products,
126-128, 137-139
main store page,
128-130
names of, 120-121
product categories,
125-126
favorite product categories
(customized ads), 307
default.asp page modi-
fications, 315-316
displaying featured
products, 313-315
retrieving, 310-311
saving, 311-312
selecting, 308-310
storing, 307
updating, 312

list of featured products,
143-144
displaying on Web
page, 146-149
optimizing display,
149-152
selecting products for,
144-146
multiple-page product
listings, 134-137
pictures of, 140
Products directory, 158
Products table
adding records to, 95
addProduct.asp page,
97-100
INSERT INTO state-
ment, 95-96
variables, 96-97
columns, 91
creating, 92-93
**product_briefDesc column
(Products table), 91**
**product_category column
(Products table), 91**
**product_fulldesc column
(Products table), 91**
**product_id column
(Products table), 91**
**product_name column
(Products table), 91**
**product_picture column
(Products table), 91**
**product_price column
(Products table), 91**
**product_status column
(Products table), 91**
program listings. *See* listings
promoting sites. *See*
publicity

properties
FileSystemObject object,
80
iisCARTship component,
265-266
NCSA Common Log File
format, 445
Recordset object
AbsolutePage, 134
CursorType, 122-123
LockType, 200-201
PageCount, 134
PageSize, 134
RecordCount, 122-123
W3C Extended Log File
format, 452-454
Protocol Version property
(W3C Extended Log File
format), 453
protocols
client-server, 387
FTP (File Transport
Protocol) Service, 385
anonymous access, 386
configuring, 386-387
CuteFTP, 389
file uploads, 387-389
installing, 385-386
IP (Internet Protocol)
addresses
retrieving, 41-42
second IP addresses,
347-349
SMTP Service
configuring, 411-413
installing, 412
proxy servers, 456
publicity, 495-496
Ad Rotator component,
514-515
implementing, 516-517
redirection files, 515
schedule files, 515-516

ad targeting, 513
affiliate programs, 514
banner ads, 510
link exchanges,
510-512
purchasing, 513
bulk mailings, 428
marketing, 438
message composition,
432-435
recipients, 429-432
sending messages,
435-437
reward/loyalty programs,
513-514
search engines, 496
listing sites with,
496-508
spidering process, 496
Web rings
definition of, 508
example of, 508-510
purchases. *See* **orders**

Q-R

query strings, 286-287
example of, 28
retrieving, 28-29
special characters, 30-31
variables, 30
passing, 29
retrieving, 38-39
quotation marks (")
Access databases and,
102-104
displaying, 24-25
HTML forms and,
112-113

radio buttons, 33
Rate Our Store form, 32-33
Read method, 80
ReadAll method, 80
reading
cookies, 49-52
text files, 79-80
ReadLine method, 80
RecordCount property
(Recordset object),
122-123
records
adding, 95
AddNew method,
201-202
addProduct.asp page,
97-100
INSERT INTO
statement, 95-96
variables, 96-97
updating
Delete method,
203-204
Update method,
202-203
UPDATE statement,
104-105
updateProduct.asp
page, 109-112
Recordset object, 119
adding records to, 201-202
cursors, 122-123
deleting records, 203-204
displaying records in,
119-121
locking, 200-201
methods
AddNew, 201-202
Delete, 203
GetRows, 148-149
Update, 202-203
opening, 121-122

paging through, 134-137
properties
    AbsolutePage, 134
    CursorType, 122-123
    LockType, 200-201
    PageCount, 134
    PageSize, 134
    RecordCount, 122-123
updating, 202-203
Redirect method, 75
redirection, 75
    alternatives to, 76
    disadvantages of, 75-76
    example of, 75
redirection files, 515
**redisplaying form fields,
35-37**
**Referrer property (W3C
Extended Log File for-
mat), 454**
REFERRER variable, 41
**register.asp page, 174-175,
477-480**
registering customers, 172
    cart.asp page, 172-174
    error handling, 181-183
    register.asp page, 174-175
    security (SSL), 183-185
        in ASPs (Active Server
        Pages), 187-188
        Certificate Request
        Files, 185-186
        enabling, 185
        server certificates,
        186-187
    storefuncs.asp page, 176
        addCookie method,
        181
        addUser method,
        176-178
        alreadyUser method,
        180

cleanCCNum method,
    180
invalidEmail method,
    178
validCCNumber
    method, 179
**registering domain names,
326**
    Control Panel settings,
    327-328
    domain name registrars,
    327
    foreign domains, 326-327
registration forms, 172
    cart.asp page, 172-174
    error handling, 181-183
    register.asp page, 174-175
    security (SSL), 183-185
        Certificate Request
        Files, 185-186
        enabling, 185
        in ASPs (Active Server
        Pages), 187-188
        server certificates,
        186-187
    storefuncs.asp page, 176
        addCookie method,
        181
        addUser method,
        176-178
        alreadyUser method,
        180
        cleanCCNum method,
        180
        invalidEmail method,
        178
        validCCNumber
        method, 179
**registration pages (database
authentication), 278**
relevance metrics, 498-499

**Reliability Program (Better
Business Bureau), 338-339**
remote administration. *See*
**Internet Service Manager
(HTML)**
**REMOTE_ADDR variable,
41-42**
Remove method, 61
RemoveAll method, 62
reports. *See* **site usage logs**
Request objects, 15, 27
    forms, 31
        credit card form, 37
        empty fields, 33-35
        radio buttons, 33
        Rate Our Store form,
        32-33
        redisplaying field data
        in, 35-37
        retrieving information
        from, 31-32
        simple HTML form
        example, 31
        variables, 38-39
    query strings, 28
        example of, 28
        retrieving, 28-29
        special characters,
        30-31
        variables, 29-30, 38-39
    server variables, 39
        PATH_TRANSLAT-
        ED, 40-41
        REFERRER, 41
        REMOTE_ADDR,
        41-42
        SCRIPT_NAME,
        39-40
        USER_AGENT, 42-43
**Resellers Subscription Sales
service, 238**

Response objects, 15-16, 22, 75

  dynamic content, displaying, 22

    date/time, 22

    long strings, 23

    output delimiters, 26

    quotation marks ("), 24-25

    special characters, 23-24

    Write method, 22-23

  script execution, ending, 26-27

retrieveFavorites method, 310-311

retrieving database records, 106-108

reward programs, 513-514

RollbackTrans method, 218

S

s-computername element (W3C Extended Log Files), 453

s-ip element (W3C Extended Log Files), 453

s-port element (W3C Extended Log Files), 453

s-sitename element (W3C Extended Log Files), 453

sales promotions, list of featured products, 143-144

  displaying on Web page, 146-149

  optimizing display, 149-152

  selecting products for, 144-146

savefavorites.asp page, 311-312

saving form data, 85-86

sc-bytes element (W3C Extended Log Files), 453

sc-status element (W3C Extended Log Files), 453

sc-win32-status element (W3C Extended Log Files), 453

scalability (online stores), 137-139

  testing for, 372-374

schedule files, 515-516

scripting languages, 14

SCRIPT_NAME variable, 39-40

search engines, 496

  listing sites with, 496-497

    optimization specialists, 498

    PageRank, 508

    popularity algorithms, 507-508

    relevance metrics, 498-499

    spider pages, 502-507

    titles/meta tags, 500

    URL submission pages, 500-501

  spidering process, 496

search pages, 152

  creating, 152-157

  optimizing, 157

searching online stores

  search pages, 152

    creating, 152-157

    optimizing, 157

  search tips, 160

Secure Electronic Transaction (SET) standard, 256

Secure Sockets Layer. *See* **SSL**

security

  ASPs (Active Server Pages), 428-429

  Better Business Bureau services

    Children's Advertising Review Uni, 342-343

    Reliability Program, 338-339

  CyberCash, 256

  databases, 337-338

  domain names, registering, 326

    Control Panel settings, 327-328

    domain name registrars, 327

    foreign domains, 326-327

  Internet Service Manager (HTML), 379-384

  Luhn check, 189

  privacy policies, 340-341

  privacy seal programs, 339-341

    BBBOnline, 341

    CPA WebTrust, 341

    TRUSTe, 341

  servers, 329

    Administrator accounts, 331-332

    firewalls, 334

    hot fixes, 330-331

    NTFS (NT File System), 332-333

    physical access, 334

    service packs, 330-331

    Windows NT Server, 329-330

SET (Secure Electronic
Transaction) standard,
256
SSL (Secure Sockets
Layer), 183-185,
335-337
in ASPs (Active Server
Pages), 187-188
Certificate Request
Files, 185-186
enabling, 185
server certificates,
186-187
**security information, pass-
ing from page to page, 285**
cookies, 286
hidden form fields, 287
query strings, 286-287
Session variables, 286
seeding, 341
**SELECT statement, 121,
152**
**SELECT...CASE statement,
74-76**
selectCust.asp page, 429-431
Send method, 415-416
SendCCServer method, 247
**sending email from ASPs
(Active Server Pages), 415**
CDONTS constants,
417-419
on errors, 419-420
HTML mail, 423-428
Newmail.Send method,
415-416
to new users, 421-422
verbose option, 416-417
sendMsg.asp page, 435-437
**sendNewUserMail method,
421-422, 426-428**

**separating development and
production systems,
346-347**
deploying application,
350-353
IP (Internet Protocol)
addresses, 347, 349
Web sites, 349-350
server certificates
applying for, 186-187
installing, 187
**Server IP property (W3C
Extended Log File for-
mat), 453**
**Server Name property
(W3C Extended Log File
format), 453**
Server object, 15, 77
**Server Port property (W3C
Extended Log File for-
mat), 453**
server processes, 387
server variables, 39
PATH_TRANSLATED,
40-41
REFERRER, 41
REMOTE_ADDR, 41-42
SCRIPT_NAME, 39-40
USER_AGENT, 42-43
server-side components
Ad Rotator, 16
Browser Capabilities, 16
Content Linking, 16
definition of, 15
File Access, 16
server-side wallets, 471
general server-side wal-
lets, 472-473
single-site wallets,
471-472

servers, 10
development servers,
346-347
deploying applications
to, 350-353
IP (Internet Protocol)
addresses, 347-349
Web sites, 349-350
IIS. *See* IIS (Internet
Information Server)
Microsoft Index Server,
157
outsourcing operations,
329, 335
Personal Web Server, 10
production servers,
361-372
proxy servers, 456
security, 329-330
SQL Server, 11-12
Windows 2000 Advanced
Server, 11
**ServerVariables collection,
39.** *See also* **server variables**
**Service Name property
(W3C Extended Log File
format), 453**
service packs, 330-331
Session arrays, 198-199
changing value of, 55
creating, 54-55
session cookies, 48
Session objects, 15
**Session variables, 52-53,
286.** *See also* **cookies**
alternatives to, 66
creating, 53, 362-364
debugging routines,
364-366
deleting, 192
displaying, 53-54

SessionIDs, 56
shopping carts, creating,
    191
    advantages, 211
    disadvantages, 192-193
    Product.asp page, 193
    sessionCart.asp page,
        193-199
storing arrays in, 54-55
user sessions, ending,
    56-57
sessionCart.asp page
    code listing, 193-196
    FOR...NEXT loop, 198
    isArray method, 198
    localCart array, 198
    Session array, 198-199
**SessionID property (Session
    object), 56**
Session_OnEnd event, 63
Session_OnStart event, 63
**SET (Secure Electronic
    Transaction) standard, 256**
SetAbort method, 218
SetComplete method, 218
**settling credit card transac-
    tions (CyberCash),
    254-256**
setup fees (banks), 241
ShipCalc method, 266-267
ShipInfo collection, 267
**Shipped status (order pro-
    cessing), 226**
shipping costs, calculating
    iisCARTship component,
        264
        installing, 265
        instantiating, 265
        methods, 266-269
        properties, 265-266
        ShipInfo collection,
            267
        troubleshooting, 272

sample application,
    269-271
shopping carts, 191
checkout pages, 213
    order completion,
        219-220
    order processing, 226
    processOrders.asp
        page, 227-234
    retrieving customer
        information, 220-221
    transferring items to
        Orders table, 224-226
    updating customer
        information, 221-224
creating with database
    tables, 204
    addCart.asp page,
        206-211
    Cart table, 205
    cart.asp page, 205
    Product.asp page, 205
creating with Session vari-
    ables, 191
    advantages, 211
    disadvantages, 192-193
    Product.asp page, 193
    sessionCart.asp page,
        193-199
**showorders.asp page
    (Account page), 262-263**
**showOrderStatus method,
    263-264**
showtime.asp page, 13-14
single-site wallets, 471-472
Site Server Express 3.0, 464
site usage logs, 441-444
    analyzing, 455
    ASPs (Active Server
        Pages), 462-464
    commercial log-analy-
        sis tools, 464

enumerating, 457-459
    limitations of, 456
    loading into databases,
        460-461
    Microsoft IIS Log File
        format, 449
        naming conventions,
            449
        sample entry, 450-451
    NCSA Common Log File
        format, 444
        properties, 445
        sample entry, 446
    ODBC Logging format,
        446-449
    W3C Extended Log File
        format, 451
        naming conventions,
            451-452
        properties, 452-454
        sample entry, 454-455
Skip method, 80
SkipLine method, 80
SmartCards, 474
SMTP Service
    configuring, 411-413
    installing, 412
**Socket component
    (CyberCash), 245**
sockets
    CyberCash Socket compo-
        nent, 245
    SSL (Secure Sockets
        Layer), 183-185,
        335-337
        in ASPs (Active Server
            Pages), 187-188
        Certificate Request
            Files, 185-186
        enabling, 185
        server certificates,
            186-187

software
electronic wallets. *See*
wallets
ICVerify, 239
SonicWALL Web site, 334
source code listings. *See* **list-**
ings
Source parameter
CopyFile method, 81
MoveFile method, 82
spamming, 160
special characters
displaying, 23-24
query strings, 30-31
spider pages, 502
creating
crawler.asp, 506-507
CreateStaticPage
method, 502-505
potential problems, 502
spidering (search engines),
456, 496
spoofing, 336
SQL (Standard Query
Language)
SQL Server, 11-12
statements
INSERT INTO, 95-96
LIKE operator, 152
SELECT, 121-122, 152
UPDATE, 104-105
Transact-SQL, 219
SSL (Secure Sockets Layer),
183-185, 335-337
in ASPs (Active Server
Pages), 187-188
Certificate Request Files,
185-186
enabling, 185
server certificates
applying for, 186-187
installing, 187

standardfooter.asp file, 71
standardfuncs.asp file, 73
standardheader.asp file, 71
starting Access, 90
statements
FOR...NEXT, 198
INSERT INTO, 95-96
looping. *See* loops
SELECT, 121-122, 152
SELECT...CASE, 74-76
UPDATE, 104-105
WHILE...WEND, 120,
210
static cursors, 122-123
stopping
ADO (Active Data Object)
transactions, 218
script execution, 26-27
storeDB database. *See* **prod-**
uct catalog database
storefuncs.asp page, 176
addCookie method, 181
addUser method, 176-178
alreadyUser method, 180
cleanCCNum method, 180
storefuncs.asp page
client-side upload routine,
393
invalidEmail method, 178
validCCNumber method,
179
stores. *See* **online stores**
storing
arrays
in Application vari-
ables, 60-61
in Session variables,
54-55
cookies, 49
product lists in memory,
137-139

strings
displaying, 23
query strings, 28
example of, 28
retrieving, 28-29
special characters,
30-31
variables, 29-30, 38-39
submitting URLs to search
engines, 500-501
subscription-based sites, 273
database authentication,
276-277
Add User scripts,
281-282
example of, 284-285
login pages, 278, 280
login validation,
283-284
registration forms, 278
server load, 295
user authentication,
282
HTTP (Hypertext
Transport Protocol)
authentication, 274
basic authentication,
274, 288
digest authentication,
274
enabling, 275-276
integrated authentica-
tion, 274
when to use, 276
hybrid authentication
AUTHORIZATION
headers, 290-292
forcing password
dialogs, 288-289
hybrid.asp example,
292-294

security information, passing from page to page, 285
  cookies, 286
  hidden form fields, 287
  query strings, 286-287
  Session variables, 286
success status code (CyberCash), 247
success-duplicate status code (CyberCash), 247
survey form, 84-86
System DSNs (Data Source Names), 93

T

tables
  shopping carts, creating with, 204
    addCart.asp page, 206-209, 211
    Cart table, 205
    cart.asp page, 205
    Product.asp page, 205
  transaction database, 170-171
    Cart, 170
    Orders, 170, 224
    Products, 91-93, 95-100
    Users, 170-171
tags (HTML)
  <INPUT>, 391
  <META>, 72, 499
  <TITLE>, 499
targeted advertising (customized ads), 307
  default.asp page, 315-316
  favorites.asp page, 308-310

featured.asp page, 313-315
retrieveFavorites method, 310-311
savefavorites.asp page, 311-312
updateFavorites method, 312
TerminalCapture model (CyberCash), 255
testing for scalability, 372-374
text files. *See also* **files**
  appending, 81
  copying, 81-82
  creating, 78-79
  deleting, 82
  listing, 83-84
  moving, 82
  reading, 79-80
  verifying existance of, 83
  writing to, 79
TextStream object, 77, 80
time, displaying, 13-14, 22
time element (W3C Extended Log Files), 453
Time property (W3C Extended Log File format), 453
Time Taken property (W3C Extended Log File format), 453
time-taken element (W3C Extended Log Files), 453
<TITLE> tag (HTML), 499
tools
  Microsoft WCAT (Web Capacity Analysis Tool), 372-373
  Upsizing Tools, 11, 90

tracking customers
  Application variables, 57
    creating, 57-58
    locking, 60
    removing from memory, 61-62
    sample hit counter applications, 58-60
    storing arrays in, 60-61
  cookies, 48
    adding to customers' browsers, 50-51
    alternatives to, 66
    Cookie Central Web site, 48
    displaying, 52
    persistent cookies, 49
    reading, 49-52
    session cookies, 48
    storing, 49
    support for, 50
  Global.asa files, 62-63
    counting customers, 63-64
    displaying active customers, 64-65
  Session variables, 52-53
    alternatives to, 66
    creating, 53
    displaying, 53-54
    SessionIDs, 56
    storing arrays in, 54-55
    user sessions, ending, 56-57
tracking orders, 260
  account.asp page, 260-261
  advantages, 259-260
  packages, 272
  showorders.asp page, 262-263
  showOrderStatus method, 263-264

Transact-SQL, 219
transaction database tables, 170-171
  Cart, 170
  Orders, 170, 224
  Products
    adding records to, 95-100
    columns, 91
    creating, 92-93
  Users, 170-171
@TRANSACTION directive, 215, 234
transaction fees (banks), 241
transactions
  abandoned transactions, 467-468
  ACID test, 214
  ADO (Active Data Objects), 218-219
    beginning, 218
    disadvantages, 234
    example of, 218-219
    marking end of, 218
    stopping, 218
  ASP page transactions, 214
    error handling, 215-216, 218
    example of, 215
  business-to-business, 8
  business-to-consumer, 8
  consumer-to-consumer, 8
  credit cards. *See* credit card transactions
  database transactions, 219
  definition of, 213-214
  wallets, 469
    accepting information from, 492
    client-side, 469-471

    customizing. *See* custom store wallets
    definition of, 469
    server-side, 471-473
    SmartCards, 474
    standards, 475-476
Transfer method, 77
transferring customer items to Orders table, 224-226
troubleshooting. *See also* **debugging**
  ADO methods, 211
  database connections, 117
  iisCARTship component, 272
TRUSTe privacy program, 341

U

unauthorized disclosure, 336
Unicode parameter (CreateTextFile method), 78
unique users, 443
United States Government Electronic Commerce Policy Web site, 9
Update method, 202-203
UPDATE statement (SQL), 104-105
updateFavorites method, 312
UpdateProduct form, 109-112
updateProduct.asp page, 109-112
  debug routine, 365
  image uploads, 398-401

updateUser method, 222-223, 490-491
updating
  address/payment information, 221-224
  database records
    UPDATE statement, 104-105
    updateProduct.asp page, 109-112
  favorite product list, 312
upgrading Access databases to SQL Server, 90
upload.asp page, 393-394
uploading files
  ASPs (Active Server Pages)
    addProduct.asp page, 396-397
    updateProduct.asp page, 398-401
  FTP (File Transport Protocol) Service, 387-389
  Posting Acceptor, 391-395
UPS shipping codes, converting, 267
Upsizing Tools, 11, 90
UPSproductConversion method, 267
URI Query property (W3C Extended Log File format), 453
URI Stem property (W3C Extended Log File format), 453
URLs, submitting to search engines, 500-501
usage logs. *See* **site usage logs**

User Agent property (W3C Extended Log File format), 454
user authentication
  database authentication, 276-277
    Add User scripts, 281-282
    example of, 284-285
    login pages, 278, 280
    login validation, 283-284
    registration forms, 278
    server load, 295
    user authentication, 282
  HTTP (Hypertext Transport Protocol), 274
    basic authentication, 274, 288
    digest authentication, 274
    enabling, 275-276
    integrated authentication, 274
    when to use, 276
  hybrid authentication
    AUTHORIZATION headers, 290-292
    forcing password dialogs, 288-289
    hybrid.asp example, 292-294
  security information, passing from page to page, 285
    cookies, 286
    hidden form fields, 287
    query strings, 286-287
    Session variables, 286

User Name property (W3C Extended Log File format), 453
user settings, 297
  displaying, 300-301
  retrieving, 298-300
users. *See* **customers**
Users table, 170-171
USER_AGENT variable, 42-43
user_ccexpire field (Users table), 171
user_ccname field (Users table), 171
user_ccnumber field (Users table), 171
user_cctype field (Users table), 171
user_city field (Users table), 171
user_email field (Users table), 171
user_id field (Users table), 171
user_password field (Users table), 171
user_state field (Users table), 171
user_street field (Users table), 171
user_username field (Users table), 171
user_zip field (Users table), 171
utilities
  Disk Administrator, 332
  Disk Management, 332
  UUEncoding, 290-291

V

validatelogin method, 282-283
validating
  forms, 33-35
  logins, 282-283
validCCNumber method, 179
variables
  Application variables, 57
    creating, 57-58
    hit counter applications, 58-60
    locking, 60
    removing from memory, 61-62
    storing arrays in, 60-61
  form variables, retrieving, 38-39
  query string variables, 286-287
    passing, 29-30
    retrieving, 38-39
  server variables, 39
    PATH_TRANSLATED, 40-41
    REFERRER, 41
    REMOTE_ADDR, 41-42
    SCRIPT_NAME, 39-40
    USER_AGENT, 42-43
  Session variables, 52-53, 286. *See also* cookies
    alternatives to, 66
    creating, 53, 362-364
    debugging routines, 364-366
    deleting, 192

displaying, 53-54
SessionIDs, 56
shopping carts, creating, 191-199, 211
storing arrays in, 54-55
user sessions, ending, 56-57
verifying file existance, 83
VIRTUAL attribute (#INCLUDE directive), 70
virtual stores. *See* **online stores**
Visual InterDev, 12
applications, deploying, 350-353
debugging feature, 354
breakpoints, 357
enabling, 355
Locals window, 360-361
permissions, 356-357
watch window, 358-359

W-Z

W3C Extended Log File format, 451
naming conventions, 451-452
properties, 452-454
sample entry, 454-455
wallets, 469
accepting information from, 492
client-side, 469
advantages/disadvantages, 470-471
obtaining, 469-470

custom store wallets, 476
addUser method, 488-489
doCheckout.asp page, 481-483
ECML (E-Commerce Modeling Language) standards, 483-487
register.asp page, 477-480
updateUser method, 490-491
definition of, 469
server-side, 471
general server-side wallets, 472-473
single-site wallets, 471-472
SmartCards, 474
standards, 475-476
watch window (Visual InterDev debugger), 358-359
WCAT (Web Capacity Analysis Tool), 372-373
Web pages
indexable pages, 158-159
Internet Service Manager (HTML), 377-378
access restrictions, 379-384
installing, 378-379
remote administration tasks, 384
search pages, 152
creating, 152-157
optimizing, 157
uploading files to
ASPs (Active Server Pages), 396-401
FTP (File Transport Protocol) Service, 387-389

Posting Acceptor, 391-395
third-party upload components, 392
Web rings
definition of, 508
example of, 508-510
Web servers. *See* **servers**
Web sites. *See also* **site usage logs**
BBBOnline, 341
Certification Authorities, 336-337
client-side wallets, 470
Cookie Central, 48
CPA WebTrust, 341
development sites, 349-350
listing with search engines, 496-497
optimization specialists, 498
PageRank, 508
popularity algorithms, 507-508
relevance metrics, 498-499
spider pages, 502-507
titles.meta tags, 500
URL submission pages, 500-501
Microsoft
Personal Web Server, 10
Upsizing Tools, 90
server-side wallets, 473
SmartCards, 474
SonicWALL, 334
subscription-based sites, 273
database authentication, 276-285, 295

HTTP authentication,
274-276, 288
hybrid authentication,
288-294
security information,
passing from page to
page, 285-287
TRUSTe, 341
United States Government
Electronic Commerce
Policy, 9
URL submission pages,
500-501
**WebTrust privacy program,
341**
**Weight property
(iisCARTship component),
265**
WHERE clause (SQL), 121
WHILE...WEND loop
paging through recordsets,
120
shopping cart application,
210
wildcard (%), 153
**Win32 Status property
(W3C Extended Log File
format), 453**
**Windows 2000 Advanced
Server, 11**
Windows NT Server
installing, 330
NTFS (NT File System),
332-333
security, 329-330
Write method, 22-23, 79
**WriteBlankLines method,
79**
WriteLine method, 78-79
writing to text files, 79

Other Related Titles

Maximum Security, Second Edition
A Anonymous
ISBN: 0-672-31341-3
$49.99 USA/$70.95 CAN

Sams Teach Yourself SQL in 21 Days, Third Edition
Christoph Wille and Christian Koller
ISBN: 0-672-31674-9
$34.99 USA/$52.95 CAN

Sams Teach Yourself SQL in 10 Minutes
Ben Forta
ISBN: 0-672-31664-1
$12.99 USA/$19.95 CAN

Active Server Pages 2.0 Unleashed
Steve Walther
ISBN: 0-672-31613-7
$49.99 USA/$71.95 CAN

Sams Teach Yourself SQL Server 7.0 in 21 Days
Rick Sawtell and Richard Waymire
ISBN: 0-672-31290-5
$39.99 USA/$57.95 CAN

Building Enterprise Solutions with Visual Studio 6
G.A.Sullivan
ISBN: 0-672-31489-4
$49.99 US/$71.95 CAN

Sams Teach Yourself CGI in 24 Hours
Rafe Colburn
ISBN: 0-672-31880-6
$24.99 USA/$37.95 CAN

Sams Teach Yourself ADO 2.5 in 21 Days
Christoph Wille
ISBN: 0-672-31873-3
$39.99 USA/$59.95 CAN

F. Scott Barker's Microsoft Access 2000 Power Programming
F. Scott Barker
ISBN: 0-672-31506-8
$49.99 USA/$74.95 CAN

Sams Teach Yourself Internet Programming with Visual C++ in 21 Days
William Robison
ISBN: 0-672-31823-7
$39.99 USA/$59.95 CAN

Microsoft Windows 2000 Troubleshooting and Configuration
Robert Reinstein
ISBN: 0-672-31878-4
$49.99 USA/$74.95 CAN

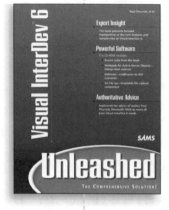

Visual InterDev 6 Unleashed
Paul Thurrott
ISBN: 0-672-31262-x
$49.99 US/$74.95 CAN

The Internet Business Guide, Second Edition
Christoph Wille and Christian Koller
ISBN: 1-57521-004-5
$25.00 US/$34.95 CAN

SAMS

www.samspublishing.com

All prices are subject to change.

What's on the Disc

The companion CD-ROM contains all of the authors' source code and samples from the book and some third-party software products.

Windows 95, Windows 98, Windows NT 4, and Windows 2000 Installation Instructions

1. Insert the CD-ROM disc into your CD-ROM drive.
2. From the desktop, double-click on the My Computer icon.
3. Double-click on the icon representing your CD-ROM drive.
4. Double-click on the icon titled START.EXE to run the installation program.
5. Follow the onscreen instructions to finish the installation.

Note

If Windows 95, Windows 98, Windows NT 4, or Windows 2000 is installed on your computer, and you have the AutoPlay feature enabled, the START.EXE program starts automatically whenever you insert the disc into your CD-ROM drive.